Dictionary of World Biography

Index

Dictionary of World Biography

The Ancient World
The Middle Ages
The Renaissance
The 17th and 18th Centuries
The 19th Century, 2 volumes
The 20th Century, 3 volumes
Index

Frank N. Magill, ***editor***

Christina J. Moose, ***managing editor***

Alison Aves, ***researcher and bibliographer***

Mark Rehn, ***acquisitions editor***

Dictionary of World Biography

Volume 10

Index

Steve Seddon, Indexer

FITZROY DEARBORN PUBLISHERS
CHICAGO • LONDON

SALEM PRESS
PASADENA • HACKENSACK, NJ

Dictionary of World Biography is a copublication of Salem Press, Inc. and Fitzroy Dearborn Publishers

For information, write to:

SALEM PRESS, INC.
P.O. Box 50062
Pasadena, California 91115

or
FITZROY DEARBORN PUBLISHERS
919 North Michigan Avenue, Suite 760
Chicago, Illinois 60611
USA

or
FITZROY DEARBORN PUBLISHERS
310 Regent Street
London W1R 5AJ
England

The paper used in this volume conforms to the American National Standard for Permanence of Paper for Printed Library Materials, Z39.48-1992.

Library of Congress Cataloging-in-Publication Data
Dictionary of world biography / editor, Frank N. Magill ; managing editor, Christina J. Moose ; researcher and bibliographer, Alison Aves ; acquisitions editor, Mark Rehn.
v. cm.
A revision and reordering, with new entries added, of the material in the thirty vols. comprising the various subsets designated "series" published under the collective title: Great lives from history, 1987-1995.
Includes bibliographical references and indexes.
Contents: v.10. Index.
ISBN 0-89356-324-2 (v. 10: alk. paper)
ISBN 0-89356-273-4 (v. 1-10 set: alk paper)
1. Biography. 2. World history. I. Magill, Frank Northen, 1907-1997. II. Moose, Christina J., 1952- . III. Aves, Alison. IV. Great lives from history.
CT104.D54 1998
920.02—dc21 97-51154
CIP

British Library Cataloguing-in-Publication Data is available.
Fitzroy Dearborn ISBN 1-57958-049-1
First Published in the U.K. and U.S., 2000
Printed by Braun-Brumfield, Inc.

Cover design by Peter Aristedes.

First Printing

CONTENTS

Area of Achievement Index 1

Geographical Location Index 49

Subject Index 83

AREA OF ACHIEVEMENT INDEX

ABOLITIONISM. ***See*** **CIVIL RIGHTS; SOCIAL REFORM**

ACTING. ***See*** **THEATER AND ENTERTAINMENT**

AERONAUTICS. ***See*** **AVIATION AND SPACE EXPLORATION; ENGINEERING**

AGRICULTURE. ***See also*** **BOTANY; HORTICULTURE**
Tull, Jethro, **IV:**1345

ALCHEMY. ***See*** **CHEMISTRY**

AMERICAN INDIAN AFFAIRS. ***See*** **NATIVE AMERICAN AFFAIRS**

ANTHROPOLOGY
Baer, Karl Ernst von, **V:**109
Benedict, Ruth, **VII:**255
Boas, Franz, **VII:**339
Breuil, Henri-Édouard-Prosper, **VII:**456
Dunham, Katherine, **VII:**984
Frobenius, Leo, **VII:**1242
Heyerdahl, Thor, **VIII:**1658
Leakey, L.S.B., **VIII:**2145
Le Bon, Gustave, **VIII:**2134
Lévi-Strauss, Claude, **VIII:**2164
Mead, Margaret, **VIII:**2468
Morgan, Lewis Henry, **VI:**1584
Rasmussen, Knud Johan Victor, **IX:**3121
Teilhard de Chardin, Pierre, **IX:**3626
Virchow, Rudolf, **VI:**2312

ARCHAEOLOGY
Ballard, Robert Duane, **VII:**180
Heyerdahl, Thor, **VIII:**1658
Raphael, **III:**642
Schliemann, Heinrich, **VI:**1980
Winckelmann, Johann Joachim, **IV:**1460

ARCHITECTURE
Aalto, Alvar, **VII:**1
Adam, James and Robert, **IV:**7
Alberti, Leon Battista, **III:**8
Arnolfo di Cambio, **II:**82
Ashurbanipal, **I:**105
Ashurnasirpal II, **I:**109
Barry, Sir Charles, **V:**138
Bernini, Gian Lorenzo, **IV:**118
Boffrand, Germain, **IV:**151
Borromini, Francesco, **IV:**167
Bramante, Donato, **III:**81
Brunelleschi, Filippo, **III:**89
Bulfinch, Charles, **V:**349
Burnham, Daniel Hudson, **V:**365
Candela, Felix, **VII:**557
Cimabue, **II:**272
Fischer von Erlach, Johann Bernhard, **IV:**473
Freyssinet, Eugène, **VII:**1228
Fuller, R. Buckminster, **VII:**1265
Garnier, Tony, **VII:**1308
Gaudí, Antonio, **VII:**1315
Giotto, **II:**388
Greenway, Francis, **V:**990
Gropius, Walter, **VIII:**1486
Guarini, Guarino, **IV:**583
Hardouin-Mansart, Jules, **IV:**901
Hawksmoor, Nicholas, **IV:**635
Hildebrandt, Johann Lucas von, **IV:**655
Imhotep, **I:**443
Jones, Inigo, **IV:**735
Latrobe, Benjamin Henry, **VI:**1327
Le Corbusier, **VIII:**2137
Lescot, Pierre, **III:**428
Lin, Maya Ying, **VIII:**2185
Mansart, François, **IV:**898
Mendelsohn, Erich, **VIII:**2487
Michelangelo, **III:**517
Mies van der Rohe, Ludwig, **VIII:**2520
Morris, William, **VI:**1588
Nash, John, **IV:**1012
Nervi, Pier Luigi, **VIII:**2720
Niemeyer, Oscar, **VIII:**2739
Oud, J.J.P., **IX:**2859
Palladio, Andrea, **III:**580
Pei, I.M., **IX:**2946
Perret, Auguste, **IX:**2976
Pugin, Augustus Welby Northmore, **VI:**1821
Raphael, **III:**642
Richardson, Henry Hobson, **VI:**1882
Sansovino, Jacopo, **III:**664
Scott, Sir George Gilbert, **VI:**2002
Siloé, Diego de, **III:**696
Street, George Edmund, **VI:**2160
Suger, **II:**859
Sullivan, Louis, **VI:**2167

Vanbrugh, Sir John, **IV:**1351
Vasari, Giorgio, **III:**743
Wren, Sir Christopher, **IV:**1480
Wright, Frank Lloyd, **IX:**4060
Xenakis, Iannis, **IX:**4075
Xerxes I, **I:**962
Zoser, **I:**978

ART. ***See also*** **PATRONAGE OF THE ARTS; PHOTOGRAPHY**
Andrea del Sarto, **III:**24
Angelico, Fra, **III:**28
Arnolfo di Cambio, **II:**82
Ashurbanipal, **I:**105
Ashurnasirpal II, **I:**109
Audubon, John James, **V:**86
Beardsley, Aubrey, **V:**161
Bellini, Giovanni, **III:**58
Bernini, Gian Lorenzo, **IV:**118
Bierstadt, Albert, **V:**233
Bingham, George Caleb, **V:**236
Blake, William, **IV:**137
Boccioni, Umberto, **VII:**342
Bonnard, Pierre, **VII:**362
Bosch, Hieronymus, **III:**70
Botticelli, Sandro, **III:**74
Brancusi, Constantin, **VII:**414
Braque, Georges, **VII:**431
Bruegel, Pieter (the Elder), **III:**85
Brunelleschi, Filippo, **III:**89
Calder, Alexander, **VII:**538
Canaletto, **IV:**242
Canova, Antonio, **V:**408
Carracci Family, The, **III:**125
Cartier-Bresson, Henri, **VII:**594
Cassatt, Mary, **V:**434
Catlin, George, **V:**443
Cellini, Benvenuto, **III:**151
Cézanne, Paul, **V:**453
Chagall, Marc, **VII:**639
Chardin, Jean Siméon, **IV:**275
Claude Lorrain, **IV:**317
Cocteau, Jean, **VII:**721
Constable, John, **V:**547
Copley, John Singleton, **IV:**356
Correggio, **III:**184
Courbet, Gustave, **V:**565
Cranach, Lucas (the Elder), **III:**200
Dalí, Salvador, **VII:**827
David, Jacques-Louis, **V:**610
Degas, Edgar, **V:**641
Delacroix, Eugène, **V:**645
Delaunay, Robert, **VII:**888
Denis, Maurice, **VII:**909
Donatello, **III:**220
Duccio di Buoninsegna, **II:**305
Duchamp, Marcel, **VII:**972
Dürer, Albrecht, **III:**230
Eakins, Thomas, **V:**732
Epstein, Sir Jacob, **VII:**1087
Ernst, Max, **VII:**1098
Eyck, Jan van, and Hubert van Eyck, **III:**250
Fragonard, Jean-Honoré, **IV:**488
Frankenthaler, Helen, **VII:**1208
Fry, Roger, **VII:**1253
Gainsborough, Thomas, **IV:**515
Gauguin, Paul, **V:**888
Geisel, Theodor Seuss, **VII:**1329
Géricault, Théodore, **V:**910
Ghiberti, Lorenzo, **III:**302
Giacometti, Alberto, **VII:**1359
Giorgione, **III:**305
Giotto, **II:**388
Gogh, Vincent van, **V:**944
Goya, Francisco de, **IV:**569
Greco, El, **III:**311
Gris, Juan, **VIII:**1483
Grünewald, Matthias, **III:**322
Hals, Frans, **IV:**604
Hiroshige, **V:**1117
Hockney, David, **VIII:**1711
Hogarth, William, **IV:**668
Hokusai, **V:**1120
Holbein, Hans, the Younger, **III:**358
Homer, Winslow, **V:**1133
Hopper, Edward, **VIII:**1740
Hsia Kuei, **II:**479
Hunt, William Holman, **V:**1168
Ingres, Jean-Auguste-Dominique, **V:**1183
Jacopo della Quercia, **III:**389
Jōchō, **II:**537
John, Augustus, **VIII:**1854
Jones, Inigo, **IV:**735
Kandinsky, Wassily, **VIII:**1903
Kauffmann, Angelica, **IV:**765
Kirchner, Ernst Ludwig, **VIII:**1991
Klee, Paul, **VIII:**2005
Kokoschka, Oskar, **VIII:**2012
Kollwitz, Käthe, **VIII:**2016
Krasner, Lee, **VIII:**2023
Kupka, František, **VIII:**2036
Lawrence, Sir Thomas, **IV:**808
Léger, Fernand, **VIII:**2154
Leonardo da Vinci, **III:**423

Lescot, Pierre, **III:**428
Lipchitz, Jacques, **VIII:**2199
Lorenzetti, Pietro, and
Ambrogio Lorenzetti, **II:**595
Lysippus, **I:**515
Ma Yüan, **II:**612
Magritte, René, **VIII:**2349
Manet, Édouard, **VI:**1471
Mantegna, Andrea, **III:**460
Marc, Franz, **VIII:**2404
Martin, Agnes, **VIII:**2437
Martini, Simone, **II:**632
Masaccio, **III:**483
Matisse, Henri, **VIII:**2452
Mi Fei, **II:**639
Michelangelo, **III:**517
Miró, Joan, **VIII:**2546
Mondrian, Piet, **VIII:**2575
Monet, Claude, **VIII:**2579
Moore, Henry, **VIII:**2609
Morris, William, **VI:**1588
Moses, Grandma, **VIII:**2633
Munch, Edvard, **VIII:**2658
Nash, Paul, **VIII:**2689
Nast, Thomas, **VI:**1627
Nevelson, Louise, **VIII:**2728
Nicholson, Ben, **VIII:**2732
Nordau, Max, **VIII:**2766
Ogata Kōrin, **IV:**1041
O'Keeffe, Georgia, **IX:**2800
Orcagna, Andrea, **II:**698
Orozco, José Clemente, **IX:**2836
Pater, Walter, **VI:**1749
Peale, Charles Willson, **IV:**1070
Phidias, **I:**624
Picasso, Pablo, **IX:**2997
Piero della Francesca, **III:**606
Pisano, Andrea, **II:**744
Pisano, Nicola and Giovanni, **II:**747
Pissarro, Camille, **VI:**1779
Pollock, Jackson, **IX:**3048
Polygnotus, **I:**676
Potter, Beatrix, **IX:**3063
Poussin, Nicolas, **IV:**1118
Praxiteles, **I:**690
Pucelle, Jean, **II:**762
Raeburn, Sir Henry, **VI:**1836
Raphael, **III:**642
Redon, Odilon, **VI:**1854
Rembrandt, **IV:**1152
Remington, Frederic, **VI:**1861
Renoir, Pierre-Auguste, **VI:**1869
Reynolds, Sir Joshua, **IV:**1160
Rivera, Diego, **IX:**3184
Rockwell, Norman, **IX:**3198
Rodin, Auguste, **VI:**1900
Romney, George, **IV:**1187
Ross, Betsy, **IV:**1191
Rouault, Georges, **IX:**3251
Rousseau, Henri, **VI:**1921
Rubens, Peter Paul, **IV:**1198
Ruskin, John, **VI:**1925
Saint-Gaudens, Augustus, **VI:**1940
Sansovino, Jacopo, **III:**664
Sargent, John Singer, **VI:**1961
Schmidt-Rottluff, Karl, **IX:**3354
Scopas, **I:**764
Sendak, Maurice, **IX:**3387
Sesshū, 679
Seurat, Georges, **VI:**2033
Siloé, Diego de, **III:**696
Sluter, Claus, **II:**832
Sōtatsu, **IV:**1257
Stuart, Gilbert, **IV:**1289
Su Tung-p'o, **II:**855
Sung Dynasty, **II:**866
Sutherland, Graham Vivian, **IX:**3587
Taine, Hippolyte-Adolphe, **VI:**2182
Thomson, Tom, **IX:**3665
Thurber, James, **IX:**3677
Tiepolo, Giovanni Battista, **IV:**1323
Tintoretto, **III:**717
Titian, **III:**721
Toulouse-Lautrec, Henri de, **VI:**2247
Turner, J.M.W., **VI:**2272
Unkei, **II:**924
Vasari, Giorgio, **III:**743
Velázquez, Diego, **IV:**1364
Vermeer, Jan, **IV:**1368
Veronese, Paolo, **III:**747
Verrocchio, Andrea del, **III:**750
Vigée-Lebrun, Élisabeth, **IV:**1376
Vuillard, Édouard, **IX:**3826
Wang Hsi-chih, **I:**946
Wang Wei, **II:**965
Warhol, Andy, **IX:**3884
Watteau, Antoine, **IV:**1413
Wedgwood, Josiah, **IV:**1421
Weyden, Rogier van der, **III:**778
Whistler, James McNeill, **VI:**2363
Whitney, Gertrude Vanderbilt, **IX:**3969
Wood, Grant, **IX:**4045
Wyeth, Andrew, **IX:**4072
Yen Li-pen, **II:**1015

ASTRONAUTICS. ***See*** **AVIATION AND SPACE EXPLORATION**

ASTROPHYSICS. ***See*** **PHYSICS**

ASTRONOMY. ***See also*** **NATURAL HISTORY; PHYSICS**

Abul Wefa, **II:**20
Alhazen, **II:**63
Ambartsumian, Viktor A., 63
Anaximander, **I:**50
Apollonius of Perga, **I:**72
Aryabhata, **II:**89
Avicenna, **II:**106
Banneker, Benjamin, **IV:**88
Battani, al-, **II:**121
Bernoulli, Jakob I, **IV:**122
Bessel, Friedrich Wilhelm, **V:**215
Brahe, Tycho, **III:**77
Brahmagupta, **II:**181
Bruno, Giordano, **III:**96
Copernicus, Nicolaus, **III:**176
Danjon, André-Louis, **VII:**837
Eudoxus of Cnidus, **I:**310
Fracastoro, Girolamo, **III:**270
Galileo, **IV:**519
Gauss, Carl Friedrich, **V:**893
Halley, Edmond, **IV:**600
Hawking, Stephen W., **VIII:**1580
Hipparchus, **I:**407
Huygens, Christiaan, **IV:**695
Kepler, Johannes, **IV:**772
Khwarizmi, al-, **II:**563
Langley, Samuel Pierpont, **VI:**1313
Laplace, Pierre-Simon, **VI:**1319
Lemaître, Georges, **VIII:**2157
Nabu-rimanni, **I:**566
Nostradamus, **III:**567
Oort, Jan Hendrik, **IX:**2827
Ptolemy, **I:**712
Pythagoras, **I:**727
Sagan, Carl, **IX:**3292
Schmidt, Bernhard Voldemar, **IX:**3351
Schwarzschild, Karl, **IX:**3366
Sosigenes, **I:**811
Tombaugh, Clyde William, **IX:**3699
Wolf, Max, **IX:**4039

ATHLETICS. ***See*** **SPORTS**

AUTO RACING. ***See*** **SPORTS**

AVIATION AND SPACE EXPLORATION

Armstrong, Neil, **VII:**110
Blériot, Louis, **VII:**325
Braun, Wernher von, **VII:**440
Byrd, Richard E., **VII:**534
Cayley, Sir George, **V:**450
Earhart, Amelia, **VII:**992
Eckener, Hugo, **VII:**1011
Gagarin, Yuri Alekseyevich, **VII:**1270
Glenn, John H., Jr., **VII:**1387
Goddard, Robert H., **VII:**1396
Heinkel, Ernst Heinrich, **VIII:**1614
Korolev, Sergei, **VIII:**2019
Langley, Samuel Pierpont, **VI:**1313
Lindbergh, Charles A., **VIII:**2193
Montgolfier, Jacques-Étienne and Joseph-Michel, **IV:**995
Oberth, Hermann, **IX:**2777
Piccard, Auguste and Jean-Felix, **IX:**3002
Prandtl, Ludwig, **IX:**3073
Ride, Sally, **IX:**3178
Santos-Dumont, Alberto, **IX:**3320
Shepard, Alan, **IX:**3405
Tereshkova, Valentina, **IX:**3639
Tsiolkovsky, Konstantin, **IX:**3749
Tupolev, Andrei Nikolayevich, **IX:**3764
Whittle, Sir Frank, **IX:**3972
Wright, Wilbur and Orville, **IX:**4064
Zeppelin, Ferdinand von, **IX:**4108

BALLET. ***See*** **DANCE**

BANKING AND FINANCE. ***See also*** **BUSINESS AND INDUSTRY; ECONOMICS**

Biddle, Nicholas, **V:**225
Bottomley, Horatio W., **VII:**382
Cooke, Jay, **V:**551
Gallatin, Albert, **V:**861
Medici, Lorenzo de', **III:**495
Morgan, J.P., **VI:**1579
Morris, Robert, **IV:**999
Necker, Jacques, **IV:**1016

BASEBALL. ***See*** **SPORTS**

BASKETBALL. ***See*** **SPORTS**

BIBLICAL FIGURES. ***See also*** **RELIGION AND THEOLOGY**

Aaron, **I:**1
Abraham, **I:**5

Darius the Great, **I:**236
David, **I:**241
Deborah, **I:**246
Ezekiel, **I:**326
Ezra, **I:**330
Herod the Great, **I:**390
Isaiah, **I:**452
Jeremiah, **I:**459
Jesus Christ, **I:**467
John the Apostle, **I:**475
John the Baptist, **I:**479
Moses, **I:**561
Nebuchadnezzar II, **I:**569
Paul, Saint, **I:**604
Peter, Saint, **I:**614
Pilate, Pontius, **I:**640
Samuel, **I:**746
Solomon, **I:**798
Stephen, Saint, **I:**822
Thomas, Saint, **I:**880
Virgin Mary, **I:**939

BIOCHEMISTRY. ***See also*** **BIOLOGY; CHEMISTRY**
Bayliss, Sir William Maddock, **VII:**217
Domagk, Gerhard, **VII:**951
Jacob, François, **VIII:**1827
Macleod, John J.R., **VIII:**2329
Oparin, Aleksandr Ivanovich, **IX:**2830
Theorell, Axel Hugo Teodor, **IX:**3654

BIOLOGY. ***See also*** **BOTANY; GENETICS; ZOOLOGY**
Baer, Karl Ernst von, **V:**109
Buffon, Comte de, **IV:**215
Calmette, Albert, **VII:**546
Cohn, Ferdinand Julius, **V:**534
Cousteau, Jacques-Yves, **VII:**778
Crick, Francis, **VII:**797
Cuvier, Georges, **V:**589
Darwin, Charles, **V:**606
Fleming, Sir Alexander, **VII:**1166
Florey, Baron, **VII:**1172
Haeckel, Ernst, **V:**1018
Harvey, William, **IV:**626
Hevesy, Georg von, **VIII:**1654
Houssay, Bernardo Alberto, **VIII:**1759
Jacob, François, **VIII:**1827
Leeuwenhoek, Antoni van, **IV:**825
Oparin, Aleksandr Ivanovich, **IX:**2830
Pasteur, Louis, **VI:**1744
Pauling, Linus, **IX:**2926
Piaget, Jean, **IX:**2990
Smith, Theobald, **IX:**3450
Spallanzani, Lazzaro, **IV:**1260
Waksman, Selman Abraham, **IX:**3833
Watson, James D., **IX:**3897
Weismann, August, **VI:**2348

BOTANY. ***See also*** **HORTICULTURE**
Bligh, William, **IV:**143
Cohn, Ferdinand Julius, **V:**534
Humboldt, Alexander von, **V:**1159
Kämpfer, Engelbert, **IV:**754
Linnaeus, **IV:**846
Malpighi, Marcello, **IV:**891
Oparin, Aleksandr Ivanovich, **IX:**2830
Vavilov, Nikolai Ivanovich, **IX:**3801

BOXING. ***See*** **SPORTS**

BROADCAST JOURNALISM. ***See*** **JOURNALISM; RADIO; TELEVISION**

BUSINESS AND INDUSTRY. ***See also*** **BANKING AND FINANCE; ECONOMICS**
Astor, John J., **V:**82
Boulton, Matthew, **IV:**182
Carnegie, Andrew, **V:**420
Chanel, Coco, **VII:**648
Citroën, André-Gustave, **VII:**695
Duke, James Buchanan, **V:**704
Du Pont, Eleuthère Irénée, **V:**718
Eads, James Buchanan, **V:**729
Eastman, George, **VII:**996
Ferrari, Enzo, **VII:**1150
Field, Marshall, **V:**783
Ford, Henry, **VII:**1184
Gadsden, James, **V:**858
Geddes, Norman Bel, **VII:**1319
Guggenheim, Daniel, **VIII:**1498
Hill, James Jerome, **IV:**659
Honda, Soichiro, **VIII:**1724
Krupp, Alfred, **VI:**1301
Lesseps, Ferdinand de, **VI:**1355
Lumière, Auguste and Louis, **VIII:**2276
Matsushita, Konosuke, **VIII:**2457
Mellon, Andrew, **VIII:**2480
Michelin, André and Édouard, **VIII:**2514
Morita, Akio, **VIII:**2622
Owen, Robert, **VI:**1708
Paterson, William, **IV:**1066
Perot, H. Ross, **IX:**2973
Pirelli Family, The, **IX:**3020

Revere, Paul, **IV:**1156
Rhodes, Cecil, **VI:**1873
Rockefeller, John D., **VI:**1896
Rolls, Charles Stewart, **IX:**3209
Rothschild Family, The, **VI:**1916
Royce, Sir Frederick Henry, **IX:**3209
Slater, Samuel, **VI:**2074
Stanford, Leland, **VI:**2096
Taylor, Frederick Winslow, **IX:**3618
Toyoda, Eiji, **IX:**3719
Vanderbilt, Cornelius, **VI:**2296
Walker, Madam C.J., **IX:**3853
Ward, Montgomery, **VI:**2331
Wedgwood, Josiah, **IV:**1421
Wilkinson, John, **IV:**1443
Winfrey, Oprah, **IX:**4029

CAESARS. ***See*** **ROMAN CAESARS**

CARTOGRAPHY. ***See also*** **GEOGRAPHY**
Lavoisier, Antoine-Laurent, **IV:**805
Mercator, Gerardus, **III:**513
Vespucci, Amerigo, **III:**758

CARTOON ILLUSTRATION. ***See*** **ART**

CHEMISTRY. ***See also*** **BIOCHEMISTRY**
Arrhenius, Svante August, **VII:**114
Avogadro, Amedeo, **V:**98
Becquerel Family, The, **V:**166
Bergius, Friedrich, **VII:**275
Bohr, Niels, **VII:**345
Boyle, Robert, **IV:**185
Cavendish, Henry, **IV:**261
Claude, Georges, **VII:**699
Curie, Pierre and Marie, **VII:**811
Dalton, John, **V:**602
Davy, Sir Humphry, **V:**621
Diels, Otto Paul Hermann, **VII:**927
Ehrlich, Paul, **VII:**1032
Faraday, Michael, **V:**767
Gay-Lussac, Joseph-Louis, **V:**897
Gibbs, Josiah Willard, **V:**923
Haber, Fritz, **VIII:**1509
Hahn, Otto, **VIII:**1513
Hevesy, Georg von, **VIII:**1654
Jabir ibn Hayyan, **II:**522
Joliot, Frédéric, and Irène Joliot-Curie, **VIII:**1870
Lavoisier, Antoine-Laurent, **IV:**805
Leblanc, Nicolas, **IV:**813
Liebig, Justus von, **VI:**1366
Lomonosov, Mikhail Vasilyevich, **IV:**860
Mendeleyev, Dmitry Ivanovich, **VI:**1529
Monge, Gaspard, **IV:**975
Natta, Giulio, **VIII:**2698
Nernst, Walther Hermann, **VIII:**2713
Ostwald, Wilhelm, **IX:**2855
Paracelsus, **III:**584
Pasteur, Louis, **VI:**1744
Pauling, Linus, **IX:**2926
Spallanzani, Lazzaro, **IV:**1260
Stahl, Georg Ernst, **IV:**1268
Staudinger, Hermann, **IX:**3497
Volta, Alessandro, **IV:**1387
Weizmann, Chaim, **IX:**3930
Wöhler, Friedrich, **VI:**2403
Woodward, Robert Burns, **IX:**4052

CHURCH GOVERNMENT. ***See also*** **CHURCH REFORM; GOVERNMENT AND POLITICS; MONASTICISM; POPES; RELIGION AND THEOLOGY**
Boniface VIII, **II:**171
Gregory VII, **II:**395

CHURCH REFORM. ***See also*** **CHURCH GOVERNMENT; MONASTICISM; RELIGION AND THEOLOGY; SOCIAL REFORM**
Bernard of Clairvaux, Saint, **II:**143
Boleyn, Anne, **III:**66
Brunner, Emil, **VII:**475
Bucer, Martin, **III:**101
Catherine of Aragon, **III:**136
Clement VII, **III:**166
Colet, John, **III:**169
Fulbert of Chartres, Saint, **II:**373
Hus, Jan, **II:**487
John XXIII, **VIII:**1858
John of the Cross, Saint, **III:**401
John Paul II, **VIII:**1862
Leo XIII, **VI:**1347
Luther, Martin, **III:**443
Marguerite of Navarre, **III:**467
Menno Simons, **III:**510
Nicholas V, **III:**559
Niemöller, Martin, **VIII:**2742
Paul VI, **IX:**2919
Philip the Magnanimous, **III:**603
Pius V, **III:**616
Ridley, Nicholas, **III:**654
Teresa of Ávila, Saint, **III:**713
Torquemada, Tomás de, **III:**725

Zinzendorf, Graf von, **IV:**1488
Zwingli, Huldrych, **III:**791

CIVIL RIGHTS. ***See also*** **SOCIAL REFORM; WOMEN'S RIGHTS**
Abernathy, Ralph David, **VII:**9
Beauvoir, Simone de, **VII:**230
Bunche, Ralph, **VII:**501
Buxton, Sir Thomas Fowell, **V:**378
Chase, Salmon P., **V:**477
Douglass, Frederick, **V:**695
du Bois, W.E.B., **VII:**963
Forten, Charlotte, **V:**807
Gandhi, Mahatma, **VII:**1282
Garvey, Marcus, **VII:**1311
Jackson, Jesse L., **VIII:**1824
Kennedy, Robert F., **VIII:**1932
King, Martin Luther, Jr., **VIII:**1971
Lincoln, Abraham, **VI:**1380
Lutuli, Albert, **VIII:**2281
Malcolm X, **VIII:**2373
Mandela, Nelson, **VIII:**2384
Parks, Rosa, **IX:**2888
Randolph, A. Philip, **IX:**3112
Robeson, Paul, **IX:**3187
Robinson, Jackie, **IX:**3193
Sakharov, Andrei, **IX:**3296
Scott, Dred, **VI:**1999
Stevens, Thaddeus, **VI:**2136
Sumner, Charles, **VI:**2170
Truth, Sojourner, **VI:**2255
Tubman, Harriet, **VI:**2264
Turner, Nat, **VI:**2276
Tutu, Desmond, **IX:**3775
Wells-Barnett, Ida B., **IX:**3941
White, Walter, **IX:**3961
Wiesel, Elie, **IX:**3980

COLONIAL ADMINISTRATION. ***See also*** **EXPLORATION AND COLONIZATION**
Carleton, Guy, **IV:**246
Césaire, Aimé, **VII:**631
Éboué, Félix, **VII:**1004
Faidherbe, Louis, **V:**763
Goldie, Sir George, **V:**953
Las Casas, Bartolomé de, **III:**413
Lawrence, First Baron, **VI:**1331
Outram, Sir James, **VI:**1705
Rhodes, Cecil, **VI:**1873

COLONIZATION. ***See*** **EXPLORATION AND COLONIZATION**

COMPUTER SCIENCE
Babbage, Charles, **V:**101
Neumann, John von, **VIII:**2724
Turing, Alan Mathison, **IX:**3768

CONQUEST. ***See*** **EXPLORATION AND COLONIZATION; WARFARE AND CONQUEST**

CONSERVATION AND ENVIRONMENTALISM
Carson, Rachel, **VII:**585
Lindbergh, Charles A., **VIII:**2193
Muir, John, **VI:**1608
Roosevelt, Theodore, **IX:**3228
Ward, Montgomery, **VI:**2331

COSMOLOGY. ***See*** **ASTRONOMY; NATURAL HISTORY; PHYSICS**

DANCE. ***See also*** **THEATER AND ENTERTAINMENT**
Astaire, Fred, **VII:**125
Balanchine, George, **VII:**155
Danilova, Alexandra, **VII:**832
de Mille, Agnes, **VII:**874
Diaghilev, Sergei, **VII:**919
Duncan, Isadora, **VII:**980
Dunham, Katherine, **VII:**984
Fonteyn, Dame Margot, **VII:**1175
Fuller, Loie, **VII:**1261
Graham, Martha, **VIII:**1455
Laban, Rudolf, **VIII:**2058
Lifar, Serge, **VIII:**2182
Massine, Léonide, **VIII:**2448
Nijinsky, Vaslav, **VIII:**2746
Pavlova, Anna, **IX:**2937
Tallchief, Maria, **IX:**3607

DENTISTRY. ***See*** **MEDICINE**

DIPLOMACY. ***See also*** **GOVERNMENT AND POLITICS**
Abbas, Ferhat, **VII:**5
Acheson, Dean, **VII:**16
Albright, Madeleine, **VII:**49
Alva, Duke of, **III:**18
Angell, Norman, **VII:**74
Bancroft, George, **V:**124
Beust, Friedrich von, **V:**222
Bevin, Ernest, **VII:**313
Bodley, Sir Thomas, **III:**62

Botha, Louis, **VII:**376
Boutros-Ghali, Boutros, **VII:**399
Bülow, Bernhard von, **VII:**494
Bunche, Ralph, **VII:**501
Burton, Sir Richard Francis, **V:**374
Castlereagh, Viscount, **V:**438
Chou En-lai, **VII:**676
Conant, James Bryant, **VII:**748
Coubertin, Pierre de, **VII:**774
Covilhã, Pêro da, **III:**197
Cushing, Caleb, **V:**581
Dulles, John Foster, **VII:**976
Eban, Abba, **VII:**1000
Eden, Anthony, **VII:**1015
Evatt, Herbert Vere, **VII:**1109
Gadsden, James, **V:**858
Hammarskjöld, Dag, **VIII:**1529
Hardenberg, Karl von, **V:**1033
Harriman, William Averell, **VIII:**1560
Hay, John, **V:**1068
Hein, Piet, **IV:**644
Herzl, Theodor, **V:**1102
Hiss, Alger, **VIII:**1683
Holstein, Friedrich von, **V:**1130
Hughes, Charles Evans, **VIII:**1766
Hull, Cordell, **VIII:**1779
Irving, Washington, **V:**1192
Kirkpatrick, Jeane, **VIII:**1994
Kissinger, Henry A., **VIII:**1998
La Fontaine, Henri-Marie, **VIII:**2051
Lesseps, Ferdinand de, **VI:**1355
Litvinov, Maksim Maksimovich, **VIII:**2208
Marlborough, First Duke of, **IV:**922
Marshall, George C., **VIII:**2429
Medici, Lorenzo de', **III:**495
Metternich, **VI:**1544
Molotov, Vyacheslav Mikhailovich, **VIII:**2571
Monnet, Jean, **VIII:**2583
Mornay, Philippe de, **III:**537
Nicholas V, **III:**559
O'Kelly, Seán T., **IX:**2804
Oldenbarnevelt, Johan van, **III:**574
Palmerston, Lord, **VI:**1719
Pandit, Vijaya Lakshmi, **IX:**2867
Pérez de Cuéllar, Javier, **IX:**2957
Perry, Matthew C., **VI:**1760
Pius XI, **IX:**3026
Pius XII, **IX:**3030
Pocahontas, **IV:**1106
Rabi, Isidor Isaac, **IX:**3101
Root, Elihu, **IX:**3232
Salisbury, First Earl of, **III:**660
Seward, William H., **VI:**2037
Stanhope, First Earl, **IV:**1277
Stimson, Henry L., **IX:**3537
Thant, U, **IX:**3646
Waldheim, Kurt, **IX:**3841
Webster, Daniel, **VI:**2344
Yamani, Ahmad Zaki, **IX:**4079

DRAMA. ***See*** **THEATER AND ENTERTAINMENT**

ECONOMICS. ***See also*** **BANKING AND FINANCE; BUSINESS AND INDUSTRY**
Beveridge, Lord, **VII:**308
Erhard, Ludwig, **VII:**1094
George, Henry, **V:**906
Greenspan, Alan, **VIII:**1471
Keynes, John Maynard, **VIII:**1952
Lassalle, Ferdinand, **VI:**1323
Malthus, Thomas Robert, **VI:**1467
Marx, Karl, **VI:**1492
Mendès-France, Pierre, **VIII:**2491
Mill, James, **VI:**1556
Mill, John Stuart, **VI:**1559
Monnet, Jean, **VIII:**2583
Myrdal, Gunnar, **VIII:**2671
Proudhon, Pierre-Joseph, **VI:**1817
Ricardo, David, **VI:**1878
Smith, Adam, **IV:**1249
Turgot, Anne-Robert-Jacques, **IV:**1348
Veblen, Thorstein, **IX:**3805
Walras, Léon, **IX:**3865
Webb, Beatrice and Sidney, **IX:**3905

EDUCATION. ***See also*** **HISTORIOGRAPHY; SCHOLARSHIP**
'Abduh, Muhammad, **V:**4
Adler, Alfred, **VII:**30
Adler, Felix, **V:**26
Agassiz, Louis, **V:**30
Ahmad Khan, Sir Sayyid, **V:**34
Albertus Magnus, Saint, **II:**37
Alcott, Bronson, **V:**37
Alcuin, **II:**44
Anthony of Padua, Saint, **II:**76
Arnold, Thomas, **V:**74
Arthur, Chester A., **V:**77
Bacon, Roger, **II:**110
Balch, Emily Greene, **VII:**160
Barnard, Henry, **V:**130
Barton, Clara, **V:**142

Basedow, Johann Bernhard, **IV:**92
Beale, Dorothea, **V:**157
Beecher, Catharine, **V:**170
Bell, Alexander Graham, **V:**185
Beneš, Edvard, **VII:**259
Beveridge, Lord, **VII:**308
Bodley, Sir Thomas, **III:**62
Brougham, Henry, **V:**314
Bunche, Ralph, **VII:**501
Butler, Nicholas Murray, **VII:**524
Butler, R.A., **VII:**529
Carver, George Washington, **VII:**602
Chang Chih-tung, **V:**466
Chu Hsi, **II:**265
Colet, John, **III:**169
Conant, James Bryant, **VII:**748
Condorcet, Marquis de, **IV:**348
Confucius, **I:**222
Dawidowicz, Lucy S., **VII:**847
Dewey, Melvil, **V:**660
Dunham, Katherine, **VII:**984
Eliot, Charles William, **V:**748
Erasmus, Desiderius, **III:**246
Fisher, Saint John, **III:**264
Flexner, Abraham, **VII:**1169
Forster, William Edward, **V:**804
Forten, Charlotte, **V:**807
Froebel, Friedrich, **V:**845
Fulbert of Chartres, Saint, **II:**373
Gentile, Giovanni, **VII:**1336
Green, Thomas Hill, **V:**987
Harper, William Rainey, **V:**1044
Howe, Samuel Gridley, **V:**1150
Hutchins, Robert M., **VIII:**1800
Isidore of Seville, Saint, **II:**518
Jiménez de Cisneros, Francisco, **III:**392
Jordan, Barbara, **VIII:**1887
Kay-Shuttleworth, First Baronet, **VIII:**1917
Keller, Helen, **VIII:**1924
Lancaster, Joseph, **VI:**1309
Langer, Susanne K., **VIII:**2087
Laski, Harold J., **VIII:**2093
Lyon, Mary, **VI:**1423
McGuffey, William Holmes, **VI:**1440
Mackinder, Sir Halford John, **VIII:**2321
Mann, Horace, **IV:**894
Mather, Increase, **IV:**938
Maurice, Frederick Denison, **VI:**1503
Melanchthon, Philipp, **III:**503
Millikan, Robert Andrews, **VIII:**2539
Montessori, Maria, **VIII:**2596
Naidu, Sarojini, **VIII:**2683
Natta, Giulio, **VIII:**2698
Neckam, Alexander, **II:**663
Palmer, Alice Freeman, **VI:**1715
Pestalozzi, Johann Heinrich, **VI:**1767
Piaget, Jean, **IX:**2990
Protagoras, **I:**705
Raman, Sir Chandrasekhara Venkata, **IX:**3109
Rousseau, Jean-Jacques, **IV:**1194
Sagan, Carl, **IX:**3292
Seaborg, Glenn Theodore, **IX:**3375
Seton, Saint Elizabeth Ann Bayley, **VI:**2029
Sidgwick, Henry, **VI:**2062
Spock, Benjamin, **IX:**3478
Stanford, Leland, **VI:**2096
Steinmetz, Charles Proteus, **VI:**2121
Stone, Harlan Fiske, **IX:**3546
Sylvester II, **II:**869
Talbot, Marion, **IX:**3603
Thayer, Sylvanus, **VI:**2223
Thorndike, Edward L., **IX:**3669
Verrius Flaccus, Marcus, **I:**930
Vincent de Paul, Saint, **IV:**1380
Webster, Noah, **IV:**1417
Willard, Emma, **VI:**2384
Willard, Frances, **VI:**2388
Wise, Isaac Mayer, **VI:**2400
Witherspoon, John, **IV:**1467

ELECTRONICS. ***See*** **COMPUTER SCIENCE; INVENTION AND TECHNOLOGY**

EMPERORS. ***See*** **ROMAN EMPERORS**

EMPIRE-BUILDING. ***See*** **COLONIAL ADMINISTRATION; EXPLORATION AND COLONIZATION; GOVERNMENT AND POLITICS; WARFARE AND CONQUEST**

ENGINEERING. ***See also*** **AVIATION AND SPACE EXPLORATION; INVENTION AND TECHNOLOGY**
Bergius, Friedrich, **VII:**275
Braun, Wernher von, **VII:**440
Brindley, James, **IV:**201
Brunel, Isambard Kingdom, **V:**335
Brunel, Marc Isambard, **V:**339
Citroën, André-Gustave, **VII:**695
Cousteau, Jacques-Yves, **VII:**778
Daimler, Gottlieb, **V:**597

Eads, James Buchanan, **V:**729
Ferrari, Enzo, **VII:**1150
Fitch, John, **IV:**476
Freyssinet, Eugène, **VII:**1228
Fuller, R. Buckminster, **VII:**1265
Fulton, Robert, **V:**854
Gadsden, James, **V:**858
Goethals, George Washington, **VIII:**1408
Hounsfield, Godfrey Newbold, **VIII:**1751
Latrobe, Benjamin Henry, **VI:**1327
Monge, Gaspard, **IV:**975
Nasmyth, James, **VI:**1624
Newcomen, Thomas, **IV:**1022
Picard, Émile, **IX:**2994
Popov, Aleksandr Stepanovich, **VI:**1806
Prandtl, Ludwig, **IX:**3073
Roebling, John Augustus, **VI:**1904
Rolls, Charles Stewart, **IX:**3209
Royce, Sir Frederick Henry, **IX:**3209
Steinmetz, Charles Proteus, **VI:**2121
Stephenson, George, **VI:**2132
Telford, Thomas, **VI:**2207
Tesla, Nikola, **VI:**2219
Thayer, Sylvanus, **VI:**2223
Trevithick, Richard, **VI:**2251
Vauban, Sébastien Le Prestre de, **IV:**1358
Whittle, Sir Frank, **IX:**3972
Xenakis, Iannis, **IX:**4075

ENTERTAINMENT. ***See*** **THEATER AND ENTERTAINMENT**

ENVIRONMENTALISM. ***See*** **CONSERVATION AND ENVIRONMENTALISM**

ETHICS. ***See*** **PHILOSOPHY; RELIGION AND THEOLOGY**

EXPLORATION AND COLONIZATION. ***See also*** **AVIATION AND SPACE EXPLORATION; COLONIAL ADMINISTRATION; WARFARE AND CONQUEST**
Alvarado, Pedro de, **III:**21
Amundsen, Roald, **VII:**66
Austin, Stephen Fuller, **V:**94
Balboa, Vasco Núñez de, **III:**45
Bering, Vitus Jonassen, **IV:**111
Bligh, William, **IV:**143
Boone, Daniel, **IV:**163
Bougainville, Louis-Antoine de, **IV:**179
Bruce, James, **IV:**208
Burton, Sir Richard Francis, **V:**374
Byrd, Richard E., **VII:**534
Cabot, John, **III:**113
Calamity Jane, **V:**390
Carpini, Giovanni da Pian del, **II:**206
Carson, Kit, **V:**429
Cartier, Jacques, **III:**129
Cavendish, Thomas, **III:**140
Champlain, Samuel de, **IV:**271
Cheng Ho, **II:**253
Citroën, André-Gustave, **VII:**695
Clark, William, **VI:**1358
Columbus, Christopher, **III:**172
Cook, Captain James, **IV:**351
Coronado, Francisco Vásquez de, **III:**180
Cortés, Hernán, **III:**188
Covilhã, Pêro da, **III:**197
Crockett, David, **V:**578
Dampier, William, **IV:**389
Davis, John, **III:**212
Dias, Bartolomeu, **III:**215
Drake, Sir Francis, **III:**224
Frémont, John C., **V:**839
Gama, Vasco da, **III:**287
Hanno, **I:**368
Hayden, Ferdinand Vandeveer, **V:**1072
Henry the Navigator, Prince, **III:**354
Heyerdahl, Thor, **VIII:**1658
Hillary, Sir Edmund, **VIII:**1662
Hsüan-tsang, **II:**482
Hudson, Henry, **IV:**680
Ibn Battutah, **II:**495
Jolliet, Louis, **IV:**732
La Salle, Sieur de, **IV:**793
Leif Eriksson, **II:**577
Lewis, Meriwether, **VI:**1358
Livingstone, David, **VI:**1399
Lugard, Lord, **VIII:**2269
Mackenzie, Sir Alexander, **IV:**879
Magellan, Ferdinand, **III:**453
Mas'udi, al-, **II:**636
Messner, Reinhold, **VIII:**2506
Muir, John, **VI:**1608
Nansen, Fridtjof, **VIII:**2686
Oglethorpe, James Edward, **IV:**1043
Park, Mungo, **VI:**1723
Peary, Robert Edwin, **IX:**2941
Pike, Zebulon Montgomery, **IV:**1094
Pinzon Brothers, The, **III:**610
Pizarro, Francisco, **III:**620
Polo, Marco, **II:**750

Ponce de Léon, Juan, **III:**629
Powell, John Wesley, **VI:**1810
Pytheas, **I:**731
Raleigh, Sir Walter, **III:**638
Rasmussen, Knud Johan Victor, **IX:**3121
Ross, Sir James Clark, **VI:**1907
Sacagawea, **VI:**1933
Smith, Jedediah Strong, **VI:**2077
Smith, John, **IV:**1253
Soto, Hernando de, **III:**699
Speke, John Hanning, **VI:**2083
Standish, Miles, **IV:**1273
Stanley, Henry Morton, **VI:**2101
Tasman, Abel Janszoon, **IV:**1313
Vancouver, George, **IV:**1355
Vespucci, Amerigo, **III:**758
Wilkes, Charles, **VI:**2381
Wilkins, Sir George Hubert, **IX:**3999
William of Rubrouck, **II:**987
Workman, Fanny Bullock, **VI:**2410

FASHION
Chanel, Coco, **VII:**648

FILM. ***See also*** **TELEVISION; THEATER AND ENTERTAINMENT**
Arzner, Dorothy, **VII:**117
Astaire, Fred, **VII:**125
Ball, Lucille, **VII:**176
Bergman, Ingmar, **VII:**278
Brando, Marlon, **VII:**424
Buñuel, Luis, **VII:**505
Chaplin, Charles, **VII:**653
Cocteau, Jean, **VII:**721
Coward, Noël, **VII:**783
Davis, Bette, **VII:**843
Demille, Cecil B., **VII:**896
Dietrich, Marlene, **VII:**930
Disney, Walt, **VII:**938
Dreyer, Carl Theodor, **VII:**959
Eisenstein, Sergei, **VII:**1047
Ephron, Nora, **VII:**1083
Fellini, Federico, **VII:**1141
Gance, Abel, **VII:**1274
Garbo, Greta, **VII:**1286
Garland, Judy, **VII:**1304
Gish, Lillian, **VII:**1383
Godard, Jean-Luc, **VII:**1391
Goldwyn, Samuel, **VIII:**1415
Griffith, D.W., **VIII:**1478
Hayworth, Rita, **VIII:**1596
Hellman, Lillian, **VIII:**1620
Henie, Sonja, **VIII:**1629
Hepburn, Katharine, **VIII:**1637
Hitchcock, Alfred, **VIII:**1687
King, Stephen, **VIII:**1977
Kurosawa, Akira, **VIII:**2043
Lang, Fritz, **VIII:**2077
Loos, Anita, **VIII:**2231
Monroe, Marilyn, **VIII:**2587
Olivier, Sir Laurence, **IX:**2808
Pickford, Mary, **IX:**3006
Ray, Satyajit, **IX:**3132
Renoir, Jean, **IX:**3157
Stewart, James, **IX:**3528
Truffaut, François, **IX:**3736
Visconti, Luchino, **IX:**3818
Wayne, John, **IX:**3901
Welles, Orson, **IX:**3934
West, Mae, **IX:**3949
Winfrey, Oprah, **IX:**4029
Zanuck, Darryl F., **IX:**4100

FINANCE. ***See*** **BANKING AND FINANCE**

GENETICS
Crick, Francis, **VII:**797
Galton, Francis, **V:**867
Jacob, François, **VIII:**1827
Mendel, Gregor Johann, **VI:**1526
Morgan, Thomas Hunt, **VIII:**2618
Muller, Hermann Joseph, **VIII:**2651
Vavilov, Nikolai Ivanovich, **IX:**3801
Watson, James D., **IX:**3897
Weismann, August, **VI:**2348

GEOGRAPHY. ***See also*** **CARTOGRAPHY**
Anaximander, **I:**50
Benjamin of Tudela, **II:**140
Braudel, Fernand, **VII:**436
Covilhã, Pêro da, **III:**197
Eratosthenes of Cyrene, **I:**303
Hipparchus, **I:**407
Humboldt, Alexander von, **V:**1159
Idrisi, al-, **II:**506
Khwarizmi, al-, **II:**563
Mackinder, Sir Halford John, **VIII:**2321
Mas'udi, al-, **II:**636
Maury, Matthew Fontaine, **VI:**1507
Mercator, Gerardus, **III:**513
Rasmussen, Knud Johan Victor, **IX:**3121
Strabo, **I:**828
Tasman, Abel Janszoon, **IV:**1313
Workman, Fanny Bullock, **VI:**2410

GEOLOGY

Agricola, Georgius, **III:**1
Baer, Karl Ernst von, **V:**109
Lyell, Sir Charles, **VI:**1418
Spallanzani, Lazzaro, **IV:**1260
Teilhard de Chardin, Pierre, **IX:**3626
Wegener, Alfred, **IX:**3918

GOLF. ***See*** **SPORTS**

GOVERNMENT AND POLITICS. ***See also*** **CHURCH GOVERNMENT; COLONIAL ADMINISTRATION; DIPLOMACY; HOLY ROMAN EMPERORS; LAW; MILITARY AFFAIRS; MONARCHY; PHARAOHS; PUBLIC ADMINISTRATION; ROMAN CAESAR; ROMAN EMPERORS; WARFARE AND CONQUEST**

Abahai, **IV:**1
Abbas, Ferhat, **VII:**5
'Abbās the Great, **IV:**4
'Abd al-Mu'min, **II:**4
'Abd-al-Rahman III al-Nasir, **II:**7
Abdelkader, **V:**1
'Abduh, Muhammad, **V:**4
Acheson, Dean, **VII:**16
Adams, John, **IV:**16
Adams, John Quincy, **V:**20
Adams, Samuel, **IV:**21
Adenauer, Konrad, **VII:**26
Afonso I, **II:**30
Agesilaus II, **I:**16
Agrippa, Marcus Vipsanius, **I:**20
Akhenaton, **I:**23
Akiba ben Joseph, **I:**27
Akihito, **VII:**41
Alboin, **II:**41
Albright, Madeleine, **VII:**49
Albuquerque, Afonso de, **III:**11
Alcibiades, **I:**31
Alexander I, **V:**44
Alexander II, **V:**48
Alexander VI, **III:**14
Alexander Nevsky, **II:**52
Alexander the Great, **I:**38
Alfonso X, **II:**56
Alp Arslan, **II:**67
Altgeld, John Peter, **V:**54
Ambrose, Saint, **I:**43
Antigonus I Monophthalmos, **I:**60
Antony, Marc, **I:**69
Aquino, Corazon, **VII:**86
Arafat, Yasir, **VII:**90
Árpád, **II:**86
Arthur, Chester A., **V:**77
Ashikaga Takauji, **II:**97
Ashurbanipal, **I:**105
Ashurnasirpal II, **I:**109
Aśoka the Great, **I:**112
Aspasia, **I:**115
Asquith, H.H., **VII:**121
Astor, Nancy, **VII:**129
Atatürk, Kemal, **VII:**133
Attila, **I:**124
Attlee, Clement, **VII:**137
Augustus, **I:**132
Aurangzeb, **IV:**69
Aurobindo, Sri, **VII:**141
Austin, Stephen Fuller, **V:**94
Azikiwe, Nnamdi, **VII:**144
Bābur, **III:**36
Bacon, Francis, **III:**41
Bacon, Nathaniel, **IV:**80
Baldwin, Robert, **V:**116
Baldwin, Stanley, **VII:**168
Balfour, Arthur, **VII:**172
Bancroft, George, **V:**124
Banerjea, Surendranath, **VII:**183
Barton, Sir Edmund, **V:**147
Basil the Macedonian, **II:**117
Baybars I, **II:**124
Bayezid II, **III:**51
Beaverbrook, Lord, **VII:**234
Begin, Menachem, **VII:**243
Ben-Gurion, David, **VII:**251
Beneš, Edvard, **VII:**259
Benton, Thomas Hart, **V:**195
Besant, Annie, **V:**211
Beust, Friedrich von, **V:**222
Bevan, Aneurin, **VII:**304
Bevin, Ernest, **VII:**313
Bismarck, Otto von, **V:**240
Blaine, James G., **V:**255
Blake, Robert, **IV:**132
Blanc, Louis, **V:**259
Blum, Léon, **VII:**335
Bolingbroke, First Viscount, **IV:**157
Bolívar, Simón, **V:**267
Bondfield, Margaret, **VII:**353
Boniface VIII, **II:**171
Borah, William E., **V:**279
Borden, Robert Laird, **VII:**365
Boris I of Bulgaria, **II:**175
Botha, Louis, **VII:**376

Bottomley, Horatio W., **VII:**382
Bourguiba, Habib, **VII:**391
Boutros-Ghali, Boutros, **VII:**399
Bradford, William, **IV:**189
Brandt, Willy, **VII:**427
Brezhnev, Leonid Ilich, **VII:**459
Bright, John, **V:**306
Brougham, Henry, **V:**314
Brown, George, **V:**318
Bruni, Leonardo, **III:**93
Brutus, Marcus Junius, **I:**140
Bryan, William Jennings, **VII:**479
Buchanan, James, **V:**346
Buckingham, First Duke of, **IV:**211
Bukharin, Nikolai Ivanovich, **VII:**491
Bulfinch, Charles, **V:**349
Bülow, Bernhard von, **VII:**494
Burgh, Hubert de, **II:**190
Burr, Aaron, **V:**369
Bush, George, **VII:**520
Butler, R.A., **VII:**529
Caesar, Julius, **I:**147
Calhoun, John C., **V:**394
Caligula, **I:**152
Calles, Plutarco Elías, **VII:**542
Cambacérès, Jean-Jacques-Régis de, **V:**398
Campbell, Kim, **VII:**549
Canning, George, **V:**405
Cárdenas, Lázaro, **VII:**571
Carlos, Don, **V:**413
Carroll, Charles, **IV:**250
Carter, Jimmy, **VII:**589
Casimir the Great, **II:**210
Cassiodorus, **II:**215
Cassius (Longinus), **I:**159
Castlereagh, Viscount, **V:**438
Castro, Fidel, **VII:**617
Catherine de Médicis, **III:**132
Catherine of Siena, Saint, **II:**218
Cato the Censor, **I:**162
Cato the Younger, **I:**166
Cavour, Count, **V:**446
Cecil, William, **III:**147
Chamberlain, Joseph, **V:**462
Chamberlain, Neville, **VII:**643
Chang Chih-tung, **V:**466
Charles V, **III:**159
Charles XIV John, **V:**474
Charles d'Orléans, **II:**232
Charles Martel, **II:**242
Charles the Bold, **III:**163
Chartier, Alain, **II:**245
Chase, Salmon P., **V:**477
Ch'en Tu-hsiu, **VII:**660
Cheng Ch'eng-kung, **IV:**297
Cheng Ho, **II:**253
Chiang Kai-shek, **VII:**664
Ch'ien-lung, **IV:**300
Ch'in Shih Huang-ti, **I:**176
Chisholm, Shirley, **VII:**668
Chou En-lai, **VII:**676
Chrétien, Jean, **VII:**680
Christophe, Henri, **V:**501
Chu Hsi, **II:**265
Chu Teh, **VII:**687
Ch'ü Yüan, **I:**187
Churchill, Sir Winston, **VII:**691
Cicero, **I:**194
Cimon, **I:**198
Claudius I, **I:**203
Clay, Henry, **V:**507
Cleisthenes of Athens, **I:**207
Clemenceau, Georges, **VII:**702
Cleomenes, **I:**214
Cleopatra VII, **I:**218
Cleveland, Grover, **V:**512
Clinton, Bill, **VII:**707
Clinton, DeWitt, **V:**517
Clinton, Hillary Rodham, **VII:**713
Clovis, **II:**274
Cobbett, William, **V:**522
Cobden, Richard, **V:**526
Collins, Michael, **VII:**733
Constantine, Baron, **VII:**759
Constantine the Great, **I:**226
Coolidge, Calvin, **VII:**762
Cornwallis, First Marquess, **IV:**367
Cosgrave, William T., **VII:**770
Croce, Benedetto, **VII:**801
Crockett, David, **V:**578
Cromwell, Oliver, **IV:**378
Cromwell, Thomas, **III:**208
Curtin, John, **VII:**816
Curzon, Lord, **VII:**819
Cushing, Caleb, **V:**581
Cyrus the Great, **I:**233
Dalhousie, First Marquess of, **V:**600
Dandolo, Enrico, **II:**282
Danton, Georges, **IV:**393
Darius the Great, **I:**236
Davis, Jefferson, **V:**614
Dayan, Moshe, **VII:**854
Deák, Ferenc, **V:**625
Deakin, Alfred, **V:**630

Debs, Eugene V., **VII:**880
de Gasperi, Alcide, **VII:**862
de Gaulle, Charles, **VII:**866
de Klerk, F.W., **VII:**870
Demosthenes, **I:**253
Deng Xiaoping, **VII:**905
Derby, Fourteenth Earl of, **V:**652
de Valera, Eamon, **VII:**877
Diocletian, **I:**263
Disraeli, Benjamin, **V:**675
Djilas, Milovan, **VII:**944
Dole, Robert J., **VII:**947
Dorgon, **IV:**421
Douglas, Stephen A., **V:**692
Draco, **I:**280
Dubcek, Alexander, **VII:**968
Dulles, John Foster, **VII:**976
Durham, First Earl of, **V:**721
Eban, Abba, **VII:**1000
Éboué, Félix, **VII:**1004
Eden, Anthony, **VII:**1015
Edward VII, **VII:**1020
Eisenhower, Dwight D., **VII:**1043
Elizabeth II, **VII:**1062
Engels, Friedrich, **V:**760
Enver Pasha, **VII:**1078
Epaminondas, **I:**290
Erhard, Ludwig, **VII:**1094
Erzberger, Matthias, **VII:**1102
Evatt, Herbert Vere, **VII:**1109
Fabius Maximus, Quintus, **I:**334
Fahd, **VII:**1115
Fairfax, Third Baron, **IV:**446
Faisal, **VII:**1118
Faisal I, **VII:**1122
Fawkes, Guy, **III:**257
Feinstein, Dianne, **VII:**1137
Ferdinand II and Isabella I, **III:**260
Ferraro, Geraldine, **VII:**1153
Fillmore, Millard, **V:**792
Ford, Gerald R., **VII:**1180
Forster, William Edward, **V:**804
Fox, Charles James, **IV:**479
Francis Ferdinand, **VII:**1197
Francis Joseph I, **V:**829
Franco, Francisco, **VII:**1200
Franklin, Benjamin, **IV:**492
Frederick William, the Great Elector, **IV:**508
Frémont, John C., **V:**839
Fujiwara Michinaga, **II:**370
Gallatin, Albert, **V:**861
Gambetta, Léon, **V:**871
Gandhi, Indira, **VII:**1278
Gandhi, Mahatma, **VII:**1282
Gardiner, Stephen, **III:**291
Garfield, James A., **V:**875
Genghis Khan, **II:**376
Genseric, **I:**342
Gentile, Giovanni, **VII:**1336
George IV, **V:**902
George V, **VII:**1339
George VI, **VII:**1343
Ghazan, Mahmud, **II:**381
Gioberti, Vincenzo, **V:**932
Gladstone, William Ewart, **V:**935
Glenn, John H., Jr., **VII:**1387
Godolphin, First Earl of, **IV:**552
Godunov, Boris Fyodorovich, **III:**308
Goebbels, Joseph, **VIII:**1404
Gorbachev, Mikhail, **VIII:**1423
Gore, Albert, **VIII:**1431
Göring, Hermann, **VIII:**1438
Gracchi, The, **I:**345
Gramsci, Antonio, **VIII:**1459
Grant, Ulysses S., **V:**975
Greenspan, Alan, **VIII:**1471
Gregory the Great, **II:**407
Grey, Second Earl, **V:**994
Grey, Sir George Edward, **V:**998
Guevara, Che, **VIII:**1494
Hadrian, **I:**356
Haile Selassie I, **VIII:**1517
Halide Edib Adivar, **VIII:**1522
Hamilton, Alexander, **IV:**608
Hammurabi, **I:**360
Hancock, John, **IV:**613
Hanna, Marcus A., **V:**1029
Hardenberg, Karl von, **V:**1033
Hardie, James Keir, **V:**1036
Harding, Warren G., **VIII:**1550
Harmsworth, Alfred and Harold, **VIII:**1554
Harriman, William Averell, **VIII:**1560
Harrison, Benjamin, **V:**1053
Harrison, William Henry, **V:**1061
Harsha, **II:**430
Harun al-Rashid, **II:**437
Hastings, Warren, **IV:**631
Hatoyama Ichiro, **VIII:**1574
Hatshepsut, **I:**371
Hatta, Mohammad, **VIII:**1577
Haya de la Torre, Víctor Raúl, **VIII:**1584
Hayes, Rutherford B., **V:**1075
Heath, Edward, **VIII:**1606
Henry IV, **III:**333

Henry, Patrick, **IV:**647
Henry the Lion, **II:**466
Heraclius, **II:**470
Herod the Great, **I:**390
Herriot, Édouard, **VIII:**1644
Himmler, Heinrich, **VIII:**1666
Hindenburg, Paul Von, **VIII:**1674
Hirohito, **VIII:**1678
Hitler, Adolf, **VIII:**1692
Hobby, Oveta Culp, **VIII:**1703
Ho Chi Minh, **VIII:**1698
Hoover, Herbert, **VIII:**1727
Hoover, J. Edgar, **VIII:**1732
Hopkins, Harry, **VIII:**1736
Houphouët-Boigny, Félix, **VIII:**1754
Houston, Sam, **V:**1137
Howe, Admiral Richard, **IV:**672
Hughes, Charles Evans, **VIII:**1766
Hughes, William Morris, **VIII:**1775
Hull, Cordell, **VIII:**1779
Humphrey, Hubert H., **VIII:**1783
Hung Hsiu-ch'üan, **V:**1165
Hunyadi, János, **III:**374
Hussein I, **VIII:**1791
Hutchinson, Thomas, **IV:**691
Ii Naosuke, **V:**1180
Ikeda, Hayato, **VIII:**1809
Innocent III, **II:**509
Innocent IV, **II:**514
İnönü, İsmet, **VIII:**1812
Itzcóatl, **III:**377
Ivan the Great, **III:**381
Ivan the Terrible, **III:**385
Jackson, Andrew, **V:**1196
Jackson, Jesse L., **VIII:**1824
Jamāl al-Dīn al-Afghānī, **V:**1207
James I, **IV:**699
James I the Conqueror, **II:**529
James II, **IV:**703
Jaurès, Jean, **V:**1221
Jefferson, Thomas, **IV:**716
Jiménez de Cisneros, Francisco, **III:**392
Jinnah, Mohammed Ali, **VIII:**1847
Joan of Arc, **III:**396
Johnson, Andrew, **V:**1232
Johnson, Lyndon B., **VIII:**1866
Jordan, Barbara, **VIII:**1887
Joséphine, **V:**1246
Juárez, Benito, **V:**1250
Justinian I, **II:**553
Kamehameha I, **VI:**1255
K'ang-Hsi, **IV:**757
Kanishka, **I:**494
Kennedy, John F., **VIII:**1928
Kennedy, Robert F., **VIII:**1932
Kenyatta, Jomo, **VIII:**1936
Kerensky, Aleksandr Fyodorovich, **VIII:**1941
Khomeini, Ruhollah, **VIII:**1957
Khosrow I, **II:**559
Khrushchev, Nikita S., **VIII:**1961
Kidd, William, **IV:**777
King, William Lyon Mackenzie, **VIII:**1981
Kirkpatrick, Jeane, **VIII:**1994
Kissinger, Henry A., **VIII:**1998
Kohl, Helmut, **VIII:**2009
Kublai Khan, **II:**566
Kuo Mo-jo, **VIII:**2033
La Follette, Robert M., **VIII:**2047
La Fontaine, Henri-Marie, **VIII:**2051
La Guardia, Fiorello Henry, **VIII:**2054
Lambert, John, **IV:**789
Lansdowne, Fifth Marquess of, **VIII:**2090
László I, Saint, **II:**574
Lathrop, Julia C., **VIII:**2096
Laurier, Sir Wilfrid, **VIII:**2100
Laval, Pierre, **VIII:**2105
Law, Bonar, **VIII:**2112
Lee Kuan Yew, **VIII:**2150
Leeds, First Duke of, **IV:**821
Lenin, Vladimir Ilich, **VIII:**2160
Leo X, **III:**419
Li Hung-chang, **VI:**1362
Li Peng, **VIII:**2178
Liebknecht, Wilhelm, **VI:**1369
Liliuokalani, **VI:**1372
Lin Piao, **VIII:**2189
Lin Tse-hsü, **VI:**1376
Lincoln, Abraham, **VI:**1380
Liu Shao-ch'i, **VIII:**2212
Liverpool, Second Earl of, **VI:**1395
Lloyd George, David, **VIII:**2216
Lodge, Henry Cabot, **VIII:**2219
Long, Huey, **VIII:**2227
Louis IX, **II:**603
Louis XI, **III:**434
Lu Hsün, **VIII:**2252
Luce, Clare Boothe, **VIII:**2256
Lugard, Lord, **VIII:**2269
Lutuli, Albert, **VIII:**2281
Lyons, Dame Enid Muriel, **VIII:**2289
Lyons, Joseph Aloysius, **VIII:**2292
Macaulay, Thomas Babington, **VI:**1427
McCarthy, Joseph R., **VIII:**2300
MacDonald, Ramsay, **VIII:**2312

Macdonald, Sir John Alexander, **VI:**1435
Machel, Samora Moisès, **VIII:**2317
Mackenzie, William Lyon, **VI:**1447
Mackinder, Sir Halford John, **VIII:**2321
McKinley, William, **VI:**1453
Macmillan, Harold, **VIII:**2340
Madero, Francisco, **VIII:**2345
Madison, Dolley, **VI:**1464
Madison, James, **IV:**886
Maecenas, Gaius, **I:**519
Mahfouz, Naguib, **VIII:**2355
Major, John, **VIII:**2369
Malenkov, Georgi M., **VIII:**2377
Malraux, André, **VIII:**2380
Mankiller, Wilma P., **VIII:**2389
Mannerheim, Carl Gustaf, **VIII:**2396
Mannix, Daniel, **VI:**1480
Mansa Mūsā, **II:**623
Mao Tse-tung, **VIII:**2400
Marat, Jean-Paul, **IV:**910
Marcos, Ferdinand E., **VIII:**2420
Marcus Aurelius, **I:**523
Margaret of Denmark, Norway, and Sweden, **II:**626
Marius, Gaius, **I:**528
Marshall, George C., **VIII:**2429
Masaryk, Tomáš, **VIII:**2440
Masinissa, **I:**535
Mason, George, **IV:**926
Massey, Vincent, **VI:**1496
Massey, William Ferguson, **VIII:**2444
Matthias I Corvinus, **III:**487
Maximilian I, **III:**491
Mazzini, Giuseppe, **VI:**1514
Medici, Lorenzo de', **III:**495
Mehmed II, **III:**499
Meir, Golda, **VIII:**2472
Melbourne, Second Viscount, **VI:**1517
Menander (Indian king), **I:**541
Mendès-France, Pierre, **VIII:**2491
Menelik II, **VI:**1537
Menes, **I:**547
Menzies, Robert Gordon, **VIII:**2497
Messalina, Valeria, **I:**550
Metternich, **VI:**1544
Miltiades the Younger, **I:**553
Mirabeau, Comte de, **IV:**963
Mithradates the Great, **I:**557
Mitterrand, François, **VIII:**2558
Mobutu Sese Seko, **VIII:**2562
Mohammad Reza Shah Pahlavi, **VIII:**2566
Mohammed I Askia, **III:**521
Molotov, Vyacheslav Mikhailovich, **VIII:**2571
Monmouth, Duke of, **IV:**980
Monnet, Jean, **VIII:**2583
Monroe, James, **VI:**1570
Montaigne, Michel de, **III:**524
Montfort, Simon V de, **II:**642
More, Sir Thomas, **III:**533
Mornay, Philippe de, **III:**537
Morris, William, **VI:**1588
Mosca, Gaetano, **VIII:**2630
Mountbatten, Louis, **VIII:**2641
Mugabe, Robert, **VIII:**2647
Muhammad, **II:**651
Muhammad 'Alī Pasha, **VI:**1604
Mulroney, Brian, **VIII:**2655
Mussolini, Benito, **VIII:**2667
Naidu, Sarojini, **VIII:**2683
Napoleon I, **VI:**1616
Napoleon III, **VI:**1620
Nasser, Gamal Abdel, **VIII:**2693
Nast, Thomas, **VI:**1627
Nebuchadnezzar II, **I:**569
Necker, Jacques, **IV:**1016
Nefertiti, **I:**573
Nehru, Jawaharlal, **VIII:**2709
Nero, **I:**577
Nezahualcóyotl, **III:**555
Nicholas I, **VI:**1650
Nikon, **IV:**1030
Nixon, Richard M., **VIII:**2758
Nizam al-Mulk, **II:**677
Nkrumah, Kwame, **VIII:**2762
Nordau, Max, **VIII:**2766
North, Lord, **IV:**1034
Nostradamus, **III:**567
Nyerere, Julius, **VIII:**2773
Oates, Titus, **IV:**1038
Obregón, Álvaro, **IX:**2781
O'Connell, Daniel, **VI:**1680
O'Connor, Sandra Day, **IX:**2789
O'Connor, Thomas Power, **IX:**2793
Oda Nobunaga, **III:**570
Odoacer, **II:**685
O'Kelly, Seán T., **IX:**2804
Olaf, Saint, **II:**691
Oldenbarnevelt, Johan van, **III:**574
Onassis, Jacqueline Kennedy, **IX:**2815
O'Neill, Thomas Philip, Jr., **IX:**2824
Orleans, Duc d', **IV:**1048
Ortega, Katherine Davalos, **IX:**2840
Osman, **II:**702
Ou-yang Hsiu, **II:**709

Oxenstierna, Axel, **IV:**1052
Pachacuti, **III:**577
Palmerston, Lord, **VI:**1719
Pandit, Vijaya Lakshmi, **IX:**2867
Papen, Franz von, **IX:**2876
Parkes, Sir Henry, **VI:**1731
Parnell, Charles Stewart, **VI:**1740
Patel, Vallabhbhai Jhaverbhai, **IX:**2903
Peel, Sir Robert, **VI:**1752
Pelham, Henry, **IV:**1074
Penn, William, **IV:**1078
Pérez de Cuéllar, Javier, **IX:**2957
Pericles, **I:**609
Perkins, Frances, **IX:**2961
Perón, Eva, **IX:**2965
Perón, Juan, **IX:**2969
Perot, H. Ross, **IX:**2973
Pétain, Philippe, **IX:**2987
Philip II of France, **II:**732
Philip II of Macedonia, **I:**628
Philip II of Spain, **III:**599
Philip IV the Fair, **II:**736
Philip the Good, **II:**740
Phillip, Arthur, **IV:**1091
Piankhi, **I:**636
Pierce, Franklin, **VI:**1775
Pilate, Pontius, **I:**640
Pirelli Family, The, **IX:**3020
Pisistratus, **I:**648
Pitt the Elder, William, **IV:**1098
Pitt the Younger, William, **IV:**1102
Pittacus of Mytilene, **I:**651
Pius II, **III:**613
Place, Francis, **VI:**1786
Pobedonostsev, Konstantin Petrovich, **VI:**1790
Poincaré, Raymond, **IX:**3044
Polk, James K., **VI:**1801
Pompey the Great, **I:**679
Pompidou, Georges, **IX:**3052
Pride, Thomas, **IV:**1126
Psamtik I, **I:**709
Psellus, Michael, **II:**758
Ptolemy Philadelphus, **I:**716
Ptolemy Soter, **I:**720
Pym, John, **IV:**1141
Qaddafi, Muammar al-, **IX:**3098
Rabanus Maurus, **II:**766
Ramses II, **I:**734
Rankin, Jeannette, **IX:**3117
Rasputin, Grigori Yefimovich, **VI:**1842
Reagan, Ronald, **IX:**3136
Reno, Janet, **IX:**3153
Revere, Paul, **IV:**1156
Rhee, Syngman, **IX:**3165
Richards, Ann, **IX:**3169
Richelieu, Cardinal de, **IV:**1165
Rienzo, Cola di, **II:**790
Robespierre, **IV:**1170
Rodney, George, **IV:**1178
Rollo, **II:**793
Roosevelt, Franklin D., **IX:**3222
Roosevelt, Theodore, **IX:**3228
Root, Elihu, **IX:**3232
Ross, Nellie Tayloe, **IX:**3243
Rurik, **II:**803
Russell, Bertrand, **IX:**3264
Russell, Lord John, **VI:**1930
Sadat, Anwar el-, **IX:**3289
Saigō Takamori, **VI:**1936
Saint-Just, Louis de, **IV:**1205
Sakharov, Andrei, **IX:**3296
Saladin, **II:**809
Salisbury, First Earl of, **III:**660
Salisbury, Third Marquess of, **VI:**1943
Samuel, **I:**746
Santa Anna, Antonio López de, **VI:**1955
Sargon II, **I:**754
Sato, Eisaku, **IX:**3336
Sauvé, Jeanne, **IX:**3344
Savonarola, Girolamo, **III:**667
Schurz, Carl, **VI:**1996
Scipio Aemilianus, **I:**757
Scipio Africanus, **I:**760
Seddon, Richard John, **VI:**2017
Seleucus I Nicator, **I:**767
Seneca the Younger, **I:**770
Senghor, Léopold, **IX:**3391
Sesostris III, **I:**774
Seward, William H., **VI:**2037
Sforza, Ludovico, **III:**682
Shaftesbury, First Earl of, **IV:**1228
Shah Jahan, **IV:**1232
Shapur II, **I:**778
Shays, Daniel, **IV:**1239
Sherman, Roger, **IV:**1242
Shōtoku Taishi, **II:**826
Sihanouk, Norodom, **IX:**3417
Sinclair, Upton, **IX:**3426
Śivajī, **IV:**1246
Smith, Alfred E., **IX:**3439
Smith, Margaret Chase, **IX:**3446
Smuts, Jan Christian, **IX:**3453
Solomon, **I:**798
Solon, **I:**803

Solzhenitsyn, Aleksandr, **IX:**3459
Spaak, Paul-Henri, **IX:**3475
Speransky, Mikhail Mikhaylovich, **VI:**2089
Ssu-ma Kuang, **II:**840
Staël, Madame de, **VI:**2092
Stalin, Joseph, **IX:**3482
Standish, Miles, **IV:**1273
Stanford, Leland, **VI:**2096
Stanhope, First Earl, **IV:**1277
Stanton, Edwin M., **VI:**2106
Stefan Du?an, **II:**843
Stein, Freiherr vom, **VI:**2115
Stephen I, **II:**851
Stephens, Alexander H., **VI:**2129
Stevens, Thaddeus, **VI:**2136
Stevenson, Adlai E., **IX:**3523
Stimson, Henry L., **IX:**3537
Strafford, First Earl of, **IV:**1285
Stresemann, Gustav, **IX:**3563
Stuyvesant, Peter, **IV:**1294
Su Tung-p'o, **II:**855
Sukarno, **IX:**3570
Süleyman the Magnificent, **III:**707
Sulla, Lucius Cornelius, **I:**833
Sumner, Charles, **VI:**2170
Sun Yat-sen, **IX:**3578
Sundjata, **II:**863
Sung Dynasty, **II:**866
Sylvester II, **II:**869
Tacitus, Cornelius, **I:**837
Taft, Robert A., **IX:**3590
Taft, William Howard, **IX:**3594
T'ai Tsung, **II:**876
Taira Kiyomori, **II:**881
Talleyrand, **VI:**2185
Tamerlane, **II:**884
Taylor, Zachary, **VI:**2194
Tereshkova, Valentina, **IX:**3639
Thatcher, Margaret, **IX:**3649
Themistocles, **I:**857
Theodora, **II:**890
Theodoric the Great, **II:**894
Theodosius the Great, **I:**868
Thiers, Adolphe, **VI:**2226
Thomas, Clarence, **IX:**3657
Thomas, Norman, **IX:**3660
Thutmose III, **I:**889
Tiberius, **I:**892
Tigranes the Great, **I:**896
Tilak, Bal Gangadhar, **IX:**3681
Tito, **IX:**3692
Tokugawa Ieyasu, **IV:**1327
Torquemada, Tomás de, **III:**725
Touré, Ahmed Sékou, **IX:**3711
Toussaint-Louverture, **IV:**1338
Toyotomi Hideyoshi, **III:**728
Trajan, **I:**899
Trotsky, Leon, **IX:**3726
Trudeau, Pierre Elliott, **IX:**3730
Truman, Harry S, **IX:**3740
Tseng Kuo-fan, **VI:**2260
Tshombe, Moïse, **IX:**3745
Tubman, William V. S., **IX:**3757
Turgot, Anne-Robert-Jacques, **IV:**1348
Tutankhamen, **I:**904
Tweed, William Marcy, **VI:**2284
Tyler, John, **VI:**2288
Ulbricht, Walter, **IX:**3779
Urban II, **II:**928
Valdemar II, **II:**932
Van Buren, Martin, **VI:**2292
Venizélos, Eleuthérios, **IX:**3808
Vercingetorix, **I:**922
Vespasian, **I:**933
Victoria, Queen, **VI:**2307
Virchow, Rudolf, **VI:**2312
Vladimir I, **II:**952
Vo Nguyen Giap, **IX:**3821
Wakefield, Edward Gibbon, **VI:**2321
Waldheim, Kurt, **IX:**3841
Walesa, Lech, **IX:**3844
Wallace, George C., **IX:**3857
Wallace, Henry A., **IX:**3860
Wallenstein, Albrecht Wenzel von, **IV:**1396
Walpole, Sir Robert, **IV:**1400
Wang An-shih, **II:**962
Wang Ching-wei, **IX:**3877
Wang Wei, **II:**965
Wang Yang-ming, **III:**771
Washington, George, **IV:**1405
Webster, Daniel, **VI:**2344
Weizmann, Chaim, **IX:**3930
Wellington, Duke of, **VI:**2351
Wentworth, W.C., **VI:**2355
Widukind, **II:**973
Wilkes, John, **IV:**1439
William II, **IX:**4003
William IV, **VI:**2392
William the Silent, **III:**781
Williams, George Washington, **VI:**2396
Wilson, Sir Harold, **IX:**4016
Wilson, Woodrow, **IX:**4020
Winthrop, John, **IV:**1463
Witherspoon, John, **IV:**1467

Władysław II Jagiełło and Jadwiga, **II:**1001
Wolsey, Cardinal Thomas, **III:**785
Yamani, Ahmad Zaki, **IX:**4079
Yeltsin, Boris N., **IX:**4082
Ypsilanti, Alexander and Demetrios, **VI:**2417
Yung-lo, **II:**1021
Zaghlūl, Sa'd, **IX:**4093
Zetkin, Clara, **IX:**4112
Zhukov, Georgy Konstantinovich, **IX:**4116
Zoser, **I:**978

HISTORIOGRAPHY. ***See also*** **EDUCATION; SCHOLARSHIP**

Acton, Lord, **V:**10
Adams, Henry, **V:**15
Alfonso X, **II:**56
Arnold, Thomas, **V:**74
Athanasius, Saint, **I:**119
Bancroft, George, **V:**124
Bayle, Pierre, **IV:**103
Beard, Charles A., **VII:**221
Bede the Venerable, Saint, **II:**132
Biruni, al-, **II:**147
Bossuet, Jacques-Bénigne, **IV:**170
Braudel, Fernand, **VII:**436
Bruni, Leonardo, **III:**93
Burckhardt, Jacob, **V:**358
Carlyle, Thomas, **V:**416
Carpini, Giovanni da Pian del, **II:**206
Cassiodorus, **II:**215
Cassirer, Ernst, **VII:**614
Celsus, Aulus Cornelius, **I:**173
Comte, Auguste, **V:**543
Croce, Benedetto, **VII:**801
Dawidowicz, Lucy S., **VII:**847
Eusebius of Caesarea, **I:**322
Froissart, Jean, **II:**366
Gibbon, Edward, **IV:**545
Gilson, Étienne, **VII:**1374
Gregory of Tours, **II:**403
Guicciardini, Francesco, **III:**325
Herodotus, **I:**394
Ibn Khaldun, **II:**502
Irving, Washington, **V:**1192
Joachim of Fiore, **II:**534
Josephus, Flavius, **I:**483
Livy, **I:**504
Lomonosov, Mikhail Vasilyevich, **IV:**860
Macaulay, Thomas Babington, **VI:**1427
Machiavelli, Niccolò, **III:**448
Mas'udi, al-, **II:**636
Michelet, Jules, **VI:**1548
Mill, James, **VI:**1556
Mommsen, Theodor, **VI:**1566
Niebuhr, Barthold Georg, **VI:**1654
Pan Ku, **I:**589
Parkman, Francis, **VI:**1735
Parrington, Vernon L., **IX:**2892
Pirenne, Henri, **IX:**3023
Polybius, **I:**673
Prescott, William Hickling, **VI:**1814
Psellus, Michael, **II:**758
Pushkin, Alexander, **VI:**1832
Ranke, Leopold von, **VI:**1839
Sallust, **I:**742
Sandburg, Carl, **IX:**3308
Saxo Grammaticus, **II:**815
Scaliger, Joseph Justus, **III:**671
Snorri Sturluson, **II:**836
Ssu-ma Ch'ien, **I:**818
Ssu-ma Kuang, **II:**840
Strabo, **I:**828
Tabari, al-, **II:**873
Tacitus, Cornelius, **I:**837
Taine, Hippolyte-Adolphe, **VI:**2182
Theophanes the Confessor, **II:**903
Thiers, Adolphe, **VI:**2226
Thucydides, **I:**885
Toynbee, Arnold, **IX:**3715
Troeltsch, Ernst, **IX:**3722
Tuchman, Barbara, **IX:**3760
Turner, Frederick Jackson, **IX:**3771
Vico, Giambattista, **IV:**1372
Villani, Giovanni, **II:**938
Vincent of Beauvais, **II:**946
Webb, Beatrice and Sidney, **IX:**3905
Williams, George Washington, **VI:**2396
Winckelmann, Johann Joachim, **IV:**1460
Yaqut, **II:**1013

HOLY ROMAN EMPERORS

Charlemagne, **II:**226
Charles IV, **II:**235
Charles V, **III:**159
Charles the Bald, **II:**239
Frederick I Barbarossa, **II:**357
Frederick II, **II:**362
Henry II the Saint, **II:**449
Henry IV (of Germany), **II:**461
Louis II the German, **II:**599
Maximilian I, **III:**491
Otto the Great, **II:**706
Rudolf I, **II:**796
Wenceslaus, **II:**969

HORTICULTURE. ***See also*** **BOTANY; LANDSCAPE ARCHITECTURE**
Appleseed, Johnny, **V:**66
Burbank, Luther, **V:**353

IMMUNOLOGY. ***See*** **MEDICINE**

INDIAN AFFAIRS. ***See*** **NATIVE AMERICAN AFFAIRS**

INDUSTRY. ***See*** **BUSINESS AND INDUSTRY**

INVENTION AND TECHNOLOGY. ***See also*** **AVIATION AND SPACE EXPLORATION; COMPUTER SCIENCE; ENGINEERING**
Archimedes, **I:**76
Arkwright, Richard, **IV:**59
Armstrong, Edwin H., **VII:**102
Babbage, Charles, **V:**101
Baskerville, John, **IV:**95
Bell, Alexander Graham, **V:**185
Benz, Carl, **V:**199
Bergius, Friedrich, **VII:**275
Bessemer, Sir Henry, **V:**218
Braille, Louis, **V:**303
Brunelleschi, Filippo, **III:**89
Carlson, Chester F., **VII:**579
Cayley, Sir George, **V:**450
Claude, Georges, **VII:**699
Colt, Samuel, **V:**540
Cooke, William Fothergill, **V:**555
Ctesibius of Alexandria, **I:**231
Daguerre, Jacques, **V:**592
Daimler, Gottlieb, **V:**597
Darby, Abraham, **IV:**396
Davy, Sir Humphry, **V:**621
de Forest, Lee, **VII:**858
Diesel, Rudolf, **V:**672
Eads, James Buchanan, **V:**729
Eastman, George, **VII:**996
Edison, Thomas Alva, **V:**743
Eupalinus of Megara, **I:**314
Fitch, John, **IV:**476
Fuller, R. Buckminster, **VII:**1265
Fulton, Robert, **V:**854
Goodyear, Charles, **V:**960
Grove, Sir William Robert, **V:**1010
Guericke, Otto von, **IV:**586
Gutenberg, Johann, **III:**328
Hargreaves, James, **IV:**623
Holland, John Philip, **V:**1123
Hounsfield, Godfrey Newbold, **VIII:**1751
Howe, Elias, **V:**1141
Huygens, Christiaan, **IV:**695
Kapitsa, Pyotr Leonidovich, **VIII:**1906
Kay, John, **IV:**769
Krupp, Alfred, **VI:**1301
Lanchester, Frederick William, **VIII:**2069
Langley, Samuel Pierpont, **VI:**1313
Lenoir, Étienne, **VI:**1343
Lippershey, Hans, **IV:**850
Lumière, Auguste and Louis, **VIII:**2276
McCormick, Cyrus Hall, **VI:**1431
Marconi, Guglielmo, **VIII:**2415
Mergenthaler, Ottmar, **VI:**1541
Michelin, André and Édouard, **VIII:**2514
Montgolfier, Jacques-Étienne and Joseph-Michel, **IV:**995
Morse, Samuel F. B., **VI:**1592
Murdock, William, **IV:**1008
Nasmyth, James, **VI:**1624
Natta, Giulio, **VIII:**2698
Newcomen, Thomas, **IV:**1022
Niépce, Nicéphore, **VI:**1657
Nobel, Alfred, **VI:**1673
Otto, Nikolaus August, **VI:**1702
Papin, Denis, **IV:**1059
Pirelli Family, The, **IX:**3020
Popov, Aleksandr Stepanovich, **VI:**1806
Roebuck, John, **IV:**1182
Rolls, Charles Stewart, **IX:**3209
Royce, Sir Frederick Henry, **IX:**3209
Santos-Dumont, Alberto, **IX:**3320
Schmidt, Bernhard Voldemar, **IX:**3351
Siemens Family, The, **VI:**2066
Swan, Joseph Wilson, **VI:**2179
Swedenborg, Emanuel, **IV:**1302
Torricelli, Evangelista, **IV:**1331
Tull, Jethro, **IV:**1345
Wankel, Felix, **IX:**3881
Watt, James, **IV:**1409
Westinghouse, George, **VI:**2358
Wheatstone, Charles, **V:**555
Whitney, Eli, **IV:**1431
Wiener, Norbert, **IX:**3976
Wright, Wilbur and Orville, **IX:**4064
Zworykin, Vladimir, **IX:**4125

IRONMAKING. ***See*** **INVENTION AND TECHNOLOGY**

JOURNALISM. ***See also*** **PUBLISHING**
'Abduh, Muhammad, **V:**4
Addison, Joseph, **IV:**26

Angell, Norman, **VII:**74
Beaverbrook, Lord, **VII:**234
Bennett, James Gordon, **V:**190
Bierce, Ambrose, **V:**230
Bottomley, Horatio W., **VII:**382
Bourke-White, Margaret, **VII:**395
Brown, George, **V:**318
Bryant, William Cullen, **V:**343
Cather, Willa, **VII:**621
Cobbett, William, **V:**522
Collins, Norman, **VII:**737
Day, Dorothy, **VII:**850
du Bois, W.E.B., **VII:**963
Ellis, Havelock, **VII:**1070
Ephron, Nora, **VII:**1083
Fuller, Margaret, **V:**849
Godkin, Edwin Lawrence, **VIII:**1400
Graham, Katharine, **VIII:**1451
Greeley, Horace, **V:**982
Hale, Sarah Josepha, **V:**1022
Harmsworth, Alfred and Harold, **VIII:**1554
Hearst, William Randolph, **VIII:**1601
Herzl, Theodor, **V:**1102
Jeffrey, Lord, **V:**1224
Johnson, Samuel, **IV:**728
Lippmann, Walter, **VIII:**2203
Luce, Clare Boothe, **VIII:**2256
Luce, Henry R., **VIII:**2260
Luxemburg, Rosa, **VIII:**2285
McCarthy, Mary, **VIII:**2304
Mackenzie, William Lyon, **VI:**1447
Marat, Jean-Paul, **IV:**910
Mencken, H. L., **VIII:**2483
Murrow, Edward R., **VIII:**2662
O'Connor, Thomas Power, **IX:**2793
Ortega y Gasset, José, **IX:**2843
Pulitzer, Joseph, **VI:**1825
Reith of Stonehaven, First Baron, **IX:**3146
Rogers, Will, **IX:**3204
Scripps, Edward Wyllis, **VI:**2014
Steinem, Gloria, **IX:**3519
Tarbell, Ida, **IX:**3614
Trotsky, Leon, **IX:**3726
Wallace, Henry A., **IX:**3860
Walter, John, II, **VI:**2324
Walters, Barbara, **IX:**3868
Wells-Barnett, Ida B., **IX:**3941
Wilkes, John, **IV:**1439
Zenger, John Peter, **IV:**1484

JURISPRUDENCE. ***See*** **LAW**

LABOR MOVEMENT. ***See also*** **SOCIAL REFORM**
Bevin, Ernest, **VII:**313
Bondfield, Margaret, **VII:**353
Debs, Eugene V., **VII:**880
Gompers, Samuel, **V:**956
Hardie, James Keir, **V:**1036
Hernandez, Aileen Clarke, **VIII:**1641
Huerta, Dolores, **VIII:**1762
Jones, Mary Harris "Mother," **VIII:**1879
Lewis, John L., **VIII:**2170
Randolph, A. Philip, **IX:**3112
Reuther, Walter P., **IX:**3161
Walesa, Lech, **IX:**3844
Zetkin, Clara, **IX:**4112

LANDSCAPE ARCHITECTURE. ***See also*** **HORTICULTURE**
Brown, Lancelot, **IV:**204
Farrand, Beatrix Jones, **VII:**1130
Le Nôtre, André, 834
Olmsted, Frederick Law, **VI:**1691

LANGUAGE AND LINGUISTICS. ***See also*** **PHILOLOGY**
Avicenna, **II:**106
Barthes, Roland, **VII:**207
Chomsky, Noam, **VII:**673
Cyril, Saint, **II:**278
Derrida, Jacques, **VII:**912
Grimm, Jacob and Wilhelm, **V:**1006
Jahiz, al-, **II:**526
Jakobson, Roman, **VIII:**1831
Lacan, Jacques, **VIII:**2061
Lévi-Strauss, Claude, **VIII:**2164
Methodius, Saint, **II:**278
Priscian, **II:**755
Saussure, Ferdinand de, **IX:**3340
Sequoyah, **VI:**2025

LAW. ***See also*** **GOVERNMENT AND POLITICS**
Abu Hanifah, **II:**16
Ahmad ibn Hanbal, **II:**33
Alfonso X, **II:**56
Arthur, Chester A., **V:**77
Avicenna, **II:**106
Barton, Sir Edmund, **V:**147
Basil the Macedonian, **II:**117
Black, Hugo L., **VII:**321

Blackstone, William, **IV:**129
Borden, Lizzie, **V:**283
Boutros-Ghali, Boutros, **VII:**399
Bracton, Henry de, **II:**178
Brandeis, Louis D., **VII:**419
Brougham, Henry, **V:**314
Burger, Warren E., **VII:**509
Burr, Aaron, **V:**369
Cambacérès, Jean-Jacques-Régis de, **V:**398
Capone, Alphonse, **VII:**563
Cardozo, Benjamin Nathan, **VII:**575
Carroll, Charles, **IV:**250
Cassin, René, **VII:**610
Chase, Salmon P., **V:**477
Chase, Samuel, **IV:**293
Ch'in Shih Huang-ti, **I:**176
Cicero, **I:**194
Cleisthenes of Athens, **I:**207
Clinton, Hillary Rodham, **VII:**713
Coke, Sir Edward, **IV:**329
Cushing, Caleb, **V:**581
Darius the Great, **I:**236
Darrow, Clarence, **VII:**839
Demosthenes, **I:**253
Draco, **I:**280
Earp, Wyatt, **V:**735
Ehrlich, Eugen, **VII:**1029
Erskine, First Baron, **IV:**439
Evatt, Herbert Vere, **VII:**1109
Field, Stephen J., **V:**787
Fortescue, Sir John, **III:**267
Frankfurter, Felix, **VII:**1212
Gentili, Alberico, **III:**295
Grotius, Hugo, **IV:**579
Grove, Sir William Robert, **V:**1010
Hale, Matthew, **IV:**596
Hammurabi, **I:**360
Hand, Learned, **VIII:**1541
Hickok, Wild Bill, **V:**1107
Hiss, Alger, **VIII:**1683
Holmes, Oliver Wendell, Jr., **VIII:**1720
Hotman, François, **III:**362
Hughes, Charles Evans, **VIII:**1766
James I the Conqueror, **II:**529
Jay, John, **IV:**711
Jeffrey, Lord, **V:**1224
Jordan, Barbara, **VIII:**1887
Justinian I, **II:**553
Kent, James, **VI:**1277
La Fontaine, Henri-Marie, **VIII:**2051
Littleton, Sir Thomas, **III:**431
Lockwood, Belva A., **VI:**1406
MacKinnon, Catharine A., **VIII:**2325
Mansfield, First Earl of, **IV:**904
Marshall, John, **VI:**1487
Marshall, Thurgood, **VIII:**2433
Nader, Ralph, **VIII:**2679
O'Connell, Daniel, **VI:**1680
O'Connor, Sandra Day, **IX:**2789
Olaf, Saint, **II:**691
Pufendorf, Samuel von, **IV:**1133
Rehnquist, William H., **IX:**3142
Reno, Janet, **IX:**3153
Sacco, Nicola, **IX:**3281
Savigny, Friedrich Karl von, **VI:**1966
Sewall, Samuel, **IV:**1225
Solon, **I:**803
Speransky, Mikhail Mikhaylovich, **VI:**2089
Stone, Harlan Fiske, **IX:**3546
Story, Joseph, **VI:**2147
Süleyman the Magnificent, **III:**707
Taft, William Howard, **IX:**3594
Taney, Roger Brooke, **VI:**2189
Van Buren, Martin, **VI:**2292
Vitoria, Francisco de, **III:**768
Warren, Earl, **IX:**3888
Webster, Daniel, **VI:**2344
Webster, Noah, **IV:**1417
Wiesenthal, Simon, **IX:**3984
Wilson, James, **IV:**1455

LINGUISTICS. ***See*** **LANGUAGE AND LINGUISTICS**

LITERATURE. ***See also*** **LANGUAGE AND LINGUISTICS; ORATORY; PHILOLOGY**

Achebe, Chinua, **VII:**13
Adam de la Halle, **II:**23
Adams, Henry, **V:**15
Addison, Joseph, **IV:**26
Aesop, **I:**13
Ahmad Khan, Sir Sayyid, **V:**34
Akhmatova, Anna, **VII:**37
Alcott, Louisa May, **V:**40
Alcuin, **II:**44
Alfonso X, **II:**56
Alger, Horatio, **V:**51
Andersen, Hans Christian, **V:**58
Angelou, Maya, **VII:**79
Apollinaire, Guillaume, **VII:**82
Ariosto, Ludovico, **III:**32
Arnold, Matthew, **V:**69
Ashurbanipal, **I:**105
Austen, Jane, **V:**90

Bakhtin, Mikhail, **VII:**152
Baldwin, James, **VII:**164
Balzac, Honoré de, **V:**120
Barnes, Djuna, **VII:**199
Barthes, Roland, **VII:**207
Baudelaire, Charles, **V:**150
Baum, L. Frank, **V:**154
Beauvoir, Simone de, **VII:**230
Beckett, Samuel, **VII:**238
Bede the Venerable, Saint, **II:**132
Bellow, Saul, **VII:**247
Benét, Stephen Vincent, **VII:**263
Benjamin, Walter, **VII:**267
Bierce, Ambrose, **V:**230
Black Hawk, **V:**247
Blake, William, **IV:**137
Blok, Aleksandr, **VII:**332
Boccaccio, Giovanni, **II:**150
Boethius, **II:**155
Böll, Heinrich, **VII:**349
Borges, Jorge Luis, **VII:**371
Bossuet, Jacques-Bénigne, **IV:**170
Boswell, James, **IV:**174
Bradstreet, Anne, **IV:**193
Brecht, Bertolt, **VII:**444
Breton, André, **VII:**448
Brontë Sisters, The, **V:**310
Browning, Elizabeth Barrett, **V:**327
Bruni, Leonardo, **III:**93
Bryant, William Cullen, **V:**343
Buber, Martin, **VII:**483
Buck, Pearl S., **VII:**486
Bunyan, John, **IV:**218
Burnett, Frances Hodgson, **V:**361
Burns, Robert, **IV:**229
Burroughs, Edgar Rice, **VII:**516
Burton, Sir Richard Francis, **V:**374
Byron, Lord, **V:**381
Caesar, Julius, **I:**147
Callimachus, **I:**156
Camões, Luís de, **III:**122
Camus, Albert, **VII:**553
Capek, Karel, **VII:**560
Capote, Truman, **VII:**567
Carlyle, Thomas, **V:**416
Carroll, Lewis, **V:**425
Carson, Rachel, **VII:**585
Casanova, Giovanni Giacomo, **IV:**254
Cather, Willa, **VII:**621
Catullus, **I:**169
Cavalcanti, Guido, **II:**223
Cædmon, **II:**198
Cellini, Benvenuto, **III:**151
Cervantes, Miguel de, **IV:**265
Césaire, Aimé, **VII:**631
Chapman, George, **III:**155
Charles d'Orléans, **II:**232
Chartier, Alain, **II:**245
Chateaubriand, **V:**481
Chaucer, Geoffrey, **II:**248
Chekhov, Anton, **V:**485
Ch'en Tu-hsiu, **VII:**660
Child, Lydia Maria, **V:**489
Chopin, Kate, **V:**497
Chrétien de Troyes, **II:**257
Christie, Agatha, **VII:**683
Christine de Pizan, **II:**260
Chuang-tzu, **I:**190
Churchill, Sir Winston, **VII:**691
Ch'ü Yüan, **I:**187
Cicero, **I:**194
Clarendon, First Earl of, **IV:**308
Cocteau, Jean, **VII:**721
Coleridge, Samuel Taylor, **V:**537
Colette, **VII:**729
Conrad, Joseph, **VII:**753
Cooper, James Fenimore, **V:**560
Crane, Hart, **VII:**789
Crane, Stephen, **V:**569
Crockett, David, **V:**578
Cruz, Sor Juana Inés de la, **IV:**382
cummings, e.e., **VII:**804
Cyrano de Bergerac, Savinien de, **IV:**385
Dante, **II:**286
Deborah, **I:**246
Defoe, Daniel, **IV:**399
Derrida, Jacques, **VII:**912
Dickens, Charles, **V:**663
Dickinson, Emily, **V:**667
Diderot, Denis, **IV:**412
Disraeli, Benjamin, **V:**675
Djilas, Milovan, **VII:**944
Donne, John, **IV:**416
Dostoevski, Fyodor, **V:**687
Doyle, Sir Arthur Conan, **V:**700
Dreiser, Theodore, **VII:**954
Dryden, John, **IV:**424
Dumas, Alexandre, *père*, **V:**708
Dunbar, Paul Laurence, **V:**714
Ehrenfels, Christian Von, **VII:**1026
Eliade, Mircea, **VII:**1055
Eliot, George, **V:**751
Eliot, T.S., **VII:**1058
Éluard, Paul, **VII:**1074

Emerson, Ralph Waldo, **V:**755
Ennius, Quintus, **I:**287
Erasmus, Desiderius, **III:**246
Eratosthenes of Cyrene, **I:**303
Erdrich, Louise, **VII:**1091
Faulkner, William, **VII:**1133
Fielding, Henry, **IV:**469
Firdusi, **II:**350
Fitzgerald, F. Scott, **VII:**1161
Flaubert, Gustave, **V:**796
Forester, C.S., **VII:**1189
Forster, E.M., **VII:**1193
Forten, Charlotte, **V:**807
Fracastoro, Girolamo, **III:**270
France, Anatole, **V:**725
Frank, Anne, **VII:**1204
Frazer, Sir James George, **VII:**1220
Frisch, Max, **VII:**1238
Frost, Robert, **VII:**1250
Fugard, Athol, **VII:**1257
García Lorca, Federico, **VII:**1290
García Márquez, Gabriel, **VII:**1293
Gardner, Erle Stanley, **VII:**1297
Geisel, Theodor Seuss, **VII:**1329
Genet, Jean, **VII:**1333
Gide, André, **VII:**1367
Giraudoux, Jean, **VII:**1379
Godwin, William, **IV:**555
Goethe, Johann Wolfgang von, **IV:**560
Gogol, Nikolai, **V:**949
Goldsmith, Oliver, **IV:**564
Gordimer, Nadine, **VIII:**1427
Gorky, Maxim, **VIII:**1442
Gottfried von Strassburg, **II:**392
Grass, Günter, **VIII:**1463
Greene, Graham, **VIII:**1467
Gregory of Nazianzus, **I:**349
Grimm, Jacob and Wilhelm, **V:**1006
H.D., **VIII:**1505
Hafiz, **II:**417
Hale, Sarah Josepha, **V:**1022
Halide Edib Adivar, **VIII:**1522
Hamsun, Knut, **VIII:**1537
Hansberry, Lorraine, **VIII:**1545
Hardy, Thomas, **V:**1040
Harris, Joel Chandler, **V:**1049
Hartmann von Aue, **II:**433
Hawthorne, Nathaniel, **V:**1064
Hayslip, Le Ly, **VIII:**1593
Heine, Heinrich, **V:**1085
Hellman, Lillian, **VIII:**1620
Hemingway, Ernest, **VIII:**1624
Henry, O., **V:**1096
Herder, Johann Gottfried, **IV:**651
Herzen, Aleksandr, **V:**1099
Hesiod, **I:**402
Hesse, Hermann, **VIII:**1650
Higginson, Thomas Wentworth, **V:**1110
Hildegard von Bingen, **II:**474
Holmes, Oliver Wendell, **V:**1126
Homer, **I:**420
Horace, **I:**424
Howe, Julia Ward, **V:**1145
Hsieh Ling-yün, **I:**429
Hsüan-tsang, **II:**482
Hughes, Langston, **VIII:**1771
Hugo, Victor, **V:**1154
Hurston, Zora Neale, **VIII:**1787
Huxley, Aldous, **VIII:**1804
Ibn Gabirol, **II:**498
Ionesco, Eugène, **VIII:**1816
Irving, Washington, **V:**1192
Isidore of Seville, Saint, **II:**518
Jackson, Helen Hunt, **V:**1200
Jahiz, al-, **II:**526
Jakobson, Roman, **VIII:**1831
James I the Conqueror, **II:**529
James, Henry, **V:**1211
Jewett, Sarah Orne, **V:**1228
John of Damascus, **II:**544
Johnson, Samuel, **IV:**728
Jonson, Ben, **IV:**744
Joyce, James, **VIII:**1891
Judah ha-Levi, **II:**548
Juvenal, **I:**488
Kafka, Franz, **VIII:**1900
Kālidāsa, **I:**491
Kämpfer, Engelbert, **IV:**754
Kawabata, Yasunari, **VIII:**1913
Kazantzakis, Nikos, **VIII:**1920
Keats, John, **VI:**1264
Kerouac, Jack, **VIII:**1945
King, Stephen, **VIII:**1977
Kipling, Rudyard, **VI:**1288
Kleist, Heinrich von, **VI:**1294
Kuo Mo-jo, **VIII:**2033
La Fontaine, Jean de, **IV:**781
Lagerlöf, Selma, **VIII:**2065
Lawrence, D.H., **VIII:**2115
Lawrence, T.E., **VIII:**2125
Laxness, Halldór, **VIII:**2131
Lazarus, Emma, **VI:**1334
Lermontov, Mikhail, **VI:**1351
Lessing, Gotthold Ephraim, **IV:**842

Lewis, C.S., **VIII:**2167
Lewis, Sinclair, **VIII:**2174
Li Ch'ing-chao, **II:**588
Li Po, **II:**591
Lomonosov, Mikhail Vasilyevich, **IV:**860
London, Jack, **VIII:**2223
Longfellow, Henry Wadsworth, **VI:**1414
Loos, Anita, **VIII:**2231
Lowell, Amy, **VIII:**2249
Lu Hsün, **VIII:**2252
Lucian, **I:**507
Lucretius, **I:**511
Lukács, György, **VIII:**2272
Lull, Raymond, **II:**608
Macaulay, Thomas Babington, **VI:**1427
McCarthy, Mary, **VIII:**2304
McCullers, Carson, **VIII:**2308
Machado de Assis, Joaquim Maria, **VI:**1444
Machaut, Guillaume de, **II:**615
Machiavelli, Niccolò, **III:**448
Maecenas, Gaius, **I:**519
Mahfouz, Naguib, **VIII:**2355
Mailer, Norman, **VIII:**2365
Malory, Sir Thomas, **III:**457
Malraux, André, **VIII:**2380
Mann, Thomas, **VIII:**2392
Manzoni, Alessandro, **VI:**1483
Marcel, Gabriel, **VIII:**2407
Marcus Aurelius, **I:**523
Marie de France, **II:**629
Martial, **I:**532
Matsuo Bashō, **IV:**942
Maupassant, Guy de, **VI:**1500
Mayakovsky, Vladimir, **VIII:**2461
Medici, Lorenzo de', **III:**495
Melville, Herman, **VI:**1520
Michener, James A., **VIII:**2517
Millay, Edna St. Vincent, **VIII:**2529
Milne, A.A., **VIII:**2543
Milton, John, **IV:**958
Mishima, Yukio, **VIII:**2551
Montagu, Mary Wortley, **IV:**983
Montaigne, Michel de, **III:**524
Montale, Eugenio, **VIII:**2592
Moore, Marianne, **VIII:**2614
Morris, William, **VI:**1588
Morrison, Toni, **VIII:**2626
Murasaki Shikibu, **II:**657
Nabokov, Vladimir, **VIII:**2675
Naidu, Sarojini, **VIII:**2683
Nashe, Thomas, **III:**548
Neruda, Pablo, **VIII:**2716
Nietzsche, Friedrich Wilhelm, **VI:**1662
Nordau, Max, **VIII:**2766
Nostradamus, **III:**567
O'Connor, Flannery, **IX:**2785
Omar Khayyám, **II:**695
Orwell, George, **IX:**2846
Ou-yang Hsiu, **II:**709
Ovid, **I:**585
Parker, Dorothy, **IX:**2884
Parrington, Vernon L., **IX:**2892
Pasternak, Boris, **IX:**2899
Pater, Walter, **VI:**1749
Paton, Alan, **IX:**2907
Petrarch, **II:**726
Phaedrus, **I:**618
Pindar, **I:**644
Pirandello, Luigi, **IX:**3013
Plath, Sylvia, **IX:**3036
Pléiade, La, **III:**623
Plutarch, **I:**670
Poe, Edgar Allan, **VI:**1794
Poggio, **III:**626
Pope, Alexander, **IV:**1115
Porter, Katherine Anne, **IX:**3059
Potter, Beatrix, **IX:**3063
Propertius, Sextus, **I:**702
Proust, Marcel, **IX:**3089
Pushkin, Alexander, **VI:**1832
Rabelais, François, **III:**633
Raleigh, Sir Walter, **III:**638
Ratramnus, **II:**773
Remarque, Erich Maria, **IX:**3150
Rilke, Rainer Maria, **IX:**3181
Rimbaud, Arthur, **VI:**1886
Ronsard, Pierre de, **III:**657
Rousseau, Jean-Jacques, **IV:**1194
Rukeyser, Muriel, **IX:**3257
Rumi, Jalal al-Din, **II:**800
Sachs, Nelly, **IX:**3285
Sa'di, **II:**806
Salimbene, **II:**812
Salinger, J.D., **IX:**3301
Sand, George, **VI:**1951
Sandburg, Carl, **IX:**3308
Santayana, George, **IX:**3317
Sappho, **I:**750
Sarraute, Nathalie, **IX:**3324
Sartre, Jean-Paul, **IX:**3327
Saxo Grammaticus, **II:**815
Scaliger, Joseph Justus, **III:**671
Schiller, Friedrich, **IV:**1217
Scott, Sir Walter, **VI:**2005

Seneca the Younger, **I:**770
Senghor, Léopold, **IX:**3391
Sexton, Anne, **IX:**3395
Shakespeare, William, **III:**686
Shaw, George Bernard, **IX:**3399
Shelley, Mary Wollstonecraft, **VI:**2048
Shelley, Percy Bysshe, **VI:**2052
Sidney, Sir Philip, **III:**691
Simonides, **I:**787
Sinclair, Upton, **IX:**3426
Skinner, B.F., **IX:**3431
Snorri Sturluson, **II:**836
Solon, **I:**803
Solzhenitsyn, Aleksandr, **IX:**3459
Sophocles, **I:**807
Soyinka, Wole, **IX:**3471
Spenser, Edmund, **III:**703
Ssu-ma Kuang, **II:**840
Staël, Madame de, **VI:**2092
Stein, Gertrude, **IX:**3511
Steinbeck, John, **IX:**3515
Stendhal, **VI:**2125
Stevenson, Robert Louis, **VI:**2139
Strindberg, August, **IX:**3566
Su Tung-p'o, **II:**855
Sung Dynasty, **II:**866
Suttner, Bertha von, **VI:**2175
Swift, Jonathan, **IV:**1305
Tagore, Rabindranath, **IX:**3598
Taine, Hippolyte-Adolphe, **VI:**2182
Tanizaki, Jun'ichiro, **IX:**3611
T'ao Ch'ien, **I:**841
Tasso, Torquato, **III:**710
Teasdale, Sara, **IX:**3622
Tennyson, Alfred, Lord, **VI:**2211
Terence, **I:**844
Tertullian, **I:**848
Theophrastus, **I:**873
Thoreau, Henry David, **VI:**2234
Thurber, James, **IX:**3677
Tolkien, J.R.R., **IX:**3696
Tolstoy, Leo, **VI:**2242
Tsvetayeva, Marina, **IX:**3753
Tu Fu, **II:**917
Turgenev, Ivan, **VI:**2268
Twain, Mark, **VI:**2279
Unamuno y Jugo, Miguel de, **IX:**3783
Valéry, Paul, **IX:**3791
Vasari, Giorgio, **III:**743
Vega Carpio, Lope de, **IV:**1361
Venette, Jean de, **II:**935
Vergil, **I:**926
Verne, Jules, **VI:**2303
Villehardouin, Geoffroi de, **II:**942
Villon, François, **III:**763
Vincent of Beauvais, **II:**946
Vitry, Philippe de, **II:**949
Voltaire, **IV:**1392
Walker, Alice, **IX:**3849
Walther von der Vogelweide, **II:**959
Wang Wei, **II:**965
Warren, Robert Penn, **IX:**3893
Wells, H.G., **IX:**3938
Wharton, Edith, **IX:**3953
Whitman, Walt, **VI:**2368
Whittier, John Greenleaf, **VI:**2374
Wiesel, Elie, **IX:**3980
Wilde, Oscar, **VI:**2377
Wilder, Laura Ingalls, **IX:**3992
Williams, Tennessee, **IX:**4007
Wilson, Edmund, **IX:**4012
Wolfe, Thomas, **IX:**4041
Wolfram von Eschenbach, **II:**1005
Wollstonecraft, Mary, **IV:**1475
Woolf, Virginia, **IX:**4056
Wordsworth, William, **VI:**2406
Xenophanes, **I:**955
Xenophon, **I:**958
Yeats, William Butler, **IX:**4082
Zola, Émile, **VI:**2420

MANUFACTURING. ***See*** **BUSINESS AND INDUSTRY; ENGINEERING; INVENTION AND TECHNOLOGY**

MATHEMATICS. ***See also*** **STATISTICS**
Abel, Niels Henrik, **V:**7
Abul Wefa, **II:**20
Alembert, Jean le Rond d', **IV:**30
Alhazen, **II:**63
Apollonius of Perga, **I:**72
Archimedes, **I:**76
Aryabhata, **II:**89
Babbage, Charles, **V:**101
Banneker, Benjamin, **IV:**88
Bernoulli, Daniel, **IV:**122
Bernoulli, Jakob I, **IV:**122
Bernoulli, Johann I, **IV:**122
Bessel, Friedrich Wilhelm, **V:**215
Brahmagupta, **II:**181
Carroll, Lewis, **V:**425
Condorcet, Marquis de, **IV:**348
Dedekind, Richard, **V:**638
Descartes, René, **IV:**403

Diophantus, **I:**272
Eratosthenes of Cyrene, **I:**303
Euclid, **I:**307
Eudoxus of Cnidus, **I:**310
Euler, Leonhard, **IV:**443
Fermat, Pierre de, **IV:**458
Fourier, Joseph, **V:**819
Frege, Gottlob, **V:**836
Galois, Èvariste, **V:**864
Gauss, Carl Friedrich, **V:**893
Hamilton, Sir William Rowan, **V:**1025
Hero of Alexandria, **I:**387
Hipparchus, **I:**407
Hypatia, **I:**436
Khwarizmi, al, **II:**563
Lagrange, Joseph-Louis, **IV:**785
Laplace, Pierre-Simon, **VI:**1319
Leibniz, Gottfried Wilhelm, **IV:**829
Lemaître, Georges, **VIII:**2157
Leonardo of Pisa, **II:**585
Lobachevsky, Nikolay Ivanovich, **VI:**1403
Maclaurin, Colin, **IV:**882
Mersenne, Marin, **IV:**949
Monge, Gaspard, **IV:**975
Napier, John, **III:**544
Neumann, John von, **VIII:**2724
Omar Khayyám, **II:**695
Pappus, **I:**593
Pascal, Blaise, **IV:**1062
Picard, Émile, **IX:**2994
Piero della Francesca, III-**III:**606
Poincaré, Henri, **VI:**1798
Ptolemy, **I:**712
Pythagoras, **I:**727
Russell, Bertrand, **IX:**3264
Sosigenes, **I:**811
Steiner, Jakob, **VI:**2118
Torricelli, Evangelista, **IV:**1331
Turing, Alan Mathison, **IX:**3768
Whitehead, Alfred North, **IX:**3965
Wiener, Norbert, **IX:**3976
Xenakis, Iannis, **IX:**4075

MEDICINE. ***See also*** **NURSING; PHYSIOLOGY; PUBLIC HEALTH; SEX RESEARCH**
Abano, Pietro d', **II:**1
Adler, Alfred, **VII:**30
Alcmaeon, **I:**34
Alhazen, **II:**63
Aretaeus of Cappadocia, **I:**81
Arnold of Villanova, **II:**79
Asclepiades of Bithynia, **I:**101
Avicenna, **II:**106
Banting, Sir Frederick Grant, **VII:**187
Barnard, Christiaan, **VII:**195
Behring, Emil von, **V:**182
Bernard, Claude, **V:**207
Bernoulli, Daniel, **IV:**122
Blackwell, Elizabeth, **V:**251
Breuer, Josef, **VII:**452
Burnet, Sir Macfarlane, **VII:**512
Calmette, Albert, **VII:**546
Celsus, Aulus Cornelius, **I:**173
Curie, Pierre and Marie, **VII:**811
Cushing, Harvey Williams, **VII:**823
Diocles of Carystus, **I:**260
Dioscorides, Pedanius, **I:**276
Domagk, Gerhard, **VII:**951
Egas Moniz, António, **VII:**1023
Ehrlich, Paul, **VII:**1032
Einthoven, Willem, **VII:**1039
Erasistratus, **I:**299
Fleming, Sir Alexander, **VII:**1166
Florey, Baron, **VII:**1172
Fowler, Lydia Folger, **V:**822
Fracastoro, Girolamo, **III:**270
Freud, Sigmund, **VII:**1224
Galen, **I:**338
Gesner, Conrad, **III:**298
Guy de Chauliac, **II:**414
Hahnemann, Samuel, **IV:**593
Harvey, William, **IV:**626
Herophilus, **I:**398
Hevesy, Georg von, **VIII:**1654
Hippocrates, **I:**411
Holmes, Oliver Wendell, **V:**1126
Hounsfield, Godfrey Newbold, **VIII:**1751
Houssay, Bernardo Alberto, **VIII:**1759
Imhotep, **I:**443
Jaspers, Karl, **VIII:**1843
Jenner, Edward, **IV:**721
Kämpfer, Engelbert, **IV:**754
Koch, Robert, **VI:**1297
Le Bon, Gustave, **VIII:**2134
Lister, Joseph, **VI:**1388
Lorenz, Konrad, **VIII:**2238
Maimonides, Moses, **II:**619
Mayo, William J. and Charles H., **VIII:**2465
Montagu, Mary Wortley, **IV:**983
Montessori, Maria, **VIII:**2596
Morton,William Thomas Green, **VI:**1596
Nostradamus, **III:**567
Osler, Sir William, **VI:**1698

Paracelsus, **III:**584
Pauling, Linus, **IX:**2926
Paul of Aegina, **II:**712
Pavlov, Ivan Petrovich, **IX:**2933
Picotte, Susan La Flesche, **IX:**3010
Razi, al-, **II:**779
Reed, Walter, **VI:**1857
Ross, Ronald, **IX:**3247
Rush, Benjamin, **IV:**1202
Salk, Jonas Edward, **IX:**3305
Santorio, Santorio, **IV:**1209
Schweitzer, Albert, **IX:**3370
Semmelweis, Ignaz Philipp, **VI:**2021
Servetus, Michael, **III:**675
Smith, Theobald, **IX:**3450
Spock, Benjamin, **IX:**3478
Stahl, Georg Ernst, **IV:**1268
Starling, Ernest Henry, **IX:**3494
Sydenham, Thomas, **IV:**1310
Vesalius, Andreas, **III:**754
Virchow, Rudolf, **VI:**2312
Waksman, Selman Abraham, **IX:**3833
Whipple, George Hoyt, **IX:**3957
Wilkins, Maurice H.F., **IX:**3995

METALLURGY
Hadfield, Sir Robert Abbott, **V:**1015

METEOROLOGY
Bjerknes, Vilhelm, **VII:**318
Dalton, John, **V:**602
Geiger, Rudolf Oskar Robert Williams, **VII:**1326
Humboldt, Alexander von, **V:**1159
Maury, Matthew Fontaine, **VI:**1507
Wilkins, Sir George Hubert, **IX:**3999

MICROBIOLOGY. ***See*** **BIOLOGY**

MILITARY AFFAIRS. ***See also*** **EXPLORATION AND COLONIZATION; GOVERNMENT AND POLITICS; WARFARE AND CONQUEST**
Abahai, **IV:**1
Abdelkader, **V:**1
Alanbrooke, First Viscount, **VII:**45
Albuquerque, Afonso de, **III:**11
Allen, Ethan, **IV:**34
Allenby, Lord, **VII:**58
Alva, Duke of, **III:**18
André, John, **IV:**42
Anson, Lord, **IV:**55
Arafat, Yasir, **VII:**90
Arnold, Benedict, **IV:**64
Atatürk, Kemal, **VII:**133
Bābur, **III:**36
Baden-Powell, Sir Robert Stephenson Smyth, **V:**105
Bayard, Chevalier de, **III:**48
Bayezid II, **III:**51
Bligh, William, **IV:**143
Blücher, Gebhard Leberecht von, **V:**263
Bolívar, Simón, **V:**267
Botha, Louis, **VII:**376
Bougainville, Louis-Antoine de, **IV:**179
Bradley, Omar N., **VII:**403
Calamity Jane, **V:**390
Carleton, Guy, **IV:**246
Carlos, Don, **V:**413
Carson, Kit, **V:**429
Charles XIV John, **V:**474
Cheng Ch'eng-kung, **IV:**297
Chu Teh, **VII:**687
Clark, George Rogers, **IV:**312
Clausewitz, Carl von, **V:**503
Clinton, Sir Henry, **IV:**321
Clive, Robert, **IV:**325
Condé, The Great, **IV:**341
Cornwallis, First Marquess, **IV:**367
Cortés, Hernán, **III:**188
Crockett, David, **V:**578
Custer, George A., **V:**585
Cyrano de Bergerac, Savinien de, **IV:**385
Dayan, Moshe, **VII:**854
Decatur, Stephen, **V:**634
de Gaulle, Charles, **VII:**866
Dewey, George, **V:**656
Dorgon, **IV:**421
Eisenhower, Dwight D., **VII:**1043
Enver Pasha, **VII:**1078
Faidherbe, Louis, **V:**763
Fairfax, Third Baron, **IV:**446
Farnese, Alessandro, **III:**254
Farragut, David G., **V:**772
Ferdinand II and Isabella I, **III:**260
Frederick Henry, **IV:**500
Gadsden, James, **V:**858
Gage, Thomas, **IV:**511
Gama, Vasco da, **III:**287
Garibaldi, Giuseppe, **V:**879
Gneisenau, August von, **V:**940
Gordon, Charles George, **V:**964
Göring, Hermann, **VIII:**1438
Grant, Ulysses S., **V:**975
Greene, Nathanael, **IV:**574
Grenville, Sir Richard, **III:**315

Guderian, Heinz, **VIII:**1490
Guevara, Che, **VIII:**1494
Halsey, William F., **VIII:**1525
Harrison, William Henry, **V:**1061
Hein, Piet, **IV:**644
Henry the Navigator, Prince, **III:**354
Hickok, Wild Bill, **V:**1107
Higginson, Thomas Wentworth, **V:**1110
Himmler, Heinrich, **VIII:**1666
Hindenburg, Paul Von, **VIII:**1674
Howe, Admiral Richard, **IV:**672
Howe, General William, **IV:**676
Huáscar, **III:**371
Hunyadi, János, **III:**374
Jackson, Andrew, **V:**1196
Jackson, Stonewall, **V:**1204
Joffre, Joseph-Jacques-Césaire, **VIII:**1851
Jones, John Paul, **IV:**738
Julius II, **III:**405
Kamehameha I, **VI:**1255
Kesselring, Albert, **VIII:**1949
Kidd, William, **IV:**777
Kitchener, Lord, **VIII:**2002
Kutuzov, Mikhail Illarionovich, **VI:**1305
Lawrence, T.E., **VIII:**2115
Lee, Robert E., **VI:**1338
Li Hung-chang, **VI:**1362
Lin Piao, **VIII:**2189
Louvois, Marquis de, **IV:**871
Ludendorff, Erich, **VIII:**2265
MacArthur, Douglas, **VIII:**2295
Machel, Samora Moisès, **VIII:**2317
Mannerheim, Carl Gustaf, **VIII:**2396
Mao Tse-tung, **VIII:**2400
Marlborough, First Duke of, **IV:**922
Marshall, George C., **VIII:**2429
Matthias I Corvinus, **III:**487
Mehmed II, **III:**499
Metacomet, **IV:**954
Mitchell, William, **VIII:**2554
Mobutu Sese Seko, **VIII:**2562
Monck, George, **IV:**971
Monmouth, Duke of, **IV:**980
Montgomery, Bernard Law, **VIII:**2601
Mornay, Philippe de, **III:**537
Mountbatten, Louis, **VIII:**2641
Muhammad ʻAlī Pasha, **VI:**1604
Napoleon I, **VI:**1616
Nasser, Gamal Abdel, **VIII:**2693
Nelson, Lord, **VI:**1634
Ney, Michel, **VI:**1646
Nimitz, Chester W., **VIII:**2750
Obregón, Álvaro, **IX:**2781
Oda Nobunaga, **III:**570
O'Higgins, Bernardo, **VI:**1688
Osceola, **VI:**1695
Outram, Sir James, **VI:**1705
Pachacuti, **III:**577
Papen, Franz von, **IX:**2876
Patton, George S., **IX:**2911
P'eng Te-huai, **IX:**2954
Perry, Matthew C., **VI:**1760
Perry, Oliver Hazard, **VI:**1764
Pershing, John J., **IX:**2983
Pétain, Philippe, **IX:**2987
Phillip, Arthur, **IV:**1091
Pike, Zebulon Montgomery, **IV:**1094
Powell, Colin L., **IX:**3070
Pride, Thomas, **IV:**1126
Revere, Paul, **IV:**1156
Rickover, Hyman G., **IX:**3171
Rochambeau, Comte de, **IV:**1174
Rodney, George, **IV:**1178
Rommel, Erwin, **IX:**3213
Root, Elihu, **IX:**3232
Rundstedt, Gerd von, **IX:**3260
San Martín, José de, **VI:**1947
Santa Anna, Antonio López de, **VI:**1955
Saragossa, La, **VI:**1958
Scharnhorst, Gerhard Johann David von, **VI:**1969
Scott, Winfield, **VI:**2009
Seeckt, Hans von, **IX:**3380
Shaka, **VI:**2041
Shays, Daniel, **IV:**1239
Sherman, William Tecumseh, **VI:**2057
Śivajī, **IV:**1246
Slim, First Viscount, **IX:**3435
Smuts, Jan Christian, **IX:**3453
Standish, Miles, **IV:**1273
Stanton, Edwin M., **VI:**2106
Stimson, Henry L., **IX:**3537
Sucre, Antonio José de, **VI:**2164
Suvorov, Aleksandr Vasilyevich, **IV:**1298
Taylor, Zachary, **VI:**2194
Thayer, Sylvanus, **VI:**2223
Tirpitz, Alfred von, **IX:**3688
Tito, **IX:**3692
Tokugawa Ieyasu, **IV:**1327
Torstenson, Lennart, **IV:**1335
Toussaint-Louverture, **IV:**1338
Toyotomi Hideyoshi, **III:**728
Tromp, Cornelius and Maarten, **IV:**1342
Trotsky, Leon, **IX:**3726

Tseng Kuo-fan, **VI:**2260
Vauban, Sébastien Le Prestre de, **IV:**1358
Villa, Pancho, **IX:**3811
Vo Nguyen Giap, **IX:**3821
Wallenstein, Albrecht Wenzel von, **IV:**1396
Warwick, Earl of, **III:**774
Wellington, Duke of, **VI:**2351
Wolfe, James, **IV:**1471
Zapata, Emiliano, **IX:**4104
Zhukov, Georgy Konstantinovich, **IX:**4116

MINISTRY. ***See*** **RELIGION AND THEOLOGY**

MOLECULAR BIOLOGY. ***See*** **BIOLOGY**

MONARCHY. ***See also*** **GOVERNMENT AND POLITICS; PHARAOHS; ROMAN EMPERORS**

Akbar, **III:**5
Alfred the Great, **II:**59
Anne, Queen, **IV:**50
Boleyn, Anne, **III:**66
Bruce, Robert, **II:**184
Canute the Great, **II:**201
Catherine of Aragon, **III:**136
Catherine the Great, **IV:**257
Charles I, **IV:**279
Charles II, **IV:**283
Charles III, **IV:**287
Charles XII, **IV:**290
Charles XIV John, **V:**474
Christina, **IV:**304
David I, **II:**291
David II, **II:**294
Diana, Princess of Wales, **VII:**923
Edward I, **II:**322
Edward II, **II:**326
Edward III, **II:**329
Edward IV, **III:**234
Edward VI, **III:**237
Edward VII, **VII:**1020
Edward the Confessor, **II:**315
Edward the Elder, **II:**319
Egbert, **II:**333
Eleanor of Aquitaine, **II:**336
Elizabeth I, **III:**241
Elizabeth II, **VII:**1062
Ethelred II, the Unready, **II:**344
Ferdinand II of Austria, **IV:**450
Ferdinand II of Spain, **III:**260
Francis I, **III:**274
Francis Joseph I, **V:**829
Frederick I, **IV:**497
Frederick the Great, **IV:**504
George I, **IV:**531
George II, **IV:**535
George III, **IV:**539
George IV, **V:**902
George V, **VII:**1339
George VI, **VII:**1343
Grey, Lady Jane, **III:**318
Gustavus II Adolphus, **IV:**589
Harold II, **II:**426
Henry I, **II:**443
Henry II, **II:**446
Henry III, **II:**453
Henry IV of England, **II:**457
Henry IV of France, **III:**333
Henry V, **III:**337
Henry VI, **III:**341
Henry VII, **III:**345
Henry VIII, **III:**349
Howard, Catherine, **III:**367
Huáscar, **III:**371
Isabella I, **III:**260
John, King, **II:**540
John III Sobieski, **IV:**725
Joseph II, **IV:**750
Leopold I, **IV:**838
Louis XIII, **IV:**863
Louis XIV, **IV:**866
Manuel I, **III:**464
Marguerite of Navarre, **III:**471
Maria Theresa, **IV:**914
Marie-Antoinette, **IV:**918
Mary, Queen of Scots, **III:**475
Mary I, **III:**479
Matthias I Corvinus, **III:**487
Menelik II, **VI:**1537
Mohammed I Askia, **III:**521
Montezuma II, **III:**528
Parr, Catherine, **III:**592
Peter III, **IV:**1087
Peter the Great, **IV:**1082
Philip the Magnanimous, **III:**603
Richard I, **II:**782
Richard II, **II:**786
Richard III, **III:**647
Shaka, **VI:**2041
Stephen, King, **II:**847
Tudor Family, The, **III:**732
Victoria, Queen, **VI:**2304
William III, **IV:**1447

William IV, **VI:**2392
William the Conqueror, **II:**997
Windsor, Duke of, **IX:**4025

MONASTICISM. ***See also*** **RELIGION AND THEOLOGY; SAINTS**
Anthony of Egypt, Saint, **I:**56
Benedict of Nursia, Saint, **II:**136
Buddha, **I:**144
Cassiodorus, **II:**215
Chuang-tzu, **I:**190
Dominic, Saint, **II:**301
Francis of Assisi, Saint, **II:**354
Gregory the Great, **II:**407
Ibn al-'Arabi, **II:**491
Jerome, Saint, **I:**463
Rabanus Maurus, **II:**766
Vardhamāna, **I:**915

MOTION PICTURES. ***See*** **FILM**

MUSIC. ***See also*** **THEATER AND ENTERTAINMENT**
Adam de la Halle, **II:**23
Alembert, Jean le Rond d', **IV:**30
Anderson, Marian, **VII:**70
Aristoxenus, **I:**98
Armstrong, Louis, **VII:**105
Bach, Johann Sebastian, **IV:**76
Barber, Samuel, **VII:**191
Bartók, Béla, **VII:**210
Beatles, The, **VII:**226
Beethoven, Ludwig van, **V:**178
Berg, Alban, **VII:**271
Berlin, Irving, **VII:**287
Berlioz, Hector, **V:**202
Bernstein, Leonard, **VII:**295
Bizet, Georges, **V:**244
Boccherini, Luigi, **IV:**147
Borodin, Aleksandr, **V:**286
Boulez, Pierre, **VII:**386
Brahms, Johannes, **V:**299
Britten, Benjamin, **VII:**466
Bruckner, Anton, **V:**331
Burney, Charles, **IV:**226
Byrd, William, **III:**105
Caruso, Enrico, **VII:**598
Casals, Pablo, **VII:**606
Charles, Ray, **VII:**657
Chopin, Frédéric, **V:**493
Coltrane, John, **VII:**741
Copland, Aaron, **VII:**766
Corelli, Arcangelo, **IV:**360
Couperin, François, **IV:**374
Coward, Noël, **VII:**783
Debussy, Claude, **VII:**884
Delibes, Léo, **V:**649
Delius, Frederick, **VII:**892
Donizetti, Gaetano, **V:**684
Dunstable, John, **III:**227
Dvořák, Antonín, **V:**725
Elgar, Sir Edward, **VII:**1051
Ellington, Duke, **VII:**1066
Falla, Manuel de, **VII:**1127
Fitzgerald, Ella, **VII:**1157
Foster, Stephen Collins, **V:**810
Franck, César, **V:**832
Franklin, Aretha, **VII:**1216
Gabrieli, Andrea, **III:**281
Gabrieli, Giovanni, **III:**284
Gershwin, George, **VII:**1347
Gershwin, Ira, **VII:**1352
Gilbert, W.S., **V:**927
Gillespie, Dizzy, **VII:**1370
Gluck, Christoph, **IV:**549
Goodman, Benny, **VIII:**1419
Gounod, Charles, **V:**967
Grieg, Edvard, **V:**1002
Guido d'Arezzo, **II:**411
Handel, George Frideric, **IV:**619
Haydn, Franz Joseph, **IV:**639
Henze, Hans Werner, **VIII:**1633
Hildegard von Bingen, **II:**474
Hindemith, Paul, **VIII:**1670
Holiday, Billie, **VIII:**1715
Horowitz, Vladimir, **VIII:**1747
Humperdinck, Engelbert, **V:**1162
Ives, Charles, **VIII:**1820
Janácek, Leoš, **VIII:**1835
Joplin, Janis, **VIII:**1883
Joplin, Scott, **V:**1239
Karajan, Herbert von, **VIII:**1910
Key, Francis Scott, **VI:**1281
Landini, Francesco, **II:**570
Lang, K.D., **VIII:**2080
Lind, Jenny, **VI:**1385
Liszt, Franz, **VI:**1391
Machaut, Guillaume de, **II:**615
Mahler, Gustav, **VIII:**2359
Mendelssohn, Felix, **VI:**1534
Menotti, Gian Carlo, **VIII:**2494
Mersenne, Marin, **IV:**949
Messiaen, Olivier, **VIII:**2503
Milhaud, Darius, **VIII:**2525

Monteverdi, Claudio, **IV:**990
Mozart, Wolfgang Amadeus, **IV:**1003
Muris, Johannes de, **II:**660
Mussorgsky, Modest, **VI:**1611
Norman, Jessye, **VIII:**2769
Offenbach, Jacques, **VI:**1684
Paganini, Niccolò, **VI:**1711
Parker, Charlie, **IX:**2880
Parton, Dolly, **IX:**2896
Pavarotti, Luciano, **IX:**2930
Pérotin, **II:**723
Pindar, **I:**644
Porter, Cole, **IX:**3055
Poulenc, Francis, **IX:**3066
Presley, Elvis, **IX:**3076
Price, Leontyne, **IX:**3081
Prokofiev, Sergei, **IX:**3085
Puccini, Giacomo, **IX:**3093
Purcell, Henry, **IV:**1137
Pythagoras, **I:**727
Rachmaninoff, Sergei, **IX:**3105
Rameau, Jean-Philippe, **IV:**1148
Ravel, Maurice, **IX:**3129
Rimsky-Korsakov, Nikolay, **VI:**1889
Robeson, Paul, **IX:**3187
Rossini, Gioacchino, **VI:**1913
Satie, Erik, **IX:**3331
Scarlatti, Alessandro, **IV:**1213
Schoenberg, Arnold, **IX:**3357
Schubert, Franz, **VI:**1988
Schumann, Robert, **VI:**1992
Schütz, Heinrich, **IV:**1221
Schweitzer, Albert, **IX:**3370
Segovia, Andrés, **IX:**3383
Shostakovich, Dmitri, **IX:**3409
Sibelius, Jean, **IX:**3413
Sinatra, Frank, **IX:**3422
Smith, Bessie, **IX:**3442
Sousa, John Philip, **IX:**3466
Stockhausen, Karlheinz, **IX:**3541
Stradivari, Antonio, **IV:**1281
Strauss, Johann, **VI:**2155
Strauss, Richard, **IX:**3555
Stravinsky, Igor, **IX:**3559
Sullivan, Sir Arthur, **V:**927
Tchaikovsky, Peter Ilich, **VI:**2198
Telemann, Georg Philipp, **IV:**1319
Thomas, Theodore, **VI:**2230
Toscanini, Arturo, **IX:**3707
Varèse, Edgard, **IX:**3794
Vaughan Williams, Ralph, **IX:**3798
Verdi, Giuseppe, **VI:**2299
Villa-Lobos, Heitor, **IX:**3815
Vitry, Philippe de, **II:**949
Vivaldi, Antonio, **IV:**1383
Wagner, Richard, **VI:**2316
Walton, Sir William, **IX:**3872
Wang Wei, **II:**965
Weber, Carl Maria von, **VI:**2340
Webern, Anton von, **IX:**3914
Weill, Kurt, **IX:**3926
Xenakis, Iannis, **IX:**4075
Zwilich, Ellen Taaffe, **IX:**4121

NATION-BUILDING. ***See*** **COLONIAL ADMINISTRATION; EXPLORATION AND COLONIZATION; GOVERNMENT AND POLITICS; WARFARE AND CONQUEST**

NATIVE AMERICAN AFFAIRS
Black Hawk, **V:**247
Brant, Joseph, **IV:**196
Carson, Kit, **V:**429
Catlin, George, **V:**443
Clark, William, **VI:**1358
Crazy Horse, **V:**573
Geronimo, **V:**915
Joseph, Chief, **V:**1242
McGillivray, Alexander, **IV:**875
Massasoit, **IV:**930
Metacomet, **IV:**954
Osceola, **VI:**1695
Pocahontas, **IV:**1106
Pontiac, **IV:**1110
Powhatan, **IV:**1122
Red Cloud, **VI:**1850
Ross, John, **VI:**1910
Sequoyah, **VI:**2025
Sitting Bull, **VI:**2070
Tecumseh, **VI:**2203
Tekakwitha, Kateri, **IV:**1316

NATURAL HISTORY. ***See also*** **ASTRONOMY; BIOLOGY; BOTANY; GENETICS; GEOLOGY; OCEANOGRAPHY; ORNITHOLOGY; PHYSICS; ZOOLOGY**
Agassiz, Louis, **V:**30
Anaxagoras, **I:**47
Anaximander, **I:**50
Aristotle, **I:**94
Bacon, Francis, **III:**41
Banks, Sir Joseph, **IV:**83
Buffon, Comte de, **IV:**215

Darwin, Charles, **V:**606
Empedocles, **I:**282
Gesner, Conrad, **III:**298
Haeckel, Ernst, **V:**1018
Hayden, Ferdinand Vandeveer, **V:**1072
Lankester, Sir Edwin Ray, **VI:**1316
Linnaeus, **IV:**846
Lucretius, **I:**511
Morgan, Lewis Henry, **VI:**1584
Peale, Charles Willson, **IV:**1070
Pliny the Elder, **I:**662
Spallanzani, Lazzaro, **IV:**1260
Weismann, August, **VI:**2348

NAVAL SERVICE. ***See also*** **MILITARY AFFAIRS**

NAVIGATION. ***See*** **EXPLORATION AND COLONIZATION**

NAVY. ***See*** **MILITARY AFFAIRS**

NURSING. ***See also*** **MEDICINE**
Barton, Clara, **V:**142
Nightingale, Florence, **VI:**1667
Tubman, Harriet, **VI:**2264
Wald, Lillian D., **IX:**3837

OCEANOGRAPHY
Ballard, Robert Duane, **VII:**180
Bjerknes, Vilhelm, **VII:**318
Maury, Matthew Fontaine, **VI:**1507
Piccard, Auguste and Jean-Felix, **IX:**3002

ORATORY. ***See also*** **LITERATURE**
Chrysostom, Saint John, **I:**184
Cicero, **I:**194
Gregory of Nazianzus, **I:**349

ORNITHOLOGY
Audubon, John James, **V:**86

PAINTING. ***See*** **ART**

PATRONAGE OF THE ARTS. ***See also*** **PHILANTHROPY**
'Abd al-Mu'min, **II:**4
Colbert, Jean-Baptiste, **IV:**336
Diaghilev, Sergei, **VII:**919
Francis I, **III:**274
Gardner, Isabella Stewart, **VII:**1300
Julius II, **III:**405
Kanishka, **I:**494
Leo X, **III:**419
Matthias I Corvinus, **III:**487
Mazarin, Jules, **IV:**945
Nero, **I:**577
Nicholas V, **III:**559
Pisistratus, **I:**648
Scipio Aemilianus, **I:**757
Sforza, Ludovico, **III:**682
Shah Jahan, **IV:**1232
Tamerlane, **II:**884
Whitney, Gertrude Vanderbilt, **IX:**3969

PEACE ADVOCACY. ***See also*** **SOCIAL REFORM**
Angell, Norman, **VII:**74
Balch, Emily Greene, **VII:**160
Cassin, René, **VII:**610
La Fontaine, Henri-Marie, **VIII:**2051
Niemöller, Martin, **VIII:**2742
Pauling, Linus, **IX:**2926
Rankin, Jeannette, **IX:**3117
Roosevelt, Eleanor, **IX:**3217
Russell, Bertrand, **IX:**3264
Sakharov, Andrei, **IX:**3296
Schweitzer, Albert, **IX:**3370
Söderblom, Nathan, **IX:**3456
Teresa, Mother, **IX:**3635
Tutu, Desmond, **IX:**3775
Wiesel, Elie, **IX:**3980

PHARAOHS
Akhenaton, **I:**23
Hatshepsut, **I:**371
Menes, **I:**547
Nefertiti, **I:**573
Psamtik I, **I:**709
Ptolemy Philadelphus, **I:**716
Ramses II, **I:**734
Sesostris III, **I:**774
Thutmose III, **I:**889
Tutankhamen, **I:**904
Zoser, **I:**978

PHILANTHROPY
Carnegie, Andrew, **V:**420
Eastman, George, **VII:**996
Field, Marshall, **V:**783
Guggenheim, Daniel, **VIII:**1498
Howe, Samuel Gridley, **V:**1150
McCormick, Cyrus Hall, **VI:**1431
Morgan, J.P., **VI:**1579

Nobel, Alfred, **VI:**1673
Rockefeller, John D., **VI:**1896

PHILOLOGY. ***See also*** **LANGUAGE AND LINGUISTICS**
Gesner, Conrad, **III:**298
Niebuhr, Barthold Georg, **VI:**1654

PHILOSOPHY. ***See also*** **RELIGION AND THEOLOGY**
Abano, Pietro d', **II:**1
Abelard, Peter, **II:**10
Alberti, Leon Battista, **III:**8
Alcmaeon, **I:**34
Alcott, Bronson, **V:**37
Alembert, Jean le Rond d', **IV:**30
Anaxagoras, **I:**47
Anaximenes of Miletus, **I:**53
Antisthenes, **I:**66
Arendt, Hannah, **VII:**98
Aristippus, **I:**85
Aristotle, **I:**94
Ash'ari, al-, **II:**93
Aspasia, **I:**115
Augustine, Saint, **I:**128
Aurobindo, Sri, **VII:**141
Averroës, **II:**100
Avicenna, **II:**106
Bacon, Francis, **III:**41
Bacon, Roger, **II:**110
Baeck, Leo, **VII:**148
Bakunin, Mikhail, **V:**112
Balfour, Arthur, **VII:**172
Bayle, Pierre, **IV:**103
Beauvoir, Simone de, **VII:**230
Bentham, Jeremy, **IV:**107
Bergson, Henri, **VII:**283
Berkeley, George, **IV:**114
Blanc, Louis, **V:**259
Boethius, **II:**155
Böhme, Jakob, **IV:**154
Bonhoeffer, Dietrich, **VII:**358
Bradley, F.H., **V:**290
Bruno, Giordano, **III:**96
Buber, Martin, **VII:**483
Buddha, **I:**144
Buridan, Jean, **II:**194
Camus, Albert, **VII:**553
Carnap, Rudolf, **VII:**582
Cassirer, Ernst, **VII:**614
Cato the Younger, **I:**166
Chu Hsi, **II:**265
Chuang-tzu, **I:**190
Cicero, **I:**194
Clausewitz, Carl von, **V:**503
Comte, Auguste, **V:**543
Condillac, Étienne Bonnot de, **IV:**344
Condorcet, Marquis de, **IV:**348
Confucius, **I:**222
Croce, Benedetto, **VII:**801
Davy, Sir Humphry, **V:**621
Democritus, **I:**249
Derrida, Jacques, **VII:**912
Descartes, René, **IV:**403
Dewey, John, **VII:**916
Diderot, Denis, **IV:**412
Diogenes, **I:**268
Djilas, Milovan, **VII:**944
Duns Scotus, John, **II:**309
Ehrenfels, Christian Von, **VII:**1026
Ehrlich, Eugen, **VII:**1029
Empedocles, **I:**282
Epicurus, **I:**295
Eucken, Rudolf Christoph, **VII:**1106
Fechner, Gustav Theodor, **V:**780
Ferguson, Adam, **IV:**454
Fichte, Johann Gottlieb, **IV:**465
Fracastoro, Girolamo, **III:**270
Galen, **I:**338
Gentile, Giovanni, **VII:**1336
Gilson, Étienne, **VII:**1374
Gioberti, Vincenzo, **V:**932
Godwin, William, **IV:**555
Green, Thomas Hill, **V:**987
Haeckel, Ernst, **V:**1018
Harrison, Frederic, **V:**1057
Hartmann, Nicolai, **VIII:**1571
Hegel, Georg Wilhelm Friedrich, **V:**1080
Heidegger, Martin, **VIII:**1610
Heraclitus of Ephesus, **I:**382
Herder, Johann Gottfried, **IV:**651
Hippolytus of Rome, **I:**415
Hobhouse, Leonard T., **VIII:**1707
Hsieh Ling-yün, **I:**429
Hsün-tzu, **I:**433
Hume, David, **IV:**683
Husserl, Edmund, **VIII:**1797
Huxley, Thomas Henry, **V:**1172
Hypatia, **I:**436
Ibn al-'Arabi, **II:**491
Ibn Gabirol, **II:**498
Isocrates, **I:**456
Jamāl al-Dīn al-Afghānī, **V:**1207
James, William, **V:**1216

Jaspers, Karl, **VIII:**1843
Judah ha-Levi, **II:**548
Kant, Immanuel, **IV:**761
Kierkegaard, Søren, **VI:**1284
Lacan, Jacques, **VIII:**2061
Langer, Susanne K., **VIII:**2087
Lao-tzu, **I:**498
Leibniz, Gottfried Wilhelm, **IV:**829
Lessing, Gotthold Ephraim, **IV:**842
Locke, John, **IV:**854
Lucretius, **I:**511
Lukács, György, **VIII:**2272
Lull, Raymond, **II:**608
Luria, Isaac ben Solomon, **III:**440
Luther, Martin, **III:**443
Luxemburg, Rosa, **VIII:**2285
Maimonides, Moses, **II:**619
Marcel, Gabriel, **VIII:**2407
Maritain, Jacques, **VIII:**2425
Marx, Karl, **VI:**1492
Masaryk, Tomáš, **VIII:**2440
Mazzini, Giuseppe, **VI:**1514
Mencius, **I:**543
Merleau-Ponty, Maurice, **VIII:**2500
Mersenne, Marin, **IV:**949
Michelet, Jules, **VI:**1548
Mill, James, **VI:**1556
Mill, John Stuart, **VI:**1559
Montaigne, Michel de, **III:**524
Montesquieu, **IV:**986
Moore, G.E., **VIII:**2605
Moses de León, **II:**648
Nicholas of Autrecourt, **II:**669
Nicholas of Cusa, **III:**563
Niebuhr, Reinhold, **VIII:**2735
Nietzsche, Friedrich Wilhelm, **VI:**1662
Nishida, Kitaro, **VIII:**2754
Ockham, William of, **II:**681
Ortega y Gasset, José, **IX:**2843
Ostwald, Wilhelm, **IX:**2855
Paracelsus, **III:**584
Parmenides, **I:**596
Pascal, Blaise, **IV:**1062
Peirce, Charles Sanders, **VI:**1756
Philo of Alexandria, **I:**632
Piaget, Jean, **IX:**2990
Planck, Max, **IX:**3033
Plato, **I:**655
Plotinus, **I:**666
Porphyry, **I:**683
Posidonius, **I:**686
Priestley, Joseph, **IV:**1129
Proclus, **I:**698
Protagoras, **I:**705
Proudhon, Pierre-Joseph, **VI:**1817
Psellus, Michael, **II:**758
Pufendorf, Samuel von, **IV:**1133
Pyrrhon of Elis, **I:**724
Pythagoras, **I:**727
Razi, al-, **II:**779
Renan, Ernest, **VI:**1865
Royce, Josiah, **IX:**3254
Russell, Bertrand, **IX:**3264
Santayana, George, **IX:**3317
Sartre, Jean-Paul, **IX:**3327
Scheler, Max, **IX:**3347
Schelling, Friedrich Wilhelm Joseph, **VI:**1972
Schiller, Friedrich, **IV:**1217
Schleiermacher, Friedrich, **VI:**1976
Schopenhauer, Arthur, **VI:**1984
Schrödinger, Erwin, **IX:**3362
Schweitzer, Albert, **IX:**3370
Seneca the Younger, **I:**770
Sidgwick, Henry, **VI:**2062
Siger of Brabant, **II:**829
Smith, Adam, **IV:**1249
Socrates, **I:**793
Sorel, Georges, **IX:**3463
Spencer, Herbert, **VI:**2086
Spinoza, Baruch, **IV:**1264
Staël, Madame de, **VI:**2092
Stein, Edith, **IX:**3506
Sung Dynasty, **II:**866
Taine, Hippolyte-Adolphe, **VI:**2182
Teilhard de Chardin, Pierre, **IX:**3626
Thales of Miletus, **I:**852
Theophrastus, **I:**873
Thomas Aquinas, Saint, **II:**911
Tillich, Paul, **IX:**3685
Troeltsch, Ernst, **IX:**3722
Valentinus, **I:**911
Valla, Lorenzo, **III:**739
Vico, Giambattista, **IV:**1372
Vitoria, Francisco de, **III:**768
Voltaire, **IV:**1392
Wang Ch'ung, **I:**943
Wang Pi, **I:**949
Wang Yang-ming, **III:**771
Weil, Simone, **IX:**3922
Whitehead, Alfred North, **IX:**3965
Wiesel, Elie, **IX:**3980
William of Auvergne, **II:**976
William of Auxerre, **II:**981
Wittgenstein, Ludwig, **IX:**4036

Xanthippe, **I:**952
Xenophanes, **I:**955
Xenophon, **I:**958
Zeno of Citium, **I:**967
Zeno of Elea, **I:**972

PHOTOGRAPHY. ***See also*** **ART**

Arbus, Diane, **VII:**95
Bourke-White, Margaret, **VII:**395
Brady, Mathew B., **V:**294
Carroll, Lewis, **V:**425
Cunningham, Imogen, **VII:**808
Daguerre, Jacques, **V:**592
Eastman, George, **VII:**996
Lange, Dorothea, **VIII:**2083
Steichen, Edward, **IX:**3501
Stieglitz, Alfred, **IX:**3532
Wilkins, Sir George Hubert, **IX:**3999

PHYSICS. ***See also*** **ASTRONOMY; NATURAL HISTORY**

Alembert, Jean le Rond d', **IV:**30
Alhazen, **II:**63
Arrhenius, Svante August, **VII:**114
Avogadro, Amedeo, **V:**98
Basov, Nikolay Gennadiyevich, **VII:**214
Becquerel Family, The, **V:**166
Bernoulli, Daniel, **IV:**122
Bernoulli, Jakob I, **IV:**122
Bethe, Hans Albrecht, **VII:**300
Bjerknes, Vilhelm, **VII:**318
Bohr, Niels, **VII:**345
Bothe, Walther, **VII:**379
Boyle, Robert, **IV:**185
Bragg, Sir Lawrence, **VII:**410
Bridgman, Percy Williams, **VII:**463
Broglie, Louis de, **VII:**472
Buridan, Jean, **II:**194
Chadwick, James, **VII:**635
Compton, Arthur Holly, **VII:**745
Curie, Pierre and Marie, **VII:**811
Dalton, John, **V:**602
Einstein, Albert, **VII:**1035
Euler, Leonhard, **IV:**443
Faraday, Michael, **V:**767
Fechner, Gustav Theodor, **V:**780
Fermi, Enrico, **VII:**1145
Fourier, Joseph, **V:**819
Galvani, Luigi, **IV:**523
Gauss, Carl Friedrich, **V:**893
Gay-Lussac, Joseph-Louis, **V:**897
Gibbs, Josiah Willard, **V:**923
Grove, Sir William Robert, **V:**1010
Guericke, Otto von, **IV:**586
Guillaume, Charles-Édouard, **VIII:**1502
Hahn, Otto, **VIII:**1513
Hamilton, Sir William Rowan, **V:**1025
Hawking, Stephen W., **VIII:**1580
Heisenberg, Werner, **VIII:**1617
Helmholtz, Hermann von, **V:**1089
Hertz, Gustav, **VIII:**1647
Hevesy, Georg von, **VIII:**1654
Huygens, Christiaan, **IV:**695
Kapitsa, Pyotr Leonidovich, **VIII:**1906
Kelvin, Lord, **VI:**1269
Kepler, Johannes, **IV:**772
Kurchatov, Igor Vasilyevich, **VIII:**2039
Landau, Lev Davidovich, **VIII:**2073
Laplace, Pierre-Simon, **VI:**1319
Lawrence, Ernest Orlando, **VIII:**2121
Lemaître, Georges, **VIII:**2157
Lockyer, Sir Joseph Norman, **VI:**1410
Lomonosov, Mikhail Vasilyevich, **IV:**860
Lorentz, Hendrik Antoon, **VIII:**2235
Maclaurin, Colin, **IV:**882
McMillan, Edwin Mattison, **VIII:**2336
Maxwell, James Clerk, **VI:**1511
Meitner, Lise, **VIII:**2476
Mersenne, Marin, **IV:**949
Michelson, Albert A., **VI:**1551
Millikan, Robert Andrews, **VIII:**2539
Monge, Gaspard, **IV:**975
Néel, Louis-Eugène-Félix, **VIII:**2705
Neumann, John von, **VIII:**2724
Newton, Sir Isaac, **IV:**1025
Oppenheimer, J. Robert, **IX:**2833
Ostwald, Wilhelm, **IX:**2855
Pauli, Wolfgang, **IX:**2923
Peregrinus de Maricourt, Petrus, **II:**719
Picard, Émile, **IX:**2994
Piccard, Auguste and Jean-Felix, **IX:**3002
Planck, Max, **IX:**3033
Poincaré, Henri, **VI:**1798
Prandtl, Ludwig, **IX:**3073
Rabi, Isidor Isaac, **IX:**3101
Raman, Sir Chandrasekhara Venkata, **IX:**3109
Rutherford, Ernest, **IX:**3277
Sakharov, Andrei, **IX:**3296
Schmidt, Bernhard Voldemar, **IX:**3351
Schrödinger, Erwin, **IX:**3362
Stark, Johannes, **IX:**3490
Teller, Edward, **IX:**3631
Torricelli, Evangelista, **IV:**1331
Volta, Alessandro, **IV:**1387

Wegener, Alfred, **IX:**3918
Wilkins, Maurice H. F., **IX:**3995
Yukawa, Hideki, **IX:**4090

PHYSIOLOGY. ***See also*** **MEDICINE**
Bayliss, Sir William Maddock, **VII:**217
Bernard, Claude, **V:**207
Breuer, Josef, **VII:**452
Eccles, Sir John Carew, **VII:**1008
Egas Moniz, António, **VII:**1023
Einthoven, Willem, **VII:**1039
Helmholtz, Hermann von, **V:**1089
Houssay, Bernardo Alberto, **VIII:**1759
Krogh, August, **VIII:**2027
Lorenz, Konrad, **VIII:**2238
Macleod, John J.R., **VIII:**2329
Malpighi, Marcello, **IV:**891
Pavlov, Ivan Petrovich, **IX:**2933
Raman, Sir Chandrasekhara Venkata, **IX:**3109
Spallanzani, Lazzaro, **IV:**1260
Swedenborg, Emanuel, **IV:**1302
Vesalius, Andreas, **III:**754
Whipple, George Hoyt, **IX:**3957
Wundt, Wilhelm, **IX:**4069

POETRY. ***See*** **LITERATURE**

POLITICAL SCIENCE. ***See also*** **GOVERNMENT AND POLITICS**
Beard, Charles A., **VII:**221
Burke, Edmund, **IV:**222
Clarendon, First Earl of, **IV:**308
Dickinson, John, **IV:**408
Godwin, William, **IV:**555
Gramsci, Antonio, **VIII:**1459
Hobbes, Thomas, **IV:**662
Hobhouse, Leonard T., **VIII:**1707
Hotman, François, **III:**362
Laski, Harold J., **VIII:**2093
Lassalle, Ferdinand, **VI:**1323
Lippmann, Walter, **VIII:**2203
Machiavelli, Niccolò, **III:**448
Marx, Karl, **VI:**1492
Montesquieu, **IV:**986
Mosca, Gaetano, **VIII:**2630
Paine, Thomas, **IV:**1055
Rousseau, Jean-Jacques, **IV:**1194
Tocqueville, Alexis de, **VI:**2238

POLITICS. ***See*** **GOVERNMENT AND POLITICS**

POPES
Adrian IV, **II:**27
Alexander III, **II:**48
Alexander VI, **III:**14
Boniface VIII, **II:**171
Clement I, **I:**210
Clement VII, **III:**166
Gregory VII, **II:**395
Gregory IX, **II:**399
Gregory the Great, **II:**407
Innocent III, **II:**509
Innocent IV, **II:**514
Julius II, **III:**405
Leo IX, **II:**581
Leo X, **III:**419
Nicholas V, **III:**559
Nicholas the Great, **II:**673
Paul III, **III:**595
Pius II, **III:**613
Pius V, **III:**616
Sergius I, Saint, **II:**823
Sylvester II, **II:**869
Urban II, **II:**928

PRINTING AND TYPEFOUNDING. ***See*** **INVENTION AND TECHNOLOGY**

PSYCHIATRY AND PSYCHOLOGY
Bleuler, Eugen, **VII:**328
Breuer, Josef, **VII:**452
Dewey, John, **VII:**916
Ehrenfels, Christian Von, **VII:**1026
Freud, Sigmund, **VII:**1224
Fromm, Erich, **VII:**1246
Gesell, Arnold, **VII:**1356
Horney, Karen, **VIII:**1744
James, William, **V:**1216
Janet, Pierre, **VIII:**1839
Jung, Carl, **VIII:**1896
Kübler-Ross, Elisabeth, **VIII:**2030
Lacan, Jacques, **VIII:**2061
Lorenz, Konrad, **VIII:**2238
Rorschach, Hermann, **IX:**3236
Skinner, B.F., **IX:**3431
Sullivan, Harry Stack, **IX:**3575
Thorndike, Edward L., **IX:**3669
Wertheimer, Max, **IX:**3945
Wundt, Wilhelm, **IX:**4069

PSYCHOLOGY. ***See*** **PSYCHIATRY AND PSYCHOLOGY**

PUBLIC ADMINISTRATION
Kay-Shuttleworth, First Baronet, **VIII:**1917

PUBLIC HEALTH. ***See also*** **MEDICINE; NURSING; SEX RESEARCH**
Gorgas, William Crawford, **VIII:**1434
Sanger, Margaret, **IX:**3313

PUBLISHING. ***See also*** **JOURNALISM; LITERATURE**
Armstrong, Edwin H., **VII:**102
Bennett, James Gordon, **V:**190
Brown, George, **V:**318
Caxton, William, **III:**143
Collins, Norman, **VII:**737
Graham, Katharine, **VIII:**1451
MacMillan, Daniel and Alexander, **VI:**1457
Morris, William, **VI:**1588
Newbery, John, **IV:**1019
O'Connor, Thomas Power, **IX:**2793

RADIO
Reith of Stonehaven, First Baron, **IX:**3146
Scripps, Edward Wyllis, **VI:**2014
Walter, John, II, **VI:**2324

RELIGION AND THEOLOGY. ***See also*** **BIBLICAL FIGURES; CHURCH GOVERNMENT; CHURCH REFORM; MONASTICISM; PHILOSOPHY; POPES; SAINTS**
Aaron, **I:**1
Abelard, Peter, **II:**10
Abraham, **I:**5
Abu Hanifah, **II:**16
Adrian IV, **II:**27
Ahmad ibn Hanbal, **II:**33
Ahmad Khan, Sir Sayyid, **V:**34
Akhenaton, **I:**23
Akiba ben Joseph, **I:**27
Alcuin, **II:**44
Alexander III, **II:**48
Alexander VI, **III:**14
Ambrose, Saint, **I:**43
Andrewes, Lancelot, **IV:**46
Anselm, Saint, **II:**72
Anthony of Egypt, Saint, **I:**56
Anthony of Padua, Saint, **II:**76
Arnold of Villanova, **II:**79
Ash'ari, al-, **II:**93
Aśoka the Great, **I:**112
Athanasius, Saint, **I:**119
Augustine, Saint, **I:**128
Aurobindo, Sri, **VII:**141
Ba'al Shem Tov, **IV:**73
Baeck, Leo, **VII:**148
Ball, John, **II:**114
Barth, Karl, **VII:**203
Becket, Thomas, **II:**128
Beecher, Henry Ward, **V:**174
Benedict of Nursia, Saint, **II:**136
Berkeley, George, **IV:**114
Bernard of Clairvaux, Saint, **II:**143
Besant, Annie, **V:**211
Biddle, John, **IV:**126
Boethius, **II:**155
Böhme, Jakob, **IV:**154
Bonaventure, Saint, **II:**163
Bonhoeffer, Dietrich, **VII:**358
Boniface, Saint, **II:**167
Boniface VIII, **II:**171
Booth, William, **V:**275
Boris I of Bulgaria, **II:**175
Bossuet, Jacques-Bénigne, **IV:**170
Brunner, Emil, **VII:**475
Buber, Martin, **VII:**483
Bucer, Martin, **III:**101
Buddha, **I:**144
Bultmann, Rudolf, **VII:**498
Bunyan, John, **IV:**218
Cabrini, Frances Xavier, **V:**386
Calvin, John, **III:**117
Cameron, Richard, **IV:**239
Campbell, Alexander, **V:**401
Carpini, Giovanni da Pian del, **II:**206
Catherine of Siena, Saint, **II:**218
Channing, William Ellery, **V:**470
Charlemagne, **II:**226
Charles V, **III:**159
Christopher, Saint, **I:**180
Chrysostom, Saint John, **I:**184
Clement I, **I:**210
Clement VII, **III:**166
Clovis, **II:**274
Colet, John, **III:**169
Comte, Auguste, **V:**543
Constantine the Great, **I:**226
Cotton, John, **IV:**371
Coverdale, Miles, **III:**193
Cranmer, Thomas, **III:**204
Cyril, Saint, **II:**278
David, **I:**241
Deborah, **I:**246

Denis, Saint, **I:**257
Diogenes, **I:**268
Dionysius Exiguus, **II:**298
Dominic, Saint, **II:**301
Duns Scotus, John, **II:**309
Eddy, Mary Baker, **V:**738
Edwards, Jonathan, **IV:**428
Eliade, Mircea, **VII:**1055
Elijah ben Solomon, **IV:**432
Eliot, John, **IV:**435
Elizabeth of Hungary, Saint, **II:**340
Erasmus, Desiderius, **III:**246
Eusebius of Caesarea, **I:**322
Ezekiel, **I:**326
Ezra, **I:**330
Fakhr al-Din al-Razi, **II:**347
Ferrar, Nicholas, **IV:**462
Fisher, Saint John, **III:**264
Fox, George, **IV:**484
Francis of Assisi, Saint, **II:**354
Gandhi, Mahatma, **VII:**1282
Gardiner, Stephen, **III:**291
Ghazzali, al-, **II:**385
Gibbons, James, **V:**919
Gilson, Étienne, **VII:**1374
Gioberti, Vincenzo, **V:**932
Graham, Billy, **VIII:**1447
Gregory VII, **II:**395
Gregory IX, **II:**399
Gregory of Nazianzus, **I:**349
Gregory of Nyssa, **I:**352
Gregory the Great, **II:**407
Hallaj, al-, **II:**421
Harnack, Adolf von, **VIII:**1557
Harsha, **II:**430
Hasan al-Basri, al-, **II:**440
Helena, Saint, **I:**375
Hildegard von Bingen, **II:**474
Hippolytus of Rome, **I:**415
Hsüan-tsang, **II:**482
Hung Hsiu-ch'üan, **V:**1165
Hus, Jan, **II:**487
Hutchinson, Anne, **IV:**687
Ibn al-'Arabi, **II:**491
Ignatius of Antioch, **I:**440
Innocent III, **II:**509
Innocent IV, **II:**514
Irenaeus, Saint, **I:**447
Isaiah, **I:**452
Isidore of Seville, Saint, **II:**518
James, William, **V:**1216
Jansen, Cornelius Otto, **IV:**707
Jeremiah, **I:**459
Jesus Christ, **I:**467
Jiménez de Cisneros, Francisco, **III:**392
Joachim of Fiore, **II:**534
Joan of Arc, **III:**396
Johanan ben Zakkai, **I:**471
John of Damascus, **II:**544
John of the Cross, Saint, **III:**401
John the Apostle, **I:**475
John the Baptist, **I:**479
Julius II, **III:**405
Kanishka, **I:**494
Khomeini, Ruhollah, **VIII:**1957
Kierkegaard, Søren, **VI:**1284
Las Casas, Bartolomé de, **III:**413
László I, Saint, **II:**574
Latimer, Hugh, **III:**416
Laud, William, **IV:**797
Laval, François, **IV:**801
Lee, Ann, **IV:**817
Leo IX, **II:**581
Leo X, **III:**419
Leo XIII, **VI:**1347
Lewis, C.S., **VIII:**2167
Livingstone, David, **VI:**1399
Louis IX, **II:**603
Loyola, Saint Ignatius of, **III:**437
Lull, Raymond, **II:**608
Luria, Isaac ben Solomon, **III:**440
Luther, Martin, **III:**443
Maimonides, Moses, **II:**619
Manning, Henry Edward, **VI:**1476
Maritain, Jacques, **VIII:**2425
Mather, Cotton, **IV:**934
Mather, Increase, **IV:**938
Maurice, Frederick Denison, **VI:**1503
Melanchthon, Philipp, **III:**503
Menander, **I:**541
Menno Simons, **III:**510
Mersenne, Marin, **IV:**949
Methodius, Saint, **II:**278
Moody, Dwight L., **VI:**1575
More, Sir Thomas, **III:**533
Mornay, Philippe de, **III:**537
Moses de León, **II:**648
Moses, **I:**561
Mott, John R., **VIII:**2637
Muhammad, **II:**651
Nānak, **III:**540
Napier, John, **III:**544
Neckam, Alexander, **II:**663

Nefertiti, **I:**573
Neri, Saint Philip, **III:**551
Newman, John Henry, **VI:**1641
Nichiren, **II:**666
Nicholas of Autrecourt, **II:**669
Nicholas of Cusa, **III:**563
Nicholas the Great, **II:**673
Niebuhr, Reinhold, **VIII:**2735
Nikon, **IV:**1030
Nishida, Kitaro, **VIII:**2754
Ockham, William of, **II:**681
Olaf, Saint, **II:**691
Olaf I, **II:**688
Origen, **I:**581
Parker, Matthew, **III:**588
Parker, Theodore, **VI:**1727
Pascal, Blaise, **IV:**1062
Patrick, Saint, **I:**600
Paul III, **III:**595
Paul VI, **IX:**2919
Pecham, John, **II:**715
Peter, Saint, **I:**614
Philip II, **III:**599
Pilate, Pontius, **I:**640
Pius II, **III:**613
Pius V, **III:**616
Pius IX, **VI:**1782
Pius XI, **IX:**3026
Pius XII, **IX:**3030
Planck, Max, **IX:**3033
Priestley, Joseph, **IV:**1129
Priscillian, **I:**694
Psellus, Michael, **II:**758
Pusey, E.B., **VI:**1828
Rabanus Maurus, **II:**766
Rāmānuja, **II:**770
Rasputin, Grigori Yefimovich, **VI:**1842
Ratramnus, **II:**773
Rauschenbusch, Walter, **IX:**3125
Ray, Rammohan, **VI:**1846
Raymond of Peñafort, **II:**776
Renan, Ernest, **VI:**1865
Ridley, Nicholas, **III:**654
Ritschl, Albrecht, **VI:**1892
Rumi, Jalal al-Din, **II:**800
Saladin, **II:**809
Samuel, **I:**746
Savonarola, Girolamo, **III:**667
Scheler, Max, **IX:**3347
Schleiermacher, Friedrich, **VI:**1976
Schweitzer, Albert, **IX:**3370
Sergius I, **II:**819
Sergius I, Saint, **II:**823
Servetus, Michael, **III:**675
Seton, Saint Elizabeth Ann Bayley, **VI:**2029
Sewall, Samuel, **IV:**1225
Shōtoku Taishi, **II:**826
Simeon Stylites, Saint, **I:**783
Siricius, Saint, **I:**790
Smith, Joseph, **VI:**2080
Söderblom, Nathan, **IX:**3456
Solomon, **I:**798
Stein, Edith, **IX:**3506
Stephen, Saint, **I:**822
Stephen I, **II:**851
Sunday, Billy, **IX:**3582
Swedenborg, Emanuel, **IV:**1302
Tabari, al-, **II:**873
Teilhard de Chardin, Pierre, **IX:**3626
Tekakwitha, Kateri, **IV:**1316
Teresa, Mother, **IX:**3635
Teresa of Ávila, Saint, **III:**713
Tertullian, **I:**848
Theodore of Mopsuestia, **I:**861
Theodoret of Cyrrhus, **I:**865
Theoleptus of Philadelphia, **II:**899
Thomas, Saint, **I:**880
Thomas à Kempis, **II:**906
Thomas Aquinas, Saint, **II:**911
Tillich, Paul, **IX:**3685
Torquemada, Tomás de, **III:**725
Troeltsch, Ernst, **IX:**3722
Turner, Nat, **VI:**2276
Tutu, Desmond, **IX:**3775
Tyndale, William, **III:**735
Ulfilas, **I:**908
Urban II, **II:**928
Valentinus, **I:**911
Valla, Lorenzo, **III:**739
Vardhamāna, **I:**915
Venette, Jean de, **II:**935
Vincent de Paul, Saint, **IV:**1380
Vincent of Lérins, Saint, **I:**936
Virgin Mary, **I:**939
Vitoria, Francisco de, **III:**768
Vladimir I, **II:**952
Wach, Joachim, **IX:**3829
Weil, Simone, **IX:**3922
Wesley, John, **IV:**1426
Widukind, **II:**973
Wiesel, Elie, **IX:**3980
William of Auxerre, **II:**981
William of Saint-Amour, **II:**990
William of Saint-Thierry, **II:**994

Williams, Roger, **IV:**1451
Wise, Isaac Mayer, **VI:**2400
Wise, Stephen Samuel, **IX:**4033
Witherspoon, John, **IV:**1467
Władysław II Jagiełło and Jadwiga, **II:**1001
Wyclif, John, **II:**1009
Xavier, Saint Francis, **III:**788
Xenophanes, **I:**955
Young, Brigham, **VI:**2414
Zoroaster, **I:**975
Zwingli, Huldrych, **III:**791

ROCKETRY. ***See*** **AVIATION AND SPACE EXPLORATION**

ROMAN CAESARS
Augustus, **I:**132
Caesar, Julius, **I:**147
Caligula, **I:**152
Claudius I, **I:**203
Tiberius, **I:**892
Vespasian, **I:**933

ROMAN EMPERORS
Constantine the Great, **I:**226
Diocletian, **I:**263
Hadrian, **I:**356
Justinian I, **II:**553
Marcus Aurelius, **I:**523
Nero, **I:**577
Theodosius the Great, **I:**868
Trajan, **I:**899

SAINTS
Albertus Magnus, Saint, **II:**37
Ambrose, Saint, **I:**43
Anselm, Saint, **II:**72
Anthony of Egypt, Saint, **I:**56
Anthony of Padua, Saint, **II:**76
Athanasius, Saint, **I:**119
Augustine, Saint, **I:**128
Bede the Venerable, Saint, **II:**132
Benedict of Nursia, Saint, **II:**136
Bernard of Clairvaux, Saint, **II:**143
Bonaventure, Saint, **II:**163
Boniface, Saint, **II:**167
Catherine of Siena, Saint, **II:**218
Christopher, Saint, **I:**180
Chrysostom, Saint John, **I:**184
Clement I, **I:**210
Cyril, Saint, **II:**278
Denis, Saint, **I:**257
Dominic, Saint, **II:**301
Elizabeth of Hungary, Saint, **II:**340
Francis of Assisi, Saint, **II:**354
Fulbert of Chartres, Saint, **II:**373
Gregory VII, **II:**395
Gregory of Nazianzus, **I:**349
Gregory of Nyssa, **I:**352
Gregory the Great, **II:**407
Helena, Saint, **I:**375
Henry II the Saint, **II:**449
Hildegard von Bingen, **II:**474
Hippolytus of Rome, **I:**415
Ignatius of Antioch, **I:**440
Irenaeus, Saint, **I:**447
Isidore of Seville, Saint, **II:**518
Jerome, Saint, **I:**463
John of Damascus, **II:**544
John the Apostle, **I:**475
John the Baptist, **I:**479
László I, Saint, **II:**574
Leo IX, **II:**581
Louis IX, **II:**603
Methodius, Saint, **II:**278
Nicholas the Great, **II:**673
Olaf, Saint, **II:**691
Patrick, Saint, **I:**600
Paul, Saint, **I:**604
Peter, Saint, **I:**614
Raymond of Peñafort, **II:**776
Sergius I, Saint, **II:**823
Simeon Stylites, Saint, **I:**783
Siricius, Saint, **I:**790
Stephen, Saint, **I:**822
Stephen I, **II:**851
Thomas, Saint, **I:**880
Vincent of Lérins, Saint, **I:**936
Vladimir I, **II:**952

SCHOLARSHIP. ***See also*** **EDUCATION; HISTORIOGRAPHY**
Averroës, **II:**100
Baeck, Leo, **VII:**148
Boccaccio, Giovanni, **II:**150
Evatt, Herbert Vere, **VII:**1109
Gregory IX, **II:**399
Harnack, Adolf von, **VIII:**1557
Jerome, Saint, **I:**463
Josephus, Flavius, **I:**483
Porphyry, **I:**683
Varro, Marcus Terentius, **I:**918
William of Moerbeke, **II:**985

SCIENCE. ***See also*** **ANTHROPOLOGY; ASTRONOMY; AVIATION AND SPACE EXPLORATION; BIOLOGY; CHEMISTRY; COMPUTER SCIENCE; ENGINEERING; GENETICS; GEOLOGY; HORTICULTURE; INVENTION AND TECHNOLOGY; MATHEMATICS; MEDICINE; METEOROLOGY; NATURAL HISTORY; OCEANOGRAPHY; ORNITHOLOGY; PHYSICS; PHYSIOLOGY; ZOOLOGY**

Abano, Pietro d', **II:**1
Abul Wefa, **II:**20
Albertus Magnus, Saint, **II:**37
Alcmaeon, **I:**34
Alhazen, **II:**63
Anaxagoras, **I:**47
Anaximander, **I:**50
Anaximenes of Miletus, **I:**53
Apollonius of Perga, **I:**72
Archimedes, **I:**76
Aretaeus of Cappadocia, **I:**81
Aristotle, **I:**94
Arnold of Villanova, **II:**79
Aryabhata, **II:**89
Asclepiades of Bithynia, **I:**101
Avicenna, **II:**106
Bacon, Roger, **II:**110
Battani, al-, **II:**121
Bell, Alexander Graham, **V:**185
Berkeley, George, **IV:**114
Biruni, al-, **II:**147
Brahmagupta, **II:**181
Bridgman, Percy Williams, **VII:**463
Buridan, Jean, **II:**194
Carver, George Washington, **VII:**602
Celsus, Aulus Cornelius, **I:**173
Conant, James Bryant, **VII:**748
Diocles of Carystus, **I:**260
Diophantus, **I:**272
Dioscorides, Pedanius, **I:**276
Empedocles, **I:**282
Erasistratus, **I:**299
Eratosthenes of Cyrene, **I:**303
Euclid, **I:**307
Eudoxus of Cnidus, **I:**310
Galen, **I:**338
Gallatin, Albert, **V:**861
Gray, Asa, **V:**979
Guy de Chauliac, **II:**414
Henry, Joseph, **V:**1093
Hero of Alexandria, **I:**387
Herophilus, **I:**398
Hipparchus, **I:**407
Hippocrates, **I:**411
Huxley, Thomas Henry, **V:**1172
Hypatia, **I:**436
Imhotep, **I:**443
Jabir ibn Hayyan, **II:**522
Jahiz, al-, **II:**526
Khwarizmi, al-, **II:**563
Leonardo of Pisa, **II:**585
Lockyer, Sir Joseph Norman, **VI:**1410
Lucretius, **I:**511
Maimonides, Moses, **II:**619
Nabu-rimanni, **I:**566
Neckam, Alexander, **II:**663
Newcomb, Simon, **VI:**1638
Omar Khayyám, **II:**695
Pappus, **I:**593
Paul of Aegina, **II:**712
Peregrinus de Maricourt, Petrus, **II:**719
Pliny the Elder, **I:**662
Powell, John Wesley, **VI:**1810
Priestley, Joseph, **IV:**1129
Ptolemy, **I:**712
Pythagoras, **I:**727
Pytheas, **I:**731
Razi, al-, **II:**779
Seaborg, Glenn Theodore, **IX:**3375
Sosigenes, **I:**811
Thales of Miletus, **I:**852
Theophrastus, **I:**873
Urey, Harold C., **IX:**3787

SCREENWRITING. ***See*** **FILM; TELEVISION**

SCULPTURE. ***See*** **ART**

SEX RESEARCH
Ellis, Havelock, **VII:**1070
Kinsey, Alfred Charles, **VIII:**1986
Stopes, Marie, **IX:**3551

SOCIAL REFORM. ***See also*** **CHURCH REFORM; CIVIL RIGHTS; LABOR MOVEMENT; PEACE ADVOCACY; WOMEN'S RIGHTS**

Abernathy, Ralph David, **VII:**9
Addams, Jane, **VII:**21
Adler, Felix, **V:**26
Angell, Norman, **VII:**74
Astor, Nancy, **VII:**129
Baden-Powell, Sir Robert Stephenson Smyth, **V:**105

Bakunin, Mikhail, **V:**112
Balch, Emily Greene, **VII:**160
Ball, John, **II:**114
Barton, Clara, **V:**142
Baxter, Richard, **IV:**98
Beale, Dorothea, **V:**157
Beauvoir, Simone de, **VII:**230
Bernstein, Eduard, **VII:**291
Besant, Annie, **V:**211
Bevan, Aneurin, **VII:**304
Beveridge, Lord, **VII:**308
Bondfield, Margaret, **VII:**353
Booth, William, **V:**275
Braille, Louis, **V:**303
Brandeis, Louis D., **VII:**419
Brown, John, **V:**321
Butler, R.A., **VII:**529
Buxton, Sir Thomas Fowell, **V:**378
Cabrini, Frances Xavier, **V:**386
Cassin, René, **VII:**610
Cayley, Sir George, **V:**450
Chadwick, Edwin, **V:**457
Child, Lydia Maria, **V:**489
Chomsky, Noam, **VII:**673
Constantine, Baron, **VII:**759
Day, Dorothy, **VII:**850
Dewey, John, **VII:**916
Diana, Princess of Wales, **VII:**923
Dix, Dorothea, **V:**680
Douglass, Frederick, **V:**695
Dunant, Jean-Henri, **V:**711
Engels, Friedrich, **V:**760
Fawcett, Dame Millicent Garrett, **V:**776
Fourier, Charles, **V:**814
Fuller, Margaret, **V:**849
Gandhi, Mahatma, **VII:**1282
Garrison, William Lloyd, **V:**883
George, Henry, **V:**906
Goldman, Emma, **VIII:**1411
Gorky, Maxim, **VIII:**1442
Greeley, Horace, **V:**982
Harrison, Frederic, **V:**1057
Hayslip, Le Ly, **VIII:**1593
Hernandez, Aileen Clarke, **VIII:**1641
Herzen, Aleksandr, **V:**1099
Higginson, Thomas Wentworth, **V:**1110
Hill, Octavia, **V:**1113
Howe, Julia Ward, **V:**1145
Hutchins, Robert M., **VIII:**1800
Jackson, Helen Hunt, **V:**1200
Jones, Mary Harris "Mother," 1879
Keller, Helen, **VIII:**1924
Kemble, Fanny, **VI:**1273
La Follette, Robert M., **VIII:**2047
Lange, Dorothea, **VIII:**2083
Las Casas, Bartolomé de, **III:**413
Lathrop, Julia C., **VIII:**2096
Lazarus, Emma, **VI:**1334
Lockwood, Belva A., **VI:**1406
Low, Juliette Gordon, **VIII:**2246
Lutuli, Albert, **VIII:**2281
Luxemburg, Rosa, **VIII:**2285
Mahfouz, Naguib, **VIII:**2355
Malcolm X, **VIII:**2373
Mandela, Nelson, **VIII:**2384
Mann, Horace, **IV:**894
Manning, Henry Edward, **VI:**1476
Montessori, Maria, **VIII:**2596
Mott, Lucretia, **VI:**1600
Nader, Ralph, **VIII:**2679
Nation, Carry, **VI:**1630
Niemöller, Martin, **VIII:**2742
O'Connell, Daniel, **VI:**1680
O'Higgins, Bernardo, **VI:**1688
Olmsted, Frederick Law, **VI:**1691
Osborne, Thomas Mott, **IX:**2852
Owen, Robert, **VI:**1708
Pankhurst, Emmeline, **IX:**2871
Paton, Alan, **IX:**2907
Phillips, Wendell, **VI:**1771
Picotte, Susan La Flesche, **IX:**3010
Pire, Dominique, **IX:**3017
Place, Francis, **VI:**1786
Potter, Beatrix, **IX:**3063
Rankin, Jeannette, **IX:**3117
Rauschenbusch, Walter, **IX:**3125
Ray, Rammohan, **VI:**1846
Reuther, Walter P., **IX:**3161
Robeson, Paul, **IX:**3187
Roosevelt, Eleanor, **IX:**3217
Ruskin, John, **VI:**1925
Sakharov, Andrei, **IX:**3296
Sanger, Margaret, **IX:**3313
Sartre, Jean-Paul, **IX:**3327
Sewall, Samuel, **IV:**1225
Sharp, Granville, **IV:**1236
Shaw, George Bernard, **IX:**3399
Sinclair, Upton, **IX:**3426
Smith, Alfred E., **IX:**3439
Söderblom, Nathan, **IX:**3456
Solzhenitsyn, Aleksandr, **IX:**3459
Sorel, Georges, **IX:**3463
Spock, Benjamin, **IX:**3478
Stanton, Elizabeth Cady, **VI:**2110

Stein, Freiherr vom, **VI:**2115
Stone, Lucy, **VI:**2143
Stopes, Marie, **IX:**3551
Stowe, Harriet Beecher, **VI:**2151
Suttner, Bertha von, **VI:**2175
Teresa, Mother, **IX:**3635
Theodora, **II:**890
Thomas, Norman, **IX:**3660
Tolstoy, Leo, **VI:**2242
Truth, Sojourner, **VI:**2255
Tutu, Desmond, **IX:**3775
Tyler, Wat, **II:**921
Vincent de Paul, Saint, **IV:**1380
Wakefield, Edward Gibbon, **VI:**2321
Wald, Lillian D., **IX:**3837
Washington, Booker T., **VI:**2335
Webb, Beatrice and Sidney, **IX:**3905
Wilberforce, William, **IV:**1435
Willard, Frances, **VI:**2388
Wise, Stephen Samuel, **IX:**4033
Zapata, Emiliano, **IX:**4104
Zetkin, Clara, **IX:**4112

SOCIAL SCIENCES. ***See also*** **ANTHROPOLOGY; ECONOMICS; EDUCATION; GEOGRAPHY; HISTORIOGRAPHY; POLITICAL SCIENCE; SEX RESEARCH; SOCIOLOGY**
Adler, Alfred, **VII:**30
Arendt, Hannah, **VII:**98
Braudel, Fernand, **VII:**436
Ellis, Havelock, **VII:**1070
Frazer, Sir James George, **VII:**1220
Kinsey, Alfred Charles, **VIII:**1986
McLuhan, Marshall, **VIII:**2332
Veblen, Thorstein, **IX:**3805

SOCIOLOGY
Comte, Auguste, **V:**543
Durkheim, Émile, **VII:**988
Hobhouse, Leonard T., **VIII:**1707
Le Bon, Gustave, **VIII:**2134
Myrdal, Gunnar, **VIII:**2671
Scheler, Max, **IX:**3347
Talbot, Marion, **IX:**3603
Tocqueville, Alexis de, **VI:**2238
Tönnies, Ferdinand Julius, **IX:**3703
Troeltsch, Ernst, **IX:**3722
Ward, Lester Frank, **VI:**2328
Webb, Beatrice and Sidney, **IX:**3905
Weber, Max, **IX:**3910

SPACE EXPLORATION. ***See*** **AVIATION AND SPACE EXPLORATION**

SPORTS
Ali, Muhammad, **VII:**53
Borg, Björn, **VII:**368
Bradman, Donald G., **VII:**407
Cobb, Ty, **VII:**717
Coe, Sebastian, **VII:**725
Constantine, Baron, **VII:**759
Coubertin, Pierre de, **VII:**774
Dempsey, Jack, **VII:**900
Dimaggio, Joe, **VII:**934
Evert, Chris, **VII:**1112
Ferrari, Enzo, **VII:**1150
Gehrig, Lou, **VII:**1322
Gibson, Althea, **VII:**1363
Grace, William Gilbert, **V:**971
Henie, Sonja, **VIII:**1629
Jones, Bobby, **VIII:**1874
Killy, Jean-Claude, **VIII:**1965
King, Billie Jean, **VIII:**1968
Laver, Rod, **VIII:**2109
Louis, Joe, **VIII:**2241
Marciano, Rocky, **VIII:**2411
Messner, Reinhold, **VIII:**2506
Navratilova, Martina, **VIII:**2702
Oakley, Annie, **VI:**1677
Oh, Sadaharu, **IX:**2796
Owens, Jesse, **IX:**2862
Pelé, **IX:**2950
Perry, Fred, **IX:**2979
Player, Gary, **IX:**3040
Robinson, Jackie, **IX:**3193
Rose, Pete, **IX:**3239
Russell, Bill, **IX:**3268
Ruth, Babe, **IX:**3273
Thorpe, Jim, **IX:**3672
Wightman, Hazel Hotchkiss, **IX:**3989
Woods, Tiger, **IX:**4049
Zaharias, "Babe" Didrikson, **IX:**4096

STATECRAFT. ***See*** **DIPLOMACY; GOVERNMENT AND POLITICS; WARFARE AND CONQUEST**

STATISTICS
Galton, Francis, **V:**867

SUFFRAGE. ***See*** **WOMEN'S RIGHTS**

SWIMMING. ***See*** **SPORTS**

TECHNOLOGY. ***See*** **INVENTION AND TECHNOLOGY**

TELEVISION. ***See also*** **THEATER AND ENTERTAINMENT**
Ball, Lucille, **VII:**176
Collins, Norman, **VII:**737
Disney, Walt, **VII:**938
Winfrey, Oprah, **IX:**4029
Zworykin, Vladimir, **IX:**4125

TENNIS. ***See*** **SPORTS**

THEATER AND ENTERTAINMENT. ***See also*** **LITERATURE; MUSIC**
Aeschylus, **I:**9
Akalaitis, Joanne, **VII:**34
Aristophanes, **I:**88
Barnum, P.T., **V:**133
Beatles, The, **VII:**226
Beaumont, Francis, **III:**54
Beckett, Samuel, **VII:**238
Bergman, Ingmar, **VII:**278
Booth, Edwin, **V:**271
Brando, Marlon, **VII:**424
Burnett, Frances Hodgson, **V:**361
Calderón de la Barca, Pedro, **IV:**235
Chapman, George, **III:**155
Chekhov, Anton, **V:**485
Cody, William Frederick, **V:**530
Corneille, Pierre, **IV:**363
Coward, Noël, **VII:**783
Crawford, Cheryl, **VII:**793
Davis, Bette, **VII:**843
Disney, Walt, **VII:**938
Dumas, Alexandre, *père*, **V:**708
Euripides, **I:**317
Fletcher, John, **III:**54
Forrest, Edwin, **V:**800
Garland, Judy, **VII:**1304
Garrick, David, **IV:**527
Geddes, Norman Bel, **VII:**1319
Gilbert, W.S., **V:**927
Gish, Lillian, **VII:**1383
Goethe, Johann Wolfgang von, **IV:**560
Hammerstein, Oscar, II, **VIII:**1533
Harsha, **II:**430
Hart, Lorenz, **VIII:**1566
Hayes, Helen, **VIII:**1588
Hellman, Lillian, **VIII:**1620
Ibsen, Henrik, **V:**1175
Irving, Henry, **V:**1187
Jonson, Ben, **IV:**744
Kean, Edmund, **VI:**1259
Kemble, Fanny, **VI:**1273
Kleist, Heinrich von, **VI:**1294
Le Gallienne, Eva, **VIII:**2141
Lessing, Gotthold Ephraim, **IV:**842
Macready, William Charles, **VI:**1460
Marlowe, Christopher, **III:**471
Menander (dramatist), **I:**538
Meyerhold, Vsevolod Yemilyevich, **VIII:**2510
Miller, Arthur, **VIII:**2533
Molière, **IV:**966
Nashe, Thomas, **III:**548
Oakley, Annie, **VI:**1677
Olivier, Sir Laurence, **IX:**2808
O'Neill, Eugene, **IX:**2819
Plautus, **I:**659
Racine, Jean, **IV:**1144
Robeson, Paul, **IX:**3187
Rodgers, Richard, **IX:**3201
Rogers, Will, **IX:**3204
Schiller, Friedrich, **IV:**1217
Shakespeare, William, **III:**686
Shaw, George Bernard, **IX:**3399
Stanislavsky, Konstantin, **IX:**3486
Stewart, James, **IX:**3528
Sullivan, Sir Arthur, **V:**927
Terry, Ellen, **VI:**2215
Terry, Megan, **IX:**3642
Thespis, **I:**877
Thurber, James, **IX:**3677
Vanbrugh, Sir John, **IV:**1351
Vega Carpio, Lope de, **IV:**1361
Visconti, Luchino, **IX:**3818
Wagner, Richard, **VI:**2316
Welles, Orson, **IX:**3934
West, Mae, **IX:**3949
Wilde, Oscar, **VI:**2377
Zeami Motokiyo, **II:**1025

THEOLOGY. ***See*** **RELIGION AND THEOLOGY**

TRACK AND FIELD. ***See*** **SPORTS**

TRADE UNIONISM. ***See*** **LABOR MOVEMENT**

URBAN DEVELOPMENT. ***See also*** **ARCHITECTURE**
Burnham, Daniel Hudson, **V:**365

VIROLOGY. ***See*** **MEDICINE**

WARFARE AND CONQUEST. ***See also*** **GOVERNMENT AND POLITICS; MILITARY AFFAIRS**

'Abd al-Mu'min, **II:**4
Agesilaus II, **I:**16
Agrippa, Marcus Vipsanius, **I:**20
Alboin, **II:**41
Alcibiades, **I:**31
Alexander Nevsky, **II:**52
Alexander the Great, **I:**38
Alp Arslan, **II:**67
Antigonus I Monophthalmos, **I:**60
Antiochus the Great, **I:**63
Antony, Marc, **I:**69
Árpád, **II:**86
Ashikaga Takauji, **II:**97
Ashurnasirpal II, **I:**109
Attila, **I:**124
Boadicca, **I:**136
Bohemond I, **II:**159
Brutus, Marcus Junius, **I:**140
Caesar, Julius, **I:**147
Cassius (Longinus), **I:**159
Charlemagne, **II:**226
Charles Martel, **II:**242
Ch'in Shih Huang-ti, **I:**176
Cid, El, **II:**268
Cimon, **I:**198
Cleomenes, **I:**214
Clovis, **II:**274
Constantine the Great, **I:**226
Cyrus the Great, **I:**233
Deborah, **I:**246
Egbert, **II:**333
Epaminondas, **I:**290
Fabius Maximus, Quintus, **I:**334
Genghis Khan, **II:**376
Genseric, **I:**342
Ghazan, Mahmud, **II:**381
Hannibal, **I:**364
Harold II, **II:**426
Harsha, **II:**430
Harun al-Rashid, **II:**437
Hengist, **I:**378
Heraclius, **II:**470
James I the Conqueror, **II:**529
Khosrow I, **II:**559
Kublai Khan, **II:**566
Leonidas, **I:**501
Marius, Gaius, **I:**528
Masinissa, **I:**535
Miltiades the Younger, **I:**553
Nebuchadnezzar II, **I:**569
Odoacer, **II:**685
Olaf I, **II:**688
Osman, **II:**702
Pheidippides, **I:**621
Philip II of Macedonia, **I:**628
Piankhi, **I:**636
Pompey the Great, **I:**679
Regulus, Marcus Atilius, **I:**739
Rollo, **II:**793
Rurik, **II:**803
Sargon II, **I:**754
Scipio Aemilianus, **I:**757
Scipio Africanus, **I:**760
Seleucus I Nicator, **I:**767
Shapur II, **I:**778
Spartacus, **I:**814
Stilicho, Flavius, **I:**825
Sulla, Lucius Cornelius, **I:**833
Tancred, **II:**887
Themistocles, **I:**857
Trajan, **I:**899
Valdemar II, **II:**932
Vercingetorix, **I:**922
Villehardouin, Geoffroi de, **II:**942
Vladimir I, **II:**952
Wallace, Sir William, **II:**955
Widukind, **II:**973
Xerxes I, **I:**962
Yo Fei, **II:**1018
Žižka, Count Jan, **II:**1030

WOMEN'S RIGHTS. ***See also*** **SOCIAL REFORM**

Adams, Abigail, **IV:**12
Anthony, Susan B., **V:**61
Beauvoir, Simone de, **VII:**230
Beecher, Catharine, **V:**170
Catt, Carrie Chapman, **VII:**627
Fawcett, Dame Millicent Garrett, **V:**776
Fowler, Lydia Folger, **V:**822
Friedan, Betty, **VII:**1231
Halide Edib Adivar, **VIII:**1522
Hernandez, Aileen Clarke, **VIII:**1641
Higginson, Thomas Wentworth, **V:**1110
Kirkpatrick, Jeane, **VIII:**1994
Lockwood, Belva A., **VI:**1406
MacKinnon, Catharine A., **VIII:**2325
Millett, Kate, **VIII:**2536

Montagu, Mary Wortley, **IV:**983
Mott, Lucretia, **VI:**1600
Naidu, Sarojini, **VIII:**2683
Paul, Alice, **IX:**2915
Shaw, Anna Howard, **VI:**2044
Stanton, Elizabeth Cady, **VI:**2110
Stein, Edith, **IX:**3506
Steinem, Gloria, **IX:**3519
Stone, Lucy, **VI:**2143
Stowe, Harriet Beecher, **VI:**2151
Talbot, Marion, **IX:**3603
Theodora, **II:**890
Wells-Barnett, Ida B., **IX:**3941
Willard, Frances, **VI:**2388
Wollstonecraft, Mary, **IV:**1475
Workman, Fanny Bullock, **VI:**2410
Zetkin, Clara, **IX:**4112

ZOOLOGY. ***See also*** **NATURAL HISTORY**

Cousteau, Jacques-Yves, **VII:**778
Frisch, Karl von, **VII:**1235
Haeckel, Ernst, **V:**1018
Kinsey, Alfred Charles, **VIII:**1986
Krogh, August, **VIII:**2027
Lankester, Sir Edwin Ray, **VI:**1316
Lorenz, Konrad, **VIII:**2238
Malpighi, Marcello, **IV:**891
Weismann, August, **VI:**2348

GEOGRAPHICAL LOCATION INDEX

AFRICA. *See* **ALEXANDRIA; ALGERIA; CARTHAGE; EAST AFRICA; EGYPT; ETHIOPIA; GABON; GHANA; GUINEA; IVORY COAST; KENYA; LIBERIA; LIBYA; MALI; MOROCCO; MOZAMBIQUE; NIGERIA; NORTH AFRICA; NUMIDIA; OTTOMAN EMPIRE; SENEGAL; SONGHAI EMPIRE; SOUTH AFRICA; TANZANIA; TUNISIA; WEST AFRICA; ZAIRE; ZIMBABWE; ZULU EMPIRE**

ALEXANDRIA. *See also* **EGYPT**
Athanasius, Saint, **I:**119
Callimachus, **I:**156
Ctesibius of Alexandria, **I:**231
Eratosthenes of Cyrene, **I:**303
Hero of Alexandria, **I:**387
Herophilus, **I:**398
Hypatia, **I:**436
Origen, **I:**581
Pappus, **I:**593
Philo of Alexandria, **I:**632
Ptolemy, **I:**712
Ptolemy Philadelphus, **I:**716
Ptolemy Soter, **I:**720
Valentinus, **I:**911

ALGERIA. *See also* **OTTOMAN EMPIRE**
Abbas, Ferhat, **VII:**5

ARABIA. *See also* **ASSYRIA; IRAN; IRAQ; MESOPOTAMIA; SYRIA**
Alp Arslan, **II:**67
Hasan al-Basri, al-, **II:**440
Lucian, **I:**507
Muhammad, **II:**651

ARGENTINA
Borges, Jorge Luis, **VII:**371
Guevara, Che, **VIII**-1494
Houssay, Bernardo Alberto, **VIII:**1759
Perón, Eva, **IX:**2965
Perón, Juan, **IX:**2969
San Martín, José de, **VI:**1947

ARMENIA
Tigranes the Great, **I:**896

ASIA. *See* **ARABIA; ARMENIA; ASIA MINOR; ASSYRIA; BABYLONIA; BITHYNIA; BURMA; BYZANTINE EMPIRE; CAMBODIA; CAPPADOCIA; CENTRAL ASIA; CHINA; CILICIA; INDIA; INDONESIA; IRAN; IRAQ; ISRAEL; JAPAN; JORDAN; KHWARIZM; KOREA; MESOPOTAMIA; MOPSUESTIA; OTTOMAN EMPIRE; PAKISTAN; PERGA; PHILIPPINES; PONTUS; RUSSIA; SINGAPORE; SOVIET UNION; SYRIA; TAIWAN; TURKEY; VIETNAM**

ASIA MINOR. *See also* **ASSYRIA; BITHYNIA; CAPPADOCIA; CILICIA; CNIDUS; COS; GREECE; MILUTUS; MOPSUESTIA; PERGA; PONTUS**
Anaxagoras, **I:**47
Aspasia, **I:**115
Christopher, Saint, **I:**180
Diogenes, **I:**268
Galen, **I:**338
Helena, Saint, **I:**375
Herodotus, **I:**394
Homer, **I:**420
Irenaeus, Saint, **I:**447
Osman, **II:**702
Rumi, Jalal al-Din, **II:**800
Theoleptus of Philadelphia, **II:**899

ASSYRIA
Ashurbanipal, **I:**105
Ashurnasirpal II, **I:**109
Sargon II, **I:**754

AUSTRALIA
Barton, Sir Edmund, **V:**147
Bradman, Donald G., **VII:**407
Bragg, Sir Lawrence, **VII:**410
Burnet, Sir Macfarlane, **VII:**512
Curtin, John, **VII:**816
Deakin, Alfred, **V:**630
Eccles, Sir John Carew, **VII:**1008
Evatt, Herbert Vere, **VII:**1109
Florey, Baron, **VII:**1172
Greenway, Francis, **V:**990
Hughes, William Morris, **VIII:**1775

Laver, Rod, **VIII:**2109
Lyons, Dame Enid Muriel, **VIII:**2289
Lyons, Joseph Aloysius, **VIII:**2292
Mannix, Daniel, **VI:**1480
Menzies, Robert Gordon, **VIII:**2497
Parkes, Sir Henry, **VI:**1731
Wentworth, W.C., **VI:**2355
Wilkins, Sir George Hubert, **IX:**3999

AUSTRIA
Adler, Alfred, **VII:**30
Berg, Alban, **VII:**271
Beust, Friedrich von, **V:**222
Breuer, Josef, **VII:**452
Bruckner, Anton, **V:**331
Buber, Martin, **VII:**483
Ehrenfels, Christian Von, **VII:**1026
Ehrlich, Eugen, **VII:**1029
Ferdinand II, **IV:**450
Fischer von Erlach, Johann Bernhard, **IV:**473
Francis Ferdinand, **VII:**1197
Francis Joseph I, **V:**829
Freud, Sigmund, **VII:**1224
Gluck, Christoph, **IV:**549
Haydn, Franz Joseph, **IV:**639
Hildebrandt, Johann Lucas von, **IV:**655
Joseph II, **IV:**750
Kafka, Franz, **VIII:**1900
Karajan, Herbert von, **VIII:**1910
Kokoschka, Oskar, **VIII:**2012
Lang, Fritz, **VIII:**2077
Leopold I, **IV:**838
Lorenz, Konrad, **VIII:**2238
Mahler, Gustav, **VIII:**2359
Maria Theresa, **IV:**914
Marie-Antoinette, **IV:**918
Maximilian I, **III:**491
Meitner, Lise, **VIII:**2476
Mendel, Gregor Johann, **VI:**1526
Metternich, **VI:**1544
Mozart, Wolfgang Amadeus, **IV:**1003
Schoenberg, Arnold, **IX:**3357
Schrödinger, Erwin, **IX:**3362
Schubert, Franz, **VI:**1988
Strauss, Johann, **VI:**2155
Suttner, Bertha von, **VI:**2175
Vivaldi, Antonio, **IV:**1383
Waldheim, Kurt, **IX:**3841
Wallenstein, Albrecht Wenzel von, **IV:**1396
Webern, Anton von, **IX:**3914
Wiesenthal, Simon, **IX:**3984

AUSTRO-HUNGARIAN EMPIRE. ***See*** **AUSTRIA; BOHEMIA; DALMATIA; HUNGARY**

AZERBAIJAN
Landau, Lev Davidovich, **VIII:**2073

BABYLONIA
Abraham, **I:**5
Hammurabi, **I:**360
Nabu-rimanni, **I:**566
Nebuchadnezzar II, **I:**569

BAVARIA. ***See*** **GERMANY**

BELGIUM
Bruegel, Pieter, the Elder, **III:**85
Eyck, Jan van, and Hubert van Eyck, **III:**250
La Fontaine, Henri-Marie, **VIII:**2051
Lemaître, Georges, **VIII:**2157
Lévi-Strauss, Claude, **VIII:**2164
Magritte, René, **VIII:**2349
Mercator, Gerardus, **III:**513
Pire, Dominique, **IX:**3017
Pirenne, Henri, **IX:**3023
Rubens, Peter Paul, **IV:**1198
Spaak, Paul-Henri, **IX:**3475
Vesalius, Andreas, **III:**754
Weyden, Rogier van der, **III:**778

BELORUSSIA
Chagall, Marc, **VII:**639

BERMERSHEIM BEI ALZEY. ***See*** **GERMANY**

BITHYNIA
Asclepiades of Bithynia, **I:**101
Hipparchus, **I:**407

BOHEMIA. ***See also*** **CZECHOSLOVIA; GERMANY**
Dvořák, Antonín, **V:**725

BOSNIA-HERZEGOVINA. ***See*** **YUGOSLAVIA**

BRAZIL
Machado de Assis, Joaquim Maria, **VI:**1444
Niemeyer, Oscar, **VIII:**2739
Pelé, **IX:**2950
Santos-Dumont, Alberto, **IX:**3320
Villa-Lobos, Heitor, **IX:**3815

BRITAIN. *See also* **GREAT BRITAIN**
Boadicca, **I:**136
Hengist, **I:**378
Patrick, Saint, **I:**600

BULGARIA
Boris I of Bulgaria, **II:**175

BURMA
Thant, U, **IX:**3646

BYZANTINE EMPIRE
Constantine the Great, **I:**226
Cyril, Saint, **II:**278
Gregory of Nyssa, **I:**352
Heraclius, **II:**470
Justinian I, **II:**553
Methodius, Saint, **II:**278
Paul of Aegina, **II:**712
Priscian, **II:**755
Proclus, **I:**698
Psellus, Michael, **II:**758
Sergius I, **II:**819
Stilicho, Flavius, **I:**825
Theodora, **II:**890
Theophanes the Confessor, **II:**903
Ulfilas, **I:**908

CAMBODIA
Sihanouk, Norodom, **IX:**3417

CANAAN. *See* **ISRAEL**

CANADA
Baldwin, Robert, **V:**116
Banting, Sir Frederick Grant, **VII:**187
Borden, Robert Laird, **VII:**365
Brown, George, **V:**318
Carleton, Guy, **IV:**246
Chrétien, Jean, **VII:**680
Clinton, Sir Henry, **IV:**321
Durham, First Earl of, **V:**721
Jolliet, Louis, **IV:**732
King, William Lyon Mackenzie, **VIII:**1981
Lansdowne, Fifth Marquess of, **VIII:**2090
Laurier, Sir Wilfrid, **VIII:**2100
Laval, François, **IV:**801
Macdonald, Sir John Alexander, **VI:**1435
Mackenzie, William Lyon, **VI:**1447
McLuhan, Marshall, **VIII:**2332
Massey, Vincent, **VI:**1496
Mulroney, Brian, **VIII:**2655
Osler, Sir William, **VI:**1698
Tekakwitha, Kateri, **IV:**1316
Thomson, Tom, **IX:**3665
Trudeau, Pierre Elliott, **IX:**3730

CAPPADOCIA
Aretaeus of Cappadocia, **I:**81
Gregory of Nazianzus, **I:**349
Heraclius, **II:**470

CARTHAGE
Genseric, **I:**342
Hannibal, **I:**364
Hanno, **I:**368
Masinissa, **I:**535
Tertullian, **I:**848

CENTRAL ASIA. *See also* **KHWARIZM**
Attila, **I:**124
Genghis Khan, **II:**376
Kublai Khan, **II:**570
Tamerlane, **II:**884

CHALDEA. *See* **BABYLONIA**

CHILE
Neruda, Pablo, **VIII:**2716
O'Higgins, Bernardo, **VI:**1688

CHINA. *See also* **TAIWAN**
Abahai, **IV:**1
Chang Chih-tung, **V:**466
Ch'en Tu-hsiu, **VII:**660
Cheng Ch'eng-kung, **IV:**297
Cheng Ho, **II:**253
Chiang Kai-shek, **VII:**664
Ch'ien-lung, **IV:**300
Ch'in Shih Huang-ti, **I:**176
Chou En-lai, **VII:**676
Chu Hsi, **II:**265
Chu Teh, **VII:**687
Ch'ü Yüan, **I:**187
Chuang-tzu, **I:**190
Confucius, **I:**222
Deng Xiaoping, **VII:**905
Dorgon, **IV:**421
Hsia Kuei, **II:**479
Hsieh Ling-yün, **I:**429
Hsüan-tsang, **II:**482
Hsün-tzu, **I:**433

Hung Hsiu-ch'üan, **V:**1165
K'ang-Hsi, **IV:**757
Kuo Mo-jo, **VIII:**2033
Lao-tzu, **I:**498
Li Ch'ing-chao, **II:**588
Li Hung-chang, **VI:**1362
Lin Piao, **VIII:**2189
Lin Tse-hsü, **VI:**1376
Li Peng, **VIII:**2178
Li Po, **II:**591
Liu Shao-ch'i, **VIII:**2212
Lu Hsün, **VIII:**2252
Mao Tse-tung, **VIII:**2400
Ma Yüan, **II:**612
Mencius, **I:**543
Mi Fei, **II:**639
Ou-yang Hsiu, **II:**709
Pan Ku, **I:**589
Peary, Robert Edwin, **IX:**2941
P'eng Te-huai, **IX:**2954
Ssu-ma Ch'ien, **I:**818
Ssu-ma Kuang, **II:**840
Sung Dynasty, **II:**866
Su Tung-p'o, **II:**855
Sun Yat-sen, **IX:**3578
T'ai Tsung, **II:**876
T'ao Ch'ien, **I:**841
Tseng Kuo-fan, **VI:**2260
Tu Fu, **II:**917
Wang An-shih, **II:**962
Wang Ching-wei, **IX:**3877
Wang Ch'ung, **I:**943
Wang Hsi-chih, **I:**946
Wang Pi, **I:**949
Wang Wei, **II:**965
Wang Yang-ming, **III:**771
Yen Li-pen, **II:**1015
Yo Fei, **II:**1018
Yung-lo, **II:**1021

CILICIA
Dioscorides, Pedanius, **I:**276
Paul, Saint, **I:**604

CNIDUS
Eudoxus of Cnidus, **I:**310

COLOMBIA
Bolívar, Simón, **V:**267
García Márquez, Gabriel, **VII:**1293

CONGO. ***See*** **ZAIRE**

COS
Hippocrates, **I:**411

CROATIA. ***See*** **YUGOSLAVIA**

CUBA
Castro, Fidel, **VII:**617
Guevara, Che, **VIII**-1494

CZECHOSLOVAKIA. ***See also*** **BOHEMIA**
Beneš, Edvard, **VII:**259
Capek, Karel, **VII:**560
Dubcek, Alexander, **VII:**968
Janácek, Leoš, **VIII:**1835
Kupka, František, **VIII:**2036
Laban, Rudolf, **VIII:**2058
Masaryk, Tomáš, **VIII:**2440
Wenceslaus, **II:**969

DALMATIA
Diocletian, **I:**263

DENMARK
Andersen, Hans Christian, **V:**58
Bering, Vitus Jonassen, **IV:**111
Bohr, Niels, **VII:**345
Brahe, Tycho, **III:**77
Dreyer, Carl Theodor, **VII:**959
Kierkegaard, Søren, **VI:**1284
Krogh, August, **VIII:**2027
Margaret of Denmark, Norway, and Sweden, **II:**626
Rasmussen, Knud Johan Victor, **IX:**3121
Saxo Grammaticus, **II:**815
Valdemar II, **II:**932

EAST AFRICA
Piankhi, **I:**636

EAST AFRICA PROTECTORATE. ***See*** **KENYA**

EAST GERMANY. ***See also*** **GERMANY**
Ulbricht, Walter, **IX:**3779

EGYPT. ***See also*** **ALEXANDRIA**
'Abduh, Muhammad, **V:**4
Akhenaton, **I:**23
Anthony of Egypt, Saint, **I:**56
Baybars I, **II:**124
Boutros-Ghali, Boutros, **VII:**399
Cleopatra VII, **I:**218

Hatshepsut, **I:**371
Imhotep, **I:**443
Mahfouz, Naguib, **VIII:**2355
Maimonides, Moses, **II:**619
Menes, **I:**547
Muhammad 'Alī Pasha, **VI:**1604
Nasser, Gamal Abdel, **VIII:**2693
Nefertiti, **I:**573
Plotinus, **I:**666
Psamtik I, **I:**709
Ramses II, **I:**734
Sadat, Anwar el-, **IX:**3289
Sesostris III, **I:**774
Thutmose III, **I:**889
Tutankhamen, **I:**904
Zaghlūl, Sa'd, **IX:**4093
Zoser, **I:**978

ELEA
Parmenides, **I:**596
Zeno of Elea, **I:**972

ENGLAND. *See also* **BRITAIN; GREAT BRITAIN**
Adrian IV, **II:**27
Alfred the Great, **II:**59
Anselm, Saint, **II:**72
Bacon, Francis, **III:**41
Bacon, Roger, **II:**110
Ball, John, **II:**114
Beaumont, Francis, **III:**54
Becket, Thomas, **II:**128
Bede the Venerable, Saint, **II:**132
Bodley, Sir Thomas, **III:**62
Boleyn, Anne, **III:**66
Bracton, Henry de, **II:**178
Burgh, Hubert de, **II:**190
Byrd, William, **III:**105
Cabot, John, **III:**113
Canute the Great, **II:**201
Catherine of Aragon, **III:**136
Cavendish, Thomas, **III:**140
Caxton, William, **III:**143
Cædmon, **II:**198
Cecil, William, **III:**147
Chapman, George, **III:**155
Chaucer, Geoffrey, **II:**248
Colet, John, **III:**169
Coverdale, Miles, **III:**193
Cranmer, Thomas, **III:**204
Cromwell, Thomas, **III:**208
Davis, John, **III:**212
Drake, Sir Francis, **III:**224
Dunstable, John, **III:**227
Edward I, **II:**322
Edward II, **II:**326
Edward III, **II:**329
Edward IV, **III:**234
Edward VI, **III:**237
Edward the Confessor, **II:**315
Edward the Elder, **II:**319
Egbert, **II:**333
Eleanor of Aquitaine, **II:**336
Elizabeth I, **III:**241
Ethelred II, the Unready, **II:**344
Fawkes, Guy, **III:**257
Fisher, Saint John, **III:**264
Fletcher, John, **III:**54
Fortescue, Sir John, **III:**267
Gardiner, Stephen, **III:**291
Grenville, Sir Richard, **III:**315
Grey, Lady Jane, **III:**318
Harold II, **II:**426
Henry I, **II:**443
Henry II, **II:**446
Henry III, **II:**453
Henry IV, **II:**457
Henry V, **III:**337
Henry VI, **III:**341
Henry VII, **III:**345
Henry VIII, **III:**349
Howard, Catherine, **III:**367
John, King, **II:**540
Latimer, Hugh, **III:**416
Littleton, Sir Thomas, **III:**431
Malory, Sir Thomas, **III:**457
Marlowe, Christopher, **III:**471
Mary, Queen of Scots, **III:**475
Mary I, **III:**479
Montfort, Simon V de, **II:**642
More, Sir Thomas, **III:**533
Nashe, Thomas, **III:**548
Ockham, William of, **II:**681
Parker, Matthew, **III:**588
Parr, Catherine, **III:**592
Pecham, John, **II:**715
Raleigh, Sir Walter, **III:**638
Richard I, **II:**782
Richard II, **II:**786
Richard III, **III:**647
Ridley, Nicholas, **III:**654
Salisbury, First Earl of, **III:**660
Shakespeare, William, **III:**686
Sidney, Sir Philip, **III:**691

Spenser, Edmund, **III:**703
Stephen, King, **II:**847
Tudor Family, The, **III:**732
Tyler, Wat, **II:**921
Tyndale, William, **III:**735
Warwick, Earl of, **III:**774
William the Conqueror, **II:**997
Wolsey, Cardinal Thomas, **III:**785
Wyclif, John, **II:**1009

ESTONIA. ***See*** **GERMANY; SOVIET UNION**

ETHIOPIA
Haile Selassie I, **VIII:**1517
Menelik II, **VI:**1537

FINLAND
Aalto, Alvar, **VII:**1
Mannerheim, Carl Gustaf, **VIII:**2396
Sibelius, Jean, **IX:**3413

FLANDERS. ***See*** **BELGIUM**

FLORENCE, REPUBIC OF. ***See*** **ITALY**

FRANCE
Abelard, Peter, **II:**10
Adam de la Halle, **II:**23
Alcuin, **II:**44
Alembert, Jean le Rond d', **IV:**30
Apollinaire, Guillaume, **VII:**82
Arnold of Villanova, **II:**79
Balzac, Honoré de, **V:**120
Barthes, Roland, **VII:**207
Baudelaire, Charles, **V:**150
Bayard, Chevalier de, **III:**48
Bayle, Pierre, **IV:**103
Beauvoir, Simone de, **VII:**230
Beckett, Samuel, **VII:**238
Becquerel Family, The, **V:**166
Benjamin, Walter, **VII:**267
Bergson, Henri, **VII:**283
Berlioz, Hector, **V:**202
Bernard, Claude, **V:**207
Bernard of Clairvaux, Saint, **II:**143
Bizet, Georges, **V:**244
Blanc, Louis, **V:**259
Blériot, Louis, **VII:**325
Blum, Léon, **VII:**335
Boffrand, Germain, **IV:**151
Bonnard, Pierre, **VII:**362
Bossuet, Jacques-Bénigne, **IV:**170
Bougainville, Louis-Antoine de, **IV:**179
Boulez, Pierre, **VII:**386
Braille, Louis, **V:**303
Brancusi, Constantin, **VII:**414
Braque, Georges, **VII:**431
Braudel, Fernand, **VII:**436
Breton, André, **VII:**448
Breuil, Henri-Édouard-Prosper, **VII:**456
Broglie, Louis de, **VII:**472
Buffon, Comte de, **IV:**215
Buridan, Jean, **II:**194
Calmette, Albert, **VII:**546
Calvin, John, **III:**117
Cambacérès, Jean-Jacques-Régis de, **V:**398
Camus, Albert, **VII:**553
Cartier, Jacques, **III:**129
Cartier-Bresson, Henri, **VII:**594
Cassin, René, **VII:**610
Catherine de Médicis, **III:**132
Césaire, Aimé, **VII:**631
Cézanne, Paul, **V:**453
Chagall, Marc, **VII:**639
Chanel, Coco, **VII:**648
Chardin, Jean Siméon, **IV:**275
Charlemagne, **II:**226
Charles XIV John, **V:**474
Charles d'Orléans, **II:**232
Charles Martel, **II:**242
Charles the Bald, **II:**239
Charles the Bold, **III:**163
Chartier, Alain, **II:**245
Chateaubriand, **V:**481
Chrétien de Troyes, **II:**257
Christine de Pizan, **II:**260
Citroën, André-Gustave, **VII:**695
Claude, Georges, **VII:**699
Claude Lorrain, **IV:**317
Clemenceau, Georges, **VII:**702
Clovis, **II:**274
Cocteau, Jean, **VII:**721
Colbert, Jean-Baptiste, **IV:**336
Colette, **VII:**729
Comte, Auguste, **V:**543
Condé, The Great, **IV:**341
Condillac, Étienne Bonnot de, **IV:**344
Condorcet, Marquis de, **IV:**348
Coubertin, Pierre de, **VII:**774
Couperin, François, **IV:**374
Courbet, Gustave, **V:**565
Cousteau, Jacques-Yves, **VII:**778
Curie, Pierre and Marie, **VII:**811
Cuvier, Georges, **V:**589

Cyrano de Bergerac, Savinien de, **IV:**385
Daguerre, Jacques, **V:**592
Danjon, André-Louis, **VII:**837
Danton, Georges, **IV:**393
David, Jacques-Louis, **V:**610
Debussy, Claude, **VII:**884
Degas, Edgar, **V:**641
de Gaulle, Charles, **VII:**866
Delacroix, Eugène, **V:**645
Delaunay, Robert, **VII:**888
Delibes, Léo, **V:**649
Denis, Maurice, **VII:**909
Denis, Saint, **I:**257
Derrida, Jacques, **VII:**912
Descartes, René, **IV:**403
Diderot, Denis, **IV:**412
Duchamp, Marcel, **VII:**972
Dumas, Alexandre, *père*, **V:**708
Durkheim, Émile, **VII:**988
Éluard, Paul, **VII:**1074
Ernst, Max, **VII:**1098
Faidherbe, Louis, **V:**763
Fermat, Pierre de, **IV:**458
Flaubert, Gustave, **V:**796
Fourier, Charles, **V:**814
Fourier, Joseph, **V:**819
Fragonard, Jean-Honoré, **IV:**488
France, Anatole, **V:**825
Francis I, **III:**274
Franck, César, **V:**832
Freyssinet, Eugène, **VII:**1228
Froissart, Jean, **II:**366
Fulbert of Chartres, Saint, **II:**373
Galois, Èvariste, **V:**864
Gambetta, Léon, **V:**871
Gance, Abel, **VII:**1274
Garnier, Tony, **VII:**1308
Gauguin, Paul, **V:**888
Gay-Lussac, Joseph-Louis, **V:**897
Genet, Jean, **VII:**1333
Géricault, Théodore, **V:**910
Gide, André, **VII:**1367
Gilson, Étienne, **VII:**1374
Giraudoux, Jean, **VII:**1379
Godard, Jean-Luc, **VIII:**1391
Gounod, Charles, **V:**967
Gregory of Tours, **II:**403
Gris, Juan, **VIII**-1483
Guy de Chauliac, **II:**414
Hahnemann, Samuel, **IV:**593
Hardouin-Mansart, Jules, **IV:**901
Henry IV, **III:**333
Herriot, Édouard, **VIII:**1644
Hotman, François, **III:**362
Hugo, Victor, **V:**1154
Ingres, Jean-Auguste-Dominique, **V:**1183
Ionesco, Eugène, **VIII:**1816
Jacob, François, **VIII:**1827
Janet, Pierre, **VIII:**1839
Jaurès, Jean, **V:**1221
Joan of Arc, **III:**396
Joffre, Joseph-Jacques-Césaire, **VIII:**1851
Joliot, Frédéric, and Irène Joliot-Curie, **VIII:**1870
Jolliet, Louis, **IV:**732
Joséphine, **V:**1246
Killy, Jean-Claude, **VIII:**1965
Lacan, Jacques, **VIII:**2061
La Fontaine, Jean de, **IV:**781
Lagrange, Joseph-Louis, **IV:**785
Laplace, Pierre-Simon, **VI:**1319
La Salle, Sieur de, **IV:**793
Laval, Pierre, **VIII:**2105
Lavoisier, Antoine-Laurent, **IV:**805
Leblanc, Nicolas, **IV:**813
Le Bon, Gustave, **VIII:**2134
Le Corbusier, **VIII:**2137
Léger, Fernand, **VIII:**2154
Lenoir, Étienne, **VI:**1343
Le Nôtre, André, **IV:**834
Lescot, Pierre, **III:**428
Lesseps, Ferdinand de, **VI:**1355
Lévi-Strauss, Claude, **VIII:**2164
Lifar, Serge, **VIII:**2182
Lipchitz, Jacques, **VIII:**2199
Louis IX, **II:**603
Louis XI, **III:**434
Louis XIII, **IV:**863
Louis XIV, **IV:**866
Louvois, Marquis de, **IV:**871
Lumière, Auguste and Louis, **VIII:**2276
Machaut, Guillaume de, **II:**615
Malraux, André, **VIII:**2380
Manet, Édouard, **VI:**1471
Mansart, François, **IV:**898
Marat, Jean-Paul, **IV:**910
Marcel, Gabriel, **VIII:**2407
Marguerite of Navarre, **III:**467
Marie-Antoinette, **IV:**918
Marie de France, **II:**629
Maritain, Jacques, **VIII:**2425
Matisse, Henri, **VIII:**2452
Maupassant, Guy de, **VI:**1500
Mazarin, Jules, **IV:**945
Mendès-France, Pierre, **VIII:**2491

Merleau-Ponty, Maurice, **VIII:**2500
Mersenne, Marin, **IV:**949
Messiaen, Olivier, **VIII:**2503
Michelet, Jules, **VI:**1548
Michelin, André and Édouard, **VIII:**2514
Milhaud, Darius, **VIII:**2525
Mirabeau, Comte de, **IV:**963
Mitterrand, François, **VIII:**2558
Molière, **IV:**966
Monet, Claude, **VIII:**2579
Monge, Gaspard, **IV:**975
Monnet, Jean, **VIII:**2583
Montaigne, Michel de, **III:**524
Montesquieu, **IV:**986
Montgolfier, Jacques-Étienne and Joseph-Michel, **IV:**995
Mornay, Philippe de, **III:**537
Muris, Johannes de, **II:**660
Napoleon I, **VI:**1616
Napoleon III, **VI:**1620
Neckam, Alexander, **II:**663
Necker, Jacques, **IV:**1016
Néel, Louis-Eugène-Félix, **VIII:**2705
Ney, Michel, **VI:**1646
Nicholas of Autrecourt, **II:**669
Niépce, Nicéphore, **VI:**1657
Nordau, Max, **VIII:**2766
Nostradamus, **III:**567
Offenbach, Jacques, **VI:**1684
Orleans, Duc d', **IV:**1048
Papin, Denis, **IV:**1059
Pascal, Blaise, **IV:**1062
Pasteur, Louis, **VI:**1744
Peregrinus de Maricourt, Petrus, **II:**719
Pérotin, **II:**723
Perret, Auguste, **IX:**2976
Pétain, Philippe, **IX:**2987
Philip II, **II:**732
Philip the Good, **II:**740
Picard, Émile, **IX:**2994
Picasso, Pablo, **IX:**2997
Pissarro, Camille, **VI:**1779
Pléiade, La, **III:**623
Poincaré, Henri, **VI:**1798
Poincaré, Raymond, **IX:**3044
Pompidou, Georges, **IX:**3052
Poulenc, Francis, **IX:**3066
Poussin, Nicolas, **IV:**1118
Proudhon, Pierre-Joseph, **VI:**1817
Proust, Marcel, **IX:**3089
Pucelle, Jean, **II:**762
Pytheas, **I:**731
Rabanus Maurus, **II:**766
Rabelais, François, **III:**633
Racine, Jean, **IV:**1144
Rameau, Jean-Philippe, **IV:**1148
Ratramnus, **II:**773
Ravel, Maurice, **IX:**3129
Redon, Odilon, **VI:**1854
Renan, Ernest, **VI:**1865
Renoir, Jean, **IX:**3157
Renoir, Pierre-Auguste, **VI:**1869
Richelieu, Cardinal de, **IV:**1165
Rimbaud, Arthur, **VI:**1886
Robespierre, **IV:**1170
Rochambeau, Comte de, **IV:**1174
Rodin, Auguste, **VI:**1900
Rollo, **II:**793
Ronsard, Pierre de, **III:**657
Rouault, Georges, **IX:**3251
Rousseau, Henri, **VI:**1921
Rousseau, Jean-Jacques, **IV:**1194
Saint-Just, Louis de, **IV:**1205
Sand, George, **VI:**1951
Sarraute, Nathalie, **IX:**3324
Sartre, Jean-Paul, **IX:**3327
Satie, Erik, **IX:**3331
Scaliger, Joseph Justus, **III:**671
Seurat, Georges, **VI:**2033
Sluter, Claus, **II:**832
Sorel, Georges, **IX:**3463
Staël, Madame de, **VI:**2092
Stendhal, **VI:**2125
Suger, **II:**859
Taine, Hippolyte-Adolphe, **VI:**2182
Talleyrand, **VI:**2185
Teilhard de Chardin, Pierre, **IX:**3626
Thiers, Adolphe, **VI:**2226
Tocqueville, Alexis de, **VI:**2238
Toulouse-Lautrec, Henri de, **VI:**2247
Toussaint-Louverture, **IV:**1338
Truffaut, François, **IX:**3736
Turgot, Anne-Robert-Jacques, **IV:**1348
Valéry, Paul, **IX:**3791
Varèse, Edgard, **IX:**3794
Vauban, Sébastien Le Prestre de, **IV:**1358
Venette, Jean de, **II:**935
Vercingetorix, **I:**922
Verne, Jules, **VI:**2303
Vigée-Lebrun, Élisabeth, **IV:**1376
Villehardouin, Geoffroi de, **II:**942
Villon, François, **III:**763
Vincent de Paul, Saint, **IV:**1380
Vincent of Beauvais, **II:**946

Vincent of Lérins, Saint, **I:**936
Vitry, Philippe de, **II:**949
Voltaire, **IV:**1392
Vuillard, Édouard, **IX:**3826
Walras, Léon, **IX:**3865
Watteau, Antoine, **IV:**1413
Weil, Simone, **IX:**3922
Wiesel, Elie, **IX:**3980
William of Auvergne, **II:**976
William of Auxerre, **II:**981
William of Moerbeke, **II:**985
William of Rubrouck, **II:**987
William of Saint-Amour, **II:**990
William of Saint-Thierry, **II:**994
Xenakis, Iannis, **IX:**4075
Zola, Émile, **VI:**2420

FRANCONIA. ***See*** **GERMANY**

FRENCH EQUATORIAL AFRICA. ***See*** **GABON**

FRENCH GUIANA
Éboué, Félix, **VII:**1004

GABON
Schweitzer, Albert, **IX:**3370

GAUL. ***See*** **FRANCE**

GERMANY. ***See also*** **EAST GERMANY; WEST GERMANY**
Agricola, Georgius, **III:**1
Albertus Magnus, Saint, **II:**37
Bach, Johann Sebastian, **IV:**76
Baeck, Leo, **VIII**-148
Baer, Karl Ernst von, **V:**109
Basedow, Johann Bernhard, **IV:**92
Beethoven, Ludwig van, **V:**178
Behring, Emil von, **V:**182
Benjamin, Walter, **VII:**267
Benz, Carl, **V:**199
Bergius, Friedrich, **VII:**275
Bernstein, Eduard, **VII:**291
Bessel, Friedrich Wilhelm, **V:**215
Bethe, Hans Albrecht, **VII:**300
Bismarck, Otto von, **V:**240
Blücher, Gebhard Leberecht von, **V:**263
Boas, Franz, **VII:**339
Böhme, Jakob, **IV:**154
Böll, Heinrich, **VII:**349
Bonhoeffer, Dietrich, **VII:**358
Boniface, Saint, **II:**167
Bothe, Walther, **VII:**379
Brahms, Johannes, **V:**299
Braun, Wernher von, **VII:**440
Brecht, Bertolt, **VII:**444
Bucer, Martin, **III:**101
Bülow, Bernhard von, **VII:**494
Bultmann, Rudolf, **VII:**498
Carnap, Rudolf, **VII:**582
Cassirer, Ernst, **VII:**614
Charles IV, **II:**235
Clausewitz, Carl von, **V:**503
Cohn, Ferdinand Julius, **V:**534
Copernicus, Nicolaus, **III:**176
Cranach, Lucas, the Elder, **III:**200
Daimler, Gottlieb, **V:**597
Dedekind, Richard, **V:**638
Diels, Otto Paul Hermann, **VII:**927
Diesel, Rudolf, **V:**672
Domagk, Gerhard, **VII:**951
Dürer, Albrecht, **III:**230
Eckener, Hugo, **VII:**1011
Ehrenfels, Christian Von, **VII:**1026
Ehrlich, Paul, **VII:**1032
Einstein, Albert, **VII:**1035
Elizabeth of Hungary, Saint, **II:**340
Engels, Friedrich, **V:**760
Ernst, Max, **VII:**1098
Erzberger, Matthias, **VII:**1102
Eucken, Rudolf Christoph, **VII:**1106
Fechner, Gustav Theodor, **V:**780
Fichte, Johann Gottlieb, **IV:**465
Frank, Anne, **VII:**1204
Frederick I, **IV:**497
Frederick I Barbarossa, **II:**357
Frederick the Great, **IV:**504
Frederick William, the Great Elector, **IV:**508
Frege, Gottlob, **V:**836
Frisch, Karl von, **VII:**1235
Frobenius, Leo, **VII:**1242
Froebel, Friedrich, **V:**845
Fromm, Erich, **VII:**1246
Gauss, Carl Friedrich, **V:**893
Geiger, Rudolf Oskar Robert Williams, **VII:**1326
Gneisenau, August von, **V:**940
Goebbels, Joseph, **VIII**-1404
Goethe, Johann Wolfgang von, **IV:**560
Göring, Hermann, **VIII**-1438
Gottfried von Strassburg, **II:**392
Grass, Günter, **VIII**-1463
Grimm, Jacob and Wilhelm, **V:**1006
Gropius, Walter, **VIII**-1486

Grünewald, Matthias, **III:**322
Guderian, Heinz, **VIII-**1490
Guericke, Otto von, **IV:**586
Gutenberg, Johann, **III:**328
Haber, Fritz, **VIII:**1509
Haeckel, Ernst, **V:**1018
Hahn, Otto, **VIII:**1513
Hahnemann, Samuel, **IV:**593
Hardenberg, Karl von, **V:**1033
Harnack, Adolf von, **VIII:**1557
Hartmann, Nicolai, **VIII:**1571
Hartmann von Aue, **II:**433
Hegel, Georg Wilhelm Friedrich, **V:**1080
Heidegger, Martin, **VIII:**1610
Heine, Heinrich, **V:**1085
Heinkel, Ernst Heinrich, **VIII:**1614
Heisenberg, Werner, **VIII:**1617
Helmholtz, Hermann von, **V:**1089
Henry II the Saint, **II:**449
Henry IV, **II:**461
Henry the Lion, **II:**466
Henze, Hans Werner, **VIII:**1633
Herder, Johann Gottfried, **IV:**651
Hertz, Gustav, **VIII:**1647
Hesse, Hermann, **VIII:**1650
Hildegard von Bingen, **II:**474
Himmler, Heinrich, **VIII:**1666
Hindemith, Paul, **VIII:**1670
Hindenburg, Paul Von, **VIII:**1674
Hitler, Adolf, **VIII:**1692
Holbein, Hans, the Younger, **III:**358
Holstein, Friedrich von, **V:**1130
Humboldt, Alexander von, **V:**1159
Humperdinck, Engelbert, **V:**1162
Husserl, Edmund, **VIII:**1797
Jaspers, Karl, **VIII:**1843
Kämpfer, Engelbert, **IV:**754
Kant, Immanuel, **IV:**761
Kepler, Johannes, **IV:**772
Kesselring, Albert, **VIII:**1949
Kirchner, Ernst Ludwig, **VIII:**1991
Kleist, Heinrich von, **VI:**1294
Koch, Robert, **VI:**1297
Kohl, Helmut, **VIII:**2009
Kollwitz, Käthe, **VIII:**2016
Krupp, Alfred, **VI:**1301
Laban, Rudolf, **VIII:**2058
Lang, Fritz, **VIII:**2077
Lassalle, Ferdinand, **VI:**1323
Leibniz, Gottfried Wilhelm, **IV:**829
Lessing, Gotthold Ephraim, **IV:**842
Liebig, Justus von, **VI:**1366
Liebknecht, Wilhelm, **VI:**1369
Louis II the German, **II:**599
Ludendorff, Erich, **VIII:**2265
Luther, Martin, **III:**443
Luxemburg, Rosa, **VIII:**2285
Mann, Thomas, **VIII:**2392
Marc, Franz, **VIII:**2404
Marx, Karl, **VI:**1492
Melanchthon, Philipp, **III:**503
Mendelsohn, Erich, **VIII:**2487
Mendelssohn, Felix, **VI:**1534
Mies Van Der Rohe, Ludwig, **VIII:**2520
Mommsen, Theodor, **VI:**1566
Nernst, Walther Hermann, **VIII:**2713
Nicholas of Cusa, **III:**563
Niebuhr, Barthold Georg, **VI:**1654
Niemöller, Martin, **VIII:**2742
Nietzsche, Friedrich Wilhelm, **VI:**1662
Oberth, Hermann, **IX:**2777
Odoacer, **II:**685
Ostwald, Wilhelm, **IX:**2855
Otto, Nikolaus August, **VI:**1702
Otto the Great, **II:**706
Papen, Franz von, **IX:**2876
Pauli, Wolfgang, **IX:**2923
Peter III, **IV:**1087
Philip the Good, **II:**740
Philip the Magnanimous, **III:**603
Planck, Max, **IX:**3033
Prandtl, Ludwig, **IX:**3073
Pufendorf, Samuel von, **IV:**1133
Ranke, Leopold von, **VI:**1839
Remarque, Erich Maria, **IX:**3150
Rilke, Rainer Maria, **IX:**3181
Ritschl, Albrecht, **VI:**1892
Rommel, Erwin, **IX:**3213
Rothschild Family, The, **VI:**1916
Rudolf I, **II:**796
Rundstedt, Gerd von, **IX:**3260
Sachs, Nelly, **IX:**3285
Savigny, Friedrich Karl von, **VI:**1966
Scharnhorst, Gerhard Johann David von, **VI:**1969
Scheler, Max, **IX:**3347
Schelling, Friedrich Wilhelm Joseph, **VI:**1972
Schleiermacher, Friedrich, **VI:**1976
Schliemann, Heinrich, **VI:**1980
Schmidt, Bernhard Voldemar, **IX:**3351
Schmidt-Rottluff, Karl, **IX:**3354
Schopenhauer, Arthur, **VI:**1984
Schumann, Robert, **VI:**1992
Schütz, Heinrich, **IV:**1221
Schwarzschild, Karl, **IX:**3366

Schweitzer, Albert, **IX:**3370
Seeckt, Hans von, **IX:**3380
Siemens Family, The, **VI:**2066
Stahl, Georg Ernst, **IV:**1268
Stark, Johannes, **IX:**3490
Staudinger, Hermann, **IX:**3497
Stein, Edith, **IX:**3506
Stein, Freiherr vom, **VI:**2115
Stockhausen, Karlheinz, **IX:**3541
Strauss, Richard, **IX:**3555
Stresemann, Gustav, **IX:**3563
Telemann, Georg Philipp, **IV:**1319
Thomas à Kempis, **II:**906
Tillich, Paul, **IX:**3685
Tirpitz, Alfred von, **IX:**3688
Tönnies, Ferdinand Julius, **IX:**3703
Troeltsch, Ernst, **IX:**3722
Virchow, Rudolf, **VI:**2312
Wach, Joachim, **IX:**3829
Wagner, Richard, **VI:**2316
Walther von der Vogelweide, **II:**959
Wankel, Felix, **IX:**3881
Weber, Carl Maria von, **VI:**2340
Weber, Max, **IX:**3910
Wegener, Alfred, **IX:**3918
Weill, Kurt, **IX:**3926
Weismann, August, **VI:**2348
Wertheimer, Max, **IX:**3945
Widukind, **II:**973
William II, **IX:**4003
Winckelmann, Johann Joachim, **IV:**1460
Wöhler, Friedrich, **VI:**2403
Wolf, Max, **IX:**4039
Wolfram von Eschenbach, **II:**1005
Wundt, Wilhelm, **IX:**4069
Zeppelin, Ferdinand von, **IX:**4108
Zetkin, Clara, **IX:**4112
Zinzendorf, Graf von, **IV:**1488
Žižka, Count Jan, **II:**1030

GHANA
Nkrumah, Kwame, **VIII:**2762

GOLD COAST. *See* **GHANA**

GREAT BRITAIN. *See also* **BRITAIN; ENGLAND; IRELAND; SCOTLAND; WALES**
Acton, Lord, **V:**10
Adam, James and Robert, **IV:**7
Addison, Joseph, **IV:**26
Alanbrooke, First Viscount, **VII:**45
Allenby, Lord, **VII:**58
Amherst, Lord, **IV:**37
André, John, **IV:**42
Andrewes, Lancelot, **IV:**46
Angell, Norman, **VII:**74
Anne, Queen, **IV:**50
Anson, Lord, **IV:**55
Arkwright, Richard, **IV:**59
Arnold, Matthew, **V:**69
Arnold, Thomas, **V:**74
Asquith, H.H., **VII:**121
Astor, Nancy, **VII:**129
Attlee, Clement, **VII:**137
Austen, Jane, **V:**90
Babbage, Charles, **V:**101
Bacon, Nathaniel, **IV:**80
Baden-Powell, Sir Robert Stephenson Smyth, **V:**105
Baldwin, Stanley, **VII:**168
Balfour, Arthur, **VII:**172
Banks, Sir Joseph, **IV:**83
Barry, Sir Charles, **V:**138
Baskerville, John, **IV:**95
Baxter, Richard, **IV:**98
Bayliss, Sir William Maddock, **VII:**217
Beale, Dorothea, **V:**157
Beardsley, Aubrey, **V:**161
Beatles, The, **VII:**226
Beaverbrook, Lord, **VII:**234
Bentham, Jeremy, **IV:**107
Besant, Annie, **V:**211
Bessemer, Sir Henry, **V:**218
Bevan, Aneurin, **VII:**304
Beveridge, Lord, **VII:**308
Bevin, Ernest, **VII:**313
Biddle, John, **IV:**126
Blackstone, William, **IV:**129
Blake, Robert, **IV:**132
Blake, William, **IV:**137
Bligh, William, **IV:**143
Bolingbroke, First Viscount, **IV:**157
Bondfield, Margaret, **VII:**353
Booth, William, **V:**275
Bottomley, Horatio W., **VII:**382
Boulton, Matthew, **IV:**182
Boyle, Robert, **IV:**185
Bradley, F.H., **V:**290
Bright, John, **V:**306
Brindley, James, **IV:**201
Britten, Benjamin, **VII:**466
Brontë Sisters, The, **V:**310
Brown, Lancelot, **IV:**204
Browning, Elizabeth Barrett, **V:**327

Brunel, Isambard Kingdom, **V:**335
Brunel, Marc Isambard, **V:**339
Buckingham, First Duke of, **IV:**211
Bunyan, John, **IV:**218
Burke, Edmund, **IV:**222
Burnett, Frances Hodgson, **V:**361
Burney, Charles, **IV:**226
Burton, Sir Richard Francis, **V:**374
Butler, R.A., **VII:**529
Buxton, Sir Thomas Fowell, **V:**378
Byron, Lord, **V:**381
Canning, George, **V:**405
Carleton, Guy, **IV:**246
Carlyle, Thomas, **V:**416
Carroll, Lewis, **V:**425
Castlereagh, Viscount, **V:**438
Cavendish, Henry, **IV:**261
Cayley, Sir George, **V:**450
Chadwick, Edwin, **V:**457
Chadwick, James, **VII:**635
Chamberlain, Joseph, **V:**462
Chamberlain, Neville, **VII:**643
Chaplin, Charles, **VII:**653
Charles I, **IV:**279
Charles II, **IV:**283
Christie, Agatha, **VII:**683
Churchill, Sir Winston, **VII:**691
Clarendon, First Earl of, **IV:**308
Clinton, Sir Henry, **IV:**321
Clive, Robert, **IV:**325
Cobbett, William, **V:**522
Cobden, Richard, **V:**526
Coe, Sebastian, **VII:**725
Coke, Sir Edward, **IV:**329
Coleridge, Samuel Taylor, **V:**537
Collins, Norman, **VII:**737
Conrad, Joseph, **VII:**753
Constable, John, **V:**547
Cook, Captain James, **IV:**351
Cooke, William Fothergill, **V:**555
Cornwallis, First Marquess, **IV:**367
Coward, Noël, **VII:**783
Crick, Francis, **VII:**797
Cromwell, Oliver, **IV:**378
Curzon, Lord, **VII:**819
Dalton, John, **V:**602
Dampier, William, **IV:**389
Darby, Abraham, **IV:**396
Darwin, Charles, **V:**606
Davy, Sir Humphry, **V:**621
Defoe, Daniel, **IV:**399
Delius, Frederick, **VII:**892
Derby, Fourteenth Earl of, **V:**652
Diana, Princess of Wales, **VII:**923
Dickens, Charles, **V:**663
Disraeli, Benjamin, **V:**675
Donne, John, **IV:**416
Doyle, Sir Arthur Conan, **V:**700
Dryden, John, **IV:**424
Durham, First Earl of, **V:**721
Eden, Anthony, **VII:**1015
Edward VII, **VII:**1020
Elgar, Sir Edward, **VII:**1051
Eliot, George, **V:**751
Eliot, John, **IV:**435
Eliot, T.S., **VII:**1058
Elizabeth II, **VII:**1062
Ellis, Havelock, **VII:**1070
Epstein, Sir Jacob, **VII:**1087
Fairfax, Third Baron, **IV:**446
Faraday, Michael, **V:**767
Fawcett, Dame Millicent Garrett, **V:**776
Ferrar, Nicholas, **IV:**462
Fielding, Henry, **IV:**469
Fonteyn, Dame Margot, **VII:**1175
Forester, C.S., **VII:**1189
Forster, E.M., **VII:**1193
Forster, William Edward, **V:**804
Fox, Charles James, **IV:**479
Fox, George, **IV:**484
Fry, Roger, **VII:**1253
Gage, Thomas, **IV:**511
Gainsborough, Thomas, **IV:**515
Galton, Francis, **V:**867
Garrick, David, **IV:**527
George I, **IV:**531
George II, **IV:**535
George III, **IV:**539
George IV, **V:**902
George V, **VII:**1339
George VI, **VII:**1343
Gibbon, Edward, **IV:**545
Gilbert, W.S., **V:**927
Gladstone, William Ewart, **V:**935
Godolphin, First Earl of, **IV:**552
Godwin, William, **IV:**555
Goldie, Sir George, **V:**953
Goldsmith, Oliver, **IV:**564
Gordon, Charles George, **V:**964
Grace, William Gilbert, **V:**971
Green, Thomas Hill, **V:**987
Greene, Graham, **VIII**-1467
Grey, Second Earl, **V:**994
Grey, Sir George Edward, **V:**998

Grove, Sir William Robert, **V:**1010
Hadfield, Sir Robert Abbott, **V:**1015
Hale, Matthew, **IV:**596
Halley, Edmond, **IV:**600
Handel, George Frideric, **IV:**619
Hardy, Thomas, **V:**1040
Hargreaves, James, **IV:**623
Harmsworth, Alfred and Harold, **VIII:**1554
Harrison, Frederic, **V:**1057
Harvey, William, **IV:**626
Hastings, Warren, **IV:**631
Hawking, Stephen W., **VIII:**1580
Hawksmoor, Nicholas, **IV:**635
Heath, Edward, **VIII:**1606
Hill, Octavia, **V:**1113
Hitchcock, Alfred, **VIII:**1687
Hobbes, Thomas, **IV:**662
Hobhouse, Leonard T., **VIII:**1707
Hockney, David, **VIII:**1711
Hogarth, William, **IV:**668
Hounsfield, Godfrey Newbold, **VIII:**1751
Howe, Admiral Richard, **IV:**672
Howe, General William, **IV:**676
Hudson, Henry, **IV:**680
Hunt, William Holman, **V:**1168
Huxley, Aldous, **VIII:**1804
Huxley, Thomas Henry, **V:**1172
Irving, Henry, **V:**1187
James I, **IV:**699
James II, **IV:**703
Jenner, Edward, **IV:**721
John, Augustus, **VIII:**1854
Johnson, Samuel, **IV:**728
Jones, Inigo, **IV:**735
Jonson, Ben, **IV:**744
Kay, John, **IV:**769
Kay-Shuttleworth, First Baronet, **VIII:**1917
Kean, Edmund, **VI:**1259
Keats, John, **VI:**1264
Keynes, John Maynard, **VIII:**1952
Kidd, William, **IV:**777
Kipling, Rudyard, **VI:**1288
Kitchener, Lord, **VIII:**2002
Lambert, John, **IV:**789
Lancaster, Joseph, **VI:**1309
Lanchester, Frederick William, **VIII:**2069
Lankester, Sir Edwin Ray, **VI:**1316
Lansdowne, Fifth Marquess of, **VIII:**2090
Laski, Harold J., **VIII:**2093
Laud, William, **IV:**797
Law, Bonar, **VIII:**2112
Lawrence, First Baron, **VI:**1331
Lawrence, D.H., **VIII:**2115
Lawrence, T.E., **VIII:**2125
Lawrence, Sir Thomas, **IV:**808
Leeds, First Duke of, **IV:**821
Lewis, C.S., **VIII:**2167
Lister, Joseph, **VI:**1388
Liverpool, Second Earl of, **VI:**1395
Lloyd George, David, **VIII:**2216
Locke, John, **IV:**854
Lockyer, Sir Joseph Norman, **VI:**1410
Lugard, Lord, **VIII:**2269
Lyell, Sir Charles, **VI:**1418
Macaulay, Thomas Babington, **VI:**1427
MacDonald, Ramsay, **VIII:**2312
Mackinder, Sir Halford John, **VIII:**2321
MacMillan, Daniel and Alexander, **VI:**1457
Macmillan, Harold, **VIII:**2340
Macready, William Charles, **VI:**1460
Major, John, **VIII:**2369
Malthus, Thomas Robert, **VI:**1467
Manning, Henry Edward, **VI:**1476
Mansfield, First Earl of, **IV:**904
Marlborough, First Duke of, **IV:**922
Maurice, Frederick Denison, **VI:**1503
Melbourne, Second Viscount, **VI:**1517
Mill, James, **VI:**1556
Mill, John Stuart, **VI:**1559
Milne, A.A., **VIII:**2543
Milton, John, **IV:**958
Monck, George, **IV:**971
Monmouth, Duke of, **IV:**980
Montagu, Mary Wortley, **IV:**983
Montgomery, Bernard Law, **VIII:**2601
Moore, G.E., **VIII:**2605
Moore, Henry, **VIII:**2609
Morris, William, **VI:**1588
Mountbatten, Louis, **VIII:**2641
Murdock, William, **IV:**1008
Nash, John, **IV:**1012
Nash, Paul, **VIII:**2689
Nelson, Lord, **VI:**1634
Newbery, John, **IV:**1019
Newcomen, Thomas, **IV:**1022
Newman, John Henry, **VI:**1641
Newton, Sir Isaac, **IV:**1025
Nicholson, Ben, **VIII:**2732
Nightingale, Florence, **VI:**1667
North, Lord, **IV:**1034
Oates, Titus, **IV:**1038
O'Connor, Thomas Power, **IX:**2793
Olivier, Sir Laurence, **IX:**2808
Orwell, George, **IX:**2846

Outram, Sir James, **VI:**1705
Palmerston, Lord, **VI:**1719
Pankhurst, Emmeline, **IX:**2871
Pater, Walter, **VI:**1749
Paterson, William, **IV:**1066
Pavlova, Anna, **IX:**2937
Peel, Sir Robert, **VI:**1752
Pelham, Henry, **IV:**1074
Perry, Fred, **IX:**2979
Phillip, Arthur, **IV:**1091
Pitt the Elder, William, **IV:**1098
Pitt the Younger, William, **IV:**1102
Place, Francis, **VI:**1786
Pope, Alexander, **IV:**1115
Potter, Beatrix, **IX:**3063
Pride, Thomas, **IV:**1126
Priestley, Joseph, **IV:**1129
Pugin, Augustus Welby Northmore, **VI:**1821
Purcell, Henry, **IV:**1137
Pusey, E.B., **VI:**1828
Pym, John, **IV:**1141
Reynolds, Sir Joshua, **IV:**1160
Rhodes, Cecil, **VI:**1873
Ricardo, David, **VI:**1878
Rodney, George, **IV:**1178
Roebuck, John, **IV:**1182
Rolls, Charles Stewart, **IX:**3209
Romney, George, **IV:**1187
Ross, Sir James Clark, **VI:**1907
Ross, Ronald, **IX:**3247
Royce, Sir Frederick Henry, **IX:**3209
Ruskin, John, **VI:**1925
Russell, Lord John, **VI:**1930
Salisbury, Third Marquess of, **VI:**1943
Scott, Sir George Gilbert, **VI:**2002
Shaftesbury, First Earl of, **IV:**1228
Sharp, Granville, **IV:**1236
Shaw, George Bernard, **IX:**3399
Shelley, Mary Wollstonecraft, **VI:**2048
Shelley, Percy Bysshe, **VI:**2052
Sidgwick, Henry, **VI:**2062
Slim, First Viscount, **IX:**3435
Speke, John Hanning, **VI:**2083
Spencer, Herbert, **VI:**2086
Stanhope, First Earl, **IV:**1277
Starling, Ernest Henry, **IX:**3494
Stephenson, George, **VI:**2132
Stopes, Marie, **IX:**3551
Strafford, First Earl of, **IV:**1285
Street, George Edmund, **VI:**2160
Sullivan, Sir Arthur, **V:**927
Sutherland, Graham Vivian, **IX:**3587
Swan, Joseph Wilson, **VI:**2179
Swift, Jonathan, **IV:**1305
Sydenham, Thomas, **IV:**1310
Tennyson, Alfred, Lord, **VI:**2211
Terry, Ellen, **VI:**2215
Thatcher, Margaret, **IX:**3649
Tolkien, J.R.R., **IX:**3696
Toynbee, Arnold, **IX:**3715
Trevithick, Richard, **VI:**2251
Tull, Jethro, **IV:**1345
Turing, Alan Mathison, **IX:**3768
Turner, J.M.W., **VI:**2272
Vanbrugh, Sir John, **IV:**1351
Vancouver, George, **IV:**1355
Vaughan Williams, Ralph, **IX:**3798
Victoria, Queen, **VI:**2307
Wakefield, Edward Gibbon, **VI:**2321
Walpole, Sir Robert, **IV:**1400
Walter, John, II, **VI:**2324
Walton, Sir William, **IX:**3872
Webb, Beatrice and Sidney, **IX:**3905
Wedgwood, Josiah, **IV:**1421
Wellington, Duke of, **VI:**2351
Wells, H.G., **IX:**3938
Wesley, John, **IV:**1426
Wheatstone, Charles, **V:**555
Whitehead, Alfred North, **IX:**3965
Whittle, Sir Frank, **IX:**3972
Wilberforce, William, **IV:**1435
Wilkes, John, **IV:**1439
Wilkins, Maurice H.F., **IX:**3995
Wilkinson, John, **IV:**1443
William III, **IV:**1447
William IV, **VI:**2392
Wilson, Sir Harold, **IX:**4016
Windsor, Duke of, **IX:**4025
Wittgenstein, Ludwig, **IX:**4036
Wolfe, James, **IV:**1471
Wollstonecraft, Mary, **IV:**1475
Woolf, Virginia, **IX:**4056
Wordsworth, William, **VI:**2406
Wren, Sir Christopher, **IV:**1480

GREECE. ***See also*** **ALEXANDRIA; ASIA MINOR; CNIDUS; COS; ELEA; MACEDONIA; MILETUS; THRACE**
Aeschylus, **I:**9
Aesop, **I:**13
Agesilaus II, **I:**16
Alcibiades, **I:**31
Alcmaeon, **I:**34
Alexander the Great, **I:**38

Anaxagoras, **I:**47
Antisthenes, **I:**66
Aristippus, **I:**85
Aristophanes, **I:**88
Aristotle, **I:**94
Aristoxenus, **I:**98
Cimon, **I:**198
Cleisthenes of Athens, **I:**207
Cleomenes, **I:**214
Cyril, Saint, **II:**278
Demosthenes, **I:**253
Diocles of Carystus, **I:**260
Diogenes, **I:**268
Diophantus, **I:**272
Draco, **I:**280
Empedocles, **I:**282
Epaminondas, **I:**290
Epicurus, **I:**295
Erasistratus, **I:**299
Euclid, **I:**307
Eupalinus of Megara, **I:**314
Euripides, **I:**317
Heraclitus of Ephesus, **I:**382
Hesiod, **I:**402
Homer, **I:**420
Isocrates, **I:**456
Kazantzakis, Nikos, **VIII:**1920
Leonidas, **I:**501
Lysippus, **I:**515
Menander (dramatist), **I:**538
Methodius, Saint, **II:**278
Miltiades the Younger, **I:**553
Paul of Aegina, **II:**712
Pericles, **I:**609
Pheidippides, **I:**621
Phidias, **I:**624
Pindar, **I:**644
Pisistratus, **I:**648
Pittacus of Mytilene, **I:**651
Plato, **I:**655
Plotinus, **I:**666
Plutarch, **I:**670
Polybius, **I:**673
Polygnotus, **I:**676
Posidonius, **I:**686
Praxiteles, **I:**690
Protagoras, **I:**705
Pyrrhon of Elis, **I:**724
Pythagoras, **I:**727
Sappho, **I:**750
Scopas, **I:**764
Simonides, **I:**787
Socrates, **I:**793
Solon, **I:**803
Sophocles, **I:**807
Themistocles, **I:**857
Theophrastus, **I:**873
Thespis, **I:**877
Thucydides, **I:**885
Venizélos, Eleuthérios, **IX:**3808
Xanthippe, **I:**952
Xenakis, Iannis, **IX:**4075
Xenophanes, **I:**955
Xenophon, **I:**958
Ypsilanti, Alexander and Demetrios, **VI:**2417
Zeno of Citium, **I:**967

GUINEA

Touré, Ahmed Sékou, **IX:**3711

HAITI

Christophe, Henri, **V:**501

HUNGARY

Árpád, **II:**86
Bartók, Béla, **VII:**210
Deák, Ferenc, **V:**625
Elizabeth of Hungary, Saint, **II:**340
Herzl, Theodor, **V:**1102
Hevesy, Georg von, **VIII:**1654
Hunyadi, János, **III:**374
László I, Saint, **II:**574
Liszt, Franz, **VI:**1391
Lukács, György, **VIII:**2272
Matthias I Corvinus, **III:**487
Neumann, John von, **VIII:**2724
Nordau, Max, **VIII:**2766
Semmelweis, Ignaz Philipp, **VI:**2021
Stephen I, **II:**851

ICELAND

Laxness, Halldór, **VIII:**2131
Leif Eriksson, **II:**577
Snorri Sturluson, **II:**836

INDIA

Ahmad Khan, Sir Sayyid, **V:**34
Akbar, **III:**6
Aryabhata, **II:**89
Aśoka the Great, **I:**112
Aurangzeb, **IV:**69
Aurobindo, Sri, **VIII**-141
Bābur, **III:**36
Banerjea, Surendranath, **VII:**183

Brahmagupta, **II:**181
Buddha, **I:**144
Curzon, Lord, **VII:**819
Gandhi, Indira, **VII:**1278
Gandhi, Mahatma, **VII:**1282
Harsha, **II:**430
Jinnah, Mohammed Ali, **VIII:**1847
Kālidāsa, **I:**491
Kanishka, **I:**494
Lansdowne, Fifth Marquess of, **VIII:**2090
Menander (Indian king), **I:**541
Mountbatten, Louis, **VIII:**2641
Naidu, Sarojini, **VIII:**2683
Nānak, **III:**540
Nehru, Jawaharlal, **VIII:**2709
Pandit, Vijaya Lakshmi, **IX:**2867
Patel, Vallabhbhai Jhaverbhai, **IX:**2903
Raman, Sir Chandrasekhara Venkata, **IX:**3109
Rāmānuja, **II:**770
Ray, Rammohan, **VI:**1846
Ray, Satyajit, **IX:**3132
Shah Jahan, **IV:**1232
Śivajī, **IV:**1246
Tagore, Rabindranath, **IX:**3598
Teresa, Mother, **IX:**3635
Thomas, Saint, **I:**880
Tilak, Bal Gangadhar, **IX:**3681
Vardhamāna, **I:**915

INDOCHINA. ***See*** **BURMA; CAMBODIA; VIETNAM**

INDONESIA
Hatta, Mohammad, **VIII:**1577
Sukarno, **IX:**3570

IONIA. ***See*** **ASIA MINOR; GREECE**

IRAN. ***See also*** **ARABIA; ASSYRIA; IRAQ; MESOPOTAMIA; SYRIA**
'Abbās the Great, **IV:**4
Abul Wefa, **II:**20
Avicenna, **II:**106
Cyrus the Great, **I:**233
Darius the Great, **I:**236
Fakhr al-Din al-Razi, **II:**347
Firdusi, **II:**350
Ghazan, Mahmud, **II:**381
Ghazzali, al-, **II:**385
Hafiz, **II:**417
Hallaj, al-, **II:**421
Harun al-Rashid, **II:**437
Jabir ibn Hayyan, **II:**522
Jamāl al-Dīn al-Afghānī, **V:**1207
Khomeini, Ruhollah, **VIII:**1957
Mohammad Reza Shah Pahlavi, **VIII:**2566
Nizam al-Mulk, **II:**677
Omar Khayyám, **II:**695
Razi, al-, **II:**779
Sa'di, **II:**806
Shapur II, **I:**778
Tabari, al-, 873
Xerxes I, **I:**962
Zoroaster, **I:**975

IRAQ. ***See also*** **ARABIA; ASSYRIA; BABYLONIA; IRAN; MESOPOTAMIA; SYRIA**
Abu Hanifah, **II:**16
Abul Wefa, **II:**20
Ahmad ibn Hanbal, **II:**33
Alhazen, **II:**63
Ash'ari, al-, **II:**93
Battani, al-, **II:**121
Faisal I, **VII:**1122
Jabir ibn Hayyan, **II:**522
Jahiz, al-, **II:**526
Khwarizmi, al-, **II:**563
Mas'udi, al-, **II:**636
Tabari, al-, **II:**873

IRELAND
Beckett, Samuel, **VII:**238
Berkeley, George, **IV:**114
Campbell, Alexander, **V:**401
Castlereagh, Viscount, **V:**438
Charles I, **IV:**279
Charles II, **IV:**283
Collins, Michael, **VII:**733
Cornwallis, First Marquess, **IV:**367
Cosgrave, William T., **VII:**770
de Valera, Eamon, **VII:**877
George I, **IV:**531
George II, **IV:**535
George III, **IV:**539
Goldsmith, Oliver, **IV:**564
Hamilton, Sir William Rowan, **V:**1025
Holland, John Philip, **V:**1123
Joyce, James, **VIII:**1891
Kelvin, Lord, **VI:**1269
Lansdowne, Fifth Marquess of, **VIII:**2090
Mannix, Daniel, **VI:**1480
O'Connell, Daniel, **VI:**1680
O'Connor, Thomas Power, **IX:**2793

O'Kelly, Seán T., **IX:**2804
Parnell, Charles Stewart, **VI:**1740
Patrick, Saint, **I:**600
Shaw, George Bernard, **IX:**3399
Swift, Jonathan, **IV:**1305
Wilde, Oscar, **VI:**2377
Yeats, William Butler, **IX:**4082

ISRAEL. ***See also*** **JUDAEA; PALESTINE**
Aaron, **I:**1
Abraham, **I:**5
Begin, Menachem, **VII:**243
Ben-Gurion, David, **VII:**251
Buber, Martin, **VII:**483
David, **I:**241
Dayan, Moshe, **VII:**854
Deborah, **I:**246
Eban, Abba, **VII:**1000
Eusebius of Caesarea, **I:**322
Ezekiel, **I:**326
Ezra, **I:**330
Jerome, Saint, **I:**463
John the Apostle, **I:**475
John the Baptist, **I:**479
Josephus, Flavius, **I:**483
Judah ha-Levi, **II:**548
Lipchitz, Jacques, **VIII:**2199
Meir, Golda, **VIII:**2472
Moses, **I:**561
Peter, Saint, **I:**614
Pilate, Pontius, **I:**640
Samuel, **I:**746
Solomon, **I:**798
Stephen, Saint, **I:**822
Thomas, Saint, **I:**880
Virgin Mary, **I:**939
Weizmann, Chaim, **IX:**3930

ITALY. ***See also*** **ELEA**
Abano, Pietro d', **II:**1
Agrippa, Marcus Vipsanius, **I:**20
Alberti, Leon Battista, **III:**8
Alboin, **II:**41
Alcmaeon, **I:**34
Alexander III, **II:**48
Alexander VI, **III:**14
Ambrose, Saint, **I:**43
Andrea del Sarto, **III:**24
Angelico, Fra, **III:**28
Anthony of Padua, Saint, **II:**76
Antony, Marc, **I:**69
Archimedes, **I:**76
Ariosto, Ludovico, **III:**32
Arnold of Villanova, **II:**79
Arnolfo di Cambio, **II:**82
Asclepiades of Bithynia, **I:**101
Attila, **I:**124
Augustus, **I:**132
Avogadro, Amedeo, **V:**98
Bellini, Giovanni, **III:**58
Benedict of Nursia, Saint, **II:**136
Bernini, Gian Lorenzo, **IV:**118
Boccaccio, Giovanni, **II:**150
Boccherini, Luigi, **IV:**147
Boccioni, Umberto, **VII:**342
Boethius, **II:**155
Bohemond I, **II:**159
Bonaventure, Saint, **II:**163
Boniface VIII, **II:**171
Borromini, Francesco, **IV:**167
Botticelli, Sandro, **III:**74
Bramante, Donato, **III:**81
Brunelleschi, Filippo, **III:**89
Bruni, Leonardo, **III:**93
Bruno, Giordano, **III:**96
Brutus, Marcus Junius, **I:**140
Cabot, John, **III:**113
Caesar, Julius, **I:**147
Caligula, **I:**152
Canaletto, **IV:**242
Canova, Antonio, **V:**408
Carpini, Giovanni da Pian del, **II:**206
Carracci Family, The, **III:**125
Caruso, Enrico, **VII:**598
Casanova, Giovanni Giacomo, **IV:**254
Cassiodorus, **II:**215
Cassius, **I:**159
Catherine of Siena, Saint, **II:**218
Cato the Censor, **I:**162
Cato the Younger, **I:**166
Catullus, **I:**169
Cavalcanti, Guido, **II:**223
Cavour, Count, **V:**446
Cellini, Benvenuto, **III:**151
Celsus, Aulus Cornelius, **I:**173
Cicero, **I:**194
Cimabue, **II:**272
Claudius I, **I:**203
Clement I, **I:**210
Clement VII, **III:**166
Constantine the Great, **I:**226
Corelli, Arcangelo, **IV:**360
Correggio, **III:**184
Croce, Benedetto, **VII:**801

Dandolo, Enrico, **II:**282
Dante, **II:**286
de Gasperi, Alcide, **VII:**862
Denis, Saint, **I:**257
Diocletian, **I:**263
Dionysius Exiguus, **II:**298
Donatello, **III:**220
Donizetti, Gaetano, **V:**684
Duccio di Buoninsegna, **II:**305
Ennius, Quintus, **I:**287
Fabius Maximus, Quintus, **I:**334
Farnese, Alessandro, **III:**254
Fellini, Federico, **VII:**1141
Fermi, Enrico, **VII:**1145
Ferrari, Enzo, **VII:**1150
Fracastoro, Girolamo, **III:**270
Francis of Assisi, Saint, **II:**354
Frederick II, **II:**362
Gabrieli, Andrea, **III:**281
Gabrieli, Giovanni, **III:**284
Galileo, **IV:**519
Galvani, Luigi, **IV:**523
Garibaldi, Giuseppe, **V:**879
Gentile, Giovanni, **VII:**1336
Gentili, Alberico, **III:**295
Ghiberti, Lorenzo, **III:**302
Gioberti, Vincenzo, **V:**932
Giorgione, **III:**305
Giotto, **II:**388
Gracchi, The, **I:**345
Gramsci, Antonio, **VIII**-1459
Gregory VII, **II:**395
Gregory IX, **II:**399
Gregory the Great, **II:**407
Guarini, Guarino, **IV:**583
Guicciardini, Francesco, **III:**325
Guido d'Arezzo, **II:**411
Hadrian, **I:**356
Hannibal, **I:**364
Hippolytus of Rome, **I:**415
Horace, **I:**424
Hus, Jan, **II:**487
Innocent III, **II:**509
Innocent IV, **II:**514
Irenaeus, Saint, **I:**447
Jacopo della Quercia, **III:**389
Jerome, Saint, **I:**463
Joachim of Fiore, **II:**534
John XXIII, **VIII:**1858
Josephus, Flavius, **I:**483
Julius II, **III:**405
Juvenal, **I:**488
Landini, Francesco, **II:**570
Leo IX, **II:**581
Leo X, **III:**419
Leo XIII, **VI:**1347
Leonardo da Vinci, **III:**423
Leonardo of Pisa, **II:**585
Livy, **I:**504
Lorenzetti, Pietro, and
  Ambrogio Lorenzetti, **II:**595
Lucian, **I:**507
Lucretius, **I:**511
Machiavelli, Niccolò, **III:**448
Maecenas, Gaius, **I:**519
Malpighi, Marcello, **IV:**891
Mantegna, Andrea, **III:**460
Manzoni, Alessandro, **VI:**1483
Marconi, Guglielmo, **VIII:**2415
Marcus Aurelius, **I:**523
Marius, Gaius, **I:**528
Martial, **I:**532
Martini, Simone, **II:**632
Masaccio, **III:**483
Mazzini, Giuseppe, **VI:**1514
Medici, Lorenzo de', **III:**495
Menotti, Gian Carlo, **VIII:**2494
Messalina, Valeria, **I:**550
Messner, Reinhold, **VIII:**2506
Michelangelo, **III:**517
Montale, Eugenio, **VIII:**2592
Montessori, Maria, **VIII:**2596
Monteverdi, Claudio, **IV:**990
Mosca, Gaetano, **VIII:**2630
Mussolini, Benito, **VIII:**2667
Natta, Giulio, **VIII:**2698
Neri, Saint Philip, **III:**551
Nero, **I:**577
Nervi, Pier Luigi, **VIII:**2720
Nicholas V, **III:**559
Nicholas the Great, **II:**673
Oberth, Hermann, **IX:**2777
Orcagna, Andrea, **II:**698
Ovid, **I:**585
Paganini, Niccolò, **VI:**1711
Palladio, Andrea, **III:**580
Paul III, **III:**595
Paul VI, **IX:**2919
Pavarotti, Luciano, **IX:**2930
Petrarch, **II:**726
Phaedrus, **I:**618
Philip IV the Fair, **II:**736
Piero della Francesca, **III:**606
Pirandello, Luigi, **IX:**3013

Pirelli Family, The, **IX:**3020
Pisano, Andrea, **II:**744
Pisano, Nicola and Giovanni, **II:**747
Pius II, **III:**613
Pius V, **III:**616
Pius IX, **VI:**1782
Pius XI, **IX:**3026
Pius XII, **IX:**3030
Plautus, **I:**659
Pliny the Elder, **I:**662
Plutarch, **I:**670
Poggio, **III:**626
Polo, Marco, **II:**750
Pompey the Great, **I:**679
Porphyry, **I:**683
Posidonius, **I:**686
Propertius, Sextus, **I:**702
Puccini, Giacomo, **IX:**3093
Raphael, **III:**642
Regulus, Marcus Atilius, **I:**739
Rienzo, Cola di, **II:**790
Rossini, Gioacchino, **VI:**1913
Salimbene, **II:**812
Sallust, **I:**742
Sansovino, Jacopo, **III:**664
Santorio, Santorio, **IV:**1209
Savonarola, Girolamo, **III:**667
Scarlatti, Alessandro, **IV:**1213
Scipio Aemilianus, **I:**757
Scipio Africanus, **I:**760
Seneca the Younger, **I:**770
Sergius I, Saint, **II:**823
Sforza, Ludovico, **III:**682
Siricius, Saint, **I:**790
Sosigenes, **I:**811
Spallanzani, Lazzaro, **IV:**1260
Spartacus, **I:**814
Stilicho, Flavius, **I:**825
Stradivari, Antonio, **IV:**1281
Sulla, Lucius Cornelius, **I:**833
Sylvester II, **II:**869
Tacitus, Cornelius, **I:**837
Tancred, **II:**887
Tasso, Torquato, **III:**710
Terence, **I:**844
Theodoret of Cyrrhus, **I:**865
Theodoric the Great, **II:**894
Theodosius the Great, **I:**868
Thomas Aquinas, Saint, **II:**911
Tiberius, **I:**892
Tiepolo, Giovanni Battista, **IV:**1323
Tintoretto, **III:**717
Titian, **III:**721
Torricelli, Evangelista, **IV:**1331
Toscanini, Arturo, **IX:**3707
Trajan, **I:**899
Urban II, **II:**928
Valentinus, **I:**911
Valla, Lorenzo, **III:**739
Varro, Marcus Terentius, **I:**918
Vasari, Giorgio, **III:**743
Verdi, Giuseppe, **VI:**2299
Vergil, **I:**926
Veronese, Paolo, **III:**747
Verrius Flaccus, Marcus, **I:**930
Verrocchio, Andrea del, **III:**750
Vespasian, **I:**933
Vespucci, Amerigo, **III:**758
Vico, Giambattista, **IV:**1372
Villani, Giovanni, **II:**938
Visconti, Luchino, **IX:**3818
Volta, Alessandro, **IV:**1387

IVORY COAST
Houphouët-Boigny, Félix, **VIII:**1754

JAPAN
Akihito, **VII:**41
Ashikaga Takauji, **II:**97
Fujiwara Michinaga, **II:**370
Hatoyama Ichiro, **VIII:**1574
Hirohito, **VIII:**1678
Hiroshige, **V:**1117
Hokusai, **V:**1120
Honda, Soichiro, **VIII:**1724
Ii Naosuke, **V:**1180
Ikeda, Hayato, **VIII:**1809
Jōchō, **II:**537
Kawabata, Yasunari, **VIII:**1913
Kurosawa, Akira, **VIII:**2043
Matsuo Bashō, **IV:**942
Matsushita, Konosuke, **VIII:**2457
Mishima, Yukio, **VIII:**2551
Morita, Akio, **VIII:**2622
Murasaki Shikibu, **II:**657
Nichiren, **II:**666
Nishida, Kitaro, **VIII:**2754
Oda Nobunaga, **III:**570
Ogata Kōrin, **IV:**1041
Oh, Sadaharu, **IX:**2796
Saigō Takamori, **VI:**1936
Sato, Eisaku, **IX:**3336
Sesshū, **III:**679
Shōtoku Taishi, **II:**826

Sōtatsu, **IV:**1257
Taira Kiyomori, **II:**881
Tanizaki, Jun'ichiro, **IX:**3611
Tokugawa Ieyasu, **IV:**1327
Toyoda, Eiji, **IX:**3719
Toyotomi Hideyoshi, **III:**728
Unkei, **II:**924
Yukawa, Hideki, **IX:**4090
Zeami Motokiyo, **II:**1025

JERUSALEM. ***See*** **ISRAEL**

JORDAN
Hussein I, **VIII:**1791

JUDAEA. ***See also*** **ISRAEL; PALESTINE**
Herod the Great, **I:**390
Isaiah, **I:**452
Jeremiah, **I:**459
Jesus Christ, **I:**467
Johanan ben Zakkai, **I:**471
Pilate, Pontius, **I:**640
Virgin Mary, **I:**939

JUDAH. ***See*** **JUDAEA**

KAMPUCHEA. ***See*** **CAMBODIA**

KAZAKHSTAN. ***See*** **SOVIET UNION**

KENYA
Kenyatta, Jomo, **VIII:**1936
Leakey, L.S.B., **VIII:**2145

KHWARIZM
Alp Arslan, **II:**67
Biruni, al-, **II:**147

KIEV
Rurik, **II:**803
Vladimir I, **II:**952

KIRGIZIA. ***See*** **SOVIET UNION**

KOREA
Rhee, Syngman, **IX:**3165

LATVIA. ***See also*** **SOVIET UNION**
Ostwald, Wilhelm, **IX:**2855

LIBERIA
Tubman, William V. S., **IX:**3757

LIBYA
Qaddafi, Muammar al-, **IX:**3098

LIMBURG-IM BREISGAU. ***See*** **GERMANY**

LITHUANIA. ***See also*** **SOVIET UNION**
Elijah ben Solomon, **IV:**432
Lipchitz, Jacques, **VIII:**2199
Władysław II Jagiełło and Jadwiga, **II:**1001

LOW COUNTRIES. ***See*** **NETHERLANDS, THE**

MACEDONIA. ***See also*** **GREECE; YUGOSLAVIA**
Alexander the Great, **I:**38
Antigonus I Monophthalmos, **I:**60
Basil the Macedonian, **II:**117
Phaedrus, **I:**618
Philip II of Macedonia, **I:**628
Seleucus I Nicator, **I:**767

MALI
Mansa Mūsā, **II:**623

MARTINIQUE
Césaire, Aimé, **VII:**631

MESOPOTAMIA. ***See also*** **ARABIA; ASSYRIA; BABYLONIA; IRAN; IRAQ; SYRIA**
Khosrow I, **II:**559
Lucian, **I:**507
Mas'udi, al-, 636

MEXICO
Calles, Plutarco Elías, **VII:**542
Candela, Felix, **VII:**557
Cárdenas, Lázaro, **VII:**571
Cruz, Sor Juana Inés de la, **IV:**382
Itzcóatl, **III:**377
Juárez, Benito, **V:**1250
Madero, Francisco, **VIII:**2345
Montezuma II, **III:**528
Nezahualcóyotl, **III:**555
Obregón, Álvaro, **IX:**2781
Orozco, José Clemente, **IX:**2836
Rivera, Diego, **IX:**3184
Santa Anna, Antonio López de, **VI:**1955
Villa, Pancho, **IX:**3811
Zapata, Emiliano, **IX:**4104

MIDDLE EAST. ***See*** **ALEXANDRIA; ARABIA; ARMENIA; ASIA MINOR; ASSYRIA; BABYLONIA; BITHYNIA; BYZANTINE EMPIRE; CAPPADOCIA; CILICIA; CNIDUS; COS; EGYPT; IRAN; IRAQ; ISRAEL; JORDAN; JUDAEA; MESOPOTAMIA; MOPSUESTIA; OTTOMAN EMPIRE; PALESTINE; PERGA; PHOENICIA; PONTUS; SYRIA; TURKEY**

MILAN, REPUBLIC OF. ***See*** **ITALY**

MILETUS
Anaximander, **I:**50
Anaximenes of Miletus, **I:**53
Thales of Miletus, **I:**852

MODENA, REPUBLIC OF. ***See*** **ITALY**

MOLDAVIA. ***See*** **SOVIET UNION**

MONGOLIA. ***See*** **CENTRAL ASIA; CHINA; SOVIET UNION**

MOPSUESTIA
Theodore of Mopsuestia, 861

MOROCCO
Averroës, **II:**100
Ibn Battutah, **II:**495
Idrisi, al-, **II:**506

MOZAMBIQUE
Machel, Samora Moisès, **VIII:**2317

MUGHAL EMPIRE. ***See*** **INDIA**

MYANMAR. ***See*** **BURMA**

NAPLES, KINGDOM OF. ***See*** **ITALY**

NETHERLANDS, THE
Bosch, Hieronymus, **III:**70
Einthoven, Willem, **VII:**1039
Erasmus, Desiderius, **III:**246
Frank, Anne, **VII:**1204
Frederick Henry, **IV:**500
Gogh, Vincent van, **V:**944
Grotius, Hugo, **IV:**579
Hals, Frans, **IV:**604
Hein, Piet, **IV:**644
Huygens, Christiaan, **IV:**695
Jansen, Cornelius Otto, **IV:**707
Leeuwenhoek, Antoni van, **IV:**825
Lippershey, Hans, **IV:**850
Lorentz, Hendrik Antoon, **VIII:**2235
Menno Simons, **III:**510
Mondrian, Piet, **VIII:**2575
Oldenbarnevelt, Johan van, **III:**574
Oort, Jan Hendrik, **IX:**2827
Oud, J.J.P., **IX:**2859
Rembrandt, **IV:**1152
Siger of Brabant, **II:**829
Sluter, Claus, **II:**832
Spinoza, Baruch, **IV:**1264
Tasman, Abel Janszoon, **IV:**1313
Tromp, Cornelius and Maarten, **IV:**1342
Vermeer, Jan, **IV:**1368
Weyden, Rogier van der, **III:**778
William the Silent, **III:**781

NEW ZEALAND
Hillary, Sir Edmund, **VIII:**1662
Massey, William Ferguson, **VIII:**2444
Rutherford, Ernest, **IX:**3277
Seddon, Richard John, **VI:**2017
Wakefield, Edward Gibbon, **VI:**2321
Wilkins, Maurice H.F., **IX:**3995

NIGERIA
Achebe, Chinua, **VII:**13
Azikiwe, Nnamdi, **VIII**-144
Soyinka, Wole, **IX:**3471

NORTH AFRICA. ***See also*** **CARTHAGE; MOROCCO; NUMIDIA; TUNISIA**
'Abd al-Mu'min, **II:**4
Masinissa, **I:**535

NORTH VIETNAM. ***See*** **VIETNAM**

NORWAY
Abel, Niels Henrik, **V:**7
Amundsen, Roald, **VII:**66
Bjerknes, Vilhelm, **VII:**318
Grieg, Edvard, **V:**1002
Hamsun, Knut, **VIII:**1537
Henie, Sonja, **VIII:**1629
Heyerdahl, Thor, **VIII:**1658
Ibsen, Henrik, **V:**1175
Margaret of Denmark, Norway, and Sweden, **II:**626
Munch, Edvard, **VIII:**2658
Nansen, Fridtjof, **VIII:**2686

Olaf I, **II:**688
Olaf, Saint, **II:**691
Rollo, **II:**793

NUMIDIA
Augustine, Saint, **I:**128
Masinissa, **I:**535

OTTOMON EMPIRE. ***See also*** **ALGERIA; EGYPT; IRAQ; PALESTINE; SAUDI ARABIA; SYRIA; TURKEY**
Abdelkader, **V:**1
Bayezid II, **III:**51
Mehmed II, **III:**499
Süleyman the Magnificent, **III:**707

PAKISTAN
Jinnah, Mohammed Ali, **VIII:**1847

PALESTINE. ***See also*** **ISRAEL; JORDAN; JUDAEA**
Akiba ben Joseph, **I:**27
Arafat, Yasir, **VII:**90
Herod the Great, **I:**390
Luria, Isaac ben Solomon, **III:**440
Pilate, Pontius, **I:**640
Thomas, Saint, **I:**880
Virgin Mary, **I:**939

PAPAL STATES. ***See*** **ITALY**

PEOPLE'S REPUBLIC OF CHINA. ***See*** **CHINA**

PERGA
Apollonius of Perga, **I:**72

PERSIA. ***See*** **IRAN**

PERSIAN EMPIRE. ***See*** **IRAN**

PERU
Bolívar, Simón, **V:**267
Haya de la Torre, Víctor Raúl, **VIII:**1584
Huáscar, **III:**371
Pachacuti, **III:**577
Pérez de Cuéllar, Javier, **IX:**2957

PHILIPPINES
Aquino, Corazon, **VII:**86
Marcos, Ferdinand E., **VIII:**2420

PHOENICIA
Porphyry, **I:**683

POLAND
Casimir the Great, **II:**210
Chopin, Frédéric, **V:**493
Conrad, Joseph, **VII:**753
Copernicus, Nicolaus, **III:**176
Curie, Marie, **VII:**811
John III Sobieski, **IV:**725
John Paul II, **VIII:**1862
Luxemburg, Rosa, **VIII:**2285
Walesa, Lech, **IX:**3844
Władysław II Jagiełło and Jadwiga, **II:**1001
Wiesenthal, Simon, **IX:**3984

PONTUS
Chrysostom, Saint John, **I:**184
Mithradates the Great, **I:**557
Strabo, **I:**828

PORTUGAL
Afonso I, **II:**30
Albuquerque, Afonso de, **III:**11
Anthony of Padua, Saint, **II:**76
Camões, Luís de, **III:**122
Covilhã, Pêro da, **III:**197
Dias, Bartolomeu, **III:**215
Egas Moniz, António, **VII:**1023
Gama, Vasco da, **III:**287
Henry the Navigator (Prince of Portugal), **III:**354
Magellan, Ferdinand, **III:**453
Manuel I, **III:**464

PORTUGUESE EAST AFRICA. ***See*** **MOZAMBIQUE**

PRUSSIA. ***See*** **GERMANY**

PUERTO RICO
Casals, Pablo, **VII:**606

RHODESIA. ***See*** **ZIMBABWE**

ROMAN EMPIRE. ***See*** **ITALY**

ROMANIA
Brancusi, Constantin, **VII:**414
Eliade, Mircea, **VII:**1055

ROME. ***See*** **ITALY**

RUPERTSBERG BEI BINGEN. *See* **GERMANY**

RUSSIA. *See also* **KIEV; KHWARIZM; SOVIET UNION; VLADIMIR-SUZDAL**
Alexander I, **V:**44
Alexander II, **V:**48
Bakunin, Mikhail, **V:**112
Balanchine, George, **VII:**155
Bering, Vitus Jonassen, **IV:**111
Borodin, Aleksandr, **V:**286
Catherine the Great, **IV:**257
Chekhov, Anton, **V:**485
Diaghilev, Sergei, **VII:**919
Dostoevski, Fyodor, **V:**687
Godunov, Boris Fyodorovich, **III:**308
Gogol, Nikolai, **V:**949
Herzen, Aleksandr, **V:**1099
Horowitz, Vladimir, **VIII:**1747
Ivan the Great, **III:**381
Ivan the Terrible, **III:**385
Jakobson, Roman, **VIII:**1831
Kutuzov, Mikhail Illarionovich, **VI:**1305
Lermontov, Mikhail, **VI:**1351
Lifar, Serge, **VIII:**2182
Lobachevsky, Nikolay Ivanovich, **VI:**1403
Lomonosov, Mikhail Vasilyevich, **IV:**860
Mendeleyev, Dmitry Ivanovich, **VI:**1529
Mussorgsky, Modest, **VI:**1611
Nabokov, Vladimir, **VIII:**2675
Nicholas I, **VI:**1650
Nijinsky, Vaslav, **VIII:**2746
Nikon, **IV:**1030
Pavlova, Anna, **IX:**2937
Peter III, **IV:**1087
Peter the Great, **IV:**1082
Pobedonostsev, Konstantin Petrovich, **VI:**1790
Popov, Aleksandr Stepanovich, **VI:**1806
Pushkin, Alexander, **VI:**1832
Rachmaninoff, Sergei, **IX:**3105
Rasputin, Grigori Yefimovich, **VI:**1842
Rimsky-Korsakov, Nikolay, **VI:**1889
Speransky, Mikhail Mikhaylovich, **VI:**2089
Stravinsky, Igor, **IX:**3559
Suvorov, Aleksandr Vasilyevich, **IV:**1298
Tchaikovsky, Peter Ilich, **VI:**2198
Tolstoy, Leo, **VI:**2242
Turgenev, Ivan, **VI:**2268
Yeltsin, Boris N., **IX:**4082
Zworykin, Vladimir, **IX:**4125

RUSSIAN FEDERATION. *See* **RUSSIA; SOVIET UNION**

SAUDI ARABIA
Fahd, **VII:**1115
Faisal, **VII:**1118
Yamani, Ahmad Zaki, **IX:**4079

SAXONY. *See* **GERMANY**

SCOTLAND
Bell, Alexander Graham, **V:**185
Boswell, James, **IV:**174
Brougham, Henry, **V:**314
Bruce, James, **IV:**208
Bruce, Robert, **II:**184
Burns, Robert, **IV:**229
Cameron, Richard, **IV:**239
Carlyle, Thomas, **V:**416
Dalhousie, First Marquess of, **V:**600
David I, **II:**291
David II, **II:**294
Doyle, Sir Arthur Conan, **V:**700
Duns Scotus, John, **II:**309
Erskine, First Baron, **IV:**439
Ferguson, Adam, **IV:**454
Fleming, Sir Alexander, **VII:**1166
Frazer, Sir James George, **VII:**1220
Hardie, James Keir, **V:**1036
Hume, David, **IV:**683
Jeffrey, Lord, **V:**1224
Kelvin, Lord, **VI:**1269
Kidd, William, **IV:**777
Livingstone, David, **VI:**1399
MacDonald, Ramsay, **VIII:**2312
Mackenzie, Sir Alexander, **IV:**879
Maclaurin, Colin, **IV:**882
Macleod, John J. R., **VIII:**2329
MacMillan, Daniel and Alexander, **VI:**1457
Maxwell, James Clerk, **VI:**1511
Mill, James, **VI:**1556
Napier, John, **III:**544
Nasmyth, James, **VI:**1624
Park, Mungo, **VI:**1723
Raeburn, Sir Henry, **VI:**1836
Reith of Stonehaven, First Baron, **IX:**3146
Scott, Sir Walter, **VI:**2005
Smith, Adam, **IV:**1249
Stevenson, Robert Louis, **VI:**2139
Telford, Thomas, **VI:**2207
Wallace, Sir William, **II:**955

Watt, James, **IV:**1409
Witherspoon, John, **IV:**1467

SENEGAL
Senghor, Léopold, **IX:**3391

SERBIA. ***See also*** **YUGOSLAVIA**
Stefan Dušan, **II:**843

SIENA, REPUBLIC OF. ***See*** **ITALY**

SILESIA. ***See*** **GERMANY**

SINGAPORE
Lee Kuan Yew, **VIII:**2150

SLOVENIA. ***See*** **YUGOSLAVIA**

SONGHAI EMPIRE
Mohammed I Askia, **III:**521

SOUTH AFRICA
Barnard, Christiaan, **VII:**195
Botha, Louis, **VII:**376
de Klerk, F.W., **VII:**870
Fugard, Athol, **VII:**1257
Gordimer, Nadine, **VIII**-1427
Lutuli, Albert, **VIII:**2281
Mandela, Nelson, **VIII:**2384
Paton, Alan, **IX:**2907
Player, Gary, **IX:**3040
Rhodes, Cecil, **VI:**1873
Smuts, Jan Christian, **IX:**3453
Tutu, Desmond, **IX:**3775

SOUTH AMERICA. ***See*** **ARGENTINA; BRAZIL; CHILE; COLOMBIA; FRENCH GUIANA; PERU**

SOUTH KOREA. ***See*** **KOREA**

SOVIET UNION. ***See also*** **ARMENIA; AZERBAIJAN; BELORUSSIA; KIEV; LATVIA; LITHUANIA; RUSSIA; TAJIKISTAN; UKRAINE**
Akhmatova, Anna, **VII:**37
Ambartsumian, Viktor A., **VII:**63
Bakhtin, Mikhail, **VII:**152
Basov, Nikolay Gennadiyevich, **VII:**214
Blok, Aleksandr, **VII:**332
Brezhnev, Leonid Ilich, **VII:**459
Bukharin, Nikolai Ivanovich, **VII:**491
Chagall, Marc, **VII:**639
Eisenstein, Sergei, **VII:**1047
Gagarin, Yuri Alekseyevich, **VII:**1270
Gorbachev, Mikhail, **VIII**-1423
Gorky, Maxim, **VIII**-1442
Kandinsky, Wassily, **VIII:**1903
Kapitsa, Pyotr Leonidovich, **VIII:**1906
Kerensky, Aleksandr Fyodorovich, **VIII:**1941
Khrushchev, Nikita S., **VIII:**1961
Korolev, Sergei, **VIII:**2019
Kurchatov, Igor Vasilyevich, **VIII:**2039
Landau, Lev Davidovich, **VIII:**2073
Lenin, Vladimir Ilich, **VIII:**2160
Litvinov, Maksim Maksimovich, **VIII:**2208
Malenkov, Georgi M., **VIII:**2377
Massine, Léonide, **VIII:**2448
Mayakovsky, Vladimir, **VIII:**2461
Meyerhold, Vsevolod Yemilyevich, **VIII:**2510
Molotov, Vyacheslav Mikhailovich, **VIII:**2571
Oparin, Aleksandr Ivanovich, **IX:**2830
Pasternak, Boris, **IX:**2899
Pavlov, Ivan Petrovich, **IX:**2933
Prokofiev, Sergei, **IX:**3085
Sakharov, Andrei, **IX:**3296
Shostakovich, Dmitri, **IX:**3409
Solzhenitsyn, Aleksandr, **IX:**3459
Stalin, Joseph, **IX:**3482
Stanislavsky, Konstantin, **IX:**3486
Tereshkova, Valentina, **IX:**3639
Trotsky, Leon, **IX:**3726
Tsiolkovsky, Konstantin, **IX:**3749
Tsvetayeva, Marina, **IX:**3753
Tupolev, Andrei Nikolayevich, **IX:**3764
Vavilov, Nikolai Ivanovich, **IX:**3801
Yeltsin, Boris N., **IX:**4082
Zhukov, Georgy Konstantinovich, **IX:**4116

SPAIN
'Abd-al-Rahman III al-Nasir, **II:**7
Alfonso X, **II:**56
Alva, Duke of, **III:**18
Alvarado, Pedro de, **III:**21
Arnold of Villanova, **II:**79
Averroës, **II:**100
Balboa, Vasco Núñez de, **III:**45
Benjamin of Tudela, **II:**140
Buñuel, Luis, **VII:**505
Calderón de la Barca, Pedro, **IV:**235
Candela, Felix, **VII:**557
Carlos, Don, **V:**413
Casals, Pablo, **VII:**606
Catherine of Aragon, **III:**136

Cervantes, Miguel de, **IV:**265
Charles III, **IV:**287
Charles V, **III:**159
Cid, El, **II:**268
Columbus, Christopher, **III:**172
Coronado, Francisco Vásquez de, **III:**180
Cortés, Hernán, **III:**188
Dalí, Salvador, **VII:**827
Dominic, Saint, **II:**301
Falla, Manuel de, **VII:**1127
Ferdinand II and Isabella I, **III:**260
Franco, Francisco, **VII:**1200
García Lorca, Federico, **VII:**1290
Gaudí, Antonio, **VII:**1315
Goya, Francisco de, **IV:**569
Greco, El, **III:**311
Gris, Juan, **VIII**-1483
Ibn al-'Arabi, **II:**491
Ibn Gabirol, **II:**498
Isidore of Seville, Saint, **II:**518
James I the Conqueror, **II:**529
Jiménez de Cisneros, Francisco, **III:**392
John of the Cross, Saint, **III:**401
Las Casas, Bartolomé de, **III:**413
Loyola, Saint Ignatius of, **III:**437
Lull, Raymond, **II:**608
Maimonides, Moses, **II:**619
Martial, **I:**532
Miró, Joan, **VIII:**2546
Moses de León, **II:**648
Ortega y Gasset, José, **IX:**2843
Philip II, **III:**599
Picasso, Pablo, **IX:**2997
Pinzón Brothers, The, **III:**610
Pizarro, Francisco, **III:**620
Ponce de Léon, Juan, **III:**629
Priscillian, **I:**694
Raymond of Peñafort, **II:**776
Saragossa, La, **VI:**1958
Segovia, Andrés, **IX:**3383
Servetus, Michael, **III:**675
Siloé, Diego de, **III:**696
Soto, Hernando de, **III:**699
Teresa of Ávila, Saint, **III:**713
Theodosius the Great, **I:**868
Torquemada, Tomás de, **III:**725
Unamuno y Jugo, Miguel de, **IX:**3783
Vega Carpio, Lope de, **IV:**1361
Velázquez, Diego, **IV:**1364
Vitoria, Francisco de, **III:**768
Xavier, Saint Francis, **III:**788

SWABIA. ***See*** **GERMANY**

SWEDEN
Arrhenius, Svante August, **VII:**114
Bergman, Ingmar, **VII:**278
Borg, Björn, **VII:**368
Charles XII, **IV:**290
Charles XIV John, **V:**474
Christina, **IV:**304
Gustavus II Adolphus, **IV:**589
Hammarskjöld, Dag, **VIII:**1529
Lagerlöf, Selma, **VIII:**2065
Lind, Jenny, **VI:**1385
Linnaeus, **IV:**846
Margaret of Denmark, Norway, and Sweden, **II:**626
Meitner, Lise, **VIII:**2476
Myrdal, Gunnar, **VIII:**2671
Nobel, Alfred, **VI:**1673
Oxenstierna, Axel, **IV:**1052
Sachs, Nelly, **IX:**3285
Söderblom, Nathan, **IX:**3456
Strindberg, August, **IX:**3566
Swedenborg, Emanuel, **IV:**1302
Theorell, Axel Hugo Teodor, **IX:**3654
Torstenson, Lennart, **IV:**1335

SWITZERLAND
Barth, Karl, **VII:**203
Bernoulli Family, The, **IV:**122
Bleuler, Eugen, **VII:**328
Brunner, Emil, **VII:**475
Burckhardt, Jacob, **V:**358
Dunant, Jean-Henri, **V:**711
Euler, Leonhard, **IV:**443
Frisch, Max, **VII:**1238
Gesner, Conrad, **III:**298
Giacometti, Alberto, **VII:**1359
Guillaume, Charles-Édouard, **VIII:**1502
Jung, Carl, **VIII:**1896
Kauffmann, Angelica, **IV:**765
Klee, Paul, **VIII:**2005
Le Corbusier, **VIII:**2137
Mann, Thomas, **VIII:**2392
Marat, Jean-Paul, **IV:**910
Paracelsus, **III:**584
Pauli, Wolfgang, **IX:**2923
Pestalozzi, Johann Heinrich, **VI:**1767
Piaget, Jean, **IX:**2990
Piccard, Auguste and Jean-Felix, **IX:**3002
Rorschach, Hermann, **IX:**3236
Saussure, Ferdinand de, **IX:**3340

Steiner, Jakob, **VI:**2118
Zwingli, Huldrych, **III:**791

SYRIA. ***See also*** **ARABIA; ASSYRIA; IRAN; IRAQ; MESOPOTAMIA**
Antiochus the Great, **I:**63
Battani, al-, **II:**121
Chrysostom, Saint John, **I:**184
Ibn al-'Arabi, **II:**491
Ignatius of Antioch, **I:**440
John of Damascus, **II:**544
Lucian, **I:**507
Saladin, **II:**809
Seleucus I Nicator, **I:**767
Simeon Stylites, Saint, **I:**783
Theodoret of Cyrrhus, **I:**865
Yaqut, **II:**1013

TAIWAN
Chiang Kai-shek, **VII:**664

TAJIKISTAN
Enver Pasha, **VII:**1078

TANGANYIKA. ***See*** **TANZANIA**

TANZANIA
Nyerere, Julius, **VIII:**2773

TENOCHTITLÁN. ***See*** **MEXICO**

TEXCOCO. ***See*** **MEXICO**

THRACE
Democritus, **I:**249

THURINGIA. ***See*** **GERMANY**

TRANSJORDAN. ***See*** **JORDAN**

TUNISIA. ***See also*** **CARTHAGE**
Bourguiba, Habib, **VII:**391
Ibn Khaldun, **II:**502

TURKEY. ***See also*** **ASIA MINOR; BITHYNIA; BYZANTINE EMPIRE; CAPPADOCIA; CILICIA; MOPSUESTIA; OTTOMAN EMPIRE; PERGA; PONTUS**
Atatürk, Kemal, **VII:**133
Enver Pasha, **VII:**1078
Halide Edib Adivar, **VIII:**1522
İnönü, İsmet, **VIII:**1812

TURKMENISTAN. ***See*** **SOVIET UNION**

UKRAINE
Ba'al Shem Tov, **IV:**73

UNITED STATES
Abernathy, Ralph David, **VII:**9
Acheson, Dean, **VII:**16
Adams, Abigail, **IV:**12
Adams, Henry, **V:**15
Adams, John, **IV:**16
Adams, John Quincy, **V:**20
Adams, Samuel, **IV:**21
Addams, Jane, **VII:**21
Adler, Felix, **V:**26
Agassiz, Louis, **V:**30
Akalaitis, Joanne, **VII:**34
Albright, Madeleine, **VII:**49
Alcott, Bronson, **V:**37
Alcott, Louisa May, **V:**40
Alger, Horatio, **V:**51
Ali, Muhammad, **VII:**53
Allen, Ethan, **IV:**34
Altgeld, John Peter, **V:**54
Anderson, Marian, **VII:**70
Angelou, Maya, **VII:**79
Anthony, Susan B., **V:**61
Appleseed, Johnny, **V:**66
Arbus, Diane, **VII:**95
Arendt, Hannah, **VII:**98
Armstrong, Edwin H., **VII:**102
Armstrong, Louis, **VII:**105
Armstrong, Neil, **VII:**110
Arnold, Benedict, **IV:**64
Arthur, Chester A., **V:**77
Arzner, Dorothy, **VII:**117
Astaire, Fred, **VII:**125
Astor, John J., **V:**82
Audubon, John James, **V:**86
Austin, Stephen Fuller, **V:**94
Balanchine, George, **VII:**155
Balch, Emily Greene, **VII:**160
Baldwin, James, **VII:**164
Ball, Lucille, **VII:**176
Ballard, Robert Duane, **VII:**180
Bancroft, George, **V:**124
Banneker, Benjamin, **IV:**88
Barber, Samuel, **VII:**191
Barnard, Henry, **V:**130
Barnes, Djuna, **VII:**199
Barnum, P.T., **V:**133
Barton, Clara, **V:**142

Baum, L. Frank, **V:**154
Beard, Charles A., **VII:**221
Beecher, Catharine, **V:**170
Beecher, Henry Ward, **V:**174
Bell, Alexander Graham, **V:**185
Bellow, Saul, **VII:**247
Benedict, Ruth, **VII:**255
Benét, Stephen Vincent, **VII:**263
Bennett, James Gordon, **V:**190
Benton, Thomas Hart, **V:**195
Berlin, Irving, **VII:**287
Bernstein, Leonard, **VII:**295
Bethe, Hans Albrecht, **VII:**300
Biddle, Nicholas, **V:**225
Bierce, Ambrose, **V:**230
Bierstadt, Albert, **V:**233
Bingham, George Caleb, **V:**236
Black, Hugo L., **VII:**321
Black Hawk, **V:**247
Blackwell, Elizabeth, **V:**251
Blaine, James G., **V:**255
Boas, Franz, **VII:**339
Boone, Daniel, **IV:**163
Booth, Edwin, **V:**271
Borah, William E., **V:**279
Borden, Lizzie, **V:**283
Bourke-White, Margaret, **VII:**395
Bradford, William, **IV:**189
Bradley, Omar N., **VII:**403
Bradstreet, Anne, **IV:**193
Brady, Mathew B., **V:**294
Brandeis, Louis D., **VII:**419
Brando, Marlon, **VII:**424
Brant, Joseph, **IV:**196
Braun, Wernher von, **VII:**440
Bridgman, Percy Williams, **VII:**463
Brown, John, **V:**321
Bryan, William Jennings, **VII:**479
Bryant, William Cullen, **V:**343
Buchanan, James, **V:**346
Buck, Pearl S., **VII:**486
Bulfinch, Charles, **V:**349
Bunche, Ralph, **VII:**501
Burbank, Luther, **V:**353
Burger, Warren E., **VII:**509
Burnett, Frances Hodgson, **V:**361
Burnham, Daniel Hudson, **V:**365
Burr, Aaron, **V:**369
Burroughs, Edgar Rice, **VII:**516
Bush, George, **VII:**520
Butler, Nicholas Murray, **VII:**524
Byrd, Richard E., **VII:**534
Cabrini, Frances Xavier, **V:**396
Calamity Jane, **V:**390
Calder, Alexander, **VII:**538
Calhoun, John C., **V:**394
Campbell, Alexander, **V:**401
Campbell, Kim, **VII:**549
Capone, Alphonse, **VII:**563
Capote, Truman, **VII:**567
Cardozo, Benjamin Nathan, **VII:**575
Carlson, Chester F., **VII:**579
Carnap, Rudolf, **VII:**582
Carnegie, Andrew, **V:**420
Carroll, Charles, **IV:**250
Carson, Kit, **V:**429
Carson, Rachel, **VII:**585
Carter, Jimmy, **VII:**589
Carver, George Washington, **VII:**602
Cassatt, Mary, **V:**434
Cather, Willa, **VII:**621
Catlin, George, **V:**443
Catt, Carrie Chapman, **VII:**627
Champlain, Samuel de, **IV:**271
Channing, William Ellery, **V:**470
Chaplin, Charles, **VII:**653
Charles, Ray, **VII:**657
Chase, Salmon P., **V:**477
Chase, Samuel, **IV:**293
Child, Lydia Maria, **V:**489
Chisholm, Shirley, **VII:**668
Chomsky, Noam, **VII:**673
Chopin, Kate, **V:**497
Clark, George Rogers, **IV:**312
Clark, William, **VI:**1358
Clay, Henry, **V:**507
Cleveland, Grover, **V:**512
Clinton, Bill, **VII:**707
Clinton, DeWitt, **V:**517
Clinton, Hillary Rodham, **VII:**713
Cobb, Ty, **VII:**717
Cody, William Frederick, **V:**530
Colt, Samuel, **V:**540
Coltrane, John, **VII:**741
Compton, Arthur Holly, **VII:**745
Conant, James Bryant, **VII:**748
Cooke, Jay, **V:**551
Coolidge, Calvin, **VII:**762
Cooper, James Fenimore, **V:**560
Copland, Aaron, **VII:**766
Copley, John Singleton, **IV:**356
Cotton, John, **IV:**371
Crane, Hart, **VII:**789
Crane, Stephen, **V:**569

Crawford, Cheryl, **VII:**793
Crazy Horse, **V:**573
Crockett, David, **V:**578
cummings, e.e., **VII:**804
Cunningham, Imogen, **VII:**808
Cushing, Caleb, **V:**581
Cushing, Harvey Williams, **VII:**823
Custer, George A., **V:**585
Danilova, Alexandra, **VII:**832
Darrow, Clarence, **VII:**839
Davis, Bette, **VII:**843
Davis, Jefferson, **V:**614
Dawidowicz, Lucy S., **VII:**847
Day, Dorothy, **VII:**850
Debs, Eugene V., **VII:**880
Decatur, Stephen, **V:**634
de Forest, Lee, **VII:**858
de Mille, Agnes, **VII:**874
Demille, Cecil B., **VII:**896
Dempsey, Jack, **VII:**900
Derrida, Jacques, **VII:**912
Dewey, George, **V:**656
Dewey, John, **VII:**916
Dewey, Melvil, **V:**660
Dickinson, Emily, **V:**667
Dickinson, John, **IV:**408
Dietrich, Marlene, **VII:**930
Dimaggio, Joe, **VII:**934
Disney, Walt, **VII:**938
Dix, Dorothea, **V:**680
Dole, Robert J., **VII:**947
Douglas, Stephen A., **V:**692
Douglass, Frederick, **V:**695
Dreiser, Theodore, **VII:**954
du Bois, W.E.B., **VII:**963
Duke, James Buchanan, **V:**704
Dulles, John Foster, **VII:**976
Dunbar, Paul Laurence, **V:**714
Duncan, Isadora, **VII:**980
Dunham, Katherine, **VII:**984
Du Pont, Eleuthère Irénée, **V:**718
Eads, James Buchanan, **V:**729
Eakins, Thomas, **V:**732
Earhart, Amelia, **VII:**992
Earp, Wyatt, **V:**735
Eastman, George, **VII:**996
Eddy, Mary Baker, **V:**738
Edison, Thomas Alva, **V:**743
Edwards, Jonathan, **IV:**428
Einstein, Albert, **VII:**1035
Eisenhower, Dwight D., **VII:**1043
Eliade, Mircea, **VII:**1055
Eliot, Charles William, **V:**748
Eliot, John, **IV:**435
Eliot, T.S., **VII:**1058
Ellington, Duke, **VII:**1066
Emerson, Ralph Waldo, **V:**755
Ephron, Nora, **VII:**1083
Epstein, Sir Jacob, **VII:**1087
Erdrich, Louise, **VII:**1091
Evert, Chris, **VII:**1112
Farragut, David G., **V:**772
Farrand, Beatrix Jones, **VII:**1130
Faulkner, William, **VII:**1133
Feinstein, Dianne, **VII:**1137
Fermi, Enrico, **VII:**1145
Ferraro, Geraldine, **VII:**1153
Field, Marshall, **V:**783
Field, Stephen J., **V:**787
Fillmore, Millard, **V:**792
Fitch, John, **IV:**476
Fitzgerald, Ella, **VII:**1157
Fitzgerald, F. Scott, **VII:**1161
Flexner, Abraham, **VII:**1169
Ford, Gerald R., **VII:**1180
Ford, Henry, **VII:**1184
Forrest, Edwin, **V:**800
Forten, Charlotte, **V:**807
Foster, Stephen Collins, **V:**810
Fowler, Lydia Folger, **V:**822
Frankenthaler, Helen, **VII:**1208
Frankfurter, Felix, **VII:**1212
Franklin, Aretha, **VII:**1216
Franklin, Benjamin, **IV:**492
Frémont, John C., **V:**839
Friedan, Betty, **VII:**1231
Frost, Robert, **VII:**1250
Fuller, Loie, **VII:**1261
Fuller, Margaret, **V:**849
Fuller, R. Buckminster, **VII:**1265
Fulton, Robert, **V:**854
Gadsden, James, **V:**858
Gallatin, Albert, **V:**861
Garbo, Greta, **VII:**1286
Gardner, Erle Stanley, **VII:**1297
Gardner, Isabella Stewart, **VII:**1300
Garfield, James A., **V:**875
Garland, Judy, **VII:**1304
Garrison, William Lloyd, **V:**883
Garvey, Marcus, **VII:**1311
Geddes, Norman Bel, **VII:**1319
Gehrig, Lou, **VII:**1322
Geisel, Theodor Seuss, **VII:**1329
George, Henry, **V:**906

Geronimo, **V:**915
Gershwin, George, **VII:**1347
Gershwin, Ira, **VII:**1352
Gesell, Arnold, **VII:**1356
Gibbons, James, **V:**919
Gibbs, Josiah Willard, **V:**923
Gibson, Althea, **VII:**1363
Gillespie, Dizzy, **VII:**1370
Gish, Lillian, **VII:**1383
Glenn, John H., Jr., **VII:**1387
Goddard, Robert H., **VIII:**1396
Godkin, Edwin Lawrence, **VIII**-1400
Goethals, George Washington, **VIII**-1408
Goldman, Emma, **VIII**-1411
Goldwyn, Samuel, **VIII**-1415
Gompers, Samuel, **V:**956
Goodman, Benny, **VIII**-1419
Goodyear, Charles, **V:**960
Gore, Albert, **VIII**-1431
Gorgas, William Crawford, **VIII**-1434
Graham, Billy, **VIII**-1447
Graham, Katharine, **VIII**-1451
Graham, Martha, **VIII**-1455
Grant, Ulysses S., **V:**975
Gray, Asa, **V:**979
Greeley, Horace, **V:**982
Greene, Nathanael, **IV:**574
Greenspan, Alan, **VIII**-1471
Griffith, D.W., **VIII**-1478
Gropius, Walter, **VIII**-1486
Guggenheim, Daniel, **VIII**-1498
Hale, Sarah Josepha, **V:**1022
Halsey, William F., **VIII:**1525
Hamilton, Alexander, **IV:**608
Hammerstein, Oscar, II, **VIII:**1533
Hancock, John, **IV:**613
Hand, Learned, **VIII:**1541
Hanna, Marcus A., **V:**1029
Hansberry, Lorraine, **VIII:**1545
Harding, Warren G., **VIII:**1550
Harper, William Rainey, **V:**1044
Harriman, William Averell, **VIII:**1560
Harris, Joel Chandler, **V:**1049
Harrison, Benjamin, **V:**1053
Harrison, William Henry, **V:**1061
Hart, Lorenz, **VIII:**1566
Hawthorne, Nathaniel, **V:**1064
Hay, John, **V:**1068
Hayden, Ferdinand Vandeveer, **V:**1072
Hayes, Helen, **VIII:**1588
Hayes, Rutherford B., **V:**1075
Hayslip, Le Ly, **VIII:**1593
Hayworth, Rita, **VIII:**1596
H.D., **VIII:**1505
Hearst, William Randolph, **VIII:**1601
Hellman, Lillian, **VIII:**1620
Hemingway, Ernest, **VIII:**1624
Henry, Joseph, **V:**1093
Henry, O, **V:**1096
Henry, Patrick, **IV:**647
Hepburn, Katharine, **VIII:**1637
Hernandez, Aileen Clarke, **VIII:**1641
Hickok, Wild Bill, **V:**1107
Higginson, Thomas Wentworth, **V:**1110
Hill, James Jerome, **IV:**659
Hiss, Alger, **VIII:**1683
Hitchcock, Alfred, **VIII:**1687
Hobby, Oveta Culp, **VIII:**1703
Holiday, Billie, **VIII:**1715
Holland, John Philip, **V:**1123
Holmes, Oliver Wendell, **V:**1126
Holmes, Oliver Wendell, Jr., **VIII:**1720
Homer, Winslow, **V:**1133
Hoover, Herbert, **VIII:**1727
Hoover, J. Edgar, **VIII:**1732
Hopkins, Harry, **VIII:**1736
Hopper, Edward, **VIII:**1740
Horney, Karen, **VIII:**1744
Horowitz, Vladimir, **VIII:**1747
Houston, Sam, **V:**1137
Howe, Elias, **V:**1141
Howe, Julia Ward, **V:**1145
Howe, Samuel Gridley, **V:**1150
Huerta, Dolores, **VIII:**1762
Hughes, Charles Evans, **VIII:**1766
Hughes, Langston, **VIII:**1771
Hull, Cordell, **VIII:**1779
Humphrey, Hubert H., **VIII:**1783
Hurston, Zora Neale, **VIII:**1787
Hutchins, Robert M., **VIII:**1800
Hutchinson, Anne, **IV:**687
Hutchinson, Thomas, **IV:**691
Irving, Washington, **V:**1192
Ives, Charles, **VIII:**1820
Jackson, Andrew, **V:**1196
Jackson, Helen Hunt, **V:**1200
Jackson, Jesse L., **VIII:**1824
Jackson, Stonewall, **V:**1204
Jakobson, Roman, **VIII:**1831
James, Henry, **V:**1211
James, William, **V:**1216
Jay, John, **IV:**711
Jefferson, Thomas, **IV:**716
Jewett, Sarah Orne, **V:**1228

Johnson, Andrew, **V:**1232
Johnson, Lyndon B., **VIII:**1866
Jones, Bobby, **VIII:**1874
Jones, John Paul, **IV:**738
Jones, Mary Harris "Mother," 1879
Joplin, Janis, **VIII:**1883
Joplin, Scott, **V:**1239
Jordan, Barbara, **VIII:**1887
Joseph, Chief, **V:**1242
Kamehameha I, **VI:**1255
Keller, Helen, **VIII:**1924
Kemble, Fanny, **VI:**1273
Kennedy, John F., **VIII:**1928
Kennedy, Robert F., **VIII:**1932
Kent, James, **VI:**1277
Kerouac, Jack, **VIII:**1945
Key, Francis Scott, **VI:**1281
King, Billie Jean, **VIII:**1968
King, Martin Luther, Jr., **VIII:**1971
King, Stephen, **VIII:**1977
Kinsey, Alfred Charles, **VIII:**1986
Kirkpatrick, Jeane, **VIII:**1994
Kissinger, Henry A., **VIII:**1998
Krasner, Lee, **VIII:**2023
Kübler-Ross, Elisabeth, **VIII:**2030
La Follette, Robert M., **VIII:**2047
La Guardia, Fiorello Henry, **VIII:**2054
Lang, Fritz, **VIII:**2077
Lang, K.D., **VIII:**2080
Lange, Dorothea, **VIII:**2083
Langer, Susanne K., **VIII:**2087
Langley, Samuel Pierpont, **VI:**1313
Lathrop, Julia C., **VIII:**2096
Latrobe, Benjamin Henry, **VI:**1327
Lawrence, Ernest Orlando, **VIII:**2121
Lazarus, Emma, **VI:**1334
Lee, Ann, **IV:**817
Lee, Robert E., **VI:**1338
Le Gallienne, Eva, **VIII:**2141
Lewis, John L., **VIII:**2170
Lewis, Meriwether, **VI:**1358
Lewis, Sinclair, **VIII:**2174
Liliuokalani, **VI:**1372
Lin, Maya Ying, **VIII:**2185
Lincoln, Abraham, **VI:**1380
Lindbergh, Charles A., **VIII:**2193
Lippmann, Walter, **VIII:**2203
Lockwood, Belva A., **VI:**1406
Lodge, Henry Cabot, **VIII:**2219
London, Jack, **VIII:**2223
Long, Huey, **VIII:**2227
Longfellow, Henry Wadsworth, **VI:**1414
Loos, Anita, **VIII:**2231
Louis, Joe, **VIII:**2241
Low, Juliette Gordon, **VIII:**2246
Lowell, Amy, **VIII:**2249
Luce, Clare Boothe, **VIII:**2256
Luce, Henry R., **VIII:**2260
Lyon, Mary, **VI:**1423
MacArthur, Douglas, **VIII:**2295
MacKinnon, Catharine A., **VIII:**2325
McCarthy, Joseph R., **VIII:**2300
McCarthy, Mary, **VIII:**2304
McCormick, Cyrus Hall, **VI:**1431
McCullers, Carson, **VIII:**2308
McGillivray, Alexander, **IV:**875
McGuffey, William Holmes, **VI:**1440
McKinley, William, **VI:**1453
McMillan, Edwin Mattison, **VIII:**2336
Madison, Dolley, **VI:**1464
Madison, James, **IV:**886
Mailer, Norman, **VIII:**2365
Malcolm X, **VIII:**2373
Mankiller, Wilma P., **VIII:**2389
Mann, Horace, **IV:**894
Marciano, Rocky, **VIII:**2411
Marshall, George C., **VIII:**2429
Marshall, John, **VI:**1487
Marshall, Thurgood, **VIII:**2433
Martin, Agnes, **VIII:**2437
Mason, George, **IV:**926
Massasoit, **IV:**930
Mather, Cotton, **IV:**934
Mather, Increase, **IV:**938
Maury, Matthew Fontaine, **VI:**1507
Mayo, William J. and Charles H., **VIII:**2465
Mead, Margaret, **VIII:**2468
Mellon, Andrew, **VIII:**2480
Melville, Herman, **VI:**1520
Mencken, H.L., **VIII:**2483
Mendelsohn, Erich, **VIII:**2487
Mergenthaler, Ottmar, **VI:**1541
Metacomet, **IV:**954
Michelson, Albert A., **VI:**1551
Michener, James A., **VIII:**2517
Mies Van Der Rohe, Ludwig, **VIII:**2520
Millay, Edna St. Vincent, **VIII:**2529
Miller, Arthur, **VIII:**2533
Millett, Kate, **VIII:**2536
Millikan, Robert Andrews, **VIII:**2539
Mitchell, William, **VIII:**2554
Monroe, James, **VI:**1570
Monroe, Marilyn, **VIII:**2587
Moody, Dwight L., **VI:**1575

Moore, Marianne, **VIII:**2614
Morgan, J.P., **VI:**1579
Morgan, Lewis Henry, **VI:**1584
Morgan, Thomas Hunt, **VIII:**2618
Morris, Robert, **IV:**999
Morrison, Toni, **VIII:**2626
Morse, Samuel F.B., **VI:**1592
Morton, William Thomas Green, **VI:**1596
Moses, Grandma, **VIII:**2633
Mott, John R., **VIII:**2637
Mott, Lucretia, **VI:**1600
Muir, John, **VI:**1608
Muller, Hermann Joseph, **VIII:**2651
Murrow, Edward R., **VIII:**2662
Nabokov, Vladimir, **VIII:**2675
Nader, Ralph, **VIII:**2679
Nast, Thomas, **VI:**1627
Nation, Carry, **VI:**1630
Navratilova, Martina, **VIII:**2702
Neumann, John von, **VIII:**2724
Nevelson, Louise, **VIII:**2728
Newcomb, Simon, **VI:**1638
Niebuhr, Reinhold, **VIII:**2735
Nimitz, Chester W., **VIII:**2750
Nixon, Richard M., **VIII:**2758
Norman, Jessye, **VIII:**2769
Oakley, Annie, **VI:**1677
O'Connor, Flannery, **IX:**2785
O'Connor, Sandra Day, **IX:**2789
Oglethorpe, James Edward, **IV:**1043
O'Keeffe, Georgia, **IX:**2800
Olmsted, Frederick Law, **VI:**1691
Onassis, Jacqueline Kennedy, **IX:**2815
O'Neill, Eugene, **IX:**2819
O'Neill, Thomas Philip, Jr., **IX:**2824
Oppenheimer, J. Robert, **IX:**2833
Ortega, Katherine Davalos, **IX:**2840
Osborne, Thomas Mott, **IX:**2852
Osceola, **VI:**1695
Owens, Jesse, **IX:**2862
Paine, Thomas, **IV:**1055
Palmer, Alice Freeman, **VI:**1715
Parker, Charlie, **IX:**2880
Parker, Dorothy, **IX:**2884
Parker, Theodore, **VI:**1727
Parkman, Francis, **VI:**1735
Parks, Rosa, **IX:**2888
Parrington, Vernon L., **IX:**2892
Parton, Dolly, **IX:**2896
Patton, George S., **IX:**2911
Paul, Alice, **IX:**2915
Pauling, Linus, **IX:**2926
Peale, Charles Willson, **IV:**1070
Peary, Robert Edwin, **IX:**2941
Pei, I.M., **IX:**2946
Peirce, Charles Sanders, **VI:**1756
Penn, William, **IV:**1078
Perkins, Frances, **IX:**2961
Perot, H. Ross, **IX:**2973
Perry, Matthew C., **VI:**1760
Perry, Oliver Hazard, **VI:**1764
Pershing, John J., **IX:**2983
Phillips, Wendell, **VI:**1771
Pickford, Mary, **IX:**3006
Picotte, Susan La Flesche, **IX:**3010
Pierce, Franklin, **VI:**1775
Pike, Zebulon Montgomery, **IV:**1094
Plath, Sylvia, **IX:**3036
Pocahontas, **IV:**1106
Poe, Edgar Allan, **VI:**1794
Polk, James K., **VI:**1801
Pollock, Jackson, **IX:**3048
Pontiac, **IV:**1110
Porter, Cole, **IX:**3055
Porter, Katherine Anne, **IX:**3059
Powell, Colin L., **IX:**3070
Powell, John Wesley, **VI:**1810
Powhatan, **IV:**1122
Prescott, William Hickling, **VI:**1814
Presley, Elvis, **IX:**3076
Price, Leontyne, **IX:**3081
Pulitzer, Joseph, **VI:**1825
Rabi, Isidor Isaac, **IX:**3101
Rachmaninoff, Sergei, **IX:**3105
Randolph, A. Philip, **IX:**3112
Rankin, Jeannette, **IX:**3117
Rauschenbusch, Walter, **IX:**3125
Reagan, Ronald, **IX:**3136
Red Cloud, **VI:**1850
Reed, Walter, **VI:**1857
Rehnquist, William H., **IX:**3142
Remington, Frederic, **VI:**1861
Reno, Janet, **IX:**3153
Reuther, Walter P., **IX:**3161
Revere, Paul, **IV:**1156
Richards, Ann, **IX:**3169
Richardson, Henry Hobson, **VI:**1882
Rickover, Hyman G., **IX:**3171
Ride, Sally, **IX:**3178
Robeson, Paul, **IX:**3187
Robinson, Jackie, **IX:**3193
Rockefeller, John D., **VI:**1896
Rockwell, Norman, **IX:**3198
Rodgers, Richard, **IX:**3201

Roebling, John Augustus, **VI:**1904
Rogers, Will, **IX:**3204
Roosevelt, Eleanor, **IX:**3217
Roosevelt, Franklin D., **IX:**3222
Roosevelt, Theodore, **IX:**3228
Root, Elihu, **IX:**3232
Rose, Pete, **IX:**3239
Ross, Betsy, **IV:**1191
Ross, John, **VI:**1910
Ross, Nellie Tayloe, **IX:**3243
Royce, Josiah, **IX:**3254
Rukeyser, Muriel, **IX:**3257
Rush, Benjamin, **IV:**1202
Russell, Bill, **IX:**3268
Ruth, Babe, **IX:**3273
Sacagawea, **VI:**1933
Sacco, Nicola, **IX:**3281
Sagan, Carl, **IX:**3292
Saint-Gaudens, Augustus, **VI:**1940
Salinger, J.D., **IX:**3301
Salk, Jonas Edward, **IX:**3305
Sandburg, Carl, **IX:**3308
Sanger, Margaret, **IX:**3313
Santayana, George, **IX:**3317
Sargent, John Singer, **VI:**1961
Sauvé, Jeanne, **IX:**3344
Schoenberg, Arnold, **IX:**3357
Schurz, Carl, **VI:**1996
Scott, Dred, **VI:**1999
Scott, Winfield, **VI:**2009
Scripps, Edward Wyllis, **VI:**2014
Seaborg, Glenn Theodore, **IX:**3375
Sendak, Maurice, **IX:**3387
Sequoyah, **VI:**2025
Seton, Saint Elizabeth Ann Bayley, **VI:**2029
Sewall, Samuel, **IV:**1225
Seward, William H., **VI:**2037
Sexton, Anne, **IX:**3395
Shaw, Anna Howard, **VI:**2044
Shays, Daniel, **IV:**1239
Shepard, Alan, **IX:**3405
Sherman, Roger, **IV:**1242
Sherman, William Tecumseh, **VI:**2057
Sinatra, Frank, **IX:**3422
Sinclair, Upton, **IX:**3426
Sitting Bull, **VI:**2070
Skinner, B.F., **IX:**3431
Slater, Samuel, **VI:**2074
Smith, Alfred E., **IX:**3439
Smith, Bessie, **IX:**3442
Smith, Jedediah Strong, **VI:**2077
Smith, John, **IV:**1253
Smith, Joseph, **VI:**2080
Smith, Margaret Chase, **IX:**3446
Smith, Theobald, **IX:**3450
Sousa, John Philip, **IX:**3466
Spock, Benjamin, **IX:**3478
Standish, Miles, **IV:**1273
Stanford, Leland, **VI:**2096
Stanton, Edwin M., **VI:**2106
Stanton, Elizabeth Cady, **VI:**2110
Steichen, Edward, **IX:**3501
Stein, Gertrude, **IX:**3511
Steinbeck, John, **IX:**3515
Steinem, Gloria, **IX:**3519
Steinmetz, Charles Proteus, **VI:**2121
Stephens, Alexander H., **VI:**2129
Stevens, Thaddeus, **VI:**2136
Stevenson, Adlai E., **IX:**3523
Stewart, James, **IX:**3528
Stieglitz, Alfred, **IX:**3532
Stimson, Henry L., **IX:**3537
Stone, Harlan Fiske, **IX:**3546
Stone, Lucy, **VI:**2143
Story, Joseph, **VI:**2147
Stowe, Harriet Beecher, **VI:**2151
Stravinsky, Igor, **IX:**3559
Stuart, Gilbert, **IV:**1289
Stuyvesant, Peter, **IV:**1294
Sullivan, Harry Stack, **IX:**3575
Sullivan, Louis, **VI:**2167
Sumner, Charles, **VI:**2170
Sunday, Billy, **IX:**3582
Taft, Robert A., **IX:**3590
Taft, William Howard, **IX:**3594
Talbot, Marion, **IX:**3603
Tallchief, Maria, **IX:**3607
Taney, Roger Brooke, **VI:**2189
Tarbell, Ida, **IX:**3614
Taylor, Frederick Winslow, **IX:**3618
Taylor, Zachary, **VI:**2194
Teasdale, Sara, **IX:**3622
Tecumseh, **VI:**2203
Tekakwitha, Kateri, **IV:**1316
Teller, Edward, **IX:**3631
Terry, Megan, **IX:**3642
Tesla, Nikola, **VI:**2219
Thayer, Sylvanus, **VI:**2223
Thomas, Clarence, **IX:**3657
Thomas, Norman, **IX:**3660
Thomas, Theodore, **VI:**2230
Thoreau, Henry David, **VI:**2234
Thorndike, Edward L., **IX:**3669

Thorpe, Jim, **IX:**3672
Thurber, James, **IX:**3677
Tillich, Paul, **IX:**3685
Tombaugh, Clyde William, **IX:**3699
Truman, Harry S, **IX:**3740
Truth, Sojourner, **VI:**2255
Tubman, Harriet, **VI:**2264
Tuchman, Barbara, **IX:**3760
Turner, Frederick Jackson, **IX:**3771
Turner, Nat, **VI:**2276
Twain, Mark, **VI:**2279
Tweed, William Marcy "Boss", **VI:**2279
Tyler, John, **VI:**2288
Urey, Harold C., **IX:**3787
Van Buren, Martin, **VI:**2292
Vanderbilt, Cornelius, **VI:**2296
Varèse, Edgard, **IX:**3794
Veblen, Thorstein, **IX:**3805
Wach, Joachim, **IX:**3829
Waksman, Selman Abraham, **IX:**3833
Wald, Lillian D., **IX:**3837
Walker, Alice, **IX:**3849
Walker, Madam C.J., **IX:**3853
Wallace, George C., **IX:**3857
Wallace, Henry A., **IX:**3860
Walters, Barbara, **IX:**3868
Ward, Lester Frank, **VI:**2328
Ward, Montgomery, **VI:**2331
Warhol, Andy, **IX:**3884
Warren, Earl, **IX:**3888
Warren, Robert Penn, **IX:**3893
Washington, Booker T., **VI:**2335
Washington, George, **IV:**1405
Watson, James D., **IX:**3897
Wayne, John, **IX:**3901
Webster, Daniel, **VI:**2344
Webster, Noah, **IV:**1417
Weill, Kurt, **IX:**3926
Welles, Orson, **IX:**3934
Wells-Barnett, Ida B., **IX:**3941
West, Mae, **IX:**3949
Westinghouse, George, **VI:**2358
Wharton, Edith, **IX:**3953
Whipple, George Hoyt, **IX:**3957
Whistler, James McNeill, **VI:**2363
White, Walter, **IX:**3961
Whitman, Walt, **VI:**2368
Whitney, Eli, **IV:**1431
Whitney, Gertrude Vanderbilt, **IX:**3969
Whittier, John Greenleaf, **VI:**2374
Wiener, Norbert, **IX:**3976
Wiesel, Elie, **IX:**3980
Wightman, Hazel Hotchkiss, **IX:**3989
Wilder, Laura Ingalls, **IX:**3992
Wilkes, Charles, **VI:**2381
Willard, Emma, **VI:**2384
Willard, Frances, **VI:**2388
Williams, George Washington, **VI:**2396
Williams, Roger, **IV:**1451
Williams, Tennessee, **IX:**4007
Wilson, Edmund, **IX:**4012
Wilson, James, **IV:**1455
Wilson, Woodrow, **IX:**4020
Winfrey, Oprah, **IX:**4029
Winthrop, John, **IV:**1463
Wise, Isaac Mayer, **VI:**2400
Wise, Stephen Samuel, **IX:**4033
Witherspoon, John, **IV:**1467
Wolfe, Thomas, **IX:**4041
Wood, Grant, **IX:**4045
Woods, Tiger, **IX:**4049
Woodward, Robert Burns, **IX:**4052
Workman, Fanny Bullock, **VI:**2410
Wright, Frank Lloyd, **IX:**4060
Wright, Wilbur and Orville, **IX:**4064
Wyeth, Andrew, **IX:**4072
Young, Brigham, **VI:**2414
Zaharias, "Babe" Didrikson, **IX:**4096
Zanuck, Darryl F., **IX:**4100
Zenger, John Peter, **IV:**1484
Zwilich, Ellen Taaffe, **IX:**4121
Zworykin, Vladimir, **IX:**4125

UZBEKISTAN. ***See*** **SOVIET UNION**

VENEZUELA
Bolívar, Simón, **V:**267
Sucre, Antonio José de, **VI:**2164

VENICE, REPUBLIC OF. ***See*** **ITALY**

VIETNAM
Ho Chi Minh, **VIII:**1698
Vo Nguyen Giap, **IX:**3821

VLADIMIR-SUZDAL
Alexander Nevsky, **II:**52

WALES
Diana, Princess of Wales, **VII:**923
Grove, Sir William Robert, **V:**1010
Owen, Robert, **VI:**1708
Russell, Bertrand, **IX:**3264
Stanley, Henry Morton, **VI:**2101

WEST AFRICA. *See also* **MALI**
Sundjata, **II:**863

WEST GERMANY. *See also* **GERMANY**
Adenauer, Konrad, **VII:**26
Brandt, Willy, **VII:**427
Erhard, Ludwig, **VII:**1094

WEST INDIES
Constantine, Baron, **VII:**759

YUGOSLAVIA. *See also* **DALMATIA; SERBIA**
Djilas, Milovan, **VII:**944
Teresa, Mother, **IX:**3635
Tito, **IX:**3692

ZAIRE
Mobutu Sese Seko, **VIII:**2562
Tshombe, Moïse, **IX:**3745

ZIMBABWE
Mugabe, Robert, **VIII:**2647
Rhodes, Cecil, **VI:**1873

ZULU EMPIRE
Shaka, **VI:**2041

SUBJECT INDEX

Aalto, Alvar, **VII:1-4**
  Turan Sanomat, VII:1
Aaron, **I:1-4**
Aaron, Hank, IX:2797, 2798
Abahai, **IV:1-3,** 421, 423
Abailard, Pierre. *See* Abelard, Peter
Abano, Pietro d', **II:1-3**
  Conciliator differentiarum philosophorum et praecipue medicorum, II:1
  De venenis eorumque remediis, II:1
Abaqa, II:381
Abbas, Ferhat, **VII:5-8**
'Abbasid empire, II:18, 67-69, 124, 126, 437-439, 522, 678
'Abbas the Great, **IV:4-6**
Abbott, Grace, VIII:2098, 2099
Abbott, Jack Henry, VIII:2367
ABC News, IX:3870
'Abd al-Mu'min, **II:4-6**
'Abd al-Qadirdir. *See* Abdelkader
'Abd-al-Rahman III al-Nasir, **II:7-9**
Abdelkader, **V:1-3**
Abdera, I:705
'Abduh, Muhammad, **V:4-6**
Abdülaziz, V:1207
Abdullah, King, VIII:1791
Abel, Niels Henrik, **V:7-9**
Abelard, Peter, **II:10-15,** 28, 50, 144, 995
  Apologia, II:14
  Dialogue of a Philosopher with a Jew and a Christian, II:14
  Ethics, II:13
  Sic et Non, II:13
  Story of My Misfortunes, The, II:13
  Tractatus de unitate et trinitate divina, II:13
Abe Masahiro, V:1181
Abercromby, Sir James, IV:37
Abernathy, Ralph David, **VII:9-12**
Abetz, Otto, VIII:2106
Abjuration, Act of, III:575
abolitionism
  Adams, V:23, 24
  Alcott, V:40
  Anthony, V:62
  Arthur, V:77
  Banneker, IV:88, 90, 91
  Beecher, Catharine, V:171
  Beecher, Henry Ward, V:174, 175
  Benton, V:196
  Brougham, V:314
  Brown, V:321, 322, 324, 325
  Bryant, V:344
  Buchanan, V:347
  Burr, V:369
  Buxton, V:378-380
  Channing, V:472
  Chase, V:477-479
  Child, V:489-491
  Clay, V:508
  Cushing, V:582, 583
  Derby, V:654
  Douglass, V:697
  Dred Scott decision, VI:1999-2001, 2189, 2191, 2192
  Dunbar, V:714
  Fillmore, V:792, 793
  Forten, V:807-809
  Fox, IV:482
  Frémont, V:840
  Garfield, V:876
  Garibaldi, V:881
  Garrison, V:883-886
  Greeley, V:984, 985
  Grey, V:996
  Higginson, V:1110-1112
  Howe, V:1151
  Kemble, VI:1275
  Lincoln, VI:1380, 1382, 1383
  Mason, IV:926, 927
  Mott, VI:1600-1602
  Oglethorpe, IV:1045
  Olmsted, VI:1691
  Parker, VI:1727-1730
  Phillips, VI:1771-1773
  Sewall, IV:1225-1227
  Seward, VI:2037-2039
  Sharp, IV:1236-1238
  Sinclair's *Manassas,* IX:3428
  Stanton, VI:2110-2112
  Stevens, VI:2137
  Stone, VI:2143
  Story, VI:2148, 2149
  Stowe, VI:2151, 2152
  Sumner, VI:2170-2173
  Toussaint-Louverture, IV:1338-1340
  Truth, VI:2255, 2257, 2258

  Tubman, VI:2264-2267
  Turner, VI:2276-2278
  Van Buren, VI:2294
  Whittier, VI:2374, 2375
  Wilberforce, IV:1435-1438
  William IV, VI:2394
Abominations, Tariff of, VI:2288, 2289
abortion
  Blackwell, V:252
  Campbell, VII:549
  Ferraro, VII:1154
  Herophilus, I:400
  John Paul II, VIII:1864
  O'Connor, IX:2790
  Reno, IX:3155
  Roe v. Wade, VII:511; IX:3143, 3144
  Sanger, IX:3313, 3314
  Steinem, IX:3519
Abraham, **I:5-8,** 564
Abraham of Beja, III:198
Absalom, I:243; II:815, 816
absolute monarchy
  Cameron, IV:240
  Colbert, IV:336
  Fortescue, III:268
  Frederick II, II:362
  Frobisher, III:275, 286
  Great Condé, IV:341-343
  Hobbes, IV:664, 665
  Richelieu, IV:1168
  Saint-Just, IV:1205, 1206
Abstract Expressionism. *See* Expressionism
Absurd, Theater of the, VIII:1816-1819
Absurdism, VII:240
Abu 'Abd Allah al-Shafi'i, II:33
Abu 'Ali al-Husain ibn 'Abdallah ibn Sina. *See* Avicenna
Abu 'Ali Hasan ibn 'Ali. *See* Nizam al-Mulk
Abu al-Qasim, II:714
Abu Hanifah, **II:16-19,** 33
Abu Hayyan al-Tawhidi, II:20
Abu Inan, II:502
Abu Ishaq al-Sahili, II:624
Abul Wefa, **II:20-22**
  Zij al-wadih, II:21
Abu Nidal, VII:92
Abu Simbel, I:737
Abu 'Ubaid al-Juzjani, II:106, 107
Abu Ya'qub Yusuf, II:100, 102
Abydos, I:736
Abyssinia, III:197-199
Academic Defense Corps, VIII:2742
Acamapichtli, III:528
Acatziri, I:125
Accademia Reale, IV:304
Acciaiuoli, Niccolò, II:150, 152
Acerbo Law, VIII:2668
Achaean League, I:215, 216, 673
Achaemenian dynastic empire, I:233-236, 238
Achaeus, I:63
Achamoth, I:912, 913
Achebe, Chinua, **VII:13-15**
  Anthills of the Savannah, VII:14
  Arrow of God, VII:13
  Beware, Soul-Brother and Other Poems, VII:14
  Chike and the River, VII:14
  Girls at War, VII:14
  Man of the People, A, VII:13
  No Longer at Ease, VII:13
  Sacrificial Egg and Other Short Stories, The, VII:13
  Things Fall Apart, VII:13, 14
Acheson, Dean, **VII:16-20**
Acheson-Lillienthal Report, IX:3102
Achilles asteroid, IX:4039
Achilli, Giacinto, VI:1643
ACLU. *See* American Civil Liberties Union
Acosta, Mercedes de
  Jeanne d'Arc, VIII:2142
acquired immune deficiency syndrome. *See* AIDS
Acre, Isaac de, II:649
Acre, siege of, II:782
Acropolis, I:280, 625, 962, 964
ACS. *See* American Colonization Society
Acte additionnel, V:611, 612
Action Committee for the United States of Europe, VIII:2585
Action Française, VIII:2425, 2427
Actium, Battle of, I:21, 133, 220
Acton, Lord, **V:10-14**
  "History of Liberty," V:11
Actors Studio, VII:424
Acts, Book of, I:243
Acts of the Apostles, I:822
adab culture, II:526, 527
Adad-nirari II, I:109
Adalbert, Saint, II:851
Adam, Adolphe-Charles, V:649
Adam, James and Robert, **IV:7-11**
  Works in Architecture, The, IV:10
Adam, William, IV:7
Adam and Eve, III:72; IV:961, 962
Adam de la Halle, **II:23-26**
  Jeu d' Adam ou de la feuillée, II:23-25

Jeu de Robin et de Marion, Le, II:24, 25
Nécrologe de la Confrérie des jongleurs et de bourgeois d' Arras, II:23
Roi de Secile, Le, II:23
Adamites, II:1031
Adam Kadmon, III:440
Adams, Abigail, **IV:12-14,** 16
Adams, Ansel, VII:809
Adams, Charles F., VI:2171
Adams, Henry, **V:15-19;** VI:1738; VIII:2219, 2220
Democracy, V:16
Education of Henry Adams, The, V:15, 16, 18
Esther, V:16
History of the United States of America, V:15, 16, 18
Mont-Saint-Michel and Chartres, II:374; V:15, 16, 18
Adams, Herbert Baxter, IX:3773
Adams, John, IV:12-14, **16-20,** 295, 315, 615, 616, 718, 719, 999
Defense of the Constitutions of Government of the United States of America, A, IV:18
Dissertation upon Parties, A, IV:161
Adams, John Quincy, **V:20-25**
Canning, V:406
Clay, V:508
Jackson, V:1197, 1198
Monroe, VI:1571, 1573
Mayflower Compact, IV:189
Polk, VI:1801
Van Buren, VI:2293
Adams, Samuel, **IV:21-25,** 691
Addams, Jane, **VII:21-25;** VIII:2097; IX:3838
Democracy and Social Ethics, VII:24
Spirit of Youth and the City Streets, The, VII:24
Twenty Years at Hull House, VII:23
Women at the Hague, VII:161
Addington, Henry, IV:1104
Addis Ababa, Treaty of, VI:1539
Addison, Joseph, **IV:26-29**
Berkeley, IV:114
Campaign, The, IV:26
Freeholder, The, IV:27
Guardian, The, IV:27, 114
Old Whig, The, IV:27
Spectator, The, IV:26-28, 566
Tatler, The, IV:26, 27
Addled Parliament, IV:1285
Adelphi scheme, IV:9
Adenauer, Konrad, **VII:26-29;** VIII:2009
Adler, Alfred, **VII:30-33,** 1226
Neurotic Constitution, The, VII:30, 31
Social Interest: A Challenge to Mankind, VII:30, 31
Study of Organ Inferiority and It's Psychical Compensation, VII:30, 31
Understanding Human Nature, VII:30
What Life Should Mean to You, VII:30
Adler, Dankmar, VI:2167, 2168
Adler, Felix, **V:26-29**
Adler, Kurt, VII:928
Admetus, I:317, 318
Administration of Justice Act, IV:616
Admirals' Revolt, VIII:2752
Admiralty Range, VI:1908
Adonijah, I:798
Adoula, Cyrille, IX:3746
Adrian II, II:279
Adrian IV, **II:27-29,** 48, 358
Laudabiliter, II:29
Adrian VI, III:166, 325
Adrianople, battle of, I:825
Adult Suffrage Society, VII:353, 354
Advancement of Women, Association for the, V:1146
Adventure Galley, IV:777, 779
Adversaria, III:673
AEA. *See* Aerial Experiment Association
AEG, VIII:2520
Aegina, Island of, I:611
Aegospotami, Battle of, I:32
Aeken, Jeroen van. *See* Bosch, Hieronymus
Aelst, Pieter Coecke van, III:85
Aenesidemus, I:725
Aerial Experiment Association, V:186
aerodynamics
Geddes, VII:1320
Lanchester, VIII:2071
Langley, VI:1313-1315
Prandtl, IX:3073-3075
Wright brothers, IX:4064-4067
aeronautics
Blériot, VII:325-327
Byrd, VII:534-536
Eckener, VII:1011-1013
Guggenheim, VIII:1500
Heinkel, VIII:1614
Korolev, VIII:2019
Santos-Dumont, IX:3320-3322
Tupolev, IX:3764-3766
Whittle, IX:3972-3974
Zeppelin, IX:4108-4110

Aeschines, I:254, 255
Aeschylus, **I:9-12,** 91, 807
Aetnae, I:10
Eumenides, I:10, 11
Glaucus Potnieus, I:10
Oresteia, I:10, 624; VIII:2525
Persians, The, I:10, 624
Phineus, I:10
Prometheus Bound, I:11
Suppliants, The, I:10, 11, 878
Aesop, **I:13-15,** 618
Fables, I:13-15; IV:857
"Frogs Who Asked for a King, The," I:14
Aetius, I:126
Aetolia, I:64
Afer, Publius Terentius. *See* Terence
Affinity Laws, V:1170
affirmative action, VII:511; IX:2790, 3143
AFL-CIO. *See* American Federation of Labor; Congress of Industrial Organizations
Afonso I, **II:30-32**
Afonso V, III:197
African American Post, VII:144
African Association, VI:1723, 1724
African Intelligence Department, VIII:2146
African National Congress
de Klerk, VII:871, 872
Lutuli, VIII:2281-2283
Machel, VIII:2318, 2319
Mandela, VIII:2384, 2386, 2387
Nyerere, VIII:2774
African Unity, Organization of, VIII:1520, 2763; IX:3758
Afrika Korps, IX:3213, 3215
Afzal Khan, IV:1246, 1247
Agakar, Gopal Ganesh, IX:3682
Agassiz, Louis, **V:30-33**
Contributions to the Natural History of the United States, V:31
Methods of Study in Natural History, V:32
Agathocles, I:716
Ageladas, I:624
Agesilaus II, **I:16-19**
Agis IV, I:215, 216
Agnadello, Battle of, III:48, 406
Agnes of Poitou, II:461
Agnew, Spiro, VIII:2759, 2760
Agnus Dei, II:823, 825
Agramonte, Aristides, VI:1858, 1859
Agram Treason Trials, VIII:2441
Agra palace-fort, IV:1234
Agricola, Georgius, **III:1-4**
Bermannus sive de re metallica dialogus, III:2
De natura fossilium, III:2
De ortu et causis subterraneorum, III:2
De re metallica libri XII, III:2
Agricultural Adjustment Act of 1933, IX:3860
Agriculture, United States Department of, VII:604
Agricus, I:377
Agrippa, Marcus Vipsanius, **I:20-22**
Agrippina, I:152, 206, 577, 772
Agrippina minor, I:550
Aguinaldo, Emiliano, V:657
Agustina, Maria. *See* Saragosa, La
Aha, I:548
Ahaz, I:453
Ahmad ibn Hanbal, **II:33-36**
Musnad, II:34
Ahmad Khan, Sir Sayyid, **V:34-36**
Asar-oos-sunnadeed, V:34
Ahmadu Tal, V:764
Ahmed ibn Arabshah, II:884
Ahmose, I:371
Ahna, Pauline de, IX:3556
Ahriman, I:976, 977
Ahura Mazda, I:237, 238
Avesta, I:975, 976
Aidh, VII:1118
Aidit, Dipa Nusantara, IX:3572
AIDS, VIII:2031, 2032; IX:3637
Aikido, IX:2797
Ailly, Pierre d', III:172
Aitken, William Maxwell. *See* Beaverbrook, Lord
Aix-la-Chappelle, Treaty of, IV:1076
Akalaitis, Joanne, **VII:34-36**
Balcony, The, VII:35
Cascando, VII:34
Cymbeline, VII:35
Dead End Kids, VII:35
Dressed Like an Egg, VII:35
Endgame, VII:35
Green Card, VII:35
Photographer, The, VII:35
Request Concert, VII:35
Screams, The, VII:35
Southern Exposure, VII:35
Through the Leaves, VII:35
Akbar, **III:5-7**
Akechi Mitsuhide, III:571
Akhenaton, **I:23-26,** 573, 575, 734, 904
Akhmatova, Anna, **VII:37-40**
Anno Domini, VII:38
"By the Seashore," VII:38

Chetki, VII:38
"Courage," VII:38
Evening, VII:37
Flight of Time, The, VII:38
Plantain, VII:38
Poem without a Hero, A, VII:38, 39
Reed, The, VII:38
Requiem, VII:38
Rosary, VII:38
Seventh Book, The, VII:38
V khvale mira, VII:38
Akiba ben Joseph, **I:27-30**
Akihito, **VII:41-44**
Akins, Zoë, VII:117, 119
Akwe clan, VIII:1754
ALA. *See* American Library Association
'Alam Khan, III:38
Alamo, Battle of the, V:578, 579
Alanbrooke, First Viscount, **VII:45-48**
Alans, I:126, 342, 343
Alarcón, Hernando de, III:180
Alaric, I:342, 826
Alaric II, II:276
Alaska
Alexander II, V:49
Arthur, V:80
Bering, IV:111, 112
Canadian boundary, V:1070
mining, VIII:1499
purchase, V:1237; VI:2172
Seward, VI:2038, 2039
Taft, IX:3596
Alaskan Boundary Tribunal, VIII:2221
Alaska Syndicate, VIII:1499
Alba, Duke of. *See* Alva, Duke of
Albanian Crisis, IX:2877
Albany Academy, V:1093
Albatenius. *See* Battani, al-
Albemarle, Duke of, IV:511
Albergati, Niccoló, III:559
Albert II, III:374
Albert, Prince, VI:2308, 2309; VII:1020
Alberti, Leon Battista, **III:8-10,** 28, 81
Architecture, The, III:9
Della tranquillità dell' anima, III:8
Family in Renaissance Florence, The, III:8, 9
Of Painting, III:8
Of Sculpture, III:8
Theogenius, III:8
Trivia Senatoria, III:9
Albert of Saxe-Coburg-Gotha, VI:1518
Albert the Bear, II:466
Albertus Magnus, Saint, **II:37-40**
Book of Minerals, II:38
De animalibus, II:38
De causis proporietatum elementorum, II:38
De vegetablilibus et plantis, II:38
Albigensian Crusade. *See* Catharist movement
Alboin, **II:41-43**
Albrecht V, III:281
Albrecht of Brandenburg, III:178
Albright, Madeleine, **VII:49-52,** 400
Albuquerque, Afonso de, **III:11-13**
Alcaeus, I:651, 652
alchemy
Agricola, III:2
Bosch, III:70
Boyle, IV:187
Jabir ibn Hayyan, II:522-524
Lavoisier, IV:805
Mersenne, IV:950
Razi, II:781
Stahl, IV:1268, 1271
Alcibiades, **I:31-33,** 795
Alcmaeon, **I:34-37**
Alcmaeonids, I:649, 803
ALCOA. *See* Aluminum Company of America
Alcott, Bronson, **V:37-39,** 40
Conversations with Children on the Gospels, V:38
Record of a School, V:38
Alcott, Louisa May, V:39, **40-43**
Eight Cousins, V:41
Flower Fables, V:40
Little Men, V:41
Little Women, V:41
Modern Mephistopheles, V:41
Old-Fashioned Girl, An, V:41
Rose in Bloom, V:41
Alcuin, **II:44-47,** 756, 766
On the Bishops, Kings, and Saints of York, II:44, 46
Aldhelm, II:824
Aldona, II:210
Aldrin, Edwin E., Jr., VII:112
Alekseyev, Konstantin Sergeyevich. *See* Stanislavsky, Konstantin
Alekseyev Circle, IX:3486
Alembert, Jean le Rond d', **IV:30-33,** 413; VI:1319
Account of the Destruction of the Jesuits in France, An, IV:32
Eléméns de musique théorique et practique suivant les principes de M. Rameau, IV:33
Essai sur les gens de lettres, IV:32

Opuscules mathématiques, IV:32
Preliminary Discourse to the Encyclopedia of Diderot, IV:31
Traité de dynamique, IV:30
Alencar, José de, VI:1445
Alenquer, Pedro de, III:217
Alesia, I:924
Aleuads, I:787
Alexander I (of Russia), **V:44-47;** VI:1306, 1307, 2089, 2307
Alexander II (of Macedonia), I:628
Alexander II (of Russia), **V:48-50;** VI:1651, 1652, 1790, 1791
Alexander III (Pope), **II:48-51**
Becket, II:128, 129
Bruce, II:184, 185
Frederick I Barbarossa, II:359
Alexander III (of Russia), VI:1790-1792; VIII:2160
Alexander IV (Pope), II:991, 992
Alexander VI (Pope), **III:14-17,** 406, 668, 669
Alexander VIII (Pope), IV:119
Alexander, Comso, IV:1289
Alexander, Franz, VIII:1745
Alexander, James, IV:1484, 1486
Alexander Nevsky, **II:52-55**
Alexander the Great, **I:38-42**
Antigonus I Monohthalmos, I:60, 61
Aristotle, I:95, 96
Demosthenes, I:255
Diogenes, I:270
Lysippus, I:515, 516
Philip II of Macedonia, I:630
Pompey the Great, I:680
Ptolemy Philadelphus, I:717
Ptolemy Soter, I:720-722
Pyrrhon of Elis, I:724, 725
Seleucus I Nicator, I:767, 768
Alexandria, Egypt
anti-Semitism, I:632
Callimachus, I:156
Cleopatra VII, I:218, 220, 221
Eratosthenes of Cyrene, I:303-305
Hypatia, I:436-438
museum, I:307
Origen, I:581
Paul of Aegina, II:712
Ptolemy Soter, I:722
Sosigenes, I:811
vivisection, I:398
Alexandria, Library of, I:303-305
Alexandrian Donations, I:70
Alexandrine War, I:149, 218
Alexis I, IV:1030, 1032
Alexius, II:159, 160
Alexius IV, II:942
Alexius V, II:429
Alfa Romeo Company, VII:1150
Alfonso X, **II:56-58**
Cántigas de Santa María, II:57
Crónica general, II:57
Siete Partidas, Las, II:57
Alfred the Great, **II:59-62,** 319, 334
Alfthryth, II:344
Algarotti, Count Francesco, IV:1324
algebra
Abel, V:7-9
Aryabhata, II:90
Diophantus, I:272-274
Galois, V:864-866
Gauss, V:893-895
Hamilton, V:1025-1027
Khwarizmi, II:563-565
Lagrange, IV:786
Leonardo of Pisa, II:586
Picard, IX:2994, 2995
Whitehead, IX:3966
Algeciras Conference of 1906, V:1131; VII:704
Alger, Horatio, **V:51-53**
Bertha's Christmas, V:51
Luck and Pluck, V:51
Paul Prescott's Charge, V:51
Ragged Dick, V:51
Tattered Tom, V:51
Algerian People, Manifesto of the, VII:5, 6
Algerian People's Union, VII:5
Algirdas, II:1001
Algonquin Round Table, IX:2884, 2885
Algren, Nelson, VII:231
Alhazen, **II:63-66**
Hay' at al-'alan, II:65
Optics, II:63-66
Ali, Muhammad, **VII:53-57;** VIII:2413
Alianza Popular Revolucionaria Americana, VIII:1584-1586
Alien and Sedition Acts
Adams, IV:19
Chase, IV:295
Jefferson, IV:718
Madison, IV:888
Alien Enemies Bureau, VIII:1732
Allahbad Municipal Board, IX:2869
Allegemeine Deutsche Erziehungsanstalt, V:845, 846

Allegheny Observatory, VI:1313, 1314
Allegri, Antonio. *See* Correggio
Allen, Ethan, **IV:34-36,** 64
Essay on the Universal Plentitude of Being, An, IV:36
Narrative of Colonel Ethan Allen's Captivity, A, IV:35
Reason the Only Oracle of Man, IV:34, 36
Allen, William Francis, IX:3772
Allenby, Lord, **VII:58-62;** IX:4094
Allende, Salvador, VIII:2718, 2759
Alliance and Friendship, Treaty of, VII:260
Alliance Israélite, VII:610, 611
All-India Conference, VII:184; IX:2867
Allison, Wilmer, IX:2981
Allouez, Father Claude-Jean, IV:732
Almanza, Battle of, IV:157
Almeida, Dom Francisco de, III:12
Almohad empire, II:4-6, 100
Almoravid dynasty, II:4, 30, 100, 268-270
Alp Arslan, **II:67-71,** 677
Alphege, Archbishop of Canterbury, II:202
Alpine skiing. *See* skiing
Alsace and Lorraine, III:164, 165; V:872, 873; VI:1622
Altenberg, Peter, VIII:2012
Alte Veste, Battle of the, IV:591
Altgeld, John Peter, **V:54-57;** VIII:2096
Our Penal Machinery and Its Victims, V:54
Altmark, Truce of, IV:590
Aluminum Company of America, VIII:2480
Alva, Duke of, III:**18-20,** 537, 782
Alvarado, Hernando de, III:181, 182
Alvarado, Pedro de, **III:21-23**
Alvares, Francisco, III:198
Aly Khan, Prince, VIII:1597
Amadism. *See* Pure Land Buddhism
Amalgamation Party, V:346
Amal kings, II:894
Amalric I, II:809
Amarna Age, I:24
Amar Quartet, VIII:1670
Amati, Nicolò, IV:1281
Ambaridi, I:755
Ambartsumian, Viktor A., **VII:63-65**
Ambrose, Saint, **I:43-46,** 416, 791, 870, 871
De fide, I:44
Ameinias, I:596
Amenhotep II, I:23, 891
Amenhotep III, I:23
Amenhotep IV. *See* Akhenaton
Amerbach, Bonifacius, III:358
American Academy of Tropical Medicine, IX:3452
American Anti-Slavery Society, V:490, 885, 886; VI:1773, 2110
American Art-Union, V:237
American Association of Petroleum Geologists, IX:3919, 3920
American Association of Social Workers, VIII:1736
American Ballet, School of, VII:835
American Ballet Company, VII:156, 296
American Bar Association, VII:421
American Biograph Studios, VIII:1480
American Civil Liberties Union, IX:3660
American Colonization Society, V:884, 885; VI:1490
American Enterprise Institute, VIII:1995
American Ethnological Society, V:861, 862
American Expeditionary Forces, VIII:1437, 2555; IX:2893-2895
American Federation of Labor, V:956-958; VII:881; VIII:2170-2172; IX:3163
American Federation of Radio Artists, VII:898
American Foundation for the Blind, VIII:1926
American Freedmen's Inquiry Commission, V:1151
American Fur Company, V:84
American Hebrew Congregations, Union of, VI:2400, 2401
American Historical Association, VII:223
American Independent Party, IX:3859
American Indians. *See* Native Americans
American Jewish Congress, IX:4034
American Journal of Sociology, The, IX:3603
American Library Association, V:660
American Magazine, The, IX:3616
American Newspaper Publishers Associatiion, VI:1542
American Party. *See* Know-Nothing Party
American Popular Revolutionary Alliance. *See* Alianza Popular Revolucionaria Americana
American Psychological Association, VIII:1989
American Railway Union, VII:881
American Red Cross, V:142, 143, 145; IX:3205, 3839
American Revolution. *See* American War of Independence
American Revolution, Daughters of the, VII:23, 72
Americans for Democratic Action, VIII:1783; IX:3162, 3163
American Smelting and Refining Company, VIII:1499, 1500
American Sociology Society, VI:2329

American States, Organization of, IX:2959
American Telephone and Telegraph Company. *See* AT&T
American Tobacco Company, V:704-706
American Type Founders Company, VI:1542
American War of Independence
Acton, V:12
Adams, John, IV:16, 18, 19
Adams, Samuel, IV:21-24
Allen, IV:34-36
André, IV:42-44
Arnold, IV:64, 66, 67
Bacon, IV:80-82
Bancroft, V:126
Blackstone, IV:130
Bolingbroke, IV:161
Boone, IV:164
Brant, IV:196, 198
Burke, IV:223, 224
Charles III, IV:288
Clark, IV:312, 314, 315
Clinton, IV:321-323
Cornwallis, IV:367
Dickinson, IV:408-411
Ferguson, IV:457
Fox, IV:481
Franklin, IV:494
Gage, IV:513
George III, IV:541, 542
Greene, IV:574-577
Hamilton, IV:608-611
Hancock, IV:617
Henry, IV:649
Howe, IV:677, 678
Hutchinson, IV:691-694
Jay, IV:711
Lewis, VI:1358
Marshall, VI:1487
Monroe, VI:1570
Morris, IV:999-1001
North, IV:1034-1036
Paine, IV:1055-1057
Peale, IV:1072
Pitt the Younger, IV:1102
Pontiac's Rebellion, IV:39, 40
Revere, IV:1156-1159
Rochambeau, IV:1174-1176
Rodney, IV:1178
Shays, IV:1239-1241
Sherman, IV:1242-1244
Washington, IV:1405-1407
Wilson, IV:1456-1458
Witherspoon, IV:1470
Wolfe, IV:1473
American Woman Suffrage Association, V:62, 64; VI:2044, 2045, 2112, 2389
American Women's Education Association, V:172
Ames Monument, VI:1883
AM-FM broadcasting, VII:102, 103
Amherst, Lord, **IV:37-41,** 512, 513, 1472
Amida, I:779, 780
Amiens, Mise of, II:454, 645
Amiens, Treaty of, IV:1104; VI:2187
Amini, Ali, VIII:2568
Amistad case, V:24, 344; VI:2148
Amman Summit, VIII:1794
Ammonites, I:748
Amon, I:23, 24, 371, 636-638, 734, 889
Amos, I:468
Amphipolis, I:629, 630
Amphitheus, I:88, 90
Amritsar Massacres, IX:2867
Amsterdam Stock Exchange, IX:2859
Amundsen, Roald, **VII:66-69,** 534; IX:3020
Amyntas, I:628
Anabaptists, III:510-512, 793
Anaconda Plan, VI:2012
anarchism
Altgeld, V:55, 56
Bakunin, V:112-114
Goldman, VIII:1411-1413
Jaurès, V:1221
Proudhon, VI:1818, 1820
Sacco and Vanzetti, IX:3281-3283
Anastasius the Librarian, II:675, 904
Anatolius, treaty of, I:124, 125
anatomy
Alcmaeon, I:35
Aretaeus of Cappadocia, I:81, 82
Brancusi, VII:414
Celsus, I:174
Cuvier, V:589-591
Diocles of Carystus, I:260-262
Eakins, V:732, 733
Empedocles, I:284
Erasistratus, I:299-302
Galen, I:338-340
Guy de Chauliac, II:414-416
Harvey, IV:628
Herophilus, I:398-400
Lankester, VI:1317
Malpighi, IV:891-893
Michelangelo, III:517, 519, 520
Vesalius, III:754-757

Anaxagoras, **I:47-49,** 609, 624
Nature, I:47
Anaxandrides, I:501
Anaximander, **I:50-52,** 53, 382
Anaximenes of Miletus, **I:53-55,** 955, 956, 972
Anazarbus, I:276
ANC. *See* African National Congress
Andersen, Hans Christian, **V:58-60**
"Emperor's New Clothes," V:59
Eventyr, V:59
Improvisatore, V:58
Little Match Girl, IX:3157
"Little Mermaid," V:59
"Nightingale," V:59
Only a Fiddler, V:58
O.T., V:58
Poet's Bazaar, V:59
"Princess and the Pea," V:59
Story of My Life, V:60
"Thumbelina," V:59
"Tinder Box," V:59
"Ugly Duckling," V:59
Anderson, Marian, **VII:70-73**
Anderson, Maxwell, IX:3928
Andersonn, Bibi, VII:278
Anderson School of Natural History, V:32
André, John, **IV:42-45,** 66
Andrea d'Agnolo. *See* Andrea del Sarto
Andrea del Sarto, **III:24-27**
Birth of the Virgin, III:24
Charity, III:26
Death of the Saint, The, III:24
Last Supper, The, III:26
Madonna and Child with Saints, III:26
Madonna del Sacco, III:26
Madonna of the Harpies, III:26
Miracles Performed by the Relics of the Saint, III:24
Saint Curing the Possessed Woman, III:24
Andrewes, Lancelot, **IV:46-49**
Manual of Private Devotions, The, IV:48
Responsio Matthaei Torti, IV:47, 48
Andrews, Samuel, VI:1897
Andronicus III, II:844
Andropov, Yuri, VIII:1423
Andros, Edmund, IV:934, 939
Angelico, Fra, **III:28-31,** 223
Altarpiece, III:28
Annunciation, The, III:28
Christ on the Cross Adored by Saint Dominic, III:29
Christ Scorned, III:29
Crucifixion, The, III:29
Presentation in the Temple, The, III:29
St. Jerome Penitent, III:28
Transfiguration, The, III:29
Angell, Norman, **VII:74-78**
After All, VII:77
Great Illusion, The, VII:74, 75, 77
Patriotism Under Three Flags, VII:74
Angelou, Maya, **VII:79-81**
Blacks, Blues, Black, VII:80
Gather Together in My Name, VII:79
I Know Why the Caged Bird Sings, VII:79, 80
Just Give Me a Cool Drink of Water 'fore I Diiie, VII:80
Oh Pray My Wings Are Gonna Fit Me Well, VII:80
"On the Pulse of Morning," VII:80
Roots, VII:80
Singin', Swingin', and Gettin' Merry Like Christmas, VII:79
Angerstein, John Julius, IV:810
Angevin Empire, II:540, 733, 849
Anglican Church. *See* England, Church of
Anglo-Dutch Wars
Blake, IV:134, 135
Monck, IV:972
Stuyvesant, IV:1296
Tromp, IV:1343, 1344
Anglo-Iranian Oil Company, VIII:2566
Anglo-Irish Agreement of 1938, VII:878
Anglo-Japanese Treaty of 1902, VIII:2091
Anglo-Saxon Chronicle, The
Alfred the Great, II:59, 60, 62
Edward the Elder, II:319, 320
Egbert, II:333, 334
Ethelred II, the Unready, II:345
Hengist, I:378, 380, 381
Olaf I, II:688
Anglo-Saxons, II:167-169, 202, 204, 333, 334
Angora, Treaty of, VII:134
Angouleme, Marguerite d'. *See* Marguerite of Navarre
Anik-C satellite, IX:3179
animal behavior. *See* ethology
Animal Industry, Bureau of, IX:3450, 3451
Anjou, Count of, II:847-849
Anjou, Duke of, III:783
An Lu-shan, II:966, 967
Annam, II:1023, 1024
Annan, Khofi, VII:400
Anna O., VII:453, 454

Annapolis, IV:293
Annapolis Convention, IV:609
Anne, Queen of England, **IV:50-54,** 531-533, 620, 922-924
Anne of Austria, IV:864, 865, 899, 945, 946, 1166
Anne of Cleves, III:205, 360
Anne of Saxony, III:781, 782
Anniceris, I:87
Annual Register, The, IV:222
Annunciation, I:941; III:28
Anselm, Saint, II:10, **72-75**
Monologion, II:72, 74
On the Procession of the Holy Spirit, II:73
Proslogion, II:72, 74
Why God Became Man, II:73
Anshan, I:236
Anshe Emet, VI:2400
Anson, Lord, **IV:55-58**
Antarctica, VI:1908, VII:66-69, 534-536
Anthanasius, Saint, **I:119-123**
Anthony, Susan B., **V:61-65;** VI:1602, 2045, 2112, 2113; VII:880; IX:2919
History of Woman Suffrage, VI:2112
Anthony of Egypt, Saint, **I:56-59,** 122
Anthony of Padua, Saint, **II:76-78**
Antichrist, II:535
Anti-Corn Law League, V:306, 307, 526-528; VI:1754
Antigonas I Monophthalmos, **I:60-62,** 721
Anti-Masonic Party, V:792; VI:2037, 2136
Antinomians, IV:688
Antioch, I:440; II:159-161, 887, 888
Antiochene school, I:861, 865, 866
Antiochus I Soter, I:299
Antiochus the Great, **I:63-65**
Anti-Party Group, VIII:2573
Anti-Pass Day, VIII:2282
Antipater, I:60, 255, 390, 392, 721
anti-Semitism
Alexandria, I:632
Ambrose, I:44
Arendt, VII:98-100
Bernstein, VII:293
Brandeis, VII:422
Butler, VII:526
Chagall, VII:641
Dewey, V:661
Dreyfus affair, VIII:2767
Goebbels, VIII:1404
Herzl, V:1104, 1105
Hitler, VIII:1692, 1694-1696
Luxemburg, VIII:2285
Malenkov, VIII:2378
Mussolini, VIII:2669
Pius XII, IX:3031
Rickover, IX:3173
Stein, IX:3508, 3509
Suttner, VI:2177
Waldheim, IX:3842, 3843
William of Auvergne, II:977, 978
See also Holocaust
Antisthenes, **I:66-68,** 270
Antonelli, Giacomo, VI:1348
Antony, Marc, **I:69-71**
Augustus, I:20, 132, 133
Brutus, I:141, 142, 160
Cicero, I:196
Cleopatra VII, I:220, 221
Dryden, IV:425
Herod the Great, I:391
Varro, I:919
Antwerp, III:85, 86
Anwendung, VII:1244
Apache Indians, V:915, 917, 918
Apama, I:767
apartheid
de Klerk, VII:870-872
Fugard, VII:1259
Gordimer, VIII:1427, 1429
Lutuli, VIII:2281-2283
Mandela, VIII:2384, 2386, 2387
Mugabe, VIII:2649
Nyerere, VIII:2774, 2775
Player, IX:3042
Rhodes, VI:1876
Tutu, IX:3775-3777
United Nations, IX:2958
Aphrodite, I:318
Apollinaire, Guillaume, VI:1922, 1923; **VII:82-85,** 448, 889; VIII:2037; IX:3066, 3067
Alcools, VII:83, 84
Breasts of Tiresias, The, VII:83
Calligrammes, VII:83, 84
Case d'armons, VII:83
"Chanson du mal-aimé, La," VII:82
Cubist Painters: Aesthetic Meditations, The, VII:83
Heresiarch and Co., The, VII:82
"Jolie Rousse, La," VII:83, 84
"Mirabeau Bridge," VII:83
Poet Assassinated, The, VII:83
"Zone," VII:83

Apollo missions
  Apollo 11, VII:110-113; VIII:2022, 2624; IX:2779
  Apollo 13, IX:3406
  Apollo 14, IX:3407
  photography, VII:781
Apollonius of Perga, **I:72-75,** 437
  Conics, I:72-75
  Epaphai, I:73
  Neyseis, I:73
  Topoi epipedoi, I:73
Apollo of Delos, I:649
Apostles
  Clement I, I:210-212
  Irenaeus, I:447, 449, 450
  Jesus Christ, I:468
  John the Apostle, I:475, 477
  Paul, I:604-606
  Peter, I:614-616
  Stephen, I:822-824
  Thomas, I:880, 882, 883
Apostles, Acts of the, I:605
Apostles Club, VI:1503, 2062
Apostles' Creed, I:449, 450
Apostolic Fathers, I:210-212, 442
Apostolic Tradition, I:415
Appian, I:160
Appleseed, Johnny, **V:66-68**
Appleton, Frances "Fanny," VI:1416
April Laws, V:626
Aqaba, Gulf of, VII:855
Aqiba ben Joseph. *See* Akiba ben Joseph
aqualung. *See* SCUBA
Aquila, I:28
Aquillus, Manius, I:558
Aquinas, Saint Thomas. *See* Thomas Aquinas, Saint
Aquino, Benigno, VII:86, 87; VIII:2422
Aquino, Corazon, **VII:86-89;** VIII:2422, 2423
Aquitaine, II:239, 782
Arab Defense Council, VIII:1793
Arabian American Oil Company, IX:4079, 4080
Arab-Israeli Wars, VIII:1791, 1794
Arab Legion, VIII:1793
Arab Socialist Union, VIII:2694, 2696
Arafat, Yasir, **VII:90-94**
  Faisal, VIII:1120
  Hussein I, VIII:1794
  Intifada, VII:92
  Nasser, VIII:2696
  Pérez de Cuéllar, IX:2958
Aragon, Louis, VIII:2351
Arakawa, Hiroshi, IX:2796, 2797
ARAMCO. *See* Arabian American Oil Company
Arango, Doroteo. *See* Villa, Pancho
Arap Moi, Daniel, VIII:1939
Aratus, I:216
Arbenz, Jacobo, VIII:1494
Arboath, Declaration of, II:188
Arbogast, I:871
Arbolancha, Don Pedro de, III:46
Arbues, Pedro, III:726
Arbus, Diane, **VII:95-97**
  "New Documents," VII:96
  "Recent Acquisitions," VII:96
  "Twins, The," VII:96
Arbuthnot, Dr. John, IV:158
Arcades Project, VII:268
Arcadia, I:293
Arcadius, I:871
Archer, William, IX:3399, 3400
Archimedes, **I:76-80**
  Equilibrium of Planes, The, I:79
  Measurement of the Circle, I:79
  Method of Mechanical Theorems, I:78
  On Conoids and Spheroids, I:78
  On Floating Bodies, I:79
  On Spirals, I:78
  On the Sphere and Cylinder, I:78
  Quadrature of the Parabola, I:78
  Sand-Reckoner, The, I:79
Arctic exploration
  Amundsen, VII:66-69
  Byrd, VII:534
  Rasmussen, IX:3121-3123
  Ross, VI:1907, 1908
  Wegener, IX:3918-3920
  Wilkins, IX:3999-4001
  See also North Pole
Ardashir I, I:778
Ardashir II, I:781
Arena Chapel, II:388, 390, 748
Arendt, Hannah, **VII:98-101**
  Between Past and Future, VII:99
  Eichmann in Jerusalem, VII:99, 100
  Human Condition, The, VII:98, 99
  Idea of Love in St. Augustine, The, VII:98
  Jew as Pariah, The, VII:100
  Life of the Mind, The, VII:100
  Men in Dark Times, VII:100
  On Revolution, VII:100
  Origins of Totalitarianism, The, VII:98, 100
Areopagus, I:199, 200, 609

Aretaeus of Cappadocia, **I:81-84**
Book on the Treatment of Acute and Chronic Diseases, I:82
On the Causes and Symptoms of Acute and Chronic Diseases, I:82
Arezzo, Guido d'. *See* Guido d'Arezzo
Argall, Captain Samuel, IV:1106, 1107
Argentine National Library, VII:374
Arghun, II:381
Argos, I:214
Argyle, Earl of, IV:283
Arianism
Ambrose, I:44
Athanasius, I:121, 122
Bruno, III:96
Clovis, II:274
Constantine the Great, I:228
Genseric, I:343
Gregory of Nyssa, I:352-354
Gregory the Great, II:408
Theodoric the Great, II:896, 897
Theodosius the Great, I:869, 870
Ulfilas, I:908-910
Ariaramnes, I:236
Ariete Division, IX:3214
Arikara tribe, VI:2077
Ariosto, Ludvico, **III:32-35**
Cinque canti, III:33
Coffer, The, III:32, 33
Lena, III:33
Necromancer, The, III:33
Orlando furioso, III:32, 33
Pretenders, The, III:33
Arispe, Miguel Ramos, V:95
Aristarchus, I:308, 409, 712
Aristippus, **I:85-87**
Ariston of Chios, I:303, 970
Aristophanes, **I:88-93**
Acharnians, The, I:88, 115
Babylonioi, I:88
Birds, The, I:88, 90
Clouds, The, I:90
Daitaleis, I:88
Ecclesiazusae, I:91, 92
Frogs, The, I:11, 91, 808, 809
Knights, The, I:90
Kokalos, I:92
Lysistrata, I:91; V:162
Plutus, I:91, 92
Thesmophoriazusae, I:91
Wasps, I:14, 90
Aristotle, **I:94-97**
Albertus Magnus, II:37-39
Alcmaeon, I:34, 36
Alexander the Great, I:38
Anaxagoras, I:48
Antisthenes, I:68
Averroës, II:102
Buridan, II:194-196
Categoriae, I:683, 685
Diocles of Carystus, I:260, 261
Ethics, VI:173
Fracastoro, III:270-272
Galen, I:339
Metaphysics, I:312, 597, 727; II:106, 983, 985
natural philosophy, II:400
Nicholas of Autrecourt, II:669-671
On the Heavens, II:195
On the Soul, I:94, 698
Poetics, I:809, 878
Politics, II:985
Polygnotus, I:677
Protreptics, I:95
Psellus, II:759
Razi, II:781
Rhetoric, I:15
Scaliger, III:671
Secretum secretorum, II:110
Solon, I:803
space, nature of, IV:586
Thales of Miletus, I:852, 854
Theophrastus, I:873-875
Thomas Aquinas, II:911, 913, 914
Valla, III:740
William of Auvergne, II:976, 978
William of Auxerre, II:981-983
William of Moerbeke, II:985, 986
Xanthippe, I:952
Zeno of Elea, I:972
Aristoxenus, **I:98-100**
Harmonics, The, I:98
Ari the Learned, II:837
Arius, I:323
Arkwright, Richard, **IV:59-63;** VI:2074, 2075
Armageddon, I:890
Armed Neutrality, League of, VI:1636
Armenia
Basil the Macedonian, II:117
Shapur II, I:779
Theodosius the Great, I:869
Tigranes the Great, I:896-898
Trajan, I:901
Arminians. *See* Remonstrants

Armory Show, VI:1855; VII:416, 973; VIII:1740
Armour, Jean, IV:231, 232
Armstrong, Duff, VI:1382
Armstrong, Louis, **VII:105-109**
"Chimes Blues," VII:105
"I Wish I Could Shimmy Like My Sister Kate," VII:105
"Mabel's Dream," VII:105
Armstrong, Neil, **VII:110-113,** 1271; IX:3766
Armstrong, Samuel C., VI:2335
Arnaz, Desi, VII:176-178
Arnim, Count Harry von, V:1130
Arnold, Benedict, IV:42-44, **64-68**
Arnold, Matthew, **V:69-73**
Culture and Anarchy, V:71
Discourses in America, V:72
Empedocles on Etna, V:71
Essays in Criticism, V:71
On Translating Homer, V:71
"Rugby Chapel," V:76
Strayed Reveller and Other Poems, The, V:70
Arnold, Thomas, V:69, **74-76**
History of Rome, V:75
Arnold of Brescia, II:28
Arnold of Villanova, **II:79-81**
Aphorismi de granibus, II:80
Regimen sanitatis, II:80
Arnolfo di Cambio, **II:82-85**
Aroostook War, VI:2011
Arouet, François-Marie. *See* Voltaire
ARPA. *See* Alianza Popular Revolucionaria Americana
Arpad, **II:86-88**
Arpinum, I:194
Arrabbiata, III:668
Arrhenius, Svante August, **VII:114-116;** VIII:2713; IX:2855
Destinies of the Stars, The, VII:116
Erde and Weltall, VII:116
Immunochemistry, VII:115
Lehrbuch der kosmischen Physik, VII:115
Life of the Universe as Conceived by Man from Earliest Ages to the Present Time, The, VII:115
Quantitative Laws in Biological Chemistry, VII:115, 116
Text-book of Electrochemistry, VII:115
Theories of Chemistry, VII:115
Theories of Solutions, VII:115
Arsames, I:236
Arshak II, I:780
Arsinoe II, I:716-718
Artabanus, I:962-964
Artaxerxes, I:331
Artek Company, VII:2
Artemidorus, I:159
Artemisium, I:764
Arthur, Chester A., **V:77-81**
Arthurian legends
Chrétien de Troyes, II:257-259
Hartmann von Aue, II:433-435
Malory, III:457, 458; V:161; VI:2213
Tennyson, VI:2213
Arthur of Wales, Prince, III:136
Articles of Confederation. *See* Confederation, Articles of
Artisans' and Laborers' Dwelling Act of 1875, V:678
Art Nouveau, VII:1263; VIII:1903
Artusi, Giovanni Mari, IV:991
Arundel, Thomas, II:787
Arverni, I:922
Arvey, Jacob M., IX:3524
Aryabhata, **II:89-92,** 181, 182
Aryabhatiya, The, II:89-91
Aryans, I:618
Arzner, Dorothy, **VII:117-120**
Anybody's Woman, VII:117, 119
Bride Wore Red, The, VII:119
Christopher Strong, VII:119
Craig's Wife, VII:119
Dance, Girl, Dance, VII:118
Fashions for Women, VII:117
First Comes Courgage, VII:118
Get Your Man, VII:117
Honor Among Lovers, VII:119
Manhattan Cocktail, VII:117
Merrily We Go to Hell, VII:119
Nana, VII:119
Sarah and Son, VII:117
Ten Modern Commandments, VII:117
Wild Party, VII:117
Working Girls, VII:119
ASARCO. *See* American Smelting and Refining Company
asceticism
Ba'al Shem Tov, IV:74, 75
Chrysostom, I:184
Diogenes, I:268
Elijah ben Solomon, IV:432
Schopenhauer, VI:1986
Simeon Stylites, I:783-785
Ascham, Roger, III:241
Asclepiades of Bithynia, **I:101-104,** 807
Concerning Common Aids, I:101

Enemata, I:101
Method of Giving Wine in Sickness, I:101
Asclepieions, I:338, 411, 445
Asdings, I:342
ASEAN. *See* Southeast Asian Nations, Association of
Ash'ari, al-, **II:93-96,** 348
Book of Highlights, II:93
Discourses of the Muslims, II:93
Elucidation of Islam's Foundation, The, II:93
Incitement to Investigation, II:93
Ashburn, Joseph, IV:1192, 1193
Ashdod, siege of, I:755
Ashdown, Battle of, II:59
Ashikaga Tadayoshi, II:97, 98
Ashikaga Takauji, **II:97-99**
Ashikaga Yoshiaki, III:571
Ashikaga Yoshimitsu, II:1025, 1026
Ashikaga Yoshimochi, II:1026
Ashikaga Yoshinori, II:1026, 1027
Ashley, Edwina, VIII:2642
Ashley, John, VI:1786
Ashley, William, VI:2077, 2078
Ashton, Frederick, VII:1175, 1177; IX:2939, 2940
Ashurbanipal, **I:105-108,** 709
Ashurnasirpal II, **I:109-111**
Asiatic Society of Bengal, VI:1846
Asoka the Great, **I:112-114**
Aspasia, **I:115-118**
Asquith, H.H., **VII:121-124;** VIII:1952, 2217
Asquith, Margot, VII:121
Associated Television Corporation, VII:739
Assumption, Church of the, I:376
Astaire, Fred, **VII:125-128**
Band Wagon, The, VII:125, 127, 128
Barkleys of Broadway, The, VII:127
Broadway Melody of 1940, VII:127
Daddy Long Legs, VII:127
Dancing Lady, VII:125
Easter Parade, VII:127
Evening with Fred Astaire, An, VII:127
Flying Down to Rio, VII:125
Funny Face, VII:127
Gay Divorcee, The, VII:125; IX:3057
Holiday Inn, VII:127, 289
Lady Be Good, VII:125, 1352
"Night and Day," VII:125
Notorious Landlady, The, VII:127
On the Beach, VII:127
Royal Wedding, VII:127, 128
Shall We Dance, VII:125, 1352
Swing Time, VII:125, 127
That's Entertainment, VII:127
Top Hat, VII:125, 127, 288
You'll Never Get Rich, VIII:1597
Astor, John J., **V:82-85**
Astor, Nancy, **VII:129-132**
Astor, Waldorf, VII:129-131
Astor House, V:84, 294
Astor Place Riot, V:802
astrology
Abano, II:1
'Abbas the Great, IV:5
Copernicus, III:179
Jabir ibn Hayyan, II:524
Hippolytus of Rome, I:415
Hypatia, I:437
Kepler, IV:772
Nostradamus, III:567, 568
Ptolemy, I:713, 714
Santorio, IV:1209, 1211
Servetus, III:676
Wallenstein, IV:1396
Astrup, Eivind, IX:2942
Aswan High Dam, VIII:2695
AT&T, VII:102, 103, 859
Atahualpa, III:371-373, 699
Atatürk, Kemal, **VII:133-136;** VIII:1812, 1813
Atenism, I:573, 575
Athalaric, II:896
Athanaric, I:908
Athanasius, Saint, I:58, **119-122**
Apology Against the Arians, An, I:122
History of the Arians, I:122
Athena Alea, temple of, I:764
Athena the Maiden, I:625, 649
Athenian Empire
Aeschylus, I:9, 10
Alcibiades, I:32
Alexander the Great, I:38
Antigonus I Monohthalmos, I:60
Aristophanes, I:90, 91
Aristotle, I:95
Cimon, I:198-201
Cleisthenes of Athens, I:207, 208
Demosthenes, I:253-255
Draco, I:280, 281
Euripides, I:317
Lysippus, I:515
Miltiades the Younger, I:553-555
Olympic Games, VII:774, 775
Pericles, I:609, 611, 612
Pheidippides, I:621-623
Phidias, I:624

Pisistratus, I:648-650
Polygnotus, I:676, 677
Socrates, I:793-796
Solon, I:803-805
Sophocles, I:809
Themistocles, I:857-859
Thucydides, I:885-887
Xanthippe, I:952-954
Xenophon, I:958-960
Atlantic Charter, VIII:2257
Atlantic Monthly, The, V:1111, 1127, 1211, 1228; VI:2375
Atlantic Records, VII:1217, 1218
Atlee, Clement, VIII:2644
Atmospheric Nuclear Test Ban Treaty, VII:302; VIII:1963
atom
Aretaeus of Cappadocia, I:81
Avogadro, V:98-100
Becquerel, V:167
Dalton, V:602-604
Einstein, VII:1035
elementary-particle physics, IX:4091
local molecular fields, VIII:2705
Lockyer, VI:1411, 1412
Ostwald, IX:2856
plastics, VIII:2698
splitting of the, VIII:1871
structure of thc, VII:379; VIII:2040; IX:2923
See also nuclear physics
atom bomb
Bethe, VII:300-303
Bothe, VII:380
Chadwick, VII:637
Compton, VII:745-747
Conant, VII:750
Einstein, VII:1036
Fermi, VII:1145, 1147, 1148
Hertz, VIII:1647, 1648
Kurchatov, VIII:2039-2041
Lawrence, VIII:2121-2123
Stimson, IX:3539
Oppenheimer, IX:2833-2835
Rabi, IX:3102
Sato, IX:3337
Seaborg, IX:3376
Teller, IX:3631, 3632
Truman, IX:3742
University of Chicago, VIII:1801
Urey, IX:3789
See also nuclear weapons
Atomic Energy Commission, VII:750; VIII:2123, 2338, 2726; IX:2834, 3377
Atomic Energy Committee, IX:3102
Aton, I:734
Attainder, Act of, III:593
Attalus III, I:346
Attianus, I:356
Attila, **I:124-127**
Attlee, Clement, **VII:137-140,** 304, 305, 310, 315, 1345
Attrition, War of, VIII:2696
Auburn Prison, IX:2853, 2854
Auckland National Association, VIII:2444
Auden, W.H., VII:466, 468, 469, 608
Audion, VII:858-860
Audran, Claude III, IV:1413
Audubon, John James, **V:86-89**
Birds of America, The, V:87, 88
Ornithological Biography, V:87
Viviparous Quadrupeds of North America, V:87
Audubon Society, V:88
Augsburg, Diet of, III:160, 505
Augsburg, League of, IV:840, 873, 1447
Augsburg, Peace of, III:161; IV:450
Augsburg Confession, III:503, 505; IV:1489
Augsburg Interim, III:103, 161
Augusta National Golf Club, VIII:1876, 1877
Augustine, Saint, **I:128-131**
Anthony of Padua, II:76
astrology, III:676
City of God, The, I:128, 129; II:726; III:533
Confessions, I:128
Jansenism, IV:707-709
On the Trinity, I:128
Plotinus, I:667
Vincent of Lérins, I:936, 937
William of Auvergne, II:976
Augustine of Hippo, Saint, II:137, 138
Augustus, **I:132-135**
Agrippa, I:20-22
Antony, I:70, 71
Brutus, I:141, 142
Caligula, I:152, 153
Cassius, I:160
Claudius I, I:203
Cleopatra VII, I:218, 220
Diocletian, I:265
Herod the Great, I:391
Horace, I:426
Livy, I:504
Maecenas, I:519, 521
Ovid, I:585-587

Phaedrus, I:618
Propertius, I:702-704
Tiberius, I:892-894
Vergil, I:926-928
Verrius Flaccus, I:930
Aulic Council, III:492, 493
Aurangzeb, **IV:69-72,** 1233, 1234, 1247
Aurobindo, Sri, **VII:141-143**
Arya, VII:142
Ausgleich, V:625, 627, 628, 830; VII:1197
Austen, Jane, **V:90-93**
Emma, V:92
Mansfield Park, V:92
Northanger Abbey, V:91
Persuasion, V:91, 92, 560
Pride and Prejudice, V:90-92; VIII:2544
Sense and Sensibility, V:90-92
Watsons, The, V:91
Austerlitz, Battle of, V:45, 475; VI:1306, 1307, 1616
Austin, James T., VI:1772
Austin, Stephen Fuller, **V:94-97**
Australian Open, VII:1112
Australopithecus boisei, VIII:2148
Austrian Baroque, IV:473, 655-657
Austrian Succession, War of
Amherst, IV:37
Carleton, IV:246
Clive, IV:325
Frederick the Great, IV:504
George II, IV:536, 537
Jenkins' Ear, IV:55
Maria Theresa, IV:914, 915
Pelham, IV:1074, 1075
Pontiac, IV:1110
Rochambeau, IV:1174
Venice, IV:243
Wolfe, IV:1471
See also Jenkins' Ear, War of
Austro-Prussian War of 1866, V:762
automobile industry
Benz, V:199-201
Citroën, VII:695-697
Daimler, V:200, 201, 597-599; IX:3881
Diesel, V:672-674
dymaxion car, VII:1266
Ferrari, VII:1150-1152
Ford, VII:1184, 1186, 1187
Geddes, VII:1321
General Motors, VII:1321; VIII:2679, 2680; IX:2974, 3162, 3881
Honda, VIII:1724-1726
Lanchester, VIII:2069-2071
Lenoir, VI:1344
Maybach, V:597-599
Michelin brothers, VIII:2514-2516
Otto, VI:1702-1704
Pirelli family, IX:3020, 3021
Rolls-Royce Limited, IX:3209-3211
Toyota Motor Company, IX:3719-3721
union labor, VIII:2171; IX:3161-3164
Wankel engine, IX:3881, 3882
Auxentius, I:909
Avars, II:41, 42, 228, 470, 471, 820
Averroes, II:1, **100-105,** 491, 830, 913
Incoherence of the Incoherence, The, II:103
Incoherence of the Philosophers, The, II:103
On the Harmony of Religion and Philosophy, II:103
Avery, Oswald, VII:797
Avicenna, II:1, **106-109**
Birr wa al-ithm, al-, II:106
Canon of Medicine, II:107
Hasil wa al-mahsul, al-, II:106
Lisan al-'Arab, II:107
Majmu, al-, II:106
Avogadro, Amedeo, **V:98-100**
Avril, Jane, VI:2248
AWSA. *See* American Woman Suffrage Association
Axis Pact, VIII:2669
Ay, I:904
Aya, I:25
Aye, I:573
Aymer of Valence. *See* Pembroke, Earl of
Ayyubid Dynasty, II:124
Azcapotzalco, III:377, 378, 555, 556
Azeglio, Massimo d', V:446
Azikiwe, Nnamdi, **VII:144-147;** VIII:2762
Aztec Empire
Alvarado, III:21-23
Cortés, III:188-191
Itzcóatl, III:377-379
Montezuma II, III:528, 529, 531
Nezahualcóyotl, III:555-557
Prescott, VI:1815
Azuma Kagami, IV:1328
Azzolino, Cardinal Decio, IV:305, 306

Baader-Meinhof group, VII:350
Ba'al Shem Tov, **IV:73-75**
Babbage, Charles, **V:101-104**
Babeuf, Grachus, IV:912
Babor, Karl, IX:3985

Babrius, I:15
Babur, **III:36-40,** 541
Babylonian Captivity, II:487, 1009
Bach, Johann Sebastian, **IV:76-79,** 227, 1321, 1383, 1385; VI:1535
Before Thy Throne I Now Appear, IV:78
Brandenburg Concertos, IV:77
Christmas Oratorio, IV:78
For Thou Wilt Not Leave My Soul in Hell, IV:76
God Is My King, IV:76
Jesu, Joy of Man's Desiring, IV:78
Pastorale in F Major, IV:76
Saint Matthew Passion, The, IV:78; VI:1534
Sheep May Safely Graze, IV:78
Well-Tempered Clavier, IV:77
Bach, Karl Philipp Emanuel, IV:227
Bachman, Richard. *See* King, Stephen
Bacon, Francis, **III:41-44,** 296, 451; IV:185, 187, 331, 332, 662, 1310
Magna Instauratio, III:43
New Atlantis, III:43
Novum Organum, III:43
Two Bookes of Francis Bacon, III:41
Bacon, Nathaniel, **IV:80-82**
Bacon, Roger, **II:110-113,** 977
Opus majus, II:112, 988
Opus tertium, II:112, 719
Bacon's Rebellion, IV:81
bacteriology
Behring, V:182-184
Burnet, VII:512-514
chromosomes, VIII:1828
Cohn, V:534, 535
Leeuwenhoek, IV:827
Koch, VI:1297-1299
Pasteur, VI:1746, 1747
Smith, IX:3450-3452
Watson, IX:3897, 3898
Bactria, I:64, 494, 541, 779
Bad Axe, Battle of, VI:2195
Baden-Powell, Sir Robert Stephenson Smyth, **V:105-108;** VIII:2246, 2247
Scouting for Boys, V:106, 107
Bad Faces, VI:1850
Badooglio, Marshal Pietro, VIII:2669
Baeck, Leo, **VII:148-151**
Essence of Judaism, The, VII:148
Pharisees, and Other Essays, The, VII:150
Romantische Religion, VII:148
This People Israel, VII:150
What Is Christianity?, VII:148
Baer, Karl Ernst von, **V:109-111**
Über Entwickelungsgeschichte der Thiere, V:110
Baffin Island, III:279
Baghdad
Benjamin of Tudela, II:141
Nizam al-Mulk, II:678
Razi, II:779
Sa'di, II:807
Tabari, II:873
Baghdad Summit Conference, VIII:1794
Bagot, Sir Charles, V:118
Bahadur Shah, IV:71
Bailey, James Anthony, V:136
Baillie, Thomas, IV:439
Bain, Alexander, V:557
Baines, Sir Edward, IV:59, 62
Baker v. Carr, VII:1214; IX:3889
Bakhtin, Mikhail, **VII:152-154**
Dialogic Imagination, The, VII:153
Problems of Dostoevsky's Poetics, VII:153
Rabelais and His World, VII:153
bakufu. *See* Tokugawa shogunate
Bakunin, Mikhail, **V:112-115,** 1100
Appeal to the Slavs, An, V:112
Balakirev, Mily, V:287; VI:1889, 2200
Balanchine, George, **VII:155-159,** 835, 921; VIII:1568, 2182, 2183; IX:3607, 3608
Agon, VII:158
Apollo, VII:156
Coppelia, VII:158
Danses Concertantes, VII:833
Don Quixote, VII:158
Four Temperaments, The, VII:156
Gods Go A-Begging, The, VII:833
Harlequinade, VII:158
Ivesiana, VII:156
Jewels, VII:158
Metamorphoses, VII:156
Midsummer Night's Dream, A, VII:158
Mozartiana, VII:833
Nutcracker, The, VII:158
Opus, VII:156
Orpheus, VII:156
Prodigal Son, The, VII:156, 833
Serenade, VII:156
Sleeping Beauty, The, VII:155
Tombeau de Couperin, Le, VII:158
Triumph of Neptune, The, VII:833
Valse, La, VII:156
Vienna Waltzes, VII:158
Western Symphony, VII:156, 158
Balboa, Vasco Núñez, de, **III:45-47**

Balch, Emily Greene, **VII:160-163**
  Approaches to the Great Settlement, VII:161
  Manual for Use in Cases of Juvenile Offenders and Other Minors in Massachusetts, VII:160
  Miracle of Living, The, VII:162
  Our Slavic Fellow Citizens, VII:160-162
  Public Assistance of the Poor in France, VII:160
  Women at the Hague, VII:160, 161
Baldwin, James, **VII:164-167**
  Amen Corner, The, VII:164
  Another Country, VII:165
  Blues for Mr. Charlie, VII:164
  Devil Finds Work, The, VII:166
  Dialogue, A, VII:166
  Evidence of Things Not Seen, The, VII:166
  Fire Next Time, The, VII:166
  Giovanni's Room, VII:164, 165
  Going to Meet the Man, VII:166
  Go Tell It on the Mountain, VII:164
  Just Above My Head, VII:166
  Nobody Knows My Name, VII:165
  Notes of a Native Son, VII:164, 165
  Price of the Ticket, The, VII:166
  Rap on Race, A, VII:166
  Tell Me How Long the Train's Been Gone, VII:166
Baldwin, Robert, **V:116-119;** VI:1451
Baldwin, Stanley, **VII:168-171,** 235, 304, 821; IX:4026
Baldwin of Flanders, II:943
Balfour, Arthur James, V:46; **VII:172-175**
  Defence of Philosophic Doubt, A, VII:172
Balfour Declaration
  Balfour, VII:174
  Ben-Gurion, VII:251, 252
  Faisal I, VII:1124
  Herzl, V:1105
  King, VIII:1982
  Lawrence, VIII:2127
  Weizmann, IX:3931
Balian de Adam. *See* Salimbene
Baline, Israel. *See* Berlin, Irving
Baliol, Edward de, II:294, 295
Baliol, John de, II:185, 294, 324, 956
Balkan Defense Pact, VII:134
Ball, John, **II:114-116,** 786, 921, 922
Ball, Lucille, VII:119, **176-179**
  I Love Lucy, VII:176, 178
  Lucy Show, The, VII:178
  Mame, VII:178
Ballance, John, VI:2018
Ballantyne, James and John, VI:2005, 2006
Ballard, Robert Duane, **VII:180-182**
Balleroy, Château de, IV:898
ballet
  Balanchine, VII:155-159
  Danilova, VII:832-835
  Degas, V:643
  Delibes, V:649-651
  de Mille, VII:874-876
  Diaghilev, VII:919-921
  Duncan, VII:980-982
  Fonteyn, VII:1175-1178
  Graham, VIII:1455-1458
  Laban, VIII:2059
  Lifar, VIII:2182-2184
  Massine, VIII:2448-2450
  musical comedy, VIII:1568
  Nijinsky, VIII:2746-2749
  Pavlova, IX:2937-2940
  Poulenc, IX:3066
  Prokofiev, IX:3085-3087
  Satie, IX:3333
  Shostakovich, IX:3409
  Stravinsky, IX:3559, 3560
  Tallchief, IX:3607-3609
  Zwilich, IX:4123
Ballet Russes
  Balanchine, VII:156
  Danilova, VII:833, 835
  Debussy, VII:885
  Diaghliev, VII:919-921
  Lifar, VIII:2182, 2183
  Massine, VIII:2448-2450
  Nijinsky, VIII:2746, 2748
  Pavlova, IX:2937
  Poulenc, IX:3066
  Satie, IX:3333
Ballinger, Richard, V:280; IX:3596
Ballot Act of 1872, V:804, 805
Ballou, Hosea, V:472
Ballou's Pictorial, V:1133
Baltimore Sermon of 1819, V:471
Baltimore *Sun,* VIII:2483, 2484
Balzac, Honoré de, **V:120-123;** VI:1901
  Chouans, Les, V:120
  Cousin Bette, V:121
  Droll Tales, V:827
  Eugénie Grandet, V:121
  Father Goriot, V:121
  Human Comedy, The, V:120, 122; VI:2183
  Magic Skin, The, V:120
  Peau de chagrin, La, V:121
  "Sarrasine," VII:208

Bancroft, George, **V:124-129**
History of the United States, V:126, 127
Martin Van Buren to the End of His Political Career, V:127
Banda, Hastings, VIII:2319
Bandinelli, Roland. *See* Alexander III (Pope)
Banerjea, Surendranath, **VII:183-186**
Bengalee, VII:183, 184
Banks, Sir Joseph, **IV:83-87,** 353; VI:1723, 1724
Banks, Nathaniel, V:1205
Banneker, Benjamin, **IV:88-91**
Pennsylvania, Delaware, Maryland and Virginia Almanack, IV:89, 90, 91
Bannockburn, Battle of, II:326
Banting, Sir Frederick Grant, **VII:187-190;** VIII:2329, 2330
Bantu Education Act, IX:3775
baptism
Anabaptists, III:510-512
Campbell, V:401-403
John the Baptist, I:478-481
Maurice, VI:1504
Pusey, VI:1829
Servetus, III:676, 677
Theodosius the Great, I:869
Barak, I:246, 247
Barbari, Jacopo de', III:201
Barbarossa, Frederick I. *See* Frederick I Barbarossa
Barbary Wars, V:634-636
Barber, Samuel, **VII:191-194**
Antony and Cleopatra, VII:191, 193; IX:3083
Canzonetta, VII:193
Hermit Songs, The, VII:193; IX:3083
Knoxville: Summer of 1915, Opus 24, VII:193
School for Scandal, The, VII:191
Vanessa, VII:193
Barbosa, Diogo, III:453
Barca, Hamilcar, I:364
Barclay, Robert H., VI:1764
Bardas, II:674
Bardot, Brigitte, VIII:1392
Barebones Parliament, IV:380, 790, 1228
Baret, Jeanne, IV:180
Barezzi, Antonio, VI:2299
Barlaam of Calabria, II:901
Barlow, Joel, V:854, 855
Barmakids, II:437, 522, 524
Barmen Confession, VII:204
Barnard, Christiaan, **VII:195-198**
Barnard, George G., VI:2284
Barnard, Henry, **V:130-132**
Barnato, Barney, VI:1874, 1875
Barner, Jacob, IV:1268
Barnes, Djuna, **VII:199-202**
Antiphon, The, VII:201
Book, A, VII:199
Book of Repulsive Women, The, VII:199, 202
Ladies Almanack, A, VII:199, 201, 202
Night Among the Horses, A, VII:199
Nightwood, VII:201, 202
"Quarry," VII:202
Ryder, VII:199, 201
Spillwax, VII:199, 201
"Walking Mort, The," VII:202
Barnes, Robert, III:193
Barnes, Thomas, VI:2325
Barnes v. Costle, VIII:2325
Barnet, Battle of, III:234, 235, 343, 649
Barnum, P.T., **V:133-137;** VI:1386, 1387
Art of Money Getting, The, V:135
Barons' Cause, II:644, 645
Barron, James, V:635, 636
Barron, Moses, VII:187
Barry, Sir Charles, **V:138-141;** VI:1823
Barth, Karl, **VII:203-206,** 358, 476
Church Dogmatics, VII:204, 205
Dogmatics in Outline, VII:204
Epistle to the Romans, The, VII:204
Barthes, Roland, **VII:207-209**
Camera Lucida: Reflections on Photography, VII:209
Empire of Signs, VII:209
Lover's Discourse: Fragments, A, VII:208
Michelet, VII:207
Mythologies, VII:208
On Racine, VII:207
Pleasure of the Text, The, VII:208
Roland Barthes by Roland Barthes, VII:208
S/Z, VII:207-209
Writing Degree Zero, VII:207
Bartholomew of Cremona, II:987
Bartlett, Bob, IX:2944
Bartók, Béla, **VII:210-213**
Bagatelles, VII:211
Concerto for Orchestra, VII:211
Duke Bluebeard's Castle, VII:211
Empire of Signs, VII:210
Hungarian Folksongs, VII:211
Kossuth Symphony, VII:210
Mikrokosmos, VII:211
Miraculous Mandarin, The, VII:211

Music for Strings, Percussion, and Celesta, VII:211
Wooden Prince, The, VII:211
Barton, Clara, **V:142-146**
Barton, Sir Edmund, **V:147-149**
Barton, Elizabeth, III:265
baseball
Cobb, VII:717-720
DiMaggio, VII:934-937
Gehrig, VII:1322-1324
Oh, IX:2796-2798
Robinson, IX:3193-3197
Rose, IX:3239-3241
Ruth, IX:3273-3276
Thorpe, IX:3675
Basedow, Johann Bernhard, **IV:92-94**
Elementarwerks erster Band, Des, IV:92
Vorstellung an Menschemfreunde und vermögende Manner über Schulen, Studien, und ihren Enfluss in die öffentliche Wohlfahrt, IV:92
Basel, Council of, III:559, 563, 564
Bashkent, Battle of, III:500
Basil of Caesarea, I:349, 350, 352
Basil the Macedonian, **II:117-120**
Basilics, II:118
Baskerville, John, **IV:95-97**
basketball, IX:3268, 3270, 3271
Basoalto, Neftali Ricardo Reyes. *See* Neruda, Pablo
Basov, Nikolay Gennadiyevich, **VII:214-216**
Bassus, Aufidius, I:663
Bastides, Don Pedro de, III:45
Bates, Edward, V:729
Bateson, Gregory, VIII:2469
Bathsheba, I:243, 798
Batista y Zaldivar, Fulgencio, VII:617, 618
Battani, al-, **II:121-123**
De scientia stellarum, II:122
Battelle Memorial Institute, VII:579, 580
Batu Khan, II:987, 988
Baudelaire, Charles, **V:150-153;** VI:1472; VII:268; IX:3792
Artificial Paradises, V:152
Fanfarlo, La, V:150
Flowers of Evil, V:150, 152; VI:1855; VIII:2530
Paris Spleen, V:152
Bauer, Georg. *See* Agricola, Georgius
Bauhaus, the
Gropius, VIII:1486-1488
Klee, VIII:2006
Marc, VIII:2406
Mies van der Rohe, VIII:2522
Pei, IX:2946, 2947
Pugin, VI:1822
Baum, L. Frank, **V:154-156**
Aunt Jane's Nieces, V:155
Dorothy and the Wizard of Oz, V:156
Dot and Tot of Merryland, V:155
Emerald City of Oz, The, V:156
Fairylogue and Radio-Plays, V:156
Father Goose, His Book, V:155
Glinda of Oz, V:156
Marvelous Land of Oz, The, V:155
Mother Goose in Prose, V:154
Ozma of Oz, V:155
Patchwork Girl, The, V:156
Road to Oz, The, V:156
Scarecrow of Oz, The, V:156
Tik-Tok Man, The, V:156
Wonderful Wizard of Oz, The, V:154-156
Baur, Ferdinand Christian, VI:1892, 1893
Bavaria, II:228, 358, 706
Baxter, Richard, **IV:98-102**
Bayard, Chevalier de, **III:48-50**
Baybars I, **II:124-127**
Baydu, II:381
Bayeu, Francisco, IV:569
Bayezid II, **III:51-53**
Bayle, Pierre, **IV:103-106**
Historical and Critical Dictionary, An, IV:104, 105
Miscellaneous Reflections Occasion'd by the Comet Which Appear'd in December, 1680, IV:103
Nouvelles de la République des Lettres, IV:103
Philosophical Commentary on These Words in the Gospel, Luke XIV, 23, IV:103
Bayliss, Sir William Maddock, **VII:217-220;** IX:3494
Nature of Enzyme Action, The, VII:219
Physiology of Food and Economy of Diet, The, VII:219
Principles of General Physiology, VII:219
Bay of Islands rebellion, V:998
Bay of Pigs invasion, VIII:1930; IX:3525
Bayram Khan, III:5
Bazille, Jean Frédéric, VI:1869
Bazin, André, VIII:1391; IX:3736, 3737
BBC. *See* British Broadcasting Corporation
Beale, Dorothea, **V:157-160**
Beanes, William, VI:1281, 1282
Beard, Charles A., **VII:221-225,** 526; IX:2893, 3762

American Foreign Policy in the Making, 1932-1940, VII:224
American Government and Politics, VII:221
American Leviathan, VII:223
American Spirit, VII:224
Balkan Pivot, VII:223
Basic History of the United States, A, VII:224
Contemporary American History, 1877-1913, VII:222
Cross Currents in Europe To-day, VII:223
Development of Modern Europe, VII:221
Economic Interpretation of the Constitution of the United States, VII:222
Economic Origins of Jeffersonian Democracy, VII:222
Idea of National Interest, The, VII:223
Industrial Revolution, The, VII:221
Open Door at Home, The, VII:223
President Roosevelt and the Coming of the War 1941, VII:224
Republic, The, VII:224
Rise of American Civilization, The, VII:222, 224
Supreme Court and the Constitution, The, VII:222
Toward Civilization, VII:223
Whither Mankind, VII:223
Beardsley, Aubrey, **V:161-165**
Story of Venus and Tannhäuser, The, V:164
Beatles, the, **VII:226-239,** 658
Abbey Road, VII:228
Beatles for Sale, VII:227
Hard Days Night, A, VII:227
Help!, VII:227
"I Want to Hold Your Hand," VII:227
Let it Be, VII:228
Magical Mystery Tour, VII:228
"Norwegian Wood," VII:228
"Penny Lane," VII:228
Please, Please Me, VII:226
Revolver, VII:228
Rubber Soul, VII:228
Sgt. Pepper's Lonely Hearts Club Band, VII:228
"Strawberry Fields Forever," VII:228
"White Album, The," VII:228
With the Beatles, VII:227
Yellow Submarine, VII:228
Beat movement, VIII:1945-1947; IX:2883
Beatrice, II:288
Beatrix, II:357
Beaufort, Henry, III:338, 341
Beaufort, Margaret, III:345, 651
Beaufort, Thomas, III:337
Beauharnais, Viscount Alexandre de, V:1246
Beauharnais v. Illinois, VII:322
Beaujeu, Sieur de, IV:794
Beaumont, Élie de, VI:1419
Beaumont, Francis, **III:54-57,** 689
Captain, The, III:56
Coxcomb, The, III:56
Cupid's Revenge, III:56
King and No King, A, III:55, 689
Knight of the Burning Pestle, The, III:54, 689
Maid's Tragedy, The, III:55
Masque of the Inner Temple and Grayes Inn, The, III:56
Philaster, III:55, 689
Salmacis and Hermaphroditus, III:54
Scornful Lady, The, III:56
Tragedy of Thierry, King of France and His Brother Theodoret, III:56
Woman Hater, The, III:54
Beaumont, George, IV:1161; V:547
Beaumont, Gustave de, VI:2238
Beauvais, Vincent of. *See* Vincent of Beauvais
Beauvoir, Simone de, **VII:230-233;** IX:3327, 3328
Adieux: A Farewell to Sartre, VII:232
Belles Images, Les, VII:232
Blood of Others, The, VII:231
Coming of Age, The, VII:232
Ethics of Ambiguity, VII:231
Mandarins, The, VII:231
Memoirs of a Dutiful Daughter, VII:230
Second Sex, The, VII:231
She Came to Stay, VII:230, 231
Woman Destroyed, The, VII:232
Beaux-Arts, École des, IX:2976, 2977
Beaverbrook, Lord, VII:76, 169, **234-237**
Bebel, August
Woman Under Socialism, VIII:2016; IX:4112
bebop, VII:1370, 1371, 1373; VIII:1718; IX:2880, 2882, 2883
Beccaria, Cesare
Essay on Crimes and Punishments, An, VI:1483
Beccaria, Giambatista, IV:523
Beccaria, Giovanni, IV:1387
Becher, Johann Joachim, IV:1269
Physica subterranea, IV:1270
Bechuanaland, VI:1874, 1876
Becker, Lydia, V:778
Becket, Thomas, **II:128-131**
Clarendon Constitutions, II:49
Eleanor of Aquitaine, II:338
Henry II, II:446, 447

Beckett, Samuel, VII:34, 201, **238-242,** 1360, 1361; IX:3091
Breath, VII:241
Cascando, VII:34
Come and Go: Dramaticule, VII:241
"Dante and the Lobster," VII:239
Endgame, VII:35, 241
Happy Days, VII:241
Krapp's Last Tape, VII:241
Malone Dies, VII:240
Molloy, VII:240
More Pricks than Kicks, VII:239
Murphy, VII:239
Not I, VII:241
Play, VII:241
Proust, VII:238
Unnamable, The, VII:240, 1361
Waiting for Godot, VII:240, 241, 1361
Watt, VII:240
Whoroscope, VII:238
Becquerel, Henry, VII:811, 812
Becquerel family, **V:166-169**
Bede the Venerable, Saint, **II:132-135,** 756, 825
Ecclesiastical History of the English People, II:132, 133, 198, 199, 378
Lives of the First Abbots of Wearmouth and Jarrow, II:133
Bedford, Earl of, IV:1141, 1142
Beecher, Catharine, **V:170-173**
American Woman's Home, The, V:172
Treatise on Domestic Economy, V:171, 172
Beecher, Harriet. *See* Stowe, Harriet Beecher
Beecher, Henry Ward, **V:174-177;** VI:2279, 2281
Yale Lectures on Preaching, V:176
Beer Hall Putsch, VIII:1694, 2266
Beethoven, Ludwig van, **V:178-181**
Boccherini, IV:149
Brahms, V:301
Choral, V:179
Creatures of Prometheus, VIII:2182
Eroica, V:179
Fidelio, V:179, 181
Haydn, IV:641
Liszt, VI:1391
Mahler, VIII:2363
Missa Solemnis, V:179, 181
Pastoral, V:179
Schiller, IV:1219
Beghards, II:906
Begin, Menachem, **VII:243-246,** 253; IX:3290
Beguines, II:906
behavior, animal. *See* ethology
behavior, human
Benedict, VII:257
Freud, VII:1226
Janet, VIII:1841
Lorenz, VIII:2239, 2240
Merleau-Ponty, VIII:2500
Muller, VIII:2652
Pavlov, VIII:2933-2935
Skinner, IX:3431-3434
Behistun Inscription, I:233
Behrens, Peter, VIII:1486, 2520
Behring, Emil von, **V:182-184;** VII:1032
Béla I, II:574
Belasco, David, IX:3006, 3094
Belaúnde Terry, Fernando, VIII:1586
Belgian Antarctic Expedition, VII:66
Belgrade, III:375
Belisarius, II:554, 555
Bell, Alexander Graham, **V:185-189**
Bell, Andrew, VI:1310
Bell, Edward, VII:383
Bell, J. Franklin, VIII:2429
Bellarmino, Roberto, IV:47, 48
Bellay, Jean du, III:633, 634
Bellini, Gentile, III:58
Bellini, Giovanni, **III:58-61,** 305, 306
Adoration of the Child, III:60
Agony in the Garden, III:59
Coronation of the Virgin, III:58,59
Enthroned Madonna and Child, III:60
Feast of the Gods, III:58, 60
Pietà with Virgin and Saint John, III:59
Portrait of Doge Leonardo Loredan, III:60
Saint Francis in Ecstasy, III:60
Bellini, Jacopo, III:58
Bellow, Saul, **VII:247-250**
Adventures of Augie March, The, VII:247, 249
Dangling Man, VII:247
Dean's December, The, VII:249
Henderson and the Rain King, VII:249
Herzog, VII:249
Humboldt's Gift, VII:249
Mosby's Memoirs and Others Stories, VII:249
Mr. Sammler's Planet, VII:249
Seize the Day, VII:247
To Jerusalem and Back, VII:249
Victim, The, VII:247
Bellum Judaicum, I:472
Belvedere Palace, IV:655-657
Bemis, Edward W., V:1046
Benavides, Oscar R., VIII:1585
Bence, Eli, V:283

Benchley, Robert, IX:2884
Benedict III, II:673
Benedict VIII, II:451
Benedict XII, II:211, 212, 671, 683
Benedict XV, IX:3026, 3030
Benedict, Ruth, **VII:255-258;** VIII:2468, 2470
  Chrysanthemum and the Sword, VII:257
  Patterns of Culture, VII:257, 258
  Race Science and Politics, VII:257
Benedict, Saint, **VII:255-258**
Benedictine Order, II:994
Benedictine Rule, II:136, 137
Benedict of Nursia, Saint, **II:136-139**
Benes, Edvard, **VII:259-262**
Benét, Stephen Vincent, **VII:263-266**
  Five Men and Pompey, VII:263
  John Brown's Body, VII:265, 266
  Western Star, VII:265, 266
Bengal Legislative Council, VII:185
Ben-Gurion, David, VII:244, 245, **251-254;** IX:3932
Benincasa, Caterina. *See* Catherine of Siena, Saint
Benito Juárez Democratic Club, VIII:2345
Benizzi, Saint Filippo, III:24
Benjamin, Walter, **VII:267-270**
  "Author as Producer, The," VII:268
  Origin of German Tragic Drama, The, VII:267
  "Theses on the Philosophy of History," VII:269
  "Work of Art in the Age of Mechanical Reproduction, The," VII:268
Benjamin of Tudela, **II:140-142**
  Itinerary of Benjamin of Tudela, The, II:140-142
Bennett, Floyd, VII:534, 535
Bennett, James Gordon, **V:190-194;** VI:2101
Benois, Aleksander, VII:919, 920
Benson, Edward White, VI:2062
Bentham, Jeremy, **IV:107-110**
  Burr, V:371
  Chadwick, V:457-460
  Condillac, IV:346
  Constitutional Code, V:460
  Fragment on Government, A, IV:108
  Introduction to the Principles of Morals and Legislation, An, IV:108
  Mill, James, VI:1556, 1557
  Mill, John Stuart, VI:1559, 1560
  Owen, VI:1709
  Rationale of Judicial Evidence, VI:1787
Bentinck, Lord George, V:653
Bentley, Thomas, IV:1422, 1423
Benton, Thomas Hart, **V:195-198,** 839; IX:3048, 3049
Bentson, Lloyd, VII:520, 521
Benz, Carl, **V:199-201**
Berardi, Giannetto, III:758
Berengar of Ivrea, II:707
Berengar of Tours, II:374
Berg, Alban, **VII:271-274,** 386, 387; IX:3359
  Five Songs with Orchestra, VII:272
  Lulu, VII:273
  Woyzeck, VII:272, 389
Bergius, Friedrich, **VII:275-277**
Bergman, Ingmar, **VII:278-282**
  After the Rehearsal, VII:280
  Autumn Sonata, VII:280
  Cries and Whispers, VII:280
  Devil's Wanton, The, VII:278
  Dream Play, A, VII:281
  Face to Face, VII:280
  Fanny and Alexander, VII:280, 281
  From the Life of the Marionettes, VII:280
  Hamlet, VII:281
  Hedda Gabler, VII:280, 281
  Hour of the Wolf, VII:280
  King Lear, VII:281
  Lesson in Love, A, VII:278
  Long Day's Journey into Night, VII:281
  Magician, The, VII:280
  Misanthrope, The, VII:281
  Naked Night, The, VII:278
  Passion of Anna, The, VII:280
  Persona, VII:280
  Scenes from a Marriage, VII:280
  Secrets of Women, VII:278
  Serpent's Egg, The, VII:280
  Seventh Seal, The, VII:278
  Shame, VII:280
  Silence, The, VII:280
  Smiles of a Summer Night, VII:278
  Three Sisters, The, VII:281
  Through a Glass Darkly, VII:280
  Torment, VII:278
  Touch, The, VII:281
  Virgin Spring, The, VII:280
  Wild Duck, The, VII:280
  Wild Strawberries, VII:278
  Winter Light, VII:280
Bergson, Henri, **VII:283-286,** 342, 343, 650, 1374; VIII:1920, 2425, 2426, 2755; IX:3090
  Annals of Mathematics, VII:283
  Creative Evolution, VII:283, 284
  "Evolution of German Imperialism, The," VII:284
  Introduction to Metaphysics, An, VII:283

Laughter, VII:283
Matter and Memory, VII:283
"Meaning of War, The," VII:284
Time and Free Will, 1910, VII:283
Two Sources of Morality and Religion, The, VII:284
Beria, Lavrenty, VIII:1961, 2377, 2378
Berigan, Bunny, VIII:1419, 1420
Bering, Vitus Jonassen, **IV:111-113**
Bering Strait, IV:111, 112
Berkeley, George, **IV:114-117,** 683, 685, 883, 884
Alciphron, IV:115
Analyst, The, IV:883
Defense of Free-thinking in Mathematics, A, IV:115
De Motu, IV:114
Essay Towards a New Theory of Vision, An, IV:114, 115
Siris, IV:115
Theory of Vision, IV:115
Three Dialogues Between Hylas and Philonous, IV:114
Treatise Concerning the Principles of Human Knowledge, A, IV:114, 344
Berkeley, Sir William, IV:80-82
Berkman, Alexander, VIII:1412, 1413, 1732
Berkshire Music Center, VII:768
Berlage, Hendrik Petrus, IX:2859
Berlin, Congress of, VI:1944
Berlin, Irving, **VII:287-290**
"Alexander's Ragtime Band," VII:287
Annie Get Your Gun, VII:289, 290; IX:3202
Call Me Madam, VII:289
Cocoanuts, The, VII:288
"Easter Parade," VII:288
"God Bless America," VII:288, 289
Holiday Inn, VII:289
Miss Liberty, VII:289
Mr. President, VII:289
"Puttin' on the Ritz," VII:288
"Supper Time," VII:289
This Is the Army, VII:289
Top Hat, VII:288
Watch Your Step, VII:288
"When I Lost You," VII:288
"White Christmas," VII:289
Yip, Yip, Yaphank, VII:288
Ziegfield Follies, VII:288
Berlin Agitation Committee, IX:4113
Berlin airlift, VII:316
Berliner Abendblätter, VI:1295
Berliner Tageblatt building, VIII:2487
Berlin Olympics of 1936, IX:2862, 2863
Berlin Party, VIII:1404
Berlin Wall, VII:428; VIII:1963; IX:3779, 3780
Berlioz, Hector, **V:202-206**
Béatrice et Bénédict, V:205
Death of Sardanapalus, The, V:203
Enfance du Christ, L', V:205
Harold in Italy, V:203, 204
Huit Scènes de Faust, V:203
Lélio, V:203, 204
Requiem, V:204, 205
Symphonie fantastique, V:203, 204; VIII:2450
Troyens, Les, V:205; VIII:2770, 2771
Bernac, Pierre, IX:3067
Bernadote, Count Folke, VII:502
Bernard, Claude, **V:207-210;** VIII:2136
Introduction to the Study of Experimental Medicine, An, V:208; VI:2420; VIII:2134
Bernard, Émile, IX:3826
Bernard of Clairvaux, Saint, II:13, 14, **143-146,** 535, 860, 994-996
Treatise on Consideration, II:144
Bernardotte, Jean-Baptiste-Jules. *See* Charles XIV John
Bernhardt, Sarah, VIII:2141
Bernini, Gian Lorenzo, **IV:118-121,** 167, 168
Aeneas, Anchises, and Ascanius Fleeing Troy, IV:118
Apollo and Daphne, IV:118
David, IV:118
Ecstasy of Saint Teresa, The, III:715; IV:119, 583
Goat Amalthea with the Infant Jupiter and a Faun, The, IV:118
Pluto and Persephone, IV:118
Tomb of Pope Urban VIII, V:408
Bernoulli family, **IV:122-125,** 443; IX:4076
Ars conjectandi, IV:122
Exercitationes quaedam mathematicae, IV:122
Hydrodynamics by Daniel Bernoulli, IV:123
Théorie de la manoeuvre des vaisseaux, IV:123
Bernstein, Carl, VII:1084
Bernstein, Eduard, **VII:291-294;** VIII:2285
Evolutionary Socialism, VII:292
Bernstein, Leonard, **VII:295-299**
Age of Anxiety, The, VII:296, 298
Candide, VII:296, 298
Clarinet Sonata, VII:295
Fancy Free, VII:296
I Hate Music, VII:295
Jeremiah Symphony, VII:295, 298
Kaddish, VII:298

Mass, VII:298
On the Waterfront, VII:296
Trouble in Tahiti, VII:296
West Side Story, VII:296
Wonderful Town, VII:296
Berny, Château de, IV:898
Berry, Joan, VII:655
Berryman, John
Homage to Mistress Bradstreet, IV:195
Berthelot, Philippe, VII:1379
Berthold, Elector of Mainz, III:491, 492
Bertholet, Alfred, VIII:2714
Berzelius, Jöns Jakob, VI:2403, 2404
Besant, Annie, **V:211-214**
Beseda, the, VIII:1835
Bessel, Friedrich Wilhelm, **V:215-217**
Fundamenta astronomiae, V:216
Refraction Tables, V:216
Bessemer, Sir Henry, **V:218-221**
Best, Charles H., VII:188, 189; VIII:2329, 2330
Best, Peter, VII:226
Betaille, Nicolas, VIII:1817
Bethany College, V:403
Bethe, Hans Albrecht, **VII:300-303**
Handbuch der Physik, VII:301
Bethlehem Steel Company, IX:3619
Bettelheim, Bruno, IX:3388
Betto Bardi, Donato di Niccolò di. *See* Donatello
Betts v. Brady, VII:322
Beust, Friedrich von, **V:222-224**
Bevan, Aneurin, **VII:304-307**
In Place of Fear, VII:306
Bevatron, VIII:2123, 2338
Beveridge, Lord, **VII:308-312**
Full Employment in a Free Society, VII:310
India Called Them, VII:311
Power and Influence, VII:311
Prices and Wages in England, VII:310
Social Insurance and Allied Services, VII:310
Unemployment, VII:308
Voluntary Action, VII:311
Bevin, Ernest, VII:138, **313-317,** 1345
Beyle, Marie-Henri. *See* Stendhal
BGEA. *See* Billy Graham Evangelistic Association
Bible. *See* New Testament; Old Testament
Biddle, John, **IV:126-128**
Confession of Faith Touching the Holy Trinity, IV:126
Testimonies Concerning That One God, and the Persons of the Holy Trinity, IV:126
Twelve Arguments Drawn Out of Scripture, IV:126
Twofold Catechism, A, IV:127
Biddle, Nicholas, **V:225-229;** VI:2077
Biedermeier, V:726
Bierce, Ambrose, **V:230-232;** VIII:1603
"Affair at Coulter's Notch, The," V:232
"Chickamauga," V:231
Cobwebs from an Empty Skull, V:230
Devil's Dictionary, The, V:231, 232
Fiend's Delight, The, V:230
In the Midst of Life, V:231, 232
"Man and the Snake, The," V:232
Nuggets and Dust Panned in California, V:230
"Occurrence at Owl Creek Bridge, An," V:231
"Suitable Surroundings, The," V:232
Bierstadt, Albert, **V:233-235**
Base of the Rocky Mountains, Laramie Peak, The, V:234
big bands, VIII:1419, 1420, 1422
big bang theory, VIII:1582, 2157-2159
Bigelow, Henry Jacob, VI:1597
Bigge, John Thomas, V:992
Bigland, Reuben, VII:385
Bildungsroman, II:1007
Billy Graham Evangelistic Association, VIII:1448, 1449
Bindusara, I:112
Binet, Alfred, V:869
Bingham, George Caleb, **V:236-239**
Fur Traders Descending the Missouri, V:237, 238
Jolly Flatboatmen, The, V:237
Order 11, V:238
Self-Portrait of the Artist, V:236
Western Boatman Ashore, V:236, 237
Bingham, William, IV:1291
Bion of Borysthenes, I:303
Biraima, Damel, V:764
Birkbeck, George, VI:1787
Birney, James G., V:477
birth control
Besant, V:211, 212
Buck, VII:488
Malthus, VI:1469
Paul VI, IX:2916, 2917
Sanger, IX:3313-3315
Stopes, IX:3551-3553
Supreme Court ruling, VII:322
Biruni, al-, **II:147-149,** 1014
Beruni's India, al-, II:147
Canon Masudicus, II:147
Chronology of Ancient Nations, The, II:147, 148

Bishapur VI, I:781
Bismarck, Otto von, **V:240-243**
Bancroft, V:127
Beust, V:222-224
Bülow, VII:494, 495
Francis Joseph I, V:830
Holstein, V:1130, 1131
Kulturkampf, VI:1783
Lassalle, VI:1324, 1325
Scharnhorst, VI:1971
Social Democrats, VI:1370
Virchow, VI:2313
William II, IX:4003, 4004
Bithynia, I:558
Bizet, Georges, **V:244-246**
Carmen, V:244-246; VI:1685; VIII:1534, 2771
Coupe du Roi de Thulé, La, V:245
Djamileh, V:245
Don Procopio, V:244
Guzla de lémir, La, V:244
Ivan IV, V:244
Jolie Fille de Perth, La, V:244
Pêcheurs de perles, Les, V:244
Vasco de Gama, V:244
Bizone, VII:1095
Bjarni Herjolfsson, II:577, 578
Bjerknes, Vilhelm, **VII:318-320**
Dynamic Meteorology and Hydrography, VII:319
On the Dynamics of the Circular Vortex, VII:319
Black, Hugo L., **VII:321-324**
Black, Joseph, IV:1184, 1409, 1411
Black Army, III:487-489
black death
Boccaccio, II:152
David II, II:295
Edward III, II:331
Ibn Battutah, II:496
Margaret of Denmark, Norway, and Sweden, II:626
Orcagna, II:700
Rienzo, II:791
Venette, II:936
Black Elk, V:576
Blackfeet Indians, V:429
Blackfish, IV:164
Blackfriars, II:1011; III:689
Black Guelfs. *See* Guelfs
Black Hand, VII:1198
Black Hawk, **V:247-250;** VI:2010
Life of Ma-ka-tai-me-she-kia-kiak, V:247
Black Hawk War, VI:1380, 2195
Black Legend, III:23, 600
Black Legion, VIII:2373
blacklisting. *See* Un-American Activities, House Committee on
Black Muslims. *See* Nation of Islam
black nationalism, VII:1314; VIII:2373
Black Panther Party, VII:298; VIII:2376
Black Power movement, VIII:1773, 1774, 1974, 2627
Black September, VII:91
Blackshirts, VIII:2668
Black Star Line, VII:1312
Blackstone, William, IV:107, 108, **129-131**
Commentaries on the Laws of England, IV:129-131, 1455; VI:1277
Blackwell, Elizabeth, **V:251-254**
Blackwell, Samuel, V:251
Blaiberg, Philip, VII:197
Blaine, James G., **V:255-258,** 513, 1054, 1055; VIII:1402, 2219
Blair, Eric Arthur. *See* Orwell, George
Blair, Robert
Grave, The, IV:138
Blair, Tony, VIII:2371
Blair Mountain, Battle of, VIII:1881
Bland-Allison Act, VI:1454
Blane, Gilbert, IV:1180
Blaise Hamlet, IV:1013
Blake, Edward, VIII:2101
Blake, Robert, **IV:132-136,** 1342-1344
Blake, William, **IV:137-142,** 1163; VIII:2689
Descriptive Catalogue, A, IV:140
French Revolution, The, IV:138
Grave, The, IV:138
Jerusalem, V:778
Original Stories from Real Life, IV:138
Poetical Sketches, IV:137, 141
Songs of Experience, IV:141
Songs of Innocence, IV:137, 138, 141
Wise and Foolish Virgins, The, IV:811
Blanc, Louis, **V:259-262**
Blanche, Jacques Émile, VII:594
Bland-Allison Act, V:1078
Blaue Reiter Almanac, The, VIII:2405
Blaue Reiter movement. *See* Blue Rider movement
Blavatsky, Helena, V:212
Bleda, I:124
Blenheim, Battle of, IV:923
Blenheim Castle, IV:635, 636, 1353; VII:691
Blenheim Park, IV:205
Blériot, Louis, **VII:325-327**

Blessed Virgin, Brotherhood of the, III:70
Bleuler, Eugen, **VII:328-331**
  Dementia Praecox, VII:329
Bligh, William, **IV:143-146**
Bliss, George, V:1143
Blitzkrieg, VIII:1949
Bloch, Ivan
  Future of War, The, VI:2177
Bloc National, VII:705
Bloc Québéc, VII:550, 551
Bloemfontein, VII:377
Blok, Aleksandr, **VII:332-334;** IX:3754
  Nechayannaya radost, VII:332
  Puppet Show, The, VII:332
  Scythians, The, VII:333
  Stikhi o prekrasnoy dame, VII:332
  Twelve, The, VII:333
  Zemlya v snegu, VII:332
blood
  anemia, IX:3957-3959
  Aretaeus of Cappadocia, I:82
  capillaries, VIII:2027-2029
  circulatory system, I:82; VIII:2027-2029; IX:2933
  Diocles of Carystus, I:261
  Empedocles, I:284
  Erasistratus, I:299-301
  Harvey, IV:626, 628,629
  Herophilus, I:399
  Hippocrates, I:412
  Malpighi, IV:891
  Servetus, III:675-677
  sickle-cell anemia, IX:2927
  Spallanzani, IV:1260-1262
Blood, Fanny, IV:1475
Blood, Princes of the, IV:1049
Bloody Assizes, IV:982
Bloody Marsh, Battle of, IV:1045, 1046
Bloody Mary. *See* Tudor, Mary
Bloomsbury Group, VII:1193, 1254; VIII:1955, 2606; IX:4056
Blow, Peter, VI:1999-2001
Bloy, Léon, VIII:2425
Blücher, Gebhard Leberecht von, **V:263-266,** 942
Blücher, Heinrich, VII:98, 100
Blue Nile, IV:208-210
Blue Rider movement, VIII:1903, 2005, 2404-2406, 2454, 2487
blues music, VII:658; IX:3442, 3444, 3445
Blum, Léon, **VII:335-338;** VIII:1699, 2491
  For All Mankind, VII:337
  Lettres sur la réforme gouvernementale, VII:335
  Stendhal et le Beyisme, VII:335
Boadicca, **I:136-139**
Boas, Franz, **VII:339-341;** VIII:2468
  Handbook of American Indian Languages, VII:339
  Mind of Primitive Man, VII:339, 340
Boavista Bank, VIII:2740
Bobadilla, Francisco de, III:174
Boccaccio, Giovanni, **II:150-154,** 730
  Book of Theseus, The, II:150
  Concerning Famous Women, II:262
  Decameron, The, II:152, 223, 470
  Filostrato, The, II:150
  Genealogia deorum gentilium, II:153
  Life of Dante, II:153
Boccherini, Luigi, **IV:147-150**
  Clementina, La, IV:148
  Tirana, La, IV:148
Bocchus, I:529, 833
Boccioni, Umberto, **VII:342-344**
  City Rises, The, VII:343
  Manifesto tecnico della scultura futurista, VII:343
  Pittura scultura futuriste (dinamismo plastico), VII:343
  States of Mind, VII:343
  Technical Manifesto of Futurist Painting, VII:342
  Unique forms of Continuity in Space, VII:343
Bodley, Sir Thomas, **III:62-65**
Boeotia, I:18, 290, 292
Boeotian League, I:611
Boerhaave, Hermann, IV:827
Boer War
  Allenby, VII:58-61
  Baden-Powell, V:105, 106
  Botha, VII:376
  Fawcett, V:778
  Hobhouse, VIII:1708
  Kitchener, VIII:2002-2004
  Lansdowne, VIII:2091
  Laurier, VIII:2102
  Rhodes, VI:1875
  Salisbury, VI:1945
  Seddon, VI:2019
  Smuts, IX:3455
Boethius, **II:155-158**
  Consolation of Philosophy, The, II:156, 157, 250, 897
  On the Trinity, II:155
Boffrand, Germain, **IV:151-153**
  Livre d'architecture, IV:151-153

Bogart, Humphrey
African Queen, The, VIII:1639
Bad Sister, VII:843
Petrified Forest, The, VII:843
Boggs, Lilburn W., VI:2415
Bogot, Father, IV:801
Bohemond I, **II:159-162**
Böhme, Jakob, **IV:154-156**
Aurora, The, IV:154
Concerning the Election of Grace, IV:155
Concerning the Three Principles of the Divine Essence, IV:155
Forty Questions of the Soul, IV:155
High and Deep Searching Out of the Threefold Life of Man, The, IV:155
Mysterium Magnun, IV:155
Signatura Rerum, IV:155
Theosophic Questions, IV:155
Way to Christ, The, IV:155
Bohr, Niels, **VII:345-348**
Bothe, VII:379
Heisenberg, VIII:1617, 1618
Hevesy, VIII:1654
Landau, VIII:2073
Meitner, VIII:2477
Rutherford, IX:3278, 3279
Teller, IX:3632
Urey, IX:3787
Bohun, Henry de, II:188
Boleslaw Chrobry, II:449, 450, 871
Boleyn, Anne, **III:66-69**
Catherine of Aragon, III:138, 139
Cranmer, III:204
Cromwell, III:208, 209
Donizetti, V:685
Henry VIII, III:351, 733
Howard, III:367-369
Mary I, III:479
More, III:535
Boleyn, Mary, III:66
Bolingbroke, First Viscount, **IV:157-162,** 1400
Dissertation upon Parties, A, IV:160, 161
Fragments, or Minutes of Essays, IV:160
Idea of a Patriot King, The, IV:159, 160
Letter on the Spirit of Patriotism, IV:159
Letter to Sir William Wyndham, A, IV:159
Bolivar, Simón, **V:267-270;** VI:2164-2166; VII:1295
Böll, Heinrich, **VII:349-352**
Acquainted with the Night, VII:349
Adam, Where Art Thou?, VII:349
Billiards at Half-Past Nine, VII:349, 350
Bread of Our Early Years, The, VII:349
Clown, The, VII:350
Group Portrait with Lady, VII:350
Lost Honor of Katharina Blum, The, VII:350
Safety Net, The, VII:351
Soldier's Legacy, A, VII:351
Train Was on Time, The, VII:349
Women in a River Landscape, VII:351
Bologna, Concordat of, III:275
Bolshevik Revolution. *See* Russian Revolution of 1917
Bolshoi Ballet, VIII:2448
Boltzmann, Ludwig, VIII:2476; IX:3362
Bolyai, János, VI:1403, 1404
Bombelli, Rafael, I:274
Bona of Savoy, III:682
Bonaparte, Louis Napoleon. *See* Napoleon III
Bonaparte, Lucien, IV:149
Bonaparte, Napoleon. *See* Napoleon I
Bonaventure, Saint, **II:163-166,** 978, 991
Breviloquium, II:163
Collations on the Six Days, II:165
Journey of the Mind to God, The, II:165
Sentences, II:163
Bondfield, Margaret, **VII:353-357**
Bo'ness. *See* Borrowstounness
Bonfini, Antonio, III:489
Bonham, Dr., IV:331
Bonhoeffer, Dietrich, **VII:358-361**
Cost of Discipleship, The, VII:359
Ethics, VII:359
Prisoner for God, VII:360
Sanctorum Communio, VII:358
Schöpfung und Fall, VII:358
Bonhomme Richard, IV:740, 741
Boniface VIII, II:79, **171-174,** 288, 738
Clericis laicos, II:172
Unum Sanctam, II:173
Boniface, Saint, **II:167-170**
Bonnard, Pierre, **VII:362-364;** IX:3826, 3827
Bonnat, Léon, VIII:2658
Bonnivet, Admiral, III:49, 50
Bonpland, Aimé, V:1160
Bonus Army, VIII:1730, 2296
Book of Changes. See *I Ching*
Boone, Daniel, **IV:163-166**
Boonesborough, IV:163, 164
Booth, Edwin, **V:271-274**
Booth, John Wilkes, V:271, 272
Booth, Junius Brutus, V:271, 272; VI:1261
Booth, William, **V:275-278**
In Darkest England and the Way Out, V:275

Borah, William E., **V:279-282**
Borah-Jones Act, V:280
Borden, Lizzie, **V:283-285**
Borden, Robert Laird, **VII:365-367;** VIII:1777
Borg, Björn, **VII:368-370;** IX:2982
Borges, Jorge Luis, **VII:371-375**
Aleph and Other Stories, The, VII:374
"Approach to al-Mu'tasism, The," VII:373
Discusión, VII:373
Ficciones, VII:374
"Library of Babel, The," VII:373
"Pierre Menard, Author of Don Quixote," VII:373
"Poem About Gifts," VII:374
Selected Poems, VII:371
"Streetcorner Man," VII:373
"Truco, El," VII:373
Universal History of Infamy, A, VII:373
Borghese, Scipione, IV:118
Borgia, Cesare, III:14-17, 405, 450, 451
Borgia, Rodrigo, III:448
Borinquén, III:629, 630
Boris I of Bulgaria, II:**175-177,** 675
Borja y Doms, Rodrigo de. *See* Alexander VI
Bork, Robert, IX:3658
Born, Max, IX:3363
Borodin, Aleksandr, **V:286-289**
Bogatiri, V:287
Petite Suite, V:288
Prince Igor, V:287
Borodino, Battle of, V:45
Borough, Edward, III:592
Boroughbridge, Battle of, II:327
Borough Road school, VI:1309, 1310
Borrell, Count, II:869
Borromeo, Charles, VIII:1858
Borromini, Francesco, **IV:167-169,** 583, 584
Borrowstounness, IV:1184
Borujerdi, Mohammad-Hussein, VIII:1957
Bosch, Carl, VII:275
Bosch, Hieronymus, **III:70-73,** 85, 86; IV:606
Adoration Triptych, III:71
Christ Carrying the Cross, III:70
Crowning with Thorns, The, III:71
Garden of Earthly Delights, The, III:70, 71
Haywain, III:70
Hell, III:70
Landloper, III:71
Saint John the Baptist, III:71
Ship of Fools, The, III:70
Boso, Guntram, II:404
Bossuet, Jacques-Bénigne, **IV:170-173**
Discourse on the History of the Whole World, A, IV:170, 172
Funeral Oration for Henrietta of England, IV:170
Sermon on Death, IV:170, 171
Sermon on Providence, IV:170
Boston Arnold Arboretum, VII:1130
Boston Celtics, IX:3268, 3270, 3271
Boston Committee of Six, VI:1729
Boston Massacre, IV:616, 693
Boston Port Act, IV:616
Boston Red Sox, IX:3273, 3274
Boston Symphony Orchestra, VI:2232; VII:767
Boston Tea Party
Adams, John, IV:16
Adams, Samuel, IV:23
Franklin, IV:494
George III, IV:541
North, IV:1035
Revere, IV:1157
Wilson, IV:1456
Witherspoon, IV:1468
Boston Vigilance Committee, VI:1729
Boswell, James, **IV:174-178**
Account of Corsica, An, IV:175
Boswell on the Grand Tour, IV:175
Boswell's London Journal, IV:174, 176, 177
Journal of a Tour to the Hebrides, The, IV:175
Life of Samuel Johnson, The, IV:174, 176, 226, 730
Boswell, Percy, VIII:2146
Bosworth Field, Battle of, III:345, 651
Botha, Louis, **VII:376-378;** IX:3453
Bothe, Walther, **VII:379-381**
Botheric, I:44
Bothwell, Fourth Earl of, III:477
Bothwell Bridge, Battle of, IV:980
Botticelli, Sandro, **III:74-76**
Adoration of the Magi, III:74, 75
Birth of Venus, The, III:75
Fortitude, III:74
Judith and Her Maid, III:74
Primavera, III:75
Saint Augustine in His Cell, III:75
Bottomley, Horatio W., **VII:382-385**
Bouchefort, IV:152
Boucher, François, IV:414, 488, 489, 1415
Boudica. *See* Boadicca
Boudin, Eugène, VIII:2579
Boudinot, Elias, VI:1911
Bougainville, Louis-Antoine de, **IV:179-181**
Boulanger, Georges, VII:703

Boulanger, Nadia, VII:766, 767
Boulez, Pierre, **VII:386-390**
Boulez on Music Today, VII:387
Deux Improvisations sur Mallarmé, VII:388,
Domaines for Clarinet Alone or with 21 Other Instruments, VII:388
. . . explosante-fixe . . . , VII:388
Livre pour cordes, VII:388
Marteau sans maître, Le, VII:387, 389
Pli selon pli, VII:388, 389
Rug Concerts, VII:389
Second Piano Sonata, VII:389
Strophes, VII:388
Third Piano Sonata, VII:388
Boulton, Matthew, **IV:182-184**
Murdock, IV:1008, 1010
Roebuck, IV:1184
Trevithick, VI:2251
Watt, IV:1411
Wilkinson, IV:1444
Bounty, H.M.S., IV:143, 145, 146
Bourbon, Charlotte de, III:783
Bourbon, House of
Catherine de Médicis, III:132, 133
Charles III, IV:287
David, V:611
Francis I, III:275
Orléans, IV:1048-1050
Bourbon Reforms, IV:287-289
Bourbon Restoration, VI:2187
Bourdon, Sébastien, IV:317
Bourguiba, Habib, **VII:391-394**
Bourke-White, Margaret, **VII:395-398**
Eyes on Russia, VII:397
North of the Danube, VII:397
Portrait of Myself, VII:397
Say, Is This the U.S.A.?, VII:397
Shooting the Russian War, VII:397
They Called It Purple Heart Valley, VII:397
You Have Seen Their Faces, VII:397
Bourne, William, IV:850
Boutros-Ghali, Boutros, VII:50, **399-402**
Bouvines, Battle of, II:734
Bovell, William, VI:1698
Bow, Clara, VII:117
Bowen, Seabury, V:283, 284
Bowles, Samuel, V:668, 669
Boxer Rebellion, V:468, VI:1365
Boyle, Robert, **IV:185-188,** 805, 855, 858, 1059
Experiments and Considerations Touching Contours, IV:186
New Experiments and Observations Touching Cold, IV:186
New Experiments Physio-Mechanicall, IV:186
Sceptical Chymist, The, IV:186
Boy Scouts, V:105-107; VIII:2246, 2247
Boys' Life magazine, IX:3198
Boxer, Barbara, VII:1139
boxing
Ali, VII:53-56
Dempsey, VII:900-903
Louis, VIII:2241-2245
Mailer, VIII:2366
Marciano, VIII:2411-2413
Bozeman Trail, VI:1851
Bracton, Henry de, **II:178-180**
De legibus et consuetudinibus Angliae, II:178-180
Braddock, Edward, IV:511
Braddock, James, VIII:2243
Braden, Spruille, IX:2970
Bradford, William, **IV:189-192,** 1274, 1484, 1485
Governor Bradford's Letter Book, IV:191
Of Plimmoth Plantation, IV:191
Bradlaugh, Charles, V:211, 212; VII:382
Bradlee, Ben, VIII:1453
Bradley, F.H., **V:290-293;** VIII:1707, 1708
Appearance and Reality, V:290
Essays on Truth and Reality, V:290
Ethical Studies, V:290
Principles of Logic, V:290
Bradley, James, V:215
Bradley, Omar N., **VII:403-406;** IX:2913
Bradley, William, III:472
Bradman, Donald G., **VII:407-409**
Bradstreet, Anne, **IV:193-195**
Four Monarchies, The, IV:194
Meditations Divine and Moral, IV:194
"Prologue, The," IV:194
Tenth Muse Lately Sprung up in America, The, IV:193, 194
Brady, Matthew B., **V:294-298**
Bragadin, Senator, IV:254, 255
Bragg, Sir Lawrence, **VII:410-413**
Brahe, Tycho, II:21; **III:77-80,** 545; IV:774
De nova et nullius aevi memoria prius visa stella, III:78
Brahmagupta, II:91, **181-183**
Brahma sphuta siddhanta, II:181-183
Brahmo Sabba, VI:1848
Brahms, Johannes, **V:299-302;** VI:2156
Choréartium, VIII:2450
Concerto No. 1 in D Minor, Op. 15, V:300
German Requiem, Op. 45, V:300

Piano Trio in B Major, Op. 8, V:300
Sonata in F Minor, Op. 5, V:300
Symphony No. 1 in C Minor, Op. 68, V:301
Braille, Louis, **V:303-305**
brain
Alcmaeon, I:35, 36
Aretaeus of Cappadocia, I:82, 83
Asclepiades, I:102
cerebral angiography, VII:1023-1025
computed tomography, VIII:1751-1753
conditioned reflexes, IX:2934
Eccles, VII:1009, 1010
Erasistratus, I:299-301
Galen, I:339
Herophilus, I:399
Malpighi, IV:891
prefrontal lobotomy, VII:1023-1025
tumors, VII:824
Bramante, Donato, **III:81-84,** 407
Christ of the Pillar, III:81
Democritus, III:81
Heraclitus, III:81
Tempietto, III:83
Bramer, Leonaert, IV:1368
Brancacci Chapel, III:485
Branch Davidians, IX:3155
Brancusi, Constantin, **VII:414-418**
Antinous of Belvedere, VII:414
Bird in Space, VII:416
Bust of a Boy, VII:416
Cock, VII:417
Endless Column, VII:417
Gate of the Kiss, VII:417
Portrait of G. Lupescu, VII:416
Pride, VII:416
Table of Silence, VII:417
Brandeis, Louis D., **VII:419-423,** 577; IX:3619
"Brandeis brief," VII:421, 423
Other People's Money, VII:421
Brandenburgischer Flugzeugwerke, VIII:1614
Brando, Marlon, **VII:424-426**
Apocalypse Now, VII:426
Chase, The, VII:426
Désirée, VII:425
Godfather, The, VII:426
Guys and Dolls, VII:425
Hannele's Way to Heaven, VII:424
I Remember Mama, VII:424
Julius Caesar, VII:425
Last Tango in Paris, VII:426
Men, The, VII:425
Mutiny on the Bounty, VII:426
One-Eyed Jacks, VII:425
On the Waterfront, VII:425, 426
Reflections in a Golden Eye, VII:426
Sayonara, VII:426
Streetcar Named Desire, A, VII:425, 426
Wild One, The, VII:425
Young Lions, The, VII:426
Brandon, Frances, III:318, 319
Brandt, Willy, **VII:427-430;** VIII:2009
Brandywine, Battle of, IV:367, 574
Braniff International Airlines, VII:540
Brant, Joseph, **IV:196-200**
Brant, Molly, IV:196, 198, 199
Braque, Georges, **VII:431-435;** IX:2998
Aria de Bach, VII:432
Bay at Antwerp, The, VII:431
Black Fish, VII:434
Doves, VII:434
Estaque, Road with two Fingers, L', VII:431
Fruit Dish and Glass, VII:432
Guédridon, Le, VII:434
Guitar and Fruit Dish, VII:432
Harbor in Normandy, VII:431
Homage to Bach, VII:432
Houses at L'Estaque, VII:431
Interior: Grey Table, The, VII:434
Landscape at Antwerp, VII:431
Musician, The, VII:432
Portuguese, The, VII:432
Ship in Harbour, Le Havre, VII:431
Standing Nude, VII:431
Still Life with Musical Instruments, VII:431
Still Life with Playing Cards, VII:432
View from the Hôtel Mistral, VII:431
Violin and Palette, VII:432
Violin and Pitcher, VII:432
Weeding, The, VII:434
Zéphere et Flore, VIII:2450
Brasilia, VIII:2740
Braudel, Fernand, **VII:436-439**
Civilization and Capitalism, VII:437
Mediterranean and Mediterranean World in the Age of Philip II, The, VII:437
Braun, Wernher von, **VII:440-443;** VIII:1615; IX:2778, 2779
Breadbasket, Operation, VIII:1824-1826
Breakspear, Nicholas. *See* Adrian IV
Brecht, Bertolt, VII:268, **444-447;** IX:3927, 3928
Baal, VII:444
Caucasian Chalk Circle, The, VII:445

Didactic Play of Baden, The, VIII:1633
Drums in the Night, VII:444
Good Woman of Setzuan, The, VII:445
In the Jungle of Cities, VII:444
Life of Galileo, VII:446
Mother, The, VII:444
Mother Courage and Her Children, VII:444, 446
Rise and Fall of the City of Mahagonny, The, IX:3927
St. Joan of the Stockyards, VII:445
Breckinridge, Sophonisba, IX:3604
Breda, Declaration of, IV:284, 310
Breda, Peace of, IV:285
Breitenfeld, Battle of, IV:1335-1337
Brennan, William J., Jr., VII:1214
Brentano, Franz, VII:1026
Bresdin, Rodolphe, VI:1854
Brest-Litovsk, Treaty of, VII:1103
Bretel, Jehan, II:23
Brétigny, Peace of, II:331
Breton, André, **VII:448-451,** 632, 829, 1075, 1099, 1100; VIII:2351, 2353, 2548
Air de l'eau, L', VII:450
Amour fou, L', VII:450
Arcane 17, VII:450
Breasts of Tiresias, The, VII:448
Champs magnétiques, Les, VII:448, 449
Fata Morgana, VII:450
Free Union, VII:450
Manifesto of Surrealism, VII:449, 450
Nadja, VII:449
Ode to Charles Fourier, VII:450
Second Manifesto of Surrealism, VII:450
Vases communicants, Les, VII:450
Bretton Woods Conference, VIII:1954
Breuer, Josef, **VII:452-455,** 1224
Breuil, Henri-Édouard-Prosper, **VII:456-458**
Brewster, Mary, IX:3837
Brezhnev, Leonid Ilich, **VII:459-462,** 969, 970; VIII:1423, 1963, 2213
bridge construction
Eads, V:729-731
Freyssinet, VII:1228-1230
Roebling, VI:1904-1906
Stanton, VI:2106
Telford, VI:2208-2210
Wilkinson, IV:1443-1445
Bridges, Calvin Blackman, VIII:2651
Bridget of Sweden, Saint, II:626
Bridgewater, Duke of, IV:201
Bridgewater Foundry, VI:1624, 1626
Bridgman, Laura, V:1150, 1152
Bridgman, Percy Williams, **VII:463-465**
Intelligent Individual and Society, The, VII:464
Logic of Modern Physics, The, VII:464
Briggs, Henry, III:545
Bright, John, **IV:306-309;** V:527, 528
Bright v. Eynon, IV:907
Brik, Osip, VIII:2461
Brill, Paul, IV:317
Brindley, James, **IV:201-203**
Brinkley, John, V:1025
Britain, Battle of, VII:234, 236; VIII:1949
Britannicus, I:551
British and Foreign Anti-Slavery Society, VI:1600
British and Foreign School Society, VI:1787
British Broadcasting Corporation
Collins, VII:737-740
Orwell, IX:2849
Reith, IX:3146-3148
British East India Company
Burke, IV:224
Burton, V:374, 375
Clive, IV:325-327
Cornwallis, IV:368, 369
George III, IV:542, 542
Hastings, IV:631-633
Kidd, IV:779
Lawrence, VI:1331
Leeds, IV:823
North, IV:1035
Outram, VI:1705, 1706
Paterson, IV:1067
British Expeditionary Force, VII:45, 46, 59
British Fourteenth Army, IX:3435-3437
British Mandate in Palestine, VIII:1791
British Medical Association building, VII:1087
British Museum, IV:85, 86
British North America Act of 1867, VI:1435, 1437; VII:681
British Open, VIII:1876, 1877; IX:3040, 3041
British South Africa Company, VI:1874
Britten, Benjamin, **VII:466-471**
Albert Herring, VII:469
Ballad of Heroes, VII:468
Billy Budd, VII:469
Boy Was Born, A, VII:466
Burning Fiery Furnance, The, VII:470
Cantata Misericordium, VII:469
Canticle II: Abraham and Issac, VII:469
Canticle III: Still Falls the Rain, VII:469
Canticle IV: The Journey of the Magi, VII:470
Ceremony of Carols, VII:468
Children's Crusade, VII:470

Curlew River, VII:469
Death in Venice, VII:470
Fairy Queen, The, VII:470
Gloriana, VII:469
Golden Vanity, The, VII:470
Hymn to St. Cecelia, A, VII:468
Midsummer Night's Dream, A, VII:469
Mont Juic, VII:468
Nocturne, VII:469
Noye's Fludde, VII:469
On This Island, VII:468
Our Hunting Fathers, VII:468
Owen Wingrave, VII:470
Paul Bunyon, VII:468
Phaedra, VII:470
Phantasy Quartet, VII:466
"Praise We Great Men," VII:470
Prince of Pogodas, The, VII:469
Prodigal Son, The, VII:470
Rape of Lucretia, The, VII:468
Rejoice in the Lamb, VII:468
Sacred and Profane, VII:470
Saint Nicolas, VII:469
Serenade, VII:468
Simple Symphony, VII:466
Sinfonietta, VII:466
Six Hölderlin Fragments, VII:469
Six Metamorphoses After Ovid, VII:469
Songs and Proverbs of William Blake, VII:470
Spring Symphony, VII:469
String Quartet in D, VII:466
Suite for Harp, VII:470
Suite on English Folk Tunes, VII:470
Turn of the Screw, The, VII:469
Variations on a Theme of Frank Bridge, VII:468
Welcome Ode, VII:470
Winter Words, VII:469
Broad Bottom cabinet, IV:1075
Broadway musicals. *See* musical theater
Brodribb, John Henry. *See* Irving, Henry
Brodsky, Joseph, VII:39
Broglie, Louis de, **VII:472-474;** IX:3363
Bronowski, Jacob, IX:3307
Bronstein, Lev Davidovich. *See* Trotsky, Leon
Brontë Anne, **V:310-313**
Agnes Grey, V:310-312
Tenant of Wildfell Hall, The, V:310
Brontë, Charlotte, **V:310-313**
Jane Eyre, V:157, 310, 312
Professor, The, V:311, 312
Shirley, V:312
Villette, V:312
Brontë, Emily, **V:310-313**
Wuthering Heights, V:310-312; VIII:1417
Brooke, Alan Francis. *See* Alanbrooke, First Viscount
Brook Farm, VI:1728
Brooklyn Bridge, VI:1905
Brooklyn Dodgers, IX:3193, 3194
Brooks, William Keith, VIII:2618
Brotherly Agreement, IV:1489
Brothers Club, IV:158
Brough, Louise, VII:1363
Brougham, Henry, **IV:314-317;** V:722; VI:1518
Inquiry into the Colonial Policy of the European Powers, An, V:314
Brown, George, **V:318-320**
Fame and Glory of England Vindicated, The, V:319
Brown, John, **V:321-326**
Benét's poem
Child, V:491
Douglass, V:697
Higginson, V:1110
Howe, V:1151
Lee, VI:1338
Parker, VI:1729
Tubman, VI:2265, 2266
Warren, IX:3894
Brown, Lancelot, **IV:204-207,** 529
Brown, Ray, VII:1159
Brown, Robert, IV:86
Browne, Sir Thomas, VIII:2690
Browning, Elizabeth Barrett, **V:327-330**
Aurora Leigh, V:329
Battle of Marathon, The, V:327
Casa Guidi Windows, V:327
"Cry of the Children, The," V:327
"Lady Geraldine's Courtship," V:327
Last Poems, V:329
Poems Before Congress, V:329
Poems, by Elizabeth Barrett Browning, V:327
"Runaway Slave at Pilgrim's Point, The," V:327
Seraphim and Other Poems, The, V:327
Sonnets from the Portuguese, V:327
Browning, Robert, V:327, 329
Strafford, VI:1461
Brownlow, Kevin, VII:1275, 1276
Brown v. Board of Education
Frankfurter, VII:1214
Hughes, VIII:1769
Hurston, VIII:1789
Marshall, VIII:2434, 2435

Myrdal, VIII:2672
Robeson, IX:3187
Stevenson, IX:3525
Warren, IX:3889
White, IX:3963
Broz, Josip. *See* Tito
Bruce, David. *See* David II
Bruce, James, **IV:208-210**
Travels to Discover the Source of the Nile, IV:209
Bruce, Robert, **II:184-189,** 294, 324, 327, 956
Bruce, Stanley M., VIII:1776
Brücke, Die, VIII:1991, 1992; IX:3354-3356
Brücke, Ernst, VII:452, 1224
Bruckner, Anton, **V:331-334;** VIII:2363
Symphony No. 1 in C Minor, V:332
Symphony No. 2 in C Minor, V:332
Symphony No. 4 in E-flat Major, V:332
Symphony No. 8, V:332
Symphony No. 9, V:332
Bruegel, Pieter the Elder, **III:85-88**
Battle Between Carnival and Lent, III:86
Blue Cloak, The, III:86
Children's Games, III:86
Cripples, The, III:86
Hunters in the Snow, III:88
Massacre of the Innocents, The, III:86
Parable of the Blind, III:86
Peasant Dance, III:86
Peasant Wedding, III:86
Road to Calvary, The, III:86
Sea Battle in the Straits of Messina, III:85
Seven Deadly Sins, III:86
Temptation of Saint Anthony, The, III:86
Brueys, Francis, VI:1636
Brugha, Cathal, VII:734
Brunel, Isambard Kingdom, **V:335-338,** 339, 341; VI:2134
Brunelleschi, Filippo, III:28, 84, **89-92,** 302, 483, 485
Brunetti, Gaetano, IV:148
Bruni, Leonardo, **III:93-95**
Concerning the Study of Literature, III:94
De militia, III:94
Dialoghi ad Petrum Paulum historum, III:93
Historiae Florentini populi, III:93
Laudatio Florentinae urbis, III:93
Rerum suo tempore gestarum commentarius, III:94
Brunner, Emil, **VII:475-478**
Christianity and Civilization, VII:476
Divine Imperative: A Study of Christian Ethics, The, VII:476
Dogmatics, VII:477
Erlebnis, Erkenntnis und Glaube, VII:475
Man in Revolt: A Christian Anthropology, VII:476
Mediator: A Study of the Central Doctrine of the Christian Faith, The, VII:476
Mystik und das Wort, Die, VII:475
Theology of Crisis, The, VII:476
Bruno, Giordano, **III:96-100;** IV:950
Cena de le Ceneri, III:97
On the Infinite Universe and Worlds, III:97
Bruno of Egisheim. *See* Leo IX
Brunswick, duke of, IV:919
Brussels, Union of, III:783
Brussels Conference, VI:1508
Brutus, Lucius Junius, I:140
Brutus, Marcus Junius, **I:140-143,** 150, 159, 160
Bryan, William Jennings, V:56, 515, 1030; VI:1454; **VII:479-482**
Bryant, William Cullen, **V:343-345**
"Embargo, The," V:343
"Forest Hymn, A," V:344
"Prairies, The," V:344
"Thanatopsis," V:343, 345
"To a Waterfowl," V:343, 345
Brzezinski, Zbigniew, VII:49, 50
Buber, Martin, **VII:483-485;** VIII:2408, 2409
For the Sake of Heaven, VII:484
Good and Evil, VII:485
Hasidism and Modern Man, VII:484
I and Thou, VII:476, 483, 484
Origin and Meaning of Hasidism, The, VII:484
Tales of the Hasidism, VII:484
bubonic plague. *See* black death
Bucareli Agreements of 1923, IX:2783
Bucer, Martin, I:883; **III:101-104,** 675
Deregno Christi, III:103
Institutes of the Christian Religion, III:103
Buchanan, James, V: 197, **346-348,** 794
Buck, Pearl S., **VII:486-490**
"America's Gunpowder Women," VII:488
"America's Medieval Women," VII:488
Bridge for Passing, A, VII:488
Child Who Never Grew, The, VII:488
Command the Morning, VII:488
Exile, The, VII:486, 489
Fighting Angel, VII:486, 489
Good, Earth, The, VII:486, 488, 489
House Divided, A, VII:486
Imperial Women, VII:488
Of Men and Women, VII:488
Sons, VII:486

This Proud Heart, VII:488
Townsman, The, VII:488
Buckingham, First Duke of, **IV:211-214**
Charles I, IV:279
Coke, IV:332, 333
James I, IV:700, 701
Laud, IV:797
Leeds, IV:821
Monck, IV:971
Buckley, William, Jr., IX:3663
Buddha, **I:144-146;** VIII:1921
Budé, Guillaume, III:274
Budge, Don, IX:2981
Buena Vista, V:615
Buen Retiro, IV:236
Buffalo Bill. *See* Cody, William Frederick
Buffon, Comte de, **IV:215-217,** 1260
Epochs of Nature, The, IV:216, 217
Natural History, General and Particular, IV:215
Buffoons, War of the, IV:1149
Bufford, John, V:1133
Bugeaud, Thomas Robert, V:2
Buggiano, Il, III:91
Bukharin, Nikolai Ivanovich, **VII:491-493**
ABC of Communism, The, VII:491
Imperialism and World Economy, VII:491
Bulan, II:550
Bulfinch, Charles, **V:349-352**
Bulganin, Nikolai, IX:4118
Bulgar Empire, II:86, 87, 175-177, 904, 952
Bulge, Battle of the, VIII:1695
Buller, Sir Redvers, VII:376
Bull Run, Battle of, V:1205; VI:2059
Bülow, Bernhard von, **VII:494-497**
Imperial Germany, VII:496
Bülow, Hans von, IX:3555
Bultmann, Rudolf, **VII:498-500**
Gospel of John, The, VII:499
History of Synoptic Tradition, The, VII:498
Jesus and the Word, VII:499
Theology of the New Testament, VII:499
Bumppo, Natty, V:562, 564
Bunche, Ralph, VII:144, **501-504**
American Dilemma, An, VII:501
Bunker Hill, Battle of, IV:677, 678, 1157, 1239
Bunsen, Robert, V:1010; VI:1530
Bunstead, Henry, VII:858
Buñuel, Luis, **VII:505-508**
Adventures of Robinson Crusoe, The, VII:506
Âge d'or, L', VII:506, 507, 829
Andalusian Dog, An, VII:505, 507, 829
Belle de jour, VII:506
Diary of a Chambermaid, VII:506
Discreet Charm of the Bourgeoisie, The, VII:506
Exterminating Angel, The, VII:506
Forgotten Ones, The, VII:506
Golden Age, The, VII:505
Land Without Bread, VII:505
Milky Way,The, VII:506
My Last Sigh, VII:506
Nazarin, VII:506
Phantom of Liberty, The, VII:506
That Obscure Object of Desire, VII:506
Tristana, VII:506
Viridiana, VII:506
Woman Without Love, A, VII:506
Bunyan, John, **IV:218-221**
Grace Abounding to the Chief of Sinners, IV:219
Holy War, The, IV:219, 220
Life and Death of Mr. Badman, The, IV:219, 220
Pilgrim's Progress, The, IV:218-220
Buoninsegna, Duccio di. *See* Duccio di Buoninsegna
Burbank, Luther, **V:353-357**
Luther Burbank: His Methods and Discoveries and Their Practical Applications, V:356
New Creations in Fruits and Flowers, V:355
Burckhardt, Jacob, III:720; **V:358-360**
Age of Constantine the Great, The, V:359
Cicerone, The, V:359
Civilization of the Renaissance in Italy, The, V:359
Burger, Warren E, **VII:509-511**
Burgess, Anthony
Cyrano, IV:387
Burgesses, House of, IV:81, 82, 647, 648
Burgh, Hubert de, **II:190-193**
Burghley, Lord. *See* Cecil, William
Burgos, III:696
Burgoyne, John, IV:677
Burgundy, Duchy of
Charles V, III:159
Charles the Bold, III:163-165
Clement VII, III:166
Henry II the Saint, II:450
Maximillian I, III:491-493
Philip the Good, II:740-742
Sluter, II:832
Warwick, III:776, 777
Buridan, Jean, **II:194-197**
Consequentie, II:194
Sophismata, II:194, 195
Summula de dialectica, II:194

Burke, Edmund, II:992; IV:160, 161, **222-225,** 481, 482, 528, 555, 556, 1035
Annual Register, The, IV:222
Appeal from the New to the Old Whigs, IV:224
Letter to a Noble Lord, A, IV:224
Philosophical Inquiry into the Origin of Our Ideas of the Sublime and Beautiful, IV:222
Reflections on the Revolution in France, IV:224, 556, 1056, 1477
Thoughts on the Cause of the Present Discontents, IV:222
Burmese Independence Army, IX:3647
Burne-Jones, Edward, V:161; VI:1288, 1588
Burnet, Sir Macfarlane, **VII:512-515**
Biological Aspects of Infectious Disease, VII:512
Immunological Surveillance, VII:514
Burnett, Frances Hodgson, **V:361-364**
Dawn of a Tomorrow, The, V:363
Little Lord Fauntleroy, V:362, 363
Little Princess, The, V:362
Lost Prince, The, V:363
My Robin, V:363
Secret Garden, The, V:363
Shuttle, The, V:362
Surly Tim and Other Stories, V:361
That Lass o' Lowrie's, V:361
Burney, Charles, **IV:226-228**
Cunning Man, The, IV:226
General History of Music, A, IV:226-228
Memoirs of the Life and Letters of the Abate Metastasio, IV:228
Present State of Music in France and Italy, The, IV:227
Present State of Music in Germany, the Netherlands, and the United Provinces, IV:227
Burnham, Daniel Hudson, **V:365-368**
Burns, Anthony, VI:1729
Burns, Lucy, IX:2919
Burns, Robert, **IV:229-234;** VI:2374; VIII:1952
"A Man's a Man for a' That," IV:231
"Cotter's Saturday Night, The," IV:231
"Holy Willie's Prayer," IV:231
"Jolly Beggars, The," IV:231
"O Wert Thou in the Cauld Blast," IV:232
Poems, Chiefly in the Scottish Dialect, IV:231, 232
"Poet's Welcome to His Love-Begotten Daughter, A," IV:231
Scots Musical Museum, The, IV:232
"Tam o'Shanter," IV:231
"Twa Dogs, The," IV:231
Burr, Aaron, IV:611, 718, 719, 1096; **V:369-373,** 507, 517
Burroughs, Edgar Rice, **VII:516-519**
Princess of Mars, A, VII:517, 519
Tarzan of the Apes, VII:517, 519
Burroughs, William, VIII:1945, 1946
Burrus, Sextus Afranius, I:772
Burton, Dan, VII:710
Burton, James, IV:1013
Burton, Sir Richard Francis, **V:374-377;** VI:2083-2085
City of the Saints, V:375
First Footsteps in Africa, V:375
Lake Regions of Central Africa, V:375
Personal Narrative of a Pilgrimage to El-Medinah and Meccah, V:375
Busby, Richard, IV:854
Bush, George, **VII:520-523**
Clinton, VII:708
Dole, VII:948
Greenspan, VIII:1472
Persian Gulf War, VIII:1432
Powell, IX:3071, 3072
Thomas, IX:3658
Walesa, IX:3847
Bushnell, Robert, V:855
Busoni, Ferruccio, IX:3794, 3926
Buss, Frances Mary, V:157, 158
Bute, Lord, IV:539, 1034
Buthos, I:912
Butler, Benjamin, V:143
Butler, Frank, VI:1677, 1678
Butler, James. *See* Ormonde, second Duke of
Butler, Nicholas Murray, **VII:524-528**
Butler, Pierce Mease, VI:1273, 1275
Butler, R.A., **VII:529-533**
Butler, Samuel
Hudibras, IV:668
Butler Act. *See* Education Act of 1944
Butt, Isaac, VI:1740
Butts, Thomas, IV:138
Buxton, Sir Thomas Fowell, **V:378-380**
Buyids, II:678
Bye and Main Plots, III:661
Bykovsky, Valeri, IX:3639, 3640
Byng, John, IV:56, 57
Byng, Lord, VIII:1982
Byrd, Richard E., **VII:534-537**
Byrd, Richard F., VIII:1784
Byrd William, **III:105-109**
"Alleluia, Confitemini Domino," III:105
"Attollite portas," III:106

Cantiones Sacrae, III:106
"Christus resurgens," III:105
"Emendemus in melius," III:106
Gradualia, III:107
"Libera me, Domine, de morte aeterna," III:106
My Ladye Nevells Booke, III:107
Ne irascaris, III:106
Parthenia, III:107
Psalmes, Sonets, and Songs of Sadness and Pietie, III:107
Songs of Sundrie Natures, III:107
Byrhtnoth, II:345
Byron, Lord, **V:381-385,** 482, 483, 646, 647; VI:1261, 2053, 2054
Beppo, V:382
Bride of Abydos, The, V:381
Childe Harold's Pilgrimage, V:381, 382, 384; VI:1959, 1960
Corsair, The, V:382
Don Juan, V:382, 384
English Bards and Scotch Reviewers, V:381
Giaour, The, V:381
Hours of Idleness, V:381
Lara, V:382
Manfred, V:382
Prisoner of Chillon, The, V:382; VI:2053
Vision of Judgment, The, V:382
Byurakan Observatory, VII:63, 64

Cabala, II:648-650; III:440, 441
Cabalists, II:500
See also Safed Cabalists
Cabell, James Branch, VIII:2484
Cabeza de Vaca, Alvar Núñez, **III:110-112,** 180, 699
Naufragios, Los, III:111
Cabot, John, **III:113-116,** 347
Cabral, Pedro Alvars, III:288, 464
Cabrini, Frances Xavier, **V:386-389**
Cadet School of Mars, IV:1207
Cadore Letter, IV:888
Cædmon, **II:198-200**
Hymm, II:199
Caedwalla, II:824
Caenis, I:933
Caesar, Gaius Julius. *See* Caligula
Caesar, Julius, **I:147-151**
Agrippa, I:20
Antony, I:69
Augustus, I:132, 133
Britain, I:136
Brutus, I:141, 142
Cassius, I:159, 160
Cato the Younger, I:166-168
Catullus, I:169, 170
Cicero, I:196
Civil Wars, The, I:147
Cleopatra VII, I:218, 220, 221
Commentaries, I:830; III:581
Conquest of Gaul, The, I:922
Gallic Wars, The, I:147
Gracchi, I:347
Herod the Great, I:390
Marius, I:528
Mommsen, VI:1567, 1568
Plutarch, I:671
Pompey the Great, I:680, 681
Sallust, I:742, 743
Sosigenes, I:811-813
Tiberius, I:892
Varro, I:918
Vercingetorix, I:922, 924
Caesarion, I:218, 220
Caetani, Benedict. *See* Boniface VIII
Cage, John, VII:387, 388
Cahiers du cinéma, VIII:1391
Cairo Agreement, VII:91
Cajamarca, III:699
Cajetan, Thomas, III:443, 445
Calamity Jane, **V:390-393**
Calced Carmelites, III:402, 714, 715
calculus
Babbage, V:101-103
Bernoulli, IV:123
Copernicus, III:178
Euler, IV:444
Lagrange, IV:787
Leibniz, IV:830
Maclaurin, IV:882-884
Caldecott, Randolph, IX:3389
Calder, Alexander, **VII:538-541**
Calder Piece, VII:540
Circus, VII:538
Frisco, VII:540
Man, VII:540
Object in Five Planes (Peace), VII:540
Plastic Interludes, VII:539
Spirale, VII:539
Universe, VII:539
Whirling Ear, VII:539
Calderón de la Barca, Pedro, **IV:235-238**
Amor, honor y poder, IV:235
Constant Prince, The, IV:235
Great Theater of the World, IV:235

Judas Macabeo, IV:235
Life Is a Dream, IV:235
Love, the Greatest Enchantment, IV:236
Phantom Lady, The, IV:235
selva confusa, La, IV:235
sitio de Breda, El, IV:235
Caldor, Louis J., VIII:2633
Caldwell, Erskine, VII:397
Caleb, I:563
Caledonian Canal, VI:2208, 2209
calendars
Brahmagupta, II:182
Chinese dynastic calendar, IV:757
Dionysius Exiguus, 298-300
Eudoxus of Cnidus, I:312
Julian calendar, I:150
Muslim calendar, II:652
Pelham, IV:1076
Rabanus Maurus, II:767
Verrius Flaccus, I:930, 931
Calhoun, John C., **V:394-397**
Benton, V:196
Discourse on the Constitution of the United States, A, V:396
Disquisition on Government, A, V:396
Gadsden Purchase, V:858, 859
Tyler, VI:2288, 2289
Caliari, Paolo. *See* Veronese, Paolo
Calico Act of 1774, IV:60
California,
Compromise of 1850, V:510
Feinstein, VII:1137-1139
Field, V:787, 789
Fillmore, V:792, 793
Frémont, V:840, 842
Jackson, V:1201, 1202
Polk, VI:1803
Reagan, IX:3138
Sinclair, IX:3428
Stanford, VI:2096-2099
Warren, IX:3888, 3889
California Welfare Reform Act of 1971, IX:3138
Caligula, **I:152-155,** 203, 632, 770
Callender, John, IV:295
Calles, Plutarco Elias, **VII:542-545**
Calley, John, IV:1022, 1023
Callias of Alopeke, I:199
calligraphy
Mi Fei, II:639, 640
Ogata Korin, IV:1041, 1042
Sotatsu, IV:1257
Wang Hsi-chi, I:946-948
Callimachus, **I:156-158**
Aetia, I:156, 157
Eratosthenes of Cyrene, I:303
Hecale, I:157
Iambi, I:156, 157
Callistus, I:417
Calloway, Cab, VII:1370
Calmette, Albert, **VII:546-548**
Caloosa Indians, III:631
Calvin, John, **III:117-121**
Institutes of the Christian Religion, III:103, 117, 118, 120, 362, 468, 676; IV:428
On Clemency, III:117
Servetus, III:676, 677
Calvinism
Catherine de Medicis, III:132, 133, 135
Gomarists, III:575
Hotman, III:362-365
Jansen, IV:707
Napier, III:544
Pym, IV:1141
Winthrop, IV:1463
See also Calvin, John; Protestant Reformation
Calzabigi, Raniero, IV:549, 550
Camacho, Manuel Ávila, VII:544
Cambacérès, Jean-Jacques-Régis de, **V:398-400**
Cambio, Arnolfo di. *See* Arnolfo di Cambio
Cambria, Treaty of, III:326
Cambridge Camden Society, VI:1822
Cambridge University
Acton, V:12, 13
Babbage, V:101, 102
Baskerville, IV:96
Cranmer, III:204
Fisher, III:265
Marlowe, III:471
Nashe, III:548
Parker, III:589
Ridley, III:654
Rothschild, VI:1918
Spenser, III:703
Cambyses II, I:236
Camden, William, IV:744
Camera Work, IX:3503, 3534
Cameron, Richard, **IV:239-241**
"Cameron's Covenant, The," IV:240
Sanquhar Declaration, IV:240
Camillus, Marcus Furius, I:505
Camões, Luís de, **III:122-124**
Filodemo, III:122,123
Lusiads, The, III: 123, 124
Lyrides, The, III:123

Campañón, Francisco, III:699
Campbell, Alan, IX:2886
Campbell, Alexander, **V:401-404**
Campbell, Kim, **VII:549-552;** VIII:2656
Campbell-Bannerman, Sir Henry, VII:121, 122
Campbell v. Hall, IV:907
Camp David Accords, VII:245, 399, 591, 592; VIII:1794; IX:3290
Campe, Joachim Heinrich, IV:93
Camperdown, Battle of, IV:145
Campin, Robert, III:778, 779
Campra, André, IV:1149, 1150
Camulodunum, I:136, 137
Camus, Albert, **VII:553-556;** IX:3327, 3328
  Caligula, VII:553
  Fall, The, VII:555
  Just Assassins, The, VII:555
  Myth of Sisyphus and Other Stories, The, VII:553, 554
  Nuptials, VII:553
  Plague, The, VII:554
  Rebel, The, VII:553, 555
  State of Siege, The, VII:555
  Stranger, The, VII:553
  Wrong Side and Right Side, The, VII:553
  Canadian Freeman, VI:1449
Canadian Pacific Railroad. *See* Northern Pacific Railway Company
Canal, Giovanni Antonio. *See* Canaletto
Canaletto, **IV:242-245**
  Bucentoro at the Molo on Ascension Day, The, IV:243
  Entrance to the Grand Canal: Looking East, IV:243
  Old Walton Bridge, IV:244
  Ponti della Pescaria and Buildings on the Quay, The, IV:243
  Portico of a Palace, IV:244
  Regatta on the Grand Canal, A, IV:243
  Stonemason's Yard, The, IV:243
  Thames and the City of London from Richmond House, The, IV:243, 244
  Whitehall and the Privy Gardens, IV:243
Canaris, Wilhelm, VIII:1616
cancer
  actinomycin D, IX:3834
  Burnet, VII:514
  Domagk, VII:952, 953
  Ehrlich, VII:1033, 1034
  Guy de Chauliac, II:415
  Hevesy, VIII:1656
  Lawrence, VIII:2121, 2122
  Razi, II:780
  vitamin C, IX:2928
  Watson, IX:3898, 3899
Candela, Felix, **VII:557-559**
Candolle, Alphonse de, V:868
Cannae, Battle of, I:760
Canning, George, **V:405-407,** 440, 904, 905; VI:1396, 1517, 2351
Cannizzaro, Stanislao, V:100
canon law
  Alexander III, II:48-50
  Boniface VIII, II:172
  Dionysius Exiguus, 298-300
  Gregory IX, II:399-401
  Raymond of Peñafort, II:776, 777
  Sergius I, II:824
Canova, Antonio, **V:408-412**
  Cupid and Psyche, V:410
  Hebe, V:410
  Pauline Borghese as Venus Victorious, V:410
  Theseus and the Minotaur, V:408
  Tomb of Archduchess Maria Christina, V:410
  Tomb of Pope Clement XIV, V:408
  Venus Italica, V:411
Cantor, Georg, V:639
Canudo, Ricciotto, VII:1274
Canute VI, II:733, 932
Canute the Great, **II:201-205,** 315, 346, 426
Canutt, Yakima, IX:3901
Cão, Diego, III:215
Capek, Josef, VII:560, 561
Capek, Karel, **VII:560-562**
  Insect Play, The, VII:560
  Krakatit, VII:561
  Makropulos Secret, The, VII:561
  Musaion, VII:560
  Pragmatismus, VII:560
  President Masaryk Tells His Story, VII:560
  Veci kolemnás, VII:560
  War with the Newts, The, VII:561
Capel, Arthur "Boy," VII:648, 650
capitalism
  Beard, VII:222
  Bernstein, VII:292
  Blanc, V:259-262
  Brandeis, VII:419
  Engels, V:760-762
  Goldman, VIII:1411-1413
  Greenspan, VIII:1471
  Keynes, VIII:1954
  Kollwitz, VIII:2016
  Laski, VIII:2093, 2094

Lenin, VIII:2161
Luxemburg, VIII:2285-2287
Malthus, VI:1468
Marx, VI:1492-1494
Morgan, VI:1579, 1581, 1582
Niebuhr, VIII:2737
Peru, VIII:1585
Randolph, IX:3113, 3114
Sinclair, IX:3428, 3429
Smith, IV:1249-1251
Veblen, IX:3805, 3806
Weber, IX:3910, 3911
Zetkin, IX:4112, 4113
capital punishment. *See* death penalty
Capodistrias, John, VI:2417, 2418
Capone, Alphonse, **VII:563-566**
Capote, Truman, **VII:567-570;** IX:3303
Answered Prayers, VII:568, 569
Beat the Devil, VII:567
Breakfast at Tiffany's, VII:567
Dogs Bark, The, VII:568
Glass House, The, VII:568
Grass Harp, The, VII:567
House of Flowers, VII:567
In Cold Blood, VII:568, 569
Innocents, The, VII:567
"Miriam" VII:567
Muses are Heard, The, VII:567
Music for Chameleons, VII:569
Other Voices, Other Rooms, VII:567
Tree of Night and Other Stories, A, VII:567
Cappadocia, I:353, 558, 896
Caprini, Palazzo. *See* Raphael, House of
Caprivi, Leo von, V:1131
Caraffa, Gian Petro, III:597
Caratacus, I:136
Caravaggio, V:610
Carbo, Gaius Papirius, I:758
Carbonari, the, VI:1514
Carcophorus, I:417
Carden, John, V:635, 636
Cárdenas, Lázaro, VII:543, **571-574**
Cárdenas, López de, III:181, 182
Cardinals, College of
Gregory VII, II:397
Innocent IV, II:516
John XXIII, VIII:1859, 1860
Paul VI, IX:2916
Urban II, II:929, 930
cardiology. *See* heart
Cardozo, Benjamin Nathan, **VII:575-578**
Growth of the Law, The, VII:576
Nature of the Judicial Process, The, VII:576
Paradoxes of Legal Science, The, VII:576
Care of Dependent Children, Conference on the, IX:3838
Carey, George Saville, VI:1259
Carey, Harry, Sr., IX:3902
Carey, Nance, VI:1259
Carib Indians, III:631
Carignano, IV:584
Carleton, Guy, **IV:246-249**
Carlevaris, Luca, IV:242
Carlism, V:414, 415
Carlos II, IV:1448
Carlos, Don, **V:413-415**
Carlson, Chester F., **VII:579-581**
Carlyle, Thomas, V:59, **416-419,** 755; VI:2370, 2371
Chartism, V:417
French Revolution, The, V:417; IX:2871
History of Friedrich II of Prussia, The, V:417
Latter-Day Pamphlets, V:417
Past and Present, V:417
Reminiscences, V:418
Sartor Resartus, V:416, 757; VI:2370
Carmelites
Cruz, IV:382
John of the Cross, III:401-403
Lorenzettis, II:595
Stein, IX:3508, 3509
Teresa of Ávila, III:714
Venette, II:935, 937
Carnap, Rudolf, **VII:582-584**
Formalization of Logic, VII:583
Introduction to Semantics, VII:583
Introduction to Symbolic Logic and Its Applications, VII:582
Logical Foundations of Probability, VII:583
Logical Syntax of Language, The, VII:583
Logische Aufblau der Welt, Der, VII:582
Meaning and Necessity, VII:583
Carnarvon, Fifth Earl of, I:905, 906
Carneades, I:725
Carnegie, Andrew, **V:420-424,** 662; VI:1898
Carnegie Corporation of New York, V:423
Carnegie Corporation Survey of the Negro, VII:501
Carnegie Endowment for International Peace, VII:525
Carnegie Foundation, V:749; VII:1169
Carnegie Steel Company, V:421; VIII:2480
Carnot, Sadi, VI:1343-1345; VIII:2714
Caroline, Fort, III:508

Caroline, Queen, IV:535; V:315, 406
Caroline Affair, VI:2011
Carolingian Empire
  Charlemagne, II:228-230
  Charles Martel, II:242-244
  Louis II the German, II:599-602
  Philip the Good, II:740
  Rabanus Maurus, II:766-768
Carolus-Duran, Charles Jurand, VI:1961
Carpenter Center for Visual Arts, VIII:2139
Carpentier, Georges, VII:902
Carpini, Giovanni da Pian del, **II:206-209**
  Historia Mongalorum quos nos Tartaros appellamus, II:208
Carr, Thomas, VI:1480
Carracci family, **III:125-128**
  Bean Eater, The, (Annibale) III:126
  History of Jason, III:125
  Last Communion of Saint Jerome, The, (Agostino) III:126
  Madonna of the Bargellini Family, (Ludovico) III:126
  Madonna with Saint John Evangelist and Saint Catherine, (Annibale) III:126
Carranza, Venustiano, VII:542; IX:2782, 3813, 4106
Carrel, Alexis, VIII:2196
Carrera, José, VI:1688
Carrillo, Alfonso, III:260
Carroll, Charles, **IV:250-253**
Carroll, James, VI:1858, 1859
Carroll, Lewis, **V:425-428**
  Alice's Adventures in Wonderland, V:427, 428; VIII:2143
  Hunting of the Snark, The, V:427
  Silvie and Bruno, V:427
  Through the Looking-Glass, V:427
Carron ironworks, IV:1183-1185
Carson, Kit, **V:429-433**
Carson, Rachel, **VII:585-588**
  Edge of the Sea, The, VII:586
  Sea Around Us, The, VII:586
  Silent Spring, VII:585-588
  "Undersea," VII:585
  Under the Sea-Wind, VII:585
Cartegena, Juan de, III:454
Carter, Howard, I:905, 906
Carter, Jimmy, **VII:589-593**
  Blood of Abraham, The, VII:591
  Bush, VII:521
  Clinton, Bill, VII:707
  Clinton, Hillary Rodham, VII:714
  Dole, VII:948
  Ford, VII:1182
  Jordan, VIII:1889
  Keeping Faith, VII:591
  Khomeini, VIII:1958, 1959
  Kirkpatrick, VIII:1995
  Presley, IX:3079
  Reagan, IX:3138
  Sadat, IX:3290
  Why Not the Best?, VII:590
Carteret, Phillip, IV:180
Cartesianism. *See* Descartes, René
Carthage
  Archimedes, I:79
  Cato the Censor, I:164
  Flaubert, V:798
  Hanno, I:368-370
  Second Punic War, I:336, 364-366, 535-537, 739-741, 761
  Third Punic War, I:757-759
Carthaginian Peace, I:366
Cartier, George Étienne, VI:1436-1438; VIII:2100
Cartier, Jacques, **III:129-131**
Cartier-Bresson, Henri, **VII:594-597**
  Decisive Moment, The, VII:595
  retour, Le, VII:595
  Victoire, VII:595
cartoons
  Geisel, VII:1329-1331
  Disney, VII:940, 941
  Nast, VI:1627-1629
  Orozco, IX:2837
  Thurber, IX:3677, 3678
Carus, I:263
Caruso, Enrico, **VII:598-601**
Carver, George Washington, **VII:602-605**
Casablanca Conference, VIII:1737, 2643
Casals, Pablo, **VII:606-609**
  Hymn to the United Nations, VII:608
Casals Festival, VII:608
Casanova, Giovanni Giacomo, **IV:254-256**
  Memoirs of Jacques Casanova de Seingalt, IV:256
Casella, Mario, II:286
Casimir the Great, **II:210-214**
Cassady, Neal, VIII:1945, 1946
Cassander, I:516
Cassatt, Mary, **V:434-437**
Cassian, John, II:137, 138
Cassin, René, **VII:610-613**
Cassini, Giovanni, IV:600

Cassino, Monte, II:137
Cassiodorus, **II:215-217**
Commentary on the Psalms, II:216
Deorthographia, II:216
Historia ecclesiastica tripartita, II:216
History of the Goths, II:215, 897
Cassirer, Ernst, **VII:614-616**
Essay on Man, An, VII:615
Kant's Life and Thought, VII:614
Language and Myth, VIII:2088
Myth of the State, The, VII:615
Philosophy of Symbolic Forms, The, VII:615
Philosophy of the Enlightenment, The, VII:615
Substance and Function, VII:614
Cassirer, Paul, VIII:2013
Cassius, I:141, 142, **159-161**
Cassius, Avidius, I:525
Castelli, Benedetto, IV:1331
Castelli, Francesco. *See* Borromini, Francesco
Castiglione, Baldassare, III:645
Castillo, Ramón S., IX:2970
Castle Howard, IV:635, 1352, 1353
Castlereagh, Viscount, V:406, **438-442;** VI:1396
Castro, Fidel, VII:**617-620**; VIII:1494-1496
Catalonia, II:79, 529
Cat and Mouse Act of 1913, IX:2873
Catesby, Robert, III:258, 259
Catharist movement, II:49, 301, 302, 511
Cathay, II:988
Cather, Willa, V:1228-1230; **VII:621-626**
Alexander's Bridge, VII:624
April Twilights, VII:623
Death Comes for the Archbishop, VII:625
My Antonia, VII:621, 624
Old Beauty and Others, The, VII:625
One of Ours, VII:621, 624
O Pioneers!, VII:624; V:1230
Professor's House, The, VII:625
Song of the Lark, VII:621, 624
Troll Garden, The, VII:623
Catherine II. *See* Catherine the Great
Catherine de Médicis, **III:132-135**
Henry IV, III:333
Mary, Queen of Scots, III:475
Medici, Lorenzo de', III:498
Mornay, III:537
Nostradamus, III:568
Catherine of Aragon, **III:136-139**
Boleyn, III:68
Clement VII, III:167
Cranmer, III:204-206
Fisher, III:264, 265
Henry VIII, III:349, 351, 732, 733
Mary I, III:479
Wolsey, III:786
Catherine of Siena, Saint, **II:218-222**
Dialogue, The, II:220
Life of Catherine of Siena, The, II:220, 221
Catherine the Great, **IV:257-260**
Alexander I, V:44
Brown, IV:206
Dickinson, IV:414
Frederick the Great, IV:505
Jones, IV:741
Joseph II, IV:752
Peter III, IV:1087, 1089
Suvorov, IV:1298, 1299
Catholic Association, VI:1681, 1683, 1753
Catholic Center Party, VII:1102-1104
Catholic Committee, VI:1680
Catholic Emancipation, V:995; VI:1680-1683
Catholic League, IV:451, 452
Catholic Liberalism, VIII:2100
Catholicon, III:330
Catholic Reformation. *See* Counter-Reformation
Catholic Revival. *See* Counter-Reformation
Catholic Worker movement, VII:850-852
Catilina, Lucius Sergius, I:196, 743
Catlin, George, V:234, **443-445**
Cato the Censor, **I:162-165**
Ad filium, I:164
De re militari, I:164
Ennius, I:287
On Agriculture, I:164
Origines, I:164
Pompey the Great, I:680, 681
Verrius Flaccus, I:930
Cato the Elder, I:759
Cato the Younger, I:140, **166-168,** 743
Cato Uticensis. *See* Cato the Younger
Catt, Carrie Chapman, VII:23, **627-630**
Cattle Problem, I:79
Catullus, **I:169-172,** 704
Cauchon, Pierre, III:398
Cauldron, Battle of the, IX:3214
Cavalcanti, Guido, **II:223-225,** 286
New Life, The, II:223
Cavalier Parliament, IV:1230
Cavalier Poets, VIII:2530
Cavelier, René-Robert. *See* La Salle, Sieur de
Cavendish, Henry, **IV:261-264,** 976
Cavendish, Thomas, **III:140-142,** 213
Cavendish, William, IV:662

Cavendish Laboratory, VII:412, 635-637, 797; IX:3277, 3279, 3897
Cavour, Count, **V:446-449;** VI:1783
Caxton, William, I:180; **III:143-146,** 457
  Arte and Crafte to Know Well to Die, The, III:143
  Canterbury Tales, The, III:144
  Dicteis or Sayenges of the Phylosophers, III:144
  Game and Playe of the Chesse, The, III:143
  Myrrour of the Worlde, The, III:144
  Recuyell of the Historyes of Troye, III:143
Cayley, Sir George, **V:450-452**
Cayor, kingdom of, V:764
Cazes, Pierre-Jacques, IV:275
CBS, VII:177; VIII:2662, 2664, 2665
CCAR. *See* Central Conference of American Rabbis
CDU. *See* Christian Democratic Union
Cecchetti, Enrico, IX:2937, 2939
Cecil, Robert. *See* Salisbury, Third Marquess of
Cecil, William, **III:147-150,** 241, 660, 661; IV:330
Celestine I, I:937
Celestine V, II:171, 173
Cellini, Benvenuto, **III:151-154,** 168
  Life Benvenuto Cellini, The, III:153,154
  Perseus, III:153
Celsus, Aulus Cornelius, **I:173-175**
  De artibus, I:173
  Eight Books of Medicine, The, I:173-175
Celtiberians, I:758
Cem, III:51, 53
Cendrars, Blaise, VII:83
censorship
  Catherine the Great, IV:260
  Cato the Censor, I:162-165
  Claudius I, I:203
  Dreiser, VII:954, 955, 958; VIII:2484
  Forster, VII:1195
  Galileo, IV:521, 522
  Joyce, VIII:1892
  Kurosawa, VIII:2043, 2044
  Lawrence, VIII:2118, 2119
  Lessing, IV:844
  Mencken, VIII:2484
  Nazi Germany, VIII:1405
  Scipio Africanus, I:761, 762
  Wang Yang-ming, III:771
  West, IX:3949, 3950
Central African Federation, VII:531
Central Conference of American Rabbis, VI:2400, 2402
Central Intelligence Agency
  Bush, VII:521
  Cuba, VII:618; VIII:1930
  Eisenhower, VII:1044
  Guatemala, VIII:1494
  Mohammad Reza Shah Pahlavi, VIII:2567
  Sihanouk, IX:3417
Central Pacific Railroad, VI:2096-2099
Central Park, V:344; VI:1691, 1692
Ceolfrid, II:132
Ceraunus, I:716
Cerchi family, II:288
Cerealis, Petillius, I:137
Ceres, V:893, 894
CERN, VIII:2338; IX:3103
Cervantes, Miguel de, **IV:265-270**
  Commerce of Algiers, The, IV:266
  Don Quixote de la Mancha, IV:265-269, 1312
  Exemplary Novels, IV:268
  Galatea, IV:265, 266
  Numantia, IV:266
  Travels of Persiles and Sigismunda, The, IV:268
  Voyage to Parnassus, The, IV:268, 269
Césaire, Aimé, **VII:631-634;** IX:3391
  Discourse on Colonialism, VII:633
  Letter to Maurice Thorez, VII:632, 633
  My Native Land, VII:631-633
  Season in the Congo, A, VII:633
  Tempest, The, VII:633
  Toussaint Louverture, VII:633
  Trajedy of King Christopher, The, VII:633
Ceuta, III:354
Cézanne, Paul, **V:453-456**
  Braque, VII:431
  Delaunay, VII:888, 889
  Denis, VII:910
  Léger, VIII:2154
  Milhaud, VIII:2528
  Monet, VIII:2581
  Picasso, IX:2998
  Poussin, IV:1120
  Renoir, VI:1870
  Self-Portrait, V:454
  Zola, VI:2420
Chacabuco, Chile, VI:1689
Chacón, Gonzalo, III:260
Chadwick, Edwin, **V:457-461**
  Internment Report, V:459
  Report on the Sanitary Condition of the Labouring Population, The, V:459
Chadwick, James, **VII:635-638;** VIII:1871, 1873
  Radiations from Radioactive Substances, VII:635
Chagall, Marc, **VII:639-642**
  Birthday, VII:639
  Double Portrait with a Glass of Wine, VII:639

Fiddler, The, VII:639
Firebird, VII:641
I and the Village, VII:639
Over the Town, VII:639
Praying Jew, The, VII:639
Rabbi of Vitebsk, VII:639
Self Portrait with Seven Fingers, VII:639
White Crucifixion, VII:641
Chaghatay tribes, II:884, 885
Chaghrï Beg, II:67, 677
Chaikin, Joseph, IX:3643
Chain, Ernst, VII:1167, 1173, 1174
Chait Singh, IV:632
Chalcedon, Council of, I:862, 863, 865, 866; II:820, 824
Chalcidian League, I:629
Chaldaean Oracles, I:684
Challenger space shuttle, VII:112, 113; IX:3179
Chalukya, II:430
Chamberlain, Austen, VII:169
Chamberlain, Joseph, **V:462-465,** 804; VII:643
Chamberlain, Neville, **VII:643-647**
Attlett, VII:138
Baldwin, VII:170
Beaverbrook, VII:236
Bevan, VII:304
Chamberlain, Joseph, V:464
Eden, VII:1016
Lyons, VIII:2294
Macmillan, VIII:2341
Reith of Stonehaven, IX:3148
Chamberlain, Wilt, IX:3271
Chamberlain of London v. Allen Evans, IV:906
chamber music
Bach, IV:78
Boccherini, IV:149
Borodin, V:286-288
Franck, V:832-834
Zwilich, IX:4121-4123
Chambers, Whittaker, VIII:1683-1685
Chambers, William, IV:206
Chambers v. Florida, VII:322
Champier, Symphorien, III:676
Champlain, Samuel de, **IV:271-274**
Champlain Canal, V:520
Chanca, III:577, 578
Chandasoka, I:112
Chanel, Coco, **VII:648-652;** VIII:2182
Chanel No. 5, VII:650, 651
Chang Chih-tung, **V:466-469**
Chang Chiu-ling, II:965, 966
Chang Lei, II:588
Chang-sun Wu-chi, II:877
Channing, William Ellery, **V:470-473;** VI:1336
Remarks on American Literature, V:472
Slavery, VI:1275
Chantelou, Paul Fréart de, IV:1119
Chanute, Octave, IX:4064
Chao Kao, I:178
Chao K'uang-yin. *See* T'ai Tsu
Chao Ming-ch'eng, II:588, 589
Chaplin, Charles, **VII:653-656,** 789; IX:3008, 3159
Circus, The, VII:654
Gold Rush, The, VII:654
Great Dictator, The, VII:654
Immigrant, The, VII:656
Jimmy the Fearless, VII:653
Kid, The, VII:653
King in New York, A, VII:655
Limelight, VII:655
Mabel's Strange Predicament, VII:653
Modern Times, VII:654
Monsieur Verdoux, VII:655
Tramp, The, VII:655, 656
Twenty Minutes of Love, VII:653
Woman of Paris, A, VII:654
Chapman, George, **III:155-158**
All Fools, III:155
Blind Beggar of Alexandria, The, III:155
Bussy D'Ambois, III:156, 157
Caesar and Pompey, III:157
Conspiracy and the Tragedy of Charles, Duke of Byron, The, III:157
Eastward Ho!, III:156
Gentleman Usher, The, III:155
Humorous Day's Mirth, An, III:155
Revenge of Bussy D' Ambois, The, III:156
Tragedy of Chabot, Admiral of France, The, III:157
Widow's Tears, The, III:156
Chapman, John. *See* Appleseed, Johnny
Chapman, J. Wilbur, IX:3583
Chapman, Leo, VII:627
Chapultepec, Battle of, VI:2011, 2012
Char, René, VII:387
Charaxus, I:750
Charbonneau, Toussaint, VI:1933
Charcot, Jean-Martin, VII:448, 1224
Chardin, Jean Siméon, **IV:275-278,** 488, 489
Chardin, Teilhard de, II:313
Charest, Jean, VII:550
Charity, Confraternity of, IV:1380, 1381
Charity, Daughters of, IV:1381
Charity, Missionaries of, IX:3636, 3637

Charity of St. Joseph, Sisters of, VI:2030, 2031
Charlemagne, **II:226-231**
  Alcuin, II:44, 46
  Augustine, I:129
  Charles the Bald, II:239, 240
  Louis II the German, II:601
  Rabanus Maurus, II:766
  Widukind, II:973-975
Charles I (of England), **IV:279-282**
  Buckingham, IV:212
  Charles II, IV:283
  Clarendon, IV:308, 309
  Coke, IV:333, 334
  Cotton, IV:372
  Cromwell, IV:378, 380
  English Civil War, IV:99, 132, 501
  Hale, IV:596
  James I, IV:700
  James II, IV:703
  Jones, IV:735-737
  Jonson, IV:748
  Lambert, IV:789, 790
  Laud, IV:797, 799
  Milton, IV:960
  Pride, IV:1126-1128
  Pym, IV:1141, 1142
  Shaftesbury, IV:1228
  Strafford, IV:1285-1288
  Winthrop, IV:1463
Charles I (of Portugal), III:453
Charles II (of England), **IV:283-286**
  Boyle, IV:187
  Clarendon, IV:309-311
  Cromwell, IV:380
  Dryden, IV:424, 425
  Godolphin, IV:552
  Hale, IV:597
  Hobbes, IV:665
  James II, IV:703, 704
  Lambert, IV:791
  Leeds, IV:821-823
  Locke, IV:855-857
  Mather, Increase, IV:938, 939
  Monck, IV:973
  Monmouth, IV:980-982
  Oates, IV:1038, 1039
  Parliament, IV:99, 219
  Pride, IV:1127
  Purcell, IV:1137, 1138
  Scotland, IV:239
  Shaftesbury, IV:1228
  Vanbrugh, IV:1351
  Virginia land grants, IV:80
  Wren, IV:1480-1482
Charles II (of France), II:24
Charles III (of Spain), IV:147, 148, **287-289,** 569, 570, 1325
Charles IV (Holy Roman Emperor), **II:235-238,** 729, 730, 791, 792, 969
Charles IV (of Spain), V:413
Charles V (Holy Roman Emperor), **III:159-162**
  Alva, III:18-20
  Alvarado, III:23
  Bucer, III:103
  Christine de Pizan, II:260, 261
  Clement VII, III:166, 167
  Coronado, III:180
  Cortés, III:190
  Edward VI, III:239
  Francis I, III:274, 275, 277
  Marguerite of Navarre, III:468
  Mary I, III:479, 480
  Paul III, III:597, 598
  Süleyman the Magnificent, III:707
  Titian, III:721
  Vesalius, III:755
  Vitoria, III:768
  Wolsey, III:786
Charles VI (of France), III:338-340
Charles VI (Holy Roman Emperor), IV:914; 1384
Charles VII (of France), III:396, 398, 399, 434
Charles VII (Holy Roman Emperor), IV:915
Charles VIII (of France), III:14, 16, 48, 405, 668, 682
Charles IX (of France), III:132, 133
Charles X (of France), VI:2226, 2238
Charles X (of Sweden), IV:304, 838
Charles XII (of Sweden), **IV:290-292,** 924, 1082, 1084
Charles XIV John (of Sweden), **V:474-476**
Charles, Prince (of England), VII:923-925, 1062, 1064; VIII:2644, 2645
Charles, Ray, **VII:657-659**
  "America the Beautiful," VII:658
  "Born to Lose," VII:658
  "Busted," VII:658
  "Crying Time," VII:658
  "Georgia on My Mind," VII:657
  "Greenbacks," VII:657
  "Hit The Road, Jack," VII:657
  "I Can't Stop Loving You," VII:658
  "I Got A Woman," VII:657
  "It Should Have Been Me," VII:657
  Message to the People, VII:658

Modern Sounds in Country and Western Music, VII:657
"One Mint Julep," VII:657
"Song for You, A," VII:658
"Unchain My Heart," VII:657
"What'd I Say?," VII:657
Charles d'Orléans, **II:232-234**
Charles Martel, II:226, **242-244**
Charles of Anjou, II:606
Charles of Austria, III:241; IV:1279
Charles River Bridge v. Warren Bridge, VI:2191
Charles the Bald, **II:239-241,** 599-601, 773
Charles the Bold, **III:163-165,** 491
Charles the Fat, II:794
Charles the Simple, II:794
Charles the Wise. *See* Charles V
Charleston, South Carolina, V:859
Charlestown Neck, Battle of. *See* Bunker Hill, Battle of
Charlier, Jean. *See* Gerson, Jean de
Charlottetown Accord, VIII:2656
Charmides, I:795
Chartier, Alain, **II:245-247**
"Belle Dame sans merci, La," II:246
Epistola de Puella, II:245
Invective Quadrilogue, The, II:246, 247
Chartreuse of Champmol, II:832
Chase, Salmon P., **V:477-480,** 551, 552
Chase, Samuel, **IV:293-296**
Chastaigner, Louis de, III:671, 672
Chateaubriand, **V:481-484**
Atala, V:482
Genius of Christianity, The, V:482, 483
Historical, Political, Moral Essay on Revolutions, An, V:482
Martyrs, The, V:482
Natchez, The, V:483
On Buonaparte and the Bourbons, V:483
René, V:482, 483
Chatham, First Earl of. *See* Pitt the Elder, William
Chaucer, Geoffrey, **II:248-252**
Boece, II:250
Book of the Duchess, II:248, 250, 251
Canterbury Tales, The, II:130, 150, 250, 251, 776; III:144; IV:138
Consolation of Philosophy, The, II:250
House of Fame, The, II:250, 251
Legend of Good Women, The, II:250
Parliament of Fowls, The, II:250
Troilus and Criseyde, II:250
Chauliac, Guy de. *See* Guy de Chauliac
Chautemps, Camille, VII:336
Chavez, César, VIII:1762-1764
Chekhov, Anton, **V:485-488;** VIII:1442, 1444
Cherry Orchard, The, V:486; IX:3403
Ostrov Sakhalin, V:486
Pystrye rasskazy, V:485
Seagull, The, V:486; IX:3487
Tales of Melpomene, V:485
Three Sisters, The, V:486; VIII:2143
Uncle Vanya, V:486
V synerkakh, V:485
Wood Demon, The, V:485
Cheltenham Ladies' College, V:157-159
Cheng Ch'eng-kung, **IV:297-299**
Cheng Chih-lung, IV:297
Cheng Ho, **II:253-256,** 1023
Cheng-shih dynasty, I:949
Ch'en-hao, III:772
Ch'en Hui, II:482
Ch'en Tu-hsiu, **VII:660-663**
Chermoye, Philip, III:763
Chernyshevsky, Nikolay, V:1100, 1101; VIII:2675
What Is to Be Done?, V:689; VI:1612; VIII:1411
Cherokee Indians
Boone, IV:163
Houston, V:1137
Lockwood, VI:1407
Mankiller, VIII:2389, 2390
Rogers, IX:3204
Ross, VI:1910-1912
Scott, VI:2011
Sequoyah, VI:2025, 2027, 2028
Cherokee Nation v. Georgia, VI:2149
Chersonese, I:254, 553, 554
Chesapeake Bay, battle in, IV:180
Chesterfield Act, IV:1076
Cheves, Langdon, V:225
Cheyenne Indians, V:575, 576
Chiang Ch'ing, VII:689; VIII:2214
Chiang Kai-shek, **VII:664-667**
Ch'en Tu-hsiu, VII:662
Chou En-lai, VII:676, 677
Chu Teh, VII:688
Ho Chi Minh, VIII:1700
Kuo Mo-jo, VIII:2034
Liu Shao-ch'i, VIII:2212
Luce, VIII:2262
P'eng Te-huai, IX:2954
Tseng Kuo-fan, VI:2262
Wang Ching-wei, IX:3878, 3879
Chicago
Addams, VII:22, 23
Altgeld, V:54-56

Burnham, V:365, 367, 368
Capone, VII:563-565
Darrow, VII:839
Field, V:783-786
meat inspection, IX:3428
Mies van der Rohe, VIII:2522, 2533
Perkins, IX:2961
Pullman Strike of 1894, VII:881
Sandburg, IX:3308, 3309
Ward, VI:2331-2334
Wells-Barnett, IX:3943, 3944
Wright, IX:4060
Chicago, University of
Eliade, VII:1056
Fermi, VII:1147
Field, V:785
Harper, V:1044-1047
Hutchins, VIII:1800-1802
Lathrop, VIII:2097
Millikan, VIII:2539
Palmer, VI:1717
Rockefeller, VI:1898
Talbot, IX:3603-3605
Veblen, IX:3806
Wach, IX:3829-3831
Chicago Lyric Opera, IX:3608
Chicago Opera Festival, VI:2167, 2168
Chicago Orchestra. *See* Chicago Symphony Orchestra
Chicago Plan of 1909, V:367
Chicago Sun-Times, V:786
Chicago Symphony Orchestra, VI:2230, 2232
Chicago White Sox, IX:3274
Chicago World's Fair of 1893. *See* World's Columbian Exposition
Chicherin, Georgi Vasilievich, VIII:2209
Chickamauga, Battle of, V:876
Chickasaw Indians, IV:1045
Ch'ien-lung, **IV:300-303**
Chien-wen, II:1022
Child, Lydia Maria, **V:489-492**
Appeal for the Indians, An, V:491
Appeal in Favor of That Class of Americans Called Africans, An, V:490, 491
Autumnal Leaves, V:491
Fact and Fiction: A Collection of Stories, V:491
First Settlers of New England, The, V:489
Freedmen's Book, The, V:491
Frugal Housewife, The, V:489
Hobomok, V:489
Juvenile Miscellany, V:489
Letters from New York, V:490, 491
Children's Bureau, United States, VIII:2096, 2097, 2099
Children's Houses, VIII:2598
children's literature
Alger, V:51-53
Andersen, V:58-60
Baum, V:154-156
Burnett, V:361-364
Calder, VII:539
Carroll, V:425, 427, 428
Geisel, VII:1329-1331
Lewis, VIII:2167-2169
Milne, VIII:2543-2545
Newbery, IV:1019-1021
Potter, IX:3063-3065
Sandburg, IX:3310
Sendak, IX:3387-3389
Stevenson, VI:2139, 2141, 2142
Tolkien, IX:3696-3698
Wilder, IX:3992-3994
Chimalpopoca, III:378
Ch'in Dynasty, I:176-179; II:1018, 1019
See also Eastern Chin Dynasty; Later Chin Dynasty
Chinese Civil War, VIII:2189, 2213
Chinese Communist Party
Ch'en Tu-hsiu, VII:660-662
Chiang Kai-shek, VII:664-667
Chou En-lai, VII:676-678
Chu Teh, VII:687-689
Deng Xiaoping, VII:905-907
Kuo Mo-jo, VIII:2033-2035
Lin Piao, VIII:2189-2191
Li Peng, VIII:2178-2180
Liu Shao-ch'i, VIII:2212-2214
Lu Hsün, VIII:2252-2254
Mao Tse-tung, VIII:2400-2402
P'eng Te-huai, IX:2954
Sun Yat-sen, IX:3579
Wang Ching-wei, IX:3879, 3879
Chinese Nationalist Party. *See* Kuomintang
Ch'ing Dynasty
Abahai, IV:1-3
Chang Chih-tung, V:466-469
Cheng Ch'eng-kung, IV:297
Ch'ien-lung, IV:300, 302
Dorgon, IV:421-423
Hung Hsiu-Ch'üan, V:1165, 1166
Li Hung-chang, VI:1362, 1354, 1365
Lin Tse-hsü, VI:1376-1379
Sun Yat-sen, IX:3578-3580

Tseng Kuo-fan, VI:2260-2262
Wang Ching-wei, IX:3879
Ching Hsiang, I:188
Ch'ing-liu, V:466
Ch'in Kuei, II:1019
Ch'in Shih Huang-ti, **I:176-179**
Chionites, I:779, 780
Chios, I:420
Chiplunkar, Vishnu Krishna, IX:3682
Chippewa, Battle of, VI:2010
Chippewa Indians, VII:1092, 1093
Chirac, Jacques, VIII:2560
Chiricahua, V:917
Chisholm, Shirley, **VII:668-672**
Chisholm v. Georgia, IV:713, 1458
chivalry
Balboa, III:45-47
Cervantes, IV:268, 269
Charles the Bold, III:163
Froissart, II:368
Henry the Navigator, III:354
Sidney, III:693
Chlorus, Constantius, I:375
Chlotsuinda, II:41
Choctaw Indians, III:700
Choeikai, IX:3337
Chogaku temple, II:924
Chomsky, Noam, **VII:673-675**
Aspects of the Theory of Syntax, VII:673
Counter-Revolutionary Violence, VII:674
Language and Mind, VII:674
Sound Pattern of English, The, VII:674
Chopin, Frédéric, **V:493-496;** VI:1392
Chopin, Kate, **V:497-500**
At Fault, V:497, 498
Awakening, The, V:497-499
Bayou Folk, V:498
Night in Acadie, A, V:498
"Story of an Hour, The," V:498
Choshu, VI:1937
Chotek, Sophie, VII:1197-1199
Chou, Duke of, I:224
Chou Dynasty, I:222-224, 544
Chou En-lai, **VII:676-679**
Chu Teh, VII:688
Deng Xiaoping, VII:906
Khrushchev, VIII:1963
Nixon, VIII:2759
Chou Shu-jên. *See* Lu Hsün
Chou Wen-chung, IX:3796
Chremonidean War, I:717
Chrétien, Jean, **VII:680-682**
Chrétien de Troyes, **II:257-259,** 1005
Cligés, II:257, 258
Erec and Enide, II:257, 258
Lancelot, II:257, 258
Perceval, II:257, 258, 1005
Yvain, II:257, 258
Christ, Church of, V:351, 401, 403
Christ, Disciples of, V:401, 403
Christ, Jesus. *See* Jesus Christ
Christian IV, III:79
Christian, Charlie, VIII:1420
Christian, Fletcher, IV:143, 145
Christian Association of Washington, V:401
Christian Baptist, V:402
Christian Connexion, IV:895
Christian Democratic Party of Italy, VII:864, 865
Christian Democratic Union, VII:27; VIII:2009, 2010
Christian Science. *See* Christ, Scientist, Church of
Christian Science Monitor, The, V:741
Christian Trade Union Movement, VII:1102
Christian Union, V:175
Christie, Agatha, **VII:683-686**
Curtain; Poirot's Last Case, VII:685
Mousetrap, The, VII:685
Murder at the Vicarage, VII:685
Murder of Roger Ackroyd, The, VII:683, 685
Murder on the Orient Express, VII:685
Mysterious Affair at Styles, The, VII:683
Mystery of the Blue Train, The, VII:683
Secret Adversary, The, VII:683
Sleeping Murder, VII:685
Ten Little Indians, VII:685
Witness for the Prosecution, VII:685
Christina, **IV:304-307,** 360, 1052, 1053, 1213; V:708
Christine de Pizan, **II:260-264**
Book of the City of Ladies, The, II:261-263
Dit de la rose, Le, II:261
"Dittié sur Jeanne d'Arc," II:263
Épistre du dieu d'amours, L', II:261
Livre de la mutacion de fortune, Le, II:261
Livre de la paix, Le, II:263
Livre des trois vertus, Le, II:262
Livre du chemin de long éstude, Le, II:261
Christophe, Henri, **V:501, 502;** VII:633
Christopher, Saint, **I:180-183**
Christy Minstrels, V:811
Chrysler Corporation, VII:112
Chrysogonus, I:195
Chrysoloras, III:93

Chrysostom, Saint John, **I:184-186,** 861
On the Priesthood, I:184
Chuang-tzu, **I:190-193**
Chu Hsi, **II:265-267,** 841
Four Books, II:266, 267
Reflections on Things at Hand, II:266
Church, Benjamin, IV:955
church and state
Acton, V:11
Ambrose, I:45
Canada, V:320
Frankfurter, VII:1214
Gibbons, V:921
Herriot, VIII:1644
O'Connell, V:1680-1683
Peter the Great, IV:1032
Pufendorf, IV:1135
Williams, IV:1451-1453
Church Council of 1666, IV:1032
Churchill, John. *See* Marlborough, First Duke of
Churchill, Lord Randolph, VI:1945; VII:691, 819
Churchill, Sarah. *See* Marlborough, Duchess of
Churchill, Sir Winston, **VII:691-694**
Alanbrooke, VII:46, 47
Asquith, VII:122, 123
Atlantic Charter, VIII:2257
Attlee, VII:138
Baldwin, VII:169, 170
Beaverbrook, VII:236
Bevan, VII:304, 306
Beveridge, VII:308
Butler, VII:530, 531
Canada, VII:365; VIII:1984
Chamberlain, VII:646
Chanel, VII:651
de Gaulle, VII:866, 867
Eden, VII:1016, 1017
George VI, VII:1344-1346
Heath, VIII:1607
History of the English Speaking Peoples, A, VII:694
Hopkins, VIII:1737, 1739
Inönü, VIII:1813
Macmillan, VIII:2341
Marshall, VIII:2431
Monnet, VIII:2583
Mountbatten, VIII:2643, 2644
Reith, IX:3147, 3148
Roosevelt, IX:3225
Second War, The, VII:694
Sutherland's portrait, IX:3588
Chu Teh, **VII:687-690**
Chu Ti. *See* Yung-lo
Ch'ü Yüan, **I:187-189**
"Great Summons," I:188
"In Praise of the Orange Tree," I:187
Li Sao, The, I:188
Nine Songs, The, I:187
"Princess of the Hsiang, The," I:187
CIA. *See* Central Intelligence Agency
Cibber, Colley, IV:1352, 1353
Cibber v. Sloper, IV:904
Cicero, **I:194-197**
Cassius, I:159
De oratore, I:787, 788
gladiators, I:814
Isocrates, I:456, 458
On Friendship, I:758
On Old Age, I:194
Philippics, I:69
Plutarch, I:671
Posidonius, I:687
Pro Archia, II:728
Pro Quinctio, I:194
Pro Roscio Amerino, I:194
Regulus, I:741
Sallust, I:743
Varro, I:918-921
Cicero, Illinois, VII:563, 564
Cid, El, **II:268-271**
Cigar-makers' Union, V:956
Cilicia, I:196
Cimabue, **II:272, 273,** 306, 388
Madonna Enthroned, II:273
Rucellai *Madonna,* II:273
Cimbri, I:529
Cimon, **I:198-202**
Aspasia, I:115
Miltiades the Younger, I:553
Pericles, I:609
Polygnotus, I:676, 677
Cinadon, I:17
Cincinnati Reds, IX:3239, 3240
Cincinnati Penny Post, VI:2015
Cinématograph, VIII:2278
Cinna, Lucius Cornelius, I:159, 160, 530, 834
CIO. *See* Congress of Industrial Organizations
Cione, Andrea di. *See* Orcagna, Andrea
Cisco Kid, V:1098
Cistercian Order, II:143-145, 534, 995
Cité Industrielle, VII:1308-1310
Citroën, André-Gustave, **VII:695-698**
City Dionysia. *See* Greater Dionysia
Civil Engineering, Institution for, VI:2209, 2210

Civilian Conservation Corps, VIII:2297
Civil Rights Act of 1866, V:1235
Civil Rights Act of 1875, V:697
Civil Rights Act of 1964
  Abernathy, VII:9, 10, 12
  Dole, VII:948
  Humphrey, VIII:1784
  Johnson, VIII:1867, 1868
  King, VIII:1971, 1973, 1974
  sexual harassment, VIII:2325
Civil Rights Commission, U.S., IX:3858
Civil Rights Memorial, VIII:2185-2187
Civil War, United States. *See* United States Civil War
Clagny, Château de, IV:901
Clairmont, Claire, VI:2048, 2053, 2054
Clairvaux, II:143-145
Clan-na-Gael, V:1123, 1124
Clanton family, V:736
Clapham Sect, IV:1435, 1436
Clare, Gilbert de. *See* Gloucester, Earl of
Clarence, Duke of, III:647, 649, 650
Clarendon, Constitutions of, II:49, 128-130, 446
Clarendon Code, IV:284, 310, 598
Clarendon, First Earl of, **IV:308-311,** 821
  Autobiography, IV:308, 310, 311
  History of the Rebellion and Civil Wars in England, IV:308, 310, 311
Clari, Robert de, II:943
Clark, George Rogers, IV:164, 198, **312-316**
Clark, Joe, VIII:2655; IX:3345, 3733
Clark, Ramsey, VIII:2435
Clark, William, V:443; **VI:1358-1361,** 1933-1935
Clarke, Arthur C., VI:2304
Clarke, Charles Cowden, VI:1264, 1266
Clarke, Samuel, IV:831
Clarksville, Indiana, IV:312, 314, 315
classical music
  Beethoven, V:178-181
  Bernstein, VII:295, 296, 298
  Gluck, IV:549-551
  Mozart, IV:1003, 1005, 1006
  Segovia, IX:3383-3386
  Telemann, IV:1319
  See also conducting, orchestral; opera; symphonies
Claude, Georges, **VII:699-701**
  Liquid Air, Oxygen, Nitrogen, VII:699
Claudel, Paul, VIII:2525, 2526
Claude Lorrain, **IV:317-320**
  Ascanius and the Stag, IV:318
  Harbor Scene, IV:318
  Liber veritatis, IV:317
  Marriage of Isaac and Rebecca, The, IV:318
  Mill, The, IV:317
Claude Neon Company, VII:700
Claudian, I:825, 826
Claudius I, **I:203-206,** 550, 551, 577, 770, 772
Claus, Daniel, IV:199
Clausewitz, Carl von, **V:503-506,** 940, 942; VI:1969, 1971; VIII:2267
  On War, V:503-505, 942
Clausius, Rudolf, VIII:2713
Clay, Cassius Marcellus, Jr.. *See* Ali, Muhammad
Clay, Henry, **V:507-511**
  Adams, John Quincy, V:22
  Cushing, V:582
  Fillmore, V:792, 793
  Jackson, V:1197
  Monroe, VI:1573
  Polk, VI:1802, 1803
  Tyler, VI:2289, 2290
Claypoole, John, IV:1193
Clazomenae, I:47
Cleanthes of Assos, I:970; IV:684
Cleisthenes of Athens, **I:207-209,** 554
Clemenceau, Georges, **VII:702-705;** IX:3045
  Grandeur and Misery of Victory, The, VII:705
Clemens, Flavius, I:210, 211
Clemens, Samuel Langhorne. *See* Twain, Mark
Clement I, **I:210-213**
  First Epistle of Clement to the Corinthians, I:211, 212
  Recognitions, I:210
  Second Epistle of Clement to the Corinthians, I:212
Clement III, II:396
Clement IV, II:112, 985
Clement V, II:790
Clement VI, II:235, 236, 790, 792
Clement VII, **III:166-168**
  Boleyn, III:66, 68
  Catherine de Médicis, III:132
  Catherine of Aragon, III:138
  Cellini, III:151, 152
  Franco-Turkish War, III:160
  Guicciardini, III:325, 326
  Machiavelli, III:450, 451
  Medici, Lorenzo de', III:498
  Michelangelo, III:519
  Paul III, III:595
  Wolsey, III:786
Clement VIII, III:334
Clement IX, IV:709

Clement XIV, V:408
Clement of Rome. *See* Clement I
Cleomenes I, **I:214-215**
Cleomenes II, **I:215**
Cleomenes III, **I:215-216**
Cleon, I:88
Cleopatra VII, **I:218-221**
  Antony, I:70, 71
  Augustus, I:133
  Caesar, I:149, 150
  Propertius, I:703, 704
Clephane, James O., VI:1541
Clerici, Palazzo, IV:1324
Clérisseau, Charles-Louis, IV:8
Clermont, Council of, II:930
Clerville, Chevalier de, IV:1358
Cleveland, Grover, **V:512-516**
  Altgeld, V:55
  Blaine, V:256
  Bryan, VII:479
  Godkin, VIII:1402
  Harrison, V:1054, 1055
  Liliuokalani, VI:1374
  Lockwood, VI:1408
  Lodge, VIII:2221
  Morgan, VI:1582
  Nast, VI:1628
  Pullman Strike of 1894, VII:881
Cleveland, Reverend James, VII:1216
Cleveland Orchestra, VII:389
Cleveland Penny Post, VI:2015
Clifford, Sir Thomas, IV:285
Cline, Patsy, VIII:2080, 2081
Clinton, Bill, **VII:707-712**
  Albright, VII:50, 51
  Boutros-Ghali, VII:400
  Bush, VII:522
  Clinton, Hillary Rodham, VII:713-715
  Dole, VII:949
  Gore, VIII:1432, 1433
  Greenspan, VIII:1472, 1473
  Hobby, VIII:1705
  Latino cabinet appointments, IX:2842
  Perot, IX:2974, 2975
  Reno, IX:3154, 3155
  speed limit, VIII:2681
Clinton, DeWitt, **V:517-521**
Clinton, George, IV:321; V:369, 370, 517
Clinton, Sir Henry, IV:66, **321-324,** 367, 368, 677, 678
Clinton, Hillary Rodham, VII:50, 707, **713-716**
Clinton, James, IV:818
Clive, Robert, **IV:325-328,** 631, 632
Clodia, I:170
Clough, Arthur Hugh, V:69, 70
Clovis, II:226, **274-277**
Cluniacs, II:144, 994
Clurman, Harold, VII:794, 795
Clyfton, Richard, IV:189
Cnemon, I:539
Cnidian Lesche, I:676, 677
Cnidus, I:310, 412, 691
coal
  Brindley, IV:201, 202
  hydrogenation, VII:275-277
  Lewis, VIII:2170-2172
  mining, V:622, VI:2251
  Stephens, VI:2130
Coalbrookdale, IV:396-398
Coal Smoke Abatement Society, V:1115
Cobb, Ty, **VII:717-720**
Cobbett, William, **V:522-524**
  Advice to Young Men, V:523
  Farmer's Friend, The, V:523
  Parliamentary History of England, V:523
  Political Register, The, V:522-524
  Poor Man's Friend, The, V:523
  Rural Rides, V:524
  Soldier's Friend, The, V:522
Cobden, Richard, V:306, 307, **525-529**
  England, Ireland, and America, V:526
  Russia and the Eastern Question, V:526
Cobden-Chevalier Treaty, V:528
Cobham, Viscount, IV:1098
Cochise, V:915, 917
Cochlaeus, Johannes, III:736
Cock, Hieronymus, III:85
Cockerill, John A., VI:1825
Cocteau, Jean, **VII:721-724;** IX:3066, 3068, 3069, 3333
  Beauty and the Beast, VII:723, 724
  Blood of a Poet, The, VII:723, 724
  Cap de Bonne-Espérance, Le, VII:721
  Children of the Game, VII:723
  Difficulty of Being, The, VII:723
  Infernal Machine, The, VII:723, 724
  Orpheus, VII:721, 723, 724
  Parade, VII:721; VIII:2449
  Thomas the Imposter, VII:721
Codex Argenteus, I:909, 910
Codex Justinianus, II:555
Cody, William Frederick, **V:530-533**
  Calamity Jane, V:392

Hickok, V:1109
Oakley, VI:1677, 1678
Sitting Bull, VI:2072
Whitney, IX:3970
Coe, Sebastian, **VII:725-728**
Coele-Syria, I:63, 64
Cognac, League of, III:166, 326
Cogswell, Joseph, V:125
Cohen, Hermann, VII:614
Cohn, Ferdinand Julius, **V:534-536;** VI:1298
Cohn, Harry, VIII:1597
coinage
Altgeld, V:55, 56
Boulton, IV:182, 183
David I, II:292
Diocletian, I:265
Kanishka, I:496
Menander, I:541
Newton, IV:1027
COINTELPRO, VIII:1733
Coke, Sir Edward, **IV:329-335,** 700
Institutes, IV:333, 334
Reports, IV:333, 334
Colbert, Claudette, VII:119
Colbert, Jean-Baptiste, **IV:336-340**
Huygens, IV:695
Louis XIV, IV:866, 868, 869
Louvois, IV:871-873
Mansart, IV:899
Mazarin, IV:946, 947
Colborne, Sir John, VI:1449
Colburn, Zerah, V:1025
Coldstream Guards, IV:973
Cold War
Attlee, VII:139
Bevin, VII:313
Bradley, VII:405
Bush, VII:522
Gorbachev, IX:4086
Hammarskjöld, VIII:1530
Harriman, VIII:1562, 1563
Hiss, VIII:1683-1685
Hitler, VIII:1696
Hoover, VIII:1733
Japan, VIII:1810
Kapitsa, VIII:1908
Lippmann, VIII:2205
Molotov, VIII:2572
Neumann, VIII:2726
Oppenheimer, IX:2834
space exploration, VII:1272
Truman, IX:3742, 3743
Colebrooke, Henry, VI:1846
Colenso, John, VI:1505
Coleridge, Samuel Taylor, IV:156; V:381, **537-539,** 1012; VI:2406, 2407
Biographia Literaria, V:538
Christabel, V:537, 538
"Dejection: An Ode," V:538
"Frost at Midnight," V:538
"Kubla Khan," V:537
Lyrical Ballads, IV:114
"Pains of Sleep, The" V:538
Rime of the Ancient Mariner, The, IV:391; V:537, 538
"To William Wordsworth," V:538
Coleridge, Stephen, IX:3495
Colet, John, **III:169-171**
Colette, **VII:729-732**
Chéri, VII:730, 731
Claudine at School, VII:729
Claudine in Paris, VII:729
Claudine Married, VII:729
Creatures Great and Small, VII:729
Gigi, VII:731
Innocent Wife, The, VII:729
Last of Chéri, The, VII:730, 731
Mitsou: Or, How Girls Grow Wise, VII:730
Vagabond, The, VII:730
Coligny, Gaspard de, III:537
College Entrance Examination Board, VII:524
Colleoni, Bartolommeo, III:751, 752
Collier, Jeremy, IV:1352
Collins, Michael (Irish leader), **VII:733-736**
Collins, Michael (U.S. astronaut), VII:112
Collins, Norman, **VII:737-740**
Bat That Flits, The, VII:738
Bond Street Story, The, VII:738
Children of the Archbishop, VII:738
Dulcimer Street, VII:738
Facts of Fiction, The, VII:737, 738
Flames Coming Out of the Top, VII:737
Governor's Lady, The, VII:738
Husband's Story, The, VII:738
I Shall Not Want, VII:737
Love in Our Time, VII:737
Penang Appointment, VII:737
Quiet Lady, VII:738
Three Friends, The, VII:737
Trinity Town, VII:737
Collip, James Bertram, VII:189
Colombo, Mattero Realdo, III:676
Colonial Advocate, VI:1449, 1450
Colonna, Pompeo, III:167

Colorado
  Hayden, V:1072-1074
  mining industry, VIII:1881
  Pike, IV:1094, 1096, 1097
  women's suffrage, VII:627
Colorado River, VI:1810, 1812, 1813
Colosimo, Big Jim, BII:563
Colt, Samuel, **V:540-542**
Coltrane, John, **VII:741-744**
  Ascension, VII:742
  Ballads, VII:742
  Blue Train, VII:741
  Coltrane, VII:741
  Crescent, VII:742
  Giant Steps, VII:741
  John Coltrane and Johnny Hartman, VII:742
  Live at the Village Vanguard, VII:742
  Love Supreme, A, VII:742
  "My Favorite Things," VII:742
Columbia Broadcasting System. *See* CBS
Columbia Players, VIII:1533
Columbia Records, VII:1217
Columbia University
  Boas, VII:339
  Butler, VII:524-527
  Research in Contemporary Cultures, VII:257, 258; VIII:2470
  School of Journalism, VI:1826
Columbus, Bartolomeo, III:217
Columbus, Christopher, **III:172-175**
  Cabot, III:113, 115, 116
  Cortés, III:188
  Dias, III:218
  Ferdinand and Isabella, III:262
  Iceland, II:579
  Ponce de Léon, III:629
  Ptolemy, I:713
  Vespucci, III:758, 759, 761
Comanche Indians, V:432
Combination Laws, VI:1787
Comenius, John Amos, IV:92
Comintern, VII:661, 662, 688; IX:3779, 4114
Commodus, I:340, 417
Commoner, The, VI:2396
common law, English. *See* English common law
Common Prayer, Book of, III:204-206, 238, 655; IV:199
Commons, House of
  abolitionism, IV:1236; V:379
  Asquith, VII:122, 123
  Astor, VII:129-131
  Attlee, VII:138
  Baldwin, VII:168, 169
  Balfour, VII:173, 174
  Bevan, VII:304
  Beveridge, VII:310
  Bright, V:306-308
  Brougham, V:314-316
  Burke, IV:223
  Butler, VII:529, 530
  Canning, V:406
  Castlereagh, V:438, 440, 441
  Catholic emancipation, VI:1681
  Chamberlain, V:462-464
  Charles I, IV:280, 281
  Clarendon, IV:308, 309
  Coke, IV:329-334
  Curzon, VII:819, 820
  Derby, V:652-654
  Disraeli, V:675, 677, 678
  Durham, V:721
  Eden, VII:1015, 1016
  Edward III, II:329, 331
  Fox, IV:479, 481, 482
  George I, IV:532
  George II, IV:535-537
  George III, IV:542
  Grey, Second Earl, V:995, 996
  Grey, Sir Edward, VIII:1475
  Henry IV, II:458
  Ireland, IV:369
  Law, VIII:2112, 2113
  Lloyd George, VIII:2216
  MacDonald, VIII:2312
  Macmillan, VIII:2340, 2343
  Mansfield, IV:904, 906
  Melbourne, VI:1517
  North, IV:1034-1036
  O'Connor, IX:2793-2795
  Palmerston, VI:1719
  Parnell, VI:1740-1742
  Pelham, IV:1074-1076
  Pitt the Elder, IV:1098-1100
  Pitt the Younger, IV:1102-1105
  Pride, IV:1126, 1127
  Reith, IX:3148
  Ricardo, VI:1879
  Russell, VI:1930
  Salisbury, VI:1943
  Scott, VI:2003
  Stanley, VI:2104
  Strafford, IV:1287
  Thatcher, IX:3649, 3651

Walpole, IV:1400-1403
Wilkes, IV:1440, 1441
William IV, VI:2392-2395
See also Parliament (English)
Commonwealth Electoral Act of 1902, VIII:2291
Commonwealth Protectorate, IV:310, 790
communism
Acheson, VII:17-19
Bukharin, VII:491-493
Castro, VII:617-619
Césaire, VII:632
Czechoslovakia, VII:261
Engels, V:760-762
Gramsci, VIII:1459-1461
Guevara, VIII:1494-1496
Harriman, VIII:1560-1563
Haya de la Torre, VIII:1584
Hiss, VIII:1683-1685
Hoover, VIII:1732, 1733
Hutchins, VIII:1801, 1802
John Paul II, VIII:1863, 1864
Khrushchev, VIII:1961-1963
Lenin, VIII:2160-2162
Liebknecht, VI:1369
Lukács, VIII:2272-2274
McCarthyism, VIII:2300-2302
Machel, VIII:2317-2319
Malthusian economics, VI:1468
Marx, VI:1492-1494
Merleau-Ponty, VIII:2501
Mill, VI:1562
Orwell, IX:2849
Randolph, IX:3114
Reagan administration, VIII:1995
Stalin, IX:3482-3484
Truman, IX:3742
See also socialism
Communist International, VIII:2315
Communist League, V:761
Communist Party of Australia, VIII:2497
Communist Party of Chile, VIII:2717, 2718
Communist Party of China. *See* Chinese Communist Party
Communist Party of France, VII:335; VIII:1698, 1755, 1872, 2559, 2560
Communist Party of Germany, IX:379
Communist Party of Indonesia, IX:3572
Communist Party of Italy, VIII:1459, 2670
Communist Party of Slovakia, VII:968
Communist Party of the Philippines, VIII:2421
Communist Party of the Soviet Union
Akhmatova, VII:38
Brezhnev, VII:459-461
Bukharin, VII:491-493
Gorbachev, VIII:1423, 1424; IX:4086, 4087
Malenkov, VIII:2377, 2378
Molotov, VIII:2571-2573
Shostakovich, IX:3410
Yeltsin, IX:4086, 4087
Zhukov, IX:4116-4119
Communists, Union of, VI:1369
Comnenus, Isaac, II:759, 760
Comnenus, Manuel, II:28, 336, 337
Compagnia dello Scalzo, III:24, 26
Comparative Zoology, Museum of, V:30, 31
Comprehensive Test Ban Treaty, VII:51; IX:3633
Compromise of 1850. *See* 1850, Compromise of
Compton, Arthur Holly, **VII:745-747**
Compton, Sir Spencer, IV:536, 1075
Comstock, Anthony, IX:3314
Comte, Auguste, **V:543-546,** 1057, 1058; VII:988; VIII:2135
Considerations sur le pouvoir spirituel, V:545
Cours de philosophie positive, V:543, 544
System of Positive Polity, V:544
Comunero Revolt, III:159
CONAKAT, IX:3745
Conant, James Bryant, **VII:748-752**
American High School Today, The, VII:751
Slums and Suburbs, VII:751
concentration camps
Baeck, VII:149
Frank, VII:1205, 1206
Himmler, VIII:1666-1668
Hitler, VIII:1694, 1695
Niemöller, VIII:2743
South African War, VIII:2003
Wiesel, IX:3980
concertos
Boccherini, IV:147-149
Corelli, IV:360-362
Schumann, VI:1993
Tchaikovsky, VI:2198, 2200, 2201
Vivaldi, IV:1383-1385
Concini, Concino, IV:863, 864
Cone Crater, IX:3407
Condé, the Great, **IV:341-343,** 872, 873, 946
Condillac, Étienne Bonnot de, **IV:344-347**
Commerce et le gouvernement considérés relativement l'un à l'autre, IV:346
Condillac's Treatise on the Sensationes, IV:345
Cours d'études pour l'instruction du prince de Parme, IV:346
Dissertation sur la liberté, IV:346

Essai sur l'origine des connaissances humaines, IV:344, 345
Traité de animaux, IV:346
Traité des systémes, IV:344
Condorcet, Marquis de, **IV:348-350;** VI:1468
Life of M. Turgot, The, IV:348
Life of Voltaire, The, IV:348
Sketch for a Historical Picture of the Progress of the Human Mind, IV:349, 350
conducting, orchestral
Bernstein, VII:295, 296, 298
Boulez, VII:386-389
Casals, VII:606-609
Karajan, VIII:1910-1912
Mahler, VIII:2360, 2361
Sibelius, IX:3414
Thomas, VI:2230-2233
Toscanini, IX:3094, 3096, 3707, 3709
Varèse, IX:3795
Villa-Lobos, IX:3817
Weber, VI:2341
Webern, IX:3915, 3916
Confederate States of America
Davis, V:614-619
Gorgas, VIII:1434
Houston, V:1138
Jackson, V:1204-1206
Johnson, V:1235
Lee, VI:1338-1341
Maury, VI:1509
Ross, VI:1911
Stephens, VI:2129-2131
Confederation, Articles of
Dickinson, IV:410
Madison, IV:886
Monroe, VI:1570
Morris, IV:999-1001
Shays, IV:1240, 1241
Sherman, IV:1243
Conféderation Générale de Travail, IX:3711
Confessing Church, VII:359, 360, 499; VIII:2742, 2743
Confucianism, I:222-224
Chang Chih-tung, V:466
Ch'ien-lung, IV:301
Chu His, II:265-267
Ch'ü Yüan, I:187-189
Hsün-tzu, I:433-435
Hung Hsiu-Ch'üan, V:1166
Legalists, I:176
Mencius, I:543-546
Ou-yang Hsui, II:709
Shih Huang-ti, I:177
Shotoku Taishi, II:826
Wang An-shih, II:963
Wang Ch'ung, I:943-945
Wang Pi, I:949-951
See also Neo-Confucianism
Confucius, **I:222-225**
Analects, I:222-224, 543, 546, 949
Book of Documents, I:224, 543
Book of Odes, I:543
Book of Songs, I:224
Lao-Tzu, I:498, 499
Spring and Autumn Annals, I:224, 819
Ssu-ma Ch'ien, I:818-820
Congo Crisis, VIII:1530
Congregationalism, IV:371, 372, 935, 938, 939; V:470-472
Congress, U.S.
antilynching laws, IX:3692
Electoral Commission, V:1076
federal election laws, V:1078
Jackson, V:1201
Luce, VIII:2256, 2257
Madison, IV:888
Mason, IV:927
Pierce, VI:1775
pocket veto, V:1198
Sherman, IV:1244
slavery, VI:2192
Smith, IX:3446-3448
Walesa, IX:3847
Washington, IV:1407
Wilson, IV:1457
See also Representatives, House of; Senate, U.S.
Congress of Industrial Organizations
Gompers, V:958
Lewis, VIII:2170-2172
Reuther, IX:3163
Congress of Racial Equality (CORE), VIII:1824
Congress Party of India, VII:1278, 1280; VIII:2709; IX:2869, 2903, 2904
Congreve, Richard, V:1057
Conkling, Roscoe, V:78, 80, 256, 1078
Conn, Billy, VIII:2243, 2244
Connecticut
Allen, IV:35
Barnard, V:130, 131
Barnum, V:133
Board of Education, VII:1356
Sherman, IV:1243, 1244
Stuyvesant, IV:1296
Connecticut Compromise, IV:1244

Conner, David, VI:1761
Connors, Jimmy, VII:1113
Conon, II:823
Conrad II, II:464
Conrad III, II:357, 358
Conrad, Joseph, **VII:753-758**
Almayer's Folly, VII:755, 756
Chance, VII:756,
Heart of Darkness, VII:757
Inheritors, The, VII:756
Lord Jim, VII:756, 757
Mirrors of the Sea, The, VII:756
Nature of a Crime, The, VII:756
Nigger of the "Narcissus," The, VII:755-757
Nostromo, VII:756, 757
One Day More, VII:756
Outcast of the Islands, An, VII:755, 756
Personal Record, A, VII:756
Romance, VII:756
Secret Agent, The, VII:756
Set of Six, A, VII:756
Suspense, VII:756
Tales of Unrest, VII:756
'Twixt Land and Sea, VII:756
Under Western Eyes, VII:756, 757
Victory, VII:756
Conrad of Marburg, II:340, 342
conscription
Canada, VII:367; VIII:1984, 2103
England, VII:124
Selective Service Act, VII:882
Conservative Party (Canada)
Borden, VII:365, 366
Chrétien, VII:681, 682
King, VIII:1982, 1983
Laurier, VIII:2101-2103
Mulroney, VIII:2656
Conservative Party (England)
Asquith, VII:122, 123
Baldwin, VII:168, 169
Balfour, VII:172, 173
Beaverbrook, VII:235
Bevan, VII:304
Butler, VII:529-531
Chamberlain, Joseph, V:462, 464
Chamberlain, Neville, VII:643, 644
Disraeli, V:675, 677, 678
Eden, VII:1016, 1017
George V, VII:1340, 1341
Gladstone, V:935, 936, 938
Heath, VIII:1606-1608
Home Rule Bill, VI:1741
Lansdowne, VIII:2091
Law, VIII:2112-2114
Lloyd George, VIII:2217
Macdonald, VI:1436
Major, VIII:2369, 2370
Pankhurst, IX:2874
Salisbury, VI:1944, 1945
Thatcher, IX:3649, 3651, 3652
See also Tory Party (England)
Constable, John, **V:547-550,** 646; VIII:2579, 2733
Hadleigh Castle, V:549
Hay Wain, The, V:549
Mouth of the Thames--morning after a stormy night, The, V:549
Salisbury: Morning, V:548
Trees Near Hampstead Church, V:549
View on Hampstead Heath, V:549
View on the Stour near Dedham, V:549
Watermeadows at Salisbury, V:549
White Horse, The, V:548
Constance, Council of, II:489, 971
Constance, Treaty of, II:358
Constantine V, II:903, 904
Constantine VI, II:437
Constantine IX, II:758, 759
Constantine, Baron, **VII:759-761**
Constantine, Donation of, II:583; III:740
Constantine the Great, **I:226-230**
Anthony of Egypt, I:58
Athanasius, I:119, 121
Eusebius of Caesarea, I:322, 324
Helena, I:375-377
Shapur II, I:779
Constantinople
Attila, I:126
Constantine the Great, I:228, 229
Fourth Crusade, II:284
Gregory of Nazianzus, I:349
Heraclius, II:470-472
Justinian I, II:554-557
Leo IX, II:582
Mehmed II, III:500
Sergius I, II:820, 821
Theoleptus of Philadelphia, II:899-901
Trullan Synod, II:824
Villehardouin, II:942
Constantinople, Council of, I:352-354, 869, 909; II:675
Constantius, I:266
Constitution, U.S.
Acton, V:12
Adams, John, IV:18, 19

Adams, Samuel, IV:24
Anthony, V:62
Bancroft, V:127
Beard, VII:222
centralization, VIII:1766
contract clause, VI:1490
Dickinson, IV:408, 410
Hamilton, IV:609, 610
Hancock, IV:617
Henry, IV:649
Jefferson, IV:718, 719
Kent, VI:1277-1280
Madison, IV:886-889
Mason, IV:926-928
Mexican Constitution, V:95
Montesquieu, IV:986-988
Revere, IV:1158
Rush, IV:1202, 1203
Shays, IV:1239-1241
Sherman, IV:1242-1244
slavery, VI:2192
Stevens, VI:2137
treason, VI:1490
Webster, Daniel, VI:2344-2346
Webster, Noah, IV:1419
Wilson, IV:1455, 1457, 1458
women's suffrage, VI:2112
Constitutional Convention, U.S.
Adams, IV:18
Dickinson, IV:410, 411
Madison, IV:889
Marshall, VI:1488
Mason, IV:927
Morris, IV:1001
Shays, IV:1239, 1240
Washington, IV:1405, 1406
consumer advocacy, VIII:2679-2681
Continental Association, IV:617
Continental Congress
Adams, John, IV:16, 18
Adams, Samuel, IV:24
Carroll, IV:251
Chase, IV:293
Franklin, IV:494
Hamilton, IV:608-610
Hancock, IV:613, 617
Henry, IV:648
Jay, IV:711
Madison, IV:886
Morris, IV:999
Sherman, IV:1243
Witherspoon, IV:1467-1470
Continuation War, VIII:2398
contraceptives. *See* birth control
Conventicle Act of 1664, IV:100, 239
Convention Parliament, IV:597
Convention People's Party, VIII:2763
Conyers, John, IX:2890
Cook, Frederick, IX:2941, 2942, 2945
Cook, Captain James, **IV:351-355**
Banks, IV:83, 85, 86
Bligh, IV:143
Dampier, IV:391
Kamehameha I, VI:1255
Vancouver, IV:1355, 1356
Cooke, Jay, **V:551-554**
Cooke, William Fothergill, **V:555-559**
Coolidge, Calvin, **VII:762-765;** VIII:1542, 1880, 2556; IX:3547
Cooper, Anthony Ashley. *See* Shaftesbury, Earl of
Cooper, Henry, VII:54
Cooper, James Fenimore, **V:560-564;** VIII:2465
American Democrat, The, V:563
Crater, The, V:563
Deerslayer, The, V:562, 563
History of the Navy of the United States, The, V:564
Home as Found, V:563
Homeward Bound, V:563
Last of the Mohicans, The, V:562
Leatherstocking Tales, V:562, 563
Letter to His Countrymen, A, V:563
Monikins, The, V:563
Notions of the Americans, V:563
Pilot, The, V:562
Pioneers, The, V:560
Precaution, V:560
Redskins, The, V:563
Spy, The, V:560, 562
Virgin Land, V:564
Coowescoowe. *See* Ross, John
Copenhagen, Battle of, IV:145
Copernicus, Nicolaus, **III:176-179**
Apollonius of Perga, I:74
Brahe, III:78, 79
Commentariolus, III:176
First Account, The, III:178
Galileo, IV:519, 521, 522
Kepler, IV:772, 775
Lobachevsky, VI:1404
Mersenne, IV:950, 951
On the Revolutions of the Celestial Spheres, III:176, 179, 755; IV:521
Pythagoras, I:729

Copland, Aaron, **VII:766-769;** VIII:1821, 2363
Appalachian Spring, VII:769
Concerto for Piano and Orchestra, VII:767
Duo for Flute and Piano, VII:768
Music for the Theater, VII:767
Passacaglia, VII:767
Salón México, El, VII:768
Second Hurricane, The, VII:768
What to Listen for in Music, VII:769
Copley, John Singleton, **IV:356-359**
Boy with a Squirrel, IV:357
Death of the Earl of Chatham, The, IV:358
Siege of Gibraltar, The, IV:358
Three Youngest Daughters of King George III, The, IV:358
Watson and the Shark, IV:358
Copperhead Democrats, VI:2401
Coquelin, Constant, IV:387
Coquillards, III:763
Coral Sea, Battle of, VIII:1525
Corazzo monastery, II:534
Corbie, abbey of, II:773
Córdoba, Treaty of, VI:1955
Cordovero, Moses, III:440
CORE. *See* Congress of Racial Equality (CORE)
Corelli, Arcangelo, **IV:360-362**
Corey, Robert B., IX:2927
Corinna of Tanagra, I:644
Corinth, League of, I:630
Corinthian Church, I:210-212, 605
Corinthians, Letters to the, I:605, 606
Corinthian War, I:18, 290
Cormack, Allan, VIII:1752
Cornaro, Alvise, III:58
Cornaro Chapel, IV:119
Corneille, Pierre, **IV:363-366,** 1120, 1145, 1146
Cid, The, IV:363, 364
Cinna, IV:364
Horace, IV:364
Illusion comique, L', IV:363, 365
Nicomède, IV:364
Pertharite, roi des Lombards, IV:364
Polyeucte, IV:364
Suréna, IV:365
Cornell University, VII:301, 395; VIII:2637, 2676
Cornet, Nicolas, IV:170
Cornish Engine, VI:2253
Corn Laws, V:306, 307, 526-528, 653, 677; VI:1396, 1879
See also Anti-Corn Law League
Cornwallis, Charles. *See* Cornwallis, First Marquess
Cornwallis, First Marquess, **IV:367-370**
Clinton, IV:323
Greene, IV:575-577
Rochambeau, IV:1175, 1176
Washington, IV:1406
Coronado, Francisco Vásquez de, **III:180-183**
Corot, Camille, VI:1779
Coroticus, I:602
Corpus Christi College, III:589, 590; VIII:1707
Corpus Juris Civilis, II:555, 557
Correggio, **III:184-187;** V:434
Adoration of the Magi, III:184
Assumption of the Virgin, III:186
Christ Taking Leave of His Mother, III:184
Danae, III:186
Deposition, The, III:186
Ganymede, III:186
Io, III:186
Leda, III:186
Loves of Jupiter, III:186
Madonna and Child with Saint Francis, III:184
Marriage of Saint Catherine, III:184
Martyrdom of Four Saints, The, III:186
Nativity, III:184
School of Love, III:186
Venus, Cupid, and Satyr, III:186
Corrèze Plateau, VII:1228
Corrigan, Michael, V:388
Cortés, Hernán, III:21-23, **188-192,** 529, 531; VI:1815
Cos, I:412
Cosby, William, IV:1484, 1485
Cosgrave, William T., **VII:770-773**
Cosmas, II:544
cosmology
Anaximander, I:51
Empedocles, I:282, 284, 285
Eudoxus of Cnidus, I:310-312
Guericke, IV:588
Heraclitus of Ephesus, I:383-385
Peregrinus de Maricourt, II:719-721
Cossacks, IV:725, 726, 1084
Costa, Lucio, VIII:2739, 2740
Coster, Dirk, VIII:1655
Costruzioni Cementizie, Societa per, VIII:2720
Coteau-Cambreis, Treaty of, III:19
Cotton, John, **IV:371-373,** 687, 938
True Constitution of a Particular Visible Church, The, IV:372

Way of the Churches of Christ in New England, The, IV:372
Way of the Congregational Churches Cleared, The, IV:372
cotton gin, IV:1431, 1433, 1434; VI:2075
cotton industry
Arkwright, IV:59-62
Hargreaves, IV:623-625
Whitney, IV:1431, 1433, 1434
Coubertin, Pierre de, **VII:774-777**
Counter-Reformation
Bernini, IV:118-120
Borromini, IV:169
Ferdinand II, IV:452
Greco, El, III:311, 313
Ignatius of Loyola, III:438
John of the Cross, III:401-403
Joseph II, IV:750, 751
Leopold I, IV:838
Neri, III:551
Paul III, III:595, 597, 598
Spanish Netherlands, IV:707-709
Tasso, III:711, 712
Teresa of Ávila, III:714, 715
Wenceslaus, II:970
country music, VII:658; VIII:2080, 2081; IX:2896-2898
Couperin, François, **IV:374-377**
Art de toucher le clavecin, L', IV:375
Concert instrumental sous le titre d'apothéose composé à la mémoire immortelle de l'incomparable Monsieur de Lully, IV:375
Concerts royaux, IV:375
Goûts-réunis, Les, IV:375
Nations, Les, IV:374, 375
Parnasse, Le, IV:375
Pièces de violes avec la basse chifrée, IV:375
Pièces d'orgues constitantes en deux messes, IV:374
Courbet, Gustave, V:434, **565-568;** VI:1473, 1869
After Dinner at Ornans, V:565
Bathers, The, V:566
Burial at Ornans, The, V:565-567
Cliffs at Étretat After the Storm, V:567
Fighting Stags, V:566
Painter's Studio, The, V:566
Stonebreakers, The, V:565, 566
Stormy Sea, The, V:567
Woman with a Parrot, V:566
Young Ladies of the Village, V:566
Cournot, Augustin, IX:3865
courtly literature
Chrétien de Troyes, II:257-259
Christine de Pizan, II:260-264
Eleanor of Aquitaine, II:338
Gottfried von Strassburg, II:392-394
Hartmann von Aue, II:433-435
Walther von der Vogelweide, II:959-961
Wolfram von Eschenbach, II:1005-1007
Cousteau, Jacques-Yves, **VII:778-782**
Living Sea, The, VII:779
Silent World, The, VII:779
World of Jacques Cousteau, The, VII:781
World Without Sun, VII:779
Couture, Thomas, VI:1471
Covenanters, IV:239, 240, 283
Covent Garden, IV:226; VI:1273, 1460, 1461
Coverdale, Miles, **III:193-196**
Covey, Edward, V:695
Covilhã, Pêro da, **III:197-199**
Coward, Noël, **VII:783-788;** VIII:1588, 2142
Ace of Clubs, VII:787
Astonished Heart, The, VII:787
Bitter Sweet, VII:785
Blithe Spirit, VII:786, 787
Brief Encounter, VII:787
Cavelcade, VII:786
Design for Living, VII:786
Easy Virtue, VII:785
Fallen Angels, VII:785
Hay Fever, VII:785, 787
High Spirits, VII:787
Home Chat, VII:785
I'll Leave It to You, VII:783
In Which We Serve, VII:787; VIII:2643
London Calling!, VII:785
"Mad Dogs and Englishmen," VII:786
Marquise, The, VII:785
Nude with Violin, VII:787
On with the Dance, VII:785
Operette, VII:786
Pacific, VII:787
Peace in Our Time, VII:787
Point Valaine, VII:786
Present Laughter, VII:786, 787
Private Lives, VII:786; IX:2808
Queen Was in the Parlour, The, VII:785
Rat Trap, The, VII:783
Relative Values, VII:787
Scoundrel, The, VII:786
Second Man, The, VII:785
Sigh No More, VII:787
Sirocco, VII:785

Suite in Three Keys, VII:787
This Happy Breed, VII:786, 787
This Was a Man, VII:785
This Year of Grace!, VII:785
Tonight at Eight-thirty, VII:786
To Step Aside, VII:786
Vortex, The, VII:785
Young Idea, The, VII:785
Cowper, Lord, VI:1719
Crabbe, George, VII:468
Crab nebula, IX:2828, 2829
Craft, Ellen and William, VI:1729
Craig, Gordon, VI:2216, 2217
Cram, Steve, VII:727, 728
Cramm, Gottfried von, IX:2981
Cranach, Hans, III:200
Cranach, Lucas, the Elder, **III:200-203**
Agony in the Garden, III:200
Allegory of Redemption, III:202
Allegory of the Law and the Gospel, III:202
Crucifixion, III:200
Dr. Johannes Scheyring, III:200
Holy Kinship Altarpiece, III:200
Judgment of Paris, The, III:200, 202
Reclining River Nymph at the Fountain, III:202
Saint Jerome in Penitence, III:200
Venus and Cupid, III:200
Venus with Cupid at the Honey-Thief, III:202
Cranach, Lucas, the Younger, III:200, 202
Cranch, Richard, IV:12
Crane, Hart, **VII:789-792**
Bridge, The, VII:791
"Chaplinesque," VII:789
"For the Marriage of Faustus and Helen," VII:789
"Voyages," VII:789
White Buildings, VII:789
Crane, Stephen, **V:569-572**
Black Riders, The, V:572
George's Mother, V:571, 572
Little Regiment and Other Episodes of the American Civil War, The, V:571
Maggie, V:569, 571, 572
Open Boat and Other Tales of Adventure, The, V:571
Red Badge of Courage, The, V:569, 571, 572
Third Violet, The, V:569, 571
Whilomville Stories, V:569
Cranmer, Thomas, **III:204-207**
Coverdale, III:193
Edward VI, III:238
Gardiner, III:292
Henry VIII, III:167
Howard, III:368, 369
Ridley, III:654-656
Crassus, Marcus Licinius, I:149, 159, 166, 168, 680, 681, 816
Crates of Thebes, I:68, 967
Crawford, Cheryl, **VII:793-796**
Crawford, Jack, IX:2981
Crawford, Joan, VII:119, 125
Crayford, battle of, I:380
Crazy Horse, **V:573-577**
Creation Society, VIII:2033, 2034
Crécy, Battle of, II:331
Credi, Lorenzo di, III:751
Credit Molilier, VI:1919
Creek Indians
Crockett, V:578
Key, VI:1283
McGillivray, IV:875-877
Osceola, VI:1695, 1697
Racine, IV:1044, 1045
Ross, VI:1910
Soto, III:700
Crelle, August Leopold, V:8, 9
Creoles, VI:2164
Crepy, Peace of, III:18
Crete, IX:3808, 3809
Crewe, John, IV:243
Crick, Francis, **VII:797-800;** IX:2927, 2928, 3897, 3898, 3996, 3997
Life Itself, VII:799
Of Molecules and Men, VII:799
"On Protein Synthesis," VII:798
cricket, V:971-973; VII:407-409, 759-761
Crimean War
Bessemer, V:219
Bright, V:307
Godkin, VIII:1400
Napoleon III, VI:1621
Nicholas I, VI:1651
Nightingale, VI:1668, 1670
Palmerston, VI:1721
Crippen, Robert L., IX:3179
Cripps, Sir Richard Stafford, VII:304, 314; VIII:2710
Crisis, The, VII:964, 965; VIII:1771
Crispus, I:376
Cristero War, VII:543
Cristobal of La Gardia, San, III:727
Critias, I:795
Crixus, I:816

Croce, Benedetto, **VII:801-803,** 1336-1338; IX:3464
Filosofia come sciensa dello spirito, VII:801
Historical Materialism and the Economics of Karl Marx, VII:801
History as the Story of Liberty, VII:802
History of Europe in the Nineteenth Century, VII:802
History of Italy, A, VII:802
"Manifesto of Anti-Fascist Intellectuals," VII:802
Crockett, David, **V:578-580**
Account of Colonel Crockett's Tour to the North and Down East, An, V:579
Life of Martin Van Buren, The, V:579
Narrative of the Life of David Crockett of the State of Tennessee, V:579
Sketches and Eccentricities of Colonel David Crockett of West Tennessee, V:580
Crocus Plain, Battle of the, I:629
Croesus, I:13, 396, 652
Croker, Richard, IX:3439
Cromeck, Robert, IV:138
Cromwell, Oliver, **IV:378-381**
Baxter, IV:99
Biddle, IV:126, 127
Charles I, IV:281
Charles II, IV:283
Clarendon, IV:310
Dryden, IV:424
Fairfax, IV:446-449
Lambert, IV:789-791
Monck, IV:972, 973
Pride, IV:1126, 1128
Scotland, IV:239
Shaftesbury, IV:1228
Cromwell, Thomas, **III:208-211**
Boleyn, III:68
Cranmer, III:204-206
Gardiner, III:292
Henry VIII, III:351
Howard, III:367, 368
Tyndale, III:736
Wolsey, III:786
Crook, George, V:575, 576, 917
Crook Factory, VIII:1626
Crosby, Bing, VII:1159
Cross Keys, battle of, V:842
Crow Indians, VI:2077
Crucifixion
Ballou, V:472
Chagall, VII:641
Giotto, II:388, 390
Grünewald, III:323
Jesus Christ, I:469
John the Apostle, I:475
Rubens, IV:1198
Sluter, II:833
Virgin Mary, I:939
Cruickshank, Bobby, VIII:1876
Crusades
Afonso I, II:31
Bohemond I, II:159-161
Dandolo, II:282, 284
Duns Scotus, II:311
Eleanor of Aquitaine, II:336
France, II:124-126
Germany, II:359, 360
Gregory IX, II:399, 400
Hartmann von Aue, II:434
Henry the Lion, II:466
Innocent III, II:511
Louis IX, II:605, 606
Raymond of Peñafort, II:776, 777
Richard I, II:782
Saladin, II:810, 811
Tancred, II:887, 888
Theoleptus of Philadelphia, II:899
Urban II, II:930
Villehardouin, II:942-945
Cruz, Joaquim, VII:727
Cruz, Sor Juana Inés de la, **IV:382-384**
Carta atenagórica, IV:383
divino Narciso, El, IV:383
Neptuno alegórico, El, IV:383
"Primero sueño," IV:383
Reply to Sor Filotea de la Cruz, IV:383
Crystal Palace Exposition, VI:2069
CSO. *See* Community Service Organization
Ctesibius of Alexandria, **I:231, 232**
Ctesiphon, I:255
Cuban Missile Crisis, VIII:1930, 1933, 1963; IX:3525
Cubism
Appolinaire, VII:82, 83
Boccioni, VII:343
Brancusi, VII:416
Braque, VII:431, 432, 434
Delaunay, VII:889
Duchamp, VII:972, 973
Gris, VIII:1483-1485
Klee, VIII:2005
Krasner, VIII:2023
Kupka, VIII:2037

Léger, VIII:2154
Lipchitz, VIII:2199-2201
Magritte, VIII:2349
Marc, VIII:2405
Miró, VIII:2546
Nevelson, VIII:2729
Picasso, IX:2997, 2998, 3000
Rivera, IX:3185
Stieglitz, IX:3534
Cujas, Jacques, III:672
Cukor, George, VIII:2232
Culpeper, Thomas, III:368, 369
Cultural Revolution
Chou En-lai, VII:678
Chu Teh, VII:689
Deng Xiaoping, VII:905, 906
Kuo Mo-jo, VIII:2033-2035
Lin Piao, VIII:2189, 2190
Li Peng, VIII:2178-2180
Liu Shao-ch'i, VIII:2212-2214
Lu Hsün, VIII:2252
Mao Tse-tung, VIII:2401, 2402
P'eng Te-huai, IX:2954, 2955
Cumans, II:574, 575
Cumberland, Duke of, IV:37, 1474
Cumberland, Earl of, III:140
cummings, e.e., **VII:804-807**
1 x 1, VII:806
XLI Poems, VII:806
50 Poems, VII:806
73 Poems, VII:806
95 Poems, VII:806
Collected Poems, VII:806
Eimi, VII:806
Enormous Room, The, VII:804
i: six nonlectures, VII:806
Is 5, VII:806
No Thanks, VII:806
Tulips and Chimneys, VII:806
Xaipe, VII:806
Cummings v. Missouri, V:788
Cunha, Tristao da, III:12
Cunimund, II:41
Cunningham, Imogen, **VII:808-810**
After Ninety, VII:809
Magnolia Blossom (Tower of Jewels), VII:809
Curchold, Suzanne, IV:1016
Curia, the, VIII:1860
Curie, Marie, V:167; VII:410, **811-815;** VIII:1870-1872
Curie, Pierre, **VII:811-815;** VIII:1870-1872
Curtin, John, **VII:816-818**
Curtis Institute of Music, VII:191, 295
Curtiss, Glenn H., IX:4066, 4067
Curzon, Lord, **VII:819-822**
Cushing, Caleb, **V:581-584**
Cushing, Harvey Williams, **VII:823-826**
Life of Sir William Osler, VII:825
Cushite dynasty, I:709, 711
Cust, Henry, V:777
Custer, George A., V:390, 574, 575, **585-588**; VI:1585, 2072
Cuvier, Georges, **V:589-591**
Cuvilliés, François, IV:152
Cuyen, IV:1
Cuzcatlán, kingdom of, III:23
Cuzco, III:577, 578, 699
Cylon, I:280
Cynaxares, I:570
Cynicism
Antisthenes, I:66-68
Aristippus, I:86
Diogenes, I:268-271
Eratosthenes of Cyrene, I:303
Menippius, I:507
Socrates, I:795
Zeno of Citium, I:967, 969
Cynosarges gymnasium, I:66, 67
Cynthia, I:702-704
Cyrano de Bergerac, **IV:385-388**
Lettres, IV:385, 386
Mort d' Agrippine, La, IV:385, 386
Other World, The, IV:385
Pédant joué, Le, IV:385-387
States and Empires of the Sun, The, IV:385
Cyrene, I:156, 303, 304
Cyril (bishop), I:437, 438
Cyril, Saint, **II:278-281**
Cyrrhus, I:865, 866
Cyrus Cylinder, I:234
Cyrus the Great, **I:233-235,** 330
Czech National Opera, V:726
Czechoslovak Communist Party, VII:968-970
Czechoslovak National Council, VII:259, 260
Czolgosz, Leon, VIII:1412, 1413

Dacian wars, I:901
Dada movement
Appolinaire, VII:83
Breton, VII:448-450
Duchamp, VII:973
Ernst, VII:1098-1100

Magritte, VIII:2351
Miró, VIII:2548
Satie, IX:3334
Daedalus Hyperboreus, IV:1302
Dagnus, I:182
Daguerre, Jacques, **V:592-596;** VI:1594, 1659, 1660
Dahl, Nikolai, IX:3105
Daily Express, VII:235
Daily Mail, VIII:1554, 1555; VII:235, 325
Daimler, Gottlieb, V:200, 201, **597-599**
Daimler Motor Company, V:599; VIII:2071; IX:3881
daimyo lords, IV:1329
Dalai Lama, VII:821; VIII:2711
Dale, Thomas, IV:1107, 1108
Dalhousie, First Marquess of, **V:600-601;** VI:1706
Dali, Salvador, VII:505, 506, **827-831,** 1075
Age of Gold, The, VII:829
Andalusian Dog, An, VII:829
Aphrodisiac Jacket, VII:829
Dream of Christopher Columbus, The, VII:829
Exploding Raphaelesque Head, VII:829
Hidden Faces, VII:829
Honey Sweeter than Blood, VII:827
Secret Life of Salvador Dali, The, VII:829
Dalton, John, V:99, **602-605**
New System of Chemical Philosophy, V:604
Damasus, I:465
Damietta, II:605
Damon, I:609
Dampier, William, **IV:389-392**
Captain Dampier's Vindication of His Voyage to the South Seas in the Ship St. George, IV:390
New Voyage 'Round the World, A, IV:389
Voyages and Descriptions, IV:389
Dana, Charles, V:984, 985
Dana, Richard Henry, Jr., VI:1522, 1601
"Discourses on Women," VI:1602
Danckelmann, Eberhard von, IV:497
Dandolo, Enrico, **II:282-285**
Danegeld, II:345
Danforth, John, IX:3657
Daniel, Book of, I:685
Daniell, John Frederic, V:1010
Danilova, Alexandra, **VII:832-836**
Apollo Musagète, VII:833
Beau Danube, Le, VII:833
Boutique fantasque, La, VII:833
Coppélia, VII:833
Firebird, The, VII:832
Gods Go A-Begging, The, VII:833
Paquita, VII:835
Prodigal Son, The, VII:833
Raymonda, VII:833
Triumph of Neptune, The, VII:833
Waltzes from Vienna, VII:833
Danis, Ida, VII:1274
Danish War of 1864, V:1130
Danjon, André-Louis, **VII:837, 838**
Danjon astrolabe, VII:837
Danley, Earl of, III:476, 477
Dannebrog, II:933
Dante, II:103, 153, **286-290,** 730; III:272
Banquet, The, II:288
Divine Comedy, The, I:440, II:223, 286, 288, 289, 768, IV:349; V:122, 646; VI:1416, 1485
Inferno, II:286, 288, 699
New Life, The, II:286, 288
Purgatorio, II:286, 288, 289
D'Anthès, Georges-Charles, VI:1833, 1834
Danton, Georges, **IV:393-395,** 1206
Dara Shukoh, IV:69, 70
Darby, Abraham, **IV:396-398,** 1443, 1444
Darcet, Jean, IV:813, 814
Dardanelles, Battle of the, VII:123, 134, 691
Dardanus, Treaty of, I:558
Dare, Virginia, III:638
Darien scheme, IV:1066-1068
Darius the Great, **I:236-240**
Alexander the Great, I:40
Behistun Inscription, I:233
Clazomenae, I:47
Herodotus, I:394
Leonidas, I:501
Miltiades the Younger, I:553, 554
Xerxes I, I:962, 964, 965
Darmstadt, Germany, VIII:1633
Darrow, Clarence, VII:481, **839-842**
Dartmouth College v. Woodward, VI:2148, 2344
Daru, Pierre, VI:2125, 2126
Darvall, Denise, VII:197
Darwin, Charles, **V:606-609**
Baer, V:110
Descent of Man and Selection in Relation to Sex, The, V:608
Le Bon, VIII:2136
London, VIII:2226
Lyell, VI:1420-1422
On the Origin of Species, V:32, 606, 608, 609, 868, 980, 1018, 1172, 1173; VI:1421, 2348; VII:283
Spencer, VI:2087
Wedgwood, IV:1422

Darwin, Erasmus
Botanic Garden, The, IV:138
Datis, I:238
Daudet, Alphonse, V:245
Davaine, Casimir-Joseph, VI;1298
David, **I:241-245,** 748, 749, 798; IV:118
David I, **II:291-293**
David II, **II:294-297**
David, Jacques-Louis, IV:490; **V:610-613,** 1183
Battle of the Romans and Sabines, The, V:611, 612
Belisarius, V:610
Brutus Receiving the Bodies of His Sons, V:611
Cupid and Psyche, V:612
Death of Socrates, The, V:611
Oath of Horatii, The, V:610
Oath of the Tennis Court, The, V:611
Telemachus and Eucharis, V:612
Davies, John, IV:174
Davies, Marion, VIII:1604
Davis, Bette, **VII:843-846**
All About Eve, VII:845
All This and Heaven Too, VII:845
Bad Sister, VII:843
Dangerous, VII:843
Dark Victory, VII:845
Great Lie, The, VII:845
Hush Hush Sweet Charlotte, VII:844
Jezebel, VII:845
Letter, The, VII:845
Little Foxes, The, VII:845
Night of the Iguana, The, VII:845
Now, Voyager, VII:845
Of Human Bondage, VII:843
Old Maid, The, VII:845
Petrified Forest, The, VII:843
Whales of August, The, VII:845
What Ever Happened to Baby Jane?, VII:845
Davis, Clive, VII:1218
Davis, Jefferson, **V:614-620**
Black Hawk, V:249
Greeley, V:985
Lee, VI:1338, 1340, 1341
Stephens, VI:2130
Davis, John, **III:212-214**
Seaman's Secrets, III:213
World's Hydrographical Description, III:213
Davis, Miles, VII:741, 742, 744; IX:2882
Davis, Theodore, I:905
Davis Cup, VII:368, 369; VIII:2109, 2110; IX:2979, 2981, 2982
Davy, Sir Humphry, **V:621-624,** 767, 768, 899
Dawidowicz, Lucy S., **VII:847-849**
Golden Tradition, The, VII:848
Holocaust and the Historians, The, VII:849
Holocaust Reader, A, VII:848
Jewish Presence, The, VII:848, 849
War Against the Jews, The, VII:848
Dawlat al-atrak, II:125
Dawlat Khan Lodi, III:38
Dawson, John William, VI:1420
Day, Dorothy, **VII:850-853**
Eleventh Virgin, The, VII:850
Day, John, VII:489
Dayan, Moshe, VII:253, **854-857**
Dayr el-Bahri, temple at, I:373
Deák, Ferenc, **V:625-629**
Deakin, Alfred, **V:630-633**
Deane, Richard, IV:132, 134, 972
Death, Union of, VII:1198
death penalty, V:379; VII:840; VIII:1574, 1864, 2099, 2435; IX:3283
DeBakey, Michael E., VII:197
De Beers Mining Company, VI:1874, 1785
Deborah, **I:246-248**
Debs, Eugene V., **VII:880-883,** 940; IX:3660, 3661
Debussy, Claude, VI:2366; **VII:884-887;** IX:3129, 3332, 3333
Afternoon of a Faun, VIII:2748
Chansons de Bilitis, VII:885
Children's Corner Suite, VII:886
Douze Préludes, VII:886
Etudes, VII:886
Fetes galantes, VII:884, 885
Images, VII:885
Jeux, VII:886
Mer, La, VII:885
Noctures, VII:885
Pelléas et Mélisande, VII:884, 885; VIII:2503
Pour le piano, VII:886
Prélude à l'aprés-midi d'un faune, VII:884, 885
Suite bergamasque, VII:886
decathlon, IX:3674
Decatur, Stephen, **V:634-637;** VI:1765
Deccan, IV:71, 1247
Deccan Education Society, IX:3682
Deceased Wife's Sister's Marriage Act, V:1170
Decebalus, I:901
Decembrist Revolt, VI:1650, 1651, 1833, 2090
De Chirico, Giorgio, VII:1098
Decianus, Catus, I:137
Decius, I:182

Declaration of Independence. *See* Independence, Declaration of
Declaratory Act, IV:367
Decretalists, II:179, 776
Dedekind, Richard, **V:638-640**
Dee, John, III:212
Defense, U.S. Department of, VIII:2752
Defense Mobilization, Office of, IX:3103
Defiance Campaign, VIII:2281, 2386
Defoe, Daniel, **IV:399-402**
Captain Singleton, IV:401
Colonel Jacque, IV:401
Consolidator, The, IV:401
Essay on Projects, An, IV:399
Family Instructor, The, IV:401
History of the Union, The, IV:401
Journal of the Plague Year, A, IV:401
Jure Divino, IV:401
Memoirs of a Cavalier, IV:401
Moll Flanders, IV:401
Robinson Crusoe, IV:390, 391, 401
Roxana, IV:401
Shortest Way with Dissenters, The, IV:399
True-Born Englishman, The, IV:399
True Relation of the Apparition of One Mrs. Veal, the Next Day After Her Death, to One Mrs. Bargrave, IV:401
de Forest, Lee, VII:102, **858-861**
Degas, Edgar, V:435, 436, **641-644,** 890, 891; VI:2247, 2249
Bellelli Family, The, V:641
Dance Class, The, V:643
Mlle. Fiocre in the Ballet "La Source," V:641
Orchestra of the Opera, The, V:643
Scene of War in the Middle Ages, V:641
Self-Portrait, V:641, 642
Steeplechase, The, V:641
Woman Bathing in a Shallow Tub, V:643
de Gasperi, Alcide, **VII:862-865**
de Gaulle, Charles, **VII:866-869**
Algeria, VII:7
Ben-Gurion, VII:254
Blum, VII:338
Cassin, VII:610, 611
French Equatorial Africa, VII:1006
Macmillan, VIII:2341
Malraux, VIII:2380, 2381
Mendès-France, VIII:2491-2493
Mitterrand, VIII:2558-2560
Pétain, IX:2988, 2989
Pompidou, IX:3052-3054
United Nations, VIII:1530
Degen, Ferdinand, V:7
degenerate art
Ernst, VII:1099
Kirchner, VIII:1993
Klee, VIII:2006
Kokoschka, VIII:2014
Kollwitz, VIII:2017
Marc, VIII:2406
Munch, VIII:2660
Webern, IX:3916
Degeorge, Frédéric, V:259
Deism, IV:412, 428, 430, 844, 1055-1057
Dekker, Thomas
Satiromastix: Or, The Untrussing of the Humorous Poet, IV:746
de Klerk, F.W., **VII:870-873;** VIII:2387
De Kruif, Paul, VIII:2175
Delacroix, Eugène, **V:645-648**
Algerian Women in Their Quarters, V:647
Arabs Skirmishing in the Mountains, V:647
Barque of Dante, The, VI:1472
Dante and Virgil Crossing the Styx, V:646
Death of Sardanapolus, The, V:646, 647
Liberty Leading the People, V:647
Lion Hunt, The, V:647
Massacre at Chios, The, V:646
Delahaye, Ernest, VI:1886
Delane, John Thaddeus, VI:2326
Delano Grape Strike, VIII:1763
Delaunay, Robert, **VII:888-891,** 1098; VIII:2405
Breton Woman, VII:888
Cities, VII:889
City of Paris, The, VII:889
Eiffel Tower, VII:889
Haystacks of Berry, VII:888
Landscape of La Ronchère, VII:888
Landscape with Disc, VII:888
Seaweed Gatherer, VII:888
Vases and Objects, VII:888
Views of Saint-Séverin, VII:889
Windows, VII:889
Delaware and Hudson Canal, VI:1904
De la Warr Pavilion, VIII:2488
Delcassé, Théophile, VII:704
Delian League, I:47, 198-200, 609, 611, 858
Delian Problem, I:305, 311
Delibes, Léo, **V:649-651**
Coppélia: Ou, La Fille aux yeux d'émail, V:649-651
Cour du roi Pétaud, La, V:649
Deux Vielles Gardes, V:649
Jean de Nivelle, V:650

Kassya, V:650, 651
Lakmé, V:650
Roi l'a dit, Le, V:650
Roi s'amuse, six airs de danse dans le style ancien, Le, V:650
Source: Ou, Naila, La, V:649
Sylvia: Ou, La Nymphe de Diane, V:650, 651
Delius, Frederick, **VII:892-895**
Appalachia, VII:893
Brigg Fair, VII:893
Eventyr, VII:893
Fennimore and Gerda, VII:893
Leute von Seldwyla, Die, VII:893
Margot la rouge, VII:892
Mass of Life, A, VII:893
North Country Sketches, VII:893
On Hearing the First Cuckoo in Spring, VII:893
Paris: The Song of a Great City, VII:893
Sea Drift, VII:893
Song of the High Hills, A, VII:893
Songs of Sunset, VII:893
String Quartet No. 2, VII:894
Summer Night on the River, VII:893
Village Romeo and Juliet, A, VII:893
della Rovere, Giuliano. *See* Julius II
Delphi, Oracle at
Cleomenes, I:501
Cylon, I:280
Demosthenes, I:254
Diogenes, I:268
Eudoxus of Cnidus, I:311
Leonidas, I:502
Pisistratid family, I:649, 650
Socrates, I:793
Xenophon, I:958
Demaratus, I:214, 215
Demarcation, Line of, III:16, 262
Demea, IV:684
Demeter, cult of, I:9
Demetrius of Phalerum, I:873
Demetrius Poliocretes, I:60
de Mille, Agnes, **VII:874-876**
Black Ritual (Obeah), VII:875
Brigadoon, VII:875
Kwamina, VII:875
Oklahoma!, VII:875, 876
Rodeo, VII:875
Texas Fourth, VII:876
DeMille, Cecil B., **VII:896-899;** VIII:14154
Cheat, The, VII:896
Cleopatra, VII:897
Crusades, The, VII:897
Greatest Show on Earth, The, VII:898
King of Kings, The, VII:897
Sign of the Cross, The, VII:897
Squaw Man, The, VII:896
Ten Commandments, The, VII:897, 898
DeMille Foundation for Political Freedom, VII:898
Demiurges, I:633, 912, 913
Democedes, I:34
democracy
Acton, V:12
Adams, IV:16
Antisthenes, I:67
Bolívar, V:268, 269
Calhoun, V:396
Carlyle, V:417
Indonesia, VIII:1578; IX:3571, 3572
Kerensky, VIII:1941-1944
Lippmann, VIII:2203-2206
Mosca, VIII:2632
Nasser, VIII:2693
Poland, IX:3847
Tocqueville, VI:2238-2240
Wallace, IX:3861
Democratic Farm-Labor Alliance, VIII:1783
Democratic Party, U.S.
Albright, VII:50, 51
Altgeld, V:55, 56
Bancroft, V:125, 126
Benton, V:197
Bryan, VII:479-481
Buchanan, V:346-348
Carter, VII:589-592
Chisholm, VII:670, 671
Cleveland, V:512, 513, 515
Clinton, VII:707-710
Cushing, V:582
Feinstein, VII:1137-1139
Ferraro, VII:1153-1155
Gore, VIII:1431-1433
Harriman, VIII:1562, 1563
Hayes, V:1078
Hearst, VIII:1603
Hobby, VIII:1704, 1705
Houston, V:1138
Humphrey, VIII:1783-1786
Jackson, V:1197
Johnson, Andrew, V:1232
Johnson, Lyndon B., VIII:1866-1868
Kansas-Nebraska Act, V:693
Kennedy, John F., VIII:1928-1931
Kennedy, Robert F., VIII:1932-1935

Kirkpatrick, VIII:1994, 1995
Kissinger, VIII:1999
Madison, IV:888
O'Neill, IX:2824-2826
organized labor, VIII:2171, 2172
Pierce, VI:1775-1777
Polk, VI:1801-1803
Reagan, IX:3138
Richards, IX:3169-3171
Roosevelt, IX:3222-3226
Ross, IX:3243, 3244
Sinclair, IX:3428
Spock, IX:3479
Stephens, VI:2129, 2131
Stevenson, IX:3523-3526
Taney, VI:2190, 2191
Truman, IX:3740, 3742, 3743
Tweed, VI:2284
Tyler, VI:2288, 2289
Wallace, George C., IX:3858, 3859
Wallace, Henry A., IX:3860-3863
Whitman, VI:2368
Wilson, IX:4020
Democratic Union of the Algerian Manifesto, VII:6, 7
Democritus, I:101, **249-252,** 511, 705
demography, II:940; VI:1467-1469, 1562, 1879; VIII:2671
Demoiselle, IX:3322
Demosthemenes, **I:253-256,** 671
"First Philippic," I:253
"Olynthiacs," I:253
"On the Chersonese," I:254
"Third Philippic," I:254
Dempsey, Jack, **VII:900-904**
Deneuve, Catherine, VII:506
Denger, Adam, VIII:2735
Deng Xiaoping, **VII:905-908**
Lee Kuan Yew, VIII:2152
Li Peng, VIII:2178, 2179
Denis, Maurice, VI:1473; **VII:909-911;** IX:3826, 3828
April, VII:909
Ascent to Calvary, The, VII:910
Battle of Jacob and the Angel, The, VII:910
Hommage à Cézanne, VII:910
Denis, Saint, **I:257-259**
Dennis v. United States, VII:322
dentistry, VI:1596-1598
deoxyribonucleic acid. *See* DNA
Deprez-d'Arsonval mirror galvanometer, VII:1040
Derain, André, VIII:2454
Derby, Fourteenth Earl of, **V:652-655,** 677, 678
Dereham, Francis, III:367-369
Derrida, Jacques, **VII:912-915**
Dissemination, VII:914
Glas, VII:914
Margins of Philosophy, VII:914
Of Grammatology, VII:912, 913
Post Card: From Socrates to Freud and Beyond, The, VII:914
Speech and Phenomena, VII:913
Truth in Painting, VII:914
Writing and Difference, VII:913
Descartes, René, IV:345, **403-407,** 978
Discourse on Method, IV:405
Fermat, IV:458-460
Geometry of Descartes, The, I:594
Gilson, VII:1374, 1376
Huygens, IV:695, 696
Leibniz, IV:830
Marcel, VIII:2407, 2408
mechanics, IV:787
Meditations on First Philosophy, IV:405
Mersenne, IV:949-952
nature of space, IV:586
Pascal, IV:1062
Passions of the Soul, The, IV:405
Rules for the Direction of the Mind, IV:403
Spinoza, IV:1264-1266
Steiner, VI:2119
Deschamps, Eustache, II:617
Deschevaux-Dumésnil, Suzanne, VII:239
desegregation, VIII:1769, 1789. *See also* segregation
Desert Shield, Operation, IX:3071
Desert Storm, Operation, VII:522, 1116; IX:3071
Desilu Productions, VII:176-178
de Sitter, Willem, VIII:2158, 2159
Desmichels, Louis Alexander, V:1, 2
Despenser, Hugh le, II:326, 327
Despenser the Younger, Hugh, II:326, 327
Dessalines, Jean-Jacques, V:501
Destour Party, VII:391
detective stories
Christie, VII:683, 685, 686
Doyle, V:700-702
Gardner, VII:1297-1299
Poe, VI:1796
Detroit Automobile Company, VII:1186
Detroit Evening News, VI:2014
Detroit Tigers, VII:717, 719
Detroit Tribune, VI:2014

Dettingen, Battle of, IV:537, 1471
Deuchar, David, VI:1836
Deuteronomy, Book of, I:563
Deutsche Gotteserkenntnis, VIII:2266
Deutsche Oper Berlin, VIII:2769, 2770
de Valera, Eamon, VI:1481; VII:734, 735, 770-772, **877-879;** IX:2805, 2806
Devereux, Robert. *See* Essex, Second Earl of
Devereux, Walter. *See* Essex, First Earl of
Devolution, War of, IV:343
De Wette, W.M.L., VI:1727, 1728
Dewey, George, **V:656-659**
Experience and Nature, VII:917
Human Nature and Conduct, VII:917
Individualism, Old and New, VII:917
Psychology, VII:916
Quest for Certainty, The, VII:917
Reconstruction in Philosophy, VII:917
School and Society, The, VII:917
Studies in Logical Theory, VII:917
Dewey, John, VI:1769; **VII:916-918**
Dewey, Melvil, **V:660-662**
Dewey, Thomas, VIII:1704; IX:3889
Dewey decimal classification system, V:660-662
diabetes, I:83
Banting, VII:187-190
Houssay, VIII:1759, 1760
Macleod, VIII:2329-2331
Diaconus, Paulus, II:41
Diaghilev, Sergei, **VII:919-922**
Afternoon of a Faun, VII:920
Apollo, VII:921
Balanchine, VII:156
Carnival, Le, VII:920
Cleopatra, VII:919
Cocteau, VII:721
Coq d'Or, Le, VII:920
Danilova, VII:833
Duncan, VII:981
Festin, Le, VII:919
Firebird, The, VII:920
Gris, VIII:1484
Legend of Joseph, The, VII:920
Lifar, VIII:2182-2184
Massine, VIII:2448, 2449
Narcisse, VII:920
Nijinsky, VIII:2746, 2748, 2749
Noces, Les, VII:921
Pavilion d'Armide, Le, VII:919
Pavlova, IX:2937
Petrushka, VII:920
Prodigal Son, The, VII:921
Prokofiev, IX:3085
Spectre de la Rose, Le, VII:920
Stravinsky, IX:3559
Swan Lake, VII:920
Sylphides, Les, VII:919
Dial, The, V:757, 849; VI:2234; VIII:2614, 2616
diamond industry, VI:1873, 1874
Diana, Princess of Wales, **VII:923-926,** 1064
Dias, Bartolomeu, **III:215-219**
Diaspora, II:549
Diaz, Porfirio, V:1253; VIII:2345, 2347; IX:3811, 4104
Díaz de Vivar, Rodrigo. *See* Cid, El
Dibbs, Sir George Richard, V:148
Dickens, Charles, V:59, **663-666;** VIII:2174, 2465
American Notes, V:663, 1150
Barnaby Rudge: A Tale of the Riots of '80, V:663
Bleak House, V:663, 665
Christmas Carol, A, V:663, 666
David Copperfield, V:663
Dombey and Son, V:663
Great Expectations, V:665
Hard Times, V:663, 665
Household Words, V:663
Little Dorrit, V:663, 665
Martin Chuzzlewit, V:663, 665
Mystery of Edwin Drood, The, V:665
Nicholas Nickleby, V:663, 666; VI:1461
Old Curiosity Shop, The, V:663
Oliver Twist, V:663, 666
Our Mutual Friend, V:665
Pickwick Papers, V:663
Sketches by Boz, V:663
Tale of Two Cities, A, V:665; VIII:2724
Dickinson, Charles, V:1196
Dickinson, Emily, **V:667-671,** 1110-1112, 1200
"Letter to the World," V:671; VIII:1458
"Master Letters," V:669
"Narrow Fellow in the Grass, A" V:668
Dickinson, John, **IV:408-411,** 1455, 1456
Late Regulations Respecting the British Colonies on the Continent of America Considered, The, IV:408
Diderot, Denis, **IV:412-415**
Alembert, IV:30-33
Condillac, IV:344, 345
Dorval, IV:413
Encyclopédie, IV:31-33, 226, 348, 413, 414
Essay on Blindness, An, IV:412
Est-il bon? Est-il méchant?, IV:414
Father of the Family, The, IV:413
Indiscreet Toys, The, IV:412

Jacques the Fatalist and His Master, IV:414
Letter on the Deaf and Dumb, IV:413
Paradox of Acting, The, IV:413
Penseés philosophiques, IV:412
Promenade du sceptique, La, IV:412
Rameau, IV:1149
Rameau's Nephew, IV:413, 414
Rousseau, IV:1194
Supplement to Bougainville's "Voyage,", IV:414
Didrikson, "Babe". *See* Zaharias, "Babe" Didrikson
Diego of Acebo, II:301, 302
Diels, Otto Paul Hermann, **VII:927-929**
Dientzenhofer, Johann, IV:656
Diepkloof, IX:2907
Dieppe raid, VIII:2602, 2643
Diesel, Rudolf, **V:672-674**
Theory and Construction of a Rational Heat Motor, V:673
Dietrich, Marlene, **VII:930-933**
Angel, VII:932
Blue Angel, The, VII:930, 932
Destry Rides Again, VII:932; IX: 3528, 3529
Dishonored, VII:932
Foreign Affair, A, VII:932
Garden of Allah, The, VII:932
Knight Without Armor, VII:932
Martin Roumaganic, VII:932
Morocco, VII:932
Scarlet Empress, The, VII:932
Seven Sinners, VII:932
Tragedy of Love, VII:930
Dieudonné, Albert, IX:3157
differential calculus
Alembert, IV:30
Dedekind, V:638
Fermat, IV:458-460
Maclaurin, IV:883
Newton, IV:1025, 1027, 1028
Torricelli, IV:1331-1333
Digambara, I:915
Dikaiopolis, I:88, 90
Dilke, Charles, V:462
Dilke, Lady Emilia, VII:353
Dill, Sir John, VII:46
DiMaggio, Joe, **VII:934-937,** 1323; VIII:2589
Dimmesdale, Arthur, V:1054, 1066
Dingiswayo, VI:2041
Dingley Act, VI:1454
Dio Cassius, I:136, 141, 142
Diocles of Carystus, **I:260-262**
Anatomy, I:261
Arkhidamos, I:260
Diokles epistole prophulakike, I:261
Directions on Health for Pleistarchos, I:261
Rhizotomika, I:261
Diocletian, I:226, **263-267**
Diodore, I:861
Diodorus of Sicily, I:547, 732
Diogenes, I:66, 68; **268-271;** 795
Dionysian festival. *See* Greater Dionysia
Dionysius, I:257, 690, 787; VI:1664
Dionysius Exiguus, **II:298-300**
"First letter written in the year of Christ 525," II:299
Paschal Tables, II:299
Dionysius the Aeropagite, Saint, I:258
Diophantus, **I:272-275;** II:20
Arithmetica, I:272-274, 437
Moriastica, I:274
Porismata, I:274
Dioscorides, Pedanius, **I:276-279**
De materia medica, I:276
Dioscuri, I:676
Dirichlet, Peter Gustav Lejeune, V:638, 639
Dirksen, Everett, VIII:2258
Discalced Carmelites, III:401, 402, 714, 715; IV:382
Discovery, IV:1355, 1356
discrimination, racial
Bunche, VII:501, 502
Constantine, VII:760
Dunham, VII:985
Garvey, VII:1311
Hernandez, VIII:1641
Myrdal, VIII:2671-2673
Parks, IX:2888-2891
Randolph, IX:3114
Walker, IX:3855
Washington, VI:2337
See also apartheid; racism; segregation
Disney, Walt, **VII:938-943**
Adventures of Ichabod and Mr. Toad, The, VII:941
Alice in Cartoonland, VII:940
Bambi, VII:941
Cinderella, VII:941
Dumbo, VII:941
Fantasia, VII:940; IX:3560
Make Mine Music, VII:941
Mary Poppins, VII:941
Mickey Mouse Club, VII:941
Old Mill, The, VII:940
Oswald the Rabbit, VII:940
Reluctant Dragon, The, VII:940

Saludos Amigos, VII:941
Snow White and the Seven Dwarfs, VII:940
So Dear to My Heart, VII:941
Song of the South, VII:941
Steamboat Willie, VII:940
Three Caballeros, VII:941
Three Little Pigs, VII:940
Tortoise and the Hare, The, VII:940
True-Life Adventure series, VII:941
Ugly Duckling, The, VII:940
Disneyland, VII:941, 942
Disraeli, Benjamin, **V:675-679**
Bright, V:307, 308
Coningsby: Or, The New Generation, V:677
Derby, V:653, 654
Forster, V:805
Gladstone, V:936, 938
O'Connor, IX:2789
Peel, VI:1754
Rothschild, VI:1918
Salisbury, VI:1944
Sybil, V:677
Victoria, VI:2308
Vivian Grey, V:675
Young Duke, The, V:675
Dissenters. *See* Radical Dissenters
di Stefano, Giuseppe, IX:2930
Divinsky, Nathan, VII:549
Dix, Dorothea, **V:680-683**
Dizé, J.J., IV:814
Djilas, Milovan, **VII:944-946**
Anatomy of a Moral, VII:944
Conversations with Stalin, VII:945
Land Without Justice, VII:945
Leper and Other Stories, The, VII:945
Montenegro, VII:945
New Class, The, VII:945
Njegos, VII:945
Stone and the Violets, The, VII:945
Under the Colors, VII:945
Unperfect Society, The, VII:945
DNA
Crick, VII:797-799
Bragg, VII:412
Jacob, VIII:1827
Pauling, IX:2927
Watson, IX:3897-3899
Wilkins, IX:3995-3997
Dnieper River, II:804
Döbereiner, Johann, VI:1532
Dobrynia, II:953
Dockers' Union, VII:313
Dodge City, V:735, 736
Doering, William, IX:4053
Dohnányi, Ernő, VII:210
Dole, Robert J., VII:400, 710, **947-950,** 1182; IX:2975
Döllinger, Johann Joseph Ignaz von, V:10, 11
Domagk, Gerhard, **VII:951-953**
Domaine Musical series, VII:387
Domesday Book, II:1000
Dominic, Saint, **II:301-304**
Dominican Order
Albertus Magnus, II:37
Angelico, III:28, 29
Bonaventure, II:163
Bruno, III:96
Bucer, III:101
Catherine of Siena, II:218, 220
Dominic, II:301-303
Inquisition, II:401
Luther, III:443
Pecham, II:717
Raymond of Peñafort, II:776, 777
Thomas Aquinas, II:911, 913, 914
Torquemada, III:725
Vincent of Beauvais, II:946
William of Moerbeke, II:985, 986
William of Saint-Amour, II:990, 991
Domitian, I:356, 488, 489, 533, 838, 839, 933
Donald III, II:291
Donatello, **III:220-223,** 303, 460, 461, 483
David (bronze), III:222
David (marble), III:220
Equestrian Monument of General Gattamelata, III:220
Feast of Herod, The, III:220
Mary Magdalene, III:220
Saint George and the Dragon, III:220
Saint John the Evangelist, III:220
Zuccone, III:220
Donati, Corso, II:286
Donatists, I:228, 344
Donatus, I:463, II:757
Ars grammatica, II:756
Donauschingen Festival, VIII:1670
Donders, Franciscus Cornelius, VII:1039
Donelson, Fort, V:976
Donizetti, Gaetano, **V:684-686**
Anna Bolena, V:685
Daughter of the Regiment, The, V:685
Don Pasquale, V:685
Elixer of Love, The, V:685; VII:599
favorite, La, V:685

Lucia di Lammermoor, V:685
Lucrezia Borgia, V:685
Marino Faliero, V:685
Roberto Devereux, V:685
zingara, La, V:684
Donnacona, III:129, 130
Donne, John, IV:48 **416-420**
Anatomy of the World, IV:418
"Canonization, The," IV:418
Devotions upon Emergent Occasions, IV:419
"Ecstasy, The," IV:416
"Flea, The," IV:416
"Good Friday, 1613, Riding Westward," IV:418
"Hymn to God My God, in My Sickness," IV:419
Of the Progress of the Soule, IV:418
Songs and Sonnets, IV:416
"Valediction, A," IV:418
Doolittle, Hilda. *See* H.D.
Doolittle, James H., VIII:1525
Doppler, Johann, IX:3490
Dorat, Jean, III:657, 671
Dorchester, Lord. *See* Carleton, Guy
Dorgon, IV:1, 2, **421-423**
Dorieus, I:214, 501
Dorris, Michael, VII:1091
Doson, I:216
Dostoevski, Fyodor, **V:687-691;** VI:2269; VII:153
Brothers Karamazov, The, V:670; VIII:2533
Crime and Punishment, V:689
Double, The, V:687
Idiot, The, V:689; VIII:2746
Notes from the Underground, V:689
Poor Folk, V:687
Possessed, The, V:689
Doubleday, Frank, VII:955
Douglas, Lord Alfred, VI:2379
Douglas, Sir Archibald, II:294
Douglas, Stephen A., V:347, 510, **692-694,** 793; VI:1382, 1383
Douglass, Frederick, **V:695-699;** VI:2257
Life and Times of Frederick Douglass, V:697
My Bondage and My Freedom, V:697
Narrative of the Life of Frederick Douglass, V:697
Douhet, Giulio, VIII:2556
Dover, Treaty of, IV:285, 1039
Dow, Arthur, IX:2800
Dow Jones Industrial Average, VIII:1472, 1473
Downs, Battle of the, IV:501
Doyen, Gabriel-François, IV:488
Doyle, Sir Arthur Conan, **V:700-703**
Adventures of Sherlock Holmes, The, V:700, 701
Case-Book of Sherlock Holmes, The, V:701
His Last Bow, V:701
History of Spiritualism, The, V:702
Hound of the Baskervilles, The, V:701
Lost World, The, V:700, 702
Return of Sherlock Holmes, The, V:701
Sign of Four, The, V:700
Study in Scarlet, A, V:700
Valley of Fear, The, V:701
War in South Africa, The, V:701
Draco, **I:280, 281**
Dragon Boat Festival, I:188
Drake, Sir Francis, **III:224-226,** 279, 315, 316, 693
Drake, H.M.S., IV:740
Draper, John William, V:294, 296
Dred Scott decision. *See* Scott, Dred
Dreisch, Hans, VIII:2619, 2620
Dreiser, Theodore, **VII:954-958**
American Tragedy, An, VII:957, 958
Bulwark, The, VII:957
Dreiser Looks at Russia, VII:957
Financier, The, VII:955
"Genius" The, VII:955; VIII:2484
Jennie Gerhardt, VII:955
Sister Carrie, VII:954, 955, 957, 958; IX:2812
Stoic, The, VII:955
Titan, The, VII:955
Drexel, Morgan, and Company, VI:1581
Dreyer, Carl Theodore, **VII:959-962**
Bride of Glomdal, The, VII:959
Day of Wrath, VII:959-961
Gertrud, VII:960
Good Mothers, VII:960
Jesus fra Nasaret, VII:960
Leaves from Satan's Book, VII:959
Love One Another, VII:959
Master of the House, VII:959
Michael, VII:959, 960
Once Upon a Time, VII:959
Ordet, VII:959-961
Parson's Widow, The, VII:959
Passion of Joan of Arc, The, VII:959, 960
President, The, VII:959
"They Caught the Ferry," VII:961
Two People, VII:960
Vampyr, VII:960
Dreyfus affair
Clemenceau, VII:703, 704
Fowler, V:825, 827
Herriot, VIII:1644
Herzl, V:1102, 1104

Jaurès, V:1222
Maritain, VIII:2425
Poincaré, IX:3044, 3045
Sorel, IX:3463
Zola, VI:2420, 2421, 2423
Drosophila, VIII:2618-2620
Drusus, I:152
Druyan, Ann, IX:3293
Dryden, John, **IV:424-427,** 1116, 1130
Absalom and Achitophel, IV:425
All for Love, IV:425, 426
Annus Mirabilis, IV:425
Astraea Redux, IV:424
Conquest of Granada by the Spaniards, The, IV:425
Essay of Dramatic Poesy, An, IV:425
Hind and the Panther, The, IV:425
Indian Emperor, The, IV:424
Indian Queen, The, IV:424
MacFlecknoe, IV:425
Religio Laici, IV:425
Wild Gallant, The, IV:424
Duarte, Eva. *See* Perón, Eva
Dubcek, Alexander, VII:460, **968-971**
Du Bois, W.E.B., VI:2258, 2338; **VII:963-967,** 1312; IX:3113, 3943
Black Reconstruction, VII:965
Philadelphia Negro, The, VII:964
Souls of Black Folk, The, VII:964, 965
Suppression of the African Slave Trade to the United States, The, VII:963
Dubos, René J., IX:3834, 3835
Du Camp, Maxime, V:796
Duccio di Buoninsegna, **II:305-308,** 632
Madonna (Crevole), II:305
Madonna (Rucellai), II:305, 306
Maestà, II:305-307
Duchamp, Marcel, **VII:972-975**
Bride Stripped Bare by Her Bachelors, Even, VII:973
Fountain, VII:973
In Advance of the Broken Arm, VII:973
Kupka, VIII:2037
Nude Descending a Staircase No. 1, VII:972
Nude Descending a Staircase No. 2, VII:973
Sad Eyed Man in a Train, VII:972
Dudley, John. *See* Northumberland, Duke of
Dudley, Robert. *See* Leicester, Earl of
Dudley, Thomas, IV:193
Duggan, Stephen Pierce, VIII:2662
Duhig, James, VI:1482
Dühring, Eugen, V:761
Duke, James Buchanan, **V:704-707**
Dulany, Daniel, IV:250
Dulles, John Foster, **VII:976-979;** IX:3663
Dumas, Alexandre, *père,* **V:708-710;** VI:2303, 2304
Black Tulip, The, V:709
Camille, VIII:2143
Catherine of Cleves, V:708
Chevalier d'Harmental, Le, V:709
Christine, V:708
Count of Monte Cristo, The, V:709; VIII:2227; IX:2819
Ladies of Saint-Cyr, The, V:1163
Marriage of Convenience, A, V:709
My Memoirs, V:710
Three Musketeers, The, IV:387; V:709
Tour de Nesle, La, V:709
Twenty Years After, V:709
Vicomte de Bragelonne, Le, V:709
Dumbarton Oaks, VII:1130, 1131
Dunant, Jean-Henri, **V:711-713**
Memory of Solferino, A, V:711
Dunbar, Battle of, IV:1127
Dunbar, Paul Laurence, **V:714-717**
Fanatics, The, V:715
Folks from Dixie, V:715
Love of Landry, The, V:715
Lyrics of Lowly Life, V:715
Lyrics of the Hearthside, V:715
Majors and Minors, V:715
Oak and Ivy, V:714, 715
"Ode to Ethiopia," V:714
Sport of Gods, The, V:717
Strength of Gideon and Other Stories, The, V:715
"Sympathy," V:714
Uncalled, The, V:715
Dunbar, Samuel, IV:1242
Duncan II, II:291
Duncan, Isadora, VII:919, **980-983,** 1263, 1264; VIII:2746
Dundee, Angelo, VII:54
Dunes, Battle of the, IV:380, 703
Dungeness, Battle off, II:134
Dunham, Katherine, **VII:984-987**
Bamboche, VII:986
Cabin in the Sky, VII:985
Carnival of Rhythm, VII:985
Green Mansions, VII:986
Journey to Accompong, VII:985, 986
Ode to Taylor Jones, VII:986
Pins and Needles, VII:985
Star Spangled Rhythm, VII:985

Stormy Weather, VII:985
Touch of Innocence, VII:986
Dunkirk, Battle of, VII:45, 46
Dunkirk House, IV:310
Dunn School of Pathology, VII:1173
Duns Scotus, John, **II:309-314;** VIII:1610
Opus Oxiniese, II:310, 313
Quaestiones quodlibetales, II:310, 313
Dunstable, John, **III:227-229**
Quam pulcra es, III:228
Rex seculorum, III:228
Veni Sancti Spiritus, III:228
Duperron, Jacques Davy, III:334
Dupes, Day of the, IV:865
Dupin, Amandine-Aurore-Lucile, Baronne Dudevant. *See* Sand, George
Duplessis, Maurice, IX:3730
Du Pont, Eleuthère Irénée, **V:718-720**
Du Pont Company. *See* E.I. Du Pont de Nemours and Company
Durbar, the, VII:820
Dürer, Albrecht, III:61, 200, 201, **230-233;** IV:975; VIII:1991
Adam and Eve, III:231
Adoration of the Magi, The, III:231
Apocalypse, III:230
Erasmus of Rotterdam, III:231, 248
Feast of the Rose Garlands, The, III:231
Four Apostles, III:231
Four Horsemen of the Apocalypse, The, III:231
Holy Family with the Butterfly, III:231
Madonna and Child, III:231
Melencolia I, III:231
Saint Jerome Curing the Lion, III:230
Self-Portrait, III:230
This Present Boke Named Shyp of Folys of the Worlde, III:230
Durham, First Earl of, V:117, **721-724;** VI:2322
Report on the Affairs of British North America, V:721-723
Durham Bull Company, V:704-706
Durkheim, Émile, **VII:988-991**
Division of Labor in Society, The, VII:988, 990
Elementary Forms of the Religious Life, The, VII:988
Montesquieu and Rousseau, VII:988
Suicide, VII:988
Dusan, Stefan. *See* Stefan Dusan
Duse, Eleonora, VIII:2141, 2142
Dutch East India Company, IV:502, 680, 681, 1313, 1314
Dutch West India Company, IV:644, 645, 1294, 1296
Dvorák, Antonín, **V:725-728;** VIII:1835-1837
Alfred, V:726
Armida, V:727
Bells of Zlonice, V:726
From the Bohemian Forest, V:726
From the New World, V:727
Hussite Overture, V:726
King and Collier, V:726
Moravian Duets, V:726
Requiem Mass, Op. 89, V:727
Rukopis kralovedvorsky, V:726
Rukopis zelenohorsky, V:726
Second Symphony in B flat major, V:726
Slavonic Dances, V:726
Spectre's Bride, The, V:726
Stabat mater, V:726
String Quartet in F minor, Op. 9, V:726
Symphonic Variations for Orchestra, V:726
Symphony in D minor, Op. 13, V:726
Symphony in F, Op. 24, V:726
Symphony in G, Op. 88, V:727
Wanda, V:726
Dworkin, Andrea, VIII:2326
Dwyer, Ada, VIII:2249
Dyrrhachium, Battle of, I:167
Dzhugashvili, Joseph Vissarionovich. *See* Stalin, Joseph

Eads, James Buchanan, **V:729-731**
Eads Bridge, V:729-731
Eakins, Thomas, **V:732-734**
John Biglin in a Single Scull, V:732
Max Schmitt in a Single Scull, V:732
Ealhmund, II:333
Earhart, Amelia, **VII:992-995**
Fun of It, The, VII:994
Twenty Hours Forty Minutes, VII:992, 994
Early Closing Act of 1904, VII:353
Earp, Wyatt, **V:735-737**
Earth
age of, IV:217
Anaximander, I:50, 51
Anaximenes of Miletus, I:54
Aryabhata, II:89-91
black holes, IX:3367
Brahe, III:78
circumference of, I:304; II:182
density of, IV:263
Empedocles, I:282, 284
Galileo, IV:519, 521, 522

Heraclitus of Ephesus, I:382-385
Kepler, IV:775
magnetic field, V:167, 897
motion of, VII:837; VIII:2236
nuclear winter, IX:3294
origins of life, VII:799; IX:2830, 2831
Peregrinus de Maricourt, II:719-721
Ptolemy, I:712
Pythagoras, I:729
East and West Association, VII:488
Eastern Chin Dynasty, II:640
Eastern Grove Monastery, I:429, 430
Eastern Han Dynasty, I:590
Eastern Orthodoxy, I:119, 121
Chrysostom, I:185
Easter, 298-300
Iconoclastic Controversy, II:544-546
Leo IX, II:583
Stefan Dusan, II:845
Theoleptus of Philadelphia, II:899-901
Trullan Synod, II:824
Vladimir I, II:952-954
Easter Uprising, VII:733, 770, 877; IX:2794, 2804, 4083
East India Act, IV:1102, 1103
Eastman, George, **VII:996-999;** VIII:1457
Eastman School of Music, VIII:1457
East Meets West Foundation, VIII:1593-1595
Eban, Abba, **VII:1000-1003**
Ebenezer Baptist Church, VIII:1971, 1973
Eberhard of Franconia, II:706
Ebers Papyrus, I:445
Eberst, Jacob. *See* Offenbach, Jacques
Ebissa, I:380
Ebner, Ferdinand, VII:476
Éboué, Felix, **VII:1004-1007**
Eccles, Sir John Crew, **VII:1008-1010**
Facing Reality, VII:1010
Neurophysicological Basis of the Mind, The, VII:1009
Physiology of Nerve Cells, The, VII:1009
Physiology of Synapses, The, VII:1009
Self and Its Brain, The, VII:1010
Ecclesiastes, I:297, 801
Ecevit, Bülent, VIII:1814
Eck, Johann, III:443, 445, 504
Eckener, Hugo, **VII:1011-1014**
Eckstine, Billy, IX:2882
École Polytechnique, IV:975, 977
ecology
Cousteau, VII:781
Geiger, VII:1327
Linnaeus, IV:848
Theophrastus, I:874, 875
Economic Journal, VIII:1953, 1954
Economic Recovery Tax Act of 1981, VII:949
Economist, The, VI:2086
Eddington, Sir Arthur Stanley, VIII:2157, 2158
Eddy, Mary Baker, **V:738-742**
Christian Healing, V:739
Science and Health, V:740, 741
Eddy, Richard M., VI:1597
Edecon, I:126; II:685
Edelman, Marian Wright, VII:713, 714
Eden, Anthony, VII:531, **1015-1019,** 1063; VIII:2342
Eden, Garden of, II:500; III:72
Eden, Robert, IV:250
Edessa, II:560
Edinburgh, Treaty of, II:184, 185, 187, 188
Edinburgh, University of, IV:9, 882
Edinburgh Review, The
Brougham, V:314
Carlyle, V:416
Jeffrey, V:1224-1226
Macauley, VI:1427-1429
Mill, James, VI:1556
Mill, John Stuart, VI:1560
Edison, Thomas Alva, **V:743-747;** VI:2180, 2219, 2360; VII:1186; VIII:2278
Edison Central Electric Station, IX:3020
Edmeston, James, VI:2002
Edo, V:1117, 1118
Education Act of 1870, V:804
Education Act of 1902, VII:173
Education Act of 1944, VII:529-532
Edward I, **II:322-325**
Boniface VIII, II:172
Bruce, II:185, 187
Circumspecte agatis, II:322
De viris religiosis, II:322
Edward II, II:326
Nisi prius, II:322
Pecham, II:715, 716
Statute of Wales, II:323
Wallace, II:955-957
Westminster II, II:322
Westminster III, II:322
Edward II, II:187, 188, **326-328,** 329
Edward III, II:294-296, **329-332,** 786
Edward IV, **III:234-236**
Fortescue, III:268
Henry VI, III:342, 343

Henry VII, III:345
Louis XI, III:434
Richard III, III:647, 649-652
Warwick, III:775, 776
Edward V, III:650
Edward VI, **III:237-240**
Coverdale, III:194
Cranmer, III:204, 205
Gardiner, III:292, 293
Grey, III:318-320
Mary I, III:479
Tudor family, III:733
Edward VII, VI:2307, 2309; **VII:1020-1022,** 1339, 1340
Edward VIII, VII:170, 1062, 1345; VIII:2641; **IX:4025-407**
Edwards, Jonathan, **IV:428-431**
Faithful Narrative of the Surprising Work of God, A, IV:429
Freedom of Will, IV:430, 431
"Nature of True Virtue, The," IV:430
"Sinners in the Hands of an Angry God," IV:429
Treatise Concerning Religious Affections, A, IV:429-431
Edward the Confessor, **II:315-318,** 426, 997
Edward the Elder, **II:319-321**
EEOC. *See* Equal Employment Opportunity Commission
Efros, Israel, II:549
Égalité, Philippe, IV:814, 815, 1050
Egas Moniz, António, **VII:1023-1025**
Egbert, **II:333-335**
Egerton, Sir Thomas, IV:418
Egyptian National Revolution, VIII:2355
Ehrenfels, Christian von, **VII:1026-1030**
Comogony, VII:1026
Kampf des Prometheus, Der, VII:1027
Mutter des Legionärs, Die, VII:1027
Sängerweihe, VII:1027
Sternenbraut, Die, VII:1027
System der Werttheorie, VII:1027
Ehrlich, Eugen, **VII:1029-1031**
Fundamental Principles of the Sociology of Law, VII:1030
Ehrlich, Paul, V:183; **VII:1032-1034**
Eichmann, Adolf, VII:99, 100; IX:3984, 3985
Eickemeyer, Rudolf, VI:2121, 2122
E.I. Du Pont de Nemours and Company, V:718-720
Eielson, Carl Ben, IX:4000
Eiffel Tower, VIII:1693
1807, Embargo of, IV:719
1809, Plan of, VI:2090
1812, War of
Benton, V:195
Biddle, V:225
Burr, V:372
Calhoun, V:394
Clay, V:507
Decatur, V:634-636
Gallatin, V:861, 862
gunpowder, V:719
Harrison, V:1062
Houston, V:1137
Jackson, V:1196
Key, VI:1281
Madison, IV:888, 889
naval weapons, V:856
Perry, VI:1764
Pike, IV:1096
Scott, VI:2009
Tecumseh, VI:2204
Thayer, VI:2223, 2225
Van Buren, VI:2292
White House attack, VI:1465
Webster, VI:2345
1830, Revolution of, VI:1817, 1917
1832, Convention of, V:96
1833, Convention of, V:96
1837, Panic of, V:226; VI:2294
1848, Revolutions of
Bakunin, V:112
Beust, V:222-224
Blanc, V:260, 261
Courbet, V:565
Lassalle, VI:1324
Michelet, VI:1549
Proudhon, VI:1818
Stein, VI:2117
Tocqueville, VI:2239
1850, Compromise of
Brown, V:322
Clay, V:510
Davis, V:615
Douglas, V:692, 693
Houston, V:1138
Seward, VI:2037
Stephens, VI:2129
Tubman, VI:2265
Webster, VI:2345
1857, Mutiny of, V:34
1868, Treaty of, VI:2070
1870, Revolution of, V:113
1873, Panic of, V:1076; VIII:2480

1893, Panic of, V:513, 515; VI:1582
1898, Generation of, IX:3784
Eighteenth Amendment, VI:1633
Eightfold Path, I:145
Eighty Years' War, IV:500-502
Einhorn, David, VI:2401
Einstein, Albert, **VII:1035-1038**
  Bohr, VII:347
  Broglie, VII:473
  Compton, VII:746
  Hawking, VIII:1580, 1582, 1583
  Lagrange, IV:785
  lasers, VII:215
  Lemaître, VIII:2157, 2159
  Lorentz, VIII:2236
  Stark, IX:3491
Einstein Tower, VIII:2487
Einthoven, Willem, **VII:1039-1042**
Eire Constitution of 1937, IX:2805
Eisenhower, Dwight D., **VII:1043-1046**
  atomic energy, IX:3103
  Bradley, VII:403, 404
  Burger, VII:509
  Conant, VII:750
  Crusade in Europe, VII:1043
  Dulles, VII:977
  Graham, VIII:1448
  Hobby, VIII:1704, 1705
  Johnson, VIII:1867
  Khrushchev, VIII:1963
  Lippmann, VIII:2205
  McCarthy, VIII:2301, 2302
  Macmillan, VIII:2341
  Marshall, VIII:2431
  Montgomery, VIII:2603
  Moses, VIII:2635
  Nehru, VIII:2711
  Nixon, VIII:2758
  Owens, IX:2863
  Rundstedt, IX:3262
  Smith, IX:3447
  Stevenson, IX:3524, 3525
  Taft, IX:3592, 3593
  Truman, IX:3743
  Warren, IX:3889
  Zhukov, IX:4117
Eisenstein, Sergei, **VII:1047-1050**
  Alexander Nevsky, VII:1048, 1049
  Behzin Meadow, VII:1048
  Die Walküre, VII:1048
  Enough Stupidity in Every Wise Man, VII:1047
  Film Sense, The, VII:1048
  General Line, The, VII:1048
  Ivan the Terrible, VII:1048, 1049; IX:3087
  October: Or Ten Days That Shook the World, VII:1048
  Potemkin, VII:1048, 1049
  Protivogazy, VII:1047
  Que viva Mexico!, VII:1048
  Romance Sentimentale, VII:1048
  Strike, VII:1047-1049
  Thunder Over Mexico, VII:1048
Elchingen, Battle of, VI:1646
Elder, Louisine, V:435
Elea, I:596, 597, 955
Eleanor of Aquitaine, **II:336-339,** 782
Eleatics, I:249-251, 955
Eleazar, I:3, 4
Eleazar ben Arariah, I:27, 28
Electrical and Musical Instruments Limited. *See* EMI
Electric Boat Company, V:1125
electric lighting
  Edison, V:743, 745, 746
  Swan, VI:2179-2181
  Westinghouse, VI:2358, 2360, 2361
electricity
  Becquerel, V:166-168
  Faraday, V:767, 768, 770
  Franklin, IV:493, 494
  Galvani, IV:523-525
  Guericke, IV:586-588
  Helmholtz, V:1091
  Henry, V:1095
  Kelvin, VI:1270
  Maxwell, VI:1512
  Picard, IX:2995
  Popov, VI:1806-1808
  Siemens family, VI:2066-2069
  Steinmetz, VI:2121, 2122, 2124
  Tesla, VI:2219, 2220, 2222
  Volta, IV:1387, 1389, 1390
Electric Telegraph Company, V:557, 558
electromagnetism
  absorption spectra, VII:214
  Becquerel, V:166-168
  Broglie, VII:472
  Faraday, V:767, 768, 770
  Hawking, VIII:1582
  Henry, V:1094
  Kelvin, VI:1271
  Lorentz, VIII:2235-2237
  Maxwell, VI:1512, 1513
  Popov, VI:1807

electron
Bohr's atomic model, VIII:1617
cyclotron development, VII:379, 380; VIII:2121
diffraction, VIII:2698
dissociation hypothesis, VI:1412
exclusion principle, IX:2923-2925
K-capture, IX:4091
phase stability, VIII:2337
photoelectric effect, VIII:2539
Sommerfeld, VII:300
theory of, VIII:2235-2237
Urey, IX:3788
wave-matter composition of, VII:472-474; IX:3363
Electronic Data Systems, IX:2973, 2974
electronic music, IX:3542, 3794-3796
Elementary Education Act of 1870, V:988
elementary-particle physics, IX:4090-4092
Eleutherius, I:257, 258, 448
Elgar, Sir Edward, **VII:1051-1054**
Black Knight, The, VII:1052
Caractacus, VII:1052
Cockaigne Overture, VII:1053
Dream Gerontius, The, VII:1052
Falstaff, VII:1053
Froissart, VII:1051
In the South, VII:1053
Light of Life, The, VII:1052
Pomp and Circumstance, VII:1053
Scenes from the Saga of King Olaf, VII:1052
Symphony No. 1 in A-flat Major, Op. 55, VII:1053
Symphony No. 2 in E-flat Major, Op. 63, VII:1053
Variations on an Original Theme ("Enigma"), VII:1052
Violin Concerto in B Minor, Op. 61, VII:1053
Eli, I:746
Eliade, Mircea, **VII:1055-1057;** IX:3831
Forbidden Forest, The, VII:1056
History of Religious Ideas, A, VII:1057
Huliganii, VII:1055
Isabel si apele diavolului, VII:1056
Sacred and the Profane, The, VII:1055
Salazar si revolutia în Portugalia, VII:1056
Elijah ben Solomon, **IV:432-434**
Be'ur ha-Gra, IV:433
Eliodoro, Stanza d', III:643
Eliot, Charles William, **V:748-750**
Eliot, George, **V:751-754**
Adam Bede, V:752, 753
Daniel Deronda, V:753
Felix Holt, Radical, V:752
Life of Jesus, The, V:751
Middlemarch, V:753
Mill on the Floss, The, V:752
Romola, V:752
Scenes of Clerical Life, V:752
Silas Marner, V:752
Spanish Gypsy, The, V:752
Eliot, John, **IV:435-438**
Bay Psalm Book, IV:435
Indian Grammar, The, IV:437
Eliot, T.S., **VII:1058-1061**
Andrewes, IV:48
Ash Wednesday, VII:1059
Barnes, VII:201
"Burnt Norton," VII:1059
Cocktail Party, The, VII:1058, 1060
Confidential Clerk, The, VII:1060
"Dry Salvages, The," VII:1059
"East Coker," VII:1059
Elder Statesman, The, VII:1060
Ezra Pound, VII:1058
Family Reunion, The, VII:1059
Fitzgerald, VII:1163
Four Quartets, VII:1059; VIII:1506
H.D., VIII:1506
"Little Gidding," VII:1059
"Love Song of J. Alfred Prufrock, The," VII:1058
Murder in the Cathedral, VII:1058, 1059
Old Possum's Book of Practical Cats, VII:1060
Pirandello, IX:3015
Prufrock and Other Observations, VII:1058
Rock, The, VII:1058
Sacred Wood, The, VII:1058
Sweeney Agonistes, VII:1058
Villon, III:766
Waste Land, The, IV:637; VII:791, 1058-1060
Elis, I:625, 626
Elisha ben Abuyah, I:28
Elizabeth I, **III:241-245**
Bacon, III:41
Catholic persecution, III:257
Cecil, III:147-149
Cranmer, III:204, 206
Cromwell, III:209
Frobisher, III:278
James I, IV:699
Mary I, III:480, 482
Mary, Queen of Scots, III:475-477
Parker, III:588-590
Raleigh, III:638, 639
Salisbury, III:660, 661

Sidney, III:691-693
Tudor family, III:733, 734
Elizabeth II, **VII:1062-1065**
Britten, VII:469
Graham, VIII:1449
Macmillan, VIII:2343
Walton, IX:3874
Elizabethan Settlement, III:148, 149
Elizabeth of Hungary, Saint, **II:340-343**
Eliezer, Israel ben. *See* Ba'al Shem Tov
Ellicott, Andrew, IV:88, 90
Ellicott, George, IV:88, 90
Ellington, Duke, **VII:1066-1069**
Black, Brown, and Beige, VII:1068
"Mood Indigo," VII:1068
"Portraits," VII:1066
"Take the A Train," VII:1068
Elliot, Charles, VI:1377, 1378
Elliot, Jesse Duncan, VI:1764, 1765
Ellis, Charles D., VII:635
Ellis, Havelock, **VII:1070-1073**
Dance of Life, The, VII:1071
My Life, VII:1070
Sexual Inversion, VII:1071
Studies in the Psychology of Sex, VII:1071
Ellis, John McTaggert, VIII:2605, 2606
Ellison, Ralph, VIII:1868
Ellsworth, Lincoln, VII:534; IX:4001
Elpinice, I:198, 676
Elsheimer, Adam, IV:317, 318
Éluard, Paul, **VII:1074-1077;** IX:3067-3069
Capital of Pain, VII:1075
Dessous d'une vie, Les, VII:1075
Devoir et l'inquiétude, Le, VII:1074
Dialogues des inutiles, VII:1074
Livre ouvert I, 1938-1940, Le, VII:1076
Mourir de ne pas mourir, VII:1075, 1076
Nécessités de la vie et les conséquences des réves, VII:1075
Phénix, Le, VII:1076
Poèmes pour la paix, VII:1074
Poésie ininterrompue, VII:1076
Poetry and Truth, VII:1076
Premiers poèmes, VII:1074
Répétitions, VII:1075
Temps déborde, Le, VII:1076
Emancipation Proclamation, V:479, 886; VI:1383, 1773, 2172
Embargo Act, IV:888; V:343; VI:2147
Embargo of 1807. *See* 1807, Embargo of
embryology
Baer, V:109-111
Diocles of Carystus, I:261
Empedocles, I:284
Harvey, IV:629
Herophilus, I:400
Lankester, VI:1316, 1317
Malpighi, IV:892
Morgan, VIII:2618
Spallanzani, IV:1261
Emergency Society for German Science, VIII:1511
Emeric, II:575
Emerson, John, VI:1999, 2000
Emerson, Ralph Waldo, **V:755-759**
Agassiz, V:31, 32
"American Scholar, The," V:757, 758
Bancroft, V:126
Boston Unitarianism, V:472
"Brahma," V:758
"Character of Socrates, The," V:755
Conduct of Life, The, V:755, 758
"Days," V:758
"Divinity School Address," V:757, 758
English Traits, V:758
Essays, V:757
Essays: Second Series, V:757
Frost, VII:1252
Fuller, V:849, 850
Lazarus, VI:1334, 1336
Letters and Social Aims, V:758
Nature, V:755, 757
Parker, VI:1730
Poems, V:758
"Poet, The," V:758
"Present State of Ethical Philosophy, The," V:758
Representative Men, V:755, 758
"Self-Reliance," V:757
"Snow Storm, The," V:758
Society and Solitude, V:758
"Sphinx, The," V:758
"Terminus," V:758
Thoreau, VI:2234
Whitman, VI:2370, 2371
Emerson, Roy Stanley, VIII:2109-2111
EMI, VIII:1751-1753
EMIDEC 1100, VIII:1751
Emin Pasha, VI:2103
Emmanuel College, IV:371
Empedocles, I:260, 261, **282-286,** 512
On Nature, I:282, 284
Purifications, I:282, 284
Empire, VI:1731, 1732

Empiricism
Aretaeus of Cappadocia, I:81
Berkeley, IV:114-116
Boyle, IV:185
Bradley, V:291
Celsus, I:173
Comte, V:543
Condillac, IV:345, 346
Duns Scotus, II:312
Green, V:987
Leibniz, IV:829
Locke, IV:854-858
Pyrrhon of Elis, I:724, 725
Empiricus, Sextus, I:725
Enabling Act of 1956, VIII:1755
Enciso, Martín Fernández de, III:45
Encyclopaedia Britannica, V:767; VII:49, 301; VII:1220; VIII:1801
Enders, John F., IX:3305
Endoradiosonde, IX:4127
Endymion, V:636
energy, conservation of
Gay-Lussac, V:898
Grove, V:1011-1013
Heimholtz, V:1089-1091
Kelvin, VI:1270
Bothe, VII:379
Planck, IX:3033
Enfantin, Prosper, VI:1355
Engelhardt, Moritz von, VIII:1557
Engels, Friedrich, **V:760-762;** VI:1324, 1325, 1492
Condition of the Working Class in England, The, V:760; VI:1369
Herr Eugen Dühring's Revolution in Science, V:761; VII:291
Origin of the Family, Private Property, and the State, The, V:761
Socialism: Utopian and Scientific, V:761
Engel v. Vitale, VII:322
England, Bank of, IV:1066-1068; VI:1396
England, Church of
Andrewes, IV:46-49
Anne, IV:50, 52, 53
Anselm, II:72-74
Baxter, IV:98, 99
Becket, II:128-130
Boleyn, III:66, 68, 69
Bolingbroke, IV:157-161
Bunyan, IV:218, 219
Charles I, IV:280
Clarendon, IV:308, 310
Cranmer, III:204-206
Cromwell, III:208, 209
Education Act of 1870, V:804
Ferrar, IV:462-464
Gardiner, III:291-293
George I, IV:533
Gladstone, V:935, 936
Henry II, II:446-448
Henry VIII, III:349, 351
James II, IV:703-705
Lancaster, VI:1310
Laud, IV:797-799
Madison, IV:886
Manning, VI:1476-1478
More, III:533-536
Newman, VI:1641, 1643, 1644
Parker, III:588-590
Pusey, VI:1828-1831
Pym, IV:1141
Ridley, III:654-656
Swift, IV:1305, 1307
Tyndale, III:736, 737
Williams, IV:1451
English Bible, III:193-195, 204-206
English Bill of Rights, IV:940
English Civil Wars
Baxter, IV:98, 99
Blake, IV:132, 134, 135
Charles I, IV:279-281
Charles II, IV:283
Cromwell, IV:380
Fairfax, IV:446-449
Frederick Henry, IV:501
Hobbes, IV:664, 665
James II, IV:703
Lambert, IV:789-792
Monck, IV:971-973
Pride, IV:1126-1128
Scotland, IV:239
Sydenham, IV:1310
Winthrop, IV:1464
English common law
Bentham, IV:107-109
Blackstone, IV:129-131
Bracton, II:178-180
Coke, IV:329-334
Hale, IV:596-598
Kent, VI:1278, 1279
Mansfield, IV:907
English Commonwealth Navy, II:132-135
English Historical Review, V:12
English Opera Group, VII:470

English Reform Bill of 1832. *See* Reform Bill of 1832
English Revolution, IV:308-311
Ennius, Quintus, **I:287-289**
Ambracia, I:288
Annals, I:288, 289
Miscellanies, I:288
Sabinae, I:288
Enrile, Juan Ponce, VIII:2421
Enryakuji, III:571
Entente Cordiale of 1904, V:1131; IX:3691
Enver Pasha, **VII:1078-1082**
Environmental Protection Agency, VII:586
Enzo, II:363, 364
EPA. *See* Environmental Protection Agency
Epaminondas, **I:290-294**
Ephesus, I:626, 941
Ephesus, Council of, I:866
Ephetae, I:281
Ephialtes, I:609
Ephraimites, I:246
Ephron, Nora, **VII:1083-1086**
All the President's Men, VII:1084
Cookie, VII:1084
Crazy Salad, VII:1084
Heartburn, VII:1084
My Blue Heaven, VII:1085
Perfect Gentlemen, VII:1084
Scribble Scribble, VII:1084
Sleepless in Seattle, VII:1085
This Is My Life, VII:1085
Wallflower at the Orgy, The, VII:1083
When Harry Met Sally, VII:1084
Epicurus, I:87, 251, **295-298,** 511, 512
On Nature, I:296
Epidus, I:926
Epinician ode, I:787
Epstein, Brian, VII:226, 228
Epstein, Sir Jacob, **VII:1087-1090**
Adam, VII:1089
Christ, VII:1088
Christ in Majesty, VII:1089
Consummatum Est, VII:1089
Ecce Homo, VII:1089
Genesis, VII:1089
Head of an Infant, VII:1087
Lazarus, VII:1089
Lucifer, VII:1089
Madonna and Child, VII:1089
Memorial to W.H. Hudson, VII:1088
Rock Drill, VII:1088
Social Consciousness, VII:1089
"Strand" statues, VII:1087, 1088
Sun God, VII:1089
T.U.C. War Memorial, VII:1089
Venus, VII:1088
Equal Employment Opportunity Commission, IX:3657, 3658
Equal Rights Amendment, VIII:2537; IX:2919, 2920, 2922, 3447; IX:3521
Erasistratus, **I:299-302**
Erasmus, Desiderius, **III:246-249**
Bucer, III:101
Colet, III:169
Colloquies of Erasmus, The, III:248
De Copia, III:247
Education of a Christian Prince, The, III:247
Holbein the Younger, III:358
Lucian, I:509
Luther, III:445, 446
Manual of the Christian Knight, The, III:246
Marguerite of Navarre, III:467
Melanchthon, III:503
More, III:533, 535
Praise of Folly, The, III:247, 248
Proverbs or Adages, III:246, 247
Scaliger, III:671
Valla, III:741
Vitoria, III:768
Zwingli, III:791
Eratosthenes of Cyrene, **I:303-306**
Ancient Comedy, I:305
Ariston, I:303
Biography of Arsinoe III, I:305
Chronological Tables, I:305
Erigone, I:303
Euclid, I:308
Geographica, I:304
Hermes, I:303
Hipparchus, I:409
On Means, I:305
On the Measurement of the Earth, I:304
Platonicus, I:303
Ercker, Lazarus, III:3
Erdrich, Louise, **VII:1091-1093**
Baptism of Desire, VII:1093
Beet Queen, The, VII:1091, 1092
Bingo Palace, The, VII:1092
Broken Cord, The, VII:1091, 1093
Crown of Columbus, The, VII:1093
Jacklight, VII:1091
Love Medicine, VII:1091, 1092
Tracks, VII:1092
Yellow Raft in Blue Water, A, VII:1093

Erfurt Program, VII:292
Ergriffenheit, VII:1244
Erhard, Ludwig, **VII:1094-1097**
Erie, Lake, VI:1764
Erie Canal, V:517, 519, 520
Eriksson. *See* Leif Eriksson
Erik the Red, II:577
Erkenntnis, VII:583
Ernst, Max, VII:1075, **1098-1101;** VIII:2548
  After Me, Sleep, VII:1100
  Coloradeau of Medusa, VII:1100
  Elephant Célèbes, The, VII:1099
  Eye of Silence, The, VII:1100
  Flowers and Fish, VII:1098
  King Playing with the Queen, The, VII:1100
  Landscape with Sun, VII:1098
  Lunar Asparagus, VII:1100
  Marriage of Heaven and Earth, The, VII:1100
  Oedipus Rex, VII:1099, 1100
  Pietà, VII:1099
  Two Children Are Menaced by a Nightingale, VII:1099
  Two Sisters, VII:1099
  Ubu Imperator, VII:1099
  Vox Angelica, VII:1100
Ernst, Wilhelm. *See* Saxe-Weimar, Duke of
Ernst Heinkel Flugzeugwerke, VIII:1614, 1615
Errors, Syllabus of, VI:1784
Erskine, First Baron, **IV:439-442**
Erzberger, Matthias, **VII:1102-1106**
Esarhaddon, I:105, 111
Eschenbach, Wolfram von. *See* Wolfram von Eschenbach
Esenin, Sergei Aleksandrovich, VII:982
Eshkol, Levi, VIII:2473, 2474
Eshnunna, I:362
Eskimos. *See* Inuits
Esma'il I, III:38, 39, 52
Esperanto, IV:385; VII:583
Esquiline Hill, I:520, 521
Esquire magazine, VII:1083, 1084
Essenes, I:467
Essex, First Earl of, III:41, 148, 149, 639, 691
Essex, Second Earl of, III:660, 661
Este, House of, III:32-34, 60, 710
Esterházy, Miklós József, IV:639
Étampes, Madame d', III:153
Etelköz, II:86, 87
Ethelflaed, II:320
Ethelred II, the Unready, II:201, 202, 315, **344-346,** 688
Ethelweard, Chronicle of, II:319
Ethelwold, II:319
Ethelwulf, II:334
Ethical Culture Society, V:26, 27, 29
Étudiant noir, L', VII:631
Euchidas, I:622
Eucken, Rudolf Christoph, **VII:1106-1108;** IX:3347
  Geschichte und Kritik der Grundbegriffe der Gegenwart, VII:1106
  Knowledge and Life, VII:1107
  Meaning and Value of Life, The, VII:1107
  Mensch und Welt, VII:1107
  Problem of Human Life, The, VII:1106
  Truth of Religion, The, VII:1106
Euclid, **I:307-309**
  Abu Wefa, II:20
  Apollonius of Perga, I:73
  Data, I:307
  Elements, I:307, 308, 310, 311, 729; II:63
  Hypatia, I:437
  Lobachevsky, VI:1403-1405
  Optics, I:308
  Phaenomena, I:308
  Sectio canonis, I:308
Euclidian geometry, VI:1403-1405
Eudemos, I:339
Eudoxus of Cnidus, **I:310-313**
  Enoptron, I:312
  Phainomena, I:312
Eugene IV, III:559
Eugene of Savoy, IV:655-657
Eugenius, I:871
Eugenius III, II:357, 358, 474
Eukles, I:622
Euler, Leonhard, **IV:443-445,** 884
  Institutiones calculi differentialis, IV:445
  Institutiones calculi integralis, IV:445
  Introductio in analysis in infinitorum, IV:445
  Letters of Euler to a German Princess, on Different Subjects in Physics and Philosophy, VII:318
  Mechanica sive motus scientia analytice exposita, IV:445
  Theoria motus corporum solidorum seu rigidorum, IV:445
Eumenes, I:60, 767
Eunomia, rule of, I:646
Eunomius, I:353
Eupalinus of Megara, **I:314-316**
Eupatrids, I:9
Euratom, VIII:2585

Euripides, **I:317-321**
Alcestis, I:317, 807
Andromache, I:318
Aristophanes, I:91
Bacchae, The, I:319
Children of Herakles, The, I:318
Electra, I:318, 808
Hecuba, I:318
Helen, I:319
Hippolytus, I:318
Ion, I:319
Iphigenia in Aulis, I:319
Iphigenia in Tauris, I:319
Medea, I:317, 318, 807
Orestes, I:319
Peliades, I:317
Suppliants, The, I:318
Trojan Women, The, I:318
Europe, Council of, VIII:1645
European Atomic Energy Community, IX:3477
European Center of Nuclear Research. *See* CERN
European Coal and Steel Community, VIII:2584, 2585; IX:3477
European Common Market, VIII:2585; IX:3053, 3054
European Court of Human Rights, VII:611
European Defense Community, VIII:2585
European Economic Commission, VIII:2672
European Economic Community
Attlee, VII:139
Heath, VIII:1606-1608
Israel, VII:1002
Major, VIII:2369-2371
Spaak, IX:3477
Wilson, IX:4017, 4018
European Economic Cooperation, Organization of, VIII:1529
European Monetary System, VIII:2585
European Nuclear Research, Center for. *See* CERN
European Recovery Program. *See* Marshall Plan
Eurydice, VI:1685
Euryphon, I:412
Eusebius of Caesarea, **I:322-325**
Chronicle, I:322; III:672, 673
Ecclesiastical History, I:322-324, 447, 448
Helena, I:375
Hippolytus of Rome, I:417, 418
Life of Constantine, I:227, 323, 375
Eustace, II:849
Eutaw Springs, Battle of, IV:576
Euthymenes, I:370
Euterpe, V:1003
evangelism
Graham, VIII:1447-1449
Moody, VI:1575-1577
Pusey, VI:1828, 1830
Sunday, IX:3582-3584
Wesley, IV:1426-1429
Wilberforce, IV:1435-1438
Evangelical Synod, VIII:2735
Evans, Mary Ann. *See* Eliot, George
Evatt, Herbert Vere, **VII:1109-1111**
Conveyancing Precedents and Forms, VII:1109
King and His Dominion Governors, The, VII:1110
Eve. *See* Adam and Eve
Everest, Mount, VIII:1662-1664, 2507
Everett, Edward, V:126; VI:1772
Evert, Chris, **VII:1112-1114;** VIII:2703
Evesham, Battle of, II:646
Evian Conference, VIII:2472
evolution, theory of
Agassiz, V:32
Baer, V:110
Beecher, V:175
Bergson, VII:283, 284
Buffon, IV:215-217
Cuvier, V:589-591
Darwin, V:606, 608, 609
Empedocles, I:284
Gray, V:979, 980
Haeckel, V:1018, 1020, 1021
Huxley, V:1172-1174
Leakey, VIII:2145-2148
Linnaeus, IV:848
Monkey Trial, VII:481, 840
Oparin, IX:2830, 2831
Spencer, VI:2087, 2088
Teilhard de Chardin, IX:3628
Tennyson, VI:2211
Weismann, VI:2350
evolutionary socialism, VI:1323, 2122
Ewing, Thomas, VI:2059
Exchequer, II:444; IV:309; VII:121, 122, 168, 532
Exclusion Crisis of 1679-1681, IV:1230
Execestides, I:803
Execration Texts, I:774
existentialism
Beauvoir, VII:230-232
Bellow, VII:247
Camus, VII:553-555
Hardy, V:1043
Heidegger, VIII:1610-1612
Hesse, VIII:1650-1653

Ibsen, V:1178
Jaspers, VIII:1843-1845
Kafka, VIII:1902
Kierkegaard, VI:1284, 1286, 1287
Kleist, VI:1294, 1295
Marcel, VIII:2407-2409
Merleau-Ponty, VIII:2500-2507
Montaigne, III:526
Ortega y Gasset, IX:2844
Parmenides, I:597, 598
psychiatry, VII:330
Rouault, IX:3251
Sartre, IX:3327, 3329, 3330
Schelling, VI:1972-1974
Teilhard de Chardin, IX:3629
Unamuno y Jugo, IX:3783-3785
Exner, Sigmund, VII:1235
Exodus, I:1, 3, 4
Expiatory Church of the Sagrada Familia, VII:1316, 1317
Explorer I, VII:111
Expressionism
Frankenthaler, VII:1208
Kandinsky, VII:1903-1905
Kirchner, VIII:1991-1993
Kokoschka, VIII:2012-2015
Krasner, VIII:2023-2025
Martin, VIII:2437-2439
Mondrian, VIII:2577
Pollock, IX:3048-3050
See also Blue Rider movement
Expressive Dance Movement, VIII:2058-2060
Extraordinary Arab Summit, VIII:1794
Eyck, Hubert van, **III:250-253**
Ghent Altarpiece, III:251, 252
Heures de Turin, III:250, 251
Three Marys at the Sepulcher, The, III:251
Eyck, Jan van, II:834; **III:250-253,** 778, 779
Arnolfini Wedding, The, III:252
Ghent Altarpiece, III:251, 252
Heures de Turin, III:250, 251
Madonna with Chancellor Rolin, III:252
Man with the Red Turban, III:250
Eylau, Battle of, VI:1646
Eymard, Pierre-Julien, VI:1900
Ezekiel, **I:326-329,** 570; II:10
Ezhov, Nikolai, VIII:2377
Ezra, **I:330-333**

Fabian, John, IX:3179
Fabian Society, V:212; VIII:1707, 1708; IX:2871, 3399, 3400, 3402, 3905-3907, 3939, 3940
Fabius, **I:334-337**, 365
fables
Aesop, I:13-15
Callimachus, I:156
Hyginus, I:398
La Fontaine, IV:781-783
Phaedrus, I:618-620
Fabricius, IV:626, 628
Fabrizi, Aldo, VII:1141
Factory Acts, V:458, 678, 996; VI:1709
Fahd, **VII:1115-1117;** IX:4080, 4081
Fahd Plan, VII:1115
Faidherbe, Louis, **V:763-766**
Fairbanks, Douglas, Jr., VIII:1638
Fair Deal, IX:3740, 3743
Fairfax, Third Baron, **IV:446-449**; 789, 790, 1126
Fairfax Resolves, IV:926
Fairhair, Harald, II:688
Fair Labor Standards Act, IX:2963
fairy tales, V:58-60, 1006-1008, 1162-1164
Faisal, **VII:1118-1121**
Faisal I, **VII:1122-1126**
Faisal II, VIII:1793, 2695
Fakhr al-Din al-Razi, **II:347-349**
Kitab al-tafsir al-kabir, II:348
Muhassal, II:348
Fa Koli, II:863, 864
Falkland, Lord, IV:308
Falkland Islands, III:213; IX:2959, 3651
Falköping, Battle of, II:627
Fall, Albert B., VIII:1551, 1552
Falla, Manuel de, **VII:1127-1129**
amor brujo, El, VII:1127, 1128
Atlántida, L', VII:1128, 1129
Four Spanish Pieces, VII:1127
Noches en los jardines de Espana, VII:1127, 1128
Three Cornered Hat, The, VII:1127
vida breve, La, VII:1127, 1128
Fallen Timbers, Battle of, VI:2204
Fallingwater, IX:4061
Fallopio, Gabriello, III:756
Fallot, VI:1817
Falloux Law, VI:2227
Falstaff, I:659, 660
FAMOUS, Project, VII:180
Famous Players-Lasky Company, VII:897; VIII:1415; IX:3006, 3008
Fan Chung-yen, II:709, 710
Fang Hsuan-ling, II:877, 879
Fan Li, II:918

Faraday, Michael, **V:767-771**
Chemical History of a Candle, The, V:768
Edison, V:743
Kelvin, VI:1269-1271
Maxwell, VI:1512, 1513
Nernst, VIII:2713
Various Forces of Nature, The, V:768
Farington, Joseph, V:547
Farinier, William, II:683
Farm Security Administration, VIII:2084, 2085; IX:3861
Farm Workers Association, VIII:1762-1764
Farnese, Alessandro, **III:254-256**
Farnese Gallery, III:126, 127
Farnsworth House, VIII:2523
Farragut, David G., V:656, **772-775**
Farrand, Beatrix Jones, **VII:1130-1132**
Farrell, Edelmiro J., IX:2970
Fars Province, II:806, 807
Fascism
Croce, VII:801, 802
De Gasperi, VII:863
Franco, VII:1201
Futurism, VII:342
Gentile, VII:1336-1338
Hellman's plays, VIII:1622
Hopkins, VIII:1736
Lukács, VIII:2274
Mann, VIII:2393
Montale, VIII:2592
Mosca, VIII:2630-2632
Mussolini, VIII:2667-2670
Pirelli, IX:3021
Sorel, IX:3464
Tunisia, VII:391
Visconti's films, IX:3818
Fatah, al-, VII:90-92, 1120
Fatamids, II:7, 68, 69
Fatimah of Cordova, II:491
Faulkner, William, VII:283, **1133-1136;** VIII:2626
Absalom, Absalom!, VII:1134
As I Lay Dying, VII:1134
Fable, A, VII:1135
Flags in the Dust, VII:1133, 1134
Go Down, Moses, VII:1135
Hamlet, The, VII:1135
Intruder in the Dust, VII:1135
Light in August, VII:1134
Mansion, The, VII:1135
Marble Faun, The, VII:1133
Mosquitoes, VII:1133
Pylon, VII:1134
Reivers, The, VII:1135
Sanctuary, VII:1134, 1135
Sartoris, VII:1134
Soldiers' Pay, VII:1133
Sound and the Fury, The, VII:1133, 1134
Town, The, VII:1135
Unvanquished, The, VII:1135
Wild Palms, The, VII:1135
Faure, Abbé Jean-Baptiste, VI:2249
Fausta, I:376
Faustus, I:159
Fauvism
Braque, VII:431
Delaunay, VII:888
Matisse, VIII:2452, 2454, 2455
Mondrian, VIII:2576
Rivera, IX:3185
Fawcett, Dame Millicent Garrett, **V:776-779**
Janet Doncaster, V:776
Political Economy for Beginners, V:776
Fawkes, Guy, **III:257-259,** 662
Faye, Antoine de la, III:96
Faysal ibn al-Husayn, VIII:2126, 2127
FBI. *See* Federal Bureau of Investigation
FDIC. *See* Federal Deposit Insurance Corporation
February House, VIII:2308
February Revolution. *See* Russian Revolution of 1917
Fechner, Gustav Theodor, **V:780-782**
Elements of Psychophysics, V:781
Nanna, V:780
Vorschule der Aesthetik, V:781
Zend-Avesta, V:780
Federal Art Project, U.S., IX:3048
Federal Bureau of Investigation, U.S., VIII:1732-1734
Federal Bureau of Prisons, U.S., VII:510
Federal Children's Bureau, U.S., IX:3838
Federal Deposit Insurance Corporation, U.S., IX:3224
Federal Emergency Relief Adminstration, U.S., VIII:1736; IX:2963
Federalist Party, U.S.
Adams, John, IV:18, 19
Adams, John Quincy, V:20
Buchanan, V:346
Burr, V:370
Chase, IV:295
Clinton, V:518
Constitution, IV:1457, 1458
Garrison, V:883
Hamilton, IV:611

Jay, IV:713, 714
Jefferson, IV:718, 719
Madison, IV:888, 889
Monroe, VI:1571, 1573
Morris, IV:1000, 1001
Federalists, Mexican, V:95
Federal Reserve System, U.S., VI:2295; VII:421; VIII:1471-1473
Federal Security Agency, U.S., VIII:1704
Federal Trade Commission, U.S., VII:421; VIII:2680
Federal Union, VII:610
Federal Works Theater Project, U.S., VII:985
Federation League, V:148
Feinstein, Diane, **VII:1137-1140,** 1154
Felician controversy, I:696, 791
Felix V, III:559, 560
Felix of Trier, I:791
Fell, Margaret, IV:485
Fellini, Federico, **VII:1141-1144**
Amarcord, VII:1142
And the Ship Sails On, VII:1143
Casanova, VII:1142
City of Women, VII:1142
dolce vita, La, VII:1142
8 1/2, VII:1142
Fellini Roma, VII:1142
Fellini Satyricon, VII:1142
Juliet of the Spirits, VII:1142
Nights of Cabiria, The, VII:1141
Strada, La, VII:1141
Variety Lights, VII:1141
White Sheik, The, VII:1141
feminism
Adams, John Quincy, V:24
Anthony, V:61-64
Arzner, VII:119
Barton, V:143
Burr, V:371
Christine de Pizan, II:262
Friedan, VII:1231, 1233
Fuller, V:849, 850, 852
Grass, VIII:1464
Horney, VIII:1746
Hutchinson, IV:689
MacKinnon, VIII:2325-2327
Millay, VIII:2529, 2530, 2532
Millett, VIII:2536-2538
Montagu, IV:984
Morrison, VIII:2628
Plato, I:657
Ross, IV:1192
Rukeyser, IX:3259
Sexton, IX:3395-3397
Spock, IX:3479
Stanton, VI:2111
Steinem, IX:3519, 3521, 3522
Terry, IX:3642-3644
Theodora, II:892
Virgin Mary, I:941
Willard, VI:2390
Wollstonecraft, IV:1475-1478
Workman, VI:2412
Zetkin, IX:4112
Feng, Marshal, VII:905
Feng Sacrifice, I:818
Feng Yün-shan, V:1165, 1166
Fenian Model, V:1124
Fenian Order, V:1123, 1124
Fenian Ram, V:1124
Fenstanton, IV:205
Fenway Court, VII:1301, 1302
Ferdinand II (Holy Roman Empire), **IV:450-453,** 1397; V:625, 626
Ferdinand II (Spain), **III:260-263**
Cabot, III:113
Catherine of Aragon, III:136
Columbus, III:172-174
Jiménez de Cisneros, III:393, 394
Manuel I, III:465
Ponce de Léon, III:630, 631
Prescott, VI:1814
Vespucci, III:759
Ferdinand III (Spain), II:56
Ferdinand V (Spain), III:45, 46, 725, 726
Ferdinand VII (Spain), V:413, 414
Fergana, III:36
Ferguson, Adam, **IV:454-457**
Essay on the History of Civil Society, An, IV:454
History of the Progress and Termination of the Roman Republic, IV:454
Institutes of Moral Philosophy, IV:454
Principles of Moral and Political Science, IV:454
Fergusson, Robert, IV:229
Fermat, Pierre de, **IV:458-461**
Fermi, Enrico, **VII:1145-1149**
Bethe, VII:300
Chadwick, VII:636
Compton, VII:747
Hahn, VIII:1514
Hevesy, VIII:1655
Meitner, VIII:2477
Fernando VII, VI:1958

Fernando Po, IX:3757
Ferrante of Naples, III:496
Ferrar, Nicholas, **IV:462-464**
Ferrara, Duchy of, III:32-34, 48, 117, 710; IV:990, 991
Ferrari, Enzo, **VII:1150-1152**
Ferraro, Geraldine, **VII:1153-1156**
Fersen, Hans Axel von, IV:919
Festus, Sextus Pompeius, I:931
Fetterman Massacre, VI:1851
Fetti, Domenico
  Ecce Homo, IV:1488
feudalism
  Alexander I, V:44
  Alexander II, V:48, 49
  Bohemia, IV:750, 751
  Edward I, II:322
  Fronde, IV:866
  Germany, II:357-360, 392, 1005
  Godunov, III:308
  Heine, V:1085-1087
  Henry II, II:447, 448
  Henry III, II:454, 646
  Henry the Lion, II:467
  Hungary, V:625-628
  Ivan the Great, III:383
  Louis IX, II:603, 605
  Louis XI, III:434, 435
  Matthias I Corvinus, III:488, 489
  Oda Nobunaga, III:570-572
  Peasants' Revolt, II:921-923
  Philip IV the Fair, II:736
  Prussia, IV:506; VI:2116
  Richard II, II:786
  Rollo, II:795
  Rudolf I, II:798
  Russia, IV:259, 1087-1089
  Saigo Takamori, VI:1936-1939
  Scandinavia, II:626
  Scharnhorst, VI:1970
  Scotland, II:184, 185, 291, 292
  Stephen, II:848
  Tokugawa Ieyasu, IV:1327-1329
  Toyotomi Hideyoshi, III:729, 730
  Turgot, IV:1350
  William the Conqueror, II:997, 998
Feuerbach, Ludwig, VI:1492
Few, William P., V:706
Fez Plan. *See* Fahd Plan
Fiammetta, II:150, 152
Fianna Fáil, VII:878; IX:2804-2806
Fibonacci, Leonardo. *See* Leonardo of Pisa
Fichte, Johann Gottlieb, **IV:465-468;** VI:1972, 1974
  Addresses to the German Nation, IV:467
  Attempt at a Critique of All Revelation, IV:465
  Beitrag zur Berichtigung der Urteile des Publikums über die französische Revolution, IV:465
  Science of Ethics as Based on the Science of Knowledge, The, IV:467
  Science of Knowledge, The, IV:465, 466
  Science of Rights, The, IV:467
  Vocation of Man, The, IV:467
  Way Towards the Blessed Life, The, IV:467
  Zurückforderung der Denkfreiheit von der Fürsten Europens, IV:465
Field, Marshall, **V:783-786**
Field, Stephen J., **V:787-791**
Fielding, Henry, **IV:469-472**
  Amelia, IV:471
  Apology for the Life of Mrs. Shamela Andrews, IV:470
  History of the Adventures of Joseph Andrews, and of His Friend Mr. Abraham Adams, IV:470
  History of the Life of the Late Mr. Jonathan Wild the Great, The, IV:470
  History of Tom Jones, A Foundling, The, IV:470, 471
  Journal of a Voyage to Lisbon, The, IV:471
  "Masquerade, The," IV:469
  Tragedy of Tragedies, The, IV:469
Fields, Annie, V:1228
Fields, Lew, VIII:1588
Fields, W.C., IX:3950
Fieschi, Sinibaldo. *See* Innocent IV
Fifth Extermination Campaign, VII:688
Fifth Republic of France, VII:866
Fifth Street Gym, VII:54
Fifth Syrian War, I:64
Filioque doctrine, II:583, 899, 900
Fillmore, Millard, **V:792-795**
Finch, Anne, IV:195
Fine Gael, VII:772
Finisterre, first battle of, IV:56, 57
Finlay, Carlos Juan, VI:1858, 1859
Finnish War for Independence, VIII:2396
Fiore, Order of, II:535
Firdusi, **II:350-353**
  Shahnamah, II:350-352
Firpo, Luis Angel, VII:903
First Aero Squadron, VIII:2554
First Amendment
  Black, VII:323
  Cardozo, VII:577

Frankfurter, VII:1214
MacKinnon, VIII:2326
Zenger, IV:1484-1486
See also freedom of speech
First Bourbon Restoration, V:611
First Carlist War, V:414
First Church of Christ, Scientist, V:740
First Five-Year Plan of the Soviet Union, IX:3483
First International, V:113
First International Women's Conference, IX:4113
First Jewish Revolt, I:880
First Manassas, Battle of, V:1205
First Mover, II:829
First National Woman's Rights Convention, VI:2143
First-Quarter Storm, VIII:2421
First Reform Bill, V:935
First Seminole War. *See* Seminole Wars
First Sikh War, VI:1331
First Syrian War, I:717
First Triumvirate, I:149, 166-168, 196, 680, 681
Fischer, Emil, VII:927; VIII:2476
Fischer von Erlach, Johann Bernhard, **IV:473-475**
Fischer von Erlach, Joseph Emanuel, IV:655, 657
Fisher, Andrew, VIII:1775
Fisher, George, V:1141
Fisher, John, V:548, 549
Fisher, Saint John, **III:264-266**
Fisk, Diamond Jim, VI:1581, 2285
Fitch, John, **IV:476-478**
Fitzgerald, Ella, **VII:1157-1160**
"Cole Porter Songbook, The," VII:1159
"Tisket, a Tasket, A," VII:1157
"You Showed Me the Way," VII:1157
Fitzgerald, F. Scott, **VII:1161-1165;** IX:4012
Beautiful and Damned, The, VII:1163
Crack-Up, The, VII:1164
Great Gatsby, The, VII:1163, 1164
Last Tycoon, The, VII:1163
Tender is the Night, VII:1162-1164
This Side of Paradise, VII:1161-1163
Three Comrades, VII:1163
Vegetable, The, VII:1163
Fitzgerald, Zelda, VII:1161-1164
Five Hundred, Council of, V:398
Flaminius, Gaius, I:334, 365
Flamsteed, John, IV:600, 601
Flaubert, Gustave, **V:796-799**
Bouvard et Pécuchet, V:798
Madame Bovary, V:796, 798; VII:569, 756; IX:3158
Over Strand and Field, V:796
Salammbô, V:798; VI:1611
Sentimental Education, A, V:798
Temptation of Saint Anthony, The, V:796
Three Tales, V:798; VIII:1816
Flaxman, John, IV:1423; V:411
Fleet, Biddy, IX:2880
Fleetwood, Charles, IV:527
Flémalle, Master of, III:779
Fleming, Sir Alexander, **VII:1166-1168,** 1172, 1174
Fletcher, Frank Jack, VIII:2751
Fletcher, John, **III:54-57,** 689
Captain, The, III:56
Cardenio, III:56
Coxcomb, The, III:56
Cupid's Revenge, III:56
Faithful Shepherdess, The, III:54
Henry VIII, III:56
King and No King, A, III:55, 689
Maid's Tragedy, The, III:55
Philaster, III:55, 689
Scornful Lady, The, III:56
Tragedy of Thierry, King of France and His Brother Theodoret, III:55
Two Noble Kinsmen, The, III:56
Fletcher v. Peck, VI:2147
Flexner, Abraham, **VII:1169-1171**
American College, The, VII:1169
Medical Education in Europe, VII:1169
Medical Education in the United States and Canada, VII:1169
Universities, VII:1170
Fliess, Wilhelm, VII:1225
Florence, Italy
Arnolfo di Cambio, II:82-84
cathedral at, III:302
Dante, II:286, 288
Giotto, II:388
Martini, II:632
Pisano, II:744
Villani, II:938, 940
Florentius, II;136, 137
Florey, Baron, VII:1167, **1172-1174**
Florida
Adams, John Quincy, V:22
Cabeza de Vaca, III:110
Gadsden, V:858-860
Menéndez de Avilés, III:507-509
Ponce de Léon, III:629-631
Soto, III:699, 700
Tyler, VI:2291
Florinus, I:448

Flowers, Gennifer, VII:714
Foch, Ferdinand, VII:705
Fokine, Michel, VII:920; VIII:2746, 2749; IX:2937, 2939
folk literature. *See* fable
folk music, IV:229; VIII:1835-1837; IX:3798, 3799, 3815-3817
Folsom, James "Big Jim," IX:3858
Fontainebleau, Edict of, IV:873
Fontana, Prospero, III:125
Fontanne, Lynn, VII:786
Fonteyn, Dame Margot, **VII:1175-1179**
  Moor's Pavane, The, VII:1178
  Ondine, VII:1177
  Paradise Lost, VII:1177
  Pelléas and Mélisande, VII:1177
  Poème d'extase, VII:1178
Foraker, Joseph B., V:1029, 1031
Ford, Gerald R., **VII:1180-1183**
  Bush, VII:521
  Carter, VII:590
  Dole, VII:948
  Greenspan, VIII:1471
  Nixon, VIII:2760
  Reagan, IX:3138
Ford, Henry, IV:1023; VI:1345; **VII:1184-1188**
Ford, John, IX:3902
Ford, Philip, IV:1080
Ford, Richard, IV:397
Ford Foundation, VII:158, 165, 1184, 1187; VIII:802
Ford Motor Company
  Ferrari, VII:1151
  Ford, VII:1184, 1186, 1187
  Fuller, VII:1268
  Lenoir, VI:1345
  Niebuhr, VIII:2735
  Reuther, IX:3162
  Toyota Motor Company, IX:3720
Fordney-McCumber Tariff, VIII:1551
Forel, Auguste, VIII:2012
Foreman, George, VII:56
Forest, Charter of the, II:329
Forester, C.S., **VII:1189-1192**
  African Queen, The, VII:1190
  Beat to Quarters, VII:1190
  Brown on Resolution, VII:1189
  Commodore Hornblower, VII:1191
  Flying Colours, VII:1191
  General, The, VII:1190
  Good Shepherd, The, VII:1191
  Gun, The, VII:1190
  Hornblower and the Crisis, VII:1191
  Lieutenant Hornblower, VII:1191
  Long Before Forty, VII:1189
  Lord Hornblower, VII:1191
  Mr. Midshipman Hornblower, VII:1191
  Paid Piper, The, VII:1190
  Pawn Among Kings, A, VII:1190
  Payment Deferred, VII:1190
  Rifleman Dodd, VII:1190
  Ship of the Line, A, VII:1191
  Ship, The, VII:1191
Forkbeard, Sven, II:688
Former Han Dynasty, I:224, 590
Forrest, Edwin, V:272, **800-803;** VI:1461
Forster, E.M., **VII:1193-1196**
  Alexandria, VII:1194
  Aspects of the Novel, VII:1195
  Maurice, VII:1194
  Passage to India, A, VII:1194, 1195
  Pharos and Pharillon, VII:1194
  Room with a View, A, VII:1193
Forster, William Edward, **V:804-806**
Forten, Charlotte, **V:807-809**
Fortescue, Sir John, **III:267-269**
  De laudibus legum Angliæ, III:268, 269
  De natura legis naturæ, III:268
  Governance of England, The, III:268
Fortunatus, Venantius, II:405
Fortune magazine, VII:395, 397
Fortune, Reo, VIII:2469
Fort Wayne, Treaty of, VI:2204
Fort William, College of, VI:1846
Fossey, Dian, VIII:2148
Foster, Stephen Collins, **V:810-813**
  "Beautiful Dreamer," V:812
  "Oh! Susanna," V:810, 811
  "Old Black Joe," V:812
  "Swanee River," V:811
Fothergill, John, IV:182, 183
Foucault, Jean-Bernard-Léon, VI:1551
Fouquet, Nicolas, IV:336, 337, 781, 782, 834, 835
Fourier, Charles, **V:814-818;** VI:1817; VII:450
  Social Destiny of Man, V:814
  Social Science, V:814
Fourier, Joseph, **V:819-821**
  Analytical Theory of Heat, The, V:820
Fourteenth Amendment
  Anthony, V:62
  Cushing, V:583
  Dred Scott decision, VI:2001
  Field, V:788, 790
  Frankfurter, VII:1214

Hayes, V:1078
Holmes, VIII:1721
Hughes, VIII:1769
Johnson, V:1235-1237
MacKinnon, VIII:2326
Marshall, VIII:2434
Stevens, VI:2137
Fourteenth Army. *See* British Fourteenth Army
Fourth Amendment, VII:422
Fourth Party, VII:172
Fourth Republic of France
Blum, VII:337
de Gaulle, VII:867
Herriot, VIII:1646
Mendès-France, VIII:2491-2493
Mitterrand, VIII:2558-2560
Four Winds, III:85, 86
Fowler, Lydia Folger, **V:822-824**
Fox, Charles James, IV:224, **479-483,** 542, 1036, 1102, 1103
Fox, George, **IV:484-486**
Foxe, John, III:655
Fox Libel Act, IV:440, 1486
Fracastoro, Girolamo, **III:270-273**
De causis criticorum dierum libellus, III:271
De contagione et contagiosis morbis et eorum curatione, III:271
De sympathia et antipathia rerum, III:271
"Fracastorius sive de anima dialogus," III:272
Homocentricorum sive de stellis, III:271
Naugerius sive de poetica dialogus, III:272
Syphilis, III:270, 271
"Turrius sive de intellectione dialogus," III:272
Fragonard, Jean-Honoré, IV:414, **488-491**
Corésus Sacrificing Himself to Save Callirhoé, IV:488
Fête at Saint-Cloud, The, IV:490
Good Mother, The, IV:489
Progress of Love, IV:489
Swing, The, IV:488, 489
Fram, VIII:2686
France, Anatole, **V:825-828**
Balthasar, V:825
Crime of Sylvestre Bonnard, The, V:825
Gods Are Athirst, The, V:828
Jocasta and the Famished Cat, V:825
Merrie Tales of Jacques Tournebroche, The, V:827
Monsieur Bergeret in Paris, V:827
Noces corinthiennes, Les, V:825
Penguin Island, V:827
Red Lily, The, V:827
Revolt of the Angels, The, V:827, 828
Seven Wives of Bluebeard and Other Marvellous Tales, The, V:827
Tales from a Mother of Pearl Casket, V:827
Thaïs, V:825
Well of Santa Clara, The, V:827
White Stone, The, V:827
Francesca, Piero della, III:59
Franciabigio, III:24
Francis I, **III:274-277**
Andrea del Sarto, III:24
Bayard, III:49
Cartier, III:129, 130
Cellini, III:152, 153
Clement VII, III:166
Francis II, III:243, 333, 475
Francis, Convers, VI:1727
Franciscan Order
Anthony of Padua, II:76, 77
Bacon, II:110, 112
Bonaventure, II:163-165
Carpini, II:206-208
Duns Scotus, II:309, 311
Francis of Assisi, II:354-356
Gregory IX, II:399, 401
Ockham, II:682
Pecham, II:715-717
Rienzo, II:791
Salimbene, II:812, 813
William of Saint-Amour, II:990, 991
Francis Ferdinand, **VII:1197-1199;** IX:4005
Francis Joseph I, V:626, 627, **829-831;** VI:2158
Francis of Assisi, Saint, **II:354-356,** 812; III:60
"Canticle of Creatures," II:354
Gregory IX, II:399
See also Franciscan Order
Franck, César, **V:832-835**
Béatitudes, Les, V:833
Djinns, Les, V:833
Éolides, Les, V:833
Quintet in F Minor for Piano and Strings, V:833
Rédemption, V:833
Ruth, V:832, 833
Sonata in A Major for Violin and Piano, V:834
String Quartet in D Major, V:834
Symphony in D Minor, V:834
Variations symphoniques, V:833
Franck, James, VIII:1647, 1648
Franckert, Hans, III:86
Franco, Francisco, **VII:1200-1203**
Blum, VII:336, 337
Buñuel, VII:506

Candela, VII:557
Garcia Lorca, VII:1291
Perón, IV:2969
François I, III:467, 468, 470
Franco-Prussian Wars
Bismarck, V:241
Bizet, V:245
Faidherbe, V:763-765
Hindenburg, VIII:1674
Kutuzov, VI:1306, 1307
Liebknecht, VI:1369, 1370
Pius IX, VI:1783
Poincaré, IX:3044
Redon, VI:1855
Thiers, VI:2228
Franco-Russian Alliance of 1893-1894, V:1131
Franco-Turkish War, III:159, 160
Frank, Anne, **VII:1204-1207**
Diary of Anne Frank, The, VII:1204-1206
Frankenthaler, Helen, **VII:1208-1211**
Mountains and Sea, VII:1208
Frankfurter, Felix, VII:17, 323, **1212-1215**
Case of Sacco and Vanzetti, The, VII:1212
Frank Leslie's Illustrated Newspaper, VI:1627
Franklin, Aretha, **VII:1216-1219**
Amazing Grace, VII:1217
Aretha Live at Fillmore West, VII:1217
Aretha Now, VII:1217
I Never Loved a Man (the Way I Loved You), VII:1217
Lady Soul, VII:1217
"Respect," VII:1217
Young, Gifted, and Black, VII:1217
Franklin, Benjamin, **IV:492-496**
Adams, IV:18, 19
André, IV:42
Edwards, IV:430
electricity, IV:523
Fitch, IV:476, 477
Hutchinson, IV:693
Poor Richard's Almanack, IV:493
Volta, IV:1387
Franklin, John, VI:1908
Franklin, Rosalind, VII:797; IX:3996, 3997
Franz Joseph, VII:1197, 1198
Fraser, John, VIII:2110
Fraser, Neale Andrew, VIII:2109
Frateschi, III:669
Frazer, Sir James George, **VII:1220-1223**
Anthologia Anthropologica, VII:1221
Belief in Immortality and the Worship of the Dead, The, VII:1221
Fear of the Dead in Primitive Religion, The, VII:1221
Folk-Lore of the Old Testament, VII:1221
Golden Bough, The, VII:1220-1223
Lectures on the Early History of the Kingship, VII:1221
Totemica, VII:1221
Totemism and Exogamy, VII:1221
Worship of Nature, The, VII:1222
Frazier, Joe, VII:56
Frazier-Lemke Act, IX:3548
Frederick I, **IV:497-499**
Frederick I Barbarossa, **II:357-361**
Adrian IV, II:28, 48
Alexander III, II:49, 50
Henry the Lion, II:467, 468
Rudolf I, II:797
Treaty of Constance, II:358
Frederick II of Saxony, III:443, 445
Frederick II of Sicily, **II:362-365,** 399-401, 510, 514, 605
Frederick III (Holy Roman Emperor), III:164, 375, 487, 488, 491
Frederick V (Holy Roman Emperor), IV:451
Frederick Henry, **IV:500-503**
Fredericksburg, Battle of, V:1205
Frederick the Great, IV:32, 444, **504-507,** 1394
Frederick William II, IV:148
Frederick William III, V:940-942, 1033; VI:1969, 1970, 2115, 2116
Frederick William IV, VI:1840
Frederick William, The Great Elector, **IV:508-510**
Fredericq, Paul, IX:3023
Free Cultivator's Law, V:44
Free Democratic Party, VII:428; VIII:2009
Freedmen's Bureau, V:1151, 1235; VI:2108, 2137
Freedom Charter, VIII:2281
Freedom League, VIII:2253
freedom of speech
Adams, IV:19
Black, VII:322
Brandeis, VII:422
Bryant, V:344
Erskine, IV:440
Fichte, IV:465
Goldman, VIII:1414
Holmes, VIII:1721
Mill, VI:1562
Nazi Germany, VIII:1405
Phillips, VI:1772
pornography, VIII:2326
See also censorship; First Amendment

freedom of the press, IV:440, 1484-1486
  See also censorship; First Amendment
Free French movement, IX:3924
free jazz, VII:741, 742, 744
Freemasonry, IV:844, 1005, 1048; VI:2208; VIII:1941
Free Officers Revolution, VIII:2356
Free Officers Society, VIII:2693; IX:3098, 3289
Free Parliament, IV:284
Freer, Charles, VI:2364, 2366
Free Silver movement, VII:479
Free Society of Artists, IV:1187
Free-Soil Party, IV:895; V:322, 477, 478, 1138; VI:2294
Free Synagogue, IX:4034
free trade
  Chamberlain, V:463
  Cobden, V:526-528
  Derby, V:653
  Germany, VII:1094, 1095
  Heath, VIII:1607
  Kohl, VIII:2010
  Liverpool, VI:1397
  NAFTA, VII:522, 682, 709, VIII:2656, 2681
  Peel, VI:1754
  Smith, IV:1249-1251
Free Traders, V:631, 632
Free Unionist Officers, IX:3098, 3099
free will
  Ahmad ibn Hanbal, II:34
  Alberti, III:9
  Ash'ari, II:94
  Boethius, II:156
  Buridan, II:195
  Duns Scotus, II:312
  Edwards, IV:429
  Hartmann, VIII:1571
  Jansen, IV:708
  Kant, IV:762
  Nishida, VIII:2755
  Schopenhauer, VI:1984-1986
  Taine, VI:2182
  Theodore of Mopsuestia, I:862
  Valla, III:739
Frege, Gottlob, **V:836-838;** VII:582
  Begriffsschrift, V:836, 838
  Foundations of Arithmetic, The, V:836
  Grundgesetze der Arithmetik, V:837
Freikorps, IX:3381
FRELIMO. *See* Mozambique Liberation Front
Frémont, John C., V:77, 197, 429-432, **839-844**
French-American Mid-Ocean Undersea Study.
  See FAMOUS, Project
French and Indian War. *See* Seven Years' War
French Indochina War, VIII:2493
French National Liberation Committee, VIII:2491
French Open, VII:368, 369
French Revolution
  Acton, V:12
  Adams, John Quincy, V:20
  Blake, IV:138
  Burke, IV:224
  Castlereagh, V:438, 439
  Catherine the Great, IV:260
  Chateaubriand, V:482
  Condorcet, IV:348-350
  Danton, IV:393-395
  David, V:611
  Du Pont, V:718, 719
  Fichte, IV:467
  Fourier, V:819
  Fox, IV:482
  Gay-Lussac, V:897
  George III, IV:542
  Herder, IV:652
  Joséphine, V:1246
  Lagrange, IV:787
  Lavoisier, IV:807
  Leblanc, IV:815
  Marat, IV:910-912
  Marie-Antoinette, IV:920
  Michelet, VI:1549
  Monge, IV:975, 977
  Napoleon I, VI:1616-1618
  Necker, IV:1018
  Orléans, IV:1048-1050
  Paine, IV:1055-1057
  Pitt the Younger, IV:1104
  Priestley, IV:1130
  Robespierre, IV:1170-1173
  Saint-Just, IV:1205-1207
  Staël, VI:2093, 2094
  Taine, VI:2183
  Thiers, VI:2226
  Turgot, IV:1348, 1349
  Wollstonecraft, IV:1475, 1477
  Wordsworth, VI:2406
French Royal Gardens, IV:215
Freud, Sigmund, **VII:1224-1227**
  Adler, VII:30, 31
  Benjamin, VII:269
  Bleuler, VII:329, 330
  Breuer, VII:452-454

Fourier, V:817
Fromm, VII:1246, 1247
H.D., VIII:1506
Hesse, VIII:1652
Horney, VIII:1744-1746
Interpretation of Dreams, The, I:400; VII:829, 1225; VIII:2062
Jung, VIII:1896, 1898, 1899
Lacan, VIII:2061-2063
Le Bon, VIII:2136
Leonardo da Vinci, VII:1226
Mahler, VIII:2363
penis envy, VIII:2537
Psychopathology of Everyday Life, VII:1226
schizophrenia, IX:3576
Schopenhauer, VI:1986
sex research, VIII:1987
Studies in Hysteria, VII:1224
Three Essays on the Theory of Sexuality, VII:1225
Totem and Taboo, VII:1226
Wit and Its Relation to the Unconscious, VII:1226
Freyssinet, Eugène, **VII:1228-1230**
Friars Preachers, Order of. *See* Dominican Order
Frick, Henry Clay, V:421; VIII:1412, 2480
Fried, Alfred Hermann, VI:2177
Friedan, Betty, **VII:1231-1234;** VIII:1642
Feminine Mystique, The, VI:2154; VII:1231; VIII:1642
Fountain of Age, The, VII:1233
It Changed My Life, VII:1233
Second Stage, The, VII:1233
Friedjung, Heinrich, VIII:2441
Friedland, Battle of, VI:1646
Friedland, duchy of, IV:1397
Friendly, Fred, VIII:2664
Friends, Religious Society of. *See* Quakers
Friendship, Mutual Assistance, and Postwar Cooperation, Treaty of, VII:261
Friends of the People, Society of the, V:994, 995
Fries, John, IV:295
Frigidus River, Battle of the, I:825
Frisch, Karl von, **VII:1235-1237**
Frisch, Max, **VII:1238-1241**
Andorra, VII:1239
Biography: A Game, VII:1239
Bluebeard, VII:1239
Chinese Wall, The, VII:1239
Don Juan, VII:1238
Fire Raisers, The, VII:1238
Homo Faber, VII:1239
I'm Not Stiller, VII:1238
Man in the Holocene, VII:1239
Montauk, VII:1239
Sketchbook 1946-1949, VII:1238
Sketchbook 1966-1971, VII:1239
Wilderness of Mirrors, A, VII:1239
Frisch, Otto, VIII:2478
Frisians, I:378; II:167, 243
Fritigern, I:908
Frizer, Ingram, III:472
Froben, Johann, III:358
Frobenius, Leo, **VII:1242-1245**
Atlantis, VII:1243
Black Decameron, The, VII:1243
Erlebte Erdteile, VII:1243
Origin of African Civilization, The, VII:1242
Frobisher, Sir Martin, III:212, **278-280**
Froebel, Friedrich, **V:845-848;** VIII:2596
Education of Man, The, V:846
Pedagogics of the Kindergarten, V:847
Mother-Play and Nursery Songs, V:847
Froissart, Jean, **II:366-369**
Chronicles, II:366-369
Fromm, Erich, **VII:1246-1249**
Art of Loving, The, VII:1248
Beyond the Chains of Illusion, VII:1248
Dogma of Christ, VII:1246
Escape from Freedom, VII:1247
Man for Himself, VII:1247
Marx's Concept of Man, VII:1248
Psychoanalysis and Religion, VII:1248
Sigmund Freud's Mission, VII:1248
You Shall Be Gods, VII:1248
Zen Buddhism and Psychoanalysis, VII:1248
Fronde, IV:336, 341-343, 386, 866, 946, 1358
Fronde of the Princes, IV:342
Frontenac, Louis de Baude, VI:1736, 1737
Frost, Elihu B., V:1124, 1125
Frost, Robert, **VII:1250-1252**
Boy's Will, A, VII:1250
Further Range, A, VII:1251
"Gift Outright, The," VII:1252
In the Clearing, VII:1252
Masque of Mercy, A, VII:1252
Masque of Reason, A, VII:1252
Mountain Interval, VII:1251
New Hampshire, VII:1251
North of Boston, VII:1250
"Oven Bird," VII:1251
"Road Not Taken, The," VII:1251
Steeple Bush, VII:1252
"Trial by Existence, The," VII:1250

"Tuft of Flowers, A," VII:1250
West-Running Brook, VII:1251
Witness Tree, A, VII:1251
Fry, Roger, **VII:1253-1256**
Cézanne, VII:1255
Transformations, VII:1254
Vision and Design, VII:1254; VIII:2609
Fry, Shirley, VII:1364
Fry, W.H., V:984
Frye, Northrop, I:509
Fryxell, Eva, VIII:2065
FSA. *See* Farm Security Administration
FTC. *See* Federal Trade Commission
Fuchs, Arved, VIII:2508
Fuchs, Vivian, VIII:1663, 1664
Fugard, Athol, **VII:1257-1260**
Blood Knot, The, VII:1258
Boesman and Lena, VII:1258
Cell, The, VII:1257
Hello and Goodbye, VII:1258
Island, The, VII:1258, 1259
Klass and the Devil, VII:1257
Lesson from Aloes, A, VII:1259
"MASTER HAROLD". . . and the boys, VII:1257, 1259
My Children, My Africa, VII:1260
No-Good Friday, VII:1257
Orestes, VII:1258
Place for the Pigs, A, VII:1257
Road to Mecca, The, VII:1259
Sizwe Bansi Is Dead, VII:1257, 1259
Statements After an Arrest Under the Immorality Act, VII:1259
Tsotsi, VII:1258
Fugitive Slave Act
Brown, V:322
Chase, V:478
Fillmore, V:793
Forten, V:807
Garrison, V:886
Parker, VI:1729
Pierce, VI:1777
Story, VI:2148
Taney, VI:2191
Tubman, VI:2265
Fujisawa, Takeo, VIII:1724-1726
Fujiwara Michinaga, **II:370-372,** 537, 538
Fujiwara no Tametoki, II:657
Fukien, IV:297, 298
Fulbert of Chartres, Saint, **II:373-375**
Fulda, II:767
Full Employment Act of 1946, IX:3862
Fuller, Loie, **VII:1261-1264**
Fifteen Years of a Dancer's Life, VII:1263
"Fire Dance," VII:1263
"Serpentine Dance," VII:1261
"Shadow Ballets," VII:1263
Fuller, Margaret, **V:849-853,** 984
Papers on Literature and Art, V:850
Summer on the Lake, V:850
Women in the Nineteenth Century, V:850, 852
Fuller, R. Buckminster, **VII:1265-1269**
Fulton, Robert, IV:478; **V:854-857**
Torpedo War and Submarine Explosions, V:856
Treatise on the Improvement of Canal Navigation, V:854
Furneaux, Tobias, IV:353
Furness, Frank, VI:2167
fur trade
Astor, V:82, 84
La Salle, IV:793, 794
Lewis and Clark, VI:1359
Mackenzie, IV:879-881
Smith, VI:2077, 2078
Fuseli, Henry, IV:1477
Fusion Ministry, V:631
Fust, Johann, III:328, 329
Futa-Toro, V:763
Futurama exhibit, VII:1321
Futurism
Blok, VII:332, 333
Boccioni, VII:342-344
Duchamp, VII:972
Magritte, VIII:2349
Mayakovsky, VIII:2461, 2462
Pasternak, IX:2899
FWA. *See* Farm Workers Association

Gabbard, Battle off the, II:135
Gabbard Shoal, Battle of the, IV:1343
Gabin, Jean, VII:932
Gable, Clark, VIII:2232
Gabriel, archangel, III:28
Gabrieli, Andrea, **III:281-283**
Concerti, III:282
Psalmi Davidici, III:282
Gabrieli, Giovanni, **III:284-286;** IV:1221, 1222
Canzoni e sonate, III:285
Sacrae symphoniae, III:285
Gaddi, Palazzo, III:664
Gadsden, James, **V:858-860**
Gadsden Purchase, V:583, 615, 858-860; VI:1956
Gaelic League, VII:877
Gaelic Nationalist Revival, IX:2804-2806

Gagarin, Yuri Alekseyevich, VII:111, **1270-1273;** IX:3407, 3639, 3640
Gage, Thomas, **IV:511-514**
Adams, Samuel, IV:23, 24
Carleton, IV:247
Clinton, IV:321, 322
Hancock, IV:616, 617
Howe, IV:677, 678
Gagnan, Émile, VII:779
Gaia, I:403
Gaillardet, Frédéric, V:709
Gaillieni, Joseph, VIII:1851, 1852
Gainsborough, Thomas, **IV:515-518,** 529, 1163, 1164
Gaitskill, Hugh, VII:305, 306; IX:4106
Gaius Octavius. *See* Augustus
Gale, Leonard Dunnell, VI:1593
Galen, **I:338-341**
Asclepiades, I:103
bloodletting, I:301
Celsus, I:174
Diocles of Carystus, I:262
Harvey, IV:628
Nostradamus, III:567
On the Usefulness of the Parts of the Body, I:339
Vesalius, III:754-756
Galerius, I:226, 227, 267
Galigai, Leonora, IV:863, 864
Galilee, I:472, 642, 880
Galileo, **IV:519-522**
Archimedes, I:80
Boyle, IV:185
Brecht, VII:446
Descartes, IV:403
Dialogue Concerning the Two Chief World Systems, IV:521, 951, 1331
Kepler, IV:774
Mersenne, IV:951
Milton, IV:958
parabola, IV:695
pulsilogium, IV:1209
Saggiatore, IV:521
Santorio, IV:1209, 1210
Sidereal Messenger, The, IV:521
telescope, IV:852
Gallatin, Albert, **V:861-863**
Gallaudet, Thomas, V:130
Gallic Wars, I:149
Gallienus, I:667
Gallman, Rolando, VII:86
Galloway, Joseph, IV:678
Gallus, Didius, I:136
Galois, Èvariste, **V:864-866**
Galton, Francis, **V:867-870**
Art of Travel, V:868
English Men of Science, V:868
Finger-Prints, V:869
Hereditary Genius, V:868
Inquiries into the Human Faculty and Its Development, V:869
Memories of My Life, V:867
Natural Inheritance, V:869
Record of Family Faculties, V:869
Tropical South Africa, V:868
Galvani, Luigi, **IV:523-526,** 1389
Commentary on the Effect of Electricity on Muscular Motion, IV:524, 525
Gama, Vasco da, III:117, 118, 120, 218, **287-290,** 464
Gamaliel II, I:27, 28, 473
Gambetta, Leon, **V:871-874;** VI:2103
Gance, Abel, **VII:1274-1277**
Digue, La, VII:1274
Folie du Docteur Tube, La, VII:1274, 1275
J'Accuse!, VII:1274, 1275
Life and Loves of Beethoven, The, VII:1275
Mater Dolorosa, VII:1274
Napoléon, VII:1274-1276
Roue, La, VII:1274, 1275
Gandhara, I:779
Gandhi, Indira, **VII:1278-1281;** VIII:2712; IX:2867, 2869
Gandhi, Mahatma, I:916; VII:397, 1278, **1282-1285;** VIII:1847, 2683, 2709-2711; IX:2867
Gandhi, Mohandas, VI:2235; VIII:1971
Gang of Four, VII:906; VIII:2214
Ganjojuin temple, II:924, 925
Gao, III:522
Garber, Paul, IX:3973
Garbett, Samuel, IV:1182-1184
Garbo, Greta, **VII:1286-1289**
Anna Christie, VII:1287
Anna Karenina, VII:1288
Camille, VII:1288
Conquest, VII:1288
Flesh and the Devil, VII:1286
Grand Hotel, VII:1287
Joyless Street, The, VII:1286
Ninotchka, VII:1288
Painted Veil, The, VII:1288
Queen Christina, VII:1288; IX:2808
Temptress, The, VII:1286
Torrent, The, VII:1286
Two-Faced Woman, VII:1288

Garcia, Manuel, Jr., VI:1385
Garcia Lorca, Federico, **VII:1290-1292;** VIII:2716, 2717; IX:3067
Blood Wedding, VII:1291
Gypsy Ballads of Garcia Lorca, The, VII:1290
House of Bernarda Alba, The, VII:1291
Lament for the Death of a Bullfighter, VII:1291
Poet in New York, VII:1291
Songs, VII:1290
Yerma, VII:1291
Garcia Márquez, Gabriel, **VII:1293-1296**
Clandestine in Chile, VII:1295
funerales de la Mamá Grande, Los, VII:1294
general en su laberinto, El, VII:1295
In Evil Hour, VII:1293
Leaf Storm and Other Stories, VII:1293
Love in the Time of Cholera, VII:1295
Monologue of Isabel Watching It Rain in Macondo, VII:1293
No One Writes to the Colonel and Other Stories, VII:1293
One Hundred Years of Solitude, VII:1294, 1295
Gardiner, Stephen, **III:291-294**
Episcopi de vera obedientia oratio, III:292
King's Book, III:292
Gardner, Alexander, V:296, 297
Gardner, Erle Stanley, **VII:1297-1299**
Bigger They Come, The, VII:1298
Case of the Velvet Claws, The, VII:1298
Gardner, Isabella Stewart, **VII:1300-1303**
Gardner, John
Wreckage of Agathon, The, I:952
Gardoqui, Diego, IV:713
Garfield, James, V:77, 78, 80, 81, 256, **875-878;** VI:2389
Garibaldi, Giuseppe, V:447, 447, 709, **879-882;** VI:1782, 1783
Garland, Judy, **VII:1304-1307**
Babes in Arms, VII:1305
Broadway Melody of 1938, VII:1304
Child Is Waiting, A, VII:1306
Easter Parade, VII:1305
For Me and My Girl, VII:1305
I Could Go on Singing, VII:1306
Judgment at Nuremberg, VII:1306
Star is Born, A, VII:1305, 1306, 1354
Wizard of Oz, The, VII:1305
Garnier, Tony, **VII:1308-1310**
Garrick, David, IV:226, **527-530,** 567
Lethe, IV:527
Lying Valet, The, IV:527
Ode, IV:529
Garrison, William Lloyd, V:489, 697, **883-887;** VI:1772, 1773, 2143, 2374
Garter, Order of the, II:329
Garvey, Marcus, VII: 668, **1311-1314;** VIII:2373; IX:3114
Gasherbrum I, VIII:2507, 2508
Gaskell, Elizabeth
Mary Barton, V:361
Gasmotorenfabrik Deutz, VI:1703
Gates, Horatio, IV:66, 1406
Gattoni, Giulio, IV:1387
Gaudi, Antonio, **VII:1315-1318**
Gauge War, V:336
Gauguin, Paul, V:946, **888-892;** VI:1922; VII:362, 363, 910; IX:2836
Breton Village Covered by Snow, V:890
Ia Orana Maria, V:890
Noa Noa, V:890
Talisman, The, VII:909
Vision After the Sermon, The, V:888
Where Do We Come From? What Are We? Where Are We Going?, V:890
Gaulle, Charles de. *See* de Gaulle, Charles
Gaunt, John of. *See* Lancaster, Duke of
Gauss, Carl Friedrich, **V:893-896;** VI:1403, 1404
Arithmetical Inquisitions, V:893-895
General Investigations of Curved Surfaces, V:895
Gauss, Christian, IX:4012
Gautama. *See* Buddha
Gauthier-Villars, Henri, VII:729
Gaveston, Piers, II:326
Gay, John, IV:27, 158, 668
Gay-Lussac, Joseph-Louis, V:98, **897-901**
Gdansk Lenin Shiyards, IX:3844, 3845
Gedaliah, I:461
Geddes, Norman Bel, **VII:1319-1321**
Magic Motorways, VII:1321
Gehrig, Lou, **VII:1322-1325**
Geiger, Hans, VII:379
Geiger, Rudolf Oskar Robert Williams, **VII:1326-1328**
Climate Near the Ground, The, VII:1326, 1327
Geisel, Theodor Seuss, **VII:1329-1332**
And to Think That I Saw It on Mulberry Street, VII:1329
Butter Battle Book, The, VII:1331
Cat in the Hat, The, VII:1330
5,000 Fingers of Dr. T, The, VII:1329
How the Grinch Stole Christmas!, VII:1330
Lorax, The, VII:1330, 1331
Oh, the Places You'll Go!, VII:1331

Sneetches, The, VII:1330
You're Only Old Once, VII:1331
Gembloux, Battle of, III:254
Gemeinschaft, IX:3703-3705
Gemellus, Tiberius, I:153, 154
Gemini space program, VII:111, 112; VIII:2021; IX:3405
General Education Board, VI:1898
General Electric Company, V:743; VI:2122, 2124; IX:3138
General German Workers' Association, VI:1324, 1325, 1369
General Motors, VII:1321; VIII:2679, 2680; IX:2974, 3162, 3881
General Overseas Service, VII:737
Genesis, Book of, I:5, 6; III:72; IV:215, 1303; VII:481
Genet, Edmond Charles, IV:718
Genet, Jean, **VII:1333-1335;** VIII:2537; IX:3329
Balcony, The, VII:35, 1334
Blacks, The, VII:79, 1334
Deathwatch, VII:1334
Funeral Rites, VII:1333
Maids, The, VII:1334
Miracle of the Rose, VII:1333
Our Lady of the Flowers, VII:1333
Querelle of Brest, VII:1333
Screams, The, VII:35
Screens, The, VII:1334
Thief's Journal, The, VII:1333
Geneva, Treaty of, V:143
Geneva, University of, III:118
Geneva Accords, VII:977; VIII:1701
Geneva Conventions, V:712
Genghis Khan, **II:376-380,** 381, 566; IV:2, 3
Gennadius of Marseilles, I:938
Genseric, **I:342-344**
Gensfleisch zur Laden, Johannes. *See* Gutenberg, Johann
Genshin sect, II:537
Gentile, Giovanni, **VII:1336-1338**
Gentili, Alberico, **III:295-297**
De iuris interpretibus dialogi sex, III:295
Three Books on Embassies, III:295, 296
Three Books on the Law of War, The, III:295, 296
Two Books of the Pleas of a Spanish Advocate, The, III:296
Geoffrey Martel, II:997
Geoffrey of Monmouth
History of the Kings of Britain, I:378, 380
Geoffroi de Villehardouin. *See* Villehardouin, Geoffroi de
Geological Society of London, VI:1418, 1421
Geological Survey of Territories, U.S., V:1072-1074; VI:1812, 1813, 2328
geometry
Aristoxenus, I:99
Euclid, I:308
Gauss, V:893-895
Hero of Alexandria, I:388
Leonardo of Pisa, II:586
Lobachevsky, VI:1403-1405
Maclaurin, IV:884
Monge, IV:975-978
Steiner, VI:2118-2120
George I, **IV:531-534**
Addison, IV:27
Bolingbroke, IV:159
George II, IV:535, 536
Stanhope, IV:1277-1279
Vanbrugh, IV:1352
Walpole, IV:1402, 1403
George II, **IV:535-538**
Amherst, IV:37
Cosby, IV:1485
George I, IV:532, 533
George III, IV:539
Handel, IV:621
Pelham, IV:1074
Walpole, IV:1403
George III, **IV:539-544**
Adams, Samuel, IV:24
Amherst, IV:39, 40
Anson, IV:57
Banks, IV:85
Brown, IV:206
Burke, IV:222-224
Castlereagh, V:440
Ch'ien-lung, IV:300
Copley, IV:358
Fox, IV:481, 482
George IV, V:902-904
Howe, IV:676, 677
Lawrence, IV:810
New Hampshire, IV:34
North, IV:1034-1036
Paine, IV:1057
Palmerston, VI:1719
Pennsylvania, IV:408
Pitt the Younger, IV:1102, 1104
Union, Act of, IV:369
Victoria, VI:2307, 2308

Virginia tobacco, IV:647
Wilkes, IV:1439
William IV, VI:2392
George IV, **V:902-905**
Brougham, V:315
Canning, V:406
Grey, V:995
Nash, IV:1013, 1014
Raeburn, VI:1837
Victoria, VI:2307, 2308
William IV, VI:2392
George V, VII:170, 1020, 1062; **1339-1342,** 1343, 1344; IX:4025, 4026
George VI, VII:170, 315, 595, 1062, **1343-1346;** IX:4026, 4027
George, Henry, **V:906-909**
Our Land and Land Policy, V:907
Progess and Poverty, V:907, 908
George of Transylvania, IV:838
Georgia
Carter, VII:589, 592
lynching, IX:3961
Massachusetts speculators, VI:2147
Native American removal, VI:1910, 1911
Oglethorpe, IV:1043-1046
Stephens, VI:2129-2131
Gepids, II:41, 42
Gerann of Reims, II:869
Gerard of Cremona, II:985
Gerbert of Aurillac. *See* Sylvester II
Géricault, Théodore, V:645, 646, **910-914**
African Slave Trade, V:913
Charging Chasseur, V:912
Liberation of the Prisoners of the Spanish Inquisition, V:913
Raft of the Medusa, The, V:646, 912, 913
Wounded Cuirassier, V:912
Gerlach, Adrian de, VII:66
Germain, Lord George, IV:248, 677
German Association of Engineers, IX:4109
German Evangelical Church, VIII:2742-2744
Germanic Diet, III:159
German High Seas Fleet, IX:3688-3690
Germanicus, I:152
German Inland Ice Expedition of 1930, IX:3920
German Inner-African Exploration Expedition, VII:1242
German People's Party, IX:3564
Germany, reunification of, VIII:2009-2011
Gerome, Jean-Leon, V:732; VI:1854
Geronimo, **V:915-918**
Gerousia, I:216
Gershwin, George, **VII:1347-1351,** 1352, 1354, 1355
American in Paris, An, VII:1349
Blue Monday, VII:1347
Concerto in F, VII:1349, 1350
Lady Be Good, VII:125, 1349, 1352
Of Thee I Sing, VII:1349, 1352, 1354
Porgy and Bess, VII:1347, 1349, 1354; IX:3081, 3083
Rhapsody in Blue, VII:1347, 1350
Shocking Miss Pilgrim, The, VII:1355
Strike Up the Band, VII:1349, 1354
"Swanee," VII:1347
Gershwin, Ira, VII:1347, 1349, 1350, **1352-1355**
Cover Girl, VII:1354
Girl Crazy, VII:1354
Goldwyin Follies, The, VII:1354
Lady Be Good, VII:125, 1349, 1352
Lady in the Dark, VII:1354; IX:3928
Lyrics on Several Occasions, VII:1355
"Man That Got Away, The," VII:1354
Of Thee I Sing, VII:1349, 1352, 1354
Porgy and Bess, VII:1347, 1349, 1354
Shall We Dance, VII:1354
Star is Born, A, VII:1354
Strike Up the Band, VII:1349, 1354
Sweetheart Shop, The, VII:1352
Gerson, Jean de, II:907
Gesell, Arnold, **VII:1356-1358**
Biographies of Child Development, VII:1357
Child from Five to Ten, The, VII:1357, 1358
Infant and Child in the Culture of Today, VII:1357, 1358
Infant Behavior, VII:1357
Youth, VII:1357
Gesner, Conrad, III:3, **298-301**
Bibliotheca universalis, III:298
De rerum fossilium, lapidum, et gemmarum maximé, figuris et similitudinibus liber, III:299
De tulipa Turcarum, III:299
Historia plantarum et vires, III:298
Historiae animalium, III:299
Opera botanica, III:299
Gessho, VI:1936
Gestapo
Adenauer, VII:27
Göring, VIII:1439
Niemöller, VIII:2743
Gettysburg Address, VI:1383, 2346
Géza, II:574
Ghana Shifimo, VIII:2763, 2764
Ghazan, Mahmud, **II:381-384**

Ghaznavid dynasty, II:70, 147, 677
Ghazzali, al-, **II:385-387**
Incoherence of the Philosophers, II:385
Revival of Religious Sciences, The, II:385,386
Ghent, Pacification of, III:783
Ghent, Treaty of, IV:889; V:21, 507, 862
Ghent, University of, IX:3023
Ghibellines, II:286, 288, 515
Ghiberti, Lorenzo, II:272, 745, 746; III:91, 220, **302-304**
Ghirlandaio, Domenico, III:517
Ghose, Sri Aurobindo. *See* Aurobindo, Sri
Ghost Dance, VI:1851, 2072
Giacometti, Alberto, **VII:1359-1362**
Busts of Diego, VII:1361
Composition, VII:1359
Couple (Man and Woman), The, VII:1359
Palace at 4 A.M., The, VII:1359
Spoon-Woman, The, VII:1359
Suspended Ball, VII:1359
Three Figures Outdoors, VII:1359
Giap, Vo Nguyen. *See* Vo Nguyen Giap
Gibbon, Edward, **IV:545-548,** 564
History of the Decline and Fall of the Roman Empire, The, IV:545-547; V:75; VI:1873
Gibbons, James, **V:919-922**
Faith of Our Fathers, The, V:919
Gibbons, Thomas, VI:2296
Gibbons v. Ogden, VI:1490
Gibbs, Josiah Willard, **V:923-926**
Elementary Principles in Statistical Mechanics, V:925
Gibbs, Oliver Wolcott, VI:1367
Gibson, Althea, **VII:1363-1366**
Gide, André, VII:910, **1367-1369**
Corydon, VII:1368
Counterfeiters, The, VII:1368
Fruits of the Earth, VII:1368
If It Die . . . , VII:1368
Immoralist, The, VII:1368
Lafcadio's Adventures, VII:1368
Madeleine, VII:1369
Marshlands, VII:1367
Notebooks of Andre Walter, The, VII:1367
Pastoral Symphony, VII:1368
Return from the U.S.S.R., VII:1369
Return of the Prodigal Son, The, VII:1367
Strait Is the Gate, VII:1368
Theseus, VII:1369
Urien's Voyage, VII:1367
Gideon v. Wainwright, VII:322
Gielgud, John, IX:2808, 2810, 2812
Gierek, Edward, IX:3844
Gifford, John, IV:218
Gilbert, Adrian, III:212
Gilbert, Sir Humphrey, III:315, 316, 639
Gilbert, Olive, VI:2257
Gilbert, Susan, V:668
Gilbert, William, IV:588
Gilbert, W.S., **V:927-931**
Bab Ballads, The, V:927, 930
Dulcamara, V:927
Grand Duke, The, V:929
H.M.S. Pinafore, V:929
Patience, V:929
Pirates of Penzance, The, V:927, 929
Pygmalion and Galatea, V:928
Thespis, V:928
Trial by Jury, V:929
Utopia, Limited, V:929
Gilchrist, Alexander, IV:141
Gillespie, Dizzy, **VII:1370-1373;** IX:2882
Greatest Jazz Concert Ever, The, VII:1371
Gillot, Claude, IV:1413
Gilson, Étienne, **VII:1374-1378**
Arts of the Beautiful, The, VII:1376
Being and Some Philosophers, VII:1376
Dantesques, VII:1377
Forms and Substances in the Arts, VII:1376
History of Christian Philosophy in the Middle Ages, VII:1376
Painting and Reality, VII:1376
Spirit of Medieval Philosophy, The, VII:1375
Thomis Realism and the Critique of Knowledge, VII:1376
Unity of Philosophical Experience, The, VII:1376
Gingrich, Newt, VII:709, 710
Ginsberg, Allen, VII:792; VIII:1945
Gioberti, Vincenzo, **V:932-934**
Del primato morale e civile degli italiani, V:932, 933; VI:1782
rinnovamento civile d'Italia, Il, V:933
Giorgione, **III:305-307**
Bellini, III:60
Concert Champêtre, III:306
Tempest, The, III:306
Three Philosophers, The, III:306, 307
Titian, III:721
Toilet of Venus, III:305
Giotto, II:272, 305, **388-391,** 632, 633, 698, 700, 745; III:483; VII:1359
Last Judgment, The, II:390
Life of Saint Francis, II:390

Raising of Drusiana, The, II:390
Saint John the Baptist, II:390
Giovanni di Simone Guidi, Tommaso di. *See* Masaccio
Girardon, François, IV:151
Giraudoux, Jean, **VII:1379-1382**
Amphitryon, VII:1380
Bella, VII:1379
Choix des élues, VII:1380
Combat avec l'ange, VII:1380
Eglantine, VII:1380
Electra, VII:1380
Enchanted, The, VII:1380
Madwoman of Chaillot, The, VII:1380
My Friend from Limousin, VII:1379, 1380
Ondine, VII:1380
Sigfried, VII:1380
Tiger at the Gates, VII:1379
Girl Guides. *See* Girl Scouts
Girl Scouts, V:105-107; VIII:2246-2248
Girodet, Louis, V:411
Girondins
Condorcet, IV:348-350
Danton, IV:394
Marat, IV:911, 912
Orléans, IV:1050
Robespierre, IV:1171, 1172
Saint-Just, IV:1205
Gish, Dorothy, VII:1383, 1385, 1386
Gish, Lillian, **VII:1383-1386**
Birth of a Nation, The, VII:1383
Broken Blossoms, VII:1385
Camille, VII:1385
Hamlet, VII:1385
Intolerance, VII:1383
Life With Father, VII:1385
Mothering Heart, The, VII:1383
Uncle Vanya, VII:1385
Unseen Enemy, An, VII:1383
Way down East, VII:1385
Whales of August, The, VII:845
Giza, temples at, VI:1412
Gladstone, William Ewart, **V:935-939**
Acton, V:12
Asquith, VII:121
Balfour, VII:172
Bradley, V:290
Bright, V:307, 308
Disraeli, V:677, 678
Forster, V:804, 805
Lansdowne, VIII:2090, 2091
Irish home rule, VI:1741
Khartoum, V:965
Liberal Party, V:1036
Peel, VI:1753, 1754
State in Its Relations with the Church, The, V:935
Glanville, Ranulf de, II:179, 447
glasnost, VIII:1424, 1426, 1963; IX:3299
Glass, Philip, VII:34, 35
Glaucia, Gaius, I:529
Gleichheit, Die, IX:4113, 4114
Glendower, Owen, II:459
Glen Grey Act of 1894, VI:1876
Glenn, John H., Jr., **VII:1387-1390**
Glorious Revolution of 1688
Addison, IV:26
Blackstone, IV:130
Kidd, IV:777
Locke, IV:857
Marlborough, IV:922
Mather, Cotton, IV:934
Mather, Increase, IV:939
Monmouth, IV:982
Shays, IV:1040
William III, IV:1447
Gloster Meteor, IX:3974
Gloucester, Duke of, III:341
Gloucester, Earl of, II:645, 646
Gloucester, Statute of, II:322
Gluck, Cristoph, **IV:549-551**
Alceste, IV:549, 550
Artaserse, IV:549
Don Juan, IV:549
Fausse Esclave, La, IV:549
Iphigénie en Aulide, IV:550
Orfeo ed Euridice, IV:549, 550
Paride ed Elena, IV:550
Semiramide riconosciuta, IV:549
Glyn, Elinor, V:290
G.M. *See* General Motors
Gneisenau, August von, V:264, 265, **9 40-943**
Gnosticism
Irenaeus, I:447-450
John the Apostle, I:477
Origen, I:581, 582
Rumi, II:800
Valentinus, I:911-914
Goa, III:12, 788, 799
Go Daigo, II:97
Godard, Jean-Luc, **VIII:1391-1395**
All the Boys Are Called Patrick, VIII:1391
Alphaville, VIII:1393

Band of Outsiders, VIII:1393
Breathless, VIII:1391, 1392
Carabiniers, Les, VII:1049
Contempt, VIII:1392
Detective, VIII:1393
Every Man for Himself, VIII:1393
First Name: Carmen, VIII:1392
Hail Mary, VIII:1393
Joy of Learning, The, VIII:1393
King Lear, VIII:1393
Little Soldier, The, VIII:1392
Married Woman, The, VIII:1393
Masculin-féminin, VIII:1393
My Life to Live, VIII:1392
Pierrot le fou, VIII:1393
Riflemen, The, VIII:1392
Sympathy for the Devil, VIII:1393
Weekend, VIII:1393
Woman is a Woman, A, VIII:1392
Goddard, Robert H., **VIII:1396-1399,** 1500; IX:2777
Method of Reaching Extreme Altitudes, A, VIII:1397
Rocket Development, VIII:1397
Gödel, Kurt, VIII:2725
Godey, Alexis, V:430
Godey, Louis, V:1022-1024
Godey's Lady's Book, V: 361, 1022-1024
Godkin, Edwin Lawrence, **VIII:1400-1403**
Godolphin, First Earl of, **IV:552-554**
Godse, Nathuram, VII:1284
Godunov, Boris Fyodorovich, **III:308-310**
Godwin, Edward William, VI:2215, 2216
Godwin, Mary. *See* Shelley, Mary Wollstonecraft
Godwin, William, **IV:555-559,** 1477; VI:1468, 2048, 2049, 2051, 2054
Caleb Williams, VI:2048
Cursory Strictures on the Charge Delivered by Lord Chief Justice Eyre to the Grand Jury, IV:557
Enquiry Concerning Political Justice, An, IV:555, 556, 558; VI:1787, 2053
Historical and Moral View of the Origin and Progress of the French Revolution, An, IV:57
Memoirs, IV:57
St. Leon, IV:57
Things as They Are, IV:557, 558
Vindication of the Rights of Woman, A, IV:57
Goebbels, Joseph, VII:1013; **VIII:1404-1407,** 2078
Goethals, George Washington, **VIII:1408-1410,** 1436
Goethe, Johann Wolfgang von, **IV:560-563,** 651-653, 1217, 1219; V:1020, 1159, 1160; VI:1989; VIII:2274
Autobiography of Goethe, The, IV:562
Elective Affinities, IV:562, 563; VII:267
Erlebnislyrik, IV:562, 564
Gotz von Berlichingen with the Iron Hand, IV:560
Iphigenia in Taurus, IV:560
Roman Elegies, IV:562
Sorrows of Young Werther, IV:560; VII:208
Theory of Colors, IV:562
Tragedy of Faust, The, IV:562; V:203; VI:1988, 1993
West-Eastern Divan, IV:562
Wilhelm Meister's Apprenticeship, IV:562, 563
Gogh, Vincent van, V:889, 891, **944-948;** VIII:1992, 2404; IX:3354, 3355
Potato Eaters, The, V:945
Self-Portrait, V:944, 946
Starry Night, The, V:946, 947
Gogol, Nikolai, V:687, **949-952;** VI:2268
Arabesques, V:949
Dead Souls, V:950, 951;VII:641
"Diary of a Madman," V:949; VIII:2252
Evenings on a Farm Near Dakota, V:949
Inspector General, The, V:950; VIII:2511
"Nose, The," V:950
"Overcoat, The," V:950
Petersburg Cycle, V:949
"St. John's Eve," VI:1612
Gokhale, Gopal Krishna, IX:3681-3684
Golan Heights, VII:856
Golden Bull of 1356, II:236, 237
Golden Fleece, Order of the, II:741, 742
Golden Horde, II:53, 54, 378, 382, 884, 987; III:382
Goldfisch, Samuel. *See* Goldwyn, Samuel
Goldie, Sir George, **V:953-955;** VIII:2269
Goldman, Emma, **VIII:1411-1414,** 1732
Mother Earth, VIII:1413
Goldmark, Rubin, VII:766
Goldoni, Carlo
Mistress of the Inn, The, VIII:2143
Gold Rush of 1849, VI:2060
Goldsmith, Oliver, **IV:564-568**
Citizen of the World, The, IV:565, 1020
Deserted Village, The, IV:566, 567
Enquiry into the Present State of Polite Learning in Europe, An, IV:565
Good-Natured Man, The, IV:566, 567
Goody Two-Shoes, IV:565

Grecian History, IV:564, 566
History of England, The, IV:566
History of England in a Series of Letters from a Nobleman to His Son, IV:566
History of the Earth, An, IV:564, 566, 567
Life of Richard Nash, Esq., The, IV:564, 566
Retaliation, IV:567
Roman History, The, IV:566
She Stoops to Conquer, IV:564, 567
Traveller, The, IV:564-566
Vicar of Wakefield, The, IV:564, 566, 1020; VI:2216
gold standard
Bevin, VII:314
Bryan, VII:479
Keynes, VIII:1952
MacDonald, VIII:2315
McKinley, VI:1454
Rhodes, VI:1874
Ricardo, VI:1878
Goldstein, Eugen, IX:3491
Goldwater, Barry, VII:713
Goldwyn, Samuel, VII:119, 176, 896; **VIII:1415-1418;** IX:3205
Best Years of Our Lives, The, VIII:1417
Little Foxes, The, VIII:1417
Porgy and Bess, VIII:1417
Squaw Man, The, VIII:1415
These Three, VIII:1417
Wuthering Heights, VIII:1417
Goldwyn Pictures Corporation, VIII:1417
golf
Didrikson, IX:4096-4098
Jones, VIII:1874-1877
Nicklaus, IX:3041, 4050
Palmer, IX:3041
Player, IX:3040-3042
Woods, IX:4049-4051
Goliath, I:241
Gomarists, III:575
Gompers, Samuel, V:26, **956-959;** VIII:2170
Gonatas, Antigonus, I:970
Goncharov, Ivan, VI:2269
Goncourt brothers, IV:1414
Gondi family, IV:1380
Gondomar, Count of, IV:700
Gonne, Maud, IX:4082, 4083, 4085
Gonzaga, Ludovico, III:9
Gonzaga dynasty, IV:990, 991
Gonzaga Palace, III:462
González, José Victoriano. *See* Gris, Juan
González, Pablo, IX:4106
González Prada, Manuel, VIII:1584
Goodall, Jane, VIII:2148
Good King Canute. *See* Canute the Great
Goodman, Benny, **VIII:1419-1422**
"Honeysuckle Rose," VIII:1420
"King Porter Stomp," VIII:1419
Let's Dance, VIII:1419
"Scarecrow," VIII:1420
"Sing, Sing, Sing," VIII:1420
"Stealin' Apples," VIII:1420
Good Neighbor Policy, VII:573; VIII:1729, 1768, 1780
Goodyear, Charles, **V:960-963**
G.O.P. *See* Republican Party
Gorbachev, Mikhail, **VIII:1423-1426**
Bukharin, VII:492, 493
Bush, VII:522
Dubcek, VII:970
Khrushchev, VIII:1963
Li Peng, VIII:2179
Sakharov, IX:3299
Yeltsin, IX:4086-4088
Gordimer, Nadine, **VIII:1427-1430**
Burger's Daughter, VIII:1429
Guest of Honor, A, VIII:1429
July's People, VIII:1429
Late Bourgeois World, The, VIII:1429
Lying Days, The, VIII:1427, 1429
Occasion for Loving, VIII:1429
World of Strangers, A, VIII:1429
Gordon, Anna A., VI:2388, 2389
Gordon, Charles George, V:936, **964-966**
Gordon, George. *See* Byron, Lord
Gordon Riots of 1780, IV:1237
Gore, Albert, VII:708; **VIII:1431-1433;** IX:3155
Gorenko, Anna Andreyevna. *See* Akhmatova, Anna
Gorgas, William Crawford, **VIII:1434-1437**
Gorgeous George, VII:54
Gorham, Maurice, VII:737, 738
Göring, Hermann, VII:1013; **VIII:1438-1441,** 1615, 1910, 1949, 1950
Gorky, Maxim, **VIII:1442-1446;** IX:2899
Life of Klim Samgin, The, VIII:1444
Lower Depths, The, VIII:1444, 1445
Mother, The, VIII:1444, 1445
Gorky Institute, VII:153
gospel music, VII:657, 1216
Gospel of Wealth, The, V:423
Gospels, I:56, I:450, 467-470
See also John, Gospel of; Luke, Gospel of; Matthew, Gospel of; Mark, Gospel of

Gosse, Sir Edmund, VIII:2683
Gosson, Stephen, III:692, 693
Gostling, John, IV:1138
Gotha Canal, VI:2208
Gotha Program, VI:1370
Gothardt, Matthias. *See* Grünewald, Matthias
Goths. *See* Visigoths
Gottfried von Strassberg, **II:392-394,** 435
Tristan and Isolde, II:392-394
Göttingen, University of, VIII:1797
Göttingen Observatory, V:894
Gottsched, Johann Christoph, IV:842, 843
Gough, John, V:602
Gould, Jay, V:731; VI:1581, 2285
Gould, Stephen Jay, V:609
Goulue, La, VI:2248
Gounod, Charles, **V:967-970**
Colombe, La, V:968, 969
Faust, V:968
Médecin malgré lui, Le, V:969
Messe solennelle de Sainte Cécile, V:968
Nonne sanglante, La, V:968
Philèmon et Baucis, V:969
Polyeucte, V:968, 969
Rédemption, La, V:969
Sapho, V:968
Government of India Act, VIII:1849
Goya, Francisco de, **IV:569-573;** VI:1854
Black Paintings, The, IV:571
Caprices, The, IV:571, 572
Clothed Maja, The, IV:571
Disasters of War, The, IV:571, 572; VI:1960
Duke and Duchess of Osuna, The, IV:570
Executions of May Second, The, IV:571
Executions of May Third, The, IV:571, 572
Milkmaid of Bordeaux, The, IV:571
Naked Maja, The, IV:571
Parasol, The, IV:570
Portrait of Don Manuel Orsorio, IV:570
Portrait of the Count of Floridablanca, The, IV:570
Portrait of the Family of King Charles IV, IV:571
Proverbs, The, IV:571, 572
Qué Valor, VI:1960
Washerwoman, The, IV:570
Goyathlay. *See* Geronimo
Gracchi, The, **I:345-348**
Grace, Covenant of, IV:1464
Grace, Pilgrimage of, III:205, 209
Grace, William Gilbert, **V:971-974**
Graf Zeppelin, VII:1012, 1013; IX:4111
Graham, Billy, **VIII:1447-1450**
Personal History, VIII:1452
Graham, John, VIII:2023, 2024
System and Dialectics of Art, VIII:2023
Graham, Katharine, **VIII:1451-1454**
Lower Depths, The, VIII:1444
Graham, Martha, VII:1178; **VIII:1455-1458**
Appalachian Spring, VIII:1458
Heretic, VIII:1457
Horizons, VII:539
Letter to the World, VIII:1458
Panorama, VII:539
Primitive Mysteries, VIII:1458
Revolt, VIII:1457
Vision of the Apocalypse, VIII:1457
Xochital, VIII:1455
Graham, Philip L., VIII:1451
Graham, Sheilah, VII:1163
Graham's Magazine, VI:1796
Grahn, Judy, VIII:1508
Gramsci, Antonio, **VIII:1459-1462**
Quaderni del carcere, VIII:1459, 1461
Selections from the Prison Notebooks, VIII:1459
Granada, Cathedral of, III:696, 697
Grand Alliance, War of the, IV:873, 923, 924
Grand Alliance of European powers, IV:1447, 1448
Grand Council of French Western Africa, VIII:1755
Grandfathers, War of the, V:126
Grand Prix racing, VII:1150
Grand Remonstrance, IV:309, 1142
Grands Rhétoriqueurs, II:245
Grand Trunk Railway, VIII:1981, 2102
Grant, James Augustus, VI:2084, 2085
Grant, Ulysses S., **V:975-978**
Arthur, V:78
Barnard, V:131
Blaine, V:256
Greeley, V:985
Hayes, V:1075
Johnson, V:1235
Joseph, V:1242
Michelson, VI:1551
Nast, VI:1628
Powell, VI:1810
Sherman, VI:2059, 2060
Stanton, VI:2108
Sumner, VI:2172, 2173
Granvelle, Antoine Perrenot de, III:599, 781
Granville, Earl of, IV:1074
Granz, Norman, VII:1159

Grass, Günter, **VIII:1463-1466**
Cat and Mouse, VIII:1464
Dog Years, VIII:1464
Flounder, The, VIII:1464
From the Diary of a Snail, VIII:1464
Headbirths, VIII:1464
Local Anaesthetic, VIII:1464
Meeting at Telgte, The, VIII:1464
Only Ten Minutes to Buffalo, VIII:1463
Plebeians Rehearse the Uprising, The, VIII:1464
Rat, The, VIII:1465
Show Your Tongue, VIII:1465
Tin Drum, The, VIII:1463, 1464
Grasse, François-Joseph-Paul, Comte de, IV:1175
Grassman, Hermann Günther, IX:3966
Gratian, I:44, 695, 868, 870; II:179
Gratus, Valerius, I:640
Graves, Robert
I, Claudius, I:551
gravity, I:79; IV:263
Guericke, IV:588
Hawking, VIII:1582
Huygens, IV:697
Kepler, IV:775, 775
Lagrange, IV:786
Laplace, VI:1319-1322
Maclaurin, IV:882-884
Newton, IV:601, 1025, 1027, 1028
Gray, Asa, V:32, **979-981**
Gray, Thomas
Elegy in a Country Churchyard, IV:1473
Great Awakening, IV:429, 1202; V:470; VI:1425
Great Books of the Western World, VIII:1801, 1802
Great Bouwerie, IV:1294
Great Camp of Kiangnan, VI:2261
Great Compromise. *See* Connecticut Compromise
Great Contract of 1610, III:662
Great Depression
Alger, V:52
Baldwin, VII:170
Broadway musicals, VIII:1567
Canada, VIII:1982, 1983
Catholic Worker movement, VII:851
Hoover, VIII:1727, 1729, 1730
Humphrey, VIII:1785
Japan, VIII:2458
Keynes, VIII:1954
London School of Economics, VII:309
Miller's plays, VIII:2533
Nazi Party, VIII:1405, 1676, 1694
photography, VII:397; VIII:2083, 2084
Rogers, IX:3206
Roosevelt, IX:3224, 3225
Sandburg, IX:3310
Steinbeck, IX:3515
Greater Dionysia
Aeschylus, I:10
Aristophanes, I:91
Demosthenes, I:255
Euripides, I:317
Pisistratus, I:649
Sophocles, I:10, 11, 807
Thespis, I:877-879
Great Leap Forward
Chou En-lai, VII:678
Deng Xiaoping, VII:905
Khrushchev, VIII:1962
Lin Piao, VIII:2190
Liu Shao-ch'i, VIII:2213, 2214
Mao Tse-tung, VIII:2401, 2402
P'eng Te-huai, IX:2955
Great Northern Expedition, IV:111, 112
Great Northern Railroad, IV:660, 661; VII:881
Great Northern War, IV:290-292, 533
Great Ordinance, II:606
Great Parliament, II:645
Great Persecution, I:266
Great Persian Wars. *See* Persian Wars
Great Proletarian Cultural Revolution. *See* Cultural Revolution
Great Purge, VIII:2571
Great Reform Bill. *See* Reform Bill of 1832
Great Renunciation, I:915
Great Saltash Bridge, V:337
Great Schism, II:220, 237, 760, 899, 969-971, 1009-1011
Great Service, III:107, 108
Great Sioux Reservation, VI:2070
Great Society, VII:948; VIII:1868
Great Swamp Battle, IV:955
Great Trek, V:380
Great Wall of China, I:177
Greco, El, **III:311-314**
Assumption of the Virgin, V:436
Burial of the Count of Orgaz, The, III:312
Martyrdom of Saint Maurice, The, III:311
Trinity, The, III:313
View of Toledo, V:436
Greco-Persian Wars. *See* Persian Wars
Greek mythology
Aesop, I:13-15
Antisthenes, I:67

Aristophanes, I:91
Bernini, IV:118-120
Callimachus, I:157
Dionysius, I:878
Empedocles, I:282
Epicurus, I:295
Hesiod, I:402-405
Homer, I:420-422
Ingres, V:1184, 1185
Offenbach, VI:1685, 1686
Phidias, I:624-626
Philo of Alexandria, I:632
Pindar, I:644-646
Racine, IV:1146
Ronsard, III:657-659
Scopas, I:765
Xenophanes, I:955-957
Greek Orthodox Church, I:121
Greeley, Horace, V:192, 850, **982-986;** VIII:1533
Green, Thomas Hill, **V:987-989;** VIII:1707
Greene, Ann Terry, VI:1771
Greene, Catherine, IV:1431
Greene, Graham, VII:731; **VIII:1467-1470**
Brighton Rock, VIII:1468
Dr. Fischer of Geneva, VIII:1469
Heart of the Matter, The, VIII:1468
Human Factor, The, VIII:1468
It's a Battlefield, VIII:1468
Journey without Maps, VIII:1468
Labyrinthine Ways, The, VIII:1468
Man Within, The, VIII:1467
Monsignor Quixote, IV:269; VIII:1469
Quiet American, The, VIII:1469
Shipwrecked, The, VIII:1468
Sort of Life, A, VIII:1467
Stamboul Train, VIII:1467
Greene, Nathanael, **IV:574-578,** 1406, 1431
Greene, Robert, III:548, 686, 687
Greenland
Davis, III:212, 213
Eriksson, II:577-579
Peary, IX:2941
Wegener, IX:3918-3920
Green Mountain Boys, IV:34-36
Green River, VI:1810, 1812
Greenspan, Alan, **VIII:1471-1474**
Green Spring Faction, IV:80
Greenville, Treaty of, VI:2204
Greenway, Francis, **V:990-993**
Greenwich Village Follies, VIII:1457
Gregory II, II:167, 900
Gregory III, II:243
Gregory VI, II:395
Gregory VII, **II:395-398,** 461, 462, 575, 583, 928, 929
Dictatus papae, II:396
Gregory IX, **II:399-402**
Anthony of Padua, II:77
Elizabeth of Hungary, II:342
Frederick II, II:362, 363
Innocent IV, II:514
Raymond of Peñafort, II:776, 777
William of Auvergne, II:977
William of Auxerre, II:982
Gregory X, II:165, 796, 797, 985
Gregory XI, II:220, 1010
Gregory XIII, I:813; III:552, 715
Gregory XVI, VI:1782
Gregory, William
Lectures on Experimental Philosophy, Astronomy and Chemistry, V:1093
Gregory, MacLeod, and Company, IV:879
Gregory of Nazianzus, **I:349-351,** 352, 869
On His Life, I:349
On St. Basil the Great, I:350
Theological Orations, I:349
Gregory of Nyssa, **I:352-355**
Contra Eunomium, I:353, 354
Gregory of Tours, II:274-276, **403-406**
History of the Franks, The, II:274, 403-405
Life of the Fathers, II:404
Miracles of St. Martin, The, II:403,404
Gregory the Great, II:405, **407-410**
Dialogues of Saint Gregory the Great, II:136-138
Moralia, II:407
Pastoral Care, II:408
Gregory v. Ashcroft, IX:2791
Grenadier Guards, VIII:2340
Grenville, Sir Richard, **III:315-317**
Cavendish, III:140
Raleigh, III:639
Wilkes, IV:1439
Greuze, Jean-Baptiste, IV:414
Grey, Charles. *See* Grey, Second Earl
Grey, Lady Jane, III:237, 239, **318-321,** 479, 480
Grey, Second Earl, IV:42; **V:994-997;** VI:2393
Grey, Sir Edward, **VIII:1475-1477**
Grey, Sir George Edward, **V:998-1001;** VIII:1475
Grieg, Edvard, **V:1002-1005;** VII:892-894
Peer Gynt, V:1003
Piano Concerto in A Minor, V:1003
Sörgemarsch over Rikard Nordraak, V:1003

Griffith, D.W., VII:1274; **VIII:1478-1482,** 1690, 2231, 2232, 2234; IX:3006, 3008
Birth of a Nation, The, VII:1383; VIII:1480, 1481
Broken Blossoms, VII:1385; VIII:1481
Hearts of the World, VII:783
Intolerance, VII:959, 1383; VIII:1480, 1481, 2232, 2234
Mothering Heart, The, VII:1383
One Million B.C., VIII:1481
Orphans of the Storm, VIII:1480, 1481
Struggle, The, VIII:1481
Unseen Enemy, An, VII:1383
Way Down East, VII:1385
Griffith, John, VII:798
Griffith, Richard R, III:458
Griffith, Sir Samuel, V:149
Griffiths, Ralph, IV:565
Grijalva, Juan de, III:21
Grimes, Peter, VII:471
Grimké, Angelina, V:885
Grimké, Francis, V:808
Grimké, Sarah, V:808
Grimm, Jacob and Wilhelm, **V:1006-1009;** VIII:1712
Grimm's Fairy Tales, V:1006-1008
Grindal, Edmund, III:590
Gris, Juan, VII:432; **VIII:1483-1485**
Harlequin, VIII:1484
Portrait of Picasso, VIII:1483
"Possibilités de la Peinture, Les," VIII:1484
Siphon and Bottles, VIII:1483
Griswold v. Conneticut, VII:322
Grolman, Karl, V:940-942
Gromyko, Andrei, VII:461; VIII:1424; IX:3102
Groote, Gerhard, II:906, 907
Gropius, Walter, **VIII:1486-1489**
Klee, VIII:2006
Kokoschka, VIII:2013
Mahler, VIII:2363
Grosseteste, Robert, II:110, 985
Grotius, Hugo, **IV:579-582**
Adamus Exul, The, IV:579
Christ's Passion, IV:579
Commentary on the Law of Prize and Booty, IV:579
Freedom of the Seas, The, IV:579
Gentili, III:296
international law, III:769
Introduction to Dutch Jurisprudence, IV:580
Oldenbarnevelt, III:575
On the Law of War and Peace, IV:579-581
Pufendorf, IV:1134
Group 47, VII:349
Group 64, VII:809
Group Theatre, VII:795; IX:4009, 4010
Grove, Sir William Robert, **V:1010-1014**
On the Correlation of Physical Forces, V:1012
Groves, Leslie, VII:637
Gruen, David. *See* Ben-Gurion, David
Grundy, Felix, VI:1801
Grünewald, Matthias, **III:322-324**
Isenheim altarpiece, III:322-324
Guadalcanal, VIII:1527
Guadalupe Hidalgo, Treaty of, V:859; VI:2416
Guajardo, Jesús M., IX:4106
Gualterotti, Raffaelo, IV:850
Guarini, Battista
Faithful Shepherd, The, IV:990, 991
Guarini, Guarino, **IV:583-585**
Architecttura civile, IV:584, 585
Desegni d'architettura civile e ecclesiastica, IV:584
Guderian, Heinz, **VIII:1490-1493**
Guelfs (Guelphs), II:286, 288, 515, 961; V:934
Guericke, Otto von, **IV:586-588**
Guerin, Camille, VII:547
Guerin, Pierre-Narcisse, V:645, 910
guerrilla warfare
Arafat, VII:90
Collins, VII:733, 734
Guevara, VIII:1494-1496
Lawrence, VIII:2128
Mozambique, VIII:2317
South African War, VIII:2003
Utah miners, VIII:1499
Viet Cong, VIII:1701
Vo Nguyen Giap, IX:3824
Zapata, IX:4104, 4106
Zimbabwe, VIII:2647-2649
Guesde, Jules, V:1222
Guettard, Jean-Étienne, IV:805
Guevara, Che, VII:617; **VIII:1494-1497,** 1634
Che Guevara on Guerrilla Warfare, VIII:1495, 1496
Guggenheim, Daniel, **VIII:1498-1501**
Guggenheim, Meyer, VIII:1498
Guggenheim, Peggy, IX:3048, 3049
Guggenheim Foundation, VIII:2733
Guggenheim Museum, IX:4062
Guicciardini, Francesco, **III:325-327,** 498
Accusatoria, III:326

Considerations on the Discourses of Machiavelli, III:325
Consolatoria, III:326
Cose fiorentine, III:326
Defensoria, III:326
Dialogo del reggimento di Firenze, III:325
History of Italy, The, III:326, 327
Ricordi, III:326, 327
Guido d'Arezzo, **II:411-413**
Aliae regulae, II:412
Epistola de ignoto cantu, II:412, 413
Micrologus, II:411, 412
Regulae rhythmicae in antiphonarii prologum prolate, II:412, 413
Guilbert, Yvette, VI:2248, 2249
Guillaume, Charles-Édouard, **VIII:1502-1504**
Traité practique de la thermométrie de précision, VIII:1495
Guinizelli, Guido, II:224
Guiscard, Marquis de, IV:158
Guiscard, Robert, II:159
Guise, House of
Catherine de Médicis, III:132, 133
Henry IV, III:333
Hotman, III:363-365
Mary, Queen of Scots, III:475
Mornay, III:538
Guizot, François, VI:2226, 2227
Gulf Oil, VIII:2481
Gulf Stream, III:629, 631
Gulf War. *See* Persian Gulf War
Gullichsen, Harry and Maire, VII:2
Gumilyov, Nikolai, VII:37, 38
Gumm, Frances. *See* Garland, Judy
Gundobad, II:276
gunpowder, II:988, 989; IV:1335; V:718-720; VI:1674
Gunpowder Plot, III:257-259, 662; IV:47, 700, 747
Gunpowder Women, VII:488
guns
Colt, V:540-542
Oakley, VI:1677-1679
Rehnquist, IX:3144
Gupta Dynasty, I:491
Gustavus II Adolphus, IV:304, 452, **589-592,** 1052, 1335, 1336
Gutenberg, Johann, **III:328-332**
Gutenberg Bible, III:328, 330, 331
Guthrum, II:60
Guy de Chauliac, **II:414-416**
Chirurgia magna, II:414, 415
Guyuk. *See* Kuyuk
Gyges, I:106
Gypsies, VII:210, 1128; VIII:1854-1856
Gzhantsk, VII:1272

Haakon Sigurdsson, II:688, 689
Ha'am, Ahad, IX:3930
Habeler, Peter, VIII:2507, 2508
Haber, Fritz, **VIII:1509-1512,** 1654
Habsburg, House of
Alva, III:18-20
Charles V, III:159-161
Czechoslovakia, VII:259
Ferdinand II, IV:450, 451
Ferdinand and Isabella, III:262
Fischer von Erlach, IV:473-475
Francis I, III:274, 275, 277
Francis Ferdinand, VII:1197
Frederick Henry, IV:500
Frederick the Great, IV:504
German Protestantism, IV:590
Guicciardini, III:326
Henry IV, III:335
Imperial Style, IV:655
Joseph II, IV:750-752
Leopold I, IV:838-840
Louis XIV, IV:868
Maria Theresa, IV:914-916
Marie-Antoinette, IV:918
Maximillian I, III:491, 492
Philip II, III:599, 600, 602
Richelieu, IV:1166, 1167
Rudolf I, II:796, 797
Strauss, VI:2158
Süleyman the Magnificent, III:707, 708
Titian, III:721
Wallenstein, IV:1396
Hadden, Briton, VIII:2260, 2262
Hadfield, James, IV:441
Hadfield, Sir Robert Abbott, **V:1015-1017**
Hadi, al-, II:437
Hadrian, I:28, **356-359,** 901, 902
Hadrian's Temple, I:358
Hadrian's Wall, I:358
Haeckel, Ernst, **V:1018-1021**
Evolution of Man, The, V:1021
Generelle Morphologie der Organismen, V:1020, 1021
History of Creation, The, V:1021
Report on the Deep-Sea Medusae, V:1020
Report on the Radiolara, V:1018, 1020
Riddle of the Universe, The, V:1021
Wonders of Life, The, V:1021

Hafiz, **II:417-420**
Divan, The, II:417, 418
Haganah, VII:243, 245, 251, 252, 854
Hagar, I:6
Hageladas. *See* Ageladas
Hagenau, Reinmar von, II:960
Haghia Sophia, II:556
Hague, The, III:574; IX:2860
Hague Peace Conferences, VI:2177; VIII:2051
Hahl, August, VI:1541
Hahn, Otto, **VIII:1513-1516,** 1618, 1648, 2476, 2477
Applied Radiochemistry, VIII:1516
Hahnemann, Samuel, **IV:593-595**
Organon of the Healing Art, IV:594
Haig, Douglas, VII:58, 59
Haile Selassie, **VIII:1517-1521**
Haitian Revolution, V:501, 502
Hakodate, VI:1762
Haldimand, Frederick, IV:198
Hale, Matthew, **IV:596-599**
History of the Common Law, IV:598
History of the Pleas of the Crown, IV:598
Hale, Sarah Josepha, **V:1022-1024**
Northwood, V:1022, 1023
Poems for Our Children, V:1023
Sketches of American Character, V:1022
Traits of American Life, V:1022
Woman's Record, V:1024
Haley, Sir William, VII:737, 738
Halffter, Ernesto, VII:1129
Half World's Convention, V:1110
Halicarnassus, Mausoleum of, I:764
Halide Edib Adivar, **VIII:1522-1524**
Clown and His Daughter, The, VIII:1524
Memoirs of Halide Edib, VIII:1524
Seviye Talip, VIII:1523
Shirt of Flame, The, VIII:1523
Turkish Ordeal, The, VIII:1524
Yeni Turan, VIII:1523
Halidon, Battle of, II:294
Halifax, Lord, VII:530
Halil, Candarli, III:499, 500
Hall, James, VI:1420
Hallaj, al-, **II:421-425**
Kitab al-tawasin, II:422
Riwayat, II:422
Hallam, Arthur Henry, VI:2211, 2213
Haller, Albrecht von, IV:523
Halley, Edmond, **IV:600-603,** 785, 883, 1027; V:215
Astronomie cometicae synopsis, IV:602
Catalogus Stellarum Australium, IV:600
Halley's Comet, IV:602; V:215
Haloid Corporation. *See* Xerox
Hals, Frans, **IV:604-607**
Laughing Cavalier, The, IV:605
Lute Player, The, IV:606
Seated Man Holding a Branch, IV:606
Halsey, William F., **VIII:1525-1528,** 2751
Halske, Johann Georg, VI:2067
Halsted, William, VII:823
Hamaguchi Yuko, VIII:1574
Hamann, Johann Georg, IV:651
Hamburg Opera, IV:1320, 1321
Hamilcar, I:740
Hamilton, Alexander, **IV:608-612**
Burr, V:369, 370
Federalist, The, IV:610
Federalist Party, IV:19
Jay, IV:714
Jefferson, IV:718, 719
Madison, IV:886, 888
Parrington, IX:2893, 2894
Report Relative to a Provision for the Support of Public Credit, IV:610
Hamilton, Andrew, IV:1486
Hamilton, Gavin, V:408
Hamilton, Henry, IV:314
Hamilton, Lady, IV:1188
Hamilton, Sir William Rowan, **V:1025-1028**
Hammadid kingdom, II:4
Hammarskjöld, Dag, VII:502; **VIII:1529-1532;** IX:3103, 3647, 3746, 3747
Hammerstein, Oscar, II, **VIII:1533-1536;** IX:3201, 3202
Allegro, VIII:1534
Always You, VIII:1533
Annie Get Your Gun, VII:289, 290
Carmen Jones, VIII:1534
Carousel, VIII:1534, 1536
Desert Song, VIII:1533
Flower Drum Song, VIII:1536
King and I, The, VIII:1534, 1536
Me and Juliet, VIII:1534
Music in the Air, VIII:1534
New Moon, The, VIII:1534
Oklahoma, VIII:1534, 1536
Pipe Dream, VIII:1536
Rose Marie, VIII:1533
Show Boat, VIII:1533, 1536
Sound of Music, The, VIII:1536
South Pacific, VIII:1534, 1536
State Fair, VIII:1534, 1536
Sunny, VIII:1533

Sweet Adeline, VIII:1534
Tickle Me, VIII:1533
Very Warm for May, VIII:1534
Hammett, Dashiell, VIII:1620, 1623
Hammond, John, VII:1217; VIII:1717
Hammurabi, **I:360-363,** 569
Hampton Court Conference, III:661
Hamsun, Knut, **VIII:1537-1540**
August, VIII:1538
Bjoerger, VIII:1537
Children of the Age, VIII:1538
Dreamers, VIII:1538
gaadefulde, Den, VIII:1537
Growth of the Soil, VIII:1538
Mysteries, VIII:1537
On Overgrown Paths, VIII:1538
Pan, VIII:1538
Segelfoss Town, VIII:1538
Victoria, VIII:1538
Hancock, John, IV:357, **613-618**
Hancock, Thomas, V:962
Hand, Learned, **VIII:1541-1544**
"Spirit of Liberty, The," VIII:1542
Handel, George Friederic, IV:228, **619-622**
Almira, IV:619
Deborah, VIII:2770
Fireworks Music, IV:621
Messiah, IV:621, 622, 641
Nero, IV:619
Resurrezione, La, IV:620
Rinaldo, IV:620
Rodrigo, IV:620
St. John Passion, IV:619
Han dynasty, I:178, 590, 944, 949
Han-fei-tzu, I:433
Hangchow, II:479, 612, 856
Hanging Gardens, I:569, 570
Hanks, John, VI:1380
Hanna, Marcus A., **V:1029-1032**
Hannah, I:746
Hannibal, I:334-336, **364-367,** 535, 536, 761
Hanno, **I:368-370**
Hanoverian Dynasty, IV:53, 531-538, 1277-1279
Hansberry, Lorraine, **VIII:1545-1549**
Blancs, Les, VIII:1547, 1548
Drinking Gourd, The, VIII:1547, 1548
"Negro Writer and His Roots, The," VIII:1547, 1548
Raisin in the Sun, A, VIII:1545, 1547
Sign in Sidney Brustein's Window, The, VIII:1547, 1548
To Be Young, Gifted, and Black, VIII:1548
What Use Are Flowers?, VIII:1547, 1548
Hanseatic League, II:933
Han Yu, II:709
Haoge, IV:421
Hapsburg, House of. *See* Habsburg, House of
Harbach, Otto, VIII:1533
Hard, Darlene, VII:1364
Hardenberg, Karl von, **V:1033-1035;** VI:2116
Hardie, James Keir, **V:1036-1039**
Harding, Warren G., **VII:1550-1553**
Butler, VII:525
Coolidge, VII:762, 763
Debs, VII:882
Hughes, VIII:1767
Mellon, VIII:2481
Hardinge, Lord, VI:1331
Hardouin-Mansart, Jules. *See* Mansart, Jules Hardouin-
Hardy, Thomas, **V:1040-1043;** VI:1786
Desperate Remedies, V:1040
Dynasts, The, V:1042
Far from the Madding Crowd, V:1040, 1042
Jude the Obscure, V:1042
Mayor of Casterbridge, The, V:1040, 1042
"Poor Man and the Lady, The," V:1040
Return of the Native, The, V:1040, 1042
Tess of the D'Urbervilles, V:1042
Under the Greenwood Tree, V:1040
Winter Words, V:1042
Woodlanders, The, V:1042
Hare, David
Judas Kiss, The, VI:2380
Hare, Julius Charles, VI:1457, 1458
Harewood House, V:138
Hargreaves, James, **IV:623-625,** 770
Harlem Railroad, VI:2297
Harlem Renaissance, VIII:1771-1774, 1787-1789
Harley, Robert, IV:52, 53, 157, 158, 401, 1400
Harmonists, I:99
Harmsworth, Alfred, **VIII:1554-1556**
Harmsworth, Harold, **VIII:1554-1556**
Harnack, Adolf von, **VIII:1557-1559**
Grundriss der Dogmengeschichte, VIII:1558
History of Dogma, VIII:1558
Luke the Physician, VIII:1558
What Is Christianity?, VIII:1558
Harold II, **II:426-429**
Harold Godwinson. *See* Harold II
Harper, Henry Alpert, VIII:1981
Harper, William Rainey, **V:1044-1048**
Harper's Bazaar, VIII:2310

Harper's Ferry
Brown, V:322, 324, 491, 1151
Lee, VI:1338
Parker, VI:1729
Thoreau, VI:2235
Tubman, VI:2266
Harper's Weekly
Homer, V:1133, 1134
Nast, VI:1627, 1628
Remington, VI:1861, 1862
Schurz, VI:1997
Tweed, VI:2285, 2286
Harries, Carl, IX:3497
Harriman, William Averell, **VIII:1560-1565**
Harringay Crusade, VIII:1448
Harris, Joel Chandler, **V:1049-1052**
Balaam and His Master, V:1051
Free Joe and Other Georgian Sketches, V:1050
"Free Joe and the Rest of the World," V:1051
Mingo, V:1049
Nights with Uncle Remus, V:1049
Uncle Remus, V:1049
"Where's Duncan?," V:1051
Harris, Middleton
Black Book, The, VIII:2628
Harris, Theodore, VII:489
Harris, Townshend, V:1181, 1182
Harrison, Benjamin, V:257, 513, **1053-1056**
Harrison, Francis, IV:1485
Harrison, Frederic, **V:1057-1060**
Harrison, George, VII:226-229
Harrison, John, IV:185
Harrison, Thomas, IV:789, 790
Harrison, William Henry, **V:1061-1063**
Clay, V:509
Cushing, V:582
Perry, VI:1764, 1765
Tecumseh, VI:2204
Tyler, VI:2288-2290
Webster, VI:2345
Harris Treaty, V:1182
Harris v. Forklift Systems, VIII:2326
Harsha, **II:430-432,** 484
Nágánanda, II:431
Retnavali, II:431
Hart, Lorenz, **VIII:1566-1570;** IX:3201, 3202
Babes in Arms, VIII:1568
"Bewitched, Bothered and Bewildered," VIII:1568
"Blue Room, The," VIII:1567
Boys from Syracuse, The, VIII:1568
Connecticut Yankee, The, VIII:1567, 1569
Dearest Enemy, VIII:1567
Garrick Gaieties, The, VIII:1566, 1567
Girl Friend, The, VIII:1567
"I Could Write a Book," VIII:1568
I'd Rather Be Right, VIII:1568
I Married an Angel, VIII:1568
Jumbo, VIII:1568
On Your Toes, VIII:1568
Pal Joey, VIII:1568
Peggy-Ann, VIII:1567
Hartford, Treaty of, IV:1296
Hartford Female Seminary, V:170
Harthacnut, II:315
Hart House, VI:1496
Hartmann, Nicolai, **VIII:1577-1579**
Aufbau der realen Welt, Der, VIII:1572
Ethics, VIII:1571
Grundzuge einer Metaphysik der Erkenntis, VIII:1572
Möglichkeit und Wirklichkeit, VIII:1572
New Ways of Ontology, VIII:1572
Zur Grundlegung der Ontologie, VIII:1572
Hartmann von Aue, **II:433-436**
De arme Heinrich, II:433, 434
Erec, II:433
Gregorius, II:433, 434
Iwein, II:433, 434
Klage, Die, II:433
Harty, Sir Hamilton, IX:3874
Harun al-Rashid, **II:437-439**
Harvard Botanic Garden, V:980
Harvard Law School
Frankfurter, VII:1212
Hand, VIII:1541
Holmes, VIII:1720, 1721
Marshall, VIII:2433
Richardson, VI:1883
Harvard Observatory, VI:1756
Harvard University
Adams, V:15
Agassiz, V:30, 31
Bancroft, V:124, 125
Bernstein, VII:295
Carpenter Center for Visual Arts, VIII:2139
Conant, VII:749
Du Bois, VII:963
Dumbarton Oaks, VII:1131
Eliot, V:748, 749
Emerson, V:757, 758
Fuller, VII:1265
Gray, V:979, 980
Higginson, V:1110

Kissinger, VIII:1998, 1999
Krogh, VIII:2029
Laski, VIII:2093
Lippmann, VIII:2203
Mather, Cotton, IV:935, 936
Mather, Increase, IV:941
Royce, IX:3254
Santayana, IX:3317
Whitehead, IX:3967
See also Harvard Law School; Harvard Observatory
Harvey, Gabriel, III:549
Harvey, William, **IV:626-630,** 891, 1210
Anatomical Exercises of Dr. William Harvey, The, IV:628
Anatomical Exercitations, IV:629
Circulation of the Blood, The, IV:629
De venarum ostiolis, IV:626
Hasan al-Basre, al-, **II:440-442**
Hashemite Kingdom of Transjordan, VIII:1791; IX:4079
Hasidic Judaism, IV:73-75, 432, 433; VII:484, 485
Haskalah, IV:432, 433
Hasmonaean dynasty, I:390-392
Hastings, Battle of, II:998
Hastings, Warren, IV:224, **631-634**
Hastings, William Lord, III:650
Hatoyama Ichiro, **VIII:1574-1576**
Hatshepsut, **I:371-374,** 889
Hatta, Mohammad, **VIII:1577-1579;** IX:3571
Hauptmann, Bruno Richard, VIII:2194
Haushofer, Karl, VIII:2322
Haüy, Valentin, V:303, 304
Havel, Václav, VII:970
Havelock, Sir Henry, VI:1706
Havemeyer, H.O., V:435, 436
Hawaii
Cook, IV:353, 354
Heyerdahl, VIII:1660
Kamehameha I, VI:1255, 1257
Liliuokalani, VI:1372, 1374
McKinley, VI:1455
New Zealand, VI:2019
Vancouver, IV:1355, 1356
Hawke, Sir Edward, IV:57
Hawking, Stephen W., **VIII:1580-1583**
Hawkins, John, Sir, III:224, 225
Hawksmoor, Nicholas, **IV:635-638,** 1352, 1353
Hawley-Smoot Tariff, VIII:1729, 1779, 1780
Hawthorne, Nathaniel, **V:1064-1067;** VI:1524, 1776, 1777, 1796
Blithedale Romance, The, V:1066
Fanshawe, V:1064
House of the Seven Gables, The, V:1066
Life of Franklin Pierce, The, V:1066
Marble Faun, The, I:691; V:1066
"Minister's Black Veil, The," IV:430
Mosses from an Old Manse, V:1064
Scarlet Letter, The, V:715, 1064, 1066
Twice-Told Tales, V:1064; VI:1794
Hawtrey, Charles, VII:783
Hay, John, **V:1068-1071**
Abraham Lincoln, V:1066
Bread-Winners, The, V:1066, 1070
Castilian Days, V:1068
Pike County Ballads and Other Pieces, V:1068, 1070
Haya de la Torre, Víctor Raúl, **VIII:1584-1587**
Hayden, Ferdinand Vandeveer, **V:1072-1074**
Hayden, Scott, V:1240
Haydn, Franz Joseph, **IV:639-643**
Beethoven, V:178, 179
Boccherini, IV:149
Brahms, V:301
Creation, The, IV:641
"Glorius Things of Thee Are Spoken," IV:642
Seasons, The, IV:641
Surprise Symphony, IV:639
Haydon, Benjamin Robert, VI:1266
Hayes, Helen, **VIII:1588-1592**
Airport, VIII:1591
Anastasia, VIII:1591
Bab, VIII:1588
Coquette, VIII:1588
Dear Brutus, VIII:1588
Harriet, VIII:1589
Mary of Scotland, VIII:1589
Sin of Madelon Claudet, The, VIII:1589
Victoria Regina, VIII:1589
What Every Woman Knows, VIII:1588
Hayes, Rutherford B., V:78, 80, 256, **1075-1079**
Hay-Herbert Treaty, V:1070
Hay-Herrán Treaty, V:1090
Hayley, William, IV:138, 1188
Hayman, Francis, IV:515
Haymarket Square Riot, V:54; VIII:1411
Haymes, Dick, VIII:1598
Hay-Pauncefote Treaty, V:1069
Hayslip, Le Ly, **VIII:1593-1595**
Child of War, Woman of Peace, VIII:1593
When Heaven and Earth Changed Places, VIII:1593, 1594
Hayward, Nathaniel, V:961
Haywood, William D., V:280

Hayworth, Rita, **VIII:1596-1600**
Affair in Trinidad, VIII:1598
Blood and Sand, VIII:1597
Cover Girl, VIII:1597
Gilda, VIII:1597-1599
Lady from Shanghai, The, VIII:1597
Miss Sadie Thompson, VIII:1598
Only Angels Have Wings, VIII:1597
Pal Joey, VIII:1598
Strawberry Blonde, The, VIII:1597
You'll Never Get Rich, VIII:1597
Hazlitt, William, VI:1266, 1267
H.D. (Hilda Doolittle), **VIII:1505-1508**
Choruses from the Iphigenia in Aulis, VIII:1506
Hedylus, VIII:1506
"Hermes of the Ways," VIII:1505-1508
Palimpsest, VIII:1506
Sea Garden, VIII:1506
Tribute to Freud, VIII:1506
Tribute to the Angels, VIII:1508
Trilogy, VIII:1506
Walls Do Not Fall, The, VIII:1506
Head, Sir Francis Bond, VI:1450
Health, Education, and Welfare, Department of, VIII:1704, 1705
Hearst, William Randolph, **VIII:1601-1605**
Eckener's zeppelin, VII:1012
Graham, VIII:1447
Oakley's libel suit, VI:1678
heart
Aretaeus of Cappadocia, I:82
Diocles of Carystus, I:261
electrocardiograms, VII:217, 1039-1041
Empedocles, I:284
Erasistratus, I:300
Galen, I:339
Harvey, IV:628
Starling, IX:3494-3496
transplants, VII:195, 197
Heartland Theory, VIII:2321-2323
Heath, Edward, VIII:**1606-1609;** IX:3649, 3650, 4017
Heath, John, VI:1765
Hebard, Grace Raymond, VI:1934
Hebra, Ferdinand von, VI:2021, 2023
Hegel, Georg Wilhelm Friedrich, **V:1080-1084**
Böhme, IV:155
Croce, VII:801
Dewey, VII:916, 917
Difference Between Fichte's and Schelling's Philosophy, The, V:1080
Encyclopedia of Philosophy, V:1082
Fichte, IV:468
Herzen, V:1099
Kierkegaard, VI:1284, 1286
Lassalle, VI:1323
Lectures on the Philosophy of History, V:1082
Marx, VI:1492
Moore, VIII:2605, 2606
Phenomenology of Spirit, The, V:1080, 1082, 1083; VIII:2061
Philosophy of Right, V:1083
Philosophy of the Unconscious, VI:1986
Ritschl, VI:1892
Schelling, VI:1972-1974
Schopenhauer, VI:1985
Science of Logic, V:1082
Tönnies, IX:3703
Veblen, IX:3806
Hegesias, I:87
Heidegger, Martin, II:313; VII:499, 615; **VIII:1610-1613,** 1798
Being and Time, VIII:1610-1612; VII:615
Letter on Humanism, VIII:1612
Selbstbehauptung der deutschen Universität, VIII:1611
Was ist Metaphysik?, VIII:1611
Heiler, Friedrich, IX:3829, 3830
Hein, Piet, IV:502, **644-646**
Heine, Heinrich, V:204, **1085-1088;** VI:1336
Atta Troll, V:1086
Book of Songs, V:1086
Germany: A Winter's Tale, V:1086
Pictures of Travel, V:1086
Salon, The, V:1086
Heinkel, Ernst Heinrich, **VIII:1614-1616**
Heinkel Corporation, IX:3974
Heinmot Tooyalakekt. *See* Joseph, Chief
Heisenberg, Werner, **VIII:1617-1619,** 2705
Helena, Saint, **I:375-377**
Helen of Troy, VI:1686
Helenopolis, I:228
Helfferich, Karl, VII:1104
Hellespont, I:963
Hellman, Lillian, **VIII:1620-1623;** IX:2886
Another Part of the Forest, VIII:1622
Autumn Garden, The, VIII:1622
Children's Hour, The, VIII:1620, 1622
Little Foxes, The, VII:845; VIII:1417, 1610, 1622, 1638
Toys in the Attic, VIII:1622
Watch on the Rhine, VIII:1622
Helmechis, II:42
Helots, I:17, 18

Helmasperger Instrument, III:328
Helmholtz, Hermann von, **V:1089-1092;** VIII:2713, 2714; IX:4069
On the Sensations of Tone as a Physiological Basis for the Theory of Music, V:1090
Treatise on Physiological Optics, V:1090
Héloïse, II:11, 13, 14
Helpmann, Robert, VII:1175, 1178
Helsinki Accord, VII:460, 612
hematology. *See* blood
Hemerken, Thomas. *See* Thomas à Kempis
Hemingway, Ernest, VII:1163; **VIII:1624-1628;** IX:3512, 4043
Across the River and into the Trees, VIII:1626
Death in the Afternoon, VIII:1626
Farewell to Arms, A, VIII:1589, 1626
Fifth Column, The, VIII:1626
For Whom the Bell Tolls, VIII:1626
Garden of Eden, The, VIII:1626
Green Hills of Africa, VIII:1626
In Our Time, VIII:1624, 1626
"Killers, The," VIII:1742
Moveable Feast, A, VIII:1626
Old Man and the Sea, The, VII:937; VIII:1626, 1627
Sun Also Rises, The, VIII:1626
To Have and Have Not, VIII:1626
Henderson, Arthur, VIII:2313
Henderson, Fletcher, VII:105
Henderson, Richard, IV:163, 164
Hengist, **I:378-381**
Hengstenberg, Ernst Wilhelm, VI:1828
Henie, Sonja, **VIII:1629-1632**
Sun Valley Serenade, VIII:1630
Hennebique, François, IX:2976
Henri, Robert, VIII:1740
Henrietta Anne, Princess, IV:171
Henry (of Anjou), II:292, 849
Henry (of Blois), II:847, 848
Henry (of Burgundy), II:30
Henry (of Condé), IV:863
Henry (of Navarre). *See* Henry IV (of France)
Henry (of Schwerin), II:933
Henry I (of England), **II:443-445**
Anselm, II:74
David I, II:291
Henry II, II:446
Stephen, II:847
Henry I (of France), II:997
Henry II (of England), **II:446-448**
Adrian IV, II:29
Alexander III, II:49
Becket, II:128
Eleanor of Aquitaine, II:338
John, King, II:540
Philip II, II:732
Richard I, II:782, 783
Stephen, II:850
Henry II (of France), III:756
Henry II the Saint, **II:449-452**
Henry III (of England), II:190-192, **453-456,** 581-583, 642-646
Henry III (of France), III:133, 333, 365, 538
Henry IV (of England), **II:457-460;** III:337
Henry IV (of France), III:255, **333-336**
Catherine de Médicis, III:133, 135
Champlain, IV:271, 273
Hotman, III:364, 365
Louis XIII, IV:863
Mansart, IV:898
Montaigne, III:525, 526
Mornay, III:537-539
Philip II, III:600
Richelieu, IV:1165
Henry IV (of Germany), **II:461-465**
Henry IV (of Spain), III:260
Henry V (of England), **III:337-340,** 341
Henry VI (of England), **III:341-344**
Fortescue, III:267, 268
Innocent III, II:510
Richard III, III:647
Warwick, III:774, 776
Henry VII (of England), **III:345-348**
Cabot, III:113, 115
Catherine of Aragon, III:136
Henry VIII, III:349
More, III:533
Richard III, III:651
Tudor family, III:732, 734
Warwick, III:776
Henry VIII (of England), **III:349-353**
Assertio septem sacramentorum adversus Martinum Lutherum, III:351
Boleyn, III:66, 68, 69
Catherine of Aragon, III:136, 138, 139
Clement VII, III:167, 168
Colet, III:170
Coverdale, III:193-195
Cranmer, III:204-206
Cromwell, III:208-210
Edward VI, III:237-239
Elizabeth I, III:241
Fisher, III:264, 265
Gardiner, III:291, 292

Grey, III:318
Holbein the Younger, III:358-360
Howard, III:367-369
Mary I, III:479
Mary, Queen of Scots, III:475
More, III:533-536
Parr, III:592-594
Ridley, III:654-656
Tudor family, III:732-734
Tyndale, III:736
Wolsey, III:785, 786
Henry, Charles, VI:2035
Henry, Fort, V:976
Henry, Joseph, V:103, **1093-1095;** VI:1593
Henry, O., **V:1096-1098**
Cabbages and Kings, V:1097
"Gift of the Magi, The," V:1098
"Miracle of Lava Canyon, The," V:1097
"Whistling Dick's Christmas Stocking," V:1097
Henry, Patrick, IV:312, **647-650**
Henry Street Settlement, IX:3837-3839
Henry the Lion, **II:466-469**
Lucidaris, II:468
Henry the Navigator, Prince, III:215, **354-357**
Henry the Proud, II:466
Henson, Matthew, IX:2942, 2944
Henze, Hans Werner, **VIII:1633-1636**
Bassarids, The, VIII:1634
Cimarrón, El, VIII:1634
Elegy for Young Lovers, VIII:1634
Essay on Pigs, VIII:1634
King of Harlem, The, VIII:1635
König Hirsch, VIII:1633, 1634
Novae de infinito laudes, VIII:1634
Oven, The, VIII:1635
Raft of the Medusa, The, VIII:1634
Hepburn, Katharine, VII:794; **VIII:1637-1640**
African Queen, The, VIII:1639
Bill of Divorcement, A, VIII:1638
Bringing Up Baby, VIII:1638
Christopher Strong, VII:119; VIII:1638
Guess Who's Coming to Dinner, VIII:1639
Lake, The, VIII:1638
Lion in Winter, The, VIII:1639
Little Women, VIII:1638
Long Day's Journey into Night, VIII:1639
Morning Glory, VIII:1638
On Golden Pond, VIII:1639
Philadelphia Story, The, VIII:1638; IX:3529
Stage Door, VIII:1638
Warrior's Husband, The, VIII:1637
Woman of the Year, VIII:1638
Hepburn Act, IX:3229
Hepburn v. Griswald, V:789
Hephthalite Huns, II:559, 560
Heracleopolis, I:637
Heracles, I:67, 317, 318
Heraclitus of Ephesus, I:157, **382-386,** 972
On Nature, I:382
Heraclius, **II:470-473,** 819-821
Herbert, George. *See* Carnarvon, Fifth Earl of
Herbst, Josephine, IX:3061
Hercules, I:69
Herder, Johann Gottfried, **IV:651-654**
Adrastea, IV:652
God: Some Conversations, IV:652
Kritische Wälder, IV:651
Letters for the Advancement of Humanity, IV:652
Outlines of a Philosophy of the History of Man, IV:652
Treatise upon the Origin of Language, IV:651
Über die neuere deutsche Literatur, IV:651
heresy
Abelard, II:14, 144
Ambrose, I:44
Andrewes, IV:47
Bayle, IV:103
Catharist movement, II:49
Dominic, II:301, 302
Galileo, IV:521
Gardiner, III:293
Gregory the Great, II:408
Hippolytus of Rome, I:415
Irenaeus, I:448-450
Mary I, III:480
Ockham, II:682, 683
Philip II, III:599
Priscillian, I:695, 696
Siger of Brabant, II:830
Spinoza, IV:1264
Stephen, I:823
Tertullian, I:849
Vincent of Lérins, I:936-938
Wyclif, II:1011
Hering, Ewald, VII:452
Hering-Breuer reflex, VII:452
Hermann I, II:340
Hermann, Wilhelm, VII:498
Hermarchus, I:295
Hermeias, I:95
Hermes, I:690-692
Hermeticism, IV:949-951
Hermias, I:63

Hermippus, I:115
Hermitage, the, IV:801
Hermite, Charles, IX:2994, 2995
Hermopolis, I:637
Hernandez, Aileen Clarke, **VIII:1641-1643**
Herod Antipus, I:480
Herodotus, **I:394-397**
Aesop, I:14
African exploration, I:370
Eupalinus of Megara, I:314
Hesiod, I:405
History of Herodotus, The, I:233, 394, 396, 397, 621, 622, 706
Pheidippides, I:621, 622
Pisistratus, I:650
Thucydides, I:886, 887
Herod the Great, **I:390-393**
Heron of Alexandria. *See* Hero of Alexandria
Hero of Alexandria, **I:387-389;** IV:787
Automata, I:387
Belopoeica, I:387
Catoptrica, I:387
Cheiroballistra, I:387
Dioptra, I:387
Mechanica, I:387
On Measures, I:387, 388
Pneumatics of Hero of Alexandria, The, I:387, 388
Stereometrica, I:387, 388
Herophilus, **I:398-401**
Against Common Opinions, I:400
Erasistratus, I:299-301
On Anatomy, I:398, 399
On Delivery, I:399
On Pulses, I:399
Herring, Constantine, IV:594
Herriot, Édouard, **VIII:1644-1646;** IX:3046
Herrmann, Bernard, VIII:1821
Herrnhut, IV:1488-1490
Herschel, William, IX:3701
Hertz, Gustav, **VIII:1647-1649**
Hertz, Heinrich, VI:1513, 1806, 1807; VII:318, 319; VIII:1647, 2415
Hertz, Rudolph, V:1090
Hertzog, Jan, VII:377
Herzen, Aleksandr, **V:1099-1101**
Diletantizm v nauke, V:1099
From the Other Shore, V:1100
My Past and Thoughts, V:1100
Pisma iz Frantsii i Italii, V:1099
Pisma ob izuchenii prirody, V:1099
Who Is to Blame?, V:1099
Zapski odnogo molodogo cheloveka, V:1099
Herzl, Theodor, **V:1102-1106;** VIII:2767; IX:3930, 3931
Jewish State, A, V:1104
Old-new Land, V:1105
Heseltine, Philip, IX:3873
Hesiod, **I:402-406**
Shield of Herakles, I:403
Thales of Miletus, I:852, 855
Theogony, I:402-404
Works and Days, I:15, 402-404
Hesse, Hermann, **VIII:1650-1653**
Peter Camenzind, VIII:1650, 1651
Demian, VIII:1650, 1651
Glass Bead Game, The, VIII:1650-1652
Klingsor's Last Summer, VIII:1650, 1651
Steppenwolf, VIII:1651, 1652
Prodigy, The, VIII:1651
Siddhartha, VIII:1651
Death and the Lover, VIII:1652
Journey to the East, The, VIII:1652
Hesychasm, II:899-901
Heth, Joice, V:135
Hetzel, P.J., VI:2303
Heuga, Jimmy, VIII:1965
Hevelius, Johannes, IV:600
Hevesy, Georg von, **VIII:1654-1657**
HEW. *See* Health, Education, and Welfare, Department of
Heyerdahl, Thor, **VIII:1658-1661**
Aku-Aku, VIII:1659
American Indians in the Pacific, VIII:1659
Archaeology of Easter Island, VIII:1659
Fatu-Hiva, VIII:1658
Kon-Tiki, VIII:1658
Ra Expeditions, The, VIII:1660
Hezekiah, I:454
Hicesias, I:268
Hickok, James Butler. *See* Hickok, Wild Bill
Hickok, Wild Bill, V:390, 391, **1107-1109**
Hicks, Amelia, VII:353
Hierapolis, I:784
Hiero, I:788, 789
Hieron, I:10
Hieron II, I:76, 78, 79
Hieronymus, I:79
Higginson, Thomas Wentworth, V:670, **1110-1112,** 1201
Highjump, Operation, VII:535
Highs, Thomas, IV:61, 624
Hijaz Railway, VIII:2126, 2127
Hilalians, II:5
Hilbert, David, VIII:2725

Hildebrandt, Johann Lucas von, **IV:655-658**
Hildegard von Bingen, **II:474-478**
Ordo virtutum, II:476
Scivias, II:474,476
Symphonia harmonia caelestium revelationum, II:476
Hilderic, I:344
Hill, Anita F., IX:3657, 3658
Hill, James Jerome, **IV:659-661**
Hill, Octavia, **V:1113-1116**
Hillary, Sir Edmund, **VIII:1662-1665**
Himmler, Heinrich, VII:440; VIII:1492, **1666-1669**
Hincmar of Reims, II:673
Hindemith, Paul, **VIII:1670-1673;** IX:3873
Cardillac, VII:471
Craft of Musical Composition, The, VIII:1671
Harmonie der Welt, Die, VIII:1672
Kammermusik, VIII:1671
Ludus Tonalis, VIII:1672
Mathis der Maler, VII:471; VIII:1671
Sancta Susanna, VIII:1671
Symphonic Metamorphosis of Themes by Carl Maria von Weber, VIII:1672
Wirbauen eine Stadt, VIII:1672
Hindenburg, IX:4111
Hindenburg, Paul von, **VIII:1674-1677,** 2265-2267; IX:2877
Hindustan Seva Dal, VIII:2709
Hines, Earl, VII:106, 107; IX:2882
Hinton, James, VII:1070
Hipparchus, **I:407-410,** 649, 712, 787, 813
Commentary on the Phaenomena of Eudoxus and Aratus, I:407
On Bodies Carried Down by Their Weight, I:407
Hipparete, I:31
Hippasus of Metapontum, I:728
Hippias, I:214, 649, 650, 857
Hippocrates, I:174, 175, 260, 262, 400, **411-414;** II:713, 779, 780
Ancient Medicine, I:35, 412
Corpus Hippocraticum, I:411
"Life Is short, Art long," I:413
Regimen, I:412
Hippodrome, II:890-892
Hippolytus of Rome, **I:415-419**
Apostolic Tradition of Hippolytus, The, I:417
Hiram of Tyre, I:800
Hiraoka, Kimitake. *See* Mishima, Yukio
Hirohito, **VIII:1678-1682**
Akihito, VII:41, 42
Hiroshige, **V:1117-1119,** 1121
Meisho Edo Hyakkei, V:1118
Tokaido Gojusantsugi, V:1118
Hiss, Alger, VII:18; **VIII:1683-1686,** 1733, 2758
In the Court of Public Opinion, VIII:1684
Recollections of a Life, VIII:1684
Histadrut, VII:252
Hitchcock, Alfred, **VIII:1687-1691;** IX:3736, 3738
Alfred Hitchcock Presents, VIII:1688
Blackmail, VIII:1687
Dial M for Murder, VIII:1690
Family Plot, VIII:1690
Frenzy, VIII:1690
Lifeboat, VIII:1688; VII:397
Lodger, The, VIII:1687
Man Who Knew Too Much, The, VIII:1688; IX:3530
North by Northwest, VIII:1690
Notorious, VIII:1688
Psycho, VIII:1690
Rear Window, VIII:1690; IX:3530
Rebecca, VIII:1688; IX:2810
Rope, IX:3530
Sabotage, VIII:1688
Shadow of a Doubt, VIII:1688
39 Steps, The, VIII:1688
To Catch a Thief, VIII:1690
Topaz, VIII:1690
Torn Curtain, VIII:1690
Vertigo, VIII:1690; IX:3530
Hitler, Adolf, **VIII:1692-1697**
Astor, VII:130
atom bomb, VII:380
Baldwin, VII:170
Berlin Olympics of 1936, IX:2862
Capek, VII:561
Chamberlain, VII:644-646
Chaplin, VII:654
evangelical church, VIII:2742
Finland, VIII:2398
Franco, VII:1201, 1202
Goebbels, VIII:1404-1406
Göring, VIII:1438-1441
Guderian, VIII:1490, 1492
Heinkel, VIII:1616
Henie, VIII:1631
Himmler, VIII:1666-1668
Hindenburg, VIII:1674-1676
Kesselring, VIII:1949, 1950
Lang, VIII:2078
Laval, VIII:2106, 2107

Lewis, VIII:2176
Lloyd George, VIII:2218
Luce, VIII:2262
Ludendorff, VIII:2266
Lyons, VIII:2294
Mackinder, VIII:2322
Mann, VIII:2393
Mein Kampf, VII:645; VIII:1694, 1695, 2135
Napoleon I, VI:1617, 1618
Nobel Prize policy, VII:952
Papen, VII:2876, 2877
Perón, IV:2969
Rommel, IX:3215
Rundstedt, IX:3260-3262
Wagner, VI:2319
Williams's music, IX:3799
zeppelins, VII:1013
Hittite empire, I:736, 904; VIII:2125
Hoad, Lewis A., VIII:2110
Hoare, Sir Samuel, VII:1016
Hoare-Laval Agreement, VIII:2105, 2107
Hobbes, Thomas, IV:160, **662-667,** 855, 857, 951, 1134
Behemoth, IV:665
De Sive, IV:664
Elements of Law, Natural and Politic, The, IV:662, 664
Leviathan, IV:664, 665, 855
Hobby, Oveta Culp, **VIII:1703-1706**
Hobhouse, Leonard T., **VIII:1707-1710**
Labour Movement, The, VIII:1707
Metaphysical Theory of the State, The, VIII:1709
Mind in Evolution, VIII:1709
Morals in Evolution, VIII:1709
Theory of Knowledge, The, VIII:1708
Hobomok, IV:1274
Hochhuth, Rolf
Deputy, The, IV:1219
Ho Chi Minh, **VIII:1698-1702;** IX:3821, 3823
Hockney, David, **VIII:1711-1714**
American Collectors, VIII:1712
Bigger Splash, A, VIII:1712
Boy About to Take a Shower, VIII:1712
Christopher Isherwood and Don Bachardy, VIII:1712
Doll Boy, VIII:1711
Mr. and Mrs. Clark with Percy, VIII:1712
Myself and My Heroes, VIII:1711
Rake's Progress, A, VIII:1711, 1712
Shell Garage, VIII:1712
We 2 Boys Together Clinging, VIII:1711
Hoffa, Jimmy, VIII:1933
Hoffman, Friedrich, IV:1268, 1269, 1271
Hoffmann, August Wilhelm von, VI:1367
Hoffmann, Roald, IX:4054
Hofmann, Hans, VIII:2023, 2728; IX:3049
Hofmann, Hugo von, IX:3556
Hofmeyr, Jan Hendrik, IX:2907
Hofstadter, Robert, IX:4090
Hogarth, William, **IV:668-671,** 1163; V:237
Analysis of Beauty, The, IV:669
Artist Painting the Comic Muse, The, IV:670
Bathos, The, IV:670
Harlot's Progress, A, IV:668, 669
Industry and Idleness, IV:669
Marriage à la Mode, IV:669, 670
Painter and His Pug, The, IV:669
Rake's Progress, The, IV:669; VIII:1711
Hogarth Press, IX:4056
Hogben, Lancelot, VII:309
Hogg, Thomas Jefferson, VI:2052
Högskola, VII:114, 115
Hohenheim, Philippus Aureolus Theophrastus Bombast von. *See* Paracelsus
Hohenstaufen Dynasty, II:466, 468, 531, 643, 796, 932, 961
Hohenzollern family, IV:508-510
Hojoji Muryojuin, II:537, 538
Hojo Ujimasa, IV:1327
Hokke, II:667
Hokusai, V:1118, **1120-1122**
Fugaku hyakkei, V:1121
Fugaku sanjurokkei, V:1121
Fuji Under the Wave at Kanagawa, V:1121
Mount Fuji at Dawn, V:1121
Mount Fuji in Storm, V:1121
Holbein, Hans the Younger, **III:358-361**
Body of the Dead Christ in His Tomb, The, III:360
Christiana of Denmark, Duchess of Milan, III:359
Erasmus, III:248
Fisher, III:264
Portrait of His Wife and Two Elder Children, III:359
Holbrooke, Richard, VII:51
Holder, Wesley, VII:670
Holiday, Billie, VII:1157; **VIII:1715-1719,** 1885
"Billie's Blues," VIII:1717
"God Bless the Child," VIII:1718
Lady in Satin, VIII:1718
Lady Sings the Blues, VIII:1715
"Strange Fruit," VIII:1717
Holland, John Philip, **V:1123-1125**

Holliday, Doc, V:735
Hollywood League Against Nazism, VIII:1534
Holmes, Oliver Wendell, **V:1126-1129;** VI:2022; VIII:1720
Autocrat of the Breakfast-Table, The, V:1127
Elsie Venner, V:1129
Guardian Angel, The, V:1129
"Last Leaf, The," V:1127
Medical Essays, 1842-1882, V:1126
Mortal Antipathy, A, V:1129
"Old Ironsides," V:1127
Holmes, Oliver Wendell, Jr., VII:576, 882; **VIII:1720-1723**
Common Law, The, VIII:1721
Holmes, Sherlock, V:700-702
Holocaust
Baeck, VII:149, 150
Bourke-White, VII:397
Dawidowicz, VII:847-849
Diary of Anne Frank, The, VII:1204-1206
Göring, VIII:1438-1441
Himmler, VIII:1666-1668
Hitler, VIII:1692, 1694, 1695
Niemöller, VIII:2743
Sachs, IX:3285-3287
Stein, IX:3508-3510
Wiesei, IX:3980, 3982
Wiesenthal, IX:3984-3987
Holstein, Friedrich von, **V:1130-1132**
Holy Alliance, V:46, 407, 414; V:1034
Holy Apostles, Church of the, II:556
Holy Brotherhood, III:261, 262
Holy Cross, Cathedral of the, V:351
Holy Cross, Mountain of the, V:1073, 1074
Holy League, III:407, 450, 493, 669
Holy Sepulchre, Church of the, I:375
Holy Shroud, Chapel of the, IV:584, 585
Holy Spirit
Filioque doctrine, II:583
Gregory of Nazianzus, I:349
Irenaeus, I:449
Theoleptus of Philadelphia, II:899, 900
Ulfilas, I:909
Valentinus, I:912
Holy Synod, VI:1790-1792
Holy Trinity, I:849, 869, 909, 910; III:485, 675
Biddle, IV:126, 127
Boethius, II:155
Channing, V:471
Clovis, II:275
Joachim of Fiore, II:534, 535
Russian Orthodox Church, IV:1031
Schleiermacher, VI:1978
Swedenborg, IV:1303
William of Saint-Thierry, II:995
Holzschuh, Dietrich, II:797
Home, John
Douglas, V:800
Home Monthly, VII:623
Homer, **I:420-423,** 624, 649, 852, 855, 955-957
Iliad, I:420-422, 758, 830; III:155; IV:1115; V:344, 1184; VI:1982
Odyssey, I:304, 420-422, 598, 685; III:155; IV:1116; V:344, 1184; VIII:1921, 2128
Homer, Winslow, **V:1133-1136**
Adolescence, V:1133
Carnival, The, V:1135
Driftwood, V:1135
Gulf Stream, The, V:1135
Herring Net, The, V:1134
Lookout—All's Well, V:1135
Prisoners from the Front, V:1134
Punishment for Intoxication, V:1134
Sharpshooter, The, V:1134
Skirmish in the Wilderness, A, V:1134
Wreck, The, V:1135
Home Rule Confederation of Great Britain, VI:1740
Homestead Strike of 1892, V:421, 423; VII:419
Honami Koetsu, IV:1041, 1257, 1258
Honda, Soichiro, **VIII:1724-1726**
Honda Motor Company, VIII:1724-1726
Hong Kong, VI:1378; VII:906; VIII:2270
Honnoji Incident, III:571
Honoria, I:126
Honorius, I:342, 871
Hood, John Bell, VI:2060
Hooke, Robert, IV:186, 600, 601, 825, 826, 1025
Micrographia, IV:825
Hooker, Joseph, V:608
Hooker, Richard, IV:46, 47
Hook of Holland project, IX:2860
Hoopes, Darlington, IX:3662
Hoover, Herbert, VIII:1552, **1727-1731;** IX:3224
Principles of Mining, VIII:1727
Hoover, J. Edgar, **VIII:1732-1735;** IX:3547
Hoover Moratorium, VIII:1729
Hopkey, Sophia, IV:1426, 1427
Hopkins, Gerard Manley, II:313
Hopkins, Harry, **VIII:1736-1739**
Hopkins, Samuel, V:470
Hopper, Edward, **VIII:1740-1743**
Cape Cod Evening, VIII:1742
Hotel Room, VIII:1742

House by the Railroad, VIII:1742
Mansard Roof, The, VIII:1740
Nighthawks, VIII:1742, 1743
Night on the El Train, VIII:1742
Night Windows, VIII:1742
Office at Night, VIII:1742
Summer Evening, VIII:1742
Two Comedians, VIII:1742
Horace, **I:424-428**
Art of Poetry, The, I:426; IV:1115
Carmen Saeculare, I:426
Epistles, I:425, 426
Epodes, I:425
Maecenas, I:521
Odes, I:425, 426, 520
Ovid, I:585, 587
Ronsard, III:657
Satires, I:424, 425, 926
Horemheb, I:25
Hormuz, Strait of, III:12
Hornblower, Horatio, VII:1189-1191
Horney, Karen, VII:1247; **VIII:1744-1746**
Neurosis and Human Growth, VIII:1745
Neurotic Personality of Our Time, The, VIII:1745
New Ways in Psychoanalysis, VIII:1745
Our Inner Conflicts, VIII:1745
Self-Analysis, VIII:1745
Horos, I:912, 913
Horowitz, Vladimir, **VIII:1747-1750**
Horseshoe Bend, Battle of, V:1196
Horti Sallustianai, I:743
Ho-shen, IV:302
Hotman, François, **III:362-366**
De statu primitivae ecclesiae, III:363
Franco-Gallia, III:364
Hotta Masayoshi, V:1181
Hou Hsien, II:1023
Hounsfield, Godfrey Newbold, **VIII:1751-1753**
Houphouët-Boigny, Félix, **VIII:1754-1758**
Hours, Book of, II:307
House Committee on Un-American Activities. *See* Un-American Activities, House Committee on
House of Representatives. *See* Representatives, House of
Houssay, Bernardo Alberto, **VIII:1759-1761**
Human Physiology, VIII:1760
Houston, Charles H, VIII:2433
Houston, Sam, **V:1137-1140**
Houston *Post,* VIII:1703-1705
Hoveve Zion, V:1104
Hoveyda, Amir Abbas, VIII:2568
Howard, Catherine, III:205, 209, **367-370**
Howard, Otis, V:1242, 1244
Howard, Sir Robert, IV:424
Howard, Thomas. *See* Norfolk, Duke of
Howe, Elias, **V:1141-1144**
Howe, Julia Ward, **V:1145-1149,** 1151
"Battle Hymn of the Republic, The," V:1145, 1146
Passion Flowers, V:1146
Howe, Admiral Richard, **IV:672-675**
Howe, Samuel Gridley, V:680, 681, 1145, 1146, **1150-1153**
Howe, General William, IV:322, 367, **676-679**
Howells, William Dean, V:715; IX:3806
Ho Yen, I:949
Hoyle, Fred, VIII:1580, 1582
Hsia Kuei, **II:479-481,** 613
Hsiang Hsiu, I:192
Hsiao Yi, I:948
Hsieh Hun, I:429
Hsieh Ling-yün, **I:429-432**
"On Distinguishing What Is Essential," I:430
Hsien-yang, I:177
Hsin ch'ing-nien, VII:661
Hsin Dynasty, I:590
Hsüan-tsang, **II:482-486**
Ta T'ang Hsi-yü-chi, II:484
Hsüan Tsung, II:592, 918, 965-967
Hsün-tzu, **I:433-435**
Shih chi, I:433
Hua Guofeng, VII:906
Huai Army, VI:1362
Huai Wang, I:187
Huáscar, **III:371-373**
Huayna Capac, III:371, 373
Hubble, Edwin Powell, VIII:2157, 2158
Hubertsburg, Treaty of, IV:505
Hudson, Henry, **IV:680-682**
Hudson River Railroad, VI:2297
Hudson's Bay Company, VI:1437
Huerta, Dolores, **VIII:1762-1765**
Huerta, Victoriano, VIII:2347; IX:3811, 3813, 4021, 4016
Huggins, Miller, VII:1322, 1323
Hughes, Charles Evans, VIII:1552, **1766-1770**
Hughes, Langston, **VIII:1771-1774**
Ask Your Mama, VIII:1773
Barrier, The, VIII:1773
Big Sea, The, VIII:1773
Esther, VIII:1773
Fine Clothes to the Jew, VIII:1771
I Wonder as I Wander, VIII:1773

Little Ham, VIII:1773
Montage of a Dream Deferred, VIII:1773
Mulatto, VIII:1773
Not Without Laughter, VIII:1773
Panther and the Lash, The, VIII:1773
Simple Speaks His Mind, VIII:1773
Simple's Uncle Sam, VIII:1773
Simple Takes a Wife, VIII:1773
Simply Heaven, VIII:1773
Tambourines of Glory, VIII:1773
Ways of White Folks, The, VIII:1773
Weary Blues, The, VIII:1771
Hughes, Ted, IX:3036, 3037
Hughes, Thomas
Tom Brown's School Days, V:75
Hughes, William Morris, **VIII:1775-1778,** 2292-2294
Hugh of Lusignan, II:540, 541
Hugo, Victor, **V:1154-1158;** VI:1901
Art d'être grand-père, L', V:1157
Burgraves, The, V:1155
Châtiments, Les, V:1155
Contemplations, Les, V:1155
Feuilles d'automne, Les, V:1155
Hans of Iceland, V:1154
Hernani, V:1154, 1155
Hunchback of Notre-Dame, The, V:1155, 1157
King Amuses Himself, The, V:1155
Last Day of a Condemned, The, V:1158
Legend of the Centuries, The, V:1155
Lucrezia Borgia, V:685
Misérables, Les, V:1155, 1157, 1158; VII:880
Ninety-three, V:1157
Odes et ballades, V:1154
Orientales, Les, V:1154
Préface de Cromwell, La, V:1154
Ruy Blas, V:1155
Huguccio of Pisa, II:509
Huguenots
Buckingham, IV:212, 213
Calvin, III:118
Henry IV, III:333, 334
Hotman, III:362-365
Louis XIII, IV:864
Louis XIV, IV:868
Mornay, III:537-539
Philip II, III:600
Richelieu, IV:1165, 1167
Hu Han-min, IX:3878
Hu Hao, I:178
Huitzilopochtli, cult of, III:378, 379, 528, 529, 531
Hui-yüan, I:429, 430
Hülagü, II:381
Hull, Cordell, **VIII:1779-1782**
Hull House, VII:21, 23; VIII:2096; IX:2961
human behavior. *See* behavior, human
human rights
Carter, VII:590
Evatt, VII:1110, 1111
Gorbachev, VIII:1426
Malcolm X, VIII:2375
Robeson, IX:3190
Sakharov, IX:3296, 3298, 3299
Universal Declaration of Human Rights, VII:610-612, 1110
human sexuality. *See* sexuality, human
human species, origin of. *See* evolution, theory of
Humayun, III:5
Humble Petition and Advice, IV:380, 790
Humboldt, Alexander von, V:267, 862, 898, **1159-1161;** VI:1366
Voyage aux régions équinoctales du Nouveau Continent, V:1160
Humboldt, Wilhelm von, VI:2118
Hume, David, **IV:683-686**
Berkeley, IV:114-116
Dialogues Concerning Natural Religion, IV:684, 685
Enquiries Concerning Human Understanding, IV:684
Enquiry Concerning the Principals of Morals, An, IV:684
Ferguson, IV:454
Gibbon, IV:547
Green, V:987
History of England, IV:684
Nicholas of Autrecourt, II:671
Treatise of Human Nature, A, IV:683, 684
Hume, Joseph, VI:1787, 1880
humors
Aretaeus of Cappadocia, I:82
Bradstreet, IV:194
Diocles of Carystus, I:261
Galen, I:339
Herophilus, I:399
Humperdinck, Engelbert, **V:1162-1164**
Bubschens Weihnachtstraum, V:1163
Dornröschen, V:1163, 1164
Hänsel and Gretel, V:1163, 1164
Heirat wider Willen, Die, V:1163
Königskinder, V:1163, 1164
Mirakel, Das, V:1164
sieben Geisslein, Die, V:1163

Humphrey, Hubert H., VII:670; **VIII:1783-1786,** 2758
Hunan Army, VI:2260, 2261
Hundred Flowers Campaign, VII:905
Hundred Slain, Battle of a, VI:1851
Hundred Years' War
  Charles IV, II:235, 237
  Chartier, II:245, 246
  Chaucer, II:248
  Edward III, II:329, 331
  Edward IV, III:234
  Froissart's *Chronicles,* II:366, 368
  Henry VI, III:341
  Joan of Arc, III:396
  Louis XI, III:434
  Venette, II:936
Huneric, I:344
Hungarian Revolution, VIII:1963
Hung Hsui ch'üan, **V:1165-1167**
Hung-li. *See* Ch'ien-lung
Hunkpapa tribe, VI:2070, 2072, 2073
Huns
  Attila, I:124-127
  Chionites, I:779, 780
  Khosrow I, II:559, 560
  Odoacer, II:685
  See also Avars
Hun Sen, IX:3419, 3420
Hunt, John, VIII:1663
Hunt, Leigh, VI:1266
Hunt, Walter, V:1143
Hunt, William Holman, **V:1165-1167**
  Finding of the Saviour in the Temple, The, V:1169
  Flight of Madeline and Prophyro, V:1168
  Light of the World, The, V:1169
  Scapegoat, The, V:1169
  Shadow of Death, The, V:1169, 1170
  Valentine Rescuing Sylvia from Proteus, V:1169
Hunter, John, IV:721
Hunyadi, János, **III:374-376,** 487
Hunyadi, Mátyás. *See* Matthias I Corvinus
Hur, I:1
Hurok, Solomon, VII:70
Hurons, IV:273
Hurst, Fannie, VIII:1787
Hurston, Zora Neale, **VIII:1787-1790;** IX:3849-3851
  Color Struck, VIII:1787
  "Drenched in Light," VIII:1787
  Dust Tracks on a Road, VIII:1787, 1788
  In Search of Our Mothers' Gardens, VIII:1789
  Jonah's Gourd Wine, VIII:1787, 1788
  Moses, Man of the Mountain, VIII:1788
  Mules and Men, VIII:1788
  Seraph on the Suwanee, VIII:1788, 1789
  "Spunk," VIII:1787
  Their Eyes Were Watching God, VIII:1788
Hus, Jan, **II:487-490,** 971, 1009-1011, 1030, 1031
  On the Church, II:489
Husayn ibn 'Ali, al-, VII:1122, 1124; VIII:2126
Hussein I, VII:92; **VIII:1791-1796**
Hussein, Saddam, VII:50, 1116; IX:3071
Husserl, Edmund, **VIII:1797-1799**
  Derrida, VII:913
  Heidegger, VIII:1610, 1611
  Merleau-Ponty, VIII:2501
  Scheler, IX:3347
  Stein, IX:3506-3508
Hussey, Obed, VI:1431
Hussite movement. *See* Hus, Jan
Hutchins, Robert M., **VIII:1800-1803**
  Freedom, Education, and the Fund, VIII:1800
Hutchinson, Anne, IV:371, **687-690,** 1464
Hutchinson, Thomas, IV:23, 24, 494, 617, **691-694**
  History of the Colony and Province of Massachusetts Bay, The, IV:23, 693
Huxley, Aldous, **VIII:1804-1808**
  Antic Hay, VIII:1804
  Brave New World, VII:1187; VIII:1804
  Doors of Perception, The, VIII:1807
  Ends and Means, VIII:1804
  Eyeless in Gaza, VIII:1804
  Point Counter Point, VIII:1804
  Those Barren Leaves, VIII:1804
  What Are You Going To Do About It?, VIII:1804
Huxley, Thomas Henry, V:277, 608, **1172-1174;** IX:3938
  Evidence as to Man's Place in Nature, V:1173
  Evolution and Ethics, V:1173
  Workingman Lectures, V:1173
Hu Yaobang, VIII:2178, 2179
Huygens, Christiaan, **IV:695-698,** 826, 830, 1059, 1060; VI:1343
  Discours de la cause de la pesanteur, IV:697
  Horologium, IV:695
  Horologium oscillatorium, IV:695
Hydatius of Emerita, I:694-696
Hyde, Edward. *See* Clarendon, First Earl of
Hyde Park Declaration, VIII:1983
hydrodynamics
  Bjerknes, VII:318, 319
  Prandtl, IX:3073

Torricelli, IV:1333
Landau, VIII:2074
hydrogen
Avogadro, V:99
Cavendish, IV:262
Gay-Lussac, V:898, 899
liquefaction of, VIII:1907
Lockyer, VI:1411, 1412
Urey, IX:3788
hydrogen bomb
Bethe, VII:302
Fermi, VII:1148
Kurchatov, VIII:2040
Lawrence, VIII:2123
Neumann, VIII:2726
Oppenheimer, IX:2834
Rabi, IX:3102
Sakharov, IX:3299
Teller, IX:3631, 3633
Urey, IX:3789
See also nuclear weapons
Hyginus, I:398
Hyksos, I:636
hymnody, I:157; II:409; III:658; IX:3798
Hypatia, I:74, **436-439**
On the Astronomical Canon of Diophantus, I:437
On the Conics of Apollonius, I:437
Hyrcanus, I:390, 391

IBM, IX:2973
Ibn al-'Arabi, **II:491-494**
Fusus al-hikam, II:492
Futuhat al-Makkiyah, al-, II:491, 492
Ibn Battutah, **II:495-497**
Rihlah, II:495
Ibn Gabirol, **II:498-501**
Improvement of Moral Qualities, The, II:498-500
Kingly Crown, The, II:499
Ibn Khaldun, **II:502-505,** 637
Muqaddimah, The, II:503, 504
Ibn Nagrella. *See* Samuel ha-Nagid
Ibn Rushd. *See* Averroës
Ibn Tufayl, II:100
Ibn Tumart, II:4-6
Ibo, VII:13, 145, 146
Ibsen, Henrik, V:1003, **1175-1179;** VIII:1891; IX:3400
Brand, V:1175
Burial Mound, V:1175
Catiline, V:1175
Doll's House, A, V:1176; IX:3400
Emperor and Galilean, V:1176
Ghosts, V:1176
Hedda Gabler, V:1176; VII:280, 281; VIII:2143
League of Youth, The, V:1176
Master Builder, The, V:1176; VIII:2142
Peer Gynt, V:1003, 1175
Rosmersholm, V:1176
Wild Duck, The, VII:280; IX:2821
Ibuka, Masaru, VIII:2622, 2623
ICBMs. *See* intercontinental ballistic missiles
Icelandic sagas
Greenlanders' Saga, II:577, 578
Laxness, VIII:2131, 2132
Saga of Erik the Red, II:577, 578
Snorri Sturluson, II:836-839
Iceni, I:136-138
I Ching, I:190, 224, 949-951
Iconoclastic Controversy, II:544-546, 903
Idealism, German
Baer, V:111
Eucken, VII:1107
Fichte, IV:465-468
Hegel, V:1082, 1083
Hobhouse, VIII:1707, 1709
Schelling, VI:1972-1974
Schiller, IV:1217, 1219, 1220
Idrisi, al-, **II:506-508**
Kitab nuzhat al-mushtaq fi ikhiraq al-afaq, II:506, 508
Idrisi tribe, VII:1118
Idumaea, I:390
Ifriqiya, II:5
Ignatius of Antioch, **I:440-442**
Ignatius of Loyola, Saint. *See* Loyola, Saint Ignatius of
Ii Naosuke, **V:1180-1182;** VI:1936
Ikeda, Hayato, **VIII:1809-1811**
Ikhnaton. *See* Akehnaton
Ikko. *See* Shinshu Buddhism
Ilceo, myth of, III:270
ILGWU. *See* International Ladies' Garment Workers Union
Illinois
Altgeld, V:54-56
Black Hawk, V:249
Lathrop, VIII:2096, 2097, 2099
Mormonism, VI:2081
Stevenson, IX:3524
Illinois Indians, IV:733
Illyria, I:263, 628, 629
ILP. *See* Independent Labour Party
Iltani, I:362

Ilu-bi'di, I:754
Imagist movement, VIII:1505, 1506, 1508, 2249-2251
Imhotep, **I:443-446,** 978
Imlay, Gilbert, IV:1477
immunology
Burnet, VII:512-514
Ehrlich, VII:1032, 1033
Fleming, VII:1166
Jenner, IV:723
Pasteur, VI:1744, 1747
Salk, IX:3305-3307
Smith, IX:3451, 3452
impeachment
Chase, IV:293-296
Clinton, VII:710, 715
Johnson, IV:296, 479, 1233; VII:710
Nixon, VIII:1888, 2760
Sherman, IV:1244
Strafford, IV:1287
Tyler, VI:2291
Imperial Ballet Company, VIII:2748, 2749
Imperial East Africa Company, VIII:2269
Imperial Hotel of Tokyo, IX:4061
Imperial Russian Musical Academy, VI:1891
Imphal and Kohima, battles of, IX:3437
Impressionism
Bonnard, VII:362, 363
Cassatt, V:434-436
Cézanne, V:453, 455
Debussy, VII:884, 885
Degas, V:641-643
Delaunay, VII:888
Duchamp, VII:972
fauves, VIII:1991
Gauguin, V:888-891
Goya, IV:571, 572
Hopper, VIII:1740, 1742
Léger, VIII:2154
Magritte, VIII:2349, 2352
Manet, VI:1473
Matisse, VIII:2452, 2454
Monet, VIII:2579-2581
Pissarro, VI:1779-1781
Renoir, VI:1869-1871
Sargent, VI:1961, 1963, 1964
Seurat, VI:2033-2035
Toulouse-Lautrec, VI:2247-2250
Whistler, VI:2363, 2364
immunization. *See* vaccination
Inca Empire
Heyerdahl, VIII:1660
Huáscar, III:371-373
Pachacuti, III:577-579
Prescott, VI:1815
Soto, III:699
Indemnity, Act of, IV:310
Independence, Declaration of
Adams, IV:16
Carroll, IV:250-252
Chase, IV:293
Dickinson, IV:411
Franklin, IV:494
George III, IV:541
Hancock, IV:613, 617, 618
Jefferson, IV:716
North, IV:1035
Rush, IV:1202, 1203
Sherman, IV:1243
Wilson, IV:1457
Witherspoon, IV:1467, 1469
Independent Labour Party, V:1036, 1037; VII:354; VIII:2312, 2314; IX:2849
Independent Treasury, VI:1803
Index Librorum Prohibitorum. See Prohibited Books, Index of
India Act of 1784, IV:633
India Act of 1935, VII:529
India Bill, IV:481
India Independence Act of 1947, VIII:1849
Indian Affairs, Bureau of, IX:3011
Indian Association, VII:183
Indian Mutiny of 1857, VI:1331-1333
Indian National Congress, VII:184, 1283; VIII:2683
Indian National Fund, VII:183
Indian Ocean, II:636
Indian Removal Bill, VI:1910
Indian Wars, V:374
Indochinese Communist Party, VIII:1698-1701; IX:3821
Indo-European languages, IX:3340, 3341
Indulgence, Declaration of, IV:704
Industrial Charter, VII:530
Industrial Revolution
Boulton, IV:182-184
Brindley, IV:201-203
Brunel, V:339-342
communism, V:761
cotton industry, IV:59-62
Darby, IV:396-398
Hargreaves, IV:623-625
Kay, IV:769, 770
Murdock, IV:1008-1010

Nasmyth, VI:1624-1626
Newcomen, IV:1022-1024
Owen, VI:1708-1710
Papin, IV:1059-1061
Scotland, IV:1182-1185
sewing machine, V:1141-1143
Siemens family, VI:2066-2069
telegraphy, V:555-558
textiles, VI:2074-2076
Watt, IV:1409, 1411, 1412
Wedgwood, IV:1421-1424
Western conception of history, VIII:2165
Whitney, IV:1431-1434
women, V:64
Infante, John, III:217
inflation, economic
Carter, VII:591
Ford, VII:1181
Greenspan, VIII:1471-1473
Japan, VIII:1809
Nixon, VIII:2759
Trudeau, IX:3733
Ingeborg, II:511
Ingres, Jean-Auguste-Dominique, V:411, **1183-1186;** VI:2033
Antiochus and Stratonice, V:1185
Apotheosis of Homer, The, V:1184
Baronne de Rothschild, V:1185
Bathing Woman, The, V:1185
Death of Leonardo da Vinci in the Arms of Francis, The, V:1183
Grand Odalisque, The, V:1185
Odalisque with the Slave, V:1185
Oedipus Solving the Riddle of the Sphinx, V:1184
Princess de Broglie, V:1185
Roger Freeing Angelica, V:1183
Turkish Bath, The, V:1185
Valpincon Bather, The, V:1185
Vicomtesse d'Haussonville, V:1185
Vow of Louis XIII, The, V:1183, 1184
Inner Mission of Westphalia, VIII:2742
Innocent III, II:29, 144, 301, 303, 354, 360, 399, **509-513,** 541
On the Misery of the Human Condition, II:509
Sacred Mystery of the Altar, The, II:509
Innocent IV, II:207, 363, **514-516,** 991
Innocent V, III:405
Inoocent VI, II:792
Innocent VIII, III:462, 496, 667, 668, 725
Innocent X, IV:168, 1062, 1366
Inönü, Ismet, **VIII:1812-1815**
Inquisition. *See* Roman Inquisition; Spanish Inquisition
Instantius, I:695
Institute de France, IV:338
insulin
Banting, VII:189, 190
Houssay, VIII:1759, 1760
Krogh, VIII:2029
Macleod, VIII:2329-2331
integration, racial. *See* desegregation; segregation
Intellectual Cooperation, Institute of, VIII:2052
Intercolonial Union, VIII:1699
intercontinental ballistic missiles, VIII:2020, 2021
International Association of Co-Workers of Mother Teresa, IX:3635, 3636
International Associations, Union of, VIII:2051
International Bureau of Weights and Measures, VIII:1502-1504
International Business Machines, IX:2973
International Congress of Women, VII:161
International Council of Women, VI:2045
International Encyclopedia of Unified Science, VII:583
International Geophysical Year, VIII:2020; IX:4001
International Labor Organization, VIII:1781
International Ladies' Garment Workers Union, VIII:1641
international law
Butler, VII:525
Gentili, III:295-297
Grotius, IV:579-581
Universal Declaration of Human Rights, VII:610-612, 1110, 1111
Vitoria, III:768, 769
See also United Nations
International Monetary Fund, VIII:1954, 2492
International Olympic Committee, VII:774-776; IX:3675
International Peace Bureau, VIII:2051
International Psychoanalytic Association, VII:329, 330, 1225, 1226
International Red Cross, V:143, 711, 712; VIII:1624
International Rehovot Conferences, VII:1001
International Style of architecture, VII:1-3; VIII:2487-2489, 2575; IX:2859, 2860
Interparliamentary Union, VIII:2051
Interstate Commerce Act, VI:1898
Intifada, VII:92, 93
Intolerable Acts, IV:16, 616, 617, 716
Intrepid, V:634

Inuits
    Davis, III:212, 213
    Frobisher, III:278, 279
    Peary, IX:2942, 2944
    Rasmussen, IX:3121-3123
    Ross, VI:1907
Invalides, Dome des, IV:903
Investiture Controversy, II:357, 464
Investment Canada, VIII:2655
Ionesco, Eugène, **VIII:1816-1819**
    Bald Soprano, The, VIII:1817
    Chairs, The, VIII:1818
    Exit the King, VIII:1818
    Lesson, The, VIII:1817
    Rhinoceros, VIII:1818
Ionia, I:238, 554
Ionian school of philosophy, I:855
Iophon, I:809
Iov, III:309
Ipsus, Battle of, I:60, 768
IRA. *See* Irish Republican Army
Iranian hostage crisis, VII:591; IX:3139
Iran-Iraq War, VIII:1958
IRB. *See* Irish Republican Brotherhood
Irenaeus, Saint, **I:447-451**
    Against Heresies, I:449
Irgun Z'vai Leumi, VII:243, 244, 253; IX:3932
Irish Church Reform Act of 1833, V:996
Irish Coercion Bill of 1881, V:805
Irish Free State, VII:770-772, 878; VIII:2217; IX:2805, 4085
Irish Home Rule Movement
    Asquith, VII:121
    George V, VII:1340
    Joyce, VIII:1891
    Law, VIII:2112
    Parnell, VI:1740, 1741
    Rhodes, VI:1875
    Salisbury, VI:1944, 1945
Irish Independence, War for, IX:2805
Irish Land Acts, V:308
Irish Literary Renaissance, VIII:1891
Irish Nationalist Party, VI:1740-1742
Irish National Land League, VI:1740-1742
Irish National Theatre, IX:4082
Irish potato famine, VI:1754, 1930, 1931
Irish Question, IV:1105; VI:2394; VIII:1475
Irish Rebellion, IV:1142
Irish Republican Army, VII:771, 877; VIII:2644
Irish Republican Brotherhood, VII:733, 877
Irish Volunteers, VII:770, 877; IX:2804
Iron Curtain, VII:693; VIII:1696
ironmaking, IV:396-398, 1182-1185; V:218-221
Iron Ore Company of Canada, VIII:2655
Ironsides, the, IV:378
Iroquois Indians
    Brant, IV:196, 198, 199
    Cartier, III:129-131
    Champlain, IV:273
    Jolliet, IV:733
    Laval, IV:801
    Pontiac, IV:1110
    Tekakwitha, IV:1316, 1317
Irrigation Act, V:632
Irving, Henry, **V:1187-1191;** VI:2216, 2217
    Bells, The, V:1187, 1189
Irving, Washington, **V:1192-1195**
    Astoria, V:84
    Bracebridge Hall, V:1193
    History of New York, A, V:84
    "Legend of Sleepy Hollow, The," V:1192, 1194
    "Rip Van Winkle," V:1192-1194
    Sketch Book of Geoffrey Crayon, Gent, The, V:1193
    Tales of a Traveller, V:1193
    Tour of the Prairies, A, V:1193
Irwin, Noel, IX:3437
Isaac, I:6
Isaaco, VI:1724, 1725
Isabella I, **III:260-263**
    Cabot, III:113
    Catherine of Aragon, III:136
    Columbus, III:172-174
    Jiménez de Cisneros, III:392-394
    Manuel I, III:465
    Prescott, VI:1814
    Torquemada, III:725
Isabella of Aragon. *See* Isabella I
Isabella of France, II:327, 329
Isabella of Portugal, III:163, 260, 599
Isabelle of Angoulême, II:540
Isagoras, I:214
Isaiah, **I:452-455**
Isham, Colonel Ralph, IV:177
Ishiyama Hongan-ji War, III:571
Ishmael, I:6
Ishmael ben Elisha, I:28, 29
Ishme-Dagan, I:360
Isidore of Seville, Saint, **II:518-521**
    Etymologiae, II:519
Isin, I:361
Isis, I:13
Islam, Nation of. *See* Nation of Islam

Islamic law
  Ash'ari, II:93-95
  Ghazzali, II:385
  Hanbalite school, II:33-35
  Hanifite school, II:16-18
  Tabari, II:874
Islamic Revolution of 1979, VIII:2566-2569
Islets of Langerhans, VII:187, 188
Isma'ili sect, II:522
Ismay, Sir Hastings, VII:47
Isocrates, **I:456-458**
  Against the Sophists, I:457, 458
  Antidosis, I:457
  Aristotle, I:95, 96
  Evagoras, I:457
  Panegyricus, I:456, 457
  Plataeicus, I:456
  To Philip, I:457
Isodice, I:199
isotopes
  cyclotron development, VIII:2122
  Hevesy, VIII:1654-1656
  uranium, VIII:1647-1649
  Urey, IX:3787, 3788
Ispahan, IV:5, 6
Israel, ancient
  Abraham, I:5, 7
  Deborah, I:246, 247
  Isaiah, I:453
  Moses, I:561-564
  Samuel, I:746, 748, 749
  Solomon, I:798, 800, 801
Israeli Defense Forces, VII:854-856
Israel Philharmonic, VII:296
Istanbul. *See* Constantinople
Istanbul, Treaty of, IV:4
Italian Catholic University Students, Federation of, IX:2915
Italian Wars, III:18; VI:1919
Italus, John, II:760
Ithacius, I:696
Itzcóatl, **III:377-380**
Ivan the Great, II:54; **III:381-384**
Ivan the Terrible, III:308, **385-388**
Iveragh, Ireland, VI:1680
Ives, Charles, **VIII:1820-1823**
  "I. A Contemplation of a Serious Matter," VIII:1821
  All the Way Around and Back, VIII:1821
  "Bells of Yale," VIII:1820
  "Camp Meeting, The" VIII:1820
  Celestial Country, The, VIII:1820
  Concord Sonata, VIII:1821
  Fourth of July, VIII:1821, 1822
  Fourth Symphony, VIII:1821
  "Slow March," VIII:1820
  Third Symphony, VIII:1821
  Three Places in New England, VIII:1821
Ives, George Edward, VIII:1820
Ivinskaya, Olga Vsevolodovna, IX:2900
Iwakura Tomoni, VI:1937, 1938
Iwerks, Ub, VII:938, 940
Izambard, Georges, VI:1886

Jabin, I:247
Jabir ibn Hayyan, **II:522-525**
Jabotinksy, Vladimir, VII:243
Jackson, Andrew, **V:1196-1199**
  Adams, John Quincy, V:23, 24
  Benton, V:195-198
  Biddle, V:226
  Calhoun, V:395
  Clay, V:508, 509
  Crockett, V:578, 579
  Gadsden Purchase, V:858, 859
  Harrison, V:1062
  Houston, V:1137
  Key, VI:1283
  Mackenzie, VI:1449
  Perry, VI:1760
  Polk, VI:1801, 1802
  Ross, VI:1910, 1911
  Scott, VI:2009, 2010
  Seminole Wars, VI:1695
  Taney, VI:2190
  Tyler, VI:2288, 2289
  Van Buren, VI:2293, 2294
  Webster, VI:2345
Jackson, Charles T., VI:1596-1598
Jackson, Helen Hunt, **V:1200-1203**
  Century of Dishonor, V:1201, 1202
  Ramona, V:1200-1202
Jackson, Jesse L., **VIII:1824-1826,** 2245
Jackson, Joe, VII:718
Jackson, Stonewall, **V:1204-1206**
Jacob, François, **VIII:1827-1830**
Jacobi, Carl Gustav Jacob, V:8, 9
Jacobins
  Danton, IV:394, 395
  Du Pont, V:718
  Marat, IV:911
  Marlborough, IV:922
  Mirabeau, IV:964
  Oglethorpe, IV:1043

Orléans, IV:1049
Pelham, IV:1075
Robespierre, IV:1171, 1172
Saint-Just, IV:1205-1207
Stanhope, IV:1278
Jacobs, Mike, VIII:2241, 2243, 2244
Jacopo della Quercia, **III:389-391**
Madonna and Child, III:390
Silvestri Madonna, III:389
Jadwiga, **II:1001-1004**
Jael, I:247
Ja'far al-Sadiq, II:522
Jahangir, IV:1232
Jahiz, al-, **II:526-528**
Characters of Theophrastus, II:527
Kitab al-bukhala', II:527
Kitab alhayawan, II:526
Jai Singh, IV:1247
Jakobson, Roman, **VIII:1831-1834**
Child Language, Aphasia and Phonological Universals, VIII:1832
Noveshaya russaya poeziya, VIII:1831
Preliminaries to Speech Analysis, VIII:1832
Jamahiriyah, IX:3099
Jamaica, III:173
Jamal al-Din al-Afghani, V:4, 5, **1207-1210**
James (Apostle), I:475, 616
James I (of England), **IV:699-702**
Andrewes, IV:46-48
Basilikon Doron, IV:699
Buckingham, IV:211
Coke, IV:331-334
Daemonologie, IV:699
Raleigh, III:639-641
Salisbury, III:660-662
Shakespeare, III:687
True Law of Free Monarchies, The, IV:699
James I the Conqueror, **II:529-533**
Furs, II:531
James II (of England), **IV:703-706**
Anne, IV:50, 52
Dryden, IV:425
Eliot, IV:437
Godolphin, IV:553
Kidd, IV:777
Leeds, IV:823
Locke, IV:857
Marlborough, IV:922
Mather, IV:939
Monmouth, IV:980-982
Oates, IV:1038-1040
Penn, IV:1079
Purcell, IV:1138
Roman Catholicism, IV:100
James IV (of Scotland), III:346
James VI (of Scotland), III:243, 244, 661; IV:279, 330
James, Harry, IX:3422
James, Henry, **V:1211-1215,** 1216; VI:1589; VII:625; IX:3953
Ambassadors, The, V:1213
American, The, V:1211, 1212
"Art of Fiction, The," V:1212
Bostonians, The, V:1212
Daisy Miller, V:1211, 1212
Golden Bowl, The, V:1213
Portrait of a Lady, The, V:1211, 1212
Princess Casamassima, The, V:1212
Roderick Hudson, V:1211
Tragic Muse, The, V:1212
Turn of the Screw, VII:568
Wings of the Dove, The, V:1213
James, Thomas, III:63
James, William, V:781, **1216-1220;** VI:1757; VII:560; VIII:1708
Principles of Psychology, The, V:1218, 1219; IX:3669
Varieties of Religious Experience, The, V:1218
Will to Believe, The, V:1218
Jameson, Leander Starr, VI:1875
Jameson Raid, V:463; VI:1875
Jamestown, Virginia, IV:1122-1124, 1253
Jammes, Francis, VIII:2525
Janácek, Leos, **VIII:1835-1838**
Beginning of a Romance, The, VIII:1836
From the House of the Dead, VIII:1837
Glagolitic Mass, VIII:1837
Janufa, VIII:1836
Mr. Broucek's Excursion to the Fifteenth Century, VIII:1837
Sárka, VIII:1836
Taras Bulba, VIII:1837
Jan Ch'iu, I:223
Janet, Pierre, **VIII:1839-1842**
Automatisme psychologique, L', VIII:1840
Mental State of Hystericals, The, VIII:1840
Janissaries, III:708
Jankow, Battle of, IV:1336, 1337
Jannings, Emil, VII:930
Jansen, Cornelius Otto, **IV:707-710,** 1062, 1064, 1144-1146, 1381, 1382
Augustinus, IV:707, 708
Delectatio coelestis, IV:707

Delectatio terrena, IV:707
Mars gallicus, IV:707
Jansenism. *See* Jansen, Cornelius Otto
Janssen, Pierre Jules César, VI:1411
Janssen, Zacharias, IV:850
Jardine, Douglas, VII:408
Jarring, Gunnar, VII:1001
Jarry, Alfred
Ubu Roi, VIII:1712
Jaruzelski, Wojciech, IX:3846, 3847
Jason the Argonaut, I:318
Jaspers, Karl, **VIII:1843-1846**
Future of Germany, The, VIII:1845
Future of Mankind, The, VIII:1844
General Psychopathology, VIII:1843, 1844
Great Philosophers, The, VIII:1845
Idea of the University, The, VIII:1844
Origin and Goal of History, The, VIII:1845
Philosophical Faith and Revelation, VIII:1844
Philosophy, VIII:1844
Philosophy of Existence, VIII:1844
Psychologie der Weltanschauungen, VIII:1843
Question of German Guilt, The, VIII:1844
Reason and Existenz, VIII:1844
Játiva, battle at, II:270
Jaurès, Jean, **V:1211-1215;** VII:335
Democracy and Military Service, V:1222
Jay, John, IV:315, **711-715,** 1291; VI:1277, 1278
Federalist, The, IV:610, 713
Jay Treaty, IV:713, 1407
jazz
Armstrong, VII:105-108
Charles, VII:658
Coltrane, VII:741, 742, 744
Copland, VII:767
Davis, VII:741, 742, 744; IX:2882
Ellington, VII:1066-1068
Fitzgerald, VII:1157-1160
Gershwin, VII:1347, 1349
Gillespie, VII:1370, 1371, 1373; IX:2882
Goodman, VIII:1419, 1420, 1422
Holiday, VIII:1715-1718
Hughes, VIII:1773
Milhaud, VIII:2526
Mondrian, VIII:2576
Monk, VII:741
Morrison, VIII:2628
Parker, IX:2880-2883
Shaw, VIII:1420, 1718
Jean II, II:949
Jean de Venette. *See* Venette, Jean de
Jeanneret, Charles-Édouard. *See* Le Corbusier
Jefferson, Thomas, **IV:716-720**
Adams, IV:18
Banneker, IV:91
Bayle, IV:105
Brown, IV:206
Bulfinch, V:349
Burr, V:369, 370
Chase, IV:295
Gallatin, V:861, 862
Hamilton, IV:611
Lewis, VI:1358
Madison, IV:886, 888; VI:1464
Monroe, VI:1571
Parrington, IX:2894
Summary View of the Rights of British America, A, IV:716
Jeffersonian, V:984
Jeffrey, Lord, **V:1224-1227**
Jehoiachin, I:326
Jehoiakim, I:326, 459
Jekyll, Gertrude, VII:1130, 1132
Jena, Battle of, V:940, 1033, 1080
Jena, University of, VI:1972
Jenkin, Fleeming, V:609
Jenkins' Ear, War of, IV:55, 1045, 1471
Jenkinson, Robert Banks. *See* Liverpool, Second Earl of
Jenner, Edward, **IV:721-724**
Cursory Observations on Emetic Tartar, IV:722
Inquiry into Cause and Effects of the Variolæ Vaccinæ, IV:723
Observations on the Natural History of the Cuckoo, IV:722
Jeremiah, I:328, **459-462,** 468, 569
Jeremiah II, III:308
Jerome, Saint, **I:463-466,** 511, 513
Jerome Clock Company, V:135
Jerusalem
architecture, VIII:2488
Augustine, I:129
Ezekiel, I:326, 328
Ezra, I:330-333
Hadrian, I:358
Herod the Great, I:391
Hussein I, VIII:1794
Jeremiah, I:459, 460
Nebuchadnezzar II, I:570
Pilate, I:640, 642
Tancred, II:888
tunnel, I:315
Jerusalem, Temple of
Eusebius of Caesarea, I:325

Ezekiel, I:328
Ezra, I:330
Herod the Great, I:391
Johanan ben Zakkai, I:471-473
Solomon, I:798, 800
Jervis, John, VI:1635
Jessup Wagon, VII:604
Jesuit Order
Alembert, IV:32
Bossuet, IV:170
Charles III, IV:288, 289
Counter-Reformation, III:160, 161
Ferdinand II, IV:450
Ignatius of Loyola, III:437-439
Jansen, IV:707-709
Joyce, VIII:1891
K'ang-hsi, IV:757
Laval, IV:801, 802
Pascal, IV:1062, 1064
Paul III, III:597
Teilhard de Chardin, IX:3626, 3627
Tekakwitha, IV:1316, 1317
Voltaire, IV:1392
Xavier, III:788-790
Jesup, Thomas S., VI:2195
Jesus, Society of. *See* Jesuit Order
Jesus Christ, **I:467-470**
Abraham, I:7
Anabaptists, III:510, 511
Angelico, III:29
Anthony of Egypt, I:56
Arianism, I:353
Christopher, Saint, I:180, 182
David, I:241, 243
divine grace, IV:708
divine nature, I:849, 862, 863; II:819, 820
Epstein's art, VII:1088
Eucharistic controversy, II:773
Giotto, II:388
Gospel of, VIII:1558, 1559
governmental authority, VII:360
Holbein the Younger, III:360
Islamic recognition, II:422
John the Apostle, I:475, 477
John the Baptist, I:478-481
Josephus, I:485
kerygma, VII:498, 499
Last Temptation of Christ, The, VIII:1922
Moses, I:4, 564
Nietzsche, VI:1662
Origen, I:581
Paul, I:605
Peter, I:614-616
Pilate, I:640, 642
rabbinical scholarship, VII:148
Renan's biography, VI:1865-1867
Ritschl, VI:1892-1894
Teilhard de Chardin, IX:3629
Theodoret of Cyrrhus, I:865, 866
Thomas, I:880, 882, 883
Unitarian doctrine, III:675-677
Valentinus, I:912, 913
Vergil, I:928
Virgin Mary, I:939, 941
Jesus Christ of Latter-day Saints, Church of. *See* Mormonism
Jet Scientific Research Institute, VIII:2019
Jewett, Sarah Orne, **V:1228-1231**
Country Doctor, The, V:1228
Country of the Pointed Furs, The, V:1229, 1230
Deephaven, V:1228, 1229
"Jenny Garrow's Ghost," V:1228
"Mr. Bruce," V:1228
Queen's Twin and Other Stories, The, V:1229
Tory Lover, The, V:1229
White Heron and Other Stories, A, V:1229
Jewish Colonial Trust, V:1005
Jewish Disabilities, Removal of, V:677
Jewish Documentation Center, IX:3984, 3985
Jewish National Committee, VII:484
Jewish Nationalization Act, IV:1076
Jewish Revolt, I:483-486, 880
Jiang Qing, VII:906
Jim Crow laws. *See* segregation
Jiménez de Cisneros, Francisco, III:262, **392-395**
Jinnah, Mohammed Ali, VII:1283; **VIII:1847-1850,** 2684, 2710, 2711
Jirgalang, IV:421
Joab, I:798
Joachim of Fiore, **II:534-536,** 812, 813
Liber figurarum, II:535
Psalterium decem chordarum, II:534
Joan of Arc, **III:396-400**
Joan the Mad, III:393
Job, Book of, II:407
Jocho, **II:537-539**
Jocho style, II:924
Jodenburt, IV:1264
Joffre, Joseph-Jacques-Césaire, **VIII:1851-1853**
Johanan ben Zakkai, **I:471-474**
Johann Georg I, Elector of Saxony, IV:1221-1223
Johansen, Hjalmer, VIII:2687
John (Apostle), **I:475-478**
Jesus Christ, I:467-469

Logos, I:634
Peter, I:615
Thomas, I:882
Virgin Mary, I:939
John (King of England), II:190, 510, 511, **540-543,** 643, 644
John I (of Portugal), III:354
John II (of Portugal), III:172, 173, 197, 215, 287, 464
John III Sobieski, **IV:725-727**
John VI Cantacuzenus, II:844
John XIII (Pope), II:707, 869
John XXII (Pope), II:682, 683, 950
Mater et magistra, VIII:1860
Pacem in terris, VIII:1860
John XXIII (Pope), **VIII:1854-1857;** IX:2916, 2917
John, Augustus, **VIII:1858-1861**
Chiaroscuro, VIII:1856
Finishing Touches, VIII:1856
In Memoriam Amedeo Modigliani, VIII:1855
Joseph Hone, VIII:1855
Merekli, VIII:1854
Moses and the Brazen Serpent, VIII:1854
Saints-Maries de la Mer with Sainte Sara l'Egyptienne, Les, VIII:1856
Sir Matthew Smith, VIII:1855
John, Gospel of, VII:499
John Bull, VII:382-385
John Frederick the Magnanimous, III:200, 201
John of Cappadocia, II:553, 892
John of Damascus, **II:544-547**
Exposition of the Orthodox Faith, II:546
On Holy Images, II:546
John of Lisbon, III:453
John of Luxembourg, II:211, 235, 615
John of Parma, II:163, 164
John of Ravenna, II:673, 674
John of the Cross, Saint, **III:401-404,** 714, 715; IX:3509
Ascent of Mount Carmel, The, III:403
Living Flame of Love, III:403
Spiritual Canticle of the Soul, A, III:403
John Paul II, **VIII:1862-1865**
Canadian visit, IX:3346
Tekakwitha, IV:1317
Waldheim, IX:3843
Walesa, IX:3844
John P. Holland Torpedo Boat Company, V:1124, 1125
Johnson, Andrew, **V:1232-1238**
Cushing, V:583
Grant, V:977
impeachment, IV:296; V:479, 1233
Stanton, VI:2108, 2109
Stephens, VI:2130
Stevens, VI:2137
Sumner, VI:2172
Johnson, Ben. *See* Jonson, Ben
Johnson, Charles S., VIII:1787
Johnson, Esther, IV:1307
Johnson, Guy, IV:198
Johnson, Jack, VIII:2241
Johnson, James, IV:232
Johnson, James Weldon, IX:3961
Johnson, Joseph, IV:138, 1475
Johnson, Lyndon B., **VIII:1866-1869**
Civil Rights Act, VIII:1974
Ford, VII:1181, 1182
Graham, VIII:1449
Harriman, VIII:1562, 1563
Hernandez, VIII:1641
Humphrey, VIII:1784, 1785
Kennedy, John F., VIII:1930
Kennedy, Robert F., VIII:1934
Kissinger, VIII:1999
Lippmann, VIII:2205
Marshall, VIII:2434, 2435
O'Neill, IX:2825
Stevenson, IX:3525
Wallace, IX:3863
Washington Post, VIII:1451, 1453
Johnson, Samuel, **IV:728-731**
Account of the Life of Mr. Richard Savage, An, IV:728
Addison, IV:28
Berkeley, IV:114
Boswell, IV:174-176
Bruce, IV:209
Burney, IV:226, 227
Canaletto, IV:243
Chase, IV:295
Goldsmith, IV:567
Journey to the Western Islands of Scotland, IV:175, 227
London, IV:728
Newbery, IV:1019, 1020
Plan of a Dictionary of the English Language, The, IV:728, 729
Plays of William Shakespeare, The, IV:728, 729
Pope, IV:1116
Rasselas, Prince of Abyssinia, IV:728
Reynolds, IV:1162
Swift, IV:1308

Vanity of Human Wishes, The, IV:728
Walpole, IV:1402, 1403
Johnson, W.A., VI:1698
Johnson, William, IV:198, 199
Johnson v. Transportation Agency of Santa Clara County, IX:2790
Johnson Wax Company, IX:4062
Johnston, Joseph E., V:617; VI:1340, 2060
Johnstown flood, V:143
John the Baptist, **I:479-482,** 880
Joinville, Treaty of, III:600
Joliot, Frédéric, VII:636, 815; **VIII:1870-1873,** 2039-2041
Joliot-Curie, Irène, VII:636, 812, 815; **VIII:1870-1873**
Jolliet, Louis, **IV:732-734**
Jomini, Antoine-Henri, V:504
Jonah, VI:1829
Jones, Anson, V:1138
Jones, Bobby, **VIII:1874-1878**
Jones, Don, VII:713
Jones, K.C., IX:3268, 3270, 3271
Jones, Inigo, **IV:735-737,** 747, 748
Masque of Blackness, The, IV:735, 747
Jones, John Paul, **IV:738-743**
Jones, Mary Harris "Mother," **VIII:1879-1882**
Jones, Quincy, VII:657
Jones, Wharton, VI:1388
Jones, William, V:1007; VI:1846
Jong Sumatranen Bond, VIII:1577
Jonson, Ben, **IV:744-749**
Alchemist, The, IV:747, 749
Bartholomew Fair, IV:747, 749
Beaumont and Fletcher, III:54, 56
Bunyan, IV:220
Case Is Altered, The, IV:746
Catiline, IV:747
Chapman, III:156
Devil Is an Ass, The, IV:747
Eastward Ho!, IV:747
Epicoene: Or, The Silent Woman, IV:747
Every Man in His Humour, IV:746
Isle of Dogs, The, IV:746
Jones, IV:735, 736
Masque of Blackness, The, IV:747
Nashe, III:548-550
Part of King James, IV:747
Sejanus, IV:747
Shakespeare, III:689, 690
Staple of News, The, IV:747
Tale of a Tub, A, IV:747
Volpone: Or, The Fox, III:54; IV:747, 749; V:162
Joplin, Janis, **VIII:1883-1886;** IX:3444
Cheap Thrills, VIII:1883
"Me and Bobby McGee," VIII:1884
Pearl, VIII:1884
Joplin, Scott, **V:1239-1241**
"Breeze From Alabama, A," V:1240
"Cascades, The," V:1240
"Easy Winner, The," V:1240
"Entertainer, The," V:1240
Guest of Honor, A, V:1240
"Harlem Rag," V:1240
"Maple Leaf Rag," V:1239, 1240
"Original Rag," V:1240
"Peacherine Rag," V:1240
"Picture of Her Face, A," V:1240
"Please Say You Will," V:1240
Ragtime Dance, V:1240
Treemonisha, V:1241
Jordan, Barbara, **VIII:1887-1890**
Jordan, Dorothea, VI:2392
Joseph II (of Habsburg), **IV:750-753,** 914, 916, 918
Joseph, Chief, **V:1242-1245**
Joséphine, V:**1246-1249;** VI:1617
Joseph of Lamego, III:198
Josephus, Flavius, I:247, 392, 480, **483-487,** 548
Against Apion, I:485
Antiquities of the Jews, The, I:484, 485
Jewish Revolt, The, I:484
Joshua, I:563
Joshua ben Hananiah, I:27, 28
Jotapata, I:484
Joule, James Prescott, VI:1269, 1270
journalism. *See* freedom of the press; newspapers; yellow journalism
Jouvet, Louis, VII:1380, 1381
Jovinian, I:792
Joyce, James, IV:1374; VII:238, 239; VIII:1537, **1891-1895**
Dubliners, VIII:1892
Finnegans Wake, VII:1223; VIII:1892, 1894
Portrait of the Artist as a Young Man, A, VIII:1892, 1894
Ulysses, VII:199, 1223; VIII:1891, 1892, 1894; IX:4014
Juan Carlos I, V:415
Juárez, Benito, **V:1250-1254**
Juchen, II:867, 1018; IV:3
Judah, Theodore Dehone, VI:2097
Judah ben Solomon Harizi, II:551
Judah ha-Levi, **II:548-552**
Book of the Kuzari, II:550, 551

Judd, Charlex, IX:4070
Jude, Der, VII:484
Judea, kingdom of, I:390-393; II, I:569
Judges, Book of, I:246, 247
Judson, Edward, VIII:1596, 1597
Jugendstil movement, VIII:2036
Jugurtha, I:743
Julia, I:528
Julian, I:121, 229, 509, 780
Julian calendar, I:150, 811-813; II:300
Julius II, III:16, 17, 83, 84, **405-408,** 450, 519
July Days crisis, VIII:1942
July manifesto, IV:919
July Monarchy, V:260; VI:2226-2229
July Revolution, V:865
July 26th Movement, VII:617, 618; VIII:1494
July 28, 1838, Ordinance of, V:722
Jumbo the Elephant, V:136
Junayd, al-, II:422
Jung, Carl, **VIII:1896-1899**
  Answer to Job, VIII:1898
  Bleuler, VII:329
  Breton, VII:448, 451
  collective unconscious, VIII:2134
  Freud, VII:1226
  Hesse, VIII:1652
  Psychology of the Unconscious, VIII:1898
Junian Law, I:163
Junius Letters, IV:908
Jupiter-C missile, VII:441
Jurgurthine War, I:528, 529, 833
Jurieu, Pierre, IV:103, 104
Jussieu, Bernard de, IV:805
Justin I, II:553, 559
Justin II, II:560, 561
Justinia, I:44
Justinian I, I:656; II:118, **553-558,** 560, 890-892
Justinian II, II:824
Justus of Tiberias, I:485
Jutta of Spanheim, II:474
Juvenal, **I:488-490**
  "On an Education in Avarice," I:490
  Satires, I:488, 489
  "Vanity of Human Wishes, The," I:489
juvenile literature. *See* children's literature

Kadaulatan rakyat, VIII:1578
Kadesh, Battle of, I:736
Kaffraria tribe, V:999
Kafka, Franz, VII:240, 241, 1027; VIII:1463, **1900-1902**
  Castle, The, VII:240; VIII:1901
  "In the Penal Colony," VIII:1901
  Judgment, The, VIII:1900
  Letter to His Father, VIII:1901
  Metamorphosis, The, V:950; VIII:1900; VII:373
  Trial, The, VIII:1901
Kahlenburg, Battle of, IV:726
Kahn, Otto, VIII:2142
Kahnweiler, Daniel-Henry, VIII:1483, 1484
Kaiho Yusho, IV:1257
Kaikei, II:926
Kaiser, Georg, IX:3927
Kaiserstil, IV:475, 655
Kaiser Wilhelm Institute, VIII:1510, 1511, 1514, 1618, 2476; IX:2857
Kakulima, Mount, I:369
Kalanikupule, V:1255
Kalhu, I:110
Kalidasa, **I:491-493**
  Birth of the War-God, The, I:492
  Cloud Messenger, The, I:491
  Dynasty of Raghu, The, I:492
  Rtusamhara, I:491
  Sakuntala, I:492
  Vikrama and Urvasi, I:492
Kalingas, I:112
Kalisz, Treaty of, II:212
Kallir, Otto, VIII:2633, 2635
Kalmar Union, II:626, 627
Kamakura shogunate, II:97, 882, 924-926
Kamchatka Expeditions, IV:112
Kamehameha I, **VI:1255-1258**
Kamehameha II, V:1257
Kamehameha IV, VI:1372
Kamehameha V, VI:1372
Kämpfer, Engelbert, **IV:754-756**
  Amoenitatum exoticarum, IV:755
  History of Japan, The, IV:755, 756
KAN. *See* Kenyan African Union
Kandalanu, I:106
Kandinsky, Wassily, **VIII:1903-1905,** 2005, 2006, 2038, 2404, 2405
  Black Arc, VIII:1903
  Composition VIII, VIII:1904
  Composition X, VIII:1904
  Concerning the Spiritual in Art, VIII:1903, 2037
  Fugue, VIII:1903
  Point and Line to Plane, VIII:1904
  Several Circles, VIII:1904
  Tempered Elan, VIII:1904
K'ang-hsi, **IV:757-760**
Kanishka, **I:494-497**

Kansas
  Coronado, III:180
  Dred Scott decision, VI:2000
  Earp, V:735-737
  Hickok, V:1108, 1109
  temperance movement, VI:1630, 1631
Kansas-Nebraska Act
  Benton, V:197
  Brown, V:322
  Buchanan, V:347
  Chase, V:478
  Douglas, V:692, 693
  Greeley, V:985
  Houston, V:1138
  Lincoln, VI:1382
  Pierce, VI:1777
  Stephens, VI:2129
  Sumner, VI:2171
Kant, Immanuel, **IV:761-764**
  Barth, VII:203
  Bayle, IV:105
  Cassirer, VII:614
  Critique of Judgment, The, IV:763
  Critique of Practical Reason, The, IV:762
  Critique of Pure Reason, The, IV:761; VII:449; IX:3965
  Dreams of a Spirit-Seer, IV:1303
  Duns Scotus, II:313
  Durkheim, VII:988
  Fichte, IV:465-468
  Foundations of the Metaphysics of Morals, IV:762
  Gilson, VII:1376
  Hartmann, VIII:1571
  Hegel, V:1082
  Herder, IV:651-653
  Hume, IV:685
  Kleist, VI:1294
  Leibniz, IV:832
  Moore, VIII:2606
  Nishida, VIII:2755
  Perpetual Peace, IV:763
  Religion Within the Boundaries of Pure Reason, IV:763
  Ritschl, VI:1893, 1894
  Schelling, VI:1973
  Schiller, IV:1219
  Schopenhauer, VI:1985
  Transcendentalists, V:757
KANU. *See* Kenyan African National Union
Kanze Motomasa, II:1026
Kanze Saburo, II:1026
Kao Tsung, II:1019
Kao Tzu, I:944
Kapitsa, Pyotr Leonidovich, **VIII:1906-1909,** 2074
Kapteyn, Jacobus, IX:2827
Karaite movement, II:550
Karajan, Herbert von, **VIII:1910-1912;** IX:3083
Karaji, al-
  Fakhri, I:273
Karakoram Mountains, VI:2411
Karakorum, II:987-989
Karameh, Battle of, VII:91
Karlsbad Decrees, V:1034
Karlskirche, IV:474, 475, 657
Kármán, Theodore von, IX:3074, 3075
Karnak, I:24, 547, 890, 891; VI:1412
Karno, Fred, VII:653
Kasavubu, Joseph, VIII:2562, 2563; IX:3745-3747
Kaskaskia, IV:312
Katsukawa Shunsho, V:1120
Katsushika Hokusai. *See* Hokusai
Katusky, Karl, VII:291, 292
Kauai, V:1255
Kauffmann, Angelica, **IV:765-768**
  Artist Hesitating Between the Arts of Music and Painting, The, IV:765
  Parting of Hector and Andromache, The, IV:767
Kaufmann House, IX:4061
Kaumualii, V:1257
Kautsky, Karl, VIII:2285, 2286
Kavadh, II:559
Kawabata, Yasunari, **VIII:1913-1916,** 2551
  House of Sleeping Beauties and Other Stories, The, VIII:1913
  Izu Dancer, The, VIII:1913
  Jurukosai no nikki, VIII:1913
  Master of Go, The, VIII:1914
  Shokonsai ikkei, VIII:1913
  Snow Country, VIII:1914
  Thousand Cranes, VIII:1914
  Tokyo no hito, VIII:1915
Kay, James Phillips. *See* Kay-Shuttleworth, First Baronet
Kay, John, IV:59, 61, **769-771**
Kay-Shuttleworth, First Baronet, **VIII:1917-1919**
Kazan, Battle of, III:387
Kazantzakis, Nikos, **VIII:1920-1923**
  Last Temptation of Christ, The, VIII:1922
  Odyssey: A Modern Sequel, The, VIII:1921
  Saint Francis, VIII:1922
  Saviors of God, The, VIII:1921
  Zorba the Greek, VIII:1920-1922

Kazin, Alfred, VIII:2273
Kchessinskaya, Mathilde, VIII:2746
Kean, Edmund, **VI:1259-1263,** 1460, 2215
Kearns, Jack, VII:900, 902, 903
Kearny, Stephen Watts, V:431, 840
Keating-Owen Act, VIII:2097
Keats, John, **VI:1264-1268,** 2055; VIII:2251
Endymion, VI:1266
Eve of St. Agnes, The, V:1168
Fall of Hyperion: A Dream, The, VI:1266, 1267
"Lamia," VI:1267
"Ode on a Grecian urn," VII:1196
"On First Looking into Chapman's Homer," VI:1266
"Sleep and Poetry," VI:1266
"To Autumn," VI:1267
"To Solitude," VI:1266
Keble, John, V:75; VI:1641, 1829, 1830
Kedleston House, IV:9
Keita dynasty, II:623, 624
Keller, Hellen, **VIII:1924-1927**
My Religion, VIII:1926
Out of the Dark, VIII:1924
Song of the Stone Wall, The, VIII:1924
Story of My Life, The, VIII:1924
Teacher, VIII:1926
World I Live In, The, VIII:1924
Kelley, Florence, IX:3838, 3839
Kellogg-Briand Pact, V:281; VII:525; VIII:2209
Kelly, Gene, VII:1305
Kelly, William, V:220
Kelvin, Lord, V:609, 768; **VI:1269-1272**
Kemble, Charles, VI:1273
Kemble, John Philip, IV:810; VI:1260, 1261
Kemble, Fanny, **VI:1273-1276**
Francis I, VI:1273
Journal of a Residence on a Georgian Plantation in 1838-1839, VI:1273, 1275, 1276
Kemmu Formulary of 1336, II:98
Kemmu Restoration, II:97
Kempis, Thomas à. *See* Thomas à Kempis
Kennedy, Jacqueline. *See* Onassis, Jacqueline Kennedy
Kennedy, John F., **VIII:1928-1931**
Civil Rights Act, VIII:1973
Harriman, VIII:1562
Humphrey, VIII:1784
Johnson, VIII:1867, 1868
Jordan, VIII:1887
Kennedy, Robert F., VIII:1930
Khrushchev, VIII:1963
Malcolm X, VIII:2375
Monroe, VIII:2590
Nixon, VIII:2758
Onassis, IX:2815-2817
Profiles in Courage, VIII:1928, 1933; IX:2815
space exploration, VII:1272
Stevenson, IX:3525
Thomas, IX:3663
Wallace, IX:3863
Warren Commission, IX:3890
Why England Slept, VIII:1928
Kennedy, Robert F., VIII:1764, 1785, 1930, **1932-1935**
Kenner, Hugh, VIII:2334
Kent, Edward, Duke of, VI:2307
Kent, James, V:562; **VI:1277-1280**
Commentaries on American Law, VI:1277-1280
Kent, William, IV:204
Kentucky Resolutions, IV:718
Kentucky v. Dennison, V:478
Kenya African National Union, VIII:1938
Kenya African Union, VIII:1936
Kenyatta, Jomo, **VIII:1936-1940,** 2147
Facing Mount Kenya, VIII:1936
Kenzan, IV:1041
Keokuk, V:249
Kephisodotos
Hermes Carrying the Infant, I:690
Peace and Wealth, I:690
Kepler, Johannes, **IV:772-776**
Ad Vitellionem paralipomena, quibus astronomiae pars optica traditur, IV:774
Alhazen, II:66
Apollonius of Perga, I:74
Astronomia nova, IV:774, 775
Brahe, III:78, 79
De fundamentis astrologiae certioribus, IV:774
De stella nova in pede serpentarii, IV:774
Dioptrice, IV:774
Epitome of Copernican Astronomy, IV:775
Galileo, IV:519, 521
Harmonies of the World, IV:775
Kepler's Conversation with Galileo's Sidereal Messenger, IV:774
Napier, III:545
Prodromus dissertationum mathematicarum continens mysterium cosmographicum, IV:774
Tabulae Rudolphinae, IV:775
Keppel, Augustus, IV:1160, 1161
Keppler, Wilhelm, IX:3881, 3882
Keraunos, Ptolemy, I:768, 769
Kerensky, Aleksandr Fyodorovich, **VIII:1941-1944**

Kern, Jerome, VIII:1533, 1534; IX:3201
Kerouac, Jack, **VIII:1945-1948**
Book of Dreams, VIII:1946
Desolation Angels, VIII:1947
Dharma Bums, The, VIII:1945, 1947
Doctor Sax, VIII:1945, 1946
Maggie Cassidy, VIII:1946
Mexico City Blues, VIII:1947
On the Road, VIII:1945-1947
Subterraneans, The, VIII:1946
Town and the City, The VIII:1946
Tristessa, VIII:1947
Visions of Cody, VIII:1946
Visions of Gerard, VIII:1945, 1947
Kesserling, Albert, **VIII:1949-1951**
Kestrel engine, IX:3211
Kew Observatory, V:868
Key, Francis Scott, **VI:1281-1283,** 2189, 2618
"Star Spangled Banner, The," VI:1281-1283
Key, Philip B., VI:2107
Keyes, Lawrence, IX:2880
Keynes, John Maynard, **VIII:1952-1956**
Economic Consequences of the Peace, The, VIII:1952
General Theory of Employment, Interest, and Money, VIII:1952, 1954, 1955
How to Pay for the War, VIII:1954
Indian Currency and Finance, VIII:1952
Treatise on Money, A, VIII:1954
Khadijah bint Khuwaylid, II:651, 652
Khanate, Il-, II:381
Kharijites, II:1013
Khayyám, Omar. *See* Omar Khayyám
Khazars, I:127; II:952, 953
Khedive Isma'il, V:1208
Khitans, II:866, 867
Khmer Rouge, IX:3419, 3420
Khomeini, Ruhollah, **VIII:1957-1960,** 2568
'Abbas the Great, IV:6
Islamic Government, VIII:1958
Khosrow I, **II:559-562**
Khrushchev, Nikita S., **VIII:1961-1964**
Brezhnev, VII:459, 460
Eisenhower, VII:1044
Hammarskjöld, VIII:1530, 1531
Joliot, VIII:1872
Kennedy, VIII:1930
Malenkov, VIII:2378
Molotov, VIII:2572, 2573
Pasternak, IX:2901
Sakharov, IX:3296, 3297
"Secret Speech," VIII:1962
space exploration, VIII:2020, 2021; IX:3639, 3640
Tupolev, IX:3765, 3766
Zhukov, IX:4116, 4118, 4119
Khwarizmi, al-, **II:563-569**
Algoritmi de numero indorum, II:564
Kitab al-jabr wa almuquabalah, II:563
Kitab surat al-ard, II:565
Liber ysagogarum Alchorismi in artem astronomicam a magistro A. compositus, II:564
Kiakhta, Treaty of, IV:1084
Kiangsi, III:772
Kiangsi Soviet, VIII:2189
Kidd, Billy, VIII:1965
Kidd, Thomas I., VII:839
Kidd, William, **IV:777-780**
Kierkegaard, Soren, **VI:1284-1287**
Concluding Unscientific Postscript, VI:1286, 1287
For Self-Examination, VI:1286
Philosophical Fragments, VI:1286
What Christ's Judgment Is About Official Christianity, VI:1286
Kiev Rus, Confederation of, II:803-805, 952-954
Kikuyu, VIII:1936-1939, 2145, 2147
Kikuyu Central Association, VIII:1936-1939
Killy, Jean-Claude, **VIII:1965-1967**
Kilmainham Treaty, V:805
Kilwardby, Robert, II:715-717
Kimball, William W., V:1124
Kimberly Division, VI:1873, 1874, 1876
Kim Chi-Ha, IX:3258
Kimmel, Husband E., VIII:2750
King, Billie Jean, VII:1112, 1113; **VIII:1968-1970**
King, Charles, V:562
King, Ernest J., VIII:2750-2752
King, Martin Luther, Jr., **VIII:1971-1976**
Abernathy, VII:9, 10, 12
Angelou, VII:80
Bunche, VII:503
Charles, VII:658
Civil Rights Memorial, VIII:2186
Hoover, VIII:1733
Jackson, VIII:1824-1826
Malcolm X, VIII:2375
Parker, IX:2886
King, Stephen, **VIII:1977-1980**
Carrie, VIII:1977, 1978
Danse Macabre, VIII:1978
Dead Zone, The, VIII:1978
Green Mile, The, VIII:1978
Insomnia, VIII:1978

Misery, VIII:1978
Shining, The, VIII:1978
Tommyknockers, The, VIII:1978
King, Tabitha, VIII:1977, 1979
King, William Lyon Mackenzie, **VIII:1981-1985**
Canada and the Fight for Freedom, VIII:1983
Canada at Britain's Side, VIII:1983
Industry and Humanity, VIII:1982
Secret of Heroism, The, VIII:1981
King David Hotel, bombing of, VII:244
Kingdom, Brotherhood of the, IX:3126
King Features, VIII:1604
King James Bible, III:661; IV:47, 229, 622; VI:1829
King Manuel, Ordinances of, III:464
King Philip's War, IV:437, 932, 933, 955, 956
Kings, Valley of the, I:23, 904, 905
King's Bench, Court of the, III:267; IV:332, 904, 906-908, 1440
Kingsbury, Mary, VII:160
King George's War. *See* Austrian Succession, War of
Kingsley, Charles, VI:1504, 1643
Two Years Ago, VI:1458
Westward Ho!, VI:1458
Kinney, Abbot, V:1201
Kingston, Council of, II:334
Kinsey, Alfred Charles, VII:1072; **VIII:1986-1990**
Human Sexual Response, VIII:1988
Introduction to Biology, An, VIII:1986
Sexual Behavior in the Human Female, VIII:1988, 1989
Sexual Behavior in the Human Male, VIII:1988, 1989
Kiowa Indians, V:432
Kipchak, Khanate of. *See* Golden Horde
Kipling, Rudyard, **VI:1288-1293;** VII:168, 554
Barrack-Room Ballads, VI:1290
Captains Courageous, VI:1290
Courting of Dinah Shadd, The, VI:1290
"Danny Deever," VI:1290
Departmental Ditties, VI:1288
"Gunga Din," VI:1292
Irish Guards in the Great War, VI:1290
Jungle Book, The, VI:1290; VII:517
Just So Stories, VI:1290
Kim, VI:1290, 1292
Light That Failed, The, VI:1290
"Mandalay," VI:1292
"Mary Postgate," VI:1291
Puck of Pook's Hill, VI:1290
"Recessional," VI:1290
Second Jungle Book, The, VI:1290
Soldiers Three, VI:1288
Stalky & Co., VI:1288, 1291
"Strange Ride of Morrowbie Jukes, The," VI:1288
"White Man's Burden, The," VI:1291
Kirchhoff, Robert, VI:1411
Kirchner, Ernst Ludwig, **VIII:1991-1993**
Emmy Frisch with Red Flowers, VIII:1992
Self-Portrait as a Soldier, VIII:1992
Street, Berlin, VIII:1992
View of Basel and the Rhine, VIII:1992
Kirill, Metropolitan, II:53
Kirkpatrick, Jeane, **VIII:1994-1997**
New Presidential Elite, The, VIII:1995
Political Woman, VIII:1995
Strategy of Deception, The, VIII:1994
Kirstein, Lincoln, VII:156
Kishi, Nobusuke, VIII:1575, 1809, 1810
Kissinger, Henry, **VIII:1998-2001**
Chinese relations, VIII:2191
Faisal, VIII:1120
Ford, VII:1181
Nixon, VIII:2759
Nuclear Weapons and Foreign Policy, VIII:1999
Perot, IX:2973
Walters, IX:3870
White House Years, VIII:2000
World Restored, 1812-1822, A, VIII:1998
Years of Upheaval, VIII:2000
Kitaj, Ron, VIII:1711
Kitchen Cabinet, V:196
Kitchener, Lord, VII:123, 376, 821; **VIII:2002-2004**
Kitty Hawk, IX:4066
Kiwalao, V:1255
Klangfarbenmelodie, IX:3914, 3915
Kleberg, Richard M., VIII:1866
Klee, Paul, **VIII:2005-2008,** 2406
Ad Parnassum, VIII:2007
Before the Gates of Kairouan, VIII:2006
Creative Credo, VIII:2006
Death and Fire, VIII:2006
Inventions, VIII:2005
Once Emerged from the Gray of Night, VIII:2006
Pedagogical Sketchbook, VIII:2006
Twittering Machine, VIII:2006
Klein, Johann, VI:2021-2023
Kleist, Heinrich von, **VI:1294-1296**
Amphitryon, VI:1294, 1295
Broken Jug, The, VI:1294, 1295

Cathy of Heilbronn, VI:1295
Marquise of O, The, VI:1295
Penthesilea, VI:1295
Prince of Homburg, The, VI:1295
Robert Guiskard, VI:1294, 1295
Kleisthenes, I:214
Klinger, Max, VIII:2016, 2017
Leben, Ein, VIII:2016
Knäred, Peace of, IV:589
Knidos. *See* Cnidus
Knight, Richard Payne, IV:1012
Knights' Academy, IV:76
Knights Hospitallers, II:311
Knights of Labor, V:919, 921
Knights Templars, II:144, 311, 609
Knopf, Alfred A., VII:624
Knopf, Edwin H., VIII:1637
Know-Nothing Party, V:794, 1138
Knox, Frank, IX:3524
Knox, John, **III:409-412**
Appelation of John Knox, The, III:411
First Blast of the Trumpet against the Monstrous Regiment of Women, The, III:411
First Book of Discipline, The, III:411
History of the Reformation of Religion Within the Realm of Scotland, The, III:411
Letter to the Commonalty of Scotland, III:411
Knut, II:692, 693
Kober, Arthur, VIII:1620
Kober, Tobias, IV:154
Koch, Christoph Wilhelm, VI:1544
Koch, Robert, V:535; **VI:1297-1300,** 1747; VII:1032; IX:3450, 3451
Kodály, Zoltán, VII:210
Kofi, Francis Nwia. *See* Nkrumah, Kwame
Kohl, Helmut, **VIII:2009-2011**
Kohler, Elmer Peter, VII:748
Köhler, Wolfgang, VII:1027
Kojève, Alexandre, VIII:2061, 2063
Kojo, II:537
Kokoschka, Oskar, **VIII:2012-2015**
irrende Ritter, Der, VIII:2013
Morder Hoffnung der Frauen, VIII:2012
Red Egg, VIII:2014
Self-portrait of a Degenerate Artist, VIII:2014
traeumenden Knaben, Die, VIII:2012
What We Are Fighting For, VIII:2014
Kollwitz, Käthe, **VIII:2016-2018**
Death, VIII:2017
Mourning Parents, VIII:2017
Peasant War, The, VIII:2017
Proletariat, VIII:2017
War, VIII:2017
Weavers' Revolt, A, VIII:2017
Kölreuter, Gottlieb, VI:1528
Komarov, Vladimir, VII:1271
Komitet Gosudarstvennoi Bezopasnosti. *See* KGB
Komyo, II:97
König, Franz Niklaus, V:592
Königgrätz, Battle of, V:830; VIII:1674
Konigsberg v. State Bar of California, VII:322
Ko no Moronao, II:97, 98
Kon-Tiki, VIII:1658-1660
Korah, I:3
Koran
Ash'ari, II:94, 348
Hanbalite school, II:34
Hanifite school, II:16-18
Mahfouz, VIII:2357
Muhammad, II:651-655
Tabari, II:873
Korean Provisional Government, IX:3165, 3166
Korean War
Bradley, VII:405
Chiang Kai-shek, VII:666
Glenn, VII:1387
Lin Piao, VIII:2189, 2190
Luce, VIII:2263
MacArthur, VIII:2298
Marshall, VIII:2431
Rhee, IX:3165-3167
Truman, IX:3742, 3743
Wallace, IX:3862
Korechika, II:370
Korematsu v. United States, VII:322
Kornei, Otto, VII:579, 580
Kornilov Revolt, VIII:1943
Korolev, Sergei, **VIII:2019-2022;** IX:3751
Kosovo, Battle of, II:845; III:499
Kossuth, Lajos, V:626, 627
Kostrowitzky, Guillaume Albert Wladimir Alexandre Apollinaire de. *See* Apollinaire, Guillaume
Koussevitsky, Serge, VII:212, 295, 296, 767
Krasner, Lee, **VIII:2023-2026;** IX:3048, 3049
Blue and Black, VIII:2024
Imperfect Indicative, VIII:2025
"Little Image" paintings, VIII:2024
Past Conditional, VIII:2025
Rising Green, VIII:2025
Kraus, Gregor, VII:1327
Kraus, Karl, VIII:2012
Kreisky, Bruno, IX:3986

Kremer, Gerhard. *See* Mercator, Gerardus
Krewo, Treaty of, II:1001
Krio, I:215
Krishnamurti, Jiddu, V:213
Kristallnacht, VIII:1406
Krogh, August, **VIII:2027-2029**
Anatomy and Physiology of Capillaries, The, VIII:2028
Comparative Physiology of Respiratory Mechanisms, The, VIII:2028
Kruger, Paul, VII:376
Krupa, Gene, VIII:1419, 1420
Krupp, Alfred, **VI:1301-1304**
Kubitschek, Juscelino, VIII:2740
Kublai Khan, II:378, **566-569,** 750, 868
Kübler-Ross, Elisabeth, **VIII:2030-2032**
On Death and Dying, VIII:2031
Kubrick, Stanley, VII:96
2001: A Space Odyssey, IX:3292
Kugler, Franz, V:358, 359
Kuhnau, Johann, IV:1320
Ku Klux Klan
Black, VII:321
Borah, V:281
Grant, V:977
Griffith, VIII:1480
Johnson, VIII:1866
Lin, VIII:2187
Stephens, VI:2131
Kumara, II:484
Kumin, Maxine, IX:3395-3397
Kuná Hora decree, II:971
Kunckel von Löwenstjern, Johann, IV:1269
Kundu, II:86
Kunersdorf, Battle of, IV:1298
Kung, Prince, VI:1362, 1364
K'ung Ch'iu. *See* Confucius
Kunstschau, VIII:2012
Kuo Hsiang, I:192
Kuomintang
Chiang Kai-shek, VII:664-666
Chou En-lai, VII:676, 677
Chu Teh, VII:687, 688
Lu Hsün, VIII:2253, 2254
Mao Tse-tung, VIII:2400, 2401
Sun Yat-sen, IX:3578-3580
Wang Ching-wei, IX:3877-3879
Kuo Mo-jo, **VIII:2033-2035**
Ch'u Yüan, VIII:2034
Li Pai yü Tu Fu, VIII:2034
Mo-jo wên-chi, VIII:2034
Kuo Wei, II:866
Kupka, Frantisek, **VIII:2036-2038**
Amorpha, Fugue in Two Colors, VIII:2034
Animated Lines, VIII:2034
"Girl with a Ball," VIII:2036
Newton's Discs, VIII:2034
Kurchatov, Igor Vasilyevich, **VIII:2039-2042**
Kurds, VII:134
Kurosawa, Akira, **VIII:2043-2046**
"Akira Kurosawa's Dreams," VIII:2045
Dersu Uzala, VIII:2045
Dodesukaden, VIII:2045
Drunken Angel, VIII:2044
High and Low, VIII:2045
Horses, VIII:2043
Idiot, The, VIII:2044
Ikiru, VIII:2044
I Live in Fear, VIII:2044
Kagemusha: The Shadow Warrior, VIII:2045
Most Beautiful, The, VIII:2044
Ran, VIII:2045
Rashomon, VIII:2044; VII:280
Red Beard, VIII:2045
Sanshiro Sugata, VIII:2044
Scandal, VIII:2044
Seven Samurai, The, VIII:2044
Stray Dog, VIII:2044
Throne of Blood, VIII:2045
Tora! Tora! Tora!, VIII:2045
Yojimbo, VIII:2045
Kurth, Godefroid, IX:3023
Kushan Empire, I:494-496, 636-638
Kutter, Hermann, VII:475
Kutuzov, Arseny Golenishchev, VI:1613
Kutuzov, Mikhail Illarionovich, **VI:1305-1308**
Kuyuk, II:207
Kyd, Thomas, III:471, 472
Kyrle, John, V:1114
Kyrle Society, V:1114, 1115

Laban, Rudolf, **VIII:2058-2060**
Choreutics, VIII:2059
Effort, VIII:2059
Mastery of Movement on the Stage, The, VIII:2059
Modern Educational Dance, VIII:2059
Titan, VIII:2059
Welt des Tänzers, Die, VIII:2059
La Boétie, Etienne de, III:524
Labor Action, Alliance for, IX:3163
Labor Party (Australia), VII:816-818, 1109-1111; VIII:2289-2292, 2498
Labor Party (England). *See* Labour Party

Labor Party (Israel), VIII:2474, 2475
labor unions. *See* unionism, trade
Labour and Socialist International, VIII:2313
Labour Party (England)
  Angell, VII:76, 77
  Attlee, VII:137-139
  Baldwin, VII:169
  Bevan, VII:304-306
  Bevin, VII:313-316
  Churchill, VII:693
  Fawcett, V:778
  George V, VII:1341
  George VI, VII:1345
  Hardie, V:1036-1038
  Heath, VIII:1607, 1608
  Hughes, VIII:1775, 1776
  Laski, VIII:2093-2095
  MacDonald, VIII:2312-2314
  Major, VIII:2370, 2371
  Soviet relations, VIII:1645
  Thatcher, IX:3651, 3652
  Webb, Beatrice and Sidney, IX:3907, 3908
  Wilson, IX:4016-4018
Labour Representation Committee, V:1037, 1038
Lacaille, Abbé Nicolas-Louis de, IV:805
Lacan, Jacques, **VIII:2061-2064**
  Ecrits, VIII:2062, 2063
Laclos, Choderlos de, IV:1049
Lacordaire, Père, V:967
La Cosa, Juan de, III:116
Lacy, James, IV:528
Ladies Home Journal, VII:623
Ladies Professional Golfer's Association, IX:4098
Laelius, I:758
Laertius, Diogenes, I:653, 967
La Fayette, Madame de
  Princess of Clèves, The, IV:172
Lafayette, Marquis de, IV:1175, 1176; V:562, 563
La Follette, Robert M., **VIII:2047-2050;** IX:3661
  La Follette's Weekly Magazine, VIII:2048
La Fontaine, Henri-Marie, **VIII:2051-2053**
  Great Solution: Magnissima Charter, The, VIII:2052
  International Judicature, VIII:2052
La Fontaine, Jean de, **IV:781-784**
  Adonis, IV:781, 783
  Discours à Mne de La Sablière, IV:782
  Épitre à Huet, IV:783
  Eunuque, L', IV:781
  Fables Written in Verse, IV:782
  Loves of Cupid and Psyche, The, IV:782
  Relation d'un voyage en Limousin, IV:782
  Songe de Vaux, Le, IV:781
  Tales and Short Stories in Verse, IV:782, 783
La Fontaine, Louis Hippolyte, V:118
La Gardia Trial, III:726
Lagerlöf, Selma, **VIII:2065-2068;** IX:3285, 3286
  Christ Legends, VIII:2066
  Diary of Selma Lagerlöf, The, VIII:2066
  Emperor of Portugallia, The, VIII:2066
  Further Adventures of Nils, The, VIII:2066, 2077
  Gösta Berlings Saga, VIII:2065
  Holy City: Jerusalem II, The, VIII:2066
  Jerusalem, VIII:2066
  Liliecrona's Home, VIII:2066
  Marbacka, VIII:2066
  Memories of My Childhood, VIII:2066
  Miracles of the Antichrist, The, VIII:2065
  Ring of the Löwenskölds: A Trilogy, The, VIII:2066, 2077
  Wonderful Adventures of Nils, The, VIII:2066, 2077
Lagrange, Joseph-Louis, **IV:785-788,** 885; IX:4039
  Mécanique analytique, IV:785-787
La Guardia, Fiorello Henry, **VIII:2054-2057**
La Guardia Trial. *See* La Gardia Trial
Laika, VIII:2021
laissez-faire economics
  Biddle, V:228
  Blanc, V:260
  Erhard, VII:1096
  Greenspan, VIII:1471
  Macmillan, VIII:2341
  Mill, VI:1562
  Smith, IV:1251
  Spencer, VI:2087
  Turgot, IV:1348
Lake Placid Club, V:661
Lamachos, I:90
Lamar, Mirabeau B., V:1138
Lamarckism, VI:2349
Lamb, William. *See* Melbourne, Second Viscount
Lambert, Constant, IX:3873, 3874
Lambert, John, **IV:789-792,** 972, 973
Lambton, John George. *See* Durham, First Earl of
Lamé, Series of. *See* Fibonacci sequence
Lamm, Richard, IX:2974
Lamoureaux, Charles, VII:606
Lamprocles, I:952, 953
Lancaster, Duke of, II:457, 458, 786, 1010
Lancaster, House of
  Edward II, II:326
  Edward IV, III:234, 235

Fortescue, III:267-269
Henry IV, II:457-460
Henry VI, III:341-343
Henry VII, III:345, 346
Richard III, III:647, 649-652
Warwick, III:774-777
Lancaster, Joseph, **VI:1309-1312**
Lancaster, Thomas, Earl of, II:326
Lanchester, Frederick William, **VIII:2069-2072;** IX:3074
Aerial Flight, VIII:2071
Landais, Pierre, IV:740
Landau, Lev Davidovich, **VIII:2073-2076**
Physics for Everyone, VIII:2075
Landauer, Gustav, VII:483
Landed Qualifications Act, IV:158
Landfriede, III:492, 493
Landini, Francesco, **II:570-573**
Lang, Fritz, **VIII:2077-2079**
Destiny, VII:505; VIII:2077
Dr. Mabuse the Gambler, VIII:2077
Fury, VIII:2078
Halbblut, VIII:2077
Liliom, VIII:2078
M, VIII:2077
Man Hunt, VIII:2078
Metropolis, VIII:2077, 2078
Niebelungen, Die, VIII:2077, 2078
Rancho Notorious, VIII:2078
Return of Frank James, The, VIII:2078
Scarlet Street, VIII:2078
Western Union, VIII:2078
While the City Sleeps, VIII:2078
Woman in the Window, The, VIII:2078; IX:2777
You Only Live Once, VIII:2078
Lang, K.D., **VIII:2080-2082**
Absolute Torch and Twang, VIII:2081
Angel with a Lariat, VIII:2080, 2081
"Constant Craving," VIII:2082
Ingenue, VIII:2081
Shadowland, VIII:2080, 2081
Truly Western Experience, A, VIII:2080
Lange, Dorothea, **VIII:2083-2086**
"Migrant Mother," VIII:2085
Notes from the Field, VIII:2084
"White Angel Bread Line," VIII:2084
Langen, Eugen, V:597; VI:1702, 1703
Langer, Susanne K., **VIII:2087-2089**
Cruise of the Little Dipper, and Other Fairy Tales, The, VIII:2087
Feeling and Form, VIII:2088
Introduction to Symbolic Logic, An, VIII:2087
Mind, VIII:2088
Philosophy in a New Key, VIII:2088
Practice of Philosophy, The, VIII:2087
Problems of Art, VIII:2088
Langland, William, II:114
Langley, Samuel Pierpont, **VI:1313-1315;** IX:4067
Langley's Law, VI:1314
Langton, Stephen, II:510, 511, 541, 542
Languet, Hubert, III:691
Lankester, Sir Edwin Ray, **VI:1316-1318**
La Noue, François, III:537
Lansbury, George, VII:314
Lansdowne, Fifth Marquess of, **VIII:2090-2092**
Lansing, Robert, IV:609
Lansing Declaration, VIII:2442
Lanuvinus, Luscius, I:845
Lanzmann, Claude, VII:231
Lao Ai, I:176
Lao-tzu, **I:498-500**
Tao-te Ching, I:190, 191, 498-500, 949, 951
Lapidoth, I:246
Laplace, Pierre-Simon, V:819, 820; **VI:1319-1322**
Philosophical Essay on Probabilities, A, VI:1320
Théorie analytique des probabilitiés, VI:1320
Treatise of Celestial Mechanics, A, V:1025
Laporte, Pierre, IX:3732
la Pouplinière, Le Riche de, IV:1148, 1149
Largus, Scribonius, I:277
Larichus, I:750
Larsa, I:361, 362
La Salle, Sieur de, **IV:793-796;** VI:1736, 1737
Las Casas, Bartolomé de, **III:413-415**
Apologética historia de las Indias, III:415
Del único modo, III:415
History of the Indies, III:413, 414
Relation of the First Voyages and Discoveries Made by the Spainiards in America, A, III:413
Lascaux cave paintings, VII:457
Lascelles, John, III:368
Laski, Harold J., **VIII:2093-2095**
American Democracy, The, VIII:2094
Authority in the Modern State, VIII:2093
Foundations of Sovereignty and Other Essays, The, VIII:2093
Grammar of Politics, A, VIII:2093
Studies in the Problem of Sovereignty, VIII:2093
Lasky, Jesse L., VII:896, 897; VIII:1415, 1417
Las Navas de Tolosa, Battle of, II:103
Lassalle, Ferdinand, **VI:1323-1326**
Lassalle's Open Letter to the National Labor Association of Germany, VI:1324

Lasso, Orlando di, III:107, 108, 284
LaStarza, Roland, VIII:2413
Lasus, I:787
László I, Saint, **II:574-576**
Lateran Councils, II:50, 396, 488, 511, 512, 716; III:407
Lateran Pacts, VII:1337
Lateran Palace, II:823
Later Chin Dynasty, IV:1
Later Chou Dynasty, II:866
Later Han Dynasty, I:590
Lathrop, Julia C., **VIII:2096-2099**
Hull-House Maps and Papers, VIII:2096
Lathrop, William, VIII:2096
Latimer, Hugh, **III:416-418,** 656
Latini, Brunetto, II:286
Latin language
Alcuin, II:44, 46, 47
Boniface, II:167
Cicero, I:196
Greek manuscripts, II:985, 986
Lucretius, I:511-513
Phaedrus, I:619, 620
Priscian, II:755-757
Psellus, II:759
Scaliger, III:671-673
Valla, III:740
Verrius Flaccus, I:930
Latin literature, Golden Age of, I:519-521
Latin poetry
Catullus, I:171
Cicero, I:194
Ennius, I:287-289
Latrobe, Benjamin Henry, **VI:1327-1330**
Laud, William, IV:280, **797-800,** 1142
Laue, Max von, VII:410
Laurel, Salvador, VII:88
Laurence, Saint, IV:118
Laurier, Sir Wilfrid, VIII:1981, 1982, **2100-2104**
Lausanne, Academy of, III:363
Lausanne, Treaty of, VIII:1812
Lautaro Lodge, VI:1947
Laval, François, **IV:801-804**
Laval, Pierre, **VIII:2105-2108;** IX:2988
Laver, Rod, **VIII:2109-2111**
Lavoisier, Antoine-Laurent, IV:262, **805-807;** V:718
Elements of Chemistry, in a New Systematic Order, IV:263, 806
Essays, Physical and Chemical, IV:806
Methods of Chemical Nomenclature, IV:263, 806
Lavon, Pinhas, VII:253
Law, Bonar, VII:168, 234, 235; **VIII:2112-2114**
Lawrence, D.H., V:1066; VI:1523; VII:625; VIII:1805, **2115-2120,** 2537
Aaron's Rod, VIII:2118
Birds, Beasts, and Flowers, VIII:2118
Fantasia of the Unconscious, VIII:2118
Kangaroo, VIII:2118
Lady Chatterley's Lover, VIII:2118; VII:322
Lost Girl, The, VIII:2118
Man Who Died, The, VIII:2119
Movements in European History, VIII:2118
Plumed Serpent, The, VIII:2118
Psychoanalysis and the Unconscious, VIII:2118
Rainbow, The, VIII:2117
St. Mawr: Together with the Princess, VIII:2118
Sea and Sardinia, VIII:2118
Sons and Lovers, VIII:2117
Studies in Classic American Literature, VIII:2118
Trespasser, The, VIII:2117
Twilight in Italy, VIII:2117
White Peacock, The, VIII:2115
Women in Love, VIII:2117
Lawrence, Ernest Orlando, **VIII:2121-2124,** 2336, 2338; IX:2833, 3376
Lawrence, First Baron, **VI:1331-1333**
Lawrence, Gertrude, VII:786
Lawrence, John Laird Mair. *See* Lawrence, First Baron
Lawrence, T.E., VII:1124, 1125; **VIII:2125-2130**
Crusader Castles, VIII:2125
Mint, The, VIII:2128
Seven Pillars of Wisdom: A Triumph, VIII:2127, 2128
Lawrence, Sir Thomas, **IV:808-812**
Portrait of an Actress, IV:809
Princess of Wales and Princess Charlotte, The, IV:810
Satan Summoning up His Legions, IV:810
Lawrence Berkeley Laboratory, VIII:2123
Lawrence Livermore Laboratory, IX:3633
Lawson, Nigel, VIII:2369, 2370
Laxness, Halldór, **VIII:2131-2133**
Atom Station, The, VIII:2132
Happy Warriors, The, VIII:2132
Independent People, VIII:2131
Islandsklukkan, VIII:2131
Salka Valka: A Novel of Iceland, VIII:2131
Vefarinn mikli frá Kasmir, VIII:2131
World Light, VIII:2131, 2132
Lazarists. *See* Mission, Congregation of the
Lazarus, IV:170

Lazarus, Emma, **VI:1334-1337;** VII:289
Admetus and Other Poems, VI:1334
Alide, VI:1334
"By the Waters of Babylon," VI:1336
Dance to Death, The, VI:1336
"Epistle to the Hebrews, An," VI:1336
"In the Jewish Synagogue at Newport," VI:1334
"New Colossus," VI:1334, 1336, 1337
Poems and Ballads of Heinrich Heine, VI:1336
Poems and Translations by Emma Lazarus, VI:1334
Songs of a Semite, VI:1336
Lazear, Jesse, VI:1858, 1859
LDP. *See* Liberal Democratic Party of Japan
Leach v. Three King's Messengers, IV:906
Leadership Conference on Civil Rights, IX:3115
League of Augsburg, War of the, IV:840
Leakey, L.S.B., **VIII:2145-2149**
Leander, II:518
Leary, Timothy, VIII:1807
Léaud, Jean-Pierre, IX:3737, 3738
Lebanon Civil War, VII:91
Lebed, II:86
Lebedia, II:86
Lebedev Physics Institute, VII:214, 215
Leblanc, Nicolas, **IV:813-816**
Le Bon, Gustave, **VIII:2134-2136**
Crowd, The, VIII:2134, 2135
Psychology of Peoples, The, VIII:2134, 2135
Psychology of the Great War, The, VIII:2135
Lech, Battle of, IV:1336
Leclerc, Charles-Victor-Emmanuel, IV:1340
Leclerc, Georges-Louis. *See* Buffon, Comte de
Le Corbusier, VII:1309, 1310; **VIII:2137-2140,** 2739, 2740; IX:4075-4077
Towards a New Architecture, VIII:2138
Lee, Ann, **IV:817-820**
Lee, Robert E., V:977, 1205, 1206; **VI:1338-1342**
Lee, William, IV:817-819
Leeds, First Duke of, **IV:821-824**
Lee Kuan Yew, **VIII:2150-2153**
Leeuwenhoek, Antoni van, **IV:825-828;** VI:1746
Lefèvre d'Etaples, Jacques, III:467
Le Gallienne, Eva, **VIII:2141-2144**
Legal Tender Act, IV:251
Legate, Bartholomew, IV:47
Legendre, Adrien-Marie, V:8
Léger, Fernand, **VIII:2154-2156**
Ballet mécanique, Le, VIII:2155
Constructeurs, Les, VIII:2155
Contrasts of Forms, VIII:2154
Disques, Les, VIII:2155
Eléments mécaniques, VIII:2155
Grand Déjeuner, Le, VIII:2155
Nus dans la forêt, Les, VIII:2154
Le Goulet, Treaty of, II:540
Leguia, Augusto, VIII:1584, 1585
Leibniz, Gottfried Wilhelm, **IV:829-833**
Condillac, IV:345
Duns Scotus, II:313
Frederick I, IV:498
New Essays Concerning Human Understanding, IV:831
Principles of Nature and Grace, The, IV:831
Theodicy, IV:105, 831
Leicester, Earl of, III:147, 243, 295, 693
Leicester House, IV:536
Leiden, University of, III:673; VII:1039; VIII:2235; IX:2827
Leif Eriksson, **II:577-580,** 689
Leigh, Vivian, IX:2811, 2812
Leipzig, Battle of, V:264, 475, 942
Leipzig, University of, IX:2855, 4069
Leipzig Opera, IV:1319, 1320
Leiter, Levi Z., V:783
Leith Hill Music Festival, IX:3798
Lemaître, Georges, **VIII:2157-2159**
Discussion sur l'evolution de l'univers, VIII:2158
Primeval Atom, The, VIII:2158
Lemercier, Jacques, IV:899
Lemon v. Kurtzman, VII:510
Lenaia, I:88, 91
Lend-Lease Act, VIII:1560, 1562, 1737, 1984
Lenin, Vladimir Ilich, VI:1494; **VIII:2160-2163**
Bukharin, VII:491
Gorky, VIII:1444, 1445
Gramsci, VIII:1461
Kazantzakis, VIII:1921
Kerensky, VIII:1942
Litvinov, VIII:2208, 2209
Lukács, VIII:2273
Molotov, VIII:2571
Sorel, IX:3464
Trotsky, IX:3726-3728
What Is to Be Done?, VIII:2161; IX:3726
Wilson, IX:4014
Leningrad affair, VIII:2378
Lennon, John, VII:226-229
Lenoir, Étienne, V:597; **VI:1343-1346,** 1702
Le Nôtre, André, **IV:834-83**
Lenya, Lotte, IX:3927, 3928
Leo I, I:785; II:894
Leo III, II:229, 544, 545, 903, 904

Leo IV, II:59
Leo V, II:904
Leo VI, II:86, 87, 117-119
Leo VIII, **V:1347-1350**
Leo IX, Pope, **II:581-584**
Leo X, **III:419-422**
  Andrea del Sarto, III:24
  Catherine de Médicis, III:132
  Clement VII, III:166
  Erasmus, III:247
  Guicciardini, III:325
  Luther, III:443
  Medici, Lorenzo de', III:498
  Michelangelo, III:519
Leo XIII, V:386, 919, 921; **VI:1347-1350,** 1644; VIII:2100
  Concerning Modern Errors, Socialism, Communism, Nihilism, VI:1348
  Condition of Labor, The, VI:1348
  Grande munus, VI:1349
  Human Liberty, VI:1348
  On Christian Marriage, VI:1349
  On Civil Government, VI:1348
  On the Christian Constitution of States, VI:1348
  On the Study of Scriptures, VI:1348
  Scholastic Philosophy, VI:1349
Leonardo da Vinci, **III:423-427**
  Adoration of the Magi, III:424
  Andrea del Sarto, III:24, 26
  Annunciation, The, III:423
  Battle of Anghiari, III:642
  Bramante, III:81
  Dürer, III:232
  Head of a Woman, III:424
  Last Supper, The, III:26, 81, 424, 684, IV:604
  Madonna Benois, III:424
  Madonna of the Rocks, III:424
  Mona Lisa, III:275, 425, IV:605
  Portrait of Ginevra dei Benci, III:751
  Raphael, III:642, 645
  Saint John the Baptist, III:425
  Treatise on Painting, IV:1187
  Valéry, IX:3791
  Vasari, III:745
  Verrocchio, III:750-752
  Virgin and Child with Saint Anne and the Infant Saint John, III:425
Leonardo of Pisa, **II:585-587**
  Flos, II:586
  Liber abaci, II:585, 586
  Liber quadratorum, II:586
  Practica geometriae, II:586
Leonico, III:45
Leonidas, **I:501-503,** 964
Leonidas II, I:215, 216
Leopold I, IV:498, **838-841**
Leopold II, VI:2103, 2398
Leopold, Nathan F., Jr., VII:840
Leopold of Anhalt-Dessau, IV:93
Leopold of Saxe-Coburg-Saalfeld, VI:1720
Leo the Great, I:126; II:823
Leotychides, I:16
Lepanto, Battle of, III:254; IV:265
Lepidus, Marcus Aemilius, I:132, 133, 140, 154
Lermontov, Mikhail, **VI:1351-1354**
  "Angel," VI:1352
  "Cossack Lullaby," VI:1353
  "Death of a Poet, The," VI:1352
  "Demon," VI:1352
  Hero of Our Time, A, VI:1351-1353
  "I Walk Out Alone onto the Road," VI:1353
  Masquerade, VI:1352
  "Novice, The," VI:1353
  "Parus," VI:1352
  Princess Ligovskaya, VI:1352
  Vadim, VI:1352
Leroux, Pierre, VI:1952
Lesage, Jean, IX:3730
Lesbia. *See* Clodia
Lesbos, I:651-653, 750-752
Lescot, Pierre, **III:428-430**
Leslie, Frank, VI:1627, 1629; VII:628
Lesseps, Ferdinand de, **VI:1355-1357;** VIII:1408
Lessing, Gotthold Ephraim, IV:465, **842-845;** VI:1287
  Briefe, die neueste Literatur betreffend, IV:842
  Education of the Human Race, The, IV:844
  Emilia Galotti, IV:843
  Free-thinker, The, IV:842
  Hamburg Dramaturgy, IV:843
  Jews, The, IV:842
  Laocoön, IV:843
  Masonic Dialogues, IV:844
  Minna von Barnhelm, IV:842, 843
  Miss Sara Sampson, IV:842
  Nathan the Wise, IV:842, 844
Lesslie, James, VI:1451
Le Tellier, François-Michel. *See* Louvois, Marquis de
Lethion, VI:1597, 1598
Leucippus, I:249
Leuckart, Rudolf, VI:2348
Leuctra, Battle of, I:215, 292
Leuven, Adolphe de, V:708

Levanevsky, Sigesmund, IX:4001
Levant, Oscar, VIII:1749
Levellers, IV:380
Le Vendre Bridge, VII:1229
Levesque, René, IX:3732
Lévi-Strauss, Claude, **VIII:2164-2166**
Levy, Lucien, VII:103
Lewaro, Villa, IX:3855
Lewes, Battle of, II:454, 645
Lewes, George Henry, V:751-753
Lewinsky, Monica, VII:710, 715
Lewis, C.S., **VIII:2167-2169;** IX:3696
  Allegory of Love, The, VIII:2167
  Chronicles of Narnia, VIII:2168
  Discarded Image, The, VIII:2168
  English Literature in the Sixteenth Century, VIII:2168
  Four Loves, The, VIII:2168
  Grief Observed, A, VIII:2168
  Mere Christianity, VIII:2168
  Perelandra, VIII:2168
  Problem of Pain, The, VIII:2168
  Screwtape Letters, The, VIII:2168
  Surprised by Joy, VIII:2168
  Till We Have Faces, VIII:2168
Lewis, Carl, IX:2865
Lewis, Edith, VII:624
Lewis, Eleanor Francis, IX:2884
Lewis, Gilbert N., IX:3375, 3787
Lewis, John L., **VIII:2170-2173**
Lewis, Meriwether, **VI:1358-1361,** 1933-1935
Lewis, Sinclair, **VIII:2174-2177**
  Ann Vickers, VIII:2175, 2176
  Arrowsmith, VIII:2174-2176
  Babbitt, VIII:2175, 2176, 2484
  Cass Timberlane, VIII:2176
  Dodsworth, VIII:2175
  Elmer Gantry, VIII:2175
  Free Air, VIII:2174
  Innocents, The, VIII:2174
  It Can't Happen Here, VIII:2174, 2176
  Job, The, VIII:2174
  Kingsblood Royal, VIII:2176
  Main Street, VIII:2174, 2175, 2484
  Mantrap, VIII:2175
  Our Mr. Wrenn, VIII:2174
  Prodigal Parents, The, VIII:2175
  The Man Who Knew Coolidge, VIII:2174, 2175
  Work of Art, VIII:2175
Lewis and Clark Expedition, VI:1358-1361, 1933-1935, 2077
Lex Regia, II:791
Ley Lerdo, V:1252
Leyte Gulf, Battle of, VIII:1527, 1528, 2752
Lhote, André, VII:594
Libanius, I:184
Liberal-Conservative Party (Canada), VI:1436
Liberal Democratic Party (Japan), VIII:1574, 1575, 1809-1811; IX:3336, 3337
Liberal Party (Australia), V:631; VIII:2498
Liberal Party (Canada), VII:680-682; VIII:1981-1983, 2100-2103; IX:3345
  Trudeau, IX:3731, 3733, 3734
Liberal Party (England)
  Asquith, VII:121, 122
  Beveridge, VII:310
  Brougham, V:316
  Chamberlain, Joseph, V:462, 464
  Chamberlain, Neville, VII:644
  Churchill, VII:691
  Fawcett, V:778
  Forster, V:804, 805
  George V, VII:1339, 1340
  Gladstone, V:936
  Grey, VIII:1475, 1476
  Hardie, V:1036, 1037
  Hobhouse, VIII:1709
  Home Rule Bill, VI:1741
  Lansdowne, VIII:2090, 2091
  Lloyd George, VIII:2217
  McDonald, VIII:2312, 2315
  Pankhurst, IX:2871, 2874
  Pusey, VI:1829
Liberal-Protectionist Party, V:631
Liberal Triennium, V:413
Libération du Québec, Front de, IX:3732
Liberation of Palestine, Front for the, VII:91
Liberation Rally, VIII:2693
Liberator, The, V:884, 885; VI:2143
Liberty, IV:617, 618
Liberty, Statue of, VI:1334, 1336, 1337; IX:2841
libraries
  ancient Rome, I:918, 919
  Carnegie, V:423, 662
  Córdoba, II:8
  York, II:46
Library, The, VII:623
Li Ch'ing-chao, **II:588-590**
  Chin shih lu, II:589, 590
  "Wu-his chung-hsing sung shi," II:588
Licinius, I:226-228, 346
Lie, Trygve, VIII:1529, 1530
Liebermann, Carl, VIII:1509

Liebig, Justus von, **VI:1366-1368,** 2403, 2404
Animal Chemistry, VI:1367
Organic Chemistry in Its Applications to Agriculture and Physiology, VI:1367
Liebknecht, Karl, VIII:2287
Liebknecht, Wilhelm, **VI:1369-1371**
Liège, battle of, III:163
Liège, Jacques de, II:661
Liehmann, Antonin, V:725
Li Fan Yuan, IV:2
Lifar, Serge, **VIII:2182-2184**
Bacchus et Ariadne, VIII:2183
Icare, VIII:2184
Manifeste du choregraphe, Le, VIII:2183
Life magazine, VII:397, 398; VIII:2256, 2262, 2263
Life of Aesop, The, I:13-15
Life of Saint Boniface, The, II:167, 168
Li-Fournier Agreement, V:466
Ligny, Battle of, V:942
Ligonier, John, IV:37, 38
Li Hung-chang, **VI:1362-1365**
Li Lin-fu, II:918, 966
Li Ling, I:820
Liliuokalani, **VI:1372-1375**
Lily, William, III:170
Limited Nuclear Test Ban Treaty, IX:3377, 3448
Limoges, IV:1348
Limousin, Claude, VII:1229
Lin, Maya Ying, **VIII:2185-2188**
Civil Rights Memorial, VIII:2185-2187
"Groundswell," VIII:2187
"TOPO," VIII:2187
Vietnam Veterans Memorial, VIII:2185-2187
"Women's Table," VIII:2187
Lincoln, Abraham, **VI:1380-1384**
assassination, V:272; VI:1383
Bennett, V:193
Brady, V:296
Chase, V:478-480
Douglas, V:693
Douglass, V:697
Frémont, V:842, 843
Garibaldi, V:881
Garrison, V:886
Gettysburg Address, VI:1383, 2346
Grant, V:976, 977
Greeley, V:985
Hay, V:1068, 1069
Holmes, V:1127
House Divided Speech, VI:1382
Johnson, V:1233
Parrington, IX:2894
Phillips, VI:1772, 1773
Pierce, VI:1778
Sandburg's biography, IX:3310, 3311
Saint-Gaudens, VI:1940
Schurz, VI:1996, 1997
Seward, VI:2038, 2039, 2172
Stanton, Edwin M., VI:2107-2109
Stanton, Elizabeth Cady, VI:2112
Stowe, VI:2151
Taney, VI:2192
Tarbell's biography, IX:3614
Truth, VI:2256, 2257
Whitman, VI:2371
Wilson's *Patriotic Gore,* IX:4014
Lincoln, Battle of, II:848
Lincoln, Benjamin, IV:1240, 1406
Lind, Jenny, V:59, 135; **VI:1385-1387**
Lindbergh, Charles A., VII:326; VIII:1397, 1500, **2193-2198**
Autobiography of Values, VIII:2196
Boyhood on the Upper Mississippi, VIII:2196
Culture of Organs, The, VIII:2196
Wartime Journals, VIII:2196
We, VIII:2196
Linde, Carl von, VII:699, 700
Lindsay, Vachel, VIII:1771; IX:3622, 3624, 3625
Linnaeus, IV:216, **846-849;** 589
General System of Nature, A, IV:846, 847
Species plantarum, IV:847
Linné, Carl von. *See* Linnaeus
Linnean Society, V:608; VI:1418
Lin Piao, **VIII:2189-2192,** 2401, 2402
Lin Tse-hsü, **VI:1376-1379**
Lionne, Hugues de, IV:947
Lipchitz, Jacques, **VIII:2199-2202**
Bellerophon Taming Pegasus, VIII:2201
Chimene, VIII:2201
Dancer, VIII:2199, 2200
Encounter, VIII:2199
Government of the People, VIII:2201
Half-Standing Figure, VIII:2201
Head, VIII:2201
Joy of Life, VIII:2201
Man with Guitar, VIII:2200
Mother and Children, VIII:2200
Our Tree of Life, VIII:2201
Pilgrim, VIII:2201
Sailor with Guitar, VIII:2200
Sculpture, VIII:2200
Standing Personage, VIII:2200

Woman and Gazelles, VIII:2199
Woman with Serpent, VIII:2199
Li Peng, **VIII:2178-2180**
Li Po, II:**591-594,** 918
Song of Pure Happiness, A, II:592
Lippershey, Hans, **IV:850-853**
Lippi, Fra Filippo, III:74, 460
Lippmann, Gabriel, VIII:2277
Lippmann, Walter, **VIII:2203-2207**
Cold War, VIII:2205
Drift and Mastery, VIII:2203
Essays in the Public Philosophy, VIII:2205
Good Society, The, VIII:2204
Phantom Public, The, VIII:2204
Preface to Morals, A, VIII:2204
Preface to Politics, A, VIII:2203, 2205
Public Opinion, VIII:2204, 2205
U.S. Foreign Policy, VIII:2205
U.S. War Aims, VIII:2205
Lisette Model, VII:95
Li Shih-min. *See* T'ai Tsung
Li Ssu, I:177, 433, 946
Lister, Joseph, **VI:1388-1390**
Liston, Sonny, VII:54
Liszt, Franz, V:833, 1003; **VI:1391-1394;** VII:210
Années de pèlerinage, VI:1391, 1393
Apparitions, VI:1391
Faust Symphony, A, VI:1392
"Fountains of the Villa d'Este, The," VI:1393
Mountain Symphony, VI:1392
"Nuages gris," VI:1393
Préludes, Les, VI:1392
Réminiscences de Don Juan, VI:1391
Sonata in B Minor, VI:1392
Symphony to Dante's "Divina Commedia," A, VI:1392
"Unstern," VI:1393
Via Crucis, VI:1393
literary criticism
Barthes, VII:207-209
Eliot, VII:1058
Fuller, V:852
Lessing, IV:842-844
Lukács, VIII:2272-2274
Millet, VIII:2537, 2538
Poe, VI:1794, 1796
Proust, IX:3089-3091
Wilson, IX:4012-4015
Li Tsung-jen, VII:666
Little, Malcolm. *See* Malcolm X
Little Big Horn, Battle of the, V:575, 585, 587; VI:2072
Little Galleries of the Photo-Secession, IX:3534
Little Gidding, IV:462-464
Little Steel strike, VIII:2171
Littleton, Sir Thomas, **III:431-433**
Tenures, III:432, 433
Litvinov, Maksim Maksimovich, **VIII:2208-2211,** 2571, 2572
Litvinov Protocol, VIII:2210
Li Tzu-ch'eng, IV:421, 422
Liu Chin, III:771
Liu Hsiang-shan, II:963
Liu Hsiu, I:590
Liu Pang, I:178
Liu Shao-ch'i, **VIII:2212-2215**
Liu Tzu-cheng, I:944
Liu Yï, I:429, 430
Liu Yü, I:429, 430
liver, I:82
Bernard, V:208
Erasistratus, I:300
Galen, I:339
Herophilus, I:398
Malpighi, IV:891
Livermore Radiation laboratories, VIII:2123
Liverpool, VI:2133, 2134
Liverpool, Second Earl of, **VI:1395-1398**
Livingston, Robert, V:369, 370, 855, 856
Livingstone, David, **VI:1399-1402,** 2101, 2102
Missionary Travels and Researches in South Africa, VI:1399
Narrative of an Expedition to the Zambezi and Its Tributaries, VI:1400
Livius, Peter, IV:248
Livonian War, III:387
Livy, **I:504-506**
History of Rome, The, I:504, II:728
Li Yuan, II:1015
Llewelyn ap Gruffyd, II:323
Lloyd George, David, V:778; **VIII:2216-2218**
Allenby, VII:61
Asquith, VII:122, 123
Baldwin, VII:168
Balfour, VII:174
Beaverbrook, VII:234, 235
Bevan, VII:304, 305
Chamberlain, VII:643
Cosgrave, VII:770
Curzon, VII:821
Harmsworths, VIII:1555
Hughes, VIII:1777
Imperial War Cabinet, VII:366
John, VIII:1855

Keynes, VIII:1952
Law, VIII:2112-2114
Sinn Féin, VII:877
Lobachevsky, Nikolay Ivanovich, **VI:1403-1405**
Geometriya, VI:1404
Pangéométrie, VI:1404, 1405
Lobengula, VI:1874
Local Government Act of 1888, VI:1945
Locarno, Treaty of, VII:169
Lochner v. New York, VII:421
Locke, John, **IV:854-859**
Berkeley, IV:114-116
Blackstone, IV:130
Bolingbroke, IV:160
Bradley, V:291
Condillac, IV:345
Essay Concerning Human Understanding, An, IV:344, 430, 856-858
Hume, IV:683, 685
Letter Concerning Toleration, A, IV:856, 857
Second Treatise of Government, IV:665
Shaftesbury, IV:1231
Some Thoughts Concerning Education, IV:92, 93, 1021
Third Letter for Toleration, A, IV:103
Transcendentalists, V:757
Two Treaties of Government, IV:857
Lockwood, Belva A., **VI:1406-1409**
Lockwood Bill, VI:1407
Lockyer, Sir Joseph Norman, **VI:1410-1413**
Chemistry of the Sun, The, VI:1412
Dawn of Astronomy, The, VI:1413
Inorganic Evolution as Studied by Spectrum Analysis, VI:1412
Meteoritic Hypothesis, The, VI:1412
Stonehenge and Other British Monuments Astronomically Considered, VI:1413
Sun's Place in Nature, The, VI:1412
Lodge, Henry Cabot, **VIII:2219-2222;** IX:3234
Life and Letters of George Cabot, The, VIII:2219
Senate and the League Nations, The, VIII:2221
Short History of the English Colonies in America, A, VIII:2219
Lodi, Ibrahim, III:38
Loeb, Jacques, VIII:2619, 2620
Loeb, Richard, VII:840
Log Cabin, V:984
Lok, John, III:278
Lombard, Peter, II:983
Sentences, II:163, 913; III:768
Lombard League, II:363, 364, 400
Lombardy
Alboin, II:41-43
Alexander III, II:50
Frederick I Barbarossa, II:358, 359
Gregory the Great, II:407-409
Henry II the Saint, II:450, 451
Lomonosov, Mikhail Vasilyevich, **IV:860-862**
Kratkoy rossiyskoy letopisets, IV:861
Rossiyskaya grammatika, IV:860
London, Jack, **VIII:2223-2226**
Call of the Wild, The, VIII:2223, 2225
Cruise of the Snark, The, VIII:2225
Iron Heel, The, VIII:2225
John Barleycorn, VIII:2225
Martin Eden, VIII:2223, 2225
People of the Abyss, The, VIII:2225
Sea-Wolf, The, VIII:2225
Smoke Bellew Tales, VIII:2225
Valley of the Moon, The, VIII:2225
War of the Classes, The, VIII:2225
White Fang, VIII:2225
Long, Huey, VIII:**2227-2230;** IX:3894
Longfellow, Henry Wadsworth, V:1145; **VI:1414-1417,** 1796
Ballads and Other Poems, VI:1416
Courtship of Miles Standish, The, IV:1274; VI:1416
"Cross of Snow, The," VI:1416
Evangeline, VI:1416; VIII:2229
Hyperion, VI:1416
Kavanagh, VI:1416
Outre-Mer, VI:1414
"Paul Revere's Ride," IV:1157; VI:1416
Poems on Slavery, VI:1416
Song of Hiawatha, The, VI:1416, 1862, 1863, 2370
Tales of a Wayside Inn, VI:1416
Voices of the Night, VI:1416
Longinus, Cassius, I:140, 150
Long Island, Battle of, IV:367
Long March, VII:688, 905; IX:2954, 2955
Longnon, Auguste, III:765
Long Parliament
Charles II, IV:284
Clarendon, IV:308
Lambert, IV:790
Laud, IV:799
Monck, IV:972
Pym, IV:1141-1143
Shaftesbury, IV:1228
Longus, Tiberius Sempronius, I:364
Lon Nol, IX:3419

Lono, VI:1255
Loos, Adolph, VIII:2012
Loos, Anita, **VIII:2231-2234**
  Gentlemen Prefer Blondes, VIII:2232, 2234
  His Picture in the Papers, VIII:2232
  Intolerance, VIII:2232, 2234
  Mystery of the Leaping Fish, The, VIII:2232
  New York Hat, The, VIII:2231
  Reaching for the Moon, VIII:2232
  Red-Headed Woman, VIII:2232
  Road to Plaindale, The, VIII:2231
  San Francisco, VIII:2232
  Wild and Woolly, VIII:2232
Lord, Otis Phillips, V:670
Lord Dunmore's War, IV:163, 312
Lords, House of
  Asquith, VII:122
  Beaverbrook, VII:234
  Beveridge, VII:308-311
  Brougham, V:316
  Butler, VII:531
  Byron, V:381
  Charles I, IV:281
  Constantine, VII:759, 760
  Dalhousie, V:600
  Derby, V:654
  George V, VII:1339, 1340
  Grey, V:994-996
  Lansdowne, VIII:2091
  Lawrence, VI:1332
  Lloyd George, VIII:2216
  Melbourne, VI:1517
  Pitt the Elder, IV:1099
  Pitt the Younger, IV:1102
  Pride, IV:1127
  Reith, IX:3148
  Salisbury, VI:1944, 1945
  Strafford, IV:1287
  Walpole, IV:1403
  William IV, VI:2393-2395
Lorentz, Hendrik Antoon, **VIII:2235-2237**
Lorenz, Konrad, **VIII:2238-2240**
  On Agression, VIII:2240
Lorenzetti, Ambrogio, **II:595-598**
  Good and Bad Government, II:596, 597
  Maestà, II:596
  Presentation in the Temple, II:597
  Vico l'Abate Madonna, II:595
Lorenzetti, Pietro, **II:595-598**
  Birth of the Virgin, II:596, 597
  Descent from the Cross, II:596
Lorenzo, Nicola di. *See* Rienzo, Cola di
Lorrain, Claude. *See* Claude Lorrain
Lorris, Guillaume de
  Romance of the Rose, The, II:261, 947
Los Alamos Laboratories, VII:1147, 1148; VIII:2122; IX:2833, 2834, 3632, 3633
Lot, I:5, 6
Lothar, II:239, 599-601
Lothar II, II:601, 674
Lothar III, II:466
Lotharingia, III:164, 165
Lothario of Segni. *See* Innocent III
Lotus Society, I:841
Louis II de Bourbon, Prince de Condé. *See* Condé, the Great
Louis II the German, II:239, **599-602**
Louis IV, II:235, 359
Louis VI, II:336
Louis VII, II:336-338, 732, 860, 861
Louis VIII, II:190, 603
Louis IX, **II:603-607**
  Carpini, II:208
  Crusades, II:124
  Mise of Amiens, II:454
  Montfort, II:644, 645
  Vincent of Beauvais, II:946
  William of Rubrouck, II:987, 988
Louis X, II:738
Louis XI, III:163, 164, **434-436,** 775, 776
Louis XII, III:16, 48, 49, 274, 406, 407, 683
Louis XIII, III:539; IV:273, **863-865,** 1165-1167
Louis XIV, **IV:866-870**
  Bernini, IV:119
  Boffrand, IV:151
  Bossuet, IV:171, 172
  Charles II, IV:285
  Colbert, IV:336-339
  Condé, IV:342, 343
  Couperin, IV:374
  Dover Treaty, IV:1039
  Frederick William, The Great Elector, IV:509
  George I, IV:531
  John III Sobieski, IV:726
  La Fontaine, IV:782
  Laval, IV:801, 803
  Leeds, IV:822
  Louis XIII, IV:865
  Louvois, IV:871-874
  Marie-Antoinette, IV:918-920
  Marlborough, IV:922-924
  Mazarin, IV:945-947
  Molière, IV:966, 968
  Vauban, IV:1358

Versailles Palace, IV:834-836, 901-903
Voltaire, IV:1392, 1394
William III, IV:1447, 1448
Louis XV
Marie-Antoinette, IV:919
Necker, IV:1016, 1017
Orléans, IV:1048
Rochambeau, IV:1174
Turgot, IV:1348, 1349
Louis XVI
Cambacérès, V:398
Danton, IV:393
Marat, IV:911
Marie-Antoinette, IV:919, 920
Monge, IV:977
Orléans, IV:1049, 1050
Robespierre, IV:1170, 1171
Saint-Just, IV:1205
Turgot, IV:1349
Louis XVIII, V:483; VI:1647
Louis, Joe, **VIII:2241-2245,** 2413
Louis, Morris, VII:1209
Louisiana
La Salle, IV:794, 795
Lewis and Clark, VI:1359
Long, VIII:2227-2229; IX:3894
Warren, IX:3894
See also Louisiana Purchase
Louisiana Purchase
Douglas, V:693
Jefferson, IV:719
Lewis, VI:1360
Madison, IV:888
Monroe, VI:1571
Sacagawea, VI:1933, 1934
Louis of Blois, II:943
Louis-Philippe, V:708; VI:1818, 1917, 2227
Louis the Great, II:1001
Louis the Lion. *See* Louis VIII
Louis the Pious, II:599, 600, 602, 767
Louis the Younger, II:601
Loutherbourg, Philippe Jacques de, IV:528
Louvois, Marquis de, IV:336, 338, 343, 868, 869, **871-874,** 947
Louvre, the
Apollinaire, VII:82
Cartier-Bresson, VII:595
Chagall, VII:641
Francis I, III:275
John XXIII, VIII:1854
Pei, IX:2947
Renoir, VI:1869
Lovejoy, Elijah P., V:885; VI:1772
Lovelace, Countess Ada, V:102
Low, Juliette Gordon, **VIII:2246-2248**
Low, Seth, VII:524
Low, William Mackay, VIII:2246
Lowe, George, VIII:1662-1664
Lowell, Amy, **VIII:2249-2251**
Critical Fable, A, VIII:2251
Dome of Many-Colored Glass, A, VIII:2250
Fir-Flower Tablets, VIII:2251
John Keats, VIII:2251
Legends, VIII:2251
Sword Blades and Poppy Seeds, VIII:2250
Tendencies in Modern American Poetry, VIII:2250
Lowell, James Russell, V:516, 1127
Lowell, Percival, IX:3700, 3701
Lower Creek Indians, IV:1044, 1045
Lowery, Samuel R., VI:1407
Lowie, Robert H.
Primitive Society, VIII:2164
Loyola, Saint Ignatius of, **III:437-439,** 788
Constitutions, III:438
Spiritual Exercises, The, III:437, 438
LPGA. *See* Ladies Professional Golfer's Association
LRC. *See* Labour Representation Committee
Luce, Clare Boothe, **VIII:2256-2259,** 2262
Europe in Spring, VIII:2256
Women, The, VIII:2232, 2256, 2258
Luce, Henry R., VII:395, 397; VIII:2256, **2260-2264**
Lu Chiu-yüan, II:266
Lucian, **I:507-510,** 622
Carousal, The, I:507
Dialogues of the Dead, I:507
Dialogues of the Gods, I:507, 509
Philosophies for Sale, I:508
True Story, A, I:508
Lucius, I:762
Lucius III, II:359
Lucknow Pact, VIII:1847, 1848; IX:3683, 3684
Lucretius, **I:511-514**
Democritus, I:251
On the Nature of Things, I:296, 511-513
Lucullus, Lucius, I:559
Ludendorff, Erich, **VIII:2265-2268**
Ludlow, Daniel, IV:721
Ludlow, J.M., VI:1504
Ludlow Massacre, VIII:1881
Ludwig II, VI:2317, 2319
Ludwig IV, II:682

Ludwig, Nikolaus. *See* Zinzendorf, Graf von
Luft, Sidney, VII:1305
Lufthansa, VIII:1615
Luftwaffe, VIII:1439-1441, 1949, 1950, 2262
Lugard, Lord, **VIII:2269-2271**
  Dual Mandate in British Tropical Africa, The, VIII:2270
Lugdunum, I:447
Lu Hsün, **VIII:2252-2255**
  "Diary of a Madman, The," VIII:2252
  "True Story of Ah Q, The," VIII:2252
Luis, Don, IV:148
Lukács, György, **VIII:2272-2275**
  Goethe and His Age, VIII:2273
  History and Class Consciousness, VII:268; VIII:2272, 2274
  Lenin, VIII:2273
  Soul and Form, VIII:2272, 2274
  Studies in European Realism, VIII:2273
Luke, Gospel of, I:467-469
  Bossuet, IV:170
  Harnack, VIII:1558
  John the Baptist, I:478
  Origen, I:583
  Ritschl, VI:1892
  Stephen, I:822-824
  Virgin Mary, I:939
Lull, Raymond, **II:608-611**
  Ars generalis ultima, II:609
  Blanquerna, II:609, 610
  Book of Contemplation, II:608
Lumière, Auguste, **VIII:2276-2280**
Lumière, Louis, **VIII:2276-2280**
  Arrivée du train en gare, L', VIII:2278
  Workers Leaving the Lumiére Factory, VIII:2278
Lumumba, Patrice, VII:633; VIII:2562, 2563; IX:3745-3747
Luna 2, VIII:2021
Lunar Society, IV:183
Lundula, Victor, VIII:2562
Lundy's Lane, Battle of, VI:2010, 2011
Lunéville, Château, IV:151, 152
Lunt, Alfred, VII:786, 794
Lu Pu-wei, I:176, 177
Luria, Issac ben Solomon, **III:440-442**
Luscombe Castle, IV:1013
Lutetia, I:257
Luther, Martin, **III:443-447**
  Aristippus, I:87
  Bucer, III:101, 103
  Calvin, III:117, 118, 120
  Charles V, III:159
  Commentary on St. Paul's Epistle to the Galations, IV:218
  Cranach, Lucas, the Elder, III:202
  Erasmus, III:248
  Fisher, III:264, 265
  Henry VIII, III:68, 351
  Marguerite of Navarre, III:467
  Melanchthon, III:503-505
  Zwingli, III:791-794
  See also Protestant Reformation
Lutheranism. *See* Luther, Martin; Protestant Reformation
Lutuli, Albert, **VIII:2272-2275**
Lützen, Battle of, IV:591, 1052, 1397
Luxembourg, Palace of, IV:898
Luxembourg Commission, V:261
Luxemburg, Rosa, VII:292; **VIII:2285-2288;** IX:4113, 4114
  Accumulation of Capital, The, VIII:2286
  Crisis in the German Social Democracy, The, VIII:2287
  Mass Strike, The, VIII:2286
  Reform or Revolution?, VIII:2285
  Russian Revolution, The, VIII:2286
Luxemburger family, II:969, 970
Luzon, Battle of, VIII:2297
Lwoff, André, VIII:1827-1829
Lyceum, I:94-96, 98, 260, 873
Lyceum Theatre, V:1190; VI:2216
Lycurgus, I:14
Lyell, Sir Charles, V:608; **VI:1418-1422**
  Elements of Geology, VI:1420
  Geological Evidences of the Antiquity of Man, The, VI:1421
  Principles of Geology, VI:1419-1421
  Second Visit to the United States of North America, VI:1420
  Travels in North America, VI:1420
Lyly, John, III:693
Lynceus, I:703
Lyne, Sir William, V:149
Lyon, Mary, **VI:1423-1426**
Lyons, Council of, II:165, 514-516, 531, 899, 900, 985
Lyons, Dame Enid Muriel, VIII:1777, **2289-2291,** 2292, 2293
Lyons, Israel, IV:83
Lyons, Joseph Aloysius, VIII:2289-2291, **2292-2294,** 2497
Lysander, I:16, 32
Lysandrus, I:716

Lysenko, Trofim Denisovitch, VIII:2652; IX:3802, 3803
Lysimachus, I:716
Lysippus, **I:515-518**
Apoxyomenos, I:516

Maastricht summit, VIII:2370
Ma'at, I:734
Mabou Mines, VII:34, 35
Macapagal, Diosadado, VIII:2421
Macaulay, Thomas Babington, **VI:1427-1430,** 1558
Critical and Historical Essays, VI:1429
History of England, The, VI:1427, 1429
Lays of Ancient Rome, VI:1429
McCall, Jack, V:391
MacArthur, Charles, VIII:1588, 1589, 1591
MacArthur, Douglas, **VIII:2295-2299**
Acheson, VII:18
Akihito, VII:41
Bradley, VII:405
Curtin, VII:817
Eisenhower, VII:1043
Halsey, VIII:1527
Hirohito, VIII:1680, 1681
Hoover, VIII:1730
Nimitz, VIII:2750-2752
Rhee, IX:3165
Truman, IX:3742, 3743
Macarthur, James, VI:2356
MacArthur, Mary, VII:353, 354, 357
MacCallum, William, IX:3248
McCarthy, Eugene, VIII:1784, 1785, 1934; IX:2825
McCarthy, Joseph R., **VIII:2300-2303**
Acheson, VII:18
Eisenhower, VII:1045
Hiss, VIII:1685
Kennedy, John F., VIII:1928
Kennedy, Robert F., VIII:1933
Lippmann, VIII:2205
Luce, VIII:2263
Murrow, VIII:2664, 2665
Smith's "Declaration of Conscience" speech, IX:3447
Stevenson, IX:3524
Taft, IX:3592
Truman, IX:3742
McCarthy, Justin Huntly, III:765, 766
McCarthy, Mary, **VIII:2304-2307**
Birds of America, VIII:2306
Cannibals and Missionaries, VIII:2306
Charmed Life, A, VIII:2304
Company She Keeps, The, VIII:2304
Group, The, VIII:2304, 2306
Groves of Academe, The, VIII:2304
Ideas and the Novel, VIII:2306
Mary McCarthy's Theatre Chronicles, VIII:2306
Memories of a Catholic Girlhood, VIII:2304, 2306
Oasis, The, VIII:2304
Sights and Spectacles, VIII:2306
Stones of Florence, The, VIII:2306
Venice Observed, VIII:2306
McCartney, Paul, VII:226-229
McClellan, George, V:1205; VI:1340, 2107
McClure's, VII:623, 624; IX:3614, 3616
McCormick, Cyrus Hall, **VI:1431-1434**
McCormick Seminary, VI:1432
McCullers, Carson, **VIII:2308-2311;** IX:3061
"Ballad of the Sad Café," VIII:2310
Clock Without Hands, VIII:2310
Heart is a Lonely Hunter, The, VIII:2308, 2310
Member of the Wedding, The, VIII:2310, 2311
Mortgaged Heart, The, VIII:2310
Reflections in a Golden Eye, VIII:2308, 2310
Sights and Spectacles, VIII:2308
Square Root of Wonderful, The, VIII:2310
"Sucker," VIII:2308
Macdonald, Sir John Alexander, **VI:1435-1439**
MacDonald, Ramsay, **VIII:2312-2316**
Angell, VII:75, 76
Attlee, VII:137
Baldwin, VII:170
Bevin, VII:314
Bondfield, VII:356
Bottomley, VII:384
Chamberlain, VII:644
George V, VII:1340, 1341
McDowell, Irvin, V:1205
Macedonia
Alexander the Great, I:38, 40
Antigonus I Monophthalmos, I:60, 61
Basil the Macedonian, II:117-119
Bulgarian Empire, II:175
Cato the Censor, I:164
Demosthenes, I:253-255
Philip II of Macedonia, I:628-630
Ptolemy Philadelphus, I:716
Ptolemy Soter, I:720-722
Scipio Aemilianus, I:757
Stefan Dusan, II:844
Theophrastus, I:873

Macedonian, V:636
McGillivray, Alexander, **IV:875-878**
McGovern, George, VIII:1995, 2759
McGuffey, William Holmes, **VI:1440-1443**
Eclectic Readers, VI:1440-1442
Machado de Assis, Joachim Maria, **VI:1444-1446**
Counselor Ayres' Memorial, VI:1445
Dom Casmurro, VI:1445
Epitaph of a Small Winner, VI:1445
Esau and Jacob, VI:1445
Iaia Garcia, VI:1445
Philosopher or Dog?, VI:1445
Machaut, Guillaume de, **II:615-618**
Bone pastor Guillerme, II:615
Dit dou Vergier, Le, II:617
Fonteinne amoureuse, La, II:616
Messe de Nostre Dame, La, II:616
Remède de Fortune, II:615, 617
Voir-Dit, Le, II:616, 617
Machel, Samora Moisès, **VIII:2317-2320**
McHenry, Fort, VI:1282
Machiavelli, Niccolò, III:208, 325, 326, **448-452**
Art of War, The, III:450
Discourses on the First Ten Books of Titus Livius, III:450
Florentine History, The, III:450
Mandrake, The, III:450
Prince, The, III:208, 296, 347, 450, 451
Machu Picchu, III:578
Mackenzie, Sir Alexander, **IV:879-881**
Voyages, IV:880, 881
Mackenzie, Henry, IV:231
Mackenzie, William Lyon, V:116, 117; **VI:1447-1452,** 1496-1498; VIII:1981
Mackenzie Rebellion, V:117
Mackenzie River, IV:879, 881
Mackinder, Sir Halford John, **VIII:2321-2324**
Britain and the British Seas, VIII:2321
Democratic Ideals and Reality, VIII:2321, 2322
McKinley, William, **VI:1453-1456**
Bryan, VII:480, 481
Goldman, VIII:1412
Hanna, V:1029-1031
Hay, V:1069
Hearst, VIII:1603
Roosevelt, IX:3229
Root, IX:3232
McKinley Tariff Act, VI:1374, 1453; VIII:1498, 2047
MacKinnon, Catharine A., **VIII:2325-2328**
Only Words, VIII:2326
Sexual Harassment of Working Women, VIII:2325
Macklin, Charles, IV:527
McLaughlin, James, VI:2072
Maclaurin, Colin, **IV:882-885**
Geometria Organica, IV:882
Treatise of Fluxions, IV:883, 884
McLaury family, V:736
McLean, Louis, VI:2191-2193
MacLeish, Archibald, VIII:2662
Macleod, John J.R., VII:188, 189; **VIII:2329-2331**
McLuhan, Marshall, **VIII:2332-2335**
Gutenberg Galaxy, The, VIII:2332
Mechanical Bride, The, VIII:2332
Understanding Media, VIII:2333
Macmillan, Alexander and Daniel, **VI:1457-1459**
McMillan, Edwin M., VIII:2122, 2123
Macmillan, Harold, VII:1063; VIII:1607, **2340-2344;** IX:3649
Industry and the State, VIII:2341
Middle Way, The, VIII:2341
Reconstruction, VIII:2341
Macmillan and Company, VI:1457-1459
Macmillan's Magazine, VI:1459
McNamara, James B. and John J., VII:839
MacPherson v. Buick Motor Company, VII:576
Macquarie, Luchlan, V:991, 992
McRae, Milton, VI:2015
Macready, William Charles, V:801, 802; **VI:1460-1463**
Macro, Naevius Cordus Sutorius, I:153, 154
McShann, Jay, IX:2882
Macy, John, VIII:1924, 1926
Madama, Villa, III:645
Mademoiselle magazine, IX:3036
Maderno, Carlo, IV:167, 168
Madero, Francisco, VII:571; **VIII:2345-2348;** IX:2836, 3811, 4104, 4106
partido nacional Antireeleccionista y la proxima lucha, El, VIII:2347
Presidential Succession in 1910, The, VIII:2345, 2347
Madinat al-Zahra', II:8
Madison, Dolley, **VI:1464-1466,** 1570
Madison, James, **IV:886-890**
Federalist Papers, The, IV:610, 666, 886
Jefferson, IV:718, 719
Jeffrey, V:1226
Madison, Dolley, IV:1464-1466
Marbury v. Madison, IV:296; VI:1488
Morris, IX:1000
pocket veto, V:1198

Madot, Jean, II:25
Madrid Riots, IV:287, 288
Maeandrius, I:705
Maecenas, Gaius, I:21, **519-522,** 702, 926, 928
Maenad, I:765
Mafeking, V:106
Maffia, VII:259
Magas, I:304
Magellan, Ferdinand, **III:453-456**
Magellan, Strait of, III:453-456
Magendie, François, V:207, 208
Maghrib, II:4, 5
Magna Carta, II:329, 453, 455, 540-542, 716
magnetism
  Becquerel, V:166-168
  Gay-Lussac, V:897
  Kelvin, VI:1270
  Néel, VIII:2705-2707
  Peregrinus de Maricourt, II:719-721
  von Guericke, IV:586-588
Magnum Concilium. *See* Great Council
Magnum Photos, VII:595
Magnus, Pompeius, I:551
Magritte, René, **VIII:2349-2354**
  Condition humaine I, La, VIII:2352
  jockey perdu, Le, VIII:2351
  Song of Love, The, VIII:2351
  Valeurs personelles, VIII:2352
Magyars, II:86, 706-708
Mahan, Alfred Thayer, IX:3688
Mahayana Buddhism, I:494-496, 949; II:483, 484
Mahfouz, Naguib, **VIII:2355-2358**
  'Abath al-aqdar, VIII:2355
  Children of Gebelawi, VIII:2356, 2357
  Fountain and Tomb, VIII:2356
  Kifah Tiba, VIII:2355
  Midaq Alley, VIII:2356
  Radubis, VIII:2355
  That al-mazalla, VIII:2357
  Thief in Search of His Identity, A, VIII:2357
  Thulathiyya, Al-, VIII:2356, 2257
Mahler, Alma, VIII:2013
Mahler, Gustav, **VIII:2359-2364;** IX:3357
  Kindertotenlieder, VIII:2362
  klagende Lied, Das, VIII:2359, 2361
  Lied von der Erde, Die, VIII:2362, 2363
  Songs of a Wayfarer, VIII:2361
Mahmud, II:350, 351
Mahmud II, VI:1604, 1606
Maiden, Stewart, VIII:1874
Mailer, Norman, **VIII:2365-2368,** 2537, 2589
  Advertisements for Myself, VIII:2365
  American Dream, An, VIII:2365, 2366
  Ancient Evenings, VIII:2367
  Armies of the Night, The, VIII:2366
  Barbary Shore, VIII:2365
  Cannibals and Christians, VIII:2366
  Deer Park, The, VIII:2365
  Executioner's Song, The, VIII:2367
  Faith of Graffiti, The, VIII:2366
  Gospel According to the Son, The, VIII:2367
  Harlot's Ghost, VIII:2367
  Marilyn, VIII:2366
  Naked and the Dead, The, VIII:2365
  Oswald's Tale: An American Mystery, VIII:2367
  Portrait of Picasso as a Young Man, VIII:2367
  Presidential Papers, The, VIII:2365, 2366
  Prisoner of Sex, The, VIII:2366
  Time of Our Time, The, VIII:2367
  Tough Guys Don't Dance, VIII:2367
  White Negro, The, VIII:2365
  Why Are We in Vietnam, VIII:2366
Maimonides, Moses, **II:619-622,** 648, 781
  Code of Maimonides, The, II:620
  Guide of the Perplexed, II:620
  Illumination, The, II:620
  Letter Concerning Apostasy, II:619
Maitland, William, II:130
Majd al-Din al-Jili, II:347
Majestas Carolina, II:236, 237
Major, John, **VIII:2369-2372**
Ma-ka-tai-me-she-kia-kiak. *See* Black Hawk
Makhpiya-Lúta. *See* Red Cloud
Malacca, III:12
Malachus. *See* Porphyry
Malatestano, Tempio, III:9
Malcolm III, II:291
Malcolmson, Alex, VII:1186
Malcolm X, **VIII:2373-2376**
  Autobiography of Malcolm X, The, VIII:2373, 2376
Malenkov, Georgi M., VIII:1961, 1962, **2377-2379;** IX:4118, 4119
Malevich, Kasimir, VII:639
Malgrange I, IV:152
Malgrange II, IV:152
Malian Empire, II:863-865
Malik ibn Anas, II:33
Malik Shah, II:677-679, 695
Malinowski, Bronislaw, VIII:2164, 2165
Mallarmé, Stéphane, V:890; VII:1367; IX:3791
Malmesbury Abbey, II:824

Malory, Sir Thomas, **III:457-459**
Morte d' Arthur, Le, III:457, 458; V:161; VI:2213; IX:3515
Malouine Islands, IV:179
Malpighi, Marcello, IV:826, **891-893**
Anatome plantarum, IV:891
De bombyce, IV:891, 893
De cerebro, IV:891
De ovo incubato, IV:891
De pulmonibus observationes anatomicae, IV:891
De viscerum structura exercitatio anatomica, IV:891
Dissertatio epistolica de formatione pulli in ovo, IV:891
Malplaquet, Battle of, IV:924
Malraux, André, **VIII:2380-2383**
Anti-Memoirs, VIII:2382
Conquerors, The, VIII:2380, 2381
Lunes en papier, VIII:2380
Man's Fate, VIII:2380-2382
Man's Hope, VIII:2380, 2381
Malthus, Thomas Robert, V:458; **VI:1467-1470,** 1562, 1879
Essay on the Principle of Population, An, V:606; VI:1467, 1468, 1787
Malves, Gua de, IV:31
Mamluk Dynasty, II:124-126, 382, 383
Manchester Guardian, VIII:1708, 1709
Manchester Literary and Philosophical Society, V:603
Manchukuo, IX:3879
Manchu Dynasty. *See* Ch'ing Dynasty
Mandate of Heaven, I:544; IV:422
Mandela, Nelson, VII:871, 872; VIII:2281-2283, **2384-2388**
Mandelstam, Osip, IX:2900
Mandeville, Bernard de
Fable of the Bees, VI:1458
Mandigo peoples, II:863-865
Manet, Édouard, III:313; V:453; **VI:1471-1475;** VIII:2579
Absinthe Drinker, The, VI:1472
Bar at the Folies-Bergère, A, VI:1473
Déjeuner sur l'herbe, VI:1472, 1473
Execution of Maximilian, IV:572
Good Glass of Beer, The, VI:1473
Luncheon on the Grass, VI:1780
Olympia, VI:1472, 1473
Rue Mosnier with Powers, The, VI:1473
Spanish Singer, The, VI:1472
Manetho
Aegyptica, I:547, 548
Mangu, II:566, 988
Manhattan Company, Bank of the, V:370, 372
Manhattan Project
Bridgman, VII:464
Compton, VII:747
Kurchatov, VIII:2040
McMillan, VIII:2337
Neumann, VIII:2725
Seaborg, IX:3376
Stimson, IX:3539
Teller, IX:3632
Wilkins, IX:3995
Manichaeanism, I:694-696; II:511
Manifest Destiny
Adler, V:27
Cooper, V:564
Gray, V:979
Polk, VI:1802
Taylor, VI:2196
Manila Bay, Battle of, V:656-658
Manilius, III:672
Manitoba, VI:1437
Mankiller, Wilma P., **VIII:2389-2391**
Mankiller: A Chief and Her People, VIII:2390
Manly, Charles, VI:1314
Mann, Horace, **IV:894-897**
Mann, Thomas, VIII:2274, **2392-2395**
Beloved Returns, The, VIII:2393
Betrachtungen eines Unpolitischen, VIII:2393
Buddenbrooks, VIII:2392, 2393
Confessions of Felix Krull, VIII:2394
Death in Venice, VIII:2392
Disorder and Early Sorrow, VIII:2393
Doctor Faustus, VIII:2393
"Fallen," VIII:2392
Joseph and His Brothers, VIII:2393
Magic Mountain, The, VIII:2393
Royal Highness, VIII:2392
Tonio Kröger, VIII:2392
Transposed Heads, The, VIII:2393
Mannerheim, Carl Gustaf, **VIII:2396-2399**
mannerism
Andrea del Sarto, III:24, 26
Carracci Family, III:125-127
Correggio, III:186
Greco, El, III:311-313
Tintoretto, III:717, 719, 720
Veronese, III:747
Mannheim National Theater, IV:1217
Manning, Henry Edward, **VI:1476-1479**

Mannix, Danile, **VI:1480-1482**
Manox, Henry, III:367
Mansa Musa, **II:623-625**
Mansart, François, **IV:898-900,** 901
Mansart, Jules Hardouin-, IV:151, 900, **901-903**
Mansa Uli, II:864
Mansfield, First Earl of, **IV:904-909**
Mansfield-Fondi Palace, IV:656
Manson, Sir Patrick, IX:3248, 3249
Manstein, Erich von, IX:3261
Mantegna, Andrea, III:58-60, **460-463**
Madonna Enthroned with Saints, III:461
Madonna of the Victory, III:462
Martyrdom of Saint James, III:461
Saint James Baptizing Hermogenes, III:461
Saint James Before Herod Agrippa, III:461
Saint James Led to Execution, III:461
Triumph of Caesar, III:462
Mantinea, I:293
Manuel I, III:11-13, **464-466,** 759
Manutius, Aldus, III:246
Manzikert, Battle of, II:69, 70
Manzoni, Alessandro, **VI:1483-1486**
Adelchi, VI:1484
Betrothed, The, VI:1483-1485
Maori people, VI:2322
Maori Wars, V:380, 998-1000
Mao Tse-tung, **VIII:2400-2403**
Ch'en Tu-hsiu, VII:662
Chiang Kai-shek, VII:666
Ch'in Shih Huang-ti, I:178
Chou En-lai, VII:677
Chu Teh, VII:688, 689
Deng Xiaoping, VII:905, 906
Hung Hsiu-ch'üan, V:1165, 1167
Kuo Mo-jo, VIII:2034
"Let a Hundred Flowers Bloom," VIII:2401
Lin Piao, VIII:2189-2191
Liu Shao-ch'i, VIII:2212-2214
Marx, VI:1494
Nixon, VIII:2760
P'eng Te-huai, IX:2954-2956
Mapai Party, VII:252, 253
Marat, Jean-Paul, **IV:910-913**
Ami du Peuple, L', IV:911
Chains of Slavery, IV:910
Plan of Criminal Legislation, IV:910
Maratha kingdom, IV:1246-1248
Maratha wars, IV:632, 633
Marathon, Battle of
Aeschylus, I:10
Darius the Great, I:238
Herodotus, I:396
Leonidas, I:501
Miltiades the Younger, I:553-555
Pheidippides, I:621-623
Phidias, I:624
Polygnotus, I:676
Simonides, I:788
Themistocles, I:857
Marble, Alice, VII:1363
Marburg, Colloquy of, III:102, 793
Marburg, University of, VII:614; IX:3918
Marbury v. Madison, IV:296; VI:1488
Marc, Franz, VII:1098; **VIII:2404-2406**
"Brücke, Die,"VIII:2405
Dead Sparrow, The, VIII:2404
Deer in the Woods, VIII:2405
Fate of Animals, VIII:2405, 2406
Fighting Forms, VIII:2405
Horse in Landscape, VIII:2405
Improvisation No. 30, VIII:2405
Tiger, The, VIII:2405
Tower of Blue Horses, VIII:2405
Yellow Corn, VIII:2405
Marcel, Gabriel, **VIII:2407-2410**
Existential Background of Human Dignity, The, VIII:2408
Homo Viator, VIII:2407
Men Against Humanity, VIII:2409
Metaphysical Journal, VIII:2407, 2409
Mystery of Being, The, VIII:2408
"On the Ontological Mystery," VIII:2407
Marcellina, I:43
Marcellinus, Ammianus, I:780
Marcellus, Claudius, I:335, 336
Marcet, Jane
Conversations on Chemistry, V:767
March, Fredric, VII:117, 119
Marchand, Jean-Baptiste, VIII:2002; IX:3730, 3731
Märchenoper, V:1163, 1164
March to the Sea, VI:2060; VIII:2710
Marciano, Rocky, VIII:2244, **2411-2414**
Marcion, I:582
Marconi, Guglielmo, VI:1807, 1808; **VIII:2415-2419**
Marconi Company, VIII:2217
Marco Polo. *See* Polo, Marco
Marcos, Ferdinand E., VII:86-88; **VIII:2420-2424**
"First-Quarter Storm," VIII:2421
Marcus Aurelius, **I:523-526**
Meditations, I:523, 525, 526
Marduk, I:234, 328

Marenzio, Luca, IV:990
Marfan's law, VII:547
Margaret of Anjou, III:341, 647, 774, 775
Margaret of Denmark, Norway, and Sweden, **II:626-628**
Margaret of Scotland, Saint, II:291
Marguerite of Navarre, **III:467-470,** 634
Heptameron, III:468, 469
Mirror of the Sinful Soul, The, III:594
Prisons, III:470
Mari, I:360, 362
Mariamne, I:391
Mariano Filipepi, Alessandro di. *See* Botticelli, Sandro
Maria Theresa, IV:504, 750, 751, **914-917,** 918
Marie-Antoinette, IV:915, **918-921,** 1376, 1378
Marie de France, **II:629-631**
Espurgatoire Seint Patriz, L', II:630
Fables, II:629-631
Lays, The, II:629-631
Marie Louise, IV:725, 726
Marignano, Battle of, III:274
Marine Band, IX:3466, 3467
Marine Corps. *See* United States Marine Corps
Marinetti, Emilio Filippo, VII:342, 343
Marinus of Tyre, I:713
Marion Daily Star, VIII:1550, 1552
Maritain, Jacques, VII:1377; **VIII:2425-2428**
Antimoderne, VIII:2426
Art and Scholasticism, VIII:2426
Bergsonian Philosophy and Thomism, VIII:2426
Christianity and Democracy, VIII:2427
Existence and the Existent, VIII:2426
Man and the State, VIII:2427
Peasant of the Garonne, The, VIII:2427
Person and the Common Good, The, VIII:2427
Scholasticism and Politics, VIII:2426
Things That Are Not Caesar's, The, VIII:2427
Three Reformers: Luther, Descartes, Rousseau, VIII:2426
Marius, Gaius, I:147, 347, **528-531,** 686, 743, 833, 834
Mark, Gospel of, I:467-469; VIII:1558
Marlborough, Duchess of, IV:50, 52, 53
Marlborough, First Duke of, IV:50, 52, 157, 158, 533, **922-925,** 1277
Marlowe, Christopher, **III:471-474**
Amores, III:471, 473
Dido Queen of Carthage, III:471, 473
Doctor Faustus, III:472, 473; IV:562
Edward II, III:472
Hero and Leander, III:473
Jew of Malta, The, III:472
Massacre at Paris, The, III:472, 473
Tamburlaine the Great, III:471, 472
Tamburlaine the Great, Part 2, III:472
Marly-le-Roi, Château de, IV:902
Marne, Battle of the, VIII:1851-1853
Maroto, Rafael, V:414
Marquette, Father Jacques, IV:732-734
marriage
Akiba, I:29
Anthony, V:62
Blackwell, V:251
canon law, II:50
Catullus, I:170
Chopin, V:499
Christine de Pizan, II:262
Epicurus, I:296
Fourier, V:816
Goldman, VIII:1412
Greene, VIII:1468
Henry II the Saint, II:451
Innocent III, II:510
Kinsey, VIII:1986
Lockwood, VI:1408
Millett, VIII:2536
polygamy, VI:2081, 2415, 2416
Pythagoreans, I:728
Sand, VI:1954
Stone, VI:2145
Theoleptus of Philadelphia, II:899, 900
Vanbrugh, IV:1351
Wollstonecraft, IV:1478
Marshall, Alfred, IX:3867
Marshall, Arthur, V:1240
Marshall, George C., **VIII:2429-2432**
Bradley, VII:404
Chiang Kai-shek, VII:666
Chu Teh, VII:689
Eisenhower, VII:1043, 1045
Hopkins, VIII:1737, 1739
Marshall Plan, VII:315; VIII:1529, 1562, 1696, 2205, 2258, 2431; IX:3862
Patton, IX:2913
Pershing, IX:2985
Marshall, John, **VI:1487-1491,** 2147-2149, 2191, 2192
Marshall, Thurgood, **VIII:2433-2436**
Marshall Field and Company, V:783, 785, 786; VI:1883, 1884, 2331; VII:1266
Marshall Plan
Bevin, VII:315

Hammarskjöld, VIII:1529
Harriman, VIII:1562
Hitler, VIII:1696
Lippmann, VIII:2205
Luce, VIII:2258
Marshall, VIII:2431
Wallace, IX:3862
Marsilius of Padua, II:683
Marston, John, III:156
Martial, **I:532-534**
On the Spectacles, I:532
Martin, Agnes, **VIII:2437-2439**
Martin, David, VI:1836
Martin, George, VII:226
Martin, Joe Elsby, VII:53
Martin, Pierre-Émile, VI:2067
Martinelli, Caterina, IV:992
Martinez Sierra, Gregorio
Cradle Song, The, VIII:2143
Martini, Simone, II:307, **632-635**
Annunciation, II:634
Guidoriccio da Fogliano, II:634
Madonna, II:633
Maestà, II:632, 633
Saint Louis of Toulouse, II:633
Martin of Tours, I:695; II:403-405
Martinsberg monastery, II:851
Martin v. Hunter's Lessee, VI:2147
martyrs
Anthony of Padua, II:76
Becket, II:128-130
bishops of Rome, I:257, 258
Christopher, I:180, 182
Hallaj, al-, II:423
Hus, II:487
Ignatius of Antioch, I:440-442
Joan of Arc, III:396, 398, 399
Montfort, II:646
Origen, I:581, 582
Pamphilus, I:322
Paul, I:605
Peter, I:616
Ridley, III:655, 656
Stephen, I:822-824
Tertullian, I:848
Maru-aton, I:24
Marville, Jean de, II:832
Mary (Virgin). *See* Virgin Mary
Mary I (of England), III:238, 239, 318, 319, **479-482**
Mary II (of England), IV:922, 923
Mary of Modena, IV:50, 52, 553
Mary, Queen of Scots, **III:475-478**
Catherine de Médicis, III:132
Cecil, III:147, 148
Elizabeth I, III:243
Tudor family, III:733
Marx, Karl, **VI:1492-1495**
Bakunin, V:112-114
Blanc, V:261
Brecht, VII:444, 445
Communist Manifesto, The, V:761, 1057; VI:1324, 1493
Contribution to a Critique of Political Economy, A, VI:1370; VIII:2034
Critique of the Gotha Program, VI:1370
Economic and Philosophic Manuscripts of 1844, VI:1493
Engels, V:760-762
George, V:908
German Ideology, The, VI:1370; VIII:2034
Kapital, Das, V:762; VI:1493, 2322; VII:160, 291
Lassalle, VI:1324, 1325
London, VIII:2226
Morgan, VI:1584
Proudhon, VI:1818, 1819
Stalin, IX:3482-3484
Veblen, IX:3806
Wilson, IX:4014
Marx Brothers, VII:288
Marxism. *See* communism; Marx, Karl
Masaccio, **III:483-486,** 517
Expulsion from Paradise, The, III:484
Holy Trinity with the Virgin and Saint John, III:485
Madonna and Child, III:483, 484, 744, 745
Madonna and Child with Saint Anne and Angels, III:483
Tribute Money, The, III:484, 485
Masada, I:483-486
Ma San-po. *See* Cheng Ho
Masaryk, Tomás, VII:259, 260; **VIII:2440-2443**
Ceská otázka, VIII:2440
philosophischen und sociologischen Grundlagen des Marxismus, Die, VIII:2440
Spirit of Russia, The, VIII:2440
Suicide and the Meaning of Civilization, VIII:2440
Masina, Giulietta, VII:1141-1143
Masinissa, **I:535-537,** 761
Masmuda tribes, II:5
Mason, Charlotte Osgood, VIII:1788
Mason, George, **IV:926-929**
Extracts from the Virginia Charters, IV:926

Scheme for Replevying Goods and Distress for Rent, IV:926
Mason, James, VII:1305
Mason, Perry, VII:1297-1299
Mason, William, VI:2230
Massachusetts
Adams, John, IV:16, 18, 19
Adams, Samuel, IV:21-24
Arnold, IV:64
Bancroft, V:124, 125
Bradstreet, IV:193
Cotton, IV:371
Eliot, IV:435, 437, 438
Hancock, IV:613, 615-618
Hutchinson, Anne, IV:687-689
Hutchinson, Thomas, IV:691-693
Mather, Cotton, IV:934-937
Mather, Increase, IV:938-941
O'Neill, IX:2824
Plymouth Colony, IV:191
Richardson's architecture, VI:1882-1884
Sacco and Vanzetti, IX:3283
Shays, IV:1239
Winthrop, IV:1463-1465
Massachusetts Anti-Slavery Society, VI:1771, 2143, 2265
Massachusetts Bay Government Act, IV:616
Massachusetts General Court, IV:617
Massachusetts Institute of Technology
Aalto, VII:3
Candela, VII:557
Chomsky, VII:673
Eliot, V:748
Jakobson, VIII:1832, 1833
Ravi, IX:3102
Wiener, IX:3976, 3977
Woodward, IX:4052
Massachusetts Quarterly Review, The, VI:1728
Massachusetts Suffrage Association, VI:2044
Massagetae, I:234
Massalia, I:731
Massasoit, **IV:930-933,** 954, 955, 1274
Massera, Giuseppe, VII:835
Massey, Vincent, **VI:1496-1499**
Massey, William Ferguson, **VIII:2444-2447**
Massine, Léonide, VII:833, 1177; **VIII:2448-2451**
Boutique fantasque, La, VIII:2449
Choréartium, VIII:2450
Femmes de bonne humeur, Les, VIII:2449
Matelots, Les, VIII:2450
Parade, VIII:2449
Pas d'acier, Les, VIII:2450
Présages, Les, VIII:2450
Rite of Spring, The, VIII:2449, 2450
Russian and Ludmilla, VIII:2448
Soleil de nuit, VIII:2449
Symphonie fantastique, VIII:2450
Tricorne, Le, VIII:2449
Zéphere et Flore, VIII:2449, 2450
Massinger, Philip, III:56
Masson, André, VII:1359
Mastai-Ferretti, Giovanni Maria. *See* Pius IX
Masterman, C.F.G., VII:383
Masters, Edgar Lee, VII:954
Masterson, Bat, V:736
Masters Tournament, VIII:1877; IX:3041, 3042, 4050
Mästlin, Michael, IV:772
Mas'udi, al-, **II:636-638**
Kitab al-Tanbih w'al-Ishraf, II:636
Muruj al-Dhahab wa-Ma'adin al-Jawhar, II:636
Masurian Lakes, Battle of the, VIII:1675
Matabele rebellion, VI:1875
Matchmaker's Union, V:212
Mather, Cotton, IV:372, **934-937;** IX:2893, 2894
Bonifacious, IV:936
Christian Philosopher, IV:936
Magnalia Christi Americana, IV:935
Mather, Increase, IV:934, 936, **938-941**
Cases of Conscience Concerning Evil Spirits, IV:940
Essay for the Recording of Illustrious Providences, An, IV:940
Mather, Richard, IV:938
Mathiapoulos, Margarita, VII:429
Matignon Agreements, VII:336
Matisse, Henri, VII:431; **VIII:2452-2456;** IX:3333
Dance and Music, VIII:2454
Decorative Figure, VIII:2454
Desserte, La, VIII:2452
Harmony in Red, VIII:2454
Luxe, Calm et Volupté, VIII:2452
Red Studio, The, VIII:2454
Woman with the Hat, VIII:2454
Matsudaira Takechiyo. *See* Tokugawa Ieyasu
Matsuo Basho, **IV:942-944**
Manuscript in My Knapsack, IV:943
Monkey's Raincoat, IV:943
Narrow Road to the Deep North, The, IV:943
Records of a Weather-Exposed Skeleton, The, IV:942
Saga nikki, IV:943
Visit to the Kashima Shrine, A, IV:943

Matsushita, Konosuke, **VIII:2457-2460**
Matsushita Electric Company, VIII:2457-2459
Matthew, Gospel of
  Harnack, VIII:1558
  Herod the Great, I:392
  Jesus Christ, I:467-469
  John the Apostle, I:475
  Origen, I:583
  Peter, I:616
  Virgin Mary, I:939
Matthews, James Newton, V:714
Matthews, William, III:457
Matthias I, Corvinus, III:376, **487-490**
Maud, II:847-849
Maudslay, Henry, VI:1624
Maugham, W. Somerset
  Catalina, IV:269
Maulawiyah Sufism, II:800, 801
Mau Mau Rebellion, VIII:1937, 1938, 2146, 2147, 2774
Maupassant, Guy de, V:798; **VI:1500-1502**
  "Boule de Suif," VI:1500, 1501
  "Hand, The," VI:1500
  "Horla, The," VI:1501
  "Madame Tellier's Establishment," VI:1500
  "Maison Tellier, La," VI:1501
  "Necklace, The," VI:1501
  Pierre and Jean, VI:1501
  Woman's Life, A, VI:1500
Maurice, Frederick Denison, VI:1457, 1458, **1503-1506**
  Kingdom of Christ, The, VI:1504
  Prophets and Kings of the Old Testament, VI:1458
  Subscription No Bondage, VI:1504
  Theological Essays, VI:1505
Maurice of Nassau, III:575; IV:590, 1335
Maurier, George du, VI:2366
Maurras, Charles, VIII:2425-2427
Maury, James, IV:647
Maury, Matthew Fontaine, **VI:1507-1510**
  New Theoretical and Practical Treatise on Navigation, A, VI:1507
  Physical Geography of the Sea, VI:1509
  Wind and Current Chart of the North Atlantic, VI:1508
Mauryan dynasty, I:112
Mauss, Marcel, VIII:2164
Maxentius, Marcus Aurelius Valerius, I:226, 227, 339, 340
Maximian, I:226
Maximianus, I:265, 266
Maximilian I, III:159, 406, 407, **491-494,** 682, 683
Maximilian, Ferdinand, V:1252, 1253
Maximinus, I:266
Maximus, Magnus, I:791, 870
Maximus, Quintus Fabius. *See* Fabius
Max Planck Institute for Fluid Mechanics, IX:3073, 3074
Max Planck Society for the Advancement of Science, VIII:1515, 1618, 2238; IX:3034
Maxwell, James Clerk, **VI:1511-1513**
  Faraday, V:770
  Gibbs, V:923, 924
  Kelvin, VI:1271
  Lorentz, VIII:2235
  Lumiére, VIII:2276
Mayakovsky, Vladimir, **VIII:2461-2464**
  150,000,000, VIII:2461
  About That, VIII:2462
  At the Top of My Voice, VIII:2462
  Bathhouse, The, VIII:2462
  Bedbug, The, VIII:2462
  Cloud in Paris, A, VIII:2461
  Mystery-Bouffe, VIII:2461
  Vladimir Illich Lenin, VIII:2462
  Vladimir Mayakovsky, VIII:2461
Maybach, Wilhelm, V:597-599
Mayflower, IV:1273
Mayflower Compact, IV:189
May Fourth Movement
  Ch'en Tu-hsiu, VII:660-662
  Kuo Mo-jo, VIII:2033-2035
  Lu Hsün, VIII:2252
  Mao Tse-tung, VIII:2400
Maynooth Seminary, VI:1480, 1481
Mayo, Charles H. and William J., **VIII:2465-2467**
Mayo Clinic, VIII:2465-2467; IX:2928, 3479
Ma Yüan, II:479, 480, **612-614**
Mazarin, Jules, **IV:945-948**
  Christina, IV:306
  Colbert, IV:336, 337
  Cyrano de Bergerac, IV:386
  Jansen, IV:709
  Louis XIV, IV:866
  Oxenstierna, IV:1053
  Vincent de Paul, IV:1381
Mazdakites, II:559, 561
Mazepa, Ivan Stepanovich, IV:1084
Mazzini, Giuseppe, V:447, 879, 932; **VI:1514-1516,** 1782, 1783
Mead, Margaret, VII:257; **VIII:2468-2471**
  And Keep Your Powder Dry, VIII:2470
  Coming of Age in Samoa, VIII:2468

In Male and Female, VIII:2469
Sex and Temperament in Three Primitive Societies, VIII:2469
Meany, George, IX:3163, 3164
Mecca, II:495, 496, 564, 623, 652, 654; III:521, 541
Meckel, Johann, V:110
Mecklenburg-Strelitz, Charlotte of, IV:539
Medawar, Peter, VII:512, 513
Medicaid, VII:709; VIII:1868
Medicare, VII:709; VIII:1868; IX:2973
Medici, Cosimo de', III:8, 29, 153
Medici, Ferdinando de', IV:619, 1214
Medici, Giovanni de'. *See* Leo X
Medici, Guilio de'. *See* Clement VII
Medici, Lorenzo de', III:9, 325, 450, **495-498,** 517, 667, 668
Medici, Piero de', III:496, 668
Médicis, Catherine de. *See* Catherine de Médicis
Médicis, Marie de, IV:863, 865, 1165, 1166
Medina, II:652, 654
Medvedev, Pavel Nikolayevich, VII:152, 153
Meech Lake Accord, VIII:2655, 2656
Meerssen, Treaty of, II:601
Megacles, I:648
Megara, I:314
Megarics, I:796
Megiddo, Battle of, I:890
Mehemet, VI:2227
Mehmed II, **III:499-502**
Meighen, Arthur, VIII:1982
Meiji Restoration, VIII:1680
Meir, Golda, VII:251, 253, 856; **VIII:2472-2475**
Meir, Rabbi, I:28
Meitner, Lise, VIII:1514-1516, 1648, **2476-2479**
Melanchthon, Philipp, III:446, **503-506**
Apology, III:505
Loci Communes, The, III:504
Unterricht der Visitatorn, III:505
Melbourne, Second Viscount, VI:**1517-1519,** 2394
Melbye, Fritz, VI:1779
Melchizadek, I:6
Melfi, Council of, II:930
Mellon, Andrew, VII:763; **VIII:2480-2482**
Mellon Plan, VIII:2481
Melville, Herman, **VI:1520-1525**
Battle-Pieces and Aspects of War, VI:1523
Billy Budd, Foretopman, VI:1524
Clarel, VI:1523
Confidence Man, The, VI:1523
Israel Potter, VI:1523
Mardi and a Voyage Thriller, VI:1522
Moby Dick, IV:430; V:1066; VI:1521, 1524
Omoo, VI:1522, 1524
Pierre, VI:1523
Redburn, VI:1520, 1521
Typee, VI:1521, 1522, 1524
White-Jacket, VI:1522
Memmius, Gaius, I:511
Menai Bridge, VI:2209
Menander (Greek writer), I:295, **538-540,** 845, 846
Arbitration, The, I:539
Bad-Tempered Man, The, I:539
Girl from Samos, The, I:539
Girl Who Was Shorn, The, I:539
Shield, The, I:539
Menander (Greek king), **I:541-542**
Mencius, I:433, 434, **543-546,** 944
Meng-tzu, I:543
Mencken, H.L., **VIII:2483-2486**
American Language, The, VIII:2484
George Bernard Shaw, VIII:2483
Philosophy of Friedrich Nietzsche, The, VIII:2484
Mendel, Gregor Johann, V:609; **VI:1526-1528;** VIII:2619, 2620
Mendeleyev, Dmitry Ivanovich, **VI:1529-1533**
Principles of Chemistry, The, VI:1530
Mendelsohn, Erich, **VIII:2487-2490**
Mendelssohn, Arnold, VIII:1670
Mendelssohn, Felix, **VI:1534-1536,** 1993
Hebrides, The, VI:1535
Hymns of Praise, VI:1535
Italian Symphony, VI:1535
Meeresstille und glückliche Fahrt, VI:1535
Midsummer Night's Dream, A, VI:1534, 1535
Scotch Symphony, VI:1535
Mendelssohn, Moses, IV:842
Mendès-France, Pierre, **VIII:2491-2496**
Mendicant Orders, II:163, 715, 717
Mendoza, Antonio de, III:180, 181
Mendoza, Pedro de, III:392
Menelaus of Alexandria, I:410
Menelik I, VIII:1517
Menelik II, **VI:1537-1540;** VIII:1517
Menemencioglu, Numan, VIII:1813, 1814
Menéndez de Avilés, Pedro, **III:507-509**
Menes, **I:547-549,** 979
Meng Hao-jan, I:841
Mengs, Anton Raphael, IV:569
Menippius, I:507, 509
Menninger, Karl
Man Against Himself, VII:1247
Sexual Behavior in the Human Male, VIII:1989

Menno, Simons, **III:510-512**
Christian Baptism, III:511
Foundation of Plain Instruction, A, III:511
True Christian Faith, The, III:511
Menotti, Gian Carlo, VII:191-193; **VIII:2494-2496**
Menzies, Robert Gordon, VIII:2293, 2294, **2497-2499**
Mercator, Gerardus, **III:513-516**
Chronologia, III:515
Geography, III:515
Mercator's Atlas, III:515
Mercedarians, II:776, 777
Mercer, Johnny, IX:3424
Mercer, Lucy, IX:3218
Mercers' Guild, III:169
Merchant Shipping Act of 1876, V:678
Mercia, kingdom of, II:59, 60, 62, 320, 333
Mercier, François, VII:1229
Merciless Parliament, II:787
Mercury space program, VII:111, 1387, 1388; IX:3405
Mercury Theater, IX:3934
Meretaton, I:25
Mergenthaler, Ottmar, **VI:1541-1543**
Mergenthaler Linotype Company, VI:1542
Mergenthaler Printing Company, VI:1542
Meritor Savings Bank v. Vinson, VIII:2326
Merleau-Ponty, Maurice, V:1083; **VIII:2500-2502**
Merman, Ethel, VII:289
Merodach-Baladan, I:754, 755
Merovingian dynasty, II:242-244, 274, 403-405
Merriam, Charles and George, IV:1420
Mersenne, Marin, **IV:949-953**
Harmonie universelle, IV:951
Impiété des deistes, athées, et libertins de ce temps, L', IV:950
Quaestiones celeberrimae in Genesim, IV:950
Vérité des sciences, contre les sceptiques ou Pyrrhoniens, La, IV:950
Merton, Thomas, II:313, 314
Meru, VIII:2773
Mesabi Range, VI:1898
Messallina, Valeria, **I:550-552**
Messenia, I:18, 292
Messerschmitt, Willy, VIII:1615, 1616
Messiaen, Olivier, VII:386; **VIII:2503-2505;** IX:3542, 4075
Banquet céleste, Le, VIII:2503, 2504
Chronochromie, VIII:2504
Couleurs de la cité céleste, VIII:2504
Et exspecto resurrectionem, VIII:2504
Mode de valeurs et d'intensités, VIII:2504
Pelléas et Mélisande, VIII:2503
Quantor pour la fin du temps, VIII:2504
Saint François d'Assie, VIII:2504
Transfiguration de Notre Seigneur Jesus-Christ, La, VIII:2504
Trois Petites Liturgies, VIII:2504
Turangalîla, VIII:2504
Messina, Antonello da, III:59
Messner, Reinhold, **VIII:2506-2509**
Seventh Grade, The, VIII:2506
Metacomet, IV:931, **954-957**
Metacom's War. *See* King Philip's War
Metaphysical Club, VI:1757
metaphysics
Bergson, VII:283
Böhme, IV:154, 155
Carnap, VII:583
Duns Scotus, II:313
Fichte, IV:466-468
Green, V:988
Heidegger, VIII:1610-1612
Hume, IV:685
Kant, IV:761-763
Leibniz, IV:829-832
Parmenides, I:596
Posidonius, I:688
Pythagoras, I:728
Scheler, IX:3347-3349
Whitehead, IX:3965-3968
Metcalfe, Sir Charles, V:118
Metellus, Quintus Caecilius, I:528
Methodism, IV:1426-1429
Methodius, Saint, II:176, **278-281**
Metilius, I:335
Metius, Jacob, IV:850
metric system
Guillaume, VIII:1502-1504
Lagrange, IV:787
Laplace, VI:1321
Michelson, VI:1554
Monge, IV:975, 977
Metro-Goldwyn-Mayer
Demille, VII:897
Fitzgerald, VII:1163
Garbo, VII:1286-1288
Garland, VII:1305-1306
Gish, VII:1385
Goldwyn, VIII:1417
Loos, VIII:2232
Metropolitan Museum of New York
Calder, VII:539
Fry, VII:1254

Morgan, VI:1582
Nevelson, VIII:2730
Whitney, IX:3969
Metropolitan Opera Company
Apollinaire, VII:82
Balanchine, VII:156
Barber, VII:193
Caruso, VII:599
Danilova, VII:835
Geddes, VII:1320
Karajan, VIII:1911
Menotti, VIII:2495
Norman, VIII:2771
Pavarotti, IX:2930
Price, IX:3081, 3083, 3084
Toscanini, IX:3709
Metternich, V:222, 441, 1034; **VI:1544-1547,** 1917
Meung, Jean de
Romance of the Rose, The, II:261, 992
Mexica, III:377-379, 528, 529, 556, 557
Mexican Confederation of Workers, VII:572
Mexican Constitution of 1824, V:95
Mexican Revolution
Bierce, V:231
Calles, VII:542-544
Madero, VIII:2345-2348
Obregón, IX:2781-2784
Orozco, IX:2838
Rivera, IX:3184
Villa, IX:3811-3814
Zapata, IX:4104, 4106, 4107
Mexican War
Bancroft, V:126
Calhoun, V:395
Colt, V:541
Davis, V:615
Douglas, V:692
Grant, V:975
Lincoln, VI:1382
Perry, VI:1761
Pierce, VI:1777
Pike, IV:1097
Polk, VI:1803
Scott, VI:2010, 2011
Sherman, VI:2057
Sumner, VI:2170
Taylor, VI:2194-2196
Mey, Lev, VI:1890
Meyer, Lothar, V:100; VI:1532
Meyer-Eppler, Werner, IX:3542
Meyergold, Vsevolod Yemilyevich. *See* Meyerhold, Vsevolod Yemilyevich
Meyerhold, Vsevolod Yemilyevich, VIII:2461-2463, **2510-2513**
Bathhouse, The, VIII:2511
Bed-bug, The, VIII:2511
Columbine's Scarf, VIII:2510
Inspector General, The, VIII:2511
Klop, VIII:2511
Miassin, Leonid Fyodorovich. *See* Massine, Léonide
Micah, I:468
Michal, I:241
Michael III (Byzantine emperor), II:117, 176, 279, 674, 675
Michael V (Byzantine emperor), II:758
Michael VIII Palaeologus, II:899
Michael of Cesena, II:682, 683
Michelangelo, **III:517-520**
Bramante, III:84
Correggio, III:186
Greco, El, III:311
Jacopo della Quercia, III:391
Julius II, III:407
Last Judgment, III:168
Pietà, III:16
Raphael, III:643, 645
Titian, III:723
Vasari, III:743
Michele Cione, Andrea di. *See* Verrocchio, Andrea del
Michelet, Jules, **VI:1548-1550**
History of France, The, VI:1548, 1549
History of the French Revolution, The, VI:1548, 1549
Introduction à l'histoire universelle, VI:1548
People, The, VI:1549
Michelin, André and Édouard, VII:696; **VIII:2514-2516**
Michelson, Albert A., VI:**1551-1555;** VIII:2539
Michener, James A., **VIII:2517-2519**
Bridges at Toko-Ri, The, VIII:2517
Caribbean, VIII:2519
Hawaii, VIII:2517, 2518
Poland, VIII:2518
Return to Paradise, VIII:2517
Sayonara, VIII:2517
Source, The, VIII:2518
Space, VIII:2519
Tales of the South Pacific, VIII:2517
Michinaga. *See* Fujiwara Michinaga
microscopy
Holmes, V:1126
Koch, VI:1298

Leeuwenhoek, IV:825-827
Malpighi, IV:892
Zworykin, IX:4127
Middle Stoa, I:686
Midway Island, Battle of, VIII:1525, 1527, 2750-2752
Mies van der Rohe, Ludwig, **VIII:2520-2524**
"Brick Countryhouse," VIII:2520
"Concrete Countryhouse," VIII:2520
"Concrete Office Building," VIII:2520
"Glass Skyscrapers," VIII:2520
Mi Fei, **II:639-641**
Pao-chang tai-fang lu, II:639
Shu-su t'ieh, II:639
Mighty Five, the, VI:1611, 1612, 1889, 2200
Mighty Handful, the. *See* Mighty Five, the
Mihajlovic, Draza, IX:3692
Milan, Duchy of
Alboin, II:42
Alexander VI:III:16
Ambrose, I:43, 44
Bayard, III:48, 49
Boccherini, IV:147
Clement VII:III:166
Francis I, III:274
Medici, Lorenzo de', III:496
Sforza, III:682-684
Miles, Nelson, V:575, 1244
Miletus, I:115, 852
Milhaud, Darius, **VIII:2525-2528**
Agamemnon, VIII:2525
Bœuf sur le toit, Le, VIII:2526
Brebis égarée, La, VIII:2525, 2526
Carnaval d'Aix, La, VIII:2526
Choëphores, Les, VIII:2525
Christophe Colomb, VIII:2526
Création du monde, La, VIII:2526
David, VIII:2527
Esther de Carprentras, VIII:2526
Euménides, Les, VIII:2525
Homme et son désir, L', VIII:2525
Machines agricoles, VIII:2526
Malheurs d'Orphée, VIII:2526
Maximilien, VIII:2526
Protée, VIII:2525
Milindapanha, I:541
Military Government of the United States, Office of, VII:848
Military Reconstruction Act, VI:2108
Military Reorganization Commission, V:940-942
Militia Act of 1792, IV:1407
Miliukov, P.N., VIII:1942
Mill, James, **VI:1556-1558,** 1559, 1560
History of British India, VI:1557, 1559, 1787
Mill, John Stuart, IV:108, 109; V:417, 460, 539, 776; VI:1556, 1557, **1559-1565,** 2211; VIII:2773
Autobiography, VI:1556, 1559, 1560
Essay on Liberty, IV:685
On Liberty, VI:1562, 1563, 2062
On the Subjection of Women, IV:1478; V:1059; VI:1563, 2064, 2213
Principles of Political Economy, VI:1559, 1562
System of Logic, A, VI:1560, 1562
Utilitarianism, VI:1563
Millais, John Everett, V:1168
Millay, Edna St. Vincent, VIII:2251, **2529-2532**
Aria da Capo, VIII:2530
Conversation at Midnight, VIII:2530
Flowers of Evil, VIII:2530
Miller, Arthur, **VIII:2533-2535,** 2589
After the Fall, VIII:2534
All My Sons, VIII:2533
American Clock, The, VIII:2534
Archbishop's Ceiling, The, VIII:2534
Broken Glass, VIII:2534
Creation of the World and Other Business, The, VIII:2534
Crucible, The, VIII:2534
Danger: Memory!, VIII:2534
Death of a Salesman, VIII:2533
Incident at Vichy, VIII:2534
Last Yankee, The, VIII:2534
Man Who Had All the Luck, The, VIII:2533
Memory of Two Mondays, A, VIII:2533, 2534
Mr. Peter's Connections, VIII:2534
Price, The, VIII:2534
Ride Down Mt. Morgan, The, VIII:2534
Story of G. I. Joe, The, VIII:2533
View from the Bridge, A, VIII:2534
Miller, Henry, VIII:2537
Millet, Kate, **VIII:2536-2538**
Basement, The, VIII:2537
Flying, VIII:2537
Loony-Bin Trip, The, VIII:2537
Sexual Politics, VIII:2536-2538
Three Lives, VIII:2537
Millikan, Robert Andrews, **VIII:2539-2542**
Mills, Earle, IX:3174
Milne, A.A., **VIII:2543-2545**
Days Play, The, VIII:2543
Holiday Round, The, VIII:2543
House at Pooh Corner, The, VIII:2544

It's Too Late Now, VIII:2544
Miss Elizabeth Bennett, VIII:2544
Mr. Pim Passes By, VIII:2543
Now We Are Six, VIII:2544
Once a Week, VIII:2543
Once on a Time, VIII:2543
Peace with Honour, VIII:2544
Red House Mystery, The, VIII:2543
Three Lives, VIII:2543
Toad of Toad Hall, VIII:2544
When We Were Very Young, VIII:2543
Winnie-the-Pooh, VIII:2543
Wurzel-Flummery, VIII:2543
Milner, Sir Alfred, VII:376; IX:4094
Milon, I:34
Miloslavskys, IV:1082
Miltiades the Younger, **I:553-556**
Milton, John, III:705; **IV:958-962;** IX:3258
Areopagitica, IV:961; IX:3258
Comus, IV:958, 961
De doctrina Christiana, IV:961
Of Education, IV:960
Paradise Lost, IV:641, 960-962; VII:945; IX:3258
Ready and Easy Way to Establish a Free Commonwealth, The, IV:960
Samson Agonistes, IV:961
Tenure of Kings and Magistrates, The, IV:960
Milvian Bridge, battle of the, I:227
Minamoto clan, II:882, 883, 924, 1025
Minangkabaus, VIII:1577
Ming Dynasty
Abahai, IV:1, 2
Cheng Ch'eng-kung, IV:297, 298
Cheng Ho, II:253-255
Ch'ien-lung, IV:300
Dorgon, IV:421, 422
K'ang-hsi, IV:758, 759
Yung-lo, II:1022-1024
Minims, IV:949
Minin, Nikita. *See* Nikon
mining industry
Agricola, III:1-3
Baldwin, VII:169
Boulton, IV:183
Brindley, IV:201, 202
Carmaux strike, V:1221, 1222
Darrow, VII:839
Davy lamp, V:622
Guggenheim, VIII:1498-1500
Hadfield, V:1016
Hearst, VIII:1601
Hoover, VIII:1727
methane detection, VIII:1510
Newcomen, IV:1023
Republic labor policies of 1892, V:1055
Rockefeller, VIII:1981
Roebuck, IV:1184
Rhodes, V:463
Sesostris III, I:774
Supreme Court decisions, VII:1212
Trevithick, VI:2251
United Mine Workers of America, VIII:1879-1881, 2170-2172
Mink, Ben, VIII:2081
Minkus, Ludwig, V:649
Minnedienst, II:959
Minnelli, Vincente, VII:1305, 1306
Minnesang, II:959
Minnesota
Humphrey, VIII:1783
Pike, IV:1094
Minorca, IV:56, 57
Minot, George Richards, IX:3959
Mint, U.S., IX:3243-3245
Minto Reforms, VII:184
Minucius, Lucius, I:335
Mirabeau, Comte de, **IV:963-965**
Miramar, II:608
Miranda, Francisco de, V:267
Miranda v. Arizona, IX:3890
Miriam, I:3
Mir Jafar, IV:326
Miró, Joan, VII:1099; **VIII:2546-2550,** 2732, 2733
Carbide, The, VIII:2548
Catalan Landscape (The Hunter), VIII:2548
Composition, VIII:2548
Constellations, VIII:2548
Dog Barking at the Moon, VIII:2548
Dutch Interiors, VIII:2548
Farm, The, VIII:2546
Farmer's Wife, The, VIII:2548
Harlequin Carnival, The, VIII:2548
Little Girl in Front of the Sun, VIII:2549
Montroig Landscaping, VIII:2546
Nocturne, VIII:2548
Object poétique, VIII:2548
Olive Grove, The, VIII:2546
Reaper, The, VIII:2548
Romeo and Juliet, VIII:2548
Spanish Dancer, VIII:2548
Still Life with an Old Shoe, VIII:2548
Still Life with Toy Horse, VIII:2546

Table with Rabbit, VIII:2546
Tilled Field, The, VIII:2548
Woman, VIII:2549
Mirza Reza Kermani, V:1209
Mishima, Yukio, **VIII:2551-2553**
Confessions of a Mark, VIII:2551
Death in Midsummer and Other Stories, VIII:2551
Madame de Sade, VIII:2551
"Patriotism," VIII:2551, 2552
Sea of Fertility, The, VIII:2551
Sun and Steel, VIII:2551
Mishnah, I:27-29
Mission, Congregation of the, IV:1380
Missionary Sisters of the Sacred Heart, V:386, 388
Mississippi River
Eads Bridge, V:729-731
Jolliet, IV:732-734
La Salle, IV:793-795
Louisiana Purchase, IV:719
Soto, III:699-701
Missouri
Benton, V:195, 197, 198
Bingham, V:236-238
Dred Scott decision, VI:2000
Frémont, V:842
Lewis and Clark, VI:1340
Mormonism, VI:2081, 2415
Schurz, VI:1997
Missouri Compromise, V:508, 693; VI:2191, 2192, 2288
MIT. *See* Massachusetts Institute of Technology
Mitanni, I:890
Mitchell, John, VIII:2759
Mitchell, Maria, V:822
Mitchell, William, **VIII:2554-2557**
Mithradates the Great, **I:557-560,** 680, 828, 834, 896, 897
Mitterand, François, **VIII:2558-2561**
Mobile Bay, Battle of, V:772, 774
Mobilier National Building, IX:2977
Möbius, Karl August, VI:2119
Mobutu Sese Seko, **VIII:2562-2565;** IX:3745
Mocenigo, Zuane, III:97
Mochihito, Prince, II:882
Model A automobile, VII:1186
Model T automobile, VII:1184, 1186, 1187
Modern Art, Museum of (New York)
Aalto, VII:2, 3
Arbus, VII:95-97
Brancusi, VII:417
Buñuel, VII:506
Ernst, VII:1100
Frankenthaler, VII:1209
Giacometti, VII:1361
Kupka, VIII:2037
Moses, VIII:2633
Nevelson, VIII:2729, 2730
Nicholson, VIII:2733
Orozco, IX:2838
Oud, IX:2860
Pollock, IX:3049, 3050
Rouault, IX:3253
Steichen, IX:3503
Modern Language Association, IX:4015
Modigliani, Amadeo, VII:37
Moffat, Robert, VI:1399
Moffat, W.B., VI:2002
Mohács, Battle of, III:376
Mohammad Reza Shah Pahlavi, VIII:1957-1959, **2566-2570**
Mohammed. *See* Muhammad
Mohammed I Askia, **III:521-523**
Mohawk Indians
Brant, IV:196, 198, 199
Champlain, IV:273
Metacomet, IV:955
Tekakwitha, IV:1316, 1317
Mokae, Zakes, VII:1257, 1258
Moland, John, IV:408
molecular biology
Crick, VII:797
Jacob, VIII:1827-1829
Pauling, IX:2928
Schrödinger, IX:3362
Staudinger, IX:3499
Watson, IX:3897-3899
Molière, IV:782, 783, **966-970,** 1145
Affected Young Ladies, The, IV:968
Blunderer, The, IV:968
Don Juan, IV:968
Fourberies de Scapin, Les, IV:387
Imaginary Invalid, The, IV:969
Love-Tiff, The, IV:968
Misanthrope, The, IV:968; VII:281
School for Husbands, The, IV:968
School for Wives, The, IV:968
Sganarelle, IV:968
Tartuffe, IV:968, 969
Moller, Martin, IV:154
Molnár, Ferenc
Liliom, VIII:2141, 2142
Swan, The, VIII:2142
Moloch, I:801

Molon, I:63
Molotov, Vyacheslav Mikhailovich, VII:316; VIII:1961, 1962, **2571-2574**
Molotov-Ribbentrop Pact, VIII:2572
Mommsen, Theodor, **VI:1566-1569**
  Corpus inscriptionum Latinarum, VI:1567, 1568
  History of Rome, The, VI:1566-1568
  Inscriptions regni Neapolitani Latinae, VI:1566
  Provinces of the Roman Empire from Caesar to Diocletian, The, VI:1567
  Römisches Staatsrecht, VI:1567
  Römisches Strafrecht, VI:1567
Monadnock Building, V:365
Monaldeschi, Gian Rinaldo, IV:306
Monck, George, IV:284, 791, **971-974,** 1229, 1343
Mondale, Walter, VII:949, 1153-1155
Mondino dei Liucci, II:414
Mondrian, Piet, VII:538; VIII:1904, **2575-2578,** 2732-2734; IX:2859
  Broadway Boogie Woogie, VIII:2576
  Composition in Red, Yellow and Blue, VIII:2576
  Oval Composition with Bright Colors, VIII:2576
  Victory Boogie Woogie, VIII:2576, 2577
Monet, Claude, VI:1869, 1870, 1963, 1964; VIII:1903, **2579-2582**
  Impression, Sunrise, VIII:2579
  Women in the Garden, VIII:2579
Monge, Gaspard, **IV:975-979**
  Elementary Treatise on Descriptive Geometry, An, IV:977
Mongols
  Baybars I, II:124-126
  Carpini, II:207
  K'ang-hsi, IV:758
  Khan, Genghis, II:376-378
  Khan, Kublai, II:566-568
  Nevsky, II:53
  Polo, II:750
  Sa'di, II:806, 807
  Sung Dynasty, II:868
  Tamerlane, II:884
  William of Rubrouck, II:987, 988
  Yaqut, II:1013
  Yung-lo, II:1021, 1022
Monk, Thelonious, VII:741
Monmouth, Battle of, IV:322, 368, 575, 1405
Monmouth, Duke of, IV:704, **980-982,** 1039
Monmouth, Henry of, II:459
Monmouth, Humphrey, III:736
Monnet, Jean, **VIII:2583-2586**
Monod, Jacques, VIII:1827-1829
Mononobe clan, II:826
monopolies
  Astor, V:82, 84
  British Broadcasting Corporation, VII:739; IX:3147
  German industrial cartels, VII:1094
  Goldie, V:953
  Morgan, VI:1582
  Rockefeller, VI:1896-1898
  Sherman Anti-Trust Act, IX:3229
  United Shoe Manufacturing Company, VII:419
  Vanderbilt, VI:2296
Monroe, James, **VI:1570-1574**
  Calhoun, V:395
  Clay, V:508
  Clinton, V:519
  Gadsden Purchase, V:858, 859
  Jeffrey, V:1226
  Paine, IV:1056
Monroe, Marilyn, VII:936; VIII:2534, **2587-2591**
  Bus Stop, VIII:2589
  Don't Bother to Knock, VIII:2589
  Gentlemen Prefer Blondes, VIII:2589
  How to Marry a Millionaire, VIII:2589
  Let's Make Love, VIII:2589
  Love Happy, VIII:2587, 2589
  Misfits, The, VIII:2589
  Prince and the Showgirl, The, VIII:2589
  Some Like It Hot, VIII:2589
  Something's Got to Give, VIII:2589
Monroe Doctrine
  Adams, V:22
  Canning, V:406
  Lodge, VIII:2221
  Monroe, IX:1570, 1573
  Polk, VI:1803
Monroe-Pinkey Treaty, VI:1571
Montagnais, IV:273
Montagnards, IV:394, 395
Montagu, Charles, IV:26, 1066-1068
Montagu, Edward Wortley, IV:135, 983
Montagu, Mary Wortley, **IV:983-985**
  Nonsense of Common Sense, The, IV:984
  Turkish Embassy Letters, IV:983
  Verses Addressed to the Imitator of Horace, IV:984
Montagu, Ralph, IV:822
Montaigne, Michel de, **III:524-527;** VII:723
Montale, Eugenio, **VIII:2592-2595**
  Bones of the Cuttlefish, VIII:2592
  Eugenio Montale: The Storm and Other Poems, VIII:2593

occasioni, Le, VIII:2593
Satura, VIII:2594
Montand, Yves, VIII:2588
Montauk Building, V:365
Montcalm, Louis de, IV:179
Monteagle, Lord, III:258
Monte Cassino, monastery of, II:911
Monterey Pop Festival, VIII:1883
Montespan, Madame de, IV:901
Montesquieu, **IV:986-989**
Considérations sur les causes de la grandeur des Romains et de leur décadence, IV:986
Persian Letters, IV:986
Spirit of the Laws, The, IV:986-988
Montessori, Maria, **VIII:2596-2600**
Advanced Montessori Method, The, VIII:2599
Dr. Montessori's Own Handbook, VIII:2599
Montessori Method, The, VIII:2598
Monteverdi, Claudio, **IV:990-994**
Arianna, L', IV:992
favola d'Orfeo, La, IV:991-993
finta pazza Licori, La, IV:992
incoronazione di Poppea, L', IV:992, 993
Vespers of 1610, IV:992, 993
vittoria d'amore, La, IV:992
Montezuma I, III:379, 556, 557
Montezuma II, III:22, 189, 190, **528-532**
Montfort, Simon V de, II:454, 455, **642-647**
Montgolfier, Jacques-Étienne, **IV:995-998**
Montgolfier, Joseph-Michel, **IV:995-998**
Montgomery, Bernard Law, **VIII:2601-2604;** IX:4117
Montgomery bus boycott, VII:9, 10; IX:2889, 2890, 3941
Montgomery Improvement Association, IX:2890
Montgomery Ward and Company, VI:2331-2334
Montini, Giovanni Battista. *See* Paul VI
Montojo, Patricio, V:657
Montrose, Marquess of, IV:283
Moody, Dwight, L., **VI:1575-1578,** 2388
Moody, William H., V:284
Moon
Braun, VII:440, 441
eclipse, II:121
Galileo, IV:521
Hipparchus, I:409
lunar calendars, I:811, 812
Nabu-Rimanni, I:567, 568
Posidonius, I:688
space exploration, VII:110-113; VIII:2021, 2022; IX:3405-3407
third inequality, II:21
three-body problem, IV:786
Mooney, Tom, VII:1212
Moore, Fred H., IX:3283
Moore, G.E., **VIII:2605-2608**
Commonplace Book, VIII:2607
"Ideal Utilitarianism," VIII:2606
"Nature of Judgment, The," VIII:2606
Philosophical Papers, VIII:2607
Philosophical Studies, VIII:2607
Principia Ethica, VIII:2606, 2607
"Refutation of Idealism, The," VIII:2606
Some Main Problems of Philosophy, VIII:2607
Moore, Henry, **VIII:2609-2613**
Double Oval Bronze, VIII:2612
Draped Reclining Mother and Baby, VIII:2612
Madonna and Child, VIII:2612
Mother and Child, VIII:2611
North Wind, VIII:2611
Reclining Figure, VIII:2612
Vision and Design, VIII:2609
Moore, Marianne, **VIII:2614-2617**
Nevertheless, VIII:2616
Observations, VIII:2614, 2616
Pangolin and Other Verse, The, VIII:2616
"Past is the Present, The," VIII:2616
What are Years?, VIII:2616
Moore, Thomas
Epistles, Odes, and Other Poems, V:1225
Moran, Bugsy, VII:564, 565
Moran, Thomas, V:234
Moravian Church, IV:1488-1490
Moray, Sir Andrew, II:294, 956
Mordaunt, Charles. *See* Peterborough, Third Earl of
More, Anne, IV:418
More, Sir Thomas, **III:533-536**
Erasmus, III:247
Fisher, III:264-266
Henry VIII, III:349, 351
History of King Richard the Third, The, III:234, 652
Holbein the Younger, III:358, 359
"Steelyard portraits," III:359
Tyndale, III:736
Utopia, I:509
Moreau, Gustave, VIII:2452; IX:3251
Morelli, Felice, V:388
Morgan, George, V:450
Morgan, J.P., IV:661; **VI:1579-1583,** 2220; IX:3501
Morgan, Lewis Henry, **VI:1584-1587**
American Beaver and His Works, The, VI:1586

Ancient Society, VI:1586
Houses and House-Life of the American Aborigines, VI:1586
League of the Ho-de-no-sau-nee, or Iroquois, VI:1584
Systems of Consanguinity and Affinity of the Human Family, VI:1585
Morgan, Thomas Hunt, **VIII:2618-2621,** 2651
Drosophila, VIII:2620
Mechanism of Mendelian Heredity, The, VIII:2619
Morgenthau, Henry, V:26
Morgenthau Plan, VIII:1780
Mori clan, III:571, 728, 729
Morita, Akio, **VIII:2622-2625**
Moritz, Langrave, IV:1221
Morley, Edward Williams, VI:1552
Morley, Thomas, III:105, 108
Mormonism, V:840; VI:2080-2082, 2414-2416
Mornay, Philippe de, **III:537-539**
Morning Chronicle, V:1192
Morning Courier, V:191
Morones, Luis, VII:542, 543
Morris, Charles A., V:1124, 1125
Morris, Robert, **IV:999-1002**
Morris, William, **VI:1588-1591;** IX:2892
Defence of Guenevere, The, VI:1588
Dream of John Ball, A, VI:1590
Earthly Paradise, The, VI:1589
Life and Death of Jason, The, VI:1589
News from Nowhere, VI:1590
Sigurd the Volsung, VI:1589
Story of the Glittering Plain, The, VI:1590
Morrison, Herbert, VII:304
Morrison, Toni, **VIII:2626-2629**
Beloved, VIII:2627; IX:4031
Black Book, The, VIII:2628
Bluest Eye, The, VIII:2627
Jazz, VIII:2627
Song of Solomon, VIII:2627
Sula, VIII:2627
Tar Baby, VIII:2627
Morrow, Dwight M., VII:543
Morse, John Vinnicum, V:283
Morse, Samuel, F.B., V:294, 541, 1094; **VI:1592-1595**
Congress Hall, VI:1593
Louvre, The, VI:1592, 1593
Old House of Representatives, The, VI:1592
Morse code, VI:1593, 1807
Mortimer, Lord Roger, II:327, 329
Mortimer's Cross, Battle of, III:345
Morton, John, III:650-652
Morton, Thomas, III:533; IV:418
Morton, William Thomas Green, **VI:1596-1599**
Mosaddeq, Mohammad, VIII:2567
Mosca, Gaetano, **VIII:2630-2632**
Elementi di scienza politica, VIII:2630, 2631
Storia delle dottrine politiche, VIII:2632
Moscow Art Theatre, VIII:2510; IX:3486-3488
Moscow Communist Party, VIII:1961
Moscow Group for the Study of Reactive Propulsion, VIII:2019
Moscow Human Rights Committee, IX:3298
Moscow Linguistic Circle, VIII:1831
Moseley, Henry, VI:1533
Moses, **I:561-565**
Aaron, I:1, 3, 4
Jesus Christ, I:939
Joshua, I:246
Philo of Alexandria, I:632
Pilate, I:642
Yahweh, I:7
Moses, Grandma, **VIII:2633-2636**
Eisenhower Farm, VIII:2635
Fireboard, VIII:2633
First Automobile, The, VIII:2633
Home, In the Maple Sugar, VIII:2633
July Fourth, VIII:2635, 2636
Old Oaken Bucket, The, VIII:2635
Sugaring Off, VIII:2635
Turkey Hunt, VIII:2635
Moses, Law of, I:331-333
Moses de León, **II:648-650**
Book of Herman, The, II:648
Rose of the Testimony, II:648
Zohar, II:648-650
Moses ibn Ezra, II:548
Moslem League. *See* Muslim League
Most, Johann, VIII:1412
Motley, John Lothrop, III:602
Mott, John R., **VIII:2637-2640**
Mott, Lucretia, V:822; **VI:1600-1603;** IX:2919
Moulin Rouge, VI:2248
mountain climbing, VI:2410-2412; VIII:2506-2508
Mountbatten, Louis, VII:1344, 1345; VIII:1848, **2641-2646**
In Which We Serve, VIII:2643
Mouvement National Congolais, VIII:2562
Moynier, Gustave, V:712
Mozambique Liberation Front, VIII:2317-2319, 2774
Mozambique National Resistance, VIII:2318, 2319

Mozart, Wolfgang Amadeus, IV:149, 639, **1003-1007;** V:178, 179; VI:1686
Abduction from the Seraglio, The, IV:1003
Artaserse, IV:550
Clemency of Titus, The, IV:1006
Cosi fan tutte, IV:1352
Don Giovanni, IV:1005; V:493; VI:1391; VIII:2746
Haffner, IV:1005
Idomeno, King of Crete, IV:1003
Magic Flute, The, IV:1005; VIII:2014
Marriage of Figaro, The, IV:1005
musikalischer Spass, Ein, IV:1006
Requiem, IV:1005; VI:2155
Ms. magazine, IX:3521, 3522
muckraking
Godkin, VIII:1402
McClure's magazine, VII:624
Rockefeller, VI:1898
Sinclair, IX:3426
Tarbell, IX:3616, 3617
Mugabe, Robert, VIII:2319, **2647-2650**
Mughal Dynasty
Ahmad Khan, V:35, 36
Akbar, III:5-7
Aurangzeb, IV:69-71
Babur, III:38
Shah Jahan, IV:1232-1234
Sivaji, IV:1247
Mugwumps, VI:1997; VIII:1402
Muhammad, **II:651-656**
Abraham, I:7, 564
Faisal I, VII:1122
Hasan al-Basri, II:440
Hussein I, VIII:1791
Ibn Khaldun, II:503, 504
Islamic law, II:17, 33
Moses, I:564
Muhammad XI, III:261
Muhammad, Elijah, VIII:2373, 2375, 2376
Muhammad 'Ali Pasha, **VI:1604-1607**
Muhammad ibn Tughluq, II:496
Muhlberg, Battle of, III:18
Muir, John, **VI:1608-1610**
Mukhtar, Omar, IX:3098
Muller, Hermann Joseph, **VIII:2651-2654;** IX:3033
Müller, Johannes, V:1018, 1089
Müller, Lucas. *See* Cranach, Lucas, the Elder
Müller, William, VI:1989
Muller v. Oregon, VII:421
Mulligan Letters, V:256, 257
Mulroney, Brian, VII:550, 681, 682; **VIII:2655-2657;** IX:3345, 3346
Munch, Edvard, **VIII:2658-2661**
Frieze of Life, The, VIII:2659
Morning After, The, VIII:2658
Puberty, VIII:2658
Scream, The, VIII:2658
Sick Child, The, VIII:2658
Muncke, Georg Wilhelm, V:555
Mundir I, II:498
Munemori, II:882
Munich Conference, VIII:2210
Municipal Corporation Act, VI:1788
Municipal Franchise Act, V:777
Munitions War Act of 1915, VII:309
Munro, Ed, VIII:1593
Murad II, III:499
Murasaki Shikibu, **II:657-659**
Tale of Genji, The, II:657, 658; IV:1258
Murchinson, Roderick, VI:1418
Murcia, II:56
Murdock, William, **IV:1008-1011**
Murena, Lucinius, I:166
Muret, Battle of, II:529
Muret, Marc-Antoine, III:671
Murillo, Gerardo, IX:2836
Muris, Johannes de, **II:660-662**
Ars novae musicae, II:660, 661
Musica speculativa secundum Boetium, II:660, 661
Opus quadripartitum numerorum, II:660
Murji'ism, II:18
Murphy, William P., IX:3959
Murray, William. *See* Mansfield, First Earl of
Murrow, Edward R., **VIII:2662-2666**
Hear It Now, VIII:2664
Person to Person, VIII:2664
See It Now, VIII:2635, 2664
Musa. *See* Mansa Musa
Muscle Shoals Canal, VIII:1408
Mushet, Robert Forester, V:220
musical theater
Gershwins, VII:1347, 1349, 1350
Gilbert and Sullivan, V:930
Hart, VIII:1566-1569
Porter, IX:3055, 3056
Rodgers, IX:3201, 3202
Weill, IX:3926-3929
Muskie, Edmund, VII:49, 50
Muslim Brotherhood, VII:90; VIII:2693
Muslim League, VII:1283; VIII:1847, 1848, 2710, 2711

Muspratt, James, VI:1367
Mussolini, Benito, **VIII:2667-2670**
Baldwin, VII:170
Croce, VII:801, 802
De Gasperi, VII:863
Franco, VII:1201
Gentile, VII:1336-1338
Gramsci, VIII:1459
Haile Selassie I, VIII:1519
Hoare-Laval Agreement, VIII:2105
Kesselring, VIII:1950
Luce, VIII:2262
Lyons, VIII:2294
Mosca, VIII:2631, 2632
Perón, IV:2970
Pirelli, IX:3021
Sorel, IX:3464
Tunisia, VII:391
Mussorgsky, Modest, V:288; **VI:1611-1615;** VIII:1837
Boris Gudunov, VI:1611-1614
Destruction of Sennacherib, The, VI:1612, 1613
From Memories of Childhood, VI:1612
Intermezzo in modo classico, VI:1611
Khovanshchina, VI:1613
Night on Bare Mountain, VI:1612, 1614
Nursery, The, VI:1613
Pictures from an Exhibition, VI:1613
Porte-Enseigne Polka, VI:1611
Rêverie, VI:1612
Songs of Dances of Death, VI:1613
Sunless, VI:1613
Mu'tazilites, II:34, 93-95, 526, 636
Mutual Assistance, Pact of, VIII:2150
Mutual Assured Destruction doctrine, IX:3633
Mutual Assured Survival doctrine, IX:3633
Mutual Welfare League, IX:2852-2854
Muybridge, Eadweard, VIII:2277, 2278
Muzorewa, Abel, VIII:2647, 2648
Mycenaean Greek kingdoms, I:422; VI:1982
Myrdal, Gunnar, **VIII:2671-2674**
American Dilemma, An, VIII:2671-2673
Asian Drama, VIII:2672, 2673
Challenge to World Poverty, The, VIII:2673
Rich Lands and Poor, VIII:2672
Myrick, Julian, VIII:1820
Myrsilus, I:651, 652
mysticism
Catherine of Siena, II:218, 220, 221
Francis of Assisi, II:354-356
Ghazzali, II:385, 386
Hesychasm, II:899-901
Hildegard von Bingen, II:474-477
Ibn al-'Arabi, II:491-493
John of the Cross, III:401-403
Luria, III:440, 441
Moses de León, II:648-650
Ritschl, VI:1893
mythology
Botticelli, III:75
Cassirer, VII:615
Ch'ü Yüan, I:187
Cocteau, VII:723
Cranach, III:202
Egypt, I:573
Fortescue, III:267-269
Herodotus, I:396
Lévi-Strauss, VIII:2164, 2165
Lewis, VIII:2167, 2168
Montezuma II, III:529
Ovid, I:585-587
Schelling, VI:1974
Thales of Miletus, I:852, 854, 855
Tolkien, IX:3697
Vico, IV:1373
See also Greek mythology
Mytilene, I:651
Mzali, Muhammad, VII:393

NAACP. *See* National Association for the Advancement of Colored People
Nabokov, Vladimir, **VIII:2675-2678**
Bend Sinister, VIII:2676
Defense, The, VIII:2675
Eugene Onegin, VIII:2676
Gift, The, VIII:2675, 2676
Invitation to a Beheading, VIII:2675
King, Queen, Knave, VIII:2675
Lolita, VIII:2676, 2677
Mary, VIII:2675
Pale Fire, VIII:2677; VII:374
Pnin, VIII:2677
Real Life of Sebastian Knight, The, VIII:2676
Speak, Memory, VIII:2676
Nabonidus, I:234
Nabulsi, Suleyman an-, VIII:1793
Nabu-rimanni, **I:566-569**
Nachmonides, Moses, II:649
Nacionalista Party, VIII:2421
Nader, Ralph, **VIII:2679-2682**
Unsafe at Any Speed, VIII:2679
NAFTA. *See* North American Free Trade Agreement
Nagashima, Shigeo, IX:2796, 2797

Nagashino, Battle of, III:571
Nägeli, Carl von, VI:1527
Naha, Treaty of, VI:1762
Nahrain, I:890
Naidu, Sarojini, **VIII:2683-2685**
  Bird of Time, The, VIII:2683
  Broken Wing, The, VIII:2683
  Feather of Dawn, The, VIII:2683
  Golden Threshold, VIII:2683
Najm al-Din Ayyub, II:809
Nalanda, II:483
Nalundasan, Julio, VIII:2420
Nãnak, **III:540-543**
Nandakumar, IV:632
Nanga Parbat expedition, VIII:2506, 2508
Nanking, Treaty of, VI:1376, 1378, 1379
Nanking Incident, VII:486
Nansen, Fridtjof, VII:66; **VIII:2686-2688**
  First Crossing of Greenland, VIII:2686
  Norwegian North Polar Expedition, The, VIII:2687
Nantes, Edict of
  Catherine de Médicis, III:135
  Colbert, IV:338
  Frederick William, The Great Elector, IV:509
  Henry IV, III:334
  Hotman, III:365
  Louis XIII, IV:864
  Louis XIV, IV:868
  Mornay, III:539
Napata, I:636-638
Napier, Sir Charles, V:374
Napier, John, **III:544-547**
  Construction of a Marvelous Canon of Logarithms, III:545
  Description of a Marvelous Canon of Logarithms, III:545
  Plaine Discovery of the Whole Revelation of St. John, A, III:544
  Study of Divining Rods, or Two Books of Numbering by Means of Rods, III:545
Naples, Kingdom of
  Alexander VI, III:16
  Boccaccio, II:150, 152
  Claude Lorrain, IV:317
  Ferdinand and Isabella, III:262
  Louis XII, III:48
  Scarlatti, IV:1213, 1214
  Sforza, III:682, 683
  Torquemada, III:726
Napoleon I, **VI:1616-1619**
  Alexander I, V:44-46
  Baybars I, II:126
  Blücher, V:263-265
  Cambacérès, V:398-400
  Canova, V:410
  Castlereagh, V:440, 441
  Cavour, V:447, 448
  Charles XIV John, V:474, 475
  Chateaubriand, V:482-484
  Code Napoleon, VI:1966
  David, V:611
  Du Pont, V:718
  Fourier, V:819, 820
  Fragonard, IV:490
  Gance's film, VII:1274, 1275
  Géricault, V:910, 912
  Gneisenau, V:940-942
  Hardenberg, V:1033-1035
  Haydn, IV:641, 642
  Joséphine, V:1246-1248
  Kutuzov, VI:1305-1307
  Louisiana Purchase, IV:719; VI:1571
  Metternich, VI:1544-1546
  Monge, IV:977, 978
  Napoleon III, VI:1620
  Ney, VI:1646-1648
  Nonintercourse Act of 1809, IV:888
  Pitt the Younger, IV:1104
  Pyréolophore, VI:1657
  San Martín, VI:1947
  Saragossa, VI:1958, 1959
  Staël, VI:2093, 2094
  Stein, VI:2115, 2116
  Stendhal, VI:2126
  Talleyrand, VI:2186, 2187
  Toussaint-Louverture, IV:1340
  Volta, IV:1390
  Vo Nguyen Giap, IX:3821
  Wellington, VI:2351-2353
  See also Napoleonic Wars
Napoleon III, **VI:1620-1623**
  Alexander II, V:49
  Bismarck, V:240, 241
  Clemenceau, VII:702
  Dunant, V:711
  Gambetta, V:871-873
  Juárez, V:1252
  Lesseps, VI:1355
  Palmerston, VI:1721
  Proudhon, VI:1818
  Rothschild family, VI:1918, 1919
  Thiers, VI:2227, 2228
  Tocqueville, VI:2239

Napoleonic Wars
  Alexander I, V:44-46
  Clausewitz, V:503-505
  Napoleon I, VI:1616-1618
  Niebuhr, VI:1654, 1655
  Perry, VI:1760
  Wellington, VI:2351-2353
Narbonne Lara, Louis, Vicomte de, VI:2092, 2093
Narkomindel, VIII:2209, 2210
Narmer, I:548
Narragansett Indians, IV:932, 955
Narses, I:778
Narváez, Pánfilo de, III:110
Naryshkins, IV:1082
NASA
  Armstrong, VII:111-113
  Braun, VII:441
  Eisenhower, VII:1045
  Glenn, VII:1387-1389
  Prandtl, IX:3074
  Ride, IX:3178, 3179
  Sagan, IX:3293
  Shepard, IX:3405-3407
Nascimento, Edson Arantes do. *See* Pelé
Naser od-Din, V:1209
Nash, John, **IV:1012-1015**
Nash, Paul, **VIII:2689-2692**
  Battle of Britain, The, VIII:2691
  Dawn: Sanctuary Wood, VIII:2690
  Forest, VIII:2690
  Landscape: Year of Our Lord 1917, VIII:2690
  Landscape of the Brown Fungus, VIII:2691
  Landscape of the Puff Ball, VIII:2691
  Landscape of the Red Fungus, VIII:2691
  Pyramids in the Sea, VIII:2689
  Strange Coast, VIII:2690
  Sunrise: Inverness Copse, VIII:2689, 2690
  Totes Meer, VIII:2691
  Vision at Evening, VIII:2689
  Wood Sea, VIII:2690
Nash, Richard, IV:566
Nashe, Thomas, **III:548-550**
  Almond for a Parrot, An, III:548
  Anatomie of Absurditie, The, III:548
  Christie's Tears over Jerusalem, III:549
  Isle of Dogs, The, III:549
  Nashe's Lenten Stuffe, III:549
  Pierce Penilesse, His Supplication to the Devil, III:548
  Strange Newes of the Intercepting of Certain Letters, III:549
  Summers Last Will and Testament, III:549
  Terrors of the Night, The, III:549
  Unfortunate Traveller: Or, The Life of Jack Wilton, The, III:549
Nasi, I:27-29
Nasmyth, James, **VI:1624-1626**
Naso, Publius Ovidius. *See* Ovid
Nasser, Gamal Abdel, **VIII:2693-2697**
  Dayan, VII:855, 856
  Eden, VII:1017
  Faisal, VIII:1119
  Hussein I, VIII:1793
  Qaddafi, IX:3098
  Sadat, IX:3289, 3290
Nast, Thomas, **VI:1627-1629,** 2284-2286
Nathan, I:243, 798
Nation, Carry, **VI:1630-1633**
National Advocate, V:191
National Aeronautics and Space Administration. *See* NASA
National African Company, V:954
National American Woman Suffrage Association, VI:2045, 2046; VII:627-629; IX:2919, 2920, 3118
National Anti-Slavery Standard, V:490
National Assembly (France)
  Gambetta, V:871, 872
  Herriot, VIII:1645
  Hugo, V:1157
  Marat, IV:910, 911
  Mendès-France, VIII:2491, 2492
  Mirabeau, IV:963-965
  Necker, IV:1017
  Robespierre, IV:1170, 1171
  Saint-Just, IV:1205, 1206
National Association for the Advancement of Colored People
  Carver, VII:604
  Disney, VII:941
  Du BoisVII:963-965
  Marshall, VI:2433, 2434
  Parker, IX:2886
  Price, IX:3083, 3084
  Randolph, IX:3113
  Robinson, IX:3196
  Washington, VI:2338
  Wells-Barnett, IX:3943
  White, IX:3961-3963
National Australasian Convention, V:148
National Broadcasting Corporation, IX:3709
National Catholic War Council, V:922
National Center for Atmospheric Research, IX:2946, 2947

National Child Labor Committee, VIII:2096, 2097
National Collegiate Athletic Association, IX:3270, 4049
National Constituent Assembly. *See* National Assembly (France)
National Consumers' League, IX:3118, 3838
National Convention of Nigeria and the Cameroons, VII:144-146
National Defense Education Act, VII:1045
National Economic Development Council, VIII:2343
National Education Association, VII:524
National Endowment for the Arts, VII:875
National Equal Rights Party, VI:1408
National Federation of Women Workers, VII:353, 354
National Gallery of Art, IX:2947
National Geographic Society, V:188; IX:2944, 2945
National Grange, VI:2332, 2333
National Guard, U.S., VIII:2295
National Indian Hall of Fame, IX:3675
National Industrial Recovery Act, VII:422; IX:3548
National Insurance Act of 1911, VII:308; VIII:2217
nationalism
  Acton, V:12
  Algeria, VII:6, 7
  Arab states, VIII:1795
  Argentina, IX:2971
  Austria, III:491-493; IX:3842
  Canada, V:118; VI:1496-1498; VII:365, 366
  China, VII:677
  Czechoslovakia, VII:969; VIII:2440
  Egypt, V:4-6; VIII:2355, 2356, 2695; IX:3290
  Germany, III:491-493; VII:494; VIII:1476, 1612, 1692, 2266, 2742, 2743
  India, V:211-213; VII:183-185, 308; VIII:1847-1849; IX:2869
  Indochina, VIII:1699
  Indonesia, VIII:1577-1579
  Ireland, VI:1740-1742; VII:172, 733, 877-879
  Italy, V:932-934
  Japan, II:667, 668
  Jaspers, VIII:1844
  Libya, IX:3099
  Native Americans, VI:2206
  Nigeria, VII:144-146
  Russia, IV:860, 861
  Scotland, II:184; IV:241
  Singapore, VIII:2152
  Spanish music, VII:1128
  Tunisia, VII:391, 392
  Turkey, VIII:1522-1524, 1812
  United States, V:126-128, 279-281, 395, 507, 694; VI:2038, 2039, 2346
  Zimbabwe, VIII:2647
Nationalist Party of Indonesia, IX:3570, 3571
National Labor Relations Act, IX:3224
National Liberal Federation, V:462; VI:1497
National Liberation Front of Algeria, VII:5-7
National Museum at Nairobi, VIII:2147
National Negro Business League, VI:2338
National Organization for Women, VII:1231; VIII:1641-1643
National Pact of Turkey, VII:134
National Park System, United States, VI:1608-1610
National Recovery Act, VIII:1768
National Reformer, VII:382
National Register of Historic Places Program, VI:1884
National Research Council, VII:745; VIII:2540
National Socialist Party. *See* Nazi Party
National Society for Penal Information, IX:2853
National Society for the Promotion of Industrial Education, VII:23
National Student Federation of America, VIII:2662
National Union of General and Municipal Workers, VII:354, 355
National Union of Women's Suffrage Societies, V:776, 778
National Woman's Party, VII:628; IX:2920
National Woman Suffrage Association, V:62, 64; VI:1407, 2045, 2112
National Youth Administration, VIII:1866
Nation of Islam, VII:54, VIII:2373-2376
Nations, Battle of the. *See* Leipzig, Battle of
Nations, League of
  Angell, VII:76, 77
  Balfour, VII:174
  Beaverbrook, VII:236
  Benes, VII:260
  Bergson, VII:284
  Butler, VII:525
  de Valera, VII:878
  Eden, VII:1016
  female participation, IX:2920
  Germany, VIII:1694, 2743; IX:3564, 3565
  Grey, VIII:1477
  Haile Selassie I, VIII:1519
  Hammarskjöld, VIII:1529

Harding, VIII:1550, 1551
Herriot, VIII:1645
Hughes, VIII:1777
Iraq, VII:1125
La Fontaine, VIII:2052
Liberia, IX:3757
Lorentz, VIII:2237
Lugard, VIII:2270
Monnet, VIII:2583
Nansen International Office for Refugees, VIII:2687
Nehru, VIII:2710
New Zealand, VIII:2445
palace construction, VIII:2138
Root, IX:3234
Smuts, IX:3453, 3454
Soviet Union, VIII:2210
Stimson, IX:3538
Taft, IX:3596
Turkey, VII:134
Wilson, IX:4022
Women's International League of Peace and Freedom, VII:162

Native Americans
Amherst, IV:39
ballet, IX:3607-3609
Berkeley, IV:114
Bible translation, IV:435, 437, 438
Black Hawk, V:247-250
Boas, VII:339
Boone, IV:163-165
Bougainville, IV:179
Brant, IV:196-199
Cabeza de Vaca, III:110, 111
Catlin, V:443, 444
Cartier, III:129-131
Carson, V:429-432
Charles V, III:161
Cherokees. *See* Cherokee Indians
Child, V:489
Cody's Wild West Show, VI:1677
Colt, V:541
Columbus, III:173-175
Cooper, V:562, 564
Crazy Horse, V:573-577
Crockett, V:578, 579
Custer, V:585-587
Davis, III:213
Edwards, IV:430
Erdrich, VII:1091-1093
fur trade, VI:2077, 2078
Gadsden Purchase, V:859
Georgia, IV:1044, 1045
Geronimo, V:915-918
Harrison, V:1061
Houston, V:1137
Iroquois. *See* Iroquois Indians
Jackson, V:1200-1202
Jolliet, IV:732, 733
Joseph, V:1242-1245
La Salle, IV:793-795
Laval, IV:801-803
Lewis and Clark, VI:1360
Lockwood, VI:1407
McGillivray, IV:875-877
Mankiller, VIII:2389-2391
Massasoit, IV:930-933
Metacomet, IV:954-956
Mohawks, IV:196, 198, 199
Ojibwe, VI:1585
Osceola, VI:1695-1697
Parkman, VI:1735-1739
Picotte, IX:3010-3012
Pike, IV:1094, 1096, 1097
Pilgrims, IV:190, 1273-1275
Pocahontas, IV:1106-1108, 1253-1255
Ponce de Léon, III:629-631
Pontiac's War, IV:513, 1110-1113
Powhatan, IV:1122-1125, 1253
Red Cloud, VI:1850-1853
Remington, VI:1862
Ross, VI:1910-1912
Sacagawea, VI:1933-1935
Saint Lawrence basin, IV:273, 274
Scott, VI:2010, 2011
Seneca, VI:1584
Sequoyah, VI:2025-2028
Shawnee, IV:164
Sioux. *See* Sioux Indians
Sitting Bull, VI:2070-2073
Soto, III:699-701
Stuyvesant, IV:1296
Tecumseh, VI:2203-2206
Tekakwitha, IV:1316, 1317
Thorpe, IX:3675
Virginia, IV:81
Vitoria, III:768, 769
Wesley, IV:1426, 1427

Nativity, Church of the, I:375, 376
NATO. *See* North Atlantic Treaty Organization
Natta, Giulio, **VIII:2698-2701**
natural selection
Burnet, VII:514
Darwin, V:606, 608, 609

Galton, V:870
Lucretius, I:512
Lyell, VI:1421
Teilhard de Chardin, IX:3628
Weismann, VI:2348-2350
Nautical Almanac Office, VI:1639
Nautilus, V:855, 856
Nautilus Submarine Boat Company, V:1124
Nauvoo, VI:2081
Navajo Indians, V:432
Navarino, Battle of, V:407
Navidad, III:173
Navratilova, Martina, VII:1112, 1113; **VIII:2702-2704**
Nawruz, II:381, 382
NAWSA. *See* National American Woman Suffrage Association
Nazarenes, VIII:2036
Nazi Party
Adenauer, VII:27, 28
Arendt, VII:98-100
Astor, VII:130, 131
Baeck, VII:149, 150
Barmen Confession, VII:204
Berg, VII:272
Bergius, VII:277
Bergman, VII:278
Boas, VII:340
Böll, VII:349-351
Bonhoeffer, VII:358-360
boxing, VIII:2243
Braun, VII:440
Bultmann, VII:499
Camus, VII:553, 554
Canada, IX:3986
Czechoslovakia, VII:261
Dreyer's *Day of Wrath,* VII:960
Ehrlich, VII:1030
Erhard, VII:1094
eugenics, V:870
Evangelical Church, VIII:2742-2743
French collaboration, IX:2988, 2989
Goebbels, VIII:1404-1406, 2078
Göring, VIII:1438-1441, 1910
Grass, VIII:1463, 1464
Guderian, VIII:1490-1492
Hamsun, VIII:1539
Harriman, VIII:1560, 1561
Heidegger, VIII:1611, 1612
Heisenberg, VIII:1618
Henze, VIII:1633
Himmler, VIII:1666-1668
Hindemith's operas, VIII:1671
Hindenburg, VIII:1674-1676
Hitler, VIII:1692-1696
Hollywood League Against Nazism, VIII:1534
Jaspers, VIII:1844
Joliot, VIII:1872
Joyce, VIII:1894
Kesselring, VIII:1949-1951
Le Bon, VIII:2135
Ludendorff, VIII:2265, 2266
Lukács, VIII:2273
Molotov, VIII:2572
Mussolini, VIII:2669
Olympic Games, VII:776
Papen, VII:2876-2878
Paris Opéra, VIII:2184
Pius XI, IX:3027
Pius XII, IX:3031
Rundstedt, IX:3260-3262
Stark, IX:3491, 3492
Strauss, IX:3557
Visconti's films, IX:3820
Waldheim, IX:3841-3843
Weill, IX:3927, 3928
Wiesenthal, IX:3984-3987
Windsor, IX:4026
zeppelins, VII:1013
See also degenerate art
NBC, IX:3709
NCAA, IX:3270, 4049
Nearchus of Elea, I:973
Nebraska
Bryan, VII:479, 480
Dred Scott decision, VI:2000
Omaha tribe, IX:3010, 3011
statehood, V:1236
See also Kansas-Nebraska Act
Nebraska, University of, VII:621, 623, 624
Nebuchadnezzar II, I:326, 328, 460, **569-572**
Necharsulm Strickmachinene Union, IX:3882
Necho I, I:709
Necker, Anne-Louise-Germaine. *See* Staël, Madame de
Necker, Jacques, **IV:1016-1018**
Neckham, Alexander, **II:663-665**
Commentary on Ecclesiastes, II:664, 665
Commentary on Martianus Capellus, II:663
Corrogationes Promethei, II:664
De naturis rerum, II:664, 665
De nominibus utensilium, II:663, 664
Laus sapiente divine, II:664
Novus Avianus, II:663

Novus Esopus, II:663
Sacredos ad altare, II:663
Solatium fidelis anime, II:664
Suppletio defectum, II:664
Needham, John Turberville, IV:1260, 1261
Néel, Louis-Eugène-Félix, **VIII:2705-2708**
Nefertiti, I:24, 25, **573-576**
Neferure, I:371, 373
Nefretari, I:736
Negev, the, IX:3932
Negro Factories Corporation, VII:1312
Negro Leagues, IX:3193, 3196
Negro Silent Protest parade, IX:3855
Neguib, Muhammad, VIII:2693
Nehemiah, I:330, 332
Nehru, Jawaharlal, VIII:2642, 2644, **2709-2712;** IX:2867, 2869, 2904, 2905
Discovery of India, The, VIII:2711
Glimpses of World History, VIII:2710
Jawaharial Nehru: An Autobiography, VIII:2710
Nelson, Judy, VIII:2703
Nelson, Lord, **VI:1634-1637**
Nemiroff, Robert, VIII:1546-1548
Nemirovich-Danchenko, Vladimir, IX:3486, 3487
Nennius, II:133
History of the Britons, I:378, 379
Neoclassicism
architecture, IV:10
literature, IV:1115-1117
music, VIII:1670-1672
painting, IV:765, 767, 1160; V:408, 610-612, 1185
Neo-Confucianism
Su Tung-p'o, II:857
Sung Dynasty, II:867
Tseng Kuo-fan, VI:2260-2262
Wang Yang-ming, III:771-773
Neo-Destour Party, VII:391, 392
Neo-Kantianism, VII:524, 614; VIII:1571
Neoplatonism
Augustine, I:128
Botticelli, III:75
Ghazzali, II:385, 386
Hypatia, I:437, 438
Ibn Gabirol, II:498-500
Lull, II:608
Plato, I:657
Plotinus, I:666-668
Porphyry, I:683-685
Posidonius, I:689
Proclus, I:698-700
Spenser, III:703, 704
Thomas Aquinas, II:914
William of Moerbeke, II:985
neorealist film movement, IX:3818-3820
Neo-Taoism, I:945, 949-951
Nephelokokkugia, I:91
Neptune, VI:1639; IX:3701
Nerchinsk, Treaty of, IV:758
Neri, Saint Philip, **III:551-554**
Nernst, Walther Hermann, VII:275; VIII:1510, **2713-2715**
Theoretical Chemistry, VIII:2714
Nero, **I:577-580**
Claudius I, I:206
Pliny the Elder, I:663
Prasutagus, I:137
Seneca the Younger, I:772, 773
Vespasian, I:933
Neruda, Pablo, **VIII:2716-2719**
Canto General, VIII:2717, 2618
Captain's Verses, The, VIII:2718
Crepusculario, VIII:2716
Elemental Odes, The, VIII:2718
Extravagaria, VIII:2718
Memoirs, VIII:2718
One Hundred Love Sonnets, VIII:2718
Residence on Earth and Other Poems, VIII:2716, 2717
Twenty Love Poems and a Song of Despair, VIII:2716
Nerva, Marcus Cocceius, I:28, 356, 899
Nervi, Pier Luigi, **VIII:2720-2723**
Nestorius, I:941
Netanyahu, Benjamin, VII:93
Netjerykhet, I:978
Neue Künstlervereingung, VIII:1903
Neue Rheinische Zeitung, V:761
Neue Zeit, VII:291
Neue Zeitschrift für Musik, VI:1992-1994
Neuf-Brisach, IV:1360
Neumann, Baltasar, IV:657
Neumann, John von, **VIII:2724-2727**
Computer and the Brain, The, VIII:2726, 2727
Mathematical Foundations of Quantum Mechanics, The, VIII:2725
Theory of Games and Economic Behavior, VIII:2727
Neustria, II:242
neutrons
Chadwick, VII:635-637
Fermi, VII:1145, 1147
Hahn, VIII:1514, 1515

Joliot-Curies, VIII:1871-1873
Kurchatov, VIII:2040
Lawrence, VIII:2121-2123
Teller, IX:3632
Yukawa, IX:4090
Nevelson, Louise, **VIII:2728-2731**
Atmosphere and Enviroment X, VIII:2730
Atmosphere and Enviroment XIII, VIII:2730
Canada Series I, VIII:2730
"Dawn's Wedding Feast," VIII:2729
Ice Palace I, VIII:2730
"Moon Garden + One," VIII:2729
Mrs. N's Palace, VIII:2730
Night Presense IV, VIII:2730
"Royal Tides, The," VIII:2730
"Royal Voyage, The," VIII:2729
Sky Cathedral, VIII:2729
Neville, Anne, III:649, 650
Neville, Richard. *See* Warwick, Earl of
Neville's Cross, Battle of, II:295
Nevsky, Alexander. *See* Alexander Nevsky
New Artists' Federation, VIII:2405
Newbery, John, IV:565, **1019-1021**
Little Pretty Pocket-Book, A, IV:1020
Tom Telescope, IV:1020
Newbery Award, IV:1021
Newcastle, Duke of, IV:447, 537, 539
New Christians, III:465
Newcomb, Simon, **VI:1638-1640**
New Comedy, Greek, I:88, 92, 538-540, 751, 845
Newcomen, Thomas, **IV:1022-1024,** 1061, 1409, 1411
New Deal
Altgeld, V:56
Butler, VII:525
Cardozo, VII:576, 577
Frankfurter, VII:1212
Harriman, VIII:1560
Hoover, VIII:1729, 1730
Humphrey, VIII:1783
Johnson, VIII:1866, 1868
Lippmann, VIII:2204
organized labor, VIII:2172
Reconstruction Finance Corporation, VIII:1729
Roosevelt, IX:3224, 3225
Stevenson, IX:3523
Supreme Court rulings, VII:321; IX:3548
Taft, IX:3591
Truman, IX:3740, 3742
New England Courant, The, IV:492
New England School for the Blind. *See* Perkins Institution
New England Woman's Club, V:1146
New England Woman Suffrage Association, V:1111
New Hampshire Grants, IV:34, 35
New Haven Railroad, VII:421, 422
New Industrial Cities Plan, VIII:1810
Newlands, John, VI:1532
Newman, John Henry, V:70; **VI:1641-1645,** 1829, 1830
Apologia Pro Vita Sua, VI:1643
Essay in Aid of a Grammar of Assent, An, VI:1643
Idea of a University Defined and Illustrated, The, VI:1643
New Mexico
Coronado, III:180
Fillmore, V:793
Gadsden Purchase, V:858-860
Hayden, V:1073
O'Keeffe, IX:2801
New Model Army, IV:378, 447, 1126-1128
New Orleans, Battle of, IV:889; V:1196
New Republic, The, VIII:2204; IX:4012
New South Church, V:351
newspapers
Azikiwe, VII:144
Beaverbrook, VII:234-237
Bennett, V:190-193
Bottomley, VII:382-385
Bryant, V:343-345
Dreiser, VII:954
Godkin, VIII:1400-1402
Greeley, V:982, 984-986
Harmsworths, VIII:1554-1556
Hearst, VIII:1601, 1603-1605
Herzen, V:1099, 1100
Mackenzie, VI:1447-1451
Nazi Germany, VIII:1405
O'Connor, IX:2793, 2794
political cartoons, VI:1627-1629
printing technology, VI:1541-1543
Pulitzer, VI:1825, 1826
Scripps, VI:2014-2016
Stamp Tax, VI:1788
Walter, VI:2324-2326
Newspaper Stamp Tax, VI:1788
New Statesman magazine, IX:3907
New Testament
Barth, VII:204, 205
Biddle, IV:126
Bonhoeffer, VII:360
Bultmann, VII:498-500

David, I:241
Erasmus, III:247
Harnack, VIII:1558
Hippolytus of Rome, I:416
Irenaeus, I:449, 450
John the Apostle, I:475, 477
John the Baptist, I:478-481
Luther, III:445
Paul, I:604-606
Peter, I:614-616
Pilate, I:640, 642
Renan, VI:1867
Ritschl, VI:1892-1894
Tertullian, I:849
Thomas, I:880, 882, 883
Tyndale, III:735, 737
Ulfilas, I:908
Wyclif, II:1009
Newton, Benjamin, V:668
Newton, Sir Isaac, **IV:1025-1029**
Berkeley, II:114
Boyle, IV:186, 187
Cavendish, IV:263
Dalton, V:602
De motu corporum in gyrum, IV:601
Fermat, IV:458-460
Halley, IV:600-602
Hawking, VIII:1583
Huygens, IV:697
Kepler, III:545
Kupka's painting, VIII:2037
Lagrange, IV:785, 786
law of inertia, II:195
Leibniz, IV:831
Maclaurin, IV:882-884
Mathematical Principles of Natural Philosophy, IV:601, 602, 1027
Method of Fluxions and Infinite Series, The, IV:215
Principia, IV:884
Smith, IV:1250
telescopes, IX:3351
New Wave cinema, VII:281; VIII:1391-1394; IX:3159, 3736-3739
New York Age, VI:2337
New York Bureau of Municipal Research, VII:221
New York Central Railroad, VI:2298
New York City
Cabrini, V:388
Bernstein, VII:295, 296, 298
Bryant, V:344
Central Park, VI:1691, 1692
Columbia University, VII:527
engineering projects, VIII:1410
Free Synagogue, IX:4034
George, V:908
Gorky, VIII:1444
Hearst, VIII:1603
Henry Street Settlement, IX:3837-3839
Hughes, VIII:1766
Kent, VI:1278
La Guardia, VIII:2054-2056
school system, VII:524
Smith, IX:3439
Stuyvesant, IV:1296, 1297
Tammany Hall, V:513, 520; VI:2284-2287; IX:3439, 3440
Tweed, VI:2284-2287
New York City Ballet, VII:158; IX:3607-3609, 4076, 4123
New York City Consumers' League, IX:2961
New York Committee on Safety, IX:2962
New York Customhouse, V:1076, 1078
New York Enquirer, V:191
New Yorker, The, VII:100, 567; IX:3677, 3678, 4012
New York *Evening Post,* V:343-345; VIII:1400-1402
New York Herald, V:192, 193; VI:2101, 2102
New York Mirror, VI:1796
New York Open Theatre, IX:3642-3644
New York Philharmonic
Anderson, VII:70
Barber, VII:193
Bernstein, VII:295, 296
Boulez, VII:389
Mahler, VIII:2362
Poulenc, IX:3068
Thomas, VI:2231, 2232
Zwilich, IX:4123
New York Port Authority, VIII:1410
New York Psychoanalytic Society, VIII:1745
New York Review, V:343
New York Shakespeare Festival, VII:35
New York Society for Ethical Culture, V:26, 28, 29
New York State
Allen, IV:34-36
Arthur, V:77, 78, 80
Astor, V:82, 84
Beard, VII:222
Bennett's newspapers, V:190-193
Blaine, V:256
bridges, VI:1905
Brunel, V:339

Burr, V:369, 370
Chisholm, VII:670
Cleveland, V:512, 513
Clinton, V:517-521
Great Depression unemployment, VIII:1736
Harriman, VIII:1562
Hughes, VIII:1766
James II, IV:703
Jay, IV:711, 713, 714
Kent, VI:1277-1279
prison system, IX:2852-2854
Roosevelt, IX:3222, 3224
Root, IX:3234
Sanger, IX:3314
Stuyvesant, IV:1294, 1296, 1297
Zenger, IV:1484-1486
New York State Factory Commission, IX:2962
New York State Library School, V:661
New York State Prison Reform Commission, IX:2852
New York State Theater, VII:158
New York Stock Exchange, VIII:1472, 1473
New York *Sun,* V:192
New York Times, VI:2285; VII:35, 36; VIII:1400
New York Times v. Sullivan, VII:322
New York Times v. United States, VII:322, 511
New York Tribune, V:850, 852, 982, 984-986; VI:1542
New York v. United States, IX:3143
New York Weekly Gazette, IV:1484, 1485
New York Weekly Journal, IV:1484-1486
New York World, V:741; VI:1826; VIII:1601, 2204
New York World's Fair of 1939-1940, VII:3, 1321
New York Woman's Temperance Society, V:62
New York Yankees, VII:934-937, 1322-1324; IX:3274-3276
New Zealand Company, V:722; VI:2322
Ney, Michel, **VI:1646-1649**
Nezahualcóyotl, III:378, **555-558**
Nezib, Battle of, VI:1606
Nez Perce War, V:1242, 1244, 1245
Ngengi, Kamau. *See* Kenyatta, Jomo
Ngo Dinh Diem, VIII:1701
Nguyen That Thanh. *See* Ho Chi Minh
Niagara Bridge, VI:1905
Niagara Movement, VII:964
Nicanor, I:768
Nicea, Council of
Constantine the Great, I:376
Easter, II:298, 299
Eusebius of Caesarea, I:323
Gregory of Nyssa, I:352-354
Iconoclastic Controversy, II:546
Nicene Creed
Ambrose, I:43-45
Athanasius, I:119, 121, 122
Constantine the Great, I:228, 376
Gregory of Nyssa, I:353
Theodosius the Great, I:869
Theoleptus of Philadelphia, II:899
Ulfilas, I:909
Nicephorus, II:437, 900
Nichiren, **II:666-668**
On the Establishment of the Orthodox Teaching and Peace of the Nation, II:667
Nicholas I, **VI:1650-1653**
Nicholas II, VI:1790, 1791, 1842, 1844, 1845; VIII:1942
Nicholas III, II:682, 715, 716, 797
Nicholas V, III:9, **559-562,** 564, 741
Nicholas of Autrecourt, II:194, **669-672**
Nicholas of Cusa, III:560, **563-566**
De coniecturis, III:564
Of Learned Ignorance, III:564
Nicholas the Great, **II:673-676**
Responsa Nicolai ad Consulta Bulgarorum, II:675
Nichols, Mike, VII:1084
Nicholson, Ben, **VIII:2732-2734**
August 1956, VIII:2733
1933, VIII:2732
Vertical Seconds, VIII:2734
Nicias, I:31, 32
Nicklaus, Jack, IX:3041, 4050
Niclaes, Heinrich, IV:688
Nicolet, Jean, IV:732
Nicollet, Joseph Nicolas, V:839
Nicomedes IV, I:898, 899
Nicon, I:338
Nicopolis, battle of, II:457
Nicuesa, Diego de, III:45, 46
Niebuhr, Barthold Georg, **VI:1654-1656**
Lectures on Ancient History, VI:1655
Lectures on Roman History, VI:1655
Roman History, The, VI:1655, 1839
Niebuhr, Reinhold, **VIII:2735-2738**
Beyond Tragedy, VIII:2737
Leaves of Notebook of Tamed Cynic, VIII:2735
Nature and Density of Man, The, VIII:2737
Niemeyer, Oscar, **VIII:2739-2741**
Niemöller, Martin, **VIII:2742-2745**
Niépce, Isidore, V:594, 595
Niépce, Nicéphore, V:594, 595; **VI:1657-1661**

Nietzsche, Friedrich Wilhelm, **VI:1662-1666;** VI:1986, 2319; VIII:1611, 1650, 1651, 1920, 2226
- *Birth of Tragedy Out of the Spirit of Music, The,* IV:1461; VI:1664
- *Human, All Too Human,* VI:1664
- *Joyful Wisdom, The,* VI:1665
- *Thus Spake Zarathustra,* VI:1664, 1665
- *Will to Power, The,* VI:1665

Nigerian Broadcasting Company, VII:13, 14
Nightingale, Florence, **VI:1667-1672,** 1732
Nijinska, Bronislawa, VII:921; VIII:2182, 2746
Nijinsky, Vaslav, VII:1178; VIII:2449, 2525, **2746-2749**
- *Afternoon of a Faun,* VIII:2748
- *Don Giovanni,* VIII:2746
- *Petrushka,* VIII:2748
- *Rite of Spring, The,* VIII:2748
- *Specter of a Rose,* VIII:2748

Nijmegen, Treaty of, IV:1447
Nijo Yoshimoto, II:1025
Nika Riots, II:554, 556, 892
Nikolayev, Andrian, IX:3639-3641
Nikon, **IV:1030-1033**
- *Kormchaia Kniga,* IV:1031

Nile, Battle of the, VI:1636
Nile River
- Bruce, IV:208-210
- Burton, V:375, 376
- Livingstone, VI:1400
- Sesostris, I:774, 776
- Speke, VI:2083-2085

Nimitz, Chester W., **VIII:2750-2753**
Nineteenth Amendment. *See* women's suffrage
Nineteenth Party Congress, VIII:2378, 2572
Nine Years' War, IV:1448, 1449
Nirmal Hriday Home for Dying Destitutes, IX:3636
Nisan, II:299
Nishida, Kitaro, **VIII:2754-2757**
- *Art and Morality,* VIII:2755
- *Fundamental Problem of Philosophy,* VIII:2755
- *Hataraku-mono kara mirumono,* VIII:2755
- *Ippansha no jikakuteki taikei,* VIII:2755
- *Ishiki no mondai,* VIII:2755
- *Jikaku ni okeru chokkan to hansei,* VIII:2755
- *Mu no jikakuteki gentei,* VIII:2755
- *Study of Good, A,* VIII:2754, 2755
- *Tetsugaku rombunshu,* VIII:2755

Nishida-Tanabe school of philosophy, VIII:2754
Nisibis, Peace of, I:778, 780
Nissim ben Jacob ben Nissim ibn Shahim, II:498, 499
Nitocris, I:709
Nixon, Edward, VII:9
Nixon, Richard M., **VIII:2758-2761**
- Armstrong, VII:112
- Burger, VII:509, 511
- Bush, VII:520, 521
- Clinton, VII:714
- Dole, VII:948
- Ellington, VII:1068
- enemy list, VII:675
- Ford, VII:1181, 1182
- Graham, VIII:1449
- Greenspan, VIII:1471
- Harriman, VIII:1563
- Hiss, VIII:1684, 1685
- Hoover, VIII:1733
- Humphrey, VIII:1785
- Israel, VII:856
- Kennedy, VIII:1930
- Kirkpatrick, VIII:1995
- Kissinger, VIII:1999, 2000
- Meir, VIII:2474
- Neruda, VIII:2718
- O'Neill, IX:2825
- Reagan, IX:3138
- Rehnquist, IX:3142
- Sato, IX:3338
- Smith, IX:3448
- Walters, IX:3870
- Watergate affair, VIII:1453, 1888

Nizam al-Mulk, II:67, 68, 70, 385, **677-680**
- *Book of Government: Or, Rules for Kings, The,* II:679

Nkomati Accord, VIII:2318
Nkomo, Joshua, VIII:2647-2649
Nkrumah, Kwame, **VIII:2762-2765**
Noah, Mordecai, V:191, 192
Nobel, Alfred, **VI:1673-1676,** 2175, 2177; IX:3456, 3457
Nobile, Umberto, VII:68
Nobilior, Fulvius, I:287, 288
Nobodaddy. *See* Urizen
Noche Triste, La, III:22, 190
Nodier, Charles, V:708
No drama, II:1025-1028; VIII:2552; IX:4082
Noland, Kenneth, VII:1209
non-Euclidean geometry, V:893-895
Nonintercourse Act of 1809, IV:888
Non-Proliferation Treaty of 1970, IX:3377
Non-Recognition Doctrine of 1932, IX:3538

nonviolent resistance
Gandhi, VII:1282-1284
King, VIII:1971, 1973, 1974
Lutuli, VIII:2281-2283
Luxemburg, VIII:2286
Thoreau, VI:2235
Tolstoy, VI:2245
Tutu, IX:3775, 3776
Nootka Sound Crisis, IV:1103
Nordau, Max, **VIII:2766-2768**
Conventional Lies of Our Civilization, The, VIII:2766, 2768
Degeneration, VIII:2766, 2767
Esencia de la Civilization, VIII:2768
Interpretation of History, The, VIII:2767
Morals and Evolution of Man, VIII:2768
Paradoxes, VIII:2766
Paris Sketches, VIII:2766
Paris unter der Dritten Republik, VIII:2766
Vom Kreml zur Alhambra, VIII:2766
Nordraak, Rikard, V:1002, 1003
Norfolk, Duke of, III:243, 316
Norgay, Tenzing. *See* Tenzing Norgay
Norge, VII:68
Noriega, Manuel, IX:3071
Norman, Jessye, **VIII:2769-2772**
Carmen, VIII:2771
Deborah, VIII:2770
Diva, VIII:2771
Troyens, Les, VIII:2770, 2771
Norman Conquest of 1066, II:201-204, 315-317, 426, 428, 429, 997, 998, 1000
Normandy, Battle of, VIII:2603; IX:3215
North, Council of the, IV:1285, 1286
North, Lord, **IV:1034-1037**
Burke, IV:223
Fox, IV:479, 481
George III, IV:541, 542
Pitt the Younger, IV:1102, 1103
North American Free Trade Agreement
Bush, VII:522
Chrétien, VII:681
Clinton, VII:709
Mulroney, VIII:2656
Nader, VIII:2681
North American Soccer League, IX:2952
North Atlantic Treaty Organization
Acheson, VII:16-19
Albright, VII:51
Belgium, IX:3476
Bevin, VII:316
Boutros-Ghali, VII:400
Eisenhower, VII:1043
France, VII:1096
Germany, VII:1017
Luce, VIII:2257
Montgomery, VIII:2603
Nasser, VIII:2695
Singapore, VIII:2151
Taft, IX:3592
Turkey, VIII:1814
Northcliffe, Lord, VII:74, 75, 235, 325
Northern Pacific Railway Company
Hill, IV:660
Cooke, V:552, 553
Macdonald, VI:1438
Morgan, VI:1581, 1582
Sitting Bull, VI:2072
Northern Peoples Congress, VII:145
Northern Securities Company, IV:661
Northern Shoshone Indians, VI:1933-1935
Northern Sung Dynasty, II:479, 840, 867, 868, 962, 963
Northern Virginia, Army of, VI:1340
Northern War, IV:509
North Ireland Partition, VII:878, 879
North Pole
Amundsen, VII:66-68
Byrd, VII:534, 535
Davis, III:212
Nansen, VIII:2687
Peary, IX:2941, 2942, 2944, 2945
Wilkins, IX:4001
North River Steamboat, The, V:856
Northumberland, Duke of, III:147, 206, 238, 239, 318-320, 479; VI:1787
North West Company, IV:879-881; V:82, 84
Northwest Palace of Ashurbanipal II, I:110, 111
Northwest Passage
Amundsen, VII:66-69
Davis, III:212, 213
Frobisher, III:278-280
Hudson, IV:680-682
Ross, VI:1907
Vancouver, IV:1355, 1356
Nostradamus, **III:567-569**
Centuries, III:567, 568
Notables, Assembly of, IV:964
Notre-Dame-du-Haut, Chapel, VIII:2138
Notre Dame organum, II:723
Nouveau, Germain, VI:1887
Nouveaux Cahiers, IX:3923
Nouvelle Vague. *See* New Wave cinema
Novak, Paul, IX:3951

Novgorod, II:52, 953; III:381, 382; IV:1030
Novotny, Antonin, VII:969
NOW. *See* National Organization for Women
No Water, V:574
Noy, William, IV:596
NSDAP. *See* Nazi Party
Nubian Dynasty, I:636-638, 774, 776
nuclear fission
  Hahn, VIII:1513-1516
  Kurchatov, VIII:2040
  McMillan, VIII:2336-2338
  Meitner, VIII:2476-2478
  Rabi, IX:3102
  Seaborg, IX:3375
nuclear physics
  Bethe, VII:300-303
  Bohr, VII:345, 347
  Broglie, VII:472-474
  Chadwick, VII:635-637
  Dali, VII:829
  Fermi, VII:1145, 1147, 1148
  Heisenberg, VIII:1617-1619
  Joliot-Curies, VIII:1870-1873
  Kapitsa, VIII:1906-1908
  Kennedy, VIII:1930
  Kurchatov, VIII:2039-2041
  Lawrence, VIII:2121-2123
  Meitner, VIII:2476-2478
  Neumann, VIII:2725, 2726
  Oppenheimer, IX:2833-2835
  Rutherford, IX:3277-3279
  Teller, IX:3631-3633
  Yukawa, IX:4090-4092
Nuclear Test Ban Treaty, VIII:2041; IX:2928
nuclear weapons
  Bethe, VII:300-303
  Bohr, VII:345, 347
  China, VIII:2190
  Comprehensive Test Ban Treaty, VII:51
  Gorbachev, VIII:1424
  Grass's novels, VIII:1464
  Hahn, VIII:1515
  Harriman, VIII:1562
  Khrushchev, VIII:1963
  Kissinger, VIII:1998-2000
  Kohl, VIII:2009
  Kurchatov, VIII:2039-2041
  Kurosawa's films, VIII:2044
  Lawrence, VIII:2121-2123
  McMillan, VIII:2336-2338
  Muller, VIII:2653
  Neumann, VIII:2725
  Oppenheimer, IX:2833-2835
  Pauling, IX:2928
  Sakharov, IX:3296
  Seaborg, IX:3377
  Spock, IX:3479
  Strategic Arms Limitation Treaty, VIII:2759
  Teller, IX:3631-3633
  See also atom bomb; hydrogen bomb
nullification
  Adams, V:23
  Calhoun, V:395
  Scott, VI:2010
  Tyler, VI:2288, 2289
  Webster, VI:2345
Numantine Wars, I:345, 758
number theory
  Dedekind, V:639
  Fermat, IV:458-460
  Gauss, V:893-895
  Lagrange, IV:786
  Mersenne, IV:952
Numbers, Book of, I:563
Numerian, I:263
Numidia, I:529, 535, 536, 743
Nur al-Din, II:809, 810
Nuremberg Laws, IX:3491
Nurhachi, IV:1, 3, 421, 423
Nürnberg Trials, VIII:1438, 1440, 1463, 1696; IX:2878, 3262
Nuwar, Ali Abu, VIII:1793
NUWSS. *See* National Union of Women's Suffrage Societies
NWSA. *See* National Woman Suffrage Association
Nyerere, Julius, **VIII:2773-2776**
Nyssa, I:353, 354
Nystadt, Treaty of, IV:291, 1084

Oak Lane Country Day School, VII:673
Oakley, Annie, **VI:1677-1679;** VII:289
Oates, Titus, IV:285, **1038-1040**
O'Banion, Dion, VII:564
Oberth, Hermann, VII:440; VIII:1397; **IX:2777-2780,** 3751
  Menschen im Weltraum, IX:2779
  Rakete zu den Planetenräumen, Die, IX:2777
  Stoff und Leben, IX:2779
  Ways to Spaceflight, IX:2777
Oboi, IV:757
Obra de Berco, VIII:2739
Obregón, Álvaro, VII:542, 543; **IX:2780-2784**
Occasional Conformity Bill, IV:52
Occidental Literary Club, VII:880

Occitania, II:529, 530
Occoquan Workhouse Day, VII:850
Ockham, John of, II:669
Ockham, William of, II:194-196, **681-684,** 983
Ad conditorem canonum, II:682
Consultario de causa matrimoniali, II:683
Cum inter nonnullos, II:682
Dialogus, II:683
Quia quorundam, II:682
Quodlibeta septem, II:681
O'Connell, Daniel, V:652; **VI:1680-1683,** 1753
O'Connor, Flannery, **IX:2785-2788**
Everything That Rises Must Converge, IX:2787
Good Man Is Hard to Find and Other Stories, A, IX:2785
Habit of Being, The, IX:2787
Memoir of Mary Ann, A, IX:2787
Mystery and Manners, IX:2787
Presence of Grace, The, IX:2787
Violent Bear It Away, The, IX:2787
Wise Blood, IX:2785
O'Connor, Richard, V:147, 148
O'Connor, Sandra Day, **IX:2789-2792**
O'Connor, Thomas Power, **IX:2793-2795**
Life of Lord Beaconsfield, IX:2793
Octavia, I:70
Octavian. *See* Augustus
Octavius, Marcus, I:346
October Revolution. *See* Russian Revolution of 1917
Oda Nobuhide, IV:1327
Oda Nobunaga, **III:570-573,** 728, 1327
Oddi, II:836
Odets, Clifford, VII:795
Odoacer, **II:685-687**
Odo of Lagery. *See* Urban II
Odovacar, II:894, 895
Odria, Manuel A., VIII:1586
Odysseus, I:421, 422
Oecolampadius, Johannes, III:675
Oersted, Hans Christian, V:768
Offa, II:46
Offenbach, Jacques, **VI:1684-1687,** 2156, 2158
Ba-ta-clan, VI:1685
Belle Hélène, La, VI:1686
Bonne d'enfants, La, VI:1685
Contes d'Hoffmann, Les, V:650; VI:1686
Deux Pêcheurs, Les, VI:1685
Geneviève de Brabant, VI:1686
Musiciens de l'orchèstre, Les, V:651
Orphée aux enfers, VI:1685, 1686
Papillon, Le, VI:1686
Offeros. *See* Christopher, Saint
Official Languages Act of 1969, IX:3732
Ogala tribe, VI:1850
Ogaryov, Nikolay, V:1099, 1100
Ogatai Khan, II:378
Ogata Korin, **IV:1041, 1042,** 1258, 1259
Irises, IV:1041, 1042
Red and White Plum Blossoms, IV:1041
Ogdensburg Agreement, VIII:1983
Ogé, Vincent, IV:1338
Oglala Indians, V:574-576
Oglethorpe, James Edward, **IV:1043-1047**
Oh, Sadaharu, **IX:2796-2799**
Ohain, Hans von, IX:3974
O'Hara, Maureen, IX:3903
O'Hickey, Michael, VI:1481
O'Higgins, Bernardo, **VI:1688-1691**
Ohio
Appleseed, V:66-68
Beecher, V:171
Chase, V:477, 478
Glenn, VII:1387, 1388
Hanna, V:1030
Harding, VIII:1550-1552
Hayes, V:1075, 1076
Honda Motor Company, VIII:1725
newspapers, VI:2015
Taft, IX:3590, 3591
Williams, VI:2397
Ohio Company, IV:312
Ohio Indians, IV:198
oil industry
Arab oil embargo, VII:1120
Canada, IX:3733
Cárdenas, VII:571-573
Faisal, VII:1119, 1120
Mellon, VIII:2481
Mohammad Reza Shah Pahlavi, VIII:2566, 2567
OPEC, VII:591, 1115, 1116, 1119; IX:4079-4081
Rockefeller, VI:1896-1898
Oisc, I:380, 381
Ojeda, Alonzo de, III:45
Ojibwe Indians, VI:1585
O.K. Corral, V:736
O'Keeffe, Georgia, **IX:2800-2803,** 3534
Barn with Snow, IX:2801
Black Patio Door, IX:2801
Cow's Skull: Red, White and Blue, IX:2801
Pelvis with Moon, IX:2801
Ram's Head with Hollyhock, IX:2801
Ranchos Church, IX:2801

Shelton with Sunspots, The, IX:2801
Sky Above Clouds II, IX:2801
Stables, IX:2801
Okehazama, Battle of, III:570
O'Kelly, Seán T., **IX:2804-2807**
Okubo Toshimichi, VI:1936-1938
Olaf, Saint, II:201, 626, **691-694,** 837
Olaf I, **II:688-690,** 691
Olaf II. *See* Olaf, Saint
Olbers, Wilhelm, V:215
Old Age Pensions Act of 1898, VI:2018
Oldcastle, Sir John, III:338
Old Corps Whigs, IV:1074, 1075
Oldenbarnevelt, Johan van, **III:574-576**
Old Slater Mill, VI:2075
Old Testament
Aaron, I:1-4
Abraham, I:5-7
Athanasius, I:12
Cædmon, II:198, 199
Channing, V:471
Clement I, I:210
Cyrus the Great, I:234
David, I:241-244
Deborah, I:246, 247
Eusebius of Caesarea, I:323
Ezekiel, I:326-329
Ezra, I:330-333
Irenaeus, I:449
Isaiah, I:452-454
Jesus Christ, I:468
Moses, I:561-564
Nebuchadnezzar II, I:569-571
Origen, I:581
Philo of Alexandria, I:632-634
Porphyry, I:685
Pusey, VI:1828, 1829
Samuel, I:746, 748, 749
Solomon, I:798, 800, 801
Tertullian, I:849
Tyndale, III:735, 737
Olduvai Gorge, VIII:2146, 2147
Olgierd. *See* Algirdas
O'Leary, John, VI:1740
Oliva, Treaty of, IV:508, 509
Olivares, Count-Duke of, IV:1364
Olive Branch petition, IV:617
Oliver, Andrew, IV:692, 693
Oliver, King, VII:105, 106
Olivier, Sir Laurence, **IX:2808-2814**
Antony and Cleopatra, IX:2811
As You Like It, IX:2810
Carrie, IX:2811, 2812
Hamlet, IX:2810, 2811, 3872
Henry V, IX:2810, 2811, 3872
Julius Caesar, IX:2808
King Lear, IX:2811, 2813
Macbeth, IX:2810, 2812
Midsummer Night's Dream, A, IX:2808
Othello, IX:2810, 2813
Richard III, IX:2812, 3872
Romeo and Juliet, IX:2808, 2810
Taming of the Shrew, The, IX:2808
Titus Andronicus, IX:2812
Twelfth Night, IX:2808, 2810, 2812
Ollokot, V:1244
Olmstead v. United States, VII:422
Olmsted, Frederick Law, **VI:1691-1694;** VIII:1400, 1401
Cotton Kingdom, The, VI:1691
Olod Mongols, IV:758
Olomouc, Peace of, III:488
Olympia, V:657
Olympian religion, I:507
Olympics
Alcmaeon, I:34
Ali, VII:53
Coe, VII:725-728
Coubertin, VII:774-776
Didrikson, IX:4096, 4097
Henie, VIII:1629-1631
Killy, VIII:1965-1967
Laban, VIII:2059
Nero, I:579
Nervi, VIII:2722
Owens, IV:2862-2865
Pheidippides, I:622, 623
Pindar, I:644
Russell, IX:3270
Thorpe, IX:3672, 3674, 3675
Tokyo, IX:3337
Wightman, IX:3990
Olynthus, I:629
Omaha Magic Theatre, IX:3643, 3644
Omaha tribe, IX:3010, 3011
Omai, IV:353
O'Malley, Walter, IX:3196
Omar Khayyám, II:419, **695-697,** 801
Omega Point, IX:3628
Omega Workshops, VII:1254
OMGUS. *See* Military Government of the United States, Office of
Onassis, Aristotle, IX:2817
Onassis, Jacqueline Kennedy, **IX:2815-2818,** 3870

oncology. *See* cancer
O'Neill, Eugene, **IX:2819-2824**
All God's Chillun Got Wings, IX:3189
Desire Under the Elms, IX:2820
Emperor Jones, The, IX:2819, 2820; IX:3189
Hairy Ape, The, IX:2820
Iceman Cometh, The, VIII:1445; IX:2821, 2822
Long Day's Journey Into Night, VIII:1639; VII:281; IX:2822
More Stately Mansions, IX:2820
Mourning Becomes Electra, IX:2820
Part of a Long Story, IX:2820
Straw, The, IX:2819
Tale of Possessors Self-Dispossessed, A, IX:2820
Haunted, The, IX:2820
Thirst, IX:2820
Touch of the Poet, A, IX:2820
O'Neill, Thomas Philip, Jr., VII:88; **IX:2824-2826**
Oort, Jan Hendrik, **IX:2827-2828**
Oparin, Aleksandr Ivanovich, **IX:2830-2832**
Origin of Life, The, IX:2831
OPEC. *See* Petroleum Exporting Countries, Organization of
Open Theatre, IX:3642-3644
opera
Anderson, VII:70-72
Barber, VII:191-193
Berg, VII:272
Berlioz, V:205
Bizet, V:244-246
Borodin, V:286-288
Britten, VII:466, 468-471
Caruso, VII:598-601
Debussy, VII:884-886
Delibes, V:649-651
Delius, VII:893
Donizetti, V:684-686
Gluck, IV:549-551
Henze, VIII:1633-1635
Hindemith, VIII:1670-1672
Humperdinck, V:1162-1164
Janácek, VIII:1837, 1838
Menotti, VIII:2494-2496
Messiaen, VIII:2503-2505
Milhaud, VIII:2526, 2527
Monteverdi, IV:990-993
Norman, VIII:2769-2771
Offenbach, VI:1684-1687
Pavarotti, IX:2930-2932
Price, IX:3081, 3083, 3084
Puccini, IX:3093, 3094, 3096
Purcell, IV:1137-1139
Rameau, IV:1149
Ravel, IX:3129
Rimsky-Korsakov, VI:1889-1891
Rossini, VI:1913-1915
Scarlatti, IV:1213-1215
Schütz, IV:1221-1223
Strauss, IX:3556
Stravinsky, IX:3561
Telemann, IV:1319, 1320
Verdi, VI:2299-2301
Wagner, VI:2316, 2317, 2319
Weber, VI:2340-2342
Weill, IX:3926-3929
Operation Breadbasket, VIII:1824-1826
Operation People United to Save Humanity, VIII:1825, 1826
operetta
Gilbert and Sullivan, V:927-930
Offenbach, VI:1684-1687
Strauss, VI:2155, 2156, 2158
Opet Festival, I:734
Opium War, V:1166; VI:1376-1379
Oppenheimer, J. Robert, **IX:2833-2835**
Bethe, VII:301
Bohr, VII:347
Conant, VII:750
Fermi, VII:1147
Lawrence, VIII:2122, 2123
Neumann, VIII:2726
Rabi, IX:3102
Teller, IX:3632, 3633
Oppian Law, I:163
Oprichnina, III:387
Oran, Battle of, V:1
Orange, House of, IV:500-502, 1447-1449
oratorios
Neri, III:552
Telemann, IV:1321
Thomas, VI:2231
Elgar, VII:1052
Henze, VIII:1634
Walton, IX:3873
Oratory, Congregation of the, III:551-553
Orcagna, Andrea, **II:698-701**
Christ Conferring Authority on Saints Peter and Thomas Aquinas, II:698
Ordinatio Imperii, II:599
Ordóñez, Bartholome, III:696
Ordóñez, García, II:269
Oregon Trail, V:839, 840; VI:1735, 1738, 2078
Orestes, I:437; II:685

Organic Act of 1902, IX:3233
organic chemistry
Conant, VII:749
Diels, VII:927-929
Hahn, VIII:1513-1516
Liebig, VI:1366-1368
Mendeleyev, VI:1530
Wöhler, VI:2403-2405
Woodward, IX:4052-4055
Oribasius, I:261; II:712
Origen, I:416, **581-584;** II:995
Against Celsus, I:323, 583
Hexapla, I:582
On First Principles, I:582
On Prayer, I:583
Tetrapla, I:582
Orisun Theatre group, IX:3472
Orléans, Charles d'. *See* Charles d'Orléans
Orléans, Duc d', IV:813, **1048-1051**
Orlov, Count Grigory, IV:257, 259
Ormonde, second Duke of, IV:1277, 1278
Orozco, José Clemente, **IX:2836-2839**
Catharsis, IX:2838
Coming of Quetzalcoatl, The, IX:2838
Cortes and Malinche, IX:2837
Dive Bomber, IX:2838
House of Tears, IX:2836, 2837
Man of Fire, IX:2838, 2839
Omniscience, IX:2837
Prometheus, IX:2837, 2838
Return of Quetzalcoatl, The, IX:2838
Social Revolution, IX:2837
Sorrows of War, IX:2837
Trench, The, IX:2837
Zapatistas, IX:2838
Orphans Fund of the City of London, IV:1067
Orpheus, myth of, IV:961; VI:1685
Orphic Mysteries, I:67
Orphism, VII:889; VIII:2037
Orsini, Giordano, III:563
Ortega, Katherine Davalos, **IX:2840-2842**
Ortega y Gasset, José, **IX:2843-2845**
Dehumanization of Art and Notes on the Novel, The, IX:2844
Invertebrate Spain, IX:2843, 2844
Meditations on Quixote, IX:2843
Mission of the University, IX:2844
Modern Theme, The, IX:2843
On Love, IX:2844
Revista de Occidente, La, IX:2843
Revolt of the Masses, The, IX:2844
Toward a Philosophy of History, IX:2844
Ortiz, Juan, III:700
Ortodoxo Party, VII:617
Orwell, George, **IX:2846-2851**
Animal Farm, IX:2849, 2850
Burmese Days, IX:2848
Clergyman's Daughter, A, IX:2849
Coming Up for Air, IX:2849
Down and Out in London and Paris, IX:2848
Homage to Catalonia, IX:2849
"How the Poor Die," IX:2848
Keep the Aspidistra Flying, IX:2849
Nineteen Eighty-Four, IX:2849, 2850
Road to Wigan Pier, The, IX:2849
Osage Nation, IX:3607, 3608
Osborne, Thomas. *See* Leeds, First Duke of
Osborne, Thomas Mott, **IX:2852-2854**
Osceola, **VI:1695-1697**
O'Shea, William Henry, VI:1740, 1742
Osiander, Andreas, III:178
Osler, Sir William, **VI:1698-1701**
Principles and Practice of Medicine, VI:1698, 1699
Oslo Peace Accords, VII:93
Osman, **II:702-705**
Osorio, Elena, IV:1361
Ospedale degli Innocenti, III:91
Ossining Correctional Facility, IX:2853
Ossoli, Giovanni Angelo, V:850, 852
Ostend Manifesto, V:583
Ostpolitik, VII:428; VIII:2009
Ostrogoths, II:215, 555, 755, 894-897
Ostwald, Wilhelm, V:924; VII:114; **IX:2855-2858**
Scientific Foundations of Analytical Chemistry, IX:2856
Osuna, Duchess of, IV:148
Otakar II, II:797, 798
Otis, James, IV:691, 692
Otlet, Paul, VIII:2051, 2052
Otluk Beli, Battle of, III:51
Otric of Magdeburg, II:870
Öttingen, Arthur von, IX:2855
Otto I. *See* Otto the Great
Otto II, II:870
Otto III, II:449, 871
Otto IV, II:468, 510, 797
Otto, Nikolaus August, V:597; **VI:1702-1704**
Ottoboni, Cardinal Pietro, IV:360
Otto of Brunswick, II:542
Otto of Burgundy, II:798
Otto the Great, II:**706-708,** 869
Ottowa Indians, IV:513, 1110-1113
Oubangui-Chari, VII:1004, 1005

Oud, J.J.P., **IX:2859-2861**
Oudenarde, Battle of, IV:923, 924
Oudh, IV:632, 633; VI:1706
Our Lady of Mount Carmel, Order of. *See* Carmelites
Our Lady of Ransom, Order of. *See* Mercedarians
Outram, Sir James, **VI:1705-1707**
Ou-yang Hsui, **II:709-711**
  Hsin T'ang shu, II:710
  Hsin Wu-tai shih, II:709
Ovando, Nicolás de, III:174, 629
Overreach, Sir Giles, VI:1261
Ovetari Chapel, III:460, 461
Ovett, Steve, VII:726, 727
Ovid, **I:585-588**
  Amores, I:586; III:473
  Art of Love, I:586
  Metamorphoses, I:586, 587; IV:1118
Ovidian elegies, IV:416-419
Owen, Robert, V:402, **VI:1708-1710**
Owens, Jesse, **IX:2862-2866**
Oxenstierna, Axel, IV:304, **1052-1054**
Oxford, Provisions of, II:644, 645
Oxford Economic Society, VIII:1707
Oxford University
  Arnold, V:69-71
  Bodleian Library, III:62-64
  Burney, IV:227
  Conant, VII:749
  Green, V:988
  Heath, VIII:1606
  Hobhouse, VIII:1707, 1708
  Locke, IV:854, 855
  Mackinder, VIII:2321, 2322
  Macmillan, VIII:2340
  Neckham, II:663
  Wesley, IV:1426
  Wyclif, II:1009, 1011
Ozawa, Jisaburo, VIII:1527
Ozenfant, Amédée, VIII:2137

Pace Gallery, VIII:2730
Pacelli, Eugenio Maria Giuseppe. *See* Pius XII
Pachacuti, **III:577-579**
Pacheco, Francisco, IV:1364
Pacific Islands, VIII:1658-1660
Pacific Ocean
  Balboa, III:45-47
  Ballard, VII:181
  Dampier, IV:389
  Drake, III:225
  Mackenzie, IV:879-881
  Magellan, III:453-456
  Wegener, IX:3919
Pacific Railway Company. *See* Northern Pacific Railway Company
pacifism. *See* nonviolent resistance
Paderhorn, Diet of, II:973
Padua, University of
  Abano, II:2
  Fracastoro, III:270
  Harvey, IV:626
  Nicholas of Cusa, III:563
  Santorio, IV:1209, 1210
  Vesalius, III:754, 755
Páez, Jose Antonio, V:268
Paganini, Niccolò, **VI:1711-1714**
  Violin Caprice in A Minor, IX:3106
paganism
  Abraham, I:5
  Ambrose, I:44
  Assyria, I:459
  Bulgaria, II:175, 176
  Germany, II:167-169
  Gregory of Nyssa, I:352
  Helena, I:375, 376
  Lithuania, II:1001
  Siricius, I:791
  Stephen I, II:851, 853
  Tertullian, I:848
  Theodosius the Great, I:869, 871
  Widukind, II:974
  See also Neoplatonism
Page, William, V:294
Pagspa, II:566
Paine, Thomas, II:921; **IV:1055-1058;** V:523
  Age of Reason, The, IV:440, 1056
  Case of the Officers of the Excise, The, IV:1055
  Common Sense, IV:16, 1055, 1057
  Crisis papers, IV:1055, 1057
  Dissertations on Government, IV:1056
  Public Good, The, IV:1056
  Rights of Man, The, II:921; IV:440, 556, 1056; VI:2208
Paiva, Afonso de, III:197, 198
Palafox, José de, VI:1958, 1959
Palais Royal, IV:1048, 1049
Palatinate, IV:212
Palatine Palace, II:823
Palazzetto dello Sport, VIII:2722
Palermo Stone, I:547
Palestine
  Baeck, VII:150
  Balfour, VII:174

Begin, VII:243-245
Ben-Gurion, VII:251, 252
Bevin, VII:315
Dayan, VII:854-856
Eban, VII:1000
Faisal, VIII:1118-1120
Herzl, V:1105
Hussein I, VIII:1791, 1793-1795
Lawrence, VIII:2126, 2127
Meir, VIII:2472-2475
Mendelsohn, VIII:2488
Nasser, VIII:2695, 2696
Psamtik I, I:711
United Nations, VII:91, 502; VIII:2473
World Zionist Organization, VIII:2766-2768; IX:3930-3932
Palestine Liberation Organization
Arafat, VII:90-93
Begin, VII:245
Dayan, VII:855
Fahd, VII:1115
Faisal, VIII:1120
Hussein I, VIII:1793, 1794
Meir, VIII:2474
Nasser, VIII:2696
Pérez de Cuéllar, IX:2957, 2958
Palestrina, Giovanni Pierluigi da, III:107
Palladianism, IV:8, 9, 637; V:139
Palladio, Andrea, **III:580-583;** IV:8, 152
antichità di Roma, L', III:580
commentari di C. Givlio Cesare, I, III:580
quattro libri dell'architettura, I, III:580, 581
Palladius, I:602
Pallavicino, Benedetto, IV:990, 991
Palmer, Alice Freeman, **VI:1715-1718**
Palmer, A. Mitchell, VIII:1732
Palmer, Arnold, IX:3041
Palmer, Humphrey, IV:1423
Palmer, Potter S., V:783
Palmer, William, V:1012, 1013
Palmerston, Lord, V:528, 654; **VI:1719-1722,** 1931, 2003, 2308
Palomar, Mount, IX:3352
Pamphia, I:539
Pamphili, Cardinal, IV:360
Pamphilus, I:322; IV:684
Pampulha, Lake, VIII:2739
Pan, I:539, 621
Pan Africanism
Du Bois, VII:965
Lutuli, VIII:2282
Mobutu Sese Seko, VIII:2562-2564
Nkrumah, VIII:2762, 2763
Nyerere, VIII:2774
Tshombe, IX:3745
Panama Canal
Goethals, VIII:1408-1410
Gorgas, VIII:1435, 1436
Hay, V:1069, 1070
Lesseps, VI:1355-1357
Taylor, VI:2196
Panathenaea, I:649
Pandora, I:404
Pandit, Vijaya Lakshmi, **IX:2867-2870**
Paneth, Friedrich, VIII:1654
Pangaea, IX:3919
Panhellenic League, I:501
Pan-Islamism, VII:1081; VIII:2694
Pankhurst, Emmeline, **IX:2871-2875**
Pankhurst, Richard, IX:2871
Pan Ku, **I:589-592**
Han shu, I:589-591
Pannonia, II:41, 87
Pantheon, I:21
Pan-Turkism, VII:1081
Paoli, General, IV:175
PAP. *See* Partido Aprista Peruano
Papal Curia, II:930
Papal States
Alexander VI, III:14-17
Alva, III:19
Canova, V:410
Charlemagne, II:228
Innocent III, II:510
Italian nationalism, V:933
Julius II, III:405-407
Leo IX, II:582
Mazzini, VI:1515
Nicholas V, III:559, 560
Paul III, III:597
Pius IX, VI:1782, 1783
Pius XI, IX:3026
Papen, Franz von, **IX:2876-2879**
Paperclip, Operation, VII:441
Paper Constitution of 1244, II:453
Paphlagonia, I:558
Papin, Denis, **IV:1059-1061**
Pappus, **I:593-595**
Collection, I:73, 74, 593
Paraclesus, **III:584-587;** IV:187
Against the Grain, III:585
Great Astronomy, III:585
Great Surgery Book, III:585
Opus paramirum, III:585

Paramount Pictures, VII:117, 119, 896, 897, 932; VIII:1415; IX:3950
Paravas, III:789
Parentucelli, Tommaso. *See* Nicholas V
Pareto, Vilfredo, IX:3866
Paria, Le, VIII:1699
Paris
  Blanc, V:261
  Boffrand, IV:151
  Cambacérès, V:399
  Chanel's fashions, VII:650
  Chopin, V:493-495
  Cyrano de Bergerac, IV:385
  Hammerstein, VIII:1534
  Hardouin-Mansart, IV:901-903
  Mansart, IV:898
  Mazarin, IV:946
  Napoleon III, VI:1620-1622
  Olympic Games, VII:775, 776
  Picasso, IX:2997, 2998
  skyscrapers, VIII:2137
  Toulouse-Lautrec, VI:2247-2250
  World Exhibition of 1867, VII:268
  World's Fair of 1937, IX:3252
Paris, Peace of, II:454, 957
Paris, Treaty of:
  1259, II:605, 606
  1783, IV:39, 314, 713, 926
  1856, V:49
  1898, VI:1455; VII:480
Paris Commune, V:113; VI:1819, 2228
Parisian Geographical Society, VI:1356
Paris Observatory, VII:837, 838, 1326
Paris Opéra, VIII:2182-2184, 2504
Paris Peace Conference of 1919, VIII:2052, 2221
Park, Mungo, **VI:1723-1726**
  Travels in the Interior of Africa, VI:1724
Parker, Charlie, VII:1370, 1371; **IX:2880-2883**
  "Cherokee" IX:2882
  "Yardbird Suite" IX:2882, 2883
Parker, Dorothy, **IX:2884-2887**
  Coast of Illyria, The, IX:2886
  Ladies of the Corridor, IX:2886
  Portable Dorothy Parker, The, IX:2886
  "Soldiers of the Republic," IX:2886
  Star is Born, A, IX:2886
Parker, Matthew, **III:588-591**
Parker, Theodore, **VI:1727-1730**
Parker, ColonelTom, IX:3076, 3078
Parkes, Sir Henry, **VI:1731-1734**
  Stolen Moments, VI:1731
Park Güell, VII:1316
Parkinson, Sydney, IV:83
Parkman, Francis, **VI:1735-1739**
  Book of Roses, The, VI:1738
  California and Oregon Trail, The, VI:1735, 1738, 1862
  Count Frontenac and New France Under Louis XIV, VI:1736
  Discovery of the Great West, The, VI:1736, 1737
  France and England in North America, VI:1735, 1736, 1739
  Half-Century of Conflict, A, VI:1736, 1738
  History of the Conspiracy of Pontiac, VI:1736
  Jesuits in North America in the Seventeenth Century, The, VI:1736
  Montcalm and Wolfe, VI:1736
  Old Regime in Canada, The, VI:1736
  Vassall Morton, VI:1736
Parks, Rosa, VII:9; VIII:1973; **IX:2888-2891**
Parliament, English
  Attlee, VII:137
  Blackstone, IV:130
  Bolingbroke, IV:158, 160
  Bottomley, VII:384
  Buckingham, IV:212, 213
  Burke, IV:222-224
  Catholic emancipation, VI:1681-1683
  Chadwick, V:457-460
  Charles I, IV:279-281
  Churchill, VII:691-693
  Clarendon, IV:308, 309
  Clive, IV:325, 327
  Cobbett, V:523, 524
  Cromwell, IV:378, 380, 381
  East India Company, IV:631, 633
  Edward I, II:322-324
  Edward II, II:326-328
  Edward III, II:329, 331
  Edward IV, III:234, 235
  English Civil War, IV:99
  Fairfax, IV:446-449
  Fortescue, III:267-269
  George III, IV:541
  George IV, V:902-905
  Gladstone, V:935, 936, 938
  Gundpowder Plot, III:257-259
  Hale, IV:597
  Henry IV, II:457-460
  James I, IV:700
  James II, IV:704, 705
  Johnson, IV:728
  Lambert, IV:789-791
  Leeds, IV:822

Liverpool, VI:1395
Macaulay, VI:1427-1430
Merciless Parliament, II:787
Monck, IV:971-973
Montfort, II:643-646
Oglethorpe, IV:1043
Paterson, IV:1066-1068
Pelham, IV:1074-1076
Place, VI:1788
Pugin, VI:1823
Pym, IV:1141-1143
Shaftesbury, IV:1228-1231
Strafford, IV:1285-1288
Walpole's architecture, V:138-140
Webb, IX:3908
Wilson, IV:1456-1459
See also Commons, House of; Lords, House of
Parliament, French. *See* National Assembly (France)
Parliament Act of 1911, VII:122, 123; VIII:2112; IX:2804
Parma, Cathedral of, III:186
Parma, Duchess of, III:781
Parma, Duke of, III:255, 256
Parmenides, I: 249-251,**596-599,** 972
Aletheia, I:597
Doxa, I:597
Peri physeos, I:596
Parmenio, I:40
Parnassus, VI:1334, 1336
Parnell, Charles Stewart, **VI:1740-1743;** VIII:1891; IX:2793, 2871, 2873
Parr, Catherine, III:194, 237, 241, **592-594**
Lamentation or Complaynt of a Sinner, A, III:594
Prayers and Meditations, III:594
Parrington, Vernon L., **IX:2892-2895**
Main Currents in American Thought, IX:2892-2895
Parry, Caleb, IV:721, 722
Parry, William Edward, VI:1907
Parsees, I:977
Parson's Cause of 1763, IV:647
Parsua, I:236
Parsva, I:916
Parthenon, I:609, 624-626
Parthia, I:64, 70, 159, 882, 901, 902
Parti Démocratique de Guinée, IX:3711-3713
Parti Démocratique de la Côte d'Ivoire, VIII:1754-1756
Partido Aprista Peruano, VIII:1585, 1586
Partido Komunistang Pilipinas, VIII:2421
Partido Nacional Revolucionario, VII:543, 544
Partindo, VIII:1577
Partisan Review, The, VIII:2304
Parti Socialiste Français, V:1222
Parton, Dolly, **IX:2896-2898**
Best Little Whorehouse in Texas, The, IX:2897
Coat of Many Colors, IX:2897
Dumb Blonde, IX:2896
Here You Come Again, IX:2896
My Tennessee Mountain Home, IX:2897
Nine to Five, IX:2896, 2897
Rhinestone, IX:2897
Something Fishy, IX:2896
Steel Magnolias, IX:2897
Straight Talk, IX:2897
Trio, IX:2897
Wild Texas Wind, IX:2897
Partridge, John, IV:1307
Pascal, Blaise, IV:952, **1062-1065**
Pensées, IV:1063
Provincial Letters, The, IV:1062
Paschal II, II:74, 823
Paschal III, II:359
Paschasius, II:773, 774
Passerini, Silvio, III:743
Pasternak, Boris, **IX:2899-2902,** 3754, 3755
Above the Barriers, IX:2899
Blind Beauty, The, IX:2901
Doctor Zhivago, IX:2900, 2901
I Remember, IX:2901
My Sister, Life, IX:2899
On Early Trains, IX:2900
Safe Conduct, IX:2900
Second Birth, IX:2900
Spektorsky, IX:2900
Vastness of Earth, The, IX:2900
When the Skies Clear, IX:2901
Pasteur, Louis, VI: 1317,**1744-1748**
Pasteur Institute, VII:546-548
Pastors, Company of, III:118
Pastors' Emergency League, VIII:2743
Patel, Vallabhbhai, Jhaverbhai, **IX:2903-2906**
Pater, Walter, **VI:1749-1751,** 2377
Marius the Epicurean, VI:1750
Studies in the History of the Renaissance, VI:1749
Paterson, William, **IV:1066-1069**
Paton, Alan, **IX:2907-2910**
Ah, but Your Land Is Beautiful, IX:2909
Cry the Beloved Country, IX:2908, 2909
For You Departed, IX:2909
Journey Continued, IX:2909

Long View, The, IX:2909
Too Late the Phalarope, IX:2908, 2909
Towards the Mountain, IX:2909
Patrick, Saint, **I:600-603**
Confession, I:600
Epistle to the Soldiers of Coroticus, I:600, 602
Patriotic Front, VIII:2647, 2648
Patriot King, IV:160
Patterson, Floyd, VII:54
Patton, George S., VII:403, 404; **IX:2911-2914**
Pau Casals Orchestra, VII:607
Paul, Saint, **I:604-608**
Abraham, I:7
Chrysostom, I:184
Clement I, I:210
Epicurus, I:297
Ezekiel, I:329
letter to the Romans, VII:204, 499
Peter, I:615
Renan, VI:1866
Stephen, I:823, 824
Paul I (Russian Czar), V:44
Paul I (Pope), IV:260, 1300
Paul III (Pope), III:152, 160, 519, **595-598,** 788
Paul IV (Pope), IV:583
Paul VI (Pope), II:221; III:715; VI:2031; VIII:1863; **IX:2915-2918**
Human Vitae, IX:2916
Sacerdotalis Caelibatus, IX:2917
Paul, Alice, **IX:2919-2922**
Paulesco, Nicolas, VII:189
Paulhan, Jean, VII:1074, 1075
Pauli, Wolfgang, **IX:2923-2925**
Pauling, Linus, VII:412; **IX:2926-2929,** 3655, 3898, 3996, 3997
Cancer and Vitamin C, IX:2928
Nature of the Chemical Bond and the Sructure of Molecules and Crystals, IX:2927
Vitamin C and the Common Cold, IX:2928
Paulinus, Suetonius, I:136-138
Paul of Aegina, **II:712-714**
Epitome, II:712, 713
Paul the Deacon, I:931
Paulus, Lucius Aemilius, I:335, 757
Pausanius, I:677, 691, 764
Pavarotti, Luciano, **IX:2930-2932**
Bohème, La, IX:2930, 2931
Fille du régiment, La, IX:2931
Three Tenors in Rome, IX:2931
Pavia, Battle of, III:159, 274
Pavia, Council of, II:48
Pavlov, Ivan Petrovich, **IX:2933-2936**
Pavlova, Anna, **IX:2937-2940**
Autumn Leaves, IX:2939
Dumb Girl of Portici, The, IX:2939
Giselle, IX:2939
Immortal Swan, The, IX:2939
Pavlovich, Nikolay. *See* Nicholas I
Pawnee Indians, IV:1096
Pax Romana, I:134, 585
Payne-Aldrich Tariff Act, IX:3596
Pazzi Chapel, III:91, 92
Pazzi conspiracy, III:496
PDCI. *See* Parti Démocratique de la Côte d'Ivoire
Peace, University of, IX:3018
Peace River, IV:880
Peacham, Edmund, IV:332
Peachtree Creek, battle of, V:1053
Peacock Throne, IV:1233, 1234
Peale, Charles Willson, **IV:1070-1073**
Peano, Giuseppe, IX:3966
Pearl Harbor attack
Beard, VII:224
Halsey, VIII:1525
Lewis, VIII:2172
MacArthur, VIII:2297
Roosevelt, IX:3225
Pears, Peter, VII:468, 469, 470
Pearse, Patrick, IX:2804, 2805
Pearson, Lester, VII:680; IX:3731
Peary, Robert Edwin, VII:67; **IX:2941-2945**
Peasants Revolt of 1381, II:114-116, 368, 786, 921-923, 1011
Peasants' War, III:584
Pease, Edward, VI:2132, 2133
Pecci, Vincenzo Gioacchino. *See* Leo XIII
Pecham, John, **II:715-718**
Pechenegs, II:953
Peculiar, John, II:30
Pedersen, Knut. *See* Hamsun, Knut
Pedrarias, III:46, 47, 699
Pedrell, Felipe, VII:1127
Peel, Sir Robert, **VI:1752-1755**
Canning, V:406
Catholic emancipation, VI:1681, 1682
Derby, V:653
Disraeli, V:675, 677
Gladstone, V:935, 936
Hargreaves, IV:623
Liverpool, VI:1397
Melbourne, VI:1518, 1519
Péguy, Charles, VIII:2425
Pei, I.M., **IX:2946-2949**

Peirce, Charles Sanders, II:313; **VI:1756-1759**
Peisandros, I:17
Peisistratidae clan, I:553, 554
P'ei Ti, II:966, 967
P'ei Yao-ching, II:966
Pelagianism, I:936, 938; III:505
Pelé, **IX:2950-2953**
Pelham, Henry, IV:537, **1074-1077,** 1156
Pelham, Peter, IV:356
Pelopidas, I:290, 292
Peloponnesian League, I:611, 857
Peloponnesian War
  Alcibiades, I:31-33
  Aristophanes, I:88, 91
  Aspasia, I:115
  Cimon, I:200
  Euripides, I:318
  Pericles, I:611, 612
  Plato, I:655
  theater, I:879
  Thebes, I:290
  Thucydides, I:885-887; IV:662
  Xenophon, I:960
Pembroke, Earl of, II:326
penal system
  Australia, V:992
  Bentham, IV:108, 109
  Buxton, V:378, 379
  Cat and Mouse Act of 1913, IX:2873
  Day, VII:850
  Diepkloof, IX:2907
  Federal Bureau of Prisons, VII:510
  New York, V:369
  Oglethorpe, IV:1043
  Osborne, IX:2852-2854
  Pestalozzi, VI:1768
  Phillip, IV:1092
  Tocqueville, VI:2238
Penance, Sisters of, II:218
Pendleton Act of 1883, V:877
P'eng Hsien, I:188
P'eng Te-huai, VIII:2189-2191; **IX:2954-2956**
Peninsular War, V:406; VI:1958-1960, 2351-2353
Penn, William, IV:1046, **1078-1081**
  Brief Account of the Province of Pennsylvania, A, IV:1080
  England's Present Interest Discovered, IV:1078
  Essay Towards the Present and Future Peace of Europe, An, IV:1080
  Further Account of the Province of Pennsylvania and Its Improvements, A, IV:1080
  No Cross, No Crown, IV:1078
  Quakerism, IV:1078
  Truth Exalted, IV:1078
Pennsylvania
  Allen, IV:36
  Dickinson, IV:408, 410
  Gallatin, V:861
  Paine, IV:1056
  Penn, IV:1078-1081
  Rockefeller, VI:1896
  Wilson, IV:1458
Pennsylvania Railroad, V:420, 423; VI:1313, 1904
Penrose, Roger, VIII:1580
Pensacola, Treaty of, IV:876
Pentagon Papers. *See New York Times v. United States*
Pentateuch, I:561, 822; II:648; III:736, 737
Pentheus, I:319
Penthilus, I:651
People's Action Party, VIII:2150, 2151, 2400
People's Liberation Army, VII:689; VIII:2179, 2189-2191; IX:2955
People's Will Party, V:50
People United to Save Humanity, Operation, VIII:1825, 1826
Pepin I, II:226, 228, 599, 600
Pepin II, II:239
Pepo, Bencivieni di. *See* Cimabue
Percy, Henry, III:66
Percy, Thomas, III:257-259
Perdiccas, I:60, 721, 767
Perdiccas III, I:628
Peregrinus de Maricourt, Petrus, **II:719-722**
Peres, Fernando, II:30
Peres, Shimon, VII:1002
Perez, Antonio, III:602
Pérez de Cuéllar, Javier, **IX:2957-2960**
Perfidious Albion, IV:158
Pergamon, I:338, 339, 346
Peri, Jacopo, IV:991, 992
Pericles, **I:609-613**
  Aeschylus, I:10
  Anaxagoras, I:47, 48
  Aspasia, I:115, 117
  Cimon, I:200
  Propylaea, I:677
Periplus, I:368, 369
Perkins, Frances, **IX:2961-2964**
Perkins, J. Maxwell, VII:1162
Perkins Institution, V:1150, 1151
Perón, Eva, **IX:2965-2967,** 2969-2971
Perón, Juan, VII:373, 374; VIII:1760, 1761; IX:2965-2967, **2969-2972**

Perot, H. Ross, VII:708, 710; VIII:1432; **IX:2973-2975**
Pérotin, **II:723-725**
Magnus liber organi, II:723
Perotti, Niccolò, I:618
Perret, Auguste, **IX:2976-2978**
Perrin v. Blake, IV:907
Perry, Fred, **IX:2979-2982**
Perry, Matthew C., V:1181; **VI:1760-1763,** 1764
Perry, Oliver Hazard, **VI:1764-1766**
Persepolis, I:239
Perses, I:404
Pershing, John J., VIII:2429; IX:2911, 2913, **2983-2986,** 3813, 3814
Persian Empire
Achaemenian empire, I:233-235
Aeschylus, I:9, 10
Agesilaus II, I:17, 18
Alexander the Great, I:38, 40, 41
Cimon, I:198-201
Cleomenes I, I:214
Darius the Great, I:236-239, 553, 554
Delian League, I:47
Miletus, I:115
Herodotus, I:394, 396
Jerusalem, I:330, 331
Miltiades the Younger, I:553-555
Sergius I, II:819-821
Xenophon, I:958-960
Xerxes I, I:962-965
Persian Gulf War
Bush, VII:522
Fahd, VII:1115, 1116
Gore, VIII:1432
Hussein I, VIII:1794
Pérez de Cuéllar, IX:2958
Powell, IX:3070-3072
Persian Wars
Cimon, I:199
Herodotus, I:394, 396
Leonidas, I:501-503
Pheidippides, I:621-623
Phidias, I:624
Philip II of Macedonia, I:628-630
Themistocles, I:857-859
Perutz, Max, VII:412
Peshkov, Aleksey Maksimovich. *See* Gorky, Maxim
Pestalozzi, Johann Heinrich, V:845, 846; **VI:1767-1770,** 2118, 2119; VIII:2596
Christoph und Else lesen in den abendstuden das Buch "Lienhard und Gertrud," VI:1768
Evening Hours of a Hermit, VI:1767
How Gertrude Teaches Her Children, VI:1768
Leonard and Gertrude: A Popular Story, VI:1768
Petacci, Clara, VIII:2669
Pétain, Phillippe, VIII:2106; IX:**2987-2989**
Peter II the Catholic, II:529
Peter III, IV:257, 259, **1087-1090,** 1298
Peter, Saint, I:211, 243, 475, 477, **614-617,** 790
Peterborough, Third Earl of, IV:1277
Peter of Castelnau, II:302
Peter the Great, **IV:1082-1086**
Alexander Nevsky, II:54
Charles XII, IV:290-292
church and state, IV:1032
Peter III, IV:1087
Siberian exploration, IV:111
Petheneggs, II:87
Petit, Roland, VII:1177
Petit Luxembourg Palace, IV:152
Petit Pont, II:663
Petrarch, II:93, 152, 153, **726-731,** 790, 949
Africa, II:728
Book Without a Name, II:729
Canzoniere, II:726, 730
De otio religioso, II:729
Eclogues, II:729
Epistle to Posterity, II:730
My Secret, II:728
Physicke Against Fortune, II:729
Quorundam virorum illustrium epithoma, II:728
Rerum vulgarium fragmenta, II:730
Triumphs, II:726
Pettazoni, Raffaele, VII:1055
Pettigrew, Richard F., V:1030, 1031
Petty, William. *See* Shelburne, Lord
Petty-Fitzmaurice, Henry Charles Keith. *See* Lansdowne, Fifth Marquess of
Peucestas, I:767
PGA. *See* Professional Golfers' Association
Phaedra, I:318
Phaedrus, I:15, **618-620**
Aesopic Fables of Phaedrus, The, I:618-620
Phalanx, VIII:1903
Phalereus, Demetrius, I:538
Phanar, VI:2417
Pharisees, I:467-469, 471-473, 483, 604
Pharsalus, Battle of, I:149, 159, 167, 681, 918
Pheidias, I:76
Pheidippides, **I:621-623**
Phelps, Samuel, V:1187
phenomenology
Barthes, VII:207
Derrida, VII:912

Heidegger, VIII:1610
Husserl, VIII:1797, 1798
Jaspers, VIII:1843
Marcel, VIII:2408
Merleau-Ponty, VIII:2500-2507
Peirce, VI:1758
Scheler, IX:3348, 3349
Stein, IX:3506-3510
Pherecydes of Syros, I:727
Phidias, **I:624-627**
Philadelphia Convention, IV:1455, 1457, 1458; IV:495, 609
Philadelphia Museum, IV:1070, 1072, 1073
Philadelphia Orchestra, VII:192
Philadelphia Phillies, VII:717, 719; IX:3240
Philadelphia Research and Protection Association, IX:2961
Philanthropinum, IV:93, 94
Philiki Hetairia, VI:2417, 2418
Philip II (of France) II:603, **732-735,** 985
Philip II (of Macedonia), **I:628-631**
Aristotle, I:95, 873
Demosthenes, I:253-255
Menéndez de Avilés, III:507-509
Ptolemy Soter, I:720
Philip II (of Spain), **III:599-602**
Alva, III:18-20
Augsburg, III:161
Braudel, VII:436, 437
Catherine de Médicis, III:133
Cervantes, IV:265
Drake, III:224
Farnese, III:254, 255
Greco, El, III:311
Mary I, III:479, 480
Tudor family, III:733
William the Silent, III:781-783
Philip III (of France), II:736
Philip III (of Macedonia), I:721
Philip IV the Fair (of France), **II:736-739**
Philip V (of Macedonia), I:64, 365
Philip V (of Spain), IV:287
Philip, King. *See* Metacomet
Philip Augustus, II:511, 782, 783
Philip of Hesse, III:102
Philippi, Battle of, I:69, 141, 142, 160
Philippines
Cavendish, III:141
Dewey, V:656-658
Magellan, III:453-456
Marcos, VIII:2420-2423
U.S. acquisition, VI:1455
Philippine Veterans Mission, VIII:2420
Philippino-American War, V:656-658, 1069
Philips Pavilion, IX:4076
Philip the Bold, II:740, 832, 833, 834
Philip the Good, **II:740-743;** III:250
Philip the Magnanimous, **III:603-605**
Philistines, I:241, 243, 746, 748, 749
Phillip, Arthur, **IV:1091-1093**
Phillips, Henry, III:737
Phillips, Sam, IX:3076
Phillips, Wendell, **VI:1771-1774**
Constitution a Pro-Slavery Compact, The, VI:1772
Labor Question, The, VI:1773
Philo, IV:684
Philochorus, I:317, 319
Philolaus, I:729
Philo of Alexandria, **I:632-635**
Contemplative Life, The, I:634
Creation of the World, The, I:632
Phipps, Sir William, IV:940
Phocas, II:470, 819
Photius, II:674, 675
Photo Chemical Laboratory, VIII:2043
Photo-Secessionists, IX:3503, 3533, 3534
Phrynon, I:651
Piaget, Jean, VII:674; VIII:2599; **IX:2990-2993**
Child's Conception of Physical Causality, The, IX:2991
Child's Conception of the World, The, IX:2991
Judgement and Reasoning in the Child, IX:2991
Language and Thought of the Child, The, IX:2991
Piankhi, **I:636-639**
piano music
Bartók, VII:211, 212
Beethoven, V:178-181
Brahms, V:299-301
Chopin, V:493-496
Debussy, VII:886
Horowitz, VIII:1747-1750
Liszt, VI:1391-1393
Rachmaninoff, IX:3105, 3016, 3108
Schumann, VI:1993
Weber, VI:2340-2342
Piasts, II:210, 212
Picard, Émile, **IX:2994-2996**
Traité d' analyse, IX:2995
Picasso, Pablo, **IX:2997-3001**
Appolinaire, VII:82
Braque, VII:431, 432
Cocteau, VII:721
Demoiselles d' Avignon, Les, VII:431; IX:2998

Diaghilev, VII:921
Duchamp, VII:974
Gris, VIII:1483-1485
Guernica, IX:2998
Hockney, VIII: 1711, 1713
Lipchitz, VIII: 2199
Ma Jolie, VII:432
Miró, VIII:2546
Nicholson, VIII:2732, 2733
Parade, VIII:2449
Rousseau, VI:1922, 1923
Piccard, Auguste and Jean-Felix, **IX:3002-3005**
Piccinni, Niccolò, IV:550
Pickford, Mary, V:363; VII:1383; **IX:3006-3009**
Coquette, IX:3008
Daddy Long-Legs, IX:3008
Little Lord Fauntleroy, IX:3008
Pollyanna, IX:3008
Poor Little Rich Girl, IX:3006, 3008
Rebecca of Sunnybrook Farm, IX:3008
Rosita, IX:3008
Secrets, IX:3008
Sparrows, IX:3008
Taming of the Shrew, The, IX:3008
Pickles, Samuel, IX:3497
Pico della Mirandola, Giovanni, III:667, 670
Picotte, Susan La Fresche, **IX:3010-3012**
Pierce, Franklin, V:582, 682, 693; **VI:1775-1778**
Piero della Francesca, **III:606-609**
Baptism of Christ, III:606, 607
Battista Sforza, III:608
Count Federico da Montefeltro, III:608
Flagellation of Christ, III:608
Legend of the True Cross, III:607
Nativity, III:608
Resurrection, III:607
Pierre, Jean-Baptiste, IV:1376
Pietro, Guido di. *See* Angelico, Fra
Pietro d'Abano. *See* Abano, Pietro d'
Pietro della Gondola, Andrea di. *See* Palladio, Andrea
Pietro di Bernardone, Francesco di. *See* Francis of Assisi, Saint
Pigafetta, Antonio, III:455
Pike, Zebulon Montgomery, **IV:1094-1097**
Pilate, Pontius, I:469, **640-643**
Pilatus, Leontius, II:153
Pilgrims
Bradford, IV:189-191
Massasoit, IV:930-933
navigational maps, IV:271, 273
Standish, IV:1273-1275
Pillar Edicts, I:113, 114
Pinchot, Gifford, IX:3596
Pindar, **I:644-647,** 787; III:657
Isthmian Odes, I:644
Nemean Odes, I:644
Olympian Odes, I:644
Pythian Odes, I:644
Pinkey, William, VI:1571
Pinturicchio, III:16
Pinzón Brothers, III: 172, 173, **610-612**
Pipiltin, III:528, 529, 531
Pippin II, II:242
Pi-Ramesse, I:736
Pirandello, Luigi, **IX:3013-3016**
Henry IV, IX:3014
Late Mattia Pascal, The, IX:3013
Lazarus, IX:3014
Mountain Giants, The, IX:3014
New Colony, The, IX:3014
One, None, and a Hundred Thousand, IX:3013
Right You Are (If You Think So), IX:3014
Shoot, The Notebooks of Serafino Gubbio, Cinematograph Operator, IX:3013
Six Characters in Search of an Author, IX:3014
Piranesi, Giovanni Battista, IV:8
Pire, Dominique, **IX:3017-3019**
Pirelli family, **IX:3020-3022**
Pirenne, Henri, **IX:3023-3025**
Belgian Democracy: Its Early History, IX:3024
Histoire de Belgique, IX:3024
Medieval Cities, IX:3024
Mohammed and Charlemagne, IX:3024
PIRG. *See* Public Interest Research Group
Pisa, Council of, II:971
Pisano, Andrea, **II:744-746;** III:302-305
Pisano, Giovanni, II:744, **747-749,** 762
Pisano, Nicola, II:744, **747-749**
Pisistratidae, I:649
Pisistratus, **I:648-650**
Pisper, Mount, I:56, 58
Pissarro, Camille, V:453, 455, 456, 888; **VI:1779-1781**
Pisthetairos, I:91
Pithon, I:767
Pittacus of Mytilene, **I:651-654**
Pittsburgh Pact, VIII:2442
Pitt the Elder, William, **IV:1098-1101**
George II, IV:536-538
George III, IV:539
Hutchinson, IV:691, 692
Pitt the Younger, IV:1102
Wolfe, IV:1472

Pitt the Younger, William, **IV:1102-1105**
Bolingbroke, IV:161
Castlereagh, V:438-440
Erskine, IV:440, 441
Fox, IV:481, 482
George III, IV:542
Liverpool, VI:1395
Pius, Antoninus, I:358, 359, 523
Pius II, III:564, **613-615**
Chrysis, III:613
Commentaries of Pius II, The, III:614
Decameron, The, III:613
Tale of Two Lovers, The, III:613
Pius III, III:405
Pius V, III:243, **616-619**
In Coena Domini, III:617
Regnans in Excelsis, III:618
Pius VII, V:1248; VI:1782
Pius IX, V:11, 682, 933; VI:1348, 1477, **1782-1785**
Pius X, VIII:1858, 2425; XI:3026
Pius XI, V:389; VIII:1858; **IX:3026-3028,** 3030, 3031
Divini Redemptoris, IX:3027
Mit brennender Sorge, IX:3027
Non Abbiamo Bisogno, IX:3027
Quaragesimo Anno, IX:3027
Ubi Arcano Dei, IX:3026
Pius XII, VIII:1858, 1859; IX:2915, 2916, **3030-3032**
Humani Generis, IX:3031
Mediator Dei, IX:3031
Menti Nostrae, IX:3031
Miranda Prosus, IX:3031
Munificentissimus Deus, IX:3031
Mystici Corporis Christi, IX:3031
Pixodarus Affair, I:720
Pizarro, Francisco, III:372, **620-622;** VI:1815
Pizzolo, Niccolò, III:461
Placards, Affair of the, III:468
Place, Francis, **VI:1786-1789**
Illustrations and Proofs of the Principle of Population, VI:1787
plague. *See* black death
Plains Indian Wars, VI:1862
Planck, Max, VI:1799; VII:472; VIII:2476; **IX:3033-3035,** 3491
Introduction to Theoretical Physics, IX:3035
New Science, The, IX:3035
Scientific Autobiography and Other Papers, IX:3035
Universe in the Light of Modern Physics, The, IX:3035
Planned Parenthood of Southeastern Pennsylvania v. Casey, IX:2790
Plan of 1809. *See* 1809, Plan of
Plan Seventeen, VIII:1851-1853
Plantagenet, Geoffrey. *See* Anjou, Count of
Plantagenet, Henry, II:850
Plasgraf v. Long Island R.R., VII:576
Plassey, Battle of, IV:326
Plataea, battle of, I:788
Plath, Sylvia, **IX:3036-3039,** 3396
Ariel, IX:3037, 3038
Bell Jar, The, IX:3036-3038
Colossus and Other Poems, The, IX:3036, 3038
Crossing the Water, IX:3038
Plato, **I:655-658**
Antisthenes, I:67, 68
Apology, I:656
Aristotle, I:94-96
Banquet, The, I:507
Euthyphro, I:656
Galen, I:339
Gorgias, I:656
Jewett, V:1230
Laws, I:656
Menexenos, I:117
Meno, I:656
Parmenides, I:596, 597
Phaedo, I:14, 94, 698
Philebus, I:656
Plutarch, I:670
Posidonius, I:687
Protagoras, I:705-707
Razi, II:780
Republic, I:656; II:155; VI:1458
Socrates, I:793
Sophist, I:973
Symposium, I:117, 656
Theaetetus, I:656
Timaeus, I:698, 729
Xenophanes, I:956
Zeno of Citium, I:967
See also Neoplatonism; Platonism
Platonism, I:655-658
Abelard, II:10
Democritus, I:251
Eratosthenes of Cyrene, I:303
Origen, I:582
Philo of Alexandria, I:632
Psellus, II:759
Plato's Academy, I:656
Aristotle, I:94, 95
Euclid, I:307

Eudoxus of Cnidus, I:311
Justinian I, II:557
Protagoras, I:707
Zeno of Citium, I:967
Plautius, Aulus, I:136
Plautus, I: 171, 540, **659-661**
Amphitryon, I:659
Braggart Warriori, The, I:659, 660
Fabulae Varronianae, I:919
Twin Meanaechmi, The, I:659, 660; III:687
Player, Gary, **IX:3040-3043**
Playtn, John, II:823
Plectrude, II:242
Pléiade, La, III:**623-625,** 657-659
Plekhanov, Georgy, VIII:2160
Pleroma, I:912, 913
Plessis, Armand-Jean du. *See* Richelieu, Cardinal de
Plessis-Marly, Seigneur du. *See* Mornay, Philippe de
Pleyel, Ignaz Joseph, IV:148, 149
Pliny the Elder, I:102, 368, 369, **662-665,** 764, 765
Natural History, I:662-664, 813
Studiosi, I:66
Pliny the Younger, I:533, 534, 837, 838, 901
PLO. *See* Palestine Liberation Organization
Plotinus, I:128, 634, **666-669,** 683, 684
Enneads, I:667
Plowshare, Project, IX:3633
Plutarch, **I:670-672**
Archimedes, I:76
Brutus, I:140
Cleopatra VII, I:220
Democritus, I:251
Ethica (Moralia), I:92, 541
Lives, I:14, 670-672, 814, 816; IV:1119
Lysippus, I:516
Pheidippides, I:622
Pittacus of Mytilene, I:653
Solon, I:803
Pluto, IX:3699-3701
Plymouth colony, IV:189-191, 954, 1273-1275
Poale Zion movement, VII:251; VIII:2472
Pobedonostsev, Konstantin Petrovich, **VI:1790-1793**
Kurs grazhdanskago prava, VI:1791
Reflections of a Russian Statesman, VI:1791
Podestà, Palazzo del, III:81
Pocahontas, **IV:1106-1109,** 1122-1125, 1253-1255
Poe, Edgar Allan, V:150, 152, 1127; **VI:1794-1797**
"Bells, The," IX:3106
Eureka: A Prose Poem, VI:1796
"Fall of the House of Usher," VI:1796
"Hans Phfall," VI:2304
"Ligeia," VI:1796
"Ms. Found in a Bottle," VI:1794
"Murders in the Rue Morgue," VI:1796
Narrative of Arthur Gordon Pym, The, VI:1796, 2305
"Raven, The," VI:1796
Tales of the Grotesque and Arabesque, VI:1796
Tamerlane and Other Poems, VI:1794
"William Wilson," VI:1796
Poggio, **III:626-628**
Corpus inscriptionum Latinarum, III:628
De avarita, III:627
De varietate fortunae, III:626, 627
Fables of Poge the Florentyn, The, III:627
Historiarum, Florentini populi, III:627
Poincaré, Henri, **VI:1798-1800**
Science and Method, VI:1799
Poincaré, Raymond, VII:795; **IX:3044-3047**
Poinsett, Joel, V:839
Poisson, Siméon-Denis, V:865
Poissy, Colloquy of, III:133
Poitiers, Battle of, II:295
Pokanoket, Alexander. *See* Wamsutta
Pokanoket Indians, IV:954
Pole, Reginald Cardinal, III:480
Polignac, Jules de, V:483
Polikarpov, Nikolai, IX:3765
Polish Liberation Army, VII:243
Polish Succession, War of, IV:536, 1402
Politburo
Brezhnev, VII:460
Gorbachev, VIII:1423
Khrushchev, VIII:1961, 1962
Molotov, VIII:2571
Yeltsin, IX:4086
Zhukov, IX:4114
Polk, James K., **VI:1801-1805**
Bancroft, V:126
Barnum, V:135
Benton, V:196
Buchanan, V:347
Carson, V:431
Clay, V:509
Tyler, VI:2290
Van Buren, VI:2294
Pollack, Ben, VIII:1419
Pollock, Jackson, VII:1208; VIII:2024, 2025, 2581; **IX:3048-3051**
Autumn Rhythm, IX:3049
Birds of Paradise, IX:3049

Covered Wagon, The, IX:3049
Easter and the Totem, IX:3049
Going West, IX:3049
Guardians of the Secret, IX:3049
Lavender Mist, IX:3049
Lucifer, IX:3049
Number 5, IX:3049
Number 8, IX:3049
Red, IX:3049
Scent, IX:3049
She-Wolf, The, IX:3049
Sleeping Effort, IX:3049
Threshers, IX:3048
Troubled Queen, The, IX:3049
White Light, IX:3049
Polo, Marco, II:567, **750-754**
Travels of Marco Polo, The, II:753
Poltava, Battle of, IV:290
Polybius, **I:673-675,** 731, 757-759
Histories, The, I:673, 674
Polycarp, I:447, 448
Polyclitus, I:515, 516
Polycrates, I:314, 315
Polygnotus, **I:676-678**
Illiupersis, I:676, 677
Nekyia, I:677
Pommersfelden, IV:656
Pompeius, Sextus, I:519, 681, 682
Pompeius Strabo, I:679
Pompey the Great, **I:679-682**
Brutus, I:140
Caesar, I:149
Cassius, I:159
Cato the Younger, I:166-168
Crassus, I:816
Histories, I:687
Mithradates the Great, I:559, 897
Posidonius, I:687
Varro, I:918
Pompidou, Georges, **IX:3052-3054**
Ponce de Léon, Juan, **III:629-632,** 699
Pond, James B., V:715
Pond, Peter, IV:879
Pontadera, Andrea da. *See* Pisano, Andrea
Pontiac, IV:39, 40, 513, **1110-1114;** VI:1736
Pontiac's War. *See* Pontiac
Pontian, I:417
Pontus, Kingdom of, I:557-559, 828
Poona Sarvajanik Sabha, IX:3681
Poor Clares, II:401
Poor People's March on Washington, VII:10; VIII:1974
Pop Art, IX:3884-3886
Pope, Alexander, IV:156, 158, 159, 983, 984, **1115-1117**
Dunciad, The, I:156; IV:984, 1116
Eloisa to Abelard, IV:1115
Epistle to Dr. Arbuthnot, An, IV:1116
Essay on Criticism, An, IV:1115, 1116
Essay on Man, An, IV:1116, 1440
Lock of Berenice, The, I:156
Rape of the Lock, The, I:156; IV:1115; V:162
Popham, Edward, IV:132
Popov, Aleksandr Stepanovich, **VI:1806-1809**
Poppa, II:794
Popular Front, VII:335-337; VIII:1699, 2491
Populist Party, VII:479, 480
Poquelin, Jean-Baptiste. *See* Molière
Porcia, I:140, 141
Porphyry, I:666, 667, **683-685**
De abstinentia, I:684
Isagoge, I:683, 685
Kata Christanon, I:683
Porta, Giambattista della, IV:850
Porter, Cole, VII:1159; **IX:3055-3058**
"Love For Sale," IX:3055
"Night and Day," IX:3055
"Old-Fashioned Garden," IX:3055
"True Love," IX:3055
Porter, David, V:772
Porter, Edwin S., VIII:1480
Porter, Katherine Anne, **IX:3059-3062**
"Devil and Cotton Mather, The," IX:3060
Flowering Judas and Other Stories, IX:3060
"Maria Concepcion," IX:3060
Never-Ending Wrong, The, IX:3060
"Noon Wine," IX:3059, 3060
"Old Mortality," IX:3059, 3060
"Pale Horse, Pale Rider," IX:3059, 3060
Ship of Fools, IX:3060, 3061
Porter, William Sydney. *See* Henry, O.
Port Folio, The, V:225
Port of London Authority, VIII:2216
Port Royal, IV:271, 273
Posada, José Guadalupe, IX:2836
Posidonius, **I:686-689**
On Astronomical Phenomena, I:688
On Duty, I:688
On Emotion, I:688
On Heroes and Daemones, I:688
On the Ocean, I:689
On the Soul, I:688
On the Sun, I:688
On the Void, I:688

positivism
  Comte, V:543-545
  Croce, VII:801
  Gentile, VII:1336
  Harrison, V:1057-1059
  Peirce, VI:1758
Post, Wiley, IX:3206
Posthumus, Poenius, I:138
post-Impressionism
  Bonnard, VII:362, 363
  Duchamp, VII:972
  Fry, VII:1254
  Toulouse-Lautrec, VI:2247-2250
Potemkin, Grigory Aleksandrovich, IV:1299
Potter, Beatrix, **IX:3063-3065**
  Tale of Peter Rabbit, The, IX:3063, 3064
Poulenc, Francis, **IX:3066-3069**
  Aubade, IX:3067
  Bestiaire, Le, IX:3066
  Biches, Les, IX:3066
  Cocardes, IX:3066
  Concert champêtre, IX:3067
  Concerto in D Minor for Two Pianos and Orchestra, IX:3067
  Concerto in G Minor, IX:3067
  Dialogues des carmélites, IX:3068
  Figure humaine, IX:3068
  Litanies à la vierge, IX:3067
  Mamelles de Tirésias, Les, IX:3068
  Mass in G Major, IX:3067
  Mouvements perpétuels, IX:3066
  Rapsodie nègre, IX:3066
  Sept Répons des ténèbres, IX:3068
  Sonata for Violin and Piano, IX:3067
  Voix humaine, La, IX:3068
Pound, Ezra
  Eliot, VII:1058
  Frost, VII:1252
  H.D., VIII:1505, 1508
  Hemingway, VIII:1627
  Joyce, VIII:1892
  Kipling, VI:1291, 1292
  Lowell, VIII:2251
  Testament of François Villon, The, III:766
  Yeats, IX:4082
Poussin, Nicolas, IV:317-319, **1118-1121**
  Adoration of the Golden Calf, The, IV:1119
  Arcadian Shepherds, The, IV:1119
  Four Seasons, IV:1120
  Landscape with the Gathering of the Ashes of Phocion, IV:1119
  Martyrdom of Saint Erasmus, IV:1118
  Self-Portrait, IV:1119
Powell, Colin L., **IX:3070-3072**
Powell, John Wesley, **VI:1810-1813**
  Canyons of the Colorado, VI:1812
  Introduction to the Study of Indian Languages, VI:1812
  Report on the Lands of the Arid Region of the United States, VI:1812
Power, Tyrone, VIII:1631
Power Jets Limited, IX:3973, 3974
Powhatan, IV:1106, 1107, **1122-1125,** 1253
Poyntz, Thomas, III:737
Pozzo, Cassiano del, IV:1118, 1119
Praeconinus, Stilo, I:918-920
Praeneste, I:930, 931
Praetorian Guard, I:203, 640, 893
Prague, Peace of, IV:452, 1052
Prague National Opera, VIII:1837
Prague Spring, VII:968-970
Prandtl, Ludwig, **IX:3073-3075**
Prandtl-Glaubert rule, IX:3074
Prasutagus, I:137
Pratinas, I:878
Pravda, VII:38, 491; VIII:2571; IX:3409
Praxiteles, **I:690-693;** VIII:2611
  Aphrodite of Knidos, I:690-692
  Lizard Slayer, I:690, 692
  Satyr, I:690, 691
predestination
  Augustine, I:129, 936-938
  Calvin, III:120
  Channing, V:471
  Edwards, IV:428, 430
  Grotius, IV:579
  Laud, IV:797, 798
  Melanchthon, III:505
  Pym, IV:1141
  Racine, IV:1144
  Weber, IX:3911
Pre-emption Act, VI:2290
Pre-Raphaelite Brotherhood, III:76; V:1168-1170; VI:1928, 2215
Prescott, William Hickling, **VI:1814-1816**
  History of the Conquest of Mexico, VI:1815
  History of the Conquest of Peru, VI:1815
  History of the Reign of Ferdinand and Isabella the Catholic, VI:1814
  History of the Reign of Philip the Second, King of Spain, VI:1815
presidency, U.S.
  Adams, John, IV:16-20

Adams, John Quincy, V:20-24, 508
Arthur, V:77-81
Buchanan, V:346-348, 794
Bush, VII:520-522
Carter, VII:589-593
Cleveland, V:256, 512-516, 1054, 1055
Clinton, VII:707-711
Coolidge, VII:762-764
Eisenhower, VII:1043-1045
electoral college, IV:1244; V:196
Fillmore, V:792-794
Ford, VII:1180-1182
Garfield, V:77, 78, 80, 81, 256, 875-877
Grant, V:78, 131, 256, 975-978, 1075
Harding, VIII:1550-1552
Harrison, Benjamin, V:257, 582, 1053-1056
Harrison, William Henry, V:1061-1063
Hayes, V:78, 80, 256, 1075, 1076, 1078
Hoover, VIII:1727-1730
Jackson, V:195-198, 508, 1196-1199
Johnson, Andrew, V:296, 479, 583, 1232, 1233, 1235-1237
Johnson, Lyndon B., VIII:1866-1868
Jefferson, V:369, 370
Kennedy, VIII:1928-1931; IX:2815-2817
Lincoln, V:193, 272, 296, 478-480; VI:1380-1383
Madison, IV:886-890, 1000; VI:1464-1466
McKinley, V:1029-1031, 1069; VI:1453-1456
Monroe, V:395, 519; VI:1570-1573
Nixon, VIII:2758-2760
Perot, IX:2974, 2975
Pierce, V:582, 682, 693; VI:1775-1778
Polk, V:126, 135, 196, 347, 431, 509; VI:1801-1804
Reagan, IX:3136, 3138, 3139
Roosevelt, Franklin D., IX:3218, 3220, 3222-3226
Roosevelt, Theodore, V:56, 280, 1069, 1070; IX:3228, 3229, 3231
Smith, IX:3440, 3441
Spock, IX:3479
Taft, IX:3594-3597
Taylor, V:792, 793; VI:2194-2196
Truman, IX:3740-3743
Tyler, V:582; VI:2288-2291
Van Buren, V:127, 371, 372, 509; VI:2292-2295
Wallace, George C., IX:3859
Wallace, Henry A., IX:3862
Washington, IV:1405-1407
Presley, Elvis, **IX:3076-3080**
How Great Thou Art, IX:3078
Jailhouse Rock, IX:3078
King Creole, IX:3078
Love Me Tender, IX:3078
"That's All Right Mama," IX:3076
Prester John, II:567; III:197, 198, 215, 217
Prestonpans, IV:1183, 1184
Prevention Detention Act, VIII:2764
Price, Leontyne, VII:72, 193; **IX:3081-3084**
Price, Richard, IV:1475, 1477
Price, Uvedale, IV:1012
Pride, Thomas, IV:380, **1126-1128**
Pride's Purge, IV:1126-1128
Priestley, Joseph, IV:262, 805, 806, **1129-1132,** 1445
Chart of Biography, A, IV:1129
Essay on a Course of Liberal Education for Civil and Active Life, An, IV:1129
Essay on the First Principles of Government, An, IV:1130
History and Present State of Discoveries Relating to Vision, Light, and Colours, The, IV:1130
History and Present State of Electricity, The, IV:1129
Institutes of Natural and Revealed Religions, IV:1130
Letters to the Inhabitants of Northumberland, IV:1131
Political Dialogue on the General Principles of Government, A, IV:1131
Rudiments of English Grammar, The, IV:1129
Prigg v. Pennsylvania, VI:2148, 2191
Primo de Rivera, Miguel, IX:3784
Princeton, Battle of, IV:1469
Princeton University
Arendt, VII:99
campus design, VII:1131
Fitzgerald, VII:1161
Neumann, VIII:2724
Nevelson, VIII:2730
Oppenheimer, IX:2834
Turing, IX:3768
Princip, Gavrilo, VII:1198
printing press
Caxton, III:143-145
Condorcet, IV:349
Gutenberg, III:328, 330, 331
Mergenthaler, VI:1541-1543
Walter, VI:2325
Priscian, **II:755-757**
De laude imperatoris Anastasii, II:755
De siderbus, II:756

Institutiones grammaticae, II:755, 756
Priscianus major, II:755
Priscianus minor, II:755
Priscillian, **I:694-697,** 791
Priscus, Marius, I:838
Privilegium Ottonianum, II:707
Privy Council, IV:309
Proclus, **I:698-701;** II:985
Elements of Theology, The, I:698
Procopius of Caesarea, II:897
Secret History of the Court of the Emperor Justinian, II:890, 892
Professional Golfers' Association, IX:4049, 4050
Profumo, John, VIII:2343
Progressive Conservative Party of Canada, VIII:2655-2657
Progessives, Academy of the, III:125-127
Prohibited Books, Index of, III:16, 451, 714; IV:521, 522; V:933
Prohibition (of alcohol)
Butler, VII:525
Capone, VII:563-565
Catt, VII:629
Harding, VIII:1550
Hayes, V:1078
Nation, VI:1631, 1633
New Zealand, VIII:2445
Sunday, IX:3584
Willard, VI:2389, 2390
See also temperance movement
Prokhorov, Aleksandr, VII:214, 215
Prokofiev, Sergei, **IX:3085-3088**
Alexander Nevsky, IX:3085, 3087
Buffoon, The, IX:3086
Cinderella, IX:3087
Classical, IX:3086
Gambler, The, IX:3086, 3087
Ivan the Terrible, IX:3087
Love for Three Oranges, IX:3086
On the Dnepr, IX:3087
Pas d'acier, Les, VIII:2450; IX:3087
Peter and the Wolf, IX:3085, 3087, 3088
Prodigal Son, The, VIII:2182; IX:3087
Queen of Spades, IX:3087
Romeo and Juliet, IX:3085, 3087
Scythian Suite, IX:3086
War and Peace, IX:3087
Proletkult Theater, VII:1047
Prometheus, I:404; II:664
Promised Land, I:563
Prontosil, VII:1167
Propertius, Sextus, **I:702-704**
Elegies, I:520, 702-704
prophecy
Deborah, I:246, 247
Delphi oracle, I:254, 268, 280
Ezekiel, I:326, 328, 329
Isaiah, I:452-454
Jeremiah, I:328, 459-461, 569
Johanan ben Zakkai, I:472
Nostradamus, III:567-569
Samuel, I:748
Savonarola, III:667-670
Propylaea, I:676, 677
Prosper of Aquitane, I:936, 937
Protagoras, I:317, 624, **705-708**
Contrary Arguments, I:706
On the Gods, I:706
Truth, The, I:706
Protective Tariff of 1816, VI:2075
Protestant League, IV:591
Protestant missionary movement, IV:1488-1490
Protestant Reformation
Aristippus, I:87
Bucer, III:101-103
Calvin, III:117, 118, 120
Catherine of Aragon, III:139
Charles V, III:159-161
Clement VII, III:166-168
Copernicus, III:178
Cotton, IV:372
Coverdale, III:193-195
Cranach, III:200-202
Cromwell, III:208-210
Edward VI, III:237-239
Erasmus, III:248
Eucharistic controversy, II:774
Ferdinand II, IV:450-452
France, III:333-335; IV:104
Gardiner, III:291-293
Harnack, VIII:1558
Henry IV, III:333-335
Henry VIII, III:68
Hotman, III:362-365
Hus, II:487-490
Laud, IV:797-799
Luther, III:443, 445, 446
Menno Simons, III:512
Ridley, III:654-656
Ritschl, VI:1894
Tertullian, I:850
Tyndale, III:735-737
Weber, IX:3910, 3911

Wyclif, II:1011
Zwingli, III:791-794
See also Counter-Reformation
Protestant Union, IV:451
protons
Chadwick, VII:635, 636
cyclotron development, VII:380; VIII:2123
McMillan, VIII:2336
Millikan, VIII:2541
Yukawa, IX:4090
Proudhon, Pierre-Joseph, **VI:1817-1820**
De la capacité politique des classes ouvrières, VI:1819
De la justice dans la révolution et dans l'église, VI:1818
Fédération de l'unité en Italie, La, VI:1819
General Idea of the Revolution in the Nineteenth Century, The, VI:1818
Guerre et la paix, La, VI:1819
Révolution sociale démontrée par le coup d'état du 2 décembre, La, VI:1818
System of Economic Contradictions, VI:1818
What Is Property?, VI:1817, 1818
Proust, Antonin, VI:1471
Proust, Marcel, **IX:3089-3092**
By Way of Sainte-Beuve, IX:3089
Jean Santeuil, IX:3090
Pleasures and Regrets, IX:3089
Remembrance of Things Past, IX:3090, 3091, 4013, 4014
Swann's Way, IX:3090
Time Regained, IX:3090
Prouty, Olive Higgins, IX:3036
Provincetown Players, VII:794
Prudential Assurance Company, VII:384
Prussian Academy of Arts, VIII:2017
Prussian Academy of Sciences, VIII:1557
Prussian-French War. *See* Franco-Prussian War
Pruth River, battle at the, IV:290
Prynne, Hester, V:1064, 1066
Prynne, William, IV:798, 799
Przywara, Erich, IX:3508
Psalms, Book of, I:241, 243, 244, 563; III:101; VI:1829
Psalter, VI:1829
Psamtik I, **I:709-711**
Psellus, Michael, **II:758-761**
Chronographia, II:759, 760
"Dialogue on the Operation of the Daimons," II:759
"On Teaching Miscellany," II:759
Pseudo-Dionysius, I:258, 699; II:860
Pskov, II:52
Psychical Research, Society for, VI:2063
psychoanalysis
Bleuler, VII:329, 330
Breuer, VII:452-454
Freud, VII:1224-1226
Fromm, VII:1246-1248
Horney, VIII:1744-1746
Jung, VIII:1896, 1898, 1899
Lacan, VIII:2061-2063
Piaget, IX:2990
Ptah, I:636, 637
Ptolemy, **I:712-715**
Alhazen, II:63, 65
Almagest, I:74, 407, 410, 567, 712-714; II:20, 63
Battani, II:121, 122
Copernicus, III:176, 178, 179
geocentric theory, I:409
Geography, I:713, 714; III:515, 676, 759
Harmonica, I:714
Idrisi, II:507
Tetrabiblos, I:713, 714
Ptolemy II. *See* Ptolemy Philadelphus
Ptolemy III Euergetes, I:304
Ptolemy IV, I:63, 305
Ptolemy V, I:64
Ptolemy XII Auletes, I:218
Ptolemy XIII Philopator, I:218
Ptolemy XIV, I:218, 220
Ptolemy Philadelphus, I:231, **716-719**
Ptolemy Soter, I:307, 716, 717, **720-723,** 767-769
public health
Chadwick, V:459, 460
Disraeli, V:678
Gorgas, VIII:1434-1437
Virchow, VI:2314
Public Health Act of 1848, V:460
Public Health Act of 1875, V:678
Public Interest Research Group, VIII:2680
Public Safety, Committee of, IV:394, 395, 912, 1172, 1206, 1207; V:398
Public Schools Act of 1866, VI:1732, 1734
Public Weal, League of the, III:434
Public Works Administration, IX:2963
Publius, IV:610
Puccini, Giacomo, **IX:3093-3097**
Bohème, La, VII:599; IX:2930, 3707
Edgar, IX:3093
Fanciulla, V:1163; IX:3094
Madame Butterfly, VII:599; IX:3094
Manon Lescaut, IX:3094
Mass of Glory, IX:3093

Rondine, La, IX:3094
Tosca, VII:599; IX:3094, 3158
Trittico, Il, IX:3094
Turandot, IX:3096
Villi, Le, IX:3093
Pucelle, Jean, II:307, **762-765**
Belleville Breviary, The, II:762-764
Breviary of Blanche of France, The, II:762
Hours of Jeanne d'Evreux, The, II:762, 763
Hours of Jean of Savoy, The, II:762
Pufendorf, Samuel von, **IV:1133-1136**
Elementorum jurisprudentiae universalis libri duo, IV:1133
On the Law of Nature and Nations, IV:1134
Present State of Germany, The, IV:1133
Whole Duty of Man According to the Law of Nature, The, IV:1134
Puffer Whim, VI:2252
Pugachev, Emelyan Ivanovich, VI:1833
Pugin, Augustus Welby Northmore, V:139; **VI:1821-1824,** 2002
Contrasts, VI:1822
True Principles of Pointed or Christian Architecture, VI:1822
Pujo Committee, VI:1582
Pulcher, Publius Clodius, I:196, 680, 681
Pulitzer, Joseph, V:741; **VI:1825-1827;** VIII:1601, 1603
Pullman Company, V:55; IX:3114
Pullman Strike of 1894, VII:881
Pulszky, Romola de, VIII:2748
Pulteney, William, IV:1074, 1075, 1403; VI:2208
Punch, VIII:2543
Punic Wars. *See* Second Punic War; Third Punic War
Punitive Expedition, IX:2984
Punt, kingdom of, I:373
Pupin, Michael, VIII:2539
Purcell, Henry, **IV:1137-1140;** VII:471
Dido and Aeneas, IV:1139
Dioclesian, IV:1139
Indian Queen, The, IV:1139
King Arthur, IV:1139
Purcell, John B., V:402
Pure Land Buddhism, II:537, 538, 666
Puritanism
Adams, IV:12
Andrewes, IV:46
Beaumont and Fletcher, III:56
Bradford, IV:190
Bunyan, IV:219
Cotton, IV:371, 372
Coverdale, III:193-195
Cromwell, IV:378, 1127
Edwards, IV:428-431
Eliot, IV:435
Hale, IV:597, 598
Hawthorne, V:1064, 1066
James I, IV:700
Laud, IV:798
Massasoit, IV:930
Mather, Cotton, IV:934-937
Mather, Increase, IV:938-941
Metacomet, IV:954-956
Parker, III:589
Parrington, IX:2893-2895
Pym, IV:1141, 1142
Sewall, IV:1225-1227
Standish, IV:1273-1275
Weber, IX:3911
Williams, IV:1451
Winthrop, IV:1463-1465
Pusey, E.B., **VI:1828-1831**
Daniel the Prophet, VI:1829
Doctrine of the Real Presence, The, VI:1829
Eirenicon, An, VI:1829
Historical Enquiry into the Probable Causes of the Rationalist Character, An, VI:1828
Library of Fathers of the Holy Catholic Church, VI:1829
Minor Prophets,, The, VI:1829
Real Presence, The, VI:1829
Scriptural Views of Holy Baptism, VI:1829
PUSH. *See* People United to Save Humanity, Operation
Pushkin, Alexander, VI:1352, 1353, **1832-1835**
"André Chenier," VI:1832
Boris Gudonov, VI:1833, 1834
Captain's Daughter, The, VI:1833, 1834
Count Nulin, VI:1832, 1834
Eugene Onegin, VI:1833, 1834, 2198
Gabriel: A Poem, VI:1833, 1834
Gypsies, The, VI:1832
Poltava, VI:1833
Prisoner of the Caucasus, VI:1832
Queen of Spades, The, VI:1833, 1834
Ruslan I Lyudmila, VI:1832, 1834
Tales of Belkin, The, VI:1833
Pydna, I:629
Pym, John, **IV:1141-1143,** 1287
Pyramid, Battle of the, IX:2947
Pyrenees, Treaty of the, IV:343, 947
Pyréolophore, VI:1657, 1658, 1660
Pyrgopolynices, I:660

Pyrrhon of Elis, **I:724-726**
Pyrrhonism, IV:685
Pythagoras, I:34, 35, 99, **727-730**
Pythagorean Theorem, I:729
Pytheas, **I:731-733**

Qaddafi, Muammar al-, **IX:3098-3100**
    Jamahiriyah, IX:3099
Qajar Dynasty, VIII:1957, 2566, 2567
Qandahar, III:36
Qarakhanids, II:70
Qavam, Ahmad, VIII:2566
Qavurt, II:68
Qom, VIII:1957, 1958
Quakers
    Alcott, Bronson, V:37
    Alcott, Louisa May, V:40
    Anthony, V:61
    Dalton, V:602
    Darby, IV:396, 397
    Forster, V:804, 805
    Fox, IV:484-486
    Fry, VII:1253
    Hoover, VIII:1730
    Lancaster, VI:1309
    Mott, VI:1600-1602
    Nixon, VIII:2758-2760
    Paul, IX:2919
    Penn, IV:1078-1080
    Ross, IV:1191-1193
    Truth, VI:2255
    Tubman, VI:2265
    Whittier, VI:2374
    Williams, IV:1453
quantum mechanics
    Bethe, VII:300
    Bohr, VII:345, 347
    Broglie, VII:472-474
    Einstein, VII:1035, 1036
    Hawking, VIII:1580, 1582, 1583
    Heisenberg, VIII:1617-1619
    Huygens, IV:697
    Landau, VIII:2073-2075
    Lorentz, VIII:2235-2237
    Neumann, VIII:2726
    Pauli, IX:2923-2924
    Pauling, IX:2927
    Planck, IX:3033-3035
    Poincaré, VI:1799
    Rutherford, IX:3278
    Schrödinger, IX:3362-3364
    Schwarzschild, IX:3368
    Teller, IX:3631
    Yukawa, IX:4092
Quapaw, IV:733
Quatre-Bras, Battle of, VI:1647
Quatremère de Quincy, V:411
Quayle, Dan, VII:521
Quebec
    Campbell, VII:550, 551
    Carleton, IV:246-248
    Champlain, IV:273, 274
    Chrétien, VII:680-682
    conscription, VII:367; VIII:1984
    King, VIII:1982
    Laurier, VIII:2100-2103
    Mackenzie, VI:1451
    Mulroney, VIII:2655-2657
    Official Languages Act of 1969, IX:3732
    Sauvé, IX:3344, 3345
    Trudeau, IX:3730-3732
Quebec, Battle of, IV:179, 1471-1473
Quebec Act, IV:247
Queensbury, Marquis of, VI:2379
Queenstown, Battle of, VI:2009
Quessant, battle of, IV:1048
Quetzalcóatl, III:190, 528, 529, 531
Quimby, Phineas P., V:739
Quinisext Council. *See* Second Trullan Synod
Quintana, Juan de, III:675
Quintetto Boccherini, IV:149
Quivira, III:182
Qumran, I:481
Quraysh, II:504
Qutlugh-Shah, II:383
Qutlumush ibn Arslan Israil, II:68

Rabanus, Maurus, II:756, **766-769**
    De computo, II:767
    De institution clericorum, II:766
    De laudibus sanctae crucis, II:766
    De natura rerum, II:768
    De oblatione puerorum, II:767
    De reuerentia filiorum erga patres, II:767
    De uirtuibus et uitiis, II:767
    Martyrologium, II:768
Rabelais, François, **III:633-637,** 764; VII:153
    Gargantua, III:634, 636
    Pantagruel, III:633
    Third Book, III:468
Rabi, Isidor Issac, **IX:3101-3104**
Rabin, Yitzhak, VII:93
Rachmaninoff, Sergei, **IX:3105-3108**
    Bells, The, IX:3106

Concerto No. 3 in D Minor, IX:3106
Isle of the Dead, The, IX:3105, 3108
Piano Concerto No. 2 in C Minor, IX:3105
Rhapsody on a Theme by Paganini, IX:3106
Symphonic Dances of the Op. 45, IX:3106
Symphony No. 2 in E Minor, IX:3105
Racine, Jean, IV:172, 365, **1144-1147;** VII:207, 208
Alexander the Great, IV:1145
Andromache, IV:1145
Athaliah, IV:1146
Bajazet, IV:1146
Bérénice, IV:1146
Britannicus, IV:1146
Cantiques spirituels, IV:1146
Esther, IV:1146
Litigants, The, IV:1145
Mithridates, IV:1146
Phaedra, IV:1146
Theban Brothers, The, IV:1145
racism
Anderson, VII:72
Baldwin, VII:164-166
Benedict, VII:257
Garvey, VII:1311-1313
Gordimer, VIII:1429, 1430
Hansberry, VIII:1545
Holiday, VIII:1717
Le Bon, VIII:2135
Louis, VIII:2243
Malcolm X, VIII:2373, 2375, 2376
Morrison, VIII:2626
Parks, IX:2888-2891
Robinson, IX:3193, 3194, 3196
Roosevelt, IX:3218
Woods, IX:4050
See also apartheid; discrimination, racial; segregation
Radcliffe College, V:748; VII:750
Radical Dissenters, IV:1475, 1478
Radical Republicans, VI:2137; VII:702, 703
Radical-Socialist Party, VIII:1644, 1645
Radiguet, Raymond, VII:721, 724
Radini-Tedeschi, Monsignor, VIII:1858
radio. *See* radio broadcasting; radio electronics
radioactivity
Becquerel, V:166-168
Bothe, VII:379
Chadwick, VII:635
Curies, VII:811, 812, 815
Hahn, VIII:1513-1516
Joliot, VIII:1870-1873
Meitner, VIII:2476-2478
Rutherford, IX:3278, 3279
Whipple, IX:3959
radio broadcasting
British Broadcasting Corporation, VII:737-740; IX:2849, 3146-3148
DeMille, VII:898
Murrow, VIII:2662, 2664
Rogers, IX:3206
Welles, IX:3934
Radio Corporation of America. *See* RCA
radio electronics
Armstrong, VII:102
Bjerknes, VII:319
de Forest, VII:858-861
Marconi, VIII:2415, 2417, 2418
Popov, VI:1806-1808
Tesla, VI:2220
Radio-Keith-Orpheum Pictures Corporation. *See* RKO Pictures Corporation
Raeburn, Sir Henry, **VI:1836-1838**
George Chalmers of Pittencrieff, VI:1836
MacNab, The, VI:1839
RAF. *See* Royal Air Force
Rafsanjani, Hashemi, VIII:1959
ragtime music, V:1239-1241; VII:287
Ragua Ocllo, III:371, 372
Rahv, Philip, VIII:2304
Rai Bhoi di Talvandi. *See* Nanak
railroads
black labor organizations, IX:3114
Carnegie, V:420, 423
Chang Chih-tung, V:468
Cooke, V:552-554
Debs, VII:880, 881
Field, V:789, 790
Frémont, V:843
Gadsden, V:859
Hill, IV:659-661
Krupp, VI:1301, 1303
Langley, VI:1313
Laurier, VIII:2101
Macdonald, VI:1438
Morgan, VI:1581, 1582
New Haven monopoly, VII:421
Rockefeller, VI:1897, 1898
Russia, VI:1651
Sioux Indians, VI:2070, 2072
Stanford, VI:2096-2099
steel production, V:220, 1016
Stephens, VI:2130-2132
switches, VIII:1503

telegraphy, V:558
Telford, VI:2209
Trevithick, VI:2251-2253
Tweed, VI:2285
Vanderbilt, VI:2296-2298
Westinghouse, VI:2358, 2360, 2361
Rainald of Dassel, II:358
Rainbow Coalition, VIII:1825
Rajputs, III:5
Raleigh, Sir Walter, III:140, 315, 316, **638-641,** 704; IV:700
Discovery of the Large, Rich, and Beautiful Empire of Guiana, The, III:639
History of the World, The, II:947, III:640; IV:194
Report of the Truth of the Fight About the Isles of Açores, A, III:639
Ramadan, VII:392
Raman, Sir Chandrasekhara Venkata, **IX:3109-3111**
Ramanuja, **II:770-772**
Rameau, Jean-Philippe, IV:33, **1148-1151**
Abaris: Ou, Les Boréades, IV:1150
Castor et Pollux, IV:1150
Demonstration of the Principle of Harmony, IV:1149
Hippolyte et Aricie, IV:1148-1150
New System of Music Theory, IV:1148
Nouvelles Suites de pièces de clavecin, IV:1148
Premier Livre de pièces de clavecin, IV:1148
Samson, IV:1149
Treatise on Harmony, IV:1148
Ramillies, Battle of, IV:923, 924
Ramsay, James Andrew Broun. *See* Dalhousie, First Marquess of
Ramsay, Sir William, VIII:1513
Ramses I, I:734
Ramses II, **I:734-738**
Ramses VI, I:905
Rand, Ayn, VIII:1471, 1472
Fountainhead, The, VII:1083
Rand, Walter Charles, IX:3683
Randall, John T., IX:3995, 3996
Randolph, A. Phillip, **IX:3112-3116**
Randolph, Edward, IV:938, 939
Random House, VIII:2626
Rangoon, Battle of, IX:3437
Ranke, Leopold von, V:358; **VI:1839-1841**
"Great Powers, The," VI:1840
History of England Principally in the Seventeenth Century, A, VI:1840
History of the Latin and Teutonic Nations from 1494 to 1514, VI:1839
History of the Popes During the Last Four Centuries, The, VI:1840
History of the Reformation in Germany, VI:1840
"Political Dialogue," VI:1839
Universal History, VI:1840
Rankin, Jeannette, VII:1153; **IX:3117-3120**
Raphael, III:24, 26, 186, **642-646**
Adam Tempted, IV:1163
Baldassare Castiglione, III:644
Cardinal Virtues, III:643
Dispute over the Sacrament, III:643
Expulsion of Attila, III:643
Expulsion of Heliodorus, III:643, 644
Liberation of Saint Peter, III:643
Madonna of the Meadows, III:642
Marriage of the Virgin, III:642
Mass of Bolsena, III:643
Parnassus, V:1184
St. George and the Dragon, III:642
School of Athens, III:643
Sistine Madonna, III:643
Transfiguration of Christ, III:644; IV:808
Triumph of Galatea, III:186
Raphael, House of, III:83
Rasmussen, Knud Johan Victor, **IX:3121-3124**
Rasputin, Grigori Yefimovich, **VI:1842-1845**
Rassemblement Démocratique Africain, IX:3711, 3712
Rastakhiz Party, VIII:1958
Rathbone, John, VI:1634
Rathenau, Walther, IX:3564
Ratti, Ambrogio Damiano Achille. *See* Pius XI
Ratramnus, **II:773-775**
Concerning the Body and Blood of the Lord, II:773
Contra graecorum opposita, II:774
De nativitate Christi, II:774
De praedestinatione, II:774
Rauschenbusch, Walter, **IX:3125-3128**
Christianity and the Social Crisis, IX:3126
Christianizing the Social Order, IX:3126
For God and the People: Prayers of the Social Awakening, IX:3126
Theology for the Social Gospel, A, IX:3126
Ravel, Maurice, **IX:3129-3131,** 3332, 3333, 3798
Bolero, IX:3130, 3131
Histoires naturelles, IX:3129
Rawdon, Lord Francis, IV:576
Ray, Rammohan, **VI:1846-1849**
Precepts of Jesus, The, VI:1847
Translation of an Abridgment of the "Vedant," VI:1847

Ray, Satyajit, **IX:3132-3135**
Adventures of Goopi and Bagha, The, IX:3133
Adversary, The, IX:3133
Big City, The, IX:3133
Chess Players, The, IX:3134
Company Limited, IX:3133
Coward and the Saint, The, IX:3133
Days and Nights in the Forest, IX:3133, 3134
Distant Thunder, IX:3134
Goddess, The, IX:3133
Hero, The, IX:3133
Home and the World, The, IX:3134
Kanchenjungha, IX:3133
Kingdom of Diamonds, The, IX:3133
Lonely Wife, The, IX:3133, 3134
Middleman, The, IX:3134
Music Room, The, IX:3132
Pather Panchali: Song of the Road, IX:3132
Rabindranath Tagore, IX:3133
Unvanquished, The, IX:3132
World of Apu, The, IX:3132
Rayburn, Sam T., VIII:1866; IX:2824
Raymond IV, II:159, 160
Raymond of Capua, II:220, 221
Raymond of Peñafort, II:400, **776-778**
Decretals of Gregory IX, II:400, 777
Summa de casibus poenitentiae, II:776, 777
Summa de matrimonio, II:776
Summa juris canonici, II:776
Razi, al-, **II:779-781**
Book of Secrets, The, II:781
Book of Spiritual Physick, The, II:780
Comprehensive Book, The, II:780
Philosopher's Way of Life, The, II:780
Treatise on the Smallpox and Measles, A, II:780
Upon the Circumstances Which Turn the Head of Most Men from the Reputable Physician, II:779
RCA, VIII:2418; IX:4125, 4126
Reade, Charles, VI:2216
Reagan, Ronald, **IX:3136-3141**
Albright, VII:50
Bush, VII:521
Carter, VII:591, 592
Charles, VII:658
Ferraro, VII:1153-1155
Gorbachev, VIII:1424
Greenspan, VIII:1471, 1472
Khomeini, VIII:1958
King's Row, IX:3136
Kirkpatrick, VIII:1995, 1996
Knute Rockne: All American, IX:3136
Mulroney, VIII:2656
nuclear deterrence, IX:3633
O'Connor, IX:2789
O'Neill, IX:2825
Ortega, IX:2840, 2841
Powell, IX:3071
This Is the Army, VIII:2243
Wiesenthal, IX:3986, 3987
Repeal Party, VI:1682
Reasoner, Harry, IX:3870
Rebner, Adolph, VIII:1670
Recared, II:518
Reciprocal Trade Agreements Act, VIII:1780
Reclamation Act, VI:1813
Reconciliation, Fellowship of, VIII:2735
Reconstruction era
Beecher, V:176
Blaine, V:256
Chase, V:479, 480
Godkin, VIII:1401
Greeley, V:985
Hayes, V:1075, 1076, 1078
Johnson, V:1232, 1233, 1235-1237
Stanton, VI:2108, 2109
Stephens, VI:2131
Stevens, VI:2136, 2137
Sumner, VI:2172
Reconstruction Finance Corporation, VIII:1729
Rectification Movement, VIII:2212, 2213
Rectification of Names, I:223
Recusants, III:148, 257, 259; IV:700
Redbook magazine, VIII:2470
Red Cloud, V:574, 575; **VI:1850-1853**
Red Cloud's War, V:574
Red Cross. *See* American Red Cross; International Red Cross
Red Flag Act, VIII:2070
Redon, Odilon, **VI:1854-1856;** VII:910
Eye Balloon, The, VI:1856
Hommage à Goya, VI:1854
Redstone Rocket, IX:2779
Rée, Paul, VI:1664
Reece, Carroll, VIII:1989
Reed, Joseph, IV:1001
Reed, Walter, **VI:1857-1860;** VIII:1434, 1435
Reed Commission, VIII:1435
Reform, War of the, V:1252
Reforma, La, V:1252
Reformation, Protestant. *See* Protestant Reformation
Reform Bill of 1832
Buxton, V:379

Disraeli, V:675, 577
Durham, V:722
Grey, V:994
Kay-Shuttleworth, VIII:1917
Macaulay, VI:1427, 1429
Mill, VI:1557, 1558
Pankhurst, IX:2874
Place, VI:1788
Russell, VI:1930
William IV, VI:2392-2394
Reform Bill of 1867, V:654, 777
Reform Bill of 1884, V:777
Reform Club, V:138; VIII:1917
Reformed Church. *See* Calvin, John; Protestant Reformation
Reformed Presbyterian Church, IV:239-241
Reform Judaism, VI:2400-2402; VII:148-151
Refusés, Salon de, VI:1780
Regency Crisis, IV:1103; V:902
Regensburg, Diet of, III:103
Regulating Act of 1773, IV:631
Regulus, **I:739-741**
Rehn, Frank K.M., VIII:1740
Rehnquist, William H., VII:511; **IX:3142-3145**
Reichstag
Bülow, VII:495, 496
Erzberger, VII:1102
Göring, VIII:1439
Himmler, VIII:1666-1668
Hitler, VIII:1676
naval building, IX:3689, 3690
Stresemann, IX:3563, 3564
Zetkin, IX:4114
Reichswehr, IX:3380, 3381
Reid, Sir George, V:631
Reid, Thomas, VI:2063
Reign of Terror. *See* Terror, Reign of
Reims Cathedral, II:615
Reinach, Adolf, IX:3507
Reiner, Fritz, VII:295
Reith of Stonehaven, First Baron, **IX:3146-3149**
relativity, theory of
Broglie, VII:473
dynamism, VII:343
Einstein, VII:1035, 1036, 1038
Hawking, VIII:1580, 1582, 1583
Lemaître, VIII:2157
Lorentz, VIII:2236
Meitner, VIII:2476
Michelson, VI:1554
Pauli, IX:2923
Planck, IX:3034
Poincaré, VI:1798-1800
Stark, IX:3490, 3491
Reliance Building, V:365, 367
Religion, French Wars of, IV:1165
Religious Socialist Movement, VII:475
Religious Society of Friends. *See* Quakers
Remarque, Erich Maria, **IX:3150-3152**
All Quiet on the Western Front, IX:3150-3152
Road Back, The, IX:3150
Three Comrades, IX:3150
Traumbude, Die, IX:3150
Rembrandt, III:645; IV:622, **1152-1155**
Anatomy Lesson of Dr. Tulp, The, IV:1152
Holy Family with Angels, The, IV:1154
Night Watch, The, IV:1152
Old Man Seated in an Armchair, An, IV:1154
Presentation of Jesus in the Temple, The, IV:1152
Stoning of Saint Stephen, IV:1152
Syndics of the Drapers' Guild, The, IV:1154
Two Scholars Disputing, IV:1152
Woman Bathing, IV:1154
Remington, Frederic, **VI:1861-1864**
Bronco Buster, The, VI:1862
John Ermine of the Yellowstone, VI:1862
Renaixença, VII:1315-1317
RENAMO. *See* Mozambique National Resistance
Renan, Ernest, **VI:1865-1868**
Future of Science, The, VI:1865, 1866
History of the Origins of Christianity, The, VI:1866
History of the People of Israel, VI:1867
Life of Jesus, The, VI:1866
My Sister Henrietta, VI:1865
Saint Paul, VI:1866
René II, III:164
Reno, Janet, **IX:3153-3156**
Renoir, Jean, VIII:2579, 2580; **IX:3157-3160**
Boudu Saved from Drowning, IX:3158
Chienne, La, IX:3158
Crime of Monsieur Lange, The, IX:3158
Day in the Country, A, VII:594; IX:3158
French Cancan, IX:3159
Grand Illusion, IX:3158
Joyless Life, IX:3157
Little Match Girl, The, IX:3157
Little Theatre of Jean Renoir, The, IX:3159
Lower Depths, The, IX:3158
Madame Bovary, IX:3158
Nana, IX:3157
Nuit de carrefour, La, IX:3158

River, The, IX:3159
Rules of the Game, The, VII:594; IX:3158
Tosca, IX:3158
Renoir, Pierre-Auguste, **VI:1869-1872;** IX:3157
Blacksmith (Fire), VI:1870
Dancing at the Moulin de la Galette, Montmarte, VI:1869
Diane Chassereuse, VI:1869
Grandes Baigneuses, Les, VI:1870
Grenouillière, La, VI:1869
Judgment of Paris, VI:1870
Madame Charpentier and Her Children, VI:1870
Representatives, House of
Adams, V:23, 24
Benton, V:197
Blaine, V:255-257
Buchanan, V:346
Bush, VII:520
Calhoun, V:394
Chisholm, VII:670, 671
Clay, V:507
Crockett, V:578, 579
Cushing, V:581
Davis, V:615
Dole, VII:948
Ford, VII:1180, 1181
Garfield, V:877
Gore, VIII:1431
Hearst, VIII:1603
Hull, VIII:1779
Johnson's impeachment, V:1237
Jordan, VIII:1887-1889
Kennedy, VIII:1928
La Follette, VIII:2047
La Guardia, VIII:2054
Lincoln, VI:1382
Lodge, VIII:2220
McKinley, VI:1453
O'Neill, IX:2824-2826
Rankin, IX:3118
Sherman, IV:1244
Stephens, VI:2129
Stevens, VI:2136
Tyler, VI:2288, 2291
Webster, VI:2344
See also Congress, U.S.
Reprobus. *See* Christopher, Saint
Repton, Humphrey, IV:1013
Republican Party, U.S.
Arthur, V:77, 78, 80
Benton, V:197
Blaine, V:255-257
Borah, V:279-281
Burger, VII:509
Bush, VII:520-522
Butler, VII:524
Chase, Salmon P., V:477-479
Chase, Samuel, IV:295
Clinton, Bill, VII:709
Clinton, DeWitt, V:517-519
Coolidge, VII:762-764
Cushing, V:583
Dole, VII:947-949
Eisenhower, VII:1043-1045
elephant symbol, VI:1628
Ford, VII:1180-1182
Freedmen's Bureau, V:1235
Garfield, V:875-877
Grant, V:977
Hanna, V:1029-1031
Harding, VIII:1550, 1551
Harrison, V:513, 1053-1056
Hayes, V:1075, 1076, 1078
Hobby, VIII:1704, 1705
Hoover, VIII:1727, 1729
Hughes, VIII:1766
Kansas-Nebraska Act, V:693
Kirkpatrick, VIII:1996
Kissinger, VIII:1999
La Follette, VIII:2047-2049
La Guardia, VIII:2055
Lincoln, VI:1383
Lodge, VIII:2219-2221
Luce, VIII:2257, 2258
MacArthur, VIII:2298
McCarthy, VIII:2300
McKinley, VI:1453
Madison, IV:889
Nixon, VIII:2758-2760
O'Connor, IX:2789
Ortega, IX:2840, 2841
Perot, IX:2974
Reagan, IX:3138
Rehnquist, IX:3142
Roosevelt, IX:3229, 3231
Root, IX:3232
Schurz, VI:1996, 1997
Seward, VI:2037-2039
Smith, IX:3448
Stanford, VI:2097
Stevens, VI:2136
Sumner, VI:2171
Taft, IX:3592, 3593

Van Buren, VI:2293
Williams, VI:2396, 2397
Requiter, Bridge of the. *See* Sifting Bridge
Resaca, battle of, V:1053
Resale Prices Act, VIII:1607
Residenz, IV:657
Resistance, French. *See* French Resistance
respiration
Aretaeus of Cappadocia, I:82
Breuer, VII:452
Erasistratus, I:300, 301
Herophilus, I:399
Krogh, VIII:2027-2029
Malpighi, IV:891
Spallanzani, IV:1262
Restitution, Edict of, IV:451, 452
Resurrection, Islamic concept of, II:652
Resurrection City, VII:10
retailing
Field, V:783-786
Mendelsohn's store designs, VIII:2488
Ward, VI:2331-2334
window displays, VII:1320
Reuchlin, Johannes, III:503
Reunion Association, VIII:2643
Reuther, Walter P., **IX:3161-3164**
Revelation, Book of, I:329, 338, 477; IV:1028, 1452; VI:1867
"Revelation of St. Stephen, The," I:823
Revere, Paul, **IV:1156-1159**
Revert, Eugène, VII:631
Revista Multicolor de los Sábados, VII:373
Revolution, American. *See* American War of Independence
Revolutionary Command Council, VIII:2693, 2694; IX:3289
Revolutionary Committee for Unity and Action, VII:6
Revue de progrès politique, social et litéraire, V:259
Reyes, Bernardo, VIII:2347
Reynolds, John Hamilton, VI:1266
Reynolds, Sir Joshua, **IV:1160-1164**
Colonel George Coussmaker, IV:1162
Copley, IV:357
Discourses, IV:1160-1163
Eliot Family, The, IV:1160
First Lieutenant Paul Henry Ourry, IV:1160
Gainsborough, IV:516, 517
Kauffmann, IV:765, 767
Lady Worsley, IV:1162
Lawrence, IV:809, 811
Marlborough Family, The, IV:1162
Master Crewe as Henry VIII, IV:1163
Master Hare, IV:1163
Miss Gideon and Her Brother, William, IV:1163
Mrs. Lloyd, IV:1163
Penelope Boothby, IV:1163
Raeburn, VI:1836
Rodney, IV:1179
Schoolboy, The, IV:1163
Reynolds v. Sims, IX:3890
Rex v. Almon, IV:907
Rex v. Delavel, IV:907
Rex v. Gordon, IV:907
Rex v. Webb, IV:906
RFC. *See* Reconstruction Finance Corporation
Rhee, Syngman, **IX:3165-3168**
Rheticus, Georg Joachim, III:178
rhetoric
Bossuet, IV:170-172
Cicero, I:194
Isocrates, I:456-458
Sylvester II, II:869
Valla, III:740
Rhodes, Cecil, V:463, 1291; **VI:1873-1877;** IX:3453
Ribbentrop, Joachim von, VIII:2572
Ribicoff, Abraham, VIII:2679, 2680
ribonucleic acid. *See* RNA
Ribot, Théodule, VIII:1840
Ricardo, David, VI:1559, 1562, **1878-1881**
Essay on the Influence of a Low Price of Corn on the Profits of Stock, An, VI:1879
High Price of Bullion, The, VI:1878
On the Principles of Political Economy and Taxation, VI:1559, 1879
Reply to Mr. Bosanquet's Practical Observation, A, VI:1878
Ricci, Marco, IV:242
Rice, Daddy, V:810
Rich, Frank, VII:35, 36
Richard I, II:468, 732, 733, **782-785**, 810
Richard II, **II:786-789**
Henry IV, II:457, 458
Henry V, III:337
Peasants' Revolt, II:114, 115, 921-923
Richard III, III:345, **647-653**
Richards, Ann, **IX:3169-3172**
Richards, Mira and Paul, VII:142
Richardson, Henry Hobson, **VI:1882-1885**
Richardson, Ralph, IX:2810, 2813, 2814
Richardson, Samuel
Pamela, IV:470
Richard the Lion Heart. *See* Richard I

Richelieu, Cardinal de, **IV:1165-1169**
  Condé, IV:341
  Corneille, IV:363
  Frederick Henry, IV:501
  Jansen, IV:707, 709
  Louis XIII, IV:863-865
  Mazarin, IV:945
  Poussin, IV:1119
Richter, Gregorius, IV:154, 155
Ricimer, II:685
Rickard, George L. "Tex," VII:900, 902
Ricketts, Ed, IX:3516
Rickey, Branch, IX:3193, 3194
Rickover, Hyman G., **IX:3173-3177**
Riddle, Nelson, IX:3434
Ride, Sally, **IX:3178-3180**
Ridge, John, VI:1911
Ridley, Nicholas, **III:654-656**
  Book of Common Prayer, III:655
  Treatise Against the Error of Transubstantiation, III:655
  Treatise on the Worship of Images, A, III:655
Ridley, Robert, III:654
Riel, Louis, VI:1437, 1438; VIII:2101
Riemann, Georg Friedrich Bernhard, V:638, 639
Rienzo, Cola di, **II:790-792**
Riggs, Bobby, VIII:1968-1970
Righi, Augusto, VIII:2415
Right, Petition of, IV:213, 329, 333, 334, 1285
Rights, Bill of (U.S.)
  Hancock, IV:617
  Hand, VIII:1543
  Henry, IV:649
  Hughes, VIII:1769
  Madison, IV:888
  Mason, IV:927
Rijswijk, Treaty of, IV:1448
Riley, Charles, IX:2862
Rilke, Rainer Maria, **IX:3181-3184**
  Book of Hours, The, IX:3181
  Buch der Bilder, Das, IX:3182
  Duino Elegies, IX:3182
  New Poems, IX:3182, 3183
  Notebooks of Malte Laurids Brigge, The, IX:3182
  Sonnets to Orpheus, IX:3182
  Tale of the Love and Death of Coronet Christopher Rilke, The, IX:3182
Rimbaud, Arthur, **VI:1886-1888;** VII:448, 791
  "Drunken Boat," VI:1887
  Illuminations, VI:1887
  Season in Hell, A, VI:1887
  "Seer Letter," VI:1886
Rim-Sin, I:360, 361
Rimsky-Korsakov, Nikolay, V:287, 288; VI:1613, 1614, **1889-1891**
  Christmas Eve, VI:1890
  Golden Cockerel, The, VI:1890, 1891
  Legend of the Invisible City of Kitezh and Maid Fevronia, The, VI:1890, 1891
  Maid of Pskov, The, VI:1889, 1890
  May Night, VI:1890
  Mlada, VI:1890
  Mozart and Salieri, VI:1890
  Pan Voyevods, VI:1890
  Sadko, VI:1890
  Servilia, VI:1890
  Snow Maiden, The, VI:1890
  Tale of Tsar Saltan, The, VI:1890
  Tsar's Bride, The, VI:1890
Rinuccini, Ottavio, IV:991, 992
Ripley, George, V:984
Riqueti, Honoré-Gabriel. *See* Mirabeau, Comte de
Risorgimento
  Browning, V:327
  Croce, VII:802
  Garibaldi, V:879, 881
  Gioberti, V:932-934
  Mazzini, VI:1514-1516
  Pius IX, VI:1782
  Visconti, IX:3818, 3819
Ritschl, Albrecht, **VI:1892-1895;** VIII:1557; IX:3722
  Christian Doctrine of Justification and Reconciliation, The, VI:1893, 1894
  Entsehung der altkatholischen Kirche, Die, VI:1893
  Evangelium Marcions und das Kanonische Evangelium des Lucas, Das, VI:1892
Ritschl, Friedrich Wilhelm, VI:1662
Rivera, Diego, **IX:3184-3186**
  Bandit Augustin Lorenzo, The, IX:3185
  Majorcan Landscape, IX:3185
  Vision of Alameda Central, IX:3185
RKO Pictures Corporation, IX:3934
RNA, VII:798; VIII:1827; IX:3997
Roanoke Island, III:638
Robbe-Grillet, Alain, VII:207
Robert I. *See* Bruce, Robert
Robert of Anjou, II:150
Robert of Normandy, II:443
Roberts, Clifford, VIII:1876, 1877
Robertson, Anna Mary. *See* Moses, Grandma

Robertson, William, IV:547
Robert the Steward, II:294, 296
Roberval, Gilles Personne de, IV:1332
Robeson, Paul, VIII:1546; IX:3081, **3187-3192**
All God's Chillun Got Wings, IX:3189
Emperor Jones, The, IX:3189
Native Land, IX:3189
"Ol' Man River," IX:3189
Othello, IX:3189, 3191
Proud Valley, IX:3189
Robespierre, **IV:1170-1173**
Condorcet, IV:348
Danton, IV:394, 395
Fourier, V:819
Saint-Just, IV:1205-1207
Robie House, IX:4061
Robinson, George D., V:284
Robinson, Jackie, **IX:3193-3197**
Robusti, Jacopo. *See* Tintoretto
Rochambeau, Comte de, **IV:1174-1177**
Roche, James, VIII:2679
Rochefort, Joseph J., Jr., VIII:2751
Rockefeller, John D., V:1045-1047; **VI:1896-1900;** VIII:1981
Rockefeller, Nelson, VII:1181; VIII:1999; IX:3196, 3633
Rockefeller Foundation
Frisch, VII:1236, 1237
Industrial Research Department, VIII:1981
International Center for Genetic Epistemology, IX:2992
Kinsey's sex research, VIII:1987-1989
London School of Economics, VII:309
National Research Council, VIII:2540
Rockefeller, VI:1898
rocketry
Goddard, VIII:1396-1398, 1500
Heinkel, VIII:1614-1616
Korolev, VIII:2019
Oberth, IX:2777-2779
Tsiolkovsky, IX:3749-3751
Rockingham, Lord, IV:222-224, 481, 482, 541, 542, 1035, 1036
Rockingham, Marquess of, IV:1102
rock music
Beatles, VII:226-229
Charles, VII:658
Joplin, VIII:1883-1885
Presley, IX:3076-3079
Terry, IX:3643
Rockwell Norman, **IX:3198-3200**
Art Critic, The, IX:3200
Boy with Baby Carriage, IX:3198
Connoisseur, The, IX:3200
Four Freedoms, IX:3198, 3199
New Kids in the Neighborhood, IX:3199
Ruby Bridges Goes to School, IX:3199
Saying Grace, IX:3199
Southern Justice, IX:3199
Triple Self-Portrait, IX:3200
Rocky Mountain Fur Company, VI:2078
Rocroi, Battle of, IV:341, 343, 865
Rodgers, John, VI:1760, 1764
Rodgers, Richard, VIII:1533, 1534, 1536, 1566-1569; **IX:3201-3203**
Boys from Syracuse, The, IX:3201
Carousel, IX:3202
Flower Drum Song, IX:3202
I Remember Mama, IX:3202
King and I, The, IX:3202
No Strings, IX:3202
Oklahoma!, IX:3201, 3202
On Your Toes, IX:3201
Pal Joey, IX:3201
Show Boat, IX:3201
Sound of Music, The, IX:3202
South Pacific, IX:3202
Rodin, Auguste, **VI:1900-1903;** VII:416; VIII:2017; IX:3181
Age of Bronze, The, VI:1900
Gates of Hell, The, VI:1900
Kiss, The, VI:1901
Saint John the Baptist Preaching, VI:1900
Thinker, The, VI:1900
Walking Man, VI:1901
Rodney, George, **IV:1178-1181**
Rodzevitch, Konstantin, IX:3754
Roebling, John Augustus, **VI:1904-1906**
Roebuck, John, IV:183, **1182-1186**
Roe v. Wade, VII:511; IX:3143
Roger II, II:506
Roger of Salisbury, II:848
Rogers, Buddy, IX:3008
Rogers, Ginger, VII:125, 127, 128
Rogers, Will, **IX:3204-3208**
Laughing Bill Hyde, IX:3205
Rogers, Woodes, IV:390
Rohan, Louis-René-Édouard, prince de, IV:919
Rohilla War, IV:632, 633
Rohmer, Eric, VIII:1391
Roila, I:124
Rokitansky, Karl von, VI:2021
Rolfe, John, IV:1107, 1108, 1254

Rollo, **II:793-795**
Rolls, Charles Stewart, **IX:3209-3212**
Rolls-Royce Limited, IX:3209-3211
Rolph, John, V:116, 117
Roman Catholic Relief Act of 1829, V:905
Roman Inquisition
  Abano, II:2
  Bruno, III:97, 98
  Dominic, II:303
  Gregory IX, II:401
  Veronese, III:748
Romberg, Sigmund, VIII:1533, 1534
Rome, Council of, II:675
Rommel, Erwin, VIII:1950; **IX:3213-3216,** 3261
Romney, George, **IV:1187-1190**
  Death of General Wolfe, The, IV:1187
  Death of King Edmund, The, IV:1187
Roncalli, Angelo Giuseppe. *See* John XXIII
Ronsard, Pierre de, **III:657-659**
  Amours, Les, III:657
  Bocage, Le, III:657
  Derniers Vers, Les, III:659
  Discours des misères de ce temps, III:658
  Franciade, Le, III:658
  Hymnes, Les, III:658
  Nouvelle continuation de amours, III:658
  Odes, III:657
  Remonstrance au peuple de France, III:658
  Sonnets for Helen, III:658, 659
Rooney, Mickey, VII:1305
Roosevelt, Eleanor, VII:72; **IX:3217-3221,** 3222, 3224, 3244, 3245
Roosevelt, Franklin D., **IX:3222-3227**
  Acheson, VII:17
  atom bomb development, VII:1147
  Beard, VII:223, 224
  Black, VII:321
  Butler, VII:525, 526
  Cardozo, VII:576, 577
  Churchill, VII:693
  Curtin, VII:817
  de Gaulle, VII:866, 867
  farm policy, IX:3860, 3861
  George VI, VII:1344
  Harriman, VIII:1560, 1561
  Hearst, VIII:1603
  Hindemith, VIII:1672
  Hiss, VIII:1683
  Hoover, Herbert, VIII:1729, 1730
  Hoover, J. Edgar, VIII:1733
  Hopkins, VIII:1736-1738
  Hull, VIII:1779-1781
  Johnson, VIII:1866, 1867
  King, VIII:1983, 1984
  labor legislation, VIII:2171, 2172
  La Guardia, VIII:2055, 2056
  Lippmann, VIII:2204, 2205
  Long, VIII:2228, 2229
  Luce, VIII:2256, 2257
  Lyons, VIII:2294
  Marshall, VIII:2429, 2431
  Mohammad Reza Shah Pahlavi, VIII:2567
  Nimitz, VIII:2750, 2752
  Perkins, IX:2962, 2963
  polio, IX:3307
  racial discrimination, IX:3114
  Rockwell, IX:3199
  Roosevelt, Eleanor, IX:3217, 3218, 3220
  Sinclair, IX:3428, 3429
  Smith, IX:3441
  Stimson, IX:3539
  Thomas, IX:3661
  Truman, IX:3740
  Wallace, IX:3860, 3861
  zeppelins, VII:1014
Roosevelt, Theodore, **IX:3228-3231**
  Altgeld, V:56
  Borah, V:280
  Butler, VII:525
  Canada-Alaska boundary, V:1070
  Grey, VIII:1476
  Hanna, V:1030, 1031
  Harris'sbooks, V:1051
  Hearst, VIII:1603
  Hughes, VIII:1766-1768
  Lodge, VIII:2219-2221
  Morgan, VI:1582
  Panama, V:1069; VIII:1409, 1436
  Peary, IX:2944
  Remington, VI:1862
  Roosevelt, Franklin D., IX:3222
  Root, IX:3232, 3233
  Ross, IX:3245
  Stimson, IX:3537, 3538
  Taft, IX:3594-3596
  Washington, VI:2337
Root, Elihu, **IX:3232-3235,** 3537, 3538
Root, Elisha, V:540, 541
Root, John Wellborn, V:365
Root and Branch Bill, IV:308
Rorschach, Hermann, **IX:3236-3238**
  Psychodiagnostics, IX:3236-3238
Rosamund, II:42
Rosburg, Percy, VII:368

Roscius, I:195
Rose, Pete, **IX:3239-3242**
Rosebery, Lord, VII:121; VIII:1475, 1476
Rose Law Firm, VII:714
Rosenberg, Alfred, VIII:1405
Rosenberg, Ethel and Julius, IX:3037
Rosenwald Foundation, VII:984
Roses, Wars of the
  Edward IV, III:234, 235
  Fortescue, III:267
  Henry IV, II:457
  Henry VI, III:341, 342
  Henry VII, III:345, 346
  Richard III, III:647, 651
  Tudor family, III:732
  Warwick, III:774-777
Rosewall, Kenneth R., VIII:2110
Rosicrucian sect, IX:3331, 4082
Rosing, Boris, IX:4125
Ross, Betsy, **IV:1191-1193**
Ross, Sir James Clark, **VI:1907-1909**
Ross, John, **VI:1910-1912**
Ross, Nellie Tayloe, **IX:3243-3246**
Ross, Robert, VI:1281
Ross, Ronald, **IX:3247-3250**
Rossellini, Roberto, VII:1141, IX:3736
Rossetti, Dante Gabriel, III:765; V:1168; VI:1588; VIII:2689
Rossi, Persiano, III:552
Rossini, Gioacchino, VI:1686, **1913-1915**
  Barber of Seville, The, VI:1913, 1914
  cambiale di matrimonio, La, VI:1913
  Demetrio e Polibio, VI:1913
  donna del lago, La, VI:1914, 1915
  Guillaume Tell, VI:1914, 1915
  Otello, VI:1914, 1915
  Péchés de viellesse, VI:1915
  Petite messe solennelle, VI:1915
  Stabat Mater, VI:1915
  Tancredi, VI:1913, 1914
Rostand, Edmond
  Cyrano de Bergerac, IV:385-387
Rostilav, II:279
Rota, Nino, VII:1142
Roth, Hieronymus, IV:510
Rothad of Soissons, II:673
Rothermere, First Viscount. *See* Harmsworth, Harold
Rothmere, Lord, VII:169
Rothschild Bank, VI:1916-1919
Rothschild family, **VI:1916-1920**
Rotterdam, architecture of, IV:2859, 2860
Rouault, Georges, **IX:3251-3253**
  Miserere, IX:3252, 3253
Rouelle, Guillaume, IV:805
Rouges, Les, VIII:2100
Rough Riders, IX:3228
Round Hill School for Boys, V:125, 126
Rousseau, Henri, **VI:1921-1924;** VIII:2546
  Carnival Evening, The, VI:1932
  Dream, The, VI:1932
  Football Players, The, VI:1932
  Hungry Lion, The, VI:1932
  Sleeping Gypsy, The, VI:1932
Rousseau, Jean-Jacques, **IV:1194-1197**
  Bakunin, V:112
  Boswell, IV:175, 177
  Condillac, IV:344
  Condorcet, IV:349
  Confessions of J.-J. Rousseau, The, IV:1196
  Cunning-Man, IV:1196
  Devin du village, Le, IV:226
  Dictionary of Music, IV:227
  Discourse on the Arts and Sciences, A, IV:1194
  Discourse upon Inequality Among Mankind, A, IV:1196
  Emilius and Sophia, IV:1196; VI:1767, 2092
  Fragonard, IV:489
  Machiavelli, III:451
  New Héloïse, The, IV:1196
  Robespierre, IV:1171
  Saint-Just, IV:1205
  Treatise on the Social Contract, A, IV:1196, 1205
  Voltaire, IV:1394
Royal Academy of London
  Bessemer, V:218
  Constable, V:549
  Copley, IV:358
  Gainsborough, IV:516
  Hunt, V:1169
  Kauffmann, IV:767
  Lawrence, IV:808-811
  Raeburn, VI:1837
  Reynolds, IV:1160, 1162
  Scott, VI:2003
  Stuart, IV:1290
  Turner, VI:2272, 2273
Royal Geographic Society
  Burton, V:375
  Galton, V:868
  Livingstone, VI:1399
  Mackinder, VIII:2321-2323
  Speke, VI:2084

Stanley, VI:2102
Workman, VI:2412
Royalists
Clarendon, IV:309
Cromwell, IV:380, 381
Fairfax, IV:448, 449
Hale, IV:596, 597
Hobbes, IV:664
James II, IV:703
Leeds, IV:821-823
Shaftesbury, IV:1228, 1229
Royal Marriages Act of 1772, IV:479; VII:1062
Royal Navy
Anson, IV:55-57
Barclay, VI:1764
Bligh, IV:143, 145, 146
Bonnard, VII:365
Brunel, V:339
Buckingham, IV:212
Cook, IV:354
George I, IV:533
George VI, VII:1343
Kidd, IV:777, 779
Mountbatten, VIII:2641-2645
Nelson, VI:1634-1636
Perry, VI:1764, 1766
Phillip, IV:1091, 1092
Reith, IX:3148
Rodney, IV:1178-1180
Vancouver, IV:1355, 1356
Windsor, IX:4025
Royal Niger Company, V:953, 954; VIII:2269, 2270
Royal Society of London
Audubon, V:87
Babbage, V:101, 102
Banks, IV:83, 85, 86
Boyle, IV:187
Bragg, VII:410
Cavendish, IV:261-263
Cook, IV:351, 353
Dalton, V:604
Davy, V:621-623
Dryden, IV:424
Faraday, V:767
Florey, VII:1174
Grove, V:1010-1013
Halley, IV:600-602
Huxley, V:1172, 1173
Jenner, IV:723
Kämpfer, IV:755, 756
Lanchester, VIII:2071
Lister, VI:1389, 1390
Malpighi, IV:892
Maxwell, VI:1511
Murdock, IV:1010
Newton, IV:1025, 1027
Papin, IV:1059-1061
Roebuck, IV:1185
Rutherford, IX:3279
Siemens, VI:2067
Street, VI:2162
Wedgwood, IV:1423
Wheatstone, V:558
Wren, IV:1480
Royal Supremecy, Act of, III:68, 208, 265, 351, 535, 654
Royce, Sir Frederick Henry, **IX:3209-3212**
Royce, Josiah, **IX:3254-3256**
Outlines of Psychology, IX:3254, 3255
Philosophy of Loyalty, The, IX:3255
Race Questions, Provincialism and Other American Problems, IX:3255
Roye, William, III:736
Roxborough, John, VIII:2241
Rozier, Ferdinand, V:86
RSFSR. *See* Russian Soviet Federated Soviet Republic
Rubens, Peter Paul, III:88; IV:737; **1198-1201**
Descent from the Cross, IV:1198
Elevation of the Cross, The, IV:1198
Landscape with a Rainbow, IV:1200
Landscape with a Sunset, IV:1200
Landscape with the Château De Steen, IV:1200
Portrait of the Marchesa Brigida Spinola-Doria, IV:1198
Three Graces, The, IV:1200
Tigers and Lions Hunt, IV:1200
Rubenstein, Arthur, IX:3816
Rubicon, Operation, VI:1620
Rucellai, Giovanni, III:9
Rudolf I, **II:796-799**
Rudolf IV, II:729
Rudolf of Swabia, II:462
Rudolph II, III:79, 691
Rudolph III, II:450
Rufus, Publius Sulpicius, I:834
Rufus, Tineius, I:29
Rukeyser, Muriel, **IX:3257-3259**
"Effort at Speech Between Two People," IX:3257
"Facing Sentencing," IX:3257
Gates, The, IX:3258
Theory of Flight, IX:3257
Rumagan, II:560

Rumi, Jalal al-Din, **II:800-802**
Divan-e Shams-e Tabriz, II:800
Mathnawi, The, II:800
Rumsey, James, IV:477
Rundstedt, Gerd von, **IX:3260-3263**
Runnels, Hardin, V:1138
Rupert, Prince, IV:134
Rupert III, II:970, 971
Rural Constabulary Act, V:459
Rurik, **II:803-805**
Rusas I, I:754
Rush, Benjamin, **IV:1202-1204,** 1468
Medical Inquiries and Observations upon the Diseases of the Mind, IV:1203
Rushdie, Salman
Satanic Verses, The, VIII:1959
Rusk, Dean, IX:3870
Ruskin, John, V:1113, 1169, 1170; **VI:1925-1929,** 2273, 2274, 2364, 2377; IX:3089, 3090
Fors Clavigera, VI:1928
Modern Painters, VI:1925, 1927
Munera Pulveris, VI:1927
Praeterita, VI:1928
Seven Lamps of Architecture, The, VI:1927
Stones of Venice, The, VI:1927
Unto This Last, VI:1927
Ruskin Hall, VII:221
Russell, Bertrand, V:837; VII:284, 584; VIII:2605-2607; **IX:3264-3267,** 3432
History of Western Philosophy, IX:3266
Marriage and Morals, IX:3266
Practice and Theory of Bolshevism, The, IX:3266
Principles of Mathematics, The, VII:582; VIII:2608, 2725; IX:3264, 3966
Principles of Social Reconstruction, IX:3266
Problems of Philosophy, The, IX:3264
Russell, Bill, **IX:3268-3272**
Russell, Lord John, **VI:1930-1932,** 2308
Russell, Lord William, VI:1930
Russian Orthodox Church
Alexander Nevsky, II:53, 54
Catherine the Great, IV:257, 259
Ivan the Great, III:383
Ivan the Terrible, III:386
Khrushchev, VIII:1962
Mott, VIII:2639
Nicholas I, VI:1650
Nikon, IV:1030-1032
Peter III, IV:1087-1089
Peter the Great, IV:1085
Pius XI, IX:3028
Rasputin, VI:1842
Tolstoy, VI:2243, 2245
Ypsilanti, VI:2418
Russian Revolution of 1905
Luxemburg, VIII:2285, 2286
Pobedonostsev, VI:1791, 1792
Trotsky, IX:3727
Russian Revolution of 1917
Bernstein, VII:293
Blok, VII:333
Bukharin, VII:491, 492
Gorky, VIII:1442, 1444, 1445
Gramsci, VIII:1459, 1460
Hoover, VIII:1732
Horowitz, VIII:1747, 1748
Hughes, VIII:1768
Kandinsky, VIII:1904
Kazantzakis, VIII:1920
Kerensky, VIII:1941, 1942
Lenin, VIII:2161
Litvinov, VIII:2208
Ludendorff, VIII:2266
Malenkov, VIII:2377
Masaryk, VIII:2441
Trotsky, IX:3726-3728
Tsvetayeva, IX:3753-3755
Zhukov, IX:4116
Russian Social Democratic Workers' Party, VIII:2161, 2208; IX:3726
Russian Soviet Federated Soviet Republic, IX:4086, 4087
Russian Workers, Union of, VIII:1732
Russo-German War, VIII:2398
Russo-Japanese War, VIII:2091, 2396, 2429; IX:3233
Russo-Turkish War, IV:1299; V:143, 678
Rustichello, II:751, 753
Rusticus, I:257, 258
Ruth, Babe, VII:1323; IX:2797, 2798, **3273-3276**
Ruthenia, II:212; VII:261
Rutherford, Ernest, **IX:3277-3280**
Bohr, VII:345
Bragg, VII:411, 412
Hevesy, VIII:1654-1656
Kapitsa, VIII:1906, 1907
Meitner, VIII:2477, 2478
Radiations from Radioactive Substances, VII:635
Rutherglen Declaration, IV:240
Ryder, Sir Dudley, IV:906

SA. *See* Sturm Abteilung
SAA. *See* Syndicat Agricole Africain

Sabin, Albert, IX:3306
Sabina, Poppaea, I:578, 579
Sabri, Ali, IX:3290
Sacagawea, **VI:1933-1935**
Sacco, Nicola, VII:1212; IX:2885, 3060, **3281-3284**
Saccus, Ammonius, I:666
Sacheverell, Henry, IV:52, 53, 1277
Sachs, Nelly, **IX:3285-3288**
Eli: A Mystery Play of the Sufferings of Israel, IX:3286
Fahrt ins Staublose, IX:3286
Flucht und Verwandlung, IX:3286
In den Wohnungren des Todes, IX:3286
O the Chimneys, IX:3287
Sternverdunkelung, IX:3286
Und niemand weiss weiter, IX:3286
Sachs, Sadie, IX:3313, 3314
Sac rebellion, VI:2010
Sadat, Anwar el-, **IX:3289-3291**
Boutros-Ghali, VII:399
Faisal, VIII:1119
Meir, VIII:2474, 2475
Nasser, VIII:2696
Nixon, VIII:2760
Sadducees, I:467
Sa'di, **II:806-808**
Orchard, The, II:806-808
Rose Garden, The, II:806-808
Sadler Committee, V:458
Sadler's Wells Ballet, IX:3873
Safavids, IV:4-6
Safed Cabalists, III:441
Sagan, Carl, IX:2829, **3292-3295**
Contact, IX:3294
Cosmos, IX:3293
Dragons of Eden, The, IX:3293
Sagarmartha National Park, VIII:1664
Sahle Mariam. *See* Menelik II
Sahle Selassie, VI:1537
Said, Mohammed, VI:1355, 1356
Saigo Takamori, **VI:1936-1939**
Sailer, Tony, VIII:1966
St. Albans, Battle of, III:647, 774, 775
St. Albans Monastery, II:663
Saint Bartholomew's Day Massacre, III:133, 333, 364, 537, 672, 782
St. Benedict, Rule of, II:136, 137
St. Brice's Day Massacre, II:202, 345
Saint Catherine of Mount Sinai monastery, II:556
St.-Clair-sur-Epte, Treaty of, II:794
St. Croix Island, IV:271
Saint Cyr, Château de, IV:902
St. Denis, Ruth, VII:1263, 1264
Saint-Denis monastery, II:859-861
Saint-Domingue, IV:1338-1340
Sainte-Beuve, Charles, IX:3089
Saint Francis, Church of, II:272
Saint-Gaudens, Augustus, **VI:1940-1942**
Diana, VI:1941
Grief, VI:1941
Hiawatha, VI:1940
Silence, VI:1940
St. George, Guild of, VI:1928
St. George Civic Guard Company, IV:604, 605
St. Germain, Treaty of, VII:260
St. Gervaise, Church of, IV:374
Saint Giovanni Evangelista, church of, III:184, 186
St. Jacques-aux-Pèlerins, Confraternity of, II:762
St. James Church, VI:1448
St. James the Less, church of, VI:2161
Saint Jerome, Order of, IV:382
St. John, Henry. *See* Bolingbroke, First Viscount
Saint-Julien, Baron de, IV:488
Saint-Just, Louis de, IV:395, **1205-1208**
Esprit de la révolution et de la constitution de France, IV:1205
Fragmens sur les institutions républicaines, IV:1207
St. Lawrence River, III:129-131; IV:273, 351
St. Louis Chronicle, VI:2015
St. Louis Enquirer, V:195
St. Louis Post-Dispatch, VI:1825, 1826
St. Luke, Academy of, IV:275
Saint Luke, Guild of, III:85
St. Mark, Procurators of, III:664
St. Mark's Basilica, III:284, 285
Saint Martial organum, II:723
Saint Mary Magdalene, Order of, II:401
St. Mary Woolnoth, Church of, IV:637
St. Paul, Minneapolis, and Manitoba Railroad, IV:659, 660
Saint Peter, Church of, III:83, 84, 407
Saint-Simon, Claude Henri de, IV:457; V:543, 544; VI:1369
St. Thomas Church, IV:77
St. Valentine's Day Massacre, VII:564
Saint Vincent de Paul, Society of, IV:1382
Saint Vitalis, Church of, II:556
Saisset, Bernard, II:172
Saito Tatsuoki, III:570
Sajjan, III:541
Sakai Hoitsu, IV:1042

Sakharov, Andrei, VIII:1426; **IX:3296-3300**
Sakyamuni. *See* Buddha
Saladin, II:125, 782, **809-811**
Salah al-Din Zarkub, II:801
Salamis, Battle of, I:10, 198, 803, 857-859, 965
Salem witchcraft trials, IV:934, 935, 940, 1225-1227
Salieri, Antonio, IV:550
Salih, al-, II:810
Salim, III:6
Salimbene, **II:812-814**
Chronicle of Salimbene de Adam, The, II:812-814
Salim Salim, IX:2957
Salinger, J.D., **IX:3301-3304**
Catcher in the Rye, The, VII:350; IX:3301-3303
"For Esmé—with Love and Squalor," IX:3301, 3302
Franny and Zooey, IX:3302, 3303
"Hapworth 16, 1924," IX:3303
Nine Stories, IX:3302
Raise High the Roof Beam Carpenters and Seymour: An Introduction, IX:3303
Salisbury, First Earl of, **III:660-663,** 774
Salisbury, Third Marquess of, IV:700; V:462; **VI:1943-1946**
Salk, Jonas Edward, **IX:3305-3307**
Salk Institute for Biological Studies, IX:3306, 3307
Sallust, **I:742-745**
Histories, I:743
War with Catiline, The, I:743
War with Jugurtha, The, I:743
Salmon, Daniel, IX:3450, 3451
Salmone, I:475
Salomé, Lou, VI:1664
Salomon, II:574, 575
SALT I. *See* Strategic Arms Limitation Treaties
Salto de Alvarado, III:22
Saltzmann, Christian, IV:93
Salvarsan, VII:1166
Salvation Army, V:275, 277
Salvianus, I:695
Samaritan Pentateuch, I:822
Samaritans, I:642, 822-824, 868
Samarkand, II:885; III:36, 38
Sambhaji, IV:71
Samos, I:13, 314, 315
Samoset, IV:930
Samprati, I:113
Sampson, Edith, VIII:1887
Sampson, William T., V:658
Samuel, **I:746-749**
Samuel ha-Nagid, II:498, 499
San Andrea, Church of, II:748, 762
Sanarelli, Giuseppe, VI:1858
Sánchez Cerro, Luis M., VIII:1585
Sanctorius Sanctorius. *See* Santorio Santorio
Sand, George, V:70, 494, 1099; **VI:1951-1954**
Consuelo, VI:1952
Devil's Pool, The, VI:1952
Francis the Waif, VI:1952
History of My Life, VI:1952
Indiana, VI:1951
Jacques, VI:1951
Lélia, VI:1951
Letters of a Traveller, VI:1951
Little Fadette, VI:1952
Mauprat, VI:1951
Miller of Angibault, The, VI:1952
She and He, VI:1952
Spiridion, VI:1952
Valentine, VI:1951
Sandburg, Carl, **IX:3308-3312**
Abraham Lincoln, IX:3310
Always the Young Strangers, IX:3311
American Songbag, The, IX:3310
Chicago Poems, IX:3310
Cornhuskers, IX:3310
People, Yes, The, IX:3310
Remembrance Rock, IX:3311
Sandemanians, V:767
Sander, August, VII:96
Sandwich, Earl of, IV:1440
San Francisco *Examiner,* VIII:1601
Sanger, Margaret, VII:1071; VIII:1637; **IX:3313-3316**
Family Limitation, IX:3314
Sangha, I:145
San Giuliano, church of, III:665
San Jacinto, Battle of, V:1138
Sankey, Ira, VI:1575, 1576
San Lorenzo, church of, III:519
San Marco, Piazza, III:664-666; IV:242
San Martín, José de, V:268; VI:1688, 1689, **1947-1950**
San Mateo v. Southern Pacific, V:789
San Miniato al Monte, Church of, II:83
San Petronio, Church of, III:390
San San Juku, VIII:2754
San Sebastiano, Church of, III:747
Sansovino, Andrea, III:664
Sansovino, Jacopo, **III:664-666**
Santa Ana, III:141, 142

Santa Anna, Antonio López de, V:579, 580, 615, 1138, 1250; **VI:1955-1957**
Santa Barbara Botanic Garden, VII:1131
Santa Croce, Church of, II:83
Santa Maria del Carmine, Church of, III:484
Santa Maria del Fiore, cathedral of, II:83, 84; III:89
Santa Maria la Antigua del Darién, III:45
Santa Maria Novella, Church of, II:83, 84; III:9
Santayana, George, **IX:3317-3319**
Egotism in German Philosophy, IX:3317
Life of Reason, The, IX:3317
Persons and Places, IX:3318
Realms of Being, IX:3318
Santo Domingo, V:1152
Santorio Santorio, **IV:1209-1212**
Commentaria in artem medicinalem Galeni, IV:1210
Commentaria in primam fen primi libri canonis Avicennae, IV:1211
Medicina Statica, IV:1210
Methodi vitandorum errorum omnium qui in arte medica contingunt, IV:1209
Santos-Dumont, Alberto, **IX:3320-3323**
San Xia project. *See* Three Gorges Dam
San Zeno, Church of, III:461, 462
Sanzio, Raffaello. *See* Raphael
Sappho, **I:750-753**
"Ode to Aphrodite," I:750, 751
"Seizure," I:750, 751
Sarabaitic monks, I:784
Saragosa, La, **VI:1958-1960**
Sarah, I:6
Sardanapalus, I:107
Sargent, Charles Sprague, VII:1130
Sargent, John Singer, **VI:1961-1965;** VII:1300
Ellen Terry as Lady Macbeth, VI:1962
Gassed, VI:1962
Jaleo, El, VI:1961
Lady Sassoon, VI:1962
Lord Ribblesdale, VI:1962
Madame Gautreau, VI:1961
Oyster Gatherers of Cancale, The, VI:1961
Triumph of Marie de' Medici, VI:1961
Woodrow Wilson, VI:1962
Wyndham Sisters, VI:1962
Sargon II, **I:754-756**
Saratoga, Second Battle of, IV:66
Sarnoff, David, IX:4125, 4127
Sarotti, Ambrose, IV:1059
Sarpi, Paolo, IV:1209
Sarraute, Nathalie, **IX:3324-3326**
Portrait of a Man Unknown, IX:3324, 3325
Tropisms, IX:3324, 3325
Sartach, Prince, II:987, 988
Sartre, Jean-Paul, **IX:3327-3330**
Age of Reason, The, IX:3327
Bariona, IX:3329
Beauvoir, VII:230-232
Being and Nothingness, IX:3329
Camus, VII:553, 555
Césaire, VII:631
Flies, The, IX:3329
Giraudoux, VII:1381
Grass, VIII:1465
Heidegger, VIII:1612
Merleau-Ponty, VIII:2501
Nausea, VII:1360; IX:3327
No Exit, IX:3329
Pirandello, IX:3015
Roads to Freedom, The, IX:3327
Saint Genet: Actor and Martyr, IX:3329
Sarraute, IX:3324
Situations, IX:3329
Wall and Other Stories, The, IX:3327
What Is Literature?, VII:207; IX:3329
Sassanid Dynasty, I:778-781
Sataspes, I:370
Satie, Erik, IX:3066, **3331-3335**
Relâche, IX:3333
Socrate, VII:539
Sports et divertissements, IX:3333
Trois Gnossiennes, IX:3331
Trois Gymnopédies, IX:3331, 3333, 3334
Trois Morceaux en forme de poire, IX:3332, 3333
satire
Aristophanes, I:88, 90-92
Callimachus, I:156
Capek, VII:562
Catullus, I:170
Cyrano de Bergerac, IV:386
Gilbert and Sullivan, V:930
Goya, IV:572
Hogarth, IV:668-670
Juvenal, I:488, 489
Lucian, I:507-509
Plautus, I:659, 660
Rabelais, III:633, 634, 636
Rogers, IX:3204-3207
Swift, IV:1305, 1307-1309
Weill, IX:3928
Sato, Eisaku, **IX:3336-3339**

Satsuma Rebellion, VI:1936-1939
Saturday Evening Post, The, IX:3198, 3199
Saturn, IV:695
Saturninus, Lucius Appuleius, I:529
Saturn rocket, VII:440, 441
Satyrus, I:43
Sauk Indians, V:247, 249, 250
Saul, I:241, 746, 748, 749
Saunders, Charles, IV:1473
Saunders, Otis, V:1239
Saussure, Ferdinand de, VII:913; **IX:3340-3343**
Course in General Linguistics, IX:3342
Mémoire sur le système primitif des voyelles dans les langues indo-européennes, IX:3340, 3341
Sauve, Jeanne, **IX:3344-3346**
Savage, Richard, IV:728
Savannah, IV:1044
Savery, Thomas, IV:1023, 1024, 1060
Savigny, Friedrich Karl von, **VI:1966-1968**
History of Roman Law During the Middle Ages, The, VI:1967
Juristische Methodenlehre, nach der Ausarbeitung des Jakob Grimm, VI:1967
Obligationenrecht, Das, VI:1967
Of the Vocation of Our Age for Legislation and Jurisprudence, VI:1966
System des heutigen römischen Rechts, VI:1967
Treatise on Possession, VI:1966
Vermischte Schriften, VI:1967
Savonarola, Girolamo, III:16, 448, 498, **667-670**
Saxe-Eisenach, Duke of, IV:1320
Saxe-Weimar, Duke of, IV:76
Saxo Grammaticus, **II:815-818**
History of the Danes, The, II:815-817
Saxony
Beust, V:222-224
Carpini, II:206-208
Charlemagne, II:228
Charles Martel, II:243
Henry IV, II:461
Henry the Lion, II:466-469
Sayyid Ahmad Khan. *See* Ahmad Khan, Sir Sayyid
Scala family, II:288
Scalero, Rosario, VIII:2494
Scalia, Antonin, IX:3658
Scaliger, Julius Caesar, III:671
Scaliger, Joseph Justus, **III:671-674**
Coniectanea in M. Terentium Varronem de lingua latina, III:671
De emendatione temporum, III:672
Thesaurus temporum, III:672
Scapula, Publius Ostorius, I:136
Scarlatti, Alessandro, **IV:1213-1216**
caduta de'Decemviri, La, IV:1214
Griselda, La, IV:1215
honestà negli amori, L', IV:1213
Macro Attilio Regolo, IV:1215
Mass for S Cecilia, IV:1215
Mitridate Eupatore, Il, IV:1214
Pirro e Demetrio, Il, IV:1214
Sinfonie di concerto grosso, IV:1215
Su le sponde del Tebro, IV:1215
Telemaco, IV:1215
Tigrane, Il, IV:1215
trionfo del'lonore, Il, IV:1215
Schall, Adam, IV:757
Scharnhorst, Gerhard Johann David von, V:940; **VI:1969-1971**
Scheler, Max, IX:**3347-3350,** 3507
Genius des Krieges und der deutsche Krieg, Der, IX:3348
Schelling, Friedrich Wilhelm Joseph, IV:155, 467, 468; V:1080; **VI:1972-1975**
Ages of the World, The, VI:1973
Introduction to Idealism, VI:1973
Introduction to the Philosophy of Nature, VI:1973
Of Human Freedom, VI:1973
Philosophie der Mythologie, VI:1973
Über die Möglichkeit einer Form der Philosophie überhaupt, VI:1972
Vom Ich als Prinzip der Philosophie, VI:1972
Von der Weltselle, VI:1973
Schiaparelli, Giovanni Virginio, I:311
Schiff, Jacob, IX:3837-3839
Schiller, Friedrich, IV:652, **1217-1220**
Cabal and Love, IV:1217
Don Carlos, Infante of Spain, IV:1217
Fiesco, IV:1217
Guillaume Tell, VI:1914
History of the Defection of the United Netherlands from the Spanish Empire, IV:1217
History of the Thirty Years' War, IV:1219
Robbers, The, IV:1217
Schinkel, Karl Friedrich, VIII:2520
Schleicher, Kurt von, IX:2877
Schleiermacher, Friedrich, **VI:1976-1979**
Christian Faith, The, VI:1976-1978
On Religion, VI:1976, 1977
Schleiermacher's Soliloquies, VI:1977
Schley, Winfield S., V:658
Schlick, Moritz, VII:582
Schlieffen, Count Alfred von, VIII:1674
Schlieffen Plan, VIII:2265

Schliemann, Heinrich, **VI:1980-1983**
Ilios, VI:1981
Tiryns, VI:1982
Troja, VI:1981
Troy and Its Remains, VI:1981
Schmalkaldic War, III:160
Schmeling, Max, VIII:2243
Schmidman, Jo Ann, IX:3643, 3644
Schmidt, Auguste, IX:4112
Schmidt, Bernhard Voldemar, **IX:3351-3353**
Schmidt, Carl, IX:2855
Schmidt, Helmut, VII:429; VIII:2009
Schmidt-Rottluff, Karl, **IX:3354-3356**
Houses at Night, IX:3355
Midday on the Moor, IX:3355
Portrait of a Girl, IX:3355
Schnitzler, Arthur
Call of Life, VIII:2142
Schoenberg, Arnold, VII:271, 272, 386, 387; **IX:3357-3361,** 3914-3916
Erwartung, Op 17, IX:3358
First Chamber Symphony, Op. 9, IX:3358
Jakobsleiter, Die, IX:3359
Pierrot Lunaire, VII:387
String Quartet in D Minor Op. 7 No. 1, IX:3358
Verklärte Nacht, IX:3357
Schönborn, Friedrich Carl von, IV:656, 657
Schönborn, Johann Philipp Franz von, IV:657
Schopenhaeur, Arthur, VI:1662, 1664, **1984-1987;** VIII:1650, 1651
Basis of Morality, The, VI:1985
On the Will in Nature, VI:1985
Parerga and Paralipomena, VI:1986
World as Will and Idea, The, VI:1984, 1986
Schott and Sons, VIII:1670
Schröder, Gerhard, VIII:2010
Schrödinger, Erwin, VII:473; **IX:3363-3365**
What Is Life?, IX:3364
Schubert, Franz, VI:1393, **1988-1991,** 1993; VIII:2359
"'Erlkonig," VI:1989
"'Lindenbaum, Der," VI:1989
"Schöne Müllerin, Die, VI:1989
"'Symphony in C Major," VI:1995
"Trout, VI:1988
"'Unfinished" Symphony in B Minor, VI:1989
"Winterreise, Die, VI:1989; IX:3066
"Zwillingsbrüder, Die, VI:1988
Schumann, Clara, V:299, 300
Schumann, Robert, V:299, 300; VI:1392, **1992-1995**
Genoveva, VI:1993
Rhenish, VI:1994
Spring Symphony, VI:1993
Schurz, Carl, **VI:1996-1998;** VIII:1402
Schütz, Heinrich, **IV:1221-1224**
Becker Psalter, IV:1222, 1223
Dafne, IV:1222
Geistliche Chormusik, IV:1222
Kleine geistliche Concerte, IV:1222
Psalmen Davids, IV:1221
Symphoniae sacrae, IV:1222, 1223
Schutzstaffel
Baeck, VII:149
Guderian, VIII:1491, 1492
Himmler, VIII:1666-1668
Rommel, IX:3213, 3215
Wiesenthal, IX:3985, 3986
Schuyler, Philip, IV:66; V:369, 370
Schwab, Charles, V:421
Schwann, Theodor, VI:2313
Schwarzschld, Karl, **IX:3366-3369**
Schweitzer, Albert, **IX:3370-3374**
Sciama, Dennis, VIII:1580
science fiction
Burroughs, VII:516, 517, 519
Capek, VII:560-562
Cyrano de Bergerac, IV:385
Shelley, VI:2048, 2049, 2051
Tsiolkovsky, IX:3750, 3751
Verne, VI:2303-2305
Wells, IX:3938-3940
Scipio, Metellus, I:167
Scipio, Publius Cornelius, I:364-366
Scipio Aemilianus, I:673, **757-759**
Scipio Africanus, I:287, 288, **760-763,** 844
Scipio the Elder. *See* Scipio Africanus
Scipio the Younger. *See* Scipio Aemilianus
SCLC. *See* Southern Christian Leadership Conference
Scopas, **I:764-766,** 787, 788
Scopes, John T., VII:481, 840
Scorpion, King, I:548
Scorsese, Martin, VIII:1922
Scotland Yard, IV:469, 471; VI:1752
Scots War, IV:446
Scott, Dred, **VI:1999-2001**
Bryant, V:344
Buchanan, V:347
Chase, V:478
Taney, VI:2189, 2191, 2192
Scott, Sir George Gilbert, **VI:2002-2004**
Scott, James. *See* Monmouth, Duke of
Scott, Robert Falcon, VII:67

Scott, Sir Walter, V:1225; VI:1485, 1838, **2005-2008;** VIII:2065, 2174; IX:3063
Abbot, The, VI:2006
Antiquary, The, VI:2006
Black Dwarf, The, VI:2006
Bridal of Triermain, The, VI:2006
Castle Dangerous, VI:2007
Count Robert of Paris, VI:2007
Fair Maid of Perth, The, V:244
Fortunes of Nigel, The, VI:2006
Guy Mannering, VI:2006
Harold the Dauntless, VI:2006
Heart of Midlothian, The, VI:2006
Ivanhoe, VI:2006, 2007
Kenilworth, VI:2006
Lady of the Lake, The, VI:1914, 2005, 2007
Lay of the Last Minstrel, The, VI:2005, 2007
Life of Napoleon Buonaparte, VI:2006
Lord of the Isles, The, VI:2006
Marmion: A Tale of Flodden Field, VI:2005
Minstrelsy of the Scottish Border, The, VI:2005
Monastery, The, VI:2006
Old Mortality, VI:2006
Peveril of the Peak, Quentin Durward, VI:2006
Pirate, The, V:562; VI:2006
Redgauntlet, VI:2006, 2007
Rob Roy, VI:2006
Rokeby, VI:2006
St. Ronan's Well, VI:2006
Tales of a Grandfather, VI:2006
Waverly: Or, 'Tis Sixty Years Since, VI:2005-2007
Scott, Winfield, **VI:2009-2013**
Scottish Guardians, II:955
Scottish Labour Party, V:1037
Scottish War for Independence, II:185, 187, 188
Scottsboro boys, IX:3962
Scotus, John Duns. *See* Duns Scotus, John
Scriblerus Club, IV:1115
Scribner's Magazine, V:361
Scripps, Edward Wyllis, **VI:2014-2016**
Scripps-McRae League, VI:2015
Scrovegni, Enrico, II:388, 390
SCUBA, VII:778, 779
Scuderia Ferrari, VII:1150
Scullin, James H., VIII:2292, 2293
Scythia, I:237
Seaborg, Glenn Theodore, **IX:3375-3379**
Seaton Delaval, IV:1353
Seattle SuperSonics, IX:3271
Sebond, Raymond, III:524
secession
Lincoln, VI:1383
Mississippi, V:615
Sherman, VI:2059
Stephens, VI:2130
Tennessee, V:1232, 1233
Texas, V:1138; VI:1338
Sechter, Simon, V:332
Secondat, Charles-Louis de. *See* Montesquieu
Second Bourbon Restoration, V:611
Second Carlist War, V:415
Second Cataract, I:774
Second Council of Orange, I:938
Second Dutch War, IV:310
Second Great Awakening, V:470, 884; VI:1425
Second International Congress, IX:4112, 4113
Second Mithradatic War, I:558
Second Punic War, I:334-336, 364-366, 535-537, 760-762
Second Republic of France, VI:1620-1622, 2227
Second Seminole War. *See* Seminole Wars
Second Sikh War, V:600; VI:1331
Second Syrian War, I:717
Second Triumvirate, I:69, 132, 141, 196, 220, 892
Second Trullan Synod, II:824
Second Vatican Council
Day, VII:852
John, VIII:1858-1860
Maritain, VIII:2427
Paul VI, IX:2915-2917
Pius VII, IX:3031
Virgin Mary, I:941
Section Française de L'internationale Ouvrière. *See* Socialist Party of France
Seddon, Richard John, V:1000; **VI:2017-2020;** VIII:2444, 2446
Sed Festival, I:979
Sedgmoor, Battle of, IV:982
Sedgwick, Adam, VI:1419
Sedition Act. *See* Alien and Sedition Acts
Seeckt, Hans Von, **IX:3380-3382**
Seely, Clinton Barnum, V:133
Segnatura, Stanza della, III:643
Segovia, Andrés, **IX:3383-3386**
"Chaconne," IX:3384
segregation
Abernathy, VII:9, 10, 12
baseball, IX:3193
Black, VII:322
Brown v. Board of Education, VII:1214; VIII:1769, 1789, 2434, 2435, 2672; IX:3187; IX:3525, 3889

Frankfurter, VII:1214
Hansberry, VIII:1545
Holiday, VIII:1717, 1718
King, VIII:1973
Marshall, VIII:2434
Myrdal, VIII:2671-2673
Parks, IX:2888-2891
Stevenson, IX:3525
Wallace, IX:3857-3859
Washington, VI:2337, 2338
Wells-Barnett, IX:3941, 3943, 3944
See also apartheid; racism
Seine River, II:793
Sejanus, Lucius Aelius, I:152, 618, 893
Sekigahara, Battle of, IV:1329
Selden Patent Case, VI:1345
Selective Service Act, VII:882
Seleucid Empire, I:896-898
Seleucus I Nicator, **I:767-769**
Seleucus III, I:63-65
self-contained underwater breathing apparatus. *See* SCUBA
Seligman, Joseph, V:26
Selim, III:52, 53
Selim III, VI:1604
Seljuk dynasty, II:67-70, 677-680, 695, 809
Selma, march on, VII:503; VIII:1974
Selwyn, Arch and Edgar, VIII:1415, 1417
Selznick, David, VIII:1688
Seminole Indians, V:859
See also Seminole Wars
Seminole Wars, V:541; VI:1695, 1697, 2010, 2011, 2057, 2195
Semmelweis, Ignaz Philipp, **VI:2021-2024**
Senate, U.S.
Adams, V:20-24
Benton, V:195-198
Black, VII:321
Blaine, V:256
Borah, V:279-281
Burr, V:370
Chase, V:478
Clay, V:507-509
Clinton, V:518
Dole, VII:948, 949
Douglas, V:693
Feinstein, VII:1137-1139
Fillmore, V:793
Foreign Relations Committee, VIII:2221
Frémont, V:842
Gallatin, V:861
Glenn, VII:1387, 1388
Hanna, V:1029-1031
Harding, VIII:1550
Houston, V:1138, 1140
Hull, VIII:1779
Humphrey, VIII:1784, 1785
Jackson, V:1198
Johnson, Andrew, V:1232, 1233, 1235-1237
Johnson, Lyndon B., VIII:1867
Kennedy, John F., VIII:1928
Kennedy, Robert F., VIII:1933, 1934
La Follette, VIII:2047-2049
Lodge, VIII:2220
Long, VIII:2228
McCarthy, VIII:2300-2302
Mason, IV:927
Root, IX:3234
Sherman, IV:1244
Sumner, VI:2171
Taft, IX:3590-3593
Tyler, VI:2288
Van Buren, VI:2293
Washington, IV:1406
Webster, VI:2345
See also Congress, U.S.
Sendak, Maurice, **IX:3387-3390**
Hole Is to Dig, A, IX:3387
In the Night Kitchen, IX:3389
Kenny's Window, IX:3388
Where the Wild Things Are, IX:3388, 3389
Wonderful Farm, The, IX:3387
Seneca Falls Convention, V:697; VI:2143, 2145
Seneca Indians, VI:1584
Seneca the Younger, **I:770-773**
Letters to Lucilius, I:772
Three Essays on Anger, I:772
To My Mother Helvia, I:772
Senegalese Riflemen, V:764
Senghor, Leopold, VII:631; **IX:3391-3394**
Chants d'ombre, IX:3392
Hosties noires, IX:3392
Senmut, I:373
Sennacherib, I:105, 454, 455
Sennett, Mack, VII:653
Sentiments, Declaration of, VI:2111
Sepoy Mutiny, VI:1706, 1707
Septennial Act, IV:532
Sequoyah, **VI:2025-2028**
Serafin, Tullio, VIII:2494
Serapion Brothers, VIII:1444
Serapis, I:722
Seres, II:988
Sergius I, II:471, **819-822**

Sergius I, Saint, **II:823-825**
Sergius Mansur, II:544
Serpent Players, VII:1258
Sert, Misia, VII:650
Sérusier, Paul, VII:909-911; IX:3826
Servetus, Michael, III:118, **675-678**
Apologetica discetatio pro astrologia, III:676
Christianismi restitutio, III:676, 677
De trinitatis erroribus libri septem, III:675
Dialogorum de trinitate libri duo, de justcia regni Christi capitual quatuor, III:675
Servile War, I:680
Servilia, I:140
Sesostris III, **I:774-777**
Sesshu, **III:679-681;** V:1120
Amanohashidate, III:680
Autumn and Winter Landscapes, III:680
Haboku Landscape, III:680
Huike Severing His Arm, III:680
Landscapes of the Four Seasons, III:680
Seti I, I:734
Seton, Saint Elizabeth Ann Bayley, **VI:2029-2032**
Sette, Guido, II:726
Settlement of 1701, Act of, IV:50, 157, 158, 531, 1277, 1278
Seurat, Georges, VI:1780, **2033-2036**
Bathing Place, Asnieres, A, VI:2034
Parade, La, VI:2035
Sunday on the Grand Jatte, A, VI:2034, 2035
Seven Cities of Cibola and Quivira, III:111, 180-183
Seven Sages of the Greeks, I:651-653, 804, 854
Seven Summits, VIII:2508
Seventeenth Amendment, V:280
Seven Wonders of the World, I:764
Seven Years' War
Amherst, IV:37, 39, 40
Anson, IV:56, 57
Blücher, V:263
Bougainville, IV:179
Carleton, IV:246
Carlos, V:414
Charles III, IV:287
Cornwallis, IV:367
Frederick the Great, IV:506
George II, IV:537, 538
George III, IV:539
Hutchinson, IV:691
Maria Theresa, IV:915
Peter III, IV:1088, 1089
Pitt the Elder, IV:1098-1100
Pontiac, IV:1111
Rochambeau, IV:1174
Rodney, IV:1178
Suvorov, IV:1298
Washington, IV:1405
Wilkes, IV:1439
Wolfe, IV:1471, 1472
Sever Hall, VI:1883
Severus, Septimus, I:415, 416
Sewall, Samuel, **IV:1225-1227**
Phaenomena quondam Apolcalyptica, IV:1226
Proposals Touching the Accomplishment of Prophecies, IV:1226
Selling of Joseph, The, IV:1226
Talitha Cumi, IV:1226
Seward, William H., V:792, 793, 985, 1252, 1253, **VI:2038-2041,** 2171, 2172
Sextius, I:346
Sexton, Anne, **IX:3395-3398**
All My Pretty Ones, IX:3396
Awful Rowing Towards God, The, IX:3397
Bedlam and Part Way Back, IX:3396
Book of Folly, The, IX:3397
Death Notebooks, The, IX:3397
"Double Image, The," IX:3396
Live or Die, IX:3396
Love Poems, IX:3396
Mercy Street, IX:3396
Transformations, IX:3396
Sextus, I:20
sexuality, human
Ellis, VII:1070-1072
Freud, VII:1224-1226
Kinsey, VIII:1986-1990
Lacan, VIII:2062, 2063
Stopes, IX:3551-3553
Seymour, Jane, III:68, 69, 204, 209, 237, 351, 594
Seymour, Thomas, III:241, 592, 594
SFIO. *See* Socialist Party of France
Sforza, Ludovico, **III:682-685**
Shaftesbury, First Earl of, IV:285, 856, 858, **1228-1231**
Inquiry Concerning Virtue in Two Discourses, An, IV:412
Shah Jahan, IV:69, 70, **1232-1235**
Shaka, **VI:2041-2043**
Shakers, IV:817-819
Shakespeare, William, III:56, 548-550, **686-690,** 693; IV:527-529, 728-730, 748, 749; V:203
Anthony and Cleopatra, IX:2811
As You Like It, IX:2810
Comedy of Errors, The, I:659, 660; III:687; VIII:1568
Coriolanus, I:671

Cymbeline, VII:35
Hamlet, II:816; V:272, 273, 1189; VII:281; IX:2809-2811
Henry IV, Part I, III:550; VII:35
Henry V, II:459; III:337-339; VI:1461; IX:2810-2812
Henry VI, III:653, 687
Henry VIII, III:56, 210, 687
Julius Caesar, III:689; VII:425; IX:2808
King Lear, VII:281; IX:2811
Love's Labour's Lost, III:468, 550
Macbeth, V:1189; VI:1461, 1462; VI:2299; VIII:2045, 2232; IX:2810, 3934, 3936
Merchant of Venice, The, V:1189; VI:1259, 1260, 1262, 2216; IX:2813
Merry Wives of Windsor, The, VI:2300
Midsummer Night's Dream, A, IV:1139; VII:469; IX:2808
Much Ado About Nothing, V:205
Othello, the Moor of Venice, V:801, 1189; VI:2300, 2301; IX:2813, 3189, 3891, 3935
Pericles, Prince of Tyre, III:689
Rape of Lucrece, The, III:687; VI:1832
Richard II, III:687
Richard III, III:653, 687; IV:527; V:271, 1189; VI:1260, 1262; IX:2812
Romeo and Juliet, III:687; V:1189; VI:2198, 2200; IX:2808, 2810
Taming of the Shrew, The, III:550, 687; IX:2808, 2810, 3008
Tempest, The, IV:1139, 1189; VII:633
Twelfth Night, VIII:2143; IX:2808
Two Gentlemen of Verona, V:1169
Venus and Adonis, III:687
Shamash-shum-ukin, I:105, 106
Shamshi-Adad I, I:360
Shams of Tabriz, II:800
Shankar, Uday, IX:2939
Shanti Nilaya, VIII:2031
Shapur II, **I:778-782**
Sharon, Ariel, VIII:2474
Sharp, Granville, **IV:1236-1238**
Address to the People, IV:1237
Declaration of the People's Natural Right to a Share in the Legislature, A IV:1237
Defense of the Right of the People to elect Representatives, A IV:1237
On Duelling, IV:1237
Remarks on the Uses of the Definitive Article in the Greek Text of the New Testament, IV:1237
Representation of the Injustice and Dangerous Tendency of Tolerating Society, A, IV:1236
Sharp, James, IV:240
Sharpey, William, VI:1388
Sharp Resolution, III:575
Shaw, Anna Howard, **VI:2044-2047**
Shaw, Artie, VIII:1420, 1718
Shaw, George Bernard, I:846; **IX:3399-3403**
Back to Methuselah, IX:3403
Caesar and Cleopatra, IX:3400
Candida: A Mystery, IX:3400
Cashel Byron's Profession, IX:3399
Common Sense About the War, IX:3402
Heartbreak House, IX:3403
Man and Superman, IX:3402
Mrs. Warren's Profession, IX:3400
Perfect Wagnerite, The, IX:3399
Quintessence of Ibsenism, The, IX:3400
Saint Joan, IV:1220; VIII:2142; IX:3403
Widowers' Houses, IX:3400
Shawn, Ted, VIII:1455, 1457
Shawnee Indians, IV:164; VI:2203, 2204
Shaw v. Reno, IX:2791
Shaybani Khan, III:36
Shays, Daniel, **IV:1239-1241**
Shays's Rebellion, IV:1239-1241, 1243
Shelburne, Lord, IV:108, 481, 542, 1036, 1130
Shelley, Mary Wollstonecraft, IV:1477; **VI:2048-2051**
Falkner, VI:2049
Fortunes of Perkin Warbeck, The, VI:2049
Frankenstein, VI:2048, 2049
Last Man, The, VI:2049
Lodore, VI:2049
Mathilda, VI:2049
Valperga, VI:2049
Shelley, Percy Bysshe, IV:557; V:382; VI:1264, 1266, 2048, 2049, 2051, **2052-2056;** IX:3426
Adonais: An Elegy on the Death of John Keats, VI:2055
Alastor: Or The Spirit of Solitude, and Other Poems, VI:2053
Cenci, The, VI:2054, 2055
Charles the Frist, VI:2055
Childe Harold's Pilgrimage, VI:2053
"Defence of Poetry, A," VI:2053, 2055
Epipsychidion, VI:2055
Hellas: A Lyrical Drama, VI:2055
"Hymn to Intellectual Beauty," VI:2053
Julian and Maddalo: A Conversation, VI:2054
Masque of Anarchy, The, VI:2055
Mont Blanc, VI:2053
Necessity of Atheism, The, VI:2052
"Ode to the West Wind," VI:2055

Oedipus Tyrannus: Or, Swellfoot the Tyrant, VI:2055
Original Poetry by Victor and Cazire, VI:2052
"Ozymandias," I:737
Peter Bell the Third, VI:2055
Prisoner of Chillon, The, VI:2053
Prometheus Unbound, VI:2054, 2055
Queen Mab: A Philosophical Poem, VI:2053
Revolt of Islam, The, VI:2054
Rosalind and Helen, VI:2054
Triumph of Life, The, VI:2055
Witch of Atlas, The, VI:2055
Zastrozzi: A Romance, VI:2052
Shell Oil Company, IX:2860
Shen-tsung, II:841, 962, 963
Shen Yo, I:842
Shepard, Alan, **IX:3405-3408**
Shepard, Thomas, IV:688
Sheridan, Philip, V:586, 1236
Sheridan, Richard Brinsley
School for Scandal, The, IV:529; VII:191
Sherman, John, V:1030; VI:1454, 1456
Sherman, Roger, **IV:1242-1245**
Sherman, William Tecumseh, V:586, 977; **VI:2057-2061,** 2108
Sherman Antitrust Act of 1890, VI:1898; IX:3229
Sherman Silver Purchase Act, V:515
Sherpas, VIII:1664
Sherrington, Sir Charles Scott, VII:1172
Shibasaburo Kitasato, V:182, 183
Shield Society, VIII:2552
Shiloh, Battle of, V:976; VI:1810, 2059
Shinshu Buddhism, III:571
Ship Money Case, IV:280
Shippen, Margaret "Peggy," IV:42, 66
Shipton, Eric, VIII:1663
Shirakawa II, II:881, 882
Shivaji Festival, IX:3683, 3684
Shklovsky, Viktor, VII:153
Shoda, Michiko, VII:42
Short Parliament, IV:1142, 1228, 1287
Shoshone Indians, VI:1933-1935
Shostakovich, Dmitri, **IX:3409-3412**
"Babi Yar," IX:3410
Katerina Izmailova, IX:3411
Lady Macbeth of Mtsensk, IX:3409, 3411
Shotoku Taishi, **II:826-828**
Shrewsbury, Duke of, IV:158
Shuiskys, III:385
Shulhan Arukh, IV:433
Shunrin Shuto, III:679
Shu'ubi movement, II:527
Sian Incident, VII:665
Sibelius, Jean, VII:70; **IX:3413-3416,** 3873
Fifth Symphony, IX:3415
Finlandia, IX:3414
Kullervo, IX:3413, 3414
Seventh Symphony, IX:3415
Sixth Symphony, IX:3415
Symphony No. 4, IX:3414
Tapiola, IX:3415
Sickles, Daniel E., VI:2107
Sicily
Archimedes, I:79
Frederick II, II:362-364
Idrisi, II:507
Innocent III, II:510
Innocent IV, II:515, 516
Mosca, VIII:2630
Siddhartha. *See* Buddha
Sidgwick, Henry, **VI:2062-2065**
Methods of Ethics, The, VI:2063, 2064
Outline of the History of Ethics, VI:2064
Principles of Political Economy; Elements of Politics, VI:2064
Sidney, Sir Philip, **III:691-695,** 703
Arcadia, III:692-694
Astrophel and Stella, III:691-694
Defense of Poesie, III:691-693; IV:746
Lady of May, The, III:691
Sieff Research Institute, IX:3932
Siegfried Line, VIII:2265
Siemens family, **VI:2066-2069**
Sierra Club, VI:1609
Siete Partidas, Las, II:57
Sievers, Susanne, VII:428
Sifting Bridge, I:976
Siger of Brabant, **II:829-831,** 913
Sigismund, II:1031; III:374, 564
Signal Corps. *See* United States Signal Corps
Sigrid the Proud, II:689
Sihanouk, Norodom, **IX:3417-3421**
Sikhism, III:540-542; V:600
Sikh Wars, V:600; VI:1331
Siking, II:1015, 1016
Sikkak, Battle of, V:2
Silesia, Army of, V:264
Silings, I:342
Silliman, Benjamin, VI:1592, 1593
Siloé, Diego do, **III:696-698**
Pietà, III:696
Presentation, III:696
Saint George Slaying the Dragon, III:696
Virgin and Child, III:696

Silsbee, Joseph Lyman, IX:4060
Silvester, Saint, I:375, 376
Simango, Urias, VIII:2317
Simeon Bar Kokhba, I:29
Simeon ben Azzai, I:28
Simeon ben Zoma, I:28
Simeon Stylites, Saint, **I:783-786**
Simmel, Georg, VII:614
Simon. *See* Peter, Saint
Simon Commission on India, VII:137
Simonides, **I:787-789**
Simon of Sudbury, II:114, 115
Simpson, James, VI:1390
Simpson, Wallis Warfield, IX:4025, 4026
Sims, Thomas, VI:1729
Sin, Jaime Cardinal, VII:87, 88
Sinai Agreement, IX:3290
Sinan Bey, III:501
Sinatra, Frank, IX:3078, **3422-3425**
  From Here to Eternity, IX:3424
  "I'll Never Smile Again," IX:3422
  Nice 'n' Easy, IX:3424
  Pal Joey, VIII:1598
  Robin and the 7 Hoods, IX:3424
  Songs for Young Lovers, IX:3424
Sinclair, Upton, VII:1048; VIII:2131, 2174; **IX:3426-3430**
  Boston, IX:3428
  Journal of Arthur Stirling, The, IX:3426
  Jungle, The, IX:3426, 3428, 3429
  King Coal, IX:3428
  Manassas, IX:3428
  Oil!, IX:3428
Singer, Isaac M., V:1143
Singer, Paris, VII:981
Sinn Féin, VII:733, 770, 877, 878; IX:2794, 2805
Sino-French War, V:466; VI:1364
Sino-Japanese Wars, V:468; VI:1364, 1365; IX:2954
Sino-Soviet Treaty of 1950, VIII:1961
Sintra, Convention of, VI:2352
Sioux Indians
  Crazy Horse, V:573-577
  Custer, V:586
  Parkman, VI:1735
  Pike, IV:1094
  Red Cloud, VI:1850, 1851
  Remington, VI:1862
  Sitting Bull, VI:2070-2073
Siqueiros, David, IX:2837
Siricius, Saint, **I:790-792**
Sisera, I:247
Sistene Chapel, III:84, 168, 519
Sisulu, Walter, VIII:2384, 2386
Sisyphus, VII:554
Sithole, Ndabaningi, VIII:2647
Sitting Bull, V:575, 576; VI:1677, **2070-2073**
Sitwell, Edith and Osbert, IX:3872-3874
Sivaji, IV:70, 71, **1246-1248**
Six, Les, VIII:2525, 2526; IX:3066, 3333
Six-Day War
  Begin, VII:245
  Ben-Gurion, VII:253
  Dayan, VII:856
  Eban, VII:1001
  Hussein I, VIII:1794
  Meir, VIII:2474
  Nasser, VIII:2695
  Qaddafi, IX:3099
  Wiesel, IX:3982
Six Edicts, IV:1349
Sixteenth Amendment, V:280
Sixtus IV, III:496
Sixtus V, III:334
Skelton, John, III:349
skiing, VIII:1965-1967
Skinner, B.F., **IX:3431-3434**
  About Behaviorism, IX:3433
  Behavior of Organisms, The, IX:3432
  Beyond Freedom and Dignity, IX:3433
  Walden Two, IX:3433
Skinner, John S., VI:1281, 1282
Skirmishing Fund, V:1124
Skúli, Earl, II:838
skyscrapers
  Burnham, V:365, 367, 368
  Le Corbusier, VIII:2137, 2138
  Mies van der Rohe, VIII:2523
  Pei, IX:2947
  Richardson, VI:1884
  Sullivan, VI:2167, 2168
  Wright, IX:4062
Slater, Samuel, **VI:2074-2076**
Slaughterhouse cases, V:479
slavery
  Agassiz, V:32
  Bolingbroke, IV:158
  Calhoun, V:395, 396
  Campbell, V:403
  Cornwallis, IV:367
  Davis, V:614, 617
  Douglas, V:692-694
  Douglass, V:695-698
  Drake, III:224

Ethiopia, VIII:1517
folk tales, V:1049-1052
Gadsden, V:859
Grant, V:975
Jefferson, IV:718
Jerusalem, I:460
John of Damascus, II:544
Johnson, V:1233, 1235
Judaea, I:569, 570
Livingstone, VI:1399-1401
Mamluk Dynasty, II:124
Mansfield, IV:906
medieval Islam, II:1013
Monroe, VI:1571
Morrison's novels, VIII:2627
Phaedrus, I:618-620
Pierce, VI:1776-1778
Polk, VI:1801
Ponce de Léon, III:629, 630
Pufendorf, IV:1134
Roman latifundia, I:346, 347
Saudi Arabia, VII:1119
Solon, I:805
Spartacus, I:814, 816, 817
Stephens, VI:2129, 2130
Turner's revolt, VI:2276-2278
U.S. Supreme Court, VI:1490
Virginia, IV:82
Wise, VI:2401
See also abolitionism
Slavery Abolition Act, IV:1437
Slim, First Viscount, **IX:3435-3438**
Slipher, Earl and Vesto, IX:3700
Sloan, David, VIII:2121
Sloane, Sir Hans, IV:755
Sloane, William, VII:774
Slonimsky, Nicholas, VIII:1821
Sluter, Claus, **II:832-835**
Virgin and Child, II:832
Well of Moses, The, II:833
Sluys, battle of, II:331
Small, William, IV:1184
Small Council, II:447, 448
Smart Set, The, VII:1162
Smeaton, John, VI:1327
Smeaton, Mark, III:69
Smenkhkare, I:25
Smibert, John, IV:356
Smith, Adam, IV:454, 457, 1103, **1249-1252**
Essays on Philosophical Subjects, IV:1251
Inquiry into the Nature and Causes of the Wealth of Nations, VIII:2672, 2673
Theory of Moral Sentiments, IV:174, 1249, 1251
Wealth of Nations, The, IV:1249-1251; VI:1878
Smith, Alfred E., IX:2962, **3439-3441**
Smith, Bessie, VIII:1883; **IX:3442-3445**
"Downhearted Blues," IX:3442
"Nobody Knows You When You're Down and Out," IX:3442
Smith, Clyde H., IX:3446
Smith, Emma, VI:2415
Smith, Gerrit, V:321, 325
Smith, Gladys Louise. *See* Pickford, Mary
Smith, Ian, VIII:2647, 2648
Smith, Jedediah Strong, **VI:2077-2079**
Smith, John, IV:681, 1106-1108, 1123, 1124, **1253-1256**
Smith, John Thomas, V:547
Smith, Joseph (British consul), IV:242, 243
Smith, Joseph (Mormon leader), **VI:2080-2082,** 2412
Smith, Lula Carson. *See* McCullers, Carson
Smith, Margaret Chase, **IX:3446-3449**
"Declaration of Conscience," IX:3447, 3448
Smith, Roger, IX:2974
Smith, Sydney, V:1224, 1225
Smith, Theobald, **IX:3450-3452**
Smith, William Robertson, VII:1220
Smithers, Leonard, V:162
Smithfield Bridge, VI:1904
Smith-Hughes Act, VII:23
Smithsonian Institution
Adams, V:24
Agassiz, V:31
Goddard, VIII:1397
Henry, V:1093-1095
Langley, VI:1314; IX:4067
Smoke Abatement Exhibition, V:1115
Smoot-Hawley Tariff. *See* Hawley-Smoot Tariff
Smuts, Jan Christian, VII:376-378; **IX:3453-3455**
snake venom, VII:546, 547
Snodgrass, William DeWitt, IX:3395, 3396
Snorri Sturluson, **II:836-839**
Egil's Saga, II:838
Heimskringla, The, II:837, 838
Prose Edda, The, II:837-839
Snowdon, Philip, VII:314
Soap, Charlie, VIII:2390
Soares, Lope, III:13
soccer, IX:2950-2952
Social Darwinism, VI:1469, 1738, 2086-2088; VIII:2484
Social Democratic Party of Germany
Bernstein, VII:291-293

Brandt, VII:427, 428
Kohl, VIII:2009
Lassalle, VI:1323, 1325
Liebknecht, VI:1369-1371
Luxemburg, VIII:2285-2287
Paul VI, IX:2916
Steinmetz, VI:2121
Ulbricht, IX:3779
Zetkin, IX:4112, 4113
Social Democratic Party of Poland, VIII:2285
socialism
Africa, VIII:2775
Blanc, V:259-262
Fourier, V:814, 816, 817
Goldman, VIII:1411-1413
Gompers, V:957
Gorky's propaganda, VIII:1444
Hardie, V:1037, 1038
Jaurès, V:1221-1223
Keller, VIII:1926
Kollwitz, VIII:2016, 2017
La Fontaine, VIII:2053
Laski, VIII:2093, 2094
Lassalle, VI:1323-1325
Liebknecht, VI:1369-1371
Luxemburg, VIII:2285
Morris, VI:1589, 1590
Owen, VI:1710
Sinclair, IX:3428, 3429
Steinmetz, VI:2121, 2124
Zetkin, IX:4112, 4113
See also Christian Socialism; communism
Socialist Academy, IX:3751
Socialist League, VI:1589
Socialist Party of America, VII:882; IX:3660-3663
Socialist Party of France, V:1222; VII:335, 336; VIII:2105, 2559, 2560
Socialist Party of Italy, VIII:2667, 2668
Socialist-Revolutionaries, Party of, VIII:1941
Socialist Unity Party, IX:3779-3781
Socialist Workers Party, VII:427
Social Labor Party of Germany, VI:1325
Social Security system, VII:577; VIII:1471, 1868; IX:2963, 3225
Social War, I:194, 530
Socinus, Faustus, IV:127
Socrates, **I:793-797**
Aesop, I:14
Alcibiades, I:31
Anaxagoras, I:48
Antisthenes, I:66, 67
Aristippus, I:85, 86
Aristophanes, I:90
Aspasia, I:117
Democritus, I:250
Lysippus, I:516
Plato, I:655, 657
Protagoras, I:705-707
Sorel, IX:3464
Xanthippe, I:952-954
Xenophon, I:958-960
Zeno of Elea, I:972
Soddy, Frederick, IX:3278
Söderblom, Nathan, **IX:3456-3458**
Soderini, Piero, III:448, 450
Sodom and Gomorrah, I:5, 6
Soga clan, II:826, 827
Sogdiana, I:779
Soho Manufactory, IV:182, 183
Soka gakkai, II:668
Solander, Daniel Carl, IV:83, 85
solar eclipse
Anaxagoras, I:48
Battani, II:121
Brahe, III:77
Thales of Miletus, I:854
Solari, Luigi, VIII:2415, 2417
Solferino, Battle of, V:711, 830
Solidarity, IX:3844, 3846, 3847
Sol Invictus, I:226, 227
Solomon, **I:798-802**
Book of Proverbs, I:801
Ecclesiastes, I:297, 801
Song of Songs, I:801
Solomon, Aubrey. *See* Eban, Abba
Solomon Islands, VIII:1527
Solon, I:281, 648, **803-806,** 877, 878
Solvay, Ernest, IV:815; VII:699
Solzhenitsyn, Aleksandr, VII:351; VIII:2273; **IX:3459-3462**
August 1914, IX:3459, 3461
Cancer Ward, The, IX:3460, 3461
Experiment in Literary Investigation, An, IX:3460
First Circle, The, IX:3460, 3461
Gulag Archipelago, The, IX:3460
One Day in the Life of Ivan Denisovich, IX:3461
Red Wheel, The, IX:3461
Shch-854, IX:3460, 3461
Somers, John, IV:26
Somerset, Duke of, III:237, 238, 318, 341, 342
Somerset, Earl of, IV:211
Somersett, James, IV:906, 1236
Somes, Michael, VII:1177

Sommerfeld, Arnold, VII:300, 301; IX:2923
sonatas
  Barber, VII:192
  Beethoven, V:178-181
  Bernstein, VII:296
  Brahms, V:299-301
  Corelli, IV:360-362
  Couperin, IV:374-376
  Franck, V:832-834
  Milhaud, VIII:2525
  Prokofiev, IX:3085
  Vivaldi, IV:1383
  Zwilich, IX:4121
Songhai Empire, III:521-523
"Song of Deborah," I:247
Song of Roland, II:228, 944
Sonni Ali, III:521, 522
Sonoran Dynasty, VII:542
Sony Corporation, VIII:2622-2624
Sopete, III:182
Sophia, I:912
Sophie of Bavaria, V:829, 830
Sophism
  Antisthenes, I:66
  Aristippus, I:85
  Democritus, I:250
  Euripides, I:317
  Phidias, I:624
  Plato, I:657
  Protagoras, I:705-707
Sophocles, I:10, 11, 807, **807-810,** 878
  Ajax, I:807
  Antigone, I:807, 808
  Electra, I:808
  Oedipus at Colonus, I:807, 809
  Oedipus Tyrannus, I:808, 809; III:282
  Philoctetes, I:808
  Women of Trachis, The, I:807
Sophonisba, I:535
Sophronius, II:820, 821
Sorel, Georges, **IX:3463-3465**
  Reflections on Violence, IX:3463, 3464
Sosigenes, I:150, **811-813**
Sotatsu, **IV:1257-1259**
  Bugaku Dancers, IV:1258
  Cormorants, The, IV:1258
  Flowers and Grasses of the Four Seasons, IV:1258
  Sekiya, IV:1258
  Wind and Thunder Gods, The, IV:1258
Soteris, I:43
Soto, Hernando de, **III:699-702**
soul music, VII:1216-1218
Sousa, John Philip, **IX:3466-3470**
  Gladiator, IX:3466
  Semper Fidelis, IX:3466
  Stars and Stripes Forever, The, IX:3467
  Washington Post, The, IX:3466
Sousa Concert Band, IX:3467-3469
South African Anglican Church, IX:3775-3777
South African Council of Churches, IX:3776
South African War. *See* Boer War
South Carolina
  Calhoun, V:394, 395
  Gadsden, V:859
  Oglethorpe, IV:1044
  Tyler, VI:2289
Southeast Asian Nations, Association of, VIII:2151
Southeast Asia Treaty Organization, VII:1044
Southern Africa Development Coordination Conference, VIII:2318, 2775
Southern Christian Leadership Conference, VII:10, 80; VIII:1824, 1825, 1973; IX:2890
Southern Literary Messenger, VI:1794, 1796
Southern Pacific Railroad, VI:2098
Southern Poverty Law Center, VIII:2187
Southern Sung Dynasty, II:479, 480, 612, 613, 867, 868, 1018, 1019
Southey, Robert, VI:2209
South Improvement Company, VI:1897
South Sea Company, IV:1279, 1401, 1402
South Pole, VII:66-69, 535; VIII:1662, 1664
South Sea Company, IV:158
Soviet Academy of Sciences, VIII:2020
Soviet-Chinese Friendship Meeting, VIII:2213
Soviet Writers, Union of, VIII:1445; IX:2901
Soyinka, Wole, **IX:3471-3474**
  Aké: The Years of Childhood, IX:3471, 3472
  Bacchae, The, IX:3472
  Death and the King's Horseman, IX:3472
  Interpreters, The, IX:3472
  Invention, The, IX:3471
  Jero's Metamorphosis, IX:3472
  Kongi's Harvest, IX:3472
  Lion and the Jewel, The, IX:3471
  Madmen and Specialists, IX:3472
  Myth, Literature, and the African World, IX:3473
  Opera Wonyosi, IX:3472
  Play of Giants, A, IX:3473
  Requiem for a Futurologist, IX:3473
  Road, The, IX:3472
  Season of Anomy, IX:3472

Strong Breed, The, IX:3472
Swamp Dwellers, The, IX:3471
Soyuz missions, VII:1271
Spaak, Paul-Henri, **IX:3475-3477**
Spallanzani, Lazzaro, **IV:1260-1263**
Dell' azione del cuore ne' vasi sanguigni, IV:1261
Dissertations Relative to the Natural History of Animals and Vegetables, IV:1261
Essay on Animal Reproductions, An, IV:1260
Experiments Upon the Circulation of the Blood?, IV:1261
Letters on a Supposed New Sense in Bats, IV:1262
Memoirs on Respiration, IV:1262
Saggio di osservazioni microsopiche concernenti il sistema della generazione de' signori di Needham e Buffon, IV:1260
Tracts on Animals and Vegetables, IV:1261
Spanish-American War
American Red Cross, V:145
Bryan, VII:480
Dewey, V:656-658
Goethals, VIII:1408
Hay, V:1069
Low, VIII:2246
McKinley, VI:1454-1456
Remington, VI:1862
yellow fever, VIII:1434
yellow journalism, VIII:1603
Spanish Armada, War of the
Cecil, III:148
Drake, III:225
Elizabeth I, III:243
Farnese, III:255
Frobisher, III:279
Grenville, III:315-317
Philip II, III:600
Spanish Civil War
Blum, VII:336
Buñuel, VII:506
Candela, VII:557
Casals, VII:607
Éluard, VII:1075
Franco, VII:1200-1202
Heinkel's aircraft, VIII:1615
Malraux, VIII:2381
Ortega y Gasset, IX:2843
Parker, IX:2886
Weil, IX:3923
Spanish Inquisition
Ferdinand and Isabella, III:262
Manuel I, III:465
Paul III, III:597
Raymond of Peñafort, II:777
Servetus, III:677
Spinoza, IV:1264
Teresa of Ávila, III:713-715
Torquemada, III:725-727
Spanish Succession, War of
Anne, IV:52
Bolingbroke, IV:157, 158
Charles III, IV:287
Charles XII, IV:290
Frederick I, IV:498
George I, IV:531
Godolphin, IV:553
Louis XIV, IV:868
Marlborough, IV:922, 923
Scarlatti, IV:1214
Stanhope, IV:1277
William III, IV:1448, 1449
Sparks, Chauncey, IX:3857, 3858
Sparks, Jared, V:125, 127, 471
Sparta
Alcibiades, I:31, 32
Alexander the Great, I:38
Antisthenes, I:67
Cimon, I:200, 201
Cleomenes I, I:214, 215
Cleomenes II, I:215
Cleomenes III, I:215, 216
Euripides, I:318
Lysippus, I:515
Macedonia, I:628
Pericles, I:609, 611, 612
Pheidippides, I:621, 622
Pisistratus, I:649, 650
Plato, I:655
Thebes, I:290
Themistocles, I:858, 859
Thucydides, I:885-887
Xenophon, I:959
Spartacus, **I:814-817**
Spartacus League, IX:4114
Speaker, Tris, VII:719
Spectator, The, V:1192
Speke, John Hanning, V:375, 376; VI:**2083-2085**
Spencer, Charles. *See* Sunderland, Third Earl of
Spencer, Herbert **VI:2086-2088,** 2330
Principles of Psychology, The, VI:2086, 2088
Social Statics, VI:2086
Synthetic Philosophy, The, VI:2086, 2087
Spenser, Edmund, III:244, **703-706**
Amoretti, III:703, 704

Colin Clout's Come Home Again, III:693
Epithalamion, III:704
Faerie Queen, The, III:703-705; VI:1264
Shepheardes Calender, The, III:692, 703, 704
Speransky, Mikhail Mikhaylovich, **VI:2089-2091**
Spessivtzeva, Olga, VIII:2182, 2183
Speyer, diets of, III:160, 505
Sphaerus, I:970
Spica, I:407
Spice Islands, III:453, 455
Spielberg, Steven, IX:4030
Spinks, Leon, VII:56
Spinoza, Baruch, **IV:1264-1267;** VI:2182
Ethics, IV:1266
Political Treatise, A, IV:1266
Theologico-Political Treatise, A, IV:1265, 1266
Spirit of St. Louis, The, VIII:2193, 2196
Spitsbergen, IV:680, 682
Spock, Benjamin, **IX:3478-3481**
Commonsense Book of Baby and Child Care, The, IX:3478, 3480
Spock on Spock, IX:3479
Springfield Republican, V:668
Spruance, Raymond A., VIII:2751
Sputnik, VII:1044; VIII:2019-2021; IX:3701
Squadrille, Edward F., IX:3017
Squanto, IV:930
Squarcialupi Codex, II:570
Squarcione, Francesco, III:460
Square Deal League, VIII:2229
Sri Vaisnavas sect, II:770-772
SS. *See* Schutzstaffel
Ssu-ma Ch'ien, I:176, 177, 498, **818-821;** II:613, 963
Shih chi, I:543, 590, 591, 818-820
Ssu-ma Kuang, **II:840-842**
Tzu-chih t'ung-chien, II:840
Staehlin, Jacob von, IV:1087
Staël, Madame de, **VI:2092-2095**
Corrine: Or, Italy, VI:2094
Delphine, VI:2093, 2094
Essay on Fiction, VI:2093
Germany, VI:2094
Treatise on Ancient and Modern Literature, A, VI:2093
Treatise on the Influence of the Passions upon the Happiness of Individuals and Nations, A, VI:2093
Stahl, Georg Ernst, **IV:1268-1272**
Fundamenta chymiae dogmaticae et experimentalis, IV:1271
Tehoria medica vera, IV:1269
Stalin, Joseph, **IX:3482-3485**
Astor, VII:130
Bourke-White, VII:395
Brezhnev, VII:459
Chamberlain, VII:645
Churchill, VII:693
Czechoslovakia, VII:261
Dubcek, VII:968
Gorky, VIII:1442, 1445
Harriman, VIII:1561
Kapitsa, VIII:1908
Kenyatta, VIII:1936
Khrushchev, VIII:1962, 1963
Kurchatov, VIII:2041
Lenin, VIII:2162
Litvinov, VIII:2209, 2210
Lukács, VIII:2274
Malenkov, VIII:2377, 2378
Marx, VI:1494
Marxism and the National and Colonial Question, IX:3482
Molotov, VIII:2571, 2572
Prokofiev, IX:3087
Roosevelt, IX:3225
Shostakovich, IX:3409, 3410
Solzhenitsyn, IX:3460
Tito, IX:3694
Tupolev, IX:3765
Ulbricht, IX:3779, 3780
Zhukov, IX:4116, 4117
Stamford Bridge, battle at, II:428
Stamp Act
Adams, John, IV:16
Adams, Samuel, IV:22
Cornwallis, IV:367
Dickinson, IV:408
Gage, IV:513
Hancock, IV:617
Henry, IV:647, 648
Hutchinson, IV:692, 693
Mason, IV:926
Morris, IV:999
Pitt the Elder, IV:1099
Revere, IV:1156
Rockingham, IV:222
Wilson, IV:1456
Standard Oil Company, VI:1896-1898; VIII:2228; IX:3616, 3617
Standerin, Abraham, IV:818
Standing Rock Agency, VI:2072
Standish, Miles, IV:190, 931, **1273-1276**
Stanford, Leland, **VI:2096-2100**

Stanhope, First Earl, IV:**1277-1280,** 1401-1403
Stanislavsky, Konstantin, **IX:3486-3489**
Actor Prepares, An, IX:3487
Akalaitis, VII:34
Building a Character, IX:3487
Creating a Role, IX:3487
Gorky, VIII:1442, 1444
Method acting, VII:424, 3487
My Life in Art, IX:3486, 3487
Stanislovski's Legacy, IX:3487
Stanley, Edward George Geoffrey Smith. *See* Derby, Fourteenth Earl of
Stanley, Henry Morton, VI:1400, **2101-2105**
Congo and the Founding of Its Free State, The, VI:2103
How I Found Livingstone, VI:2102
My Kalulu, VI:2102
Stanley, Thomas, Lord, III:650
Stanley, Sir William, III:257
Stanton, Edwin M., V:1236; **VI:2106-2109**
Stanton, Elizabeth Cady, I:247; V:61, 62; VI:1600-1602, **2110-2114**
History of Woman Suffrage, VI:2112
Woman's Bible, The, VI:2113
Stanton, Henry, VI:2110, 2111
Stark, Johannes, **IX:3490-3493**
Stark, John, V:1240, 1241
Starling, Ernest Henry, **IX:3494-3496**
Starr, Kenneth, VII:710; IX:3155
Starr, Ringo, VII:226-229
Star Wars program, VII:302; IX:3633
Stassen, Harold, VII:509
State Secession Convention, V:1138, 1140
Statius, Caecilius, I:844
Staudinger, Hermann, VIII:2698; **IX:3497-3500**
Staudinger's law, IX:3499
Staupitz, Johann von, III:443
Stavropol, VIII:1423
Stavrovouni Monastery, I:376
steam engine
Boulton, IV:182-184
Diesel, V:672
Ford, VII:1186
Guericke, IV:588
Lenoir, VI:1343, 1345
Murdock, IV:1008-1010
Newcomen, IV:1022-1024
Papin, IV:1059-1061
Roebuck, IV:1184
Siemens family, VI:2068
Stephenson, VI:2132
Trevithick, VI:2251-2253
Watt, IV:1409, 1411, 1412
Westinghouse, VI:2358, 2360
Wilkinson, IV:1443-1445
Steber, Eleanor, VII:193
Steele, Richard, IV:26-28, 114
Steelhouse Lane, IV:1182
steel industry
Bessemer, V:218-221
Gibbs, V:925
Hadfield, V:1015, 1016
Krupp, VI:1301, 1303
Lewis, VIII:2171
Mellon, VIII:2480
Morgan, VI:1581, 1582
Siemens family, VI:2066-2069
Taylor-White process, IX:3619
Stefan Dusan, **II:843-846**
Stefan Uros III Decanski, II:843
Steichen, Edward, **IX:3501-3505**
"Family of Man, The," IX:3503, 3504
Stein, Edith, **IX:3406-3510**
Science of the Cross, The, IX:3509
Stein, Freiherr vom, V:1034; VI:1654, 1655, **2115-2117**
Stein, Gertrude, VIII:1484, 1485, 1627; **IX:3511-3514,** 4014
Autobiography of Alice B. Toklas, IX:3513
Geography and Plays, IX:3512
Making of Americans, The, IX:3512
"Sacred Emily," IX:3512
Tender Buttons, IX:3512
Three Lives, IX:3512
Steinbeck, John, **IX:3515-3518**
America and Americans, IX:3516
Cannery Row, IX:3516, 3517
Cup of Gold, IX:3515
East of Eden, IX:3516
Grapes of Wrath, The, VIII:2084; IX:3516, 3517
In Dubious Battle, IX:3516, 3517
Log from the Sea of Cortez, IX:3516
Of Mice and Men, IX:3516, 3517
To a God Unknown, IX:3515
Tortilla Flat, IX:3515-3517
Winter of Our Discontent, The, IX:3516
Steinbus, Ferdinand von, V:597
Steinem, Gloria, VII:1155; **IX:3519-3522**
Ms. magazine, IX:3521, 3522
Outrageous Acts and Everyday Rebellions, IX:3521
Revolution from Within, IX:3521
Steiner, Jakob, **VI:2118-2120**

Steinmetz, Charles Proteus, **VI:2121-2124**
Stellaburg, III:78
Steller, Georg Wilhelm, IV:112
Stendhal, **VI:2125-2128,** 2183
Armance, VI:2127
Charterhouse of Parma, The, VI:2127
Histoire de la peinture de Italie, VI:2126
Lamiel, VI:2128
Maxims of Love, VI:2126
Memoirs of a Tourist, VI:2128
Memoirs of Rossini, VI:2127
Racine and Shakespeare, VI:2127
Red and the Black, The, VI:2127
Roman Journal, A, VI:2127
Rome, Naples, and Florence in 1817, VI:2126
Stephen I (of Hungary), II:574, 575, **851-854**
Stephen II (Pope), II:226
Stephen, King (of England), **II:847-850**
Stephen, Saint, I:605, **822-824**
Stephen of Blois, II:292, 446
Stephens, Alexander H., **VI:2129-2131**
Constitutional View of the Late War Between the States, A, VI:2130
Stephenson, George, **VI:2132-2135**
Stephenson, Robert, VI:2252
Sterling, Ernest Henry, VII:217, 218
Stern, Günther, VII:98
Stern, Otto, VIII:2336
Sternberg, Josef von, VII:930, 932
Stevens, Thaddeus, **VI:2136-2138**
Stevenson, Adlai E., VIII:1784, 1930; **IX:3523-3527,** 3743
Stevenson, Robert Louis, III:765; **VI:2139-2142**
Black Arrow, The, VI:2141
"Bottle Imp, The," VI:2141, 2142
Catriona, VI:2141
Child's Garden of Verses, A, VI:2141
David Balfour, VI:2141
Ebb-Tide, The, VI:2141, 2142
Edinburgh: Picturesque Notes, VI:2139
Inland Voyage, An, VI:2139
Island Nights' Entertainments, VI:2141
Kidnapped, VI:2141, 2142
"Lodging for the Night, A," III:765
Master of Ballantrae, The, VI:2141
Strange Case of Dr. Jekyll and Mr. Hyde, VI:2139, 2141, 2142
Travels with a Donkey in the Cévennes, VI:2139
Treasure Island, VI:2139, 2141, 2142
Weir of Hermiston, VI:2141
Wrecker, The, VI:2141
Stewart, James, **IX:3528-3531,** 3903
Anatomy of a Murder, IX:3530
Destry Rides Again, IX:3528, 3529
Harvey, IX:3530
It's a Wonderful Life, IX:3530
Man Who Knew Too Much, The, IX:3530
Mr. Smith Goes to Washington, IX:3528
Philadelphia Story, The, IX:3529
Rear Window, IX:3530
Rope, IX:3530
Shenandoah, IX:3530
Shootist, The, IX:3903
Vertigo, IX:3530
You Can't Take It With You, IX:3528
Stewart, Robert. *See* Castlereagh, Viscount
Stieglitz, Alfred, IX:2800, 2801, 3501, 3503, **3532-3536**
Stigand, II:426
Stijl, De, IX:2859, 2860
Stilicho, Flavius, I:342, **825-827**
Still, William, VI:2264
Stiller, Moritz, VII:1286
Stimson, Henry L., VII:1212; VIII:2431; **IX:3537-3540**
Stimson Doctrine, VIII:1729
Stirling Bridge, Battle of, II:324, 956
Stoa Poikile, I:676, 969
Stockbridge Indians, IV:430
Stockhausen, Karlheinz, **IX:3541-3545**
Aus den sieben Tagen, IX:3544
Carré, IX:3543
Donnerstag aus Licht, IX:3544
Electronishe Studien I and II, IX:3542
Gesang der Jünglinde, IX:3543
Gruppen, IX:3543
Hymnen, IX:3544
Kontakte, IX:3543
Kontra-Punkte, IX:3542
Licht, die sieben Tgen der Woche, IX:3544
Mantra, IX:3544
Momente, IX:3543
Samstag aus Licht, IX:3544
Stimmung, IX:3544
Zeitmasze, IX:3543
Stockholm Conference, IX:3456, 3457
Stockholm Olympics of 1912, VII:775
Stockton, Robert F., V:840
Stockton and Darlington Railway, VI:2132, 2133
Stockton-on-Tees, VIII:2340, 2341
Stoicism
Antisthenes, I:68
Cato the Younger, I:166

Eratosthenes of Cyrene, I:303
Livy, I:505
Montaigne, III:524
Montesquieu, IV:986
Philo of Alexandria, I:632, 633
Posidonius, I:686-689
Poussin, IV:1120
Seneca the Younger, I:772
Zeno of Citium, I:967, 969, 970
Stölbova, Peace of, IV:589, 1052
Stone, Harlan Fiske, VII:577; **IX:3546-3550**
Stone, Lucy, **VI:2143-2146**
Stone, Oliver
Heaven and Earth, VIII:1595
Stoner, Edmund, IX:2923
Stoner, Fed, VII:53
Stopes, Marie, **IX:3551-3554**
Married Love, IX:3552
Roman Catholic Methods of Birth Control, IX:3552
Wise Parenthood, IX:3552
Story, Joseph, **VI:2147-2150,** 2191
Commentaries, VI:2149
Story, William Wetmore, VI:2257
Stothart, Herbert, VIII:1533
Stowe, Harriet Beecher, V:170, 172, 174; **VI:2151-2154,** 2257
American Woman's Home, The, V:172
Minister's Wooing, The, VI:2152
Oldtown Folks, VI:2152
Pearl of Orr's Island, The, V:1228; VI:2152
Poganuc People, VI:2152
Uncle Tom's Cabin, VI:2151, 2152, 2177, 2268, 2270, 2375; VIII:1589
Strabo, I:731, **828-831**
Geography, I:407, 541, 566, 828, 830, 831
Historical Memoirs, I:828, 830
Strachan, John, VI:1448-1450
Strachey, Lytton, VIII:2606
Stradivari, Antonio, **IV:1281-1284**
Stradonitz, Friedrich August Kekule von, VI:1367
Strafford, First Earl of, IV:308, 1142, **1285-1288**
Stralsund, IV:291
Strand, Paul, VII:594
Strand, The, V:700, 701
Strasberg, Lee, VII:794, 795; VIII:2589; IX:3488
Strasser, Gregor and Otto, VIII:1404
Strassman, Fritz, VIII:1514, 1515, 2477
Strategic Arms Limitation Treaties, VII:590, 591; VIII:2759
Strategic Defense Initiative. *See* Star Wars program
Stratemeyer, Edward, V:52
Strato of Lampsachus, I:873
Strauss, Johann, VI:1686, **2155-2159**
Acceleration Waltz, VI:2156
Blue Danube, The, VI:2156
Fledermaus, Die, VI:2156
Kaiserwaltzer, VI:2158
Tales from the Vienna Woods, VI:2156
Zigeunerbaron, Der, VI:2158
Strauss, Richard, V:1164; **IX:3555-3558,** 3794
Ariadne auf Naxos, IX:3557
Aus Italian, IX:3555
Elektra, IX:3556
Festival March, IX:3555
Guntram, IX:3556
Heldenleben, Ein, VII:210
Rosenkavalier, Der, IX:3556, 3557
Salome, IX:3556
Serenade for Wind Instruments in Eb, IX:3555
Thus Spake Zarathusta, VII:210
Stravinsky, Igor, **IX:3559-3562**
Apollo Musagetes, VIII:2182; IX:3560
Card Party, The, IX:3560
Firebird, The, IX:3560, 3607
Oedipus Rex, VII:721; IX:3560
Perséphone, IX:3560
Petrushka, VIII:2748; IX:3560
Rake's Progress, The, VII:471; IX:3561
Rite of Spring, The, VII:387, 389; VIII:2449, 2748, 2749; IX:3086, 3560
Soldier's Tale, The, IX:3560
Symphony of Psalms, IX:3560
Straw, Jack, II:114, 116
Streep, Meryl, VII:1084
Street, George Edmund, **VI:2160-2163**
Strelow, Albert, VII:1186
Stresemann, Gustav, **IX:3563-3565**
Strindberg, August, V:890; IX:2819, **3566-3569**
Dream Play, A, IX:3566
Fröken Julie, VII:281
Great Highway, The, IX:3566
Inferno, IX:3566
To Damascus, IX:3566
string quartet
Bartók, VII:211
Beethoven, V:178-181
Boccherini, IV:147-149
Haydn, IV:639, 641, 642
Schumann, VI:1993
Zwilich, IX:4121-4123
Strong, Jonathan, IV:1236
Strutt, Jedediah, VI:2074
Stryker, Ron, VIII:2084

Stuart, Alexander, IV:576
Stuart, Charles Edward, IV:884
Stuart, Gilbert, **IV:1289-1293**
Skater, The, IV:1290
Stuart, James. *See* James I
Stuart, John Todd, VI:1382
Studd, J.E.K., VIII:2637
Student Nonviolent Coordinating Committee, VIII:1973
Studio, The, V:161
Sturlung Age, II:836, 838
Sturluson, Snorri. *See* Snorri Sturluson
Sturm, Der, VIII:2013
Sturm Abteilung, VIII:1438
Sturtevant, Alfred Henry, VIII:2651
Stuttgart Declaration of Guilt, VIII:2743
Stuyvesant, Peter, **IV:1294-1297**
Styron, William
Confessions of Nat Turner, The, VI:2277, 2278
submarines
Fulton, V:855, 856
Holland, V:1123-1125
Ludendorff, VIII:2266
Rickover, IX:3173-3176
Verne, VI:2304
Wilkins, IX:4000, 4001
Succession, Act of, III:209, 265, 654
Succession, House of, I:105
Sucre, Antonio José de, **VI:2164-2166**
Suddhodana, I:144
Sudebnik, III:383
Suess, Dr.. *See* Geisel, Theodor Seuss
Suetonius, I:928, 930, 933
Suevi, I:342
Suez Canal, VI:1355-1357, 1537; VIII:1530, 2695
Suez Canal Company, VII:1017
Suez Crisis, VII:531, 1017, 1018; VIII:1961, 2695
Suffolk, Earl of, II:232
suffrage, women's. *See* women's suffrage
Suffrage Act of 1918, VII:354
Sufism
'Abbas the Great, IV:4-6
Abdelkader, V:1
'Abduh, V:4
Hallaj, al-, II:421-424
Hasan al-Basri, II:441
Ibn al-'Arabi, II:491-493
Nanak, III:542
Rumi, II:800, 801
Sa'di, II:806
Sugar Act of 1764, IV:692
Suger, **II:859-862**
Abbot Suger on the Abbey Church of St. Denis and Its Art Treasures, II:861
Sui Dynasty, II:482, 827, 1015
Sukarno, XIII:1577, 1578; **IX:3570-3574**
Sulaiman, II:68
Süleyman the Magnificent, III:159, **707-709**
Sulla, Lucius Cornelius, **I:833-836**
Caesar, I:147
Cicero, I:194
Gracchi, I:347
Jugurthine War, I:529, 530
Mithradates the Great, I:558
Pompey the Great, I:679
Tigranes the Great, I:896, 897
Sullivan, Anne, VIII:1924, 1926
Sullivan, Sir Arthur, **V:927-931**
Contrabandistas, The, V:928
Cox and Box, V:928
Grand Duke, The, V:929
H.M.S. Pinafore, V:929
In Memoriam, V:928
Patience, V:929
Prodigal Son, The, V:928
Pygmalion and Galatea, V:928
Tempest, The, V:928
Thespis, V:928
Trial by Jury, V:929
Utopia, Limited, V:929
Sullivan, Harry Stack, VII:1247; **IX:3575-3577**
Sullivan, Louis, **VI:2167-2169;** IX:4060
Sully, Duke of, III:334
Sumanguru, II:863, 864
Sumer and Akkad, I:361, 362; VIII:1660
See also Babylonia
Sumner, Charles, V:680, 681, 1152; **VI:2170-2174**
Sumter, Fort, V:1233
Sunday, Billy, **IX:3582-3586**
Sunderland, Third Earl of, IV:1401-1403
Sundjata, **II:863-865**
Sung Dynasty, **II:866-868**
calligraphy, II:639, 640
Ou-yang Hsui, II:709, 710
Ssu-ma Kuang, II:840, 841
Su Tung-p'o, II:855-857
See also Northern Sung Dynasty; Southern Sung Dynasty
Sunila Pulp Mill, VII:2
Sunni Islam, II:385, 386, 678
Sun Records, IX:3076, 3079
Sun Yat-sen, V:1165, 1167; VII:664, 665, 676, 687; **IX:3578-3581,** 3877-3879

Supper Controversy, III:102, 103
Suppression of Vice, Society for the, IV:1436
Supreme Council of India, VI:1428
Supreme Council of the United Orders of Railroad Employees, VII:880
Supreme Court, U.S.
- Altgeld, V:55
- Black, VII:321-323
- Bork, IX:3658
- Brandeis, VII:419, 421-423
- Burger, VII:509-511
- Cardozo, VII:575-577
- Chase, Salmon P., V:477-479
- Chase, Samuel, IV:293-296
- Dred Scott decision, VI:2000, 2001
- Espionage Act, VII:882
- Field, V:787-789
- Frankfurter, VII:1212-1215
- Kent, VI:1280
- Holmes, VIII:1721
- Hughes, VIII:1766-1769
- Lockwood, VI:1407, 1408
- Marshall, John, VI:1487-1491
- Marshall, Thurgood, VIII:2433-2435
- O'Connor, IX:2789-2791
- Rehnquist, IX:3142-3144
- Roosevelt, IX:3225
- Scalia, IX:3658
- segregation. *See Brown v. Board of Education*
- sexual harassment, VIII:2326
- slavery, VI:1490
- Stone, IX:3546-3549
- Story, VI:2147-2149
- Taft, VIII:1542; IX:3594-3596
- Taney, VI:2189-2193
- Thomas, IX:3657-3658
- treason, VI:1490, 1491
- Warren, IX:3888-3891
- Wilson, IV:1458

Supremecy, Act of. *See* Royal Supremecy, Act of
Supreme War Council of France, VIII:1851
surgery
- anesthesia, VI:1596-1598
- Aretaeus of Cappadocia, I:82, 83
- Celsus, I:173-175
- Cushing, VII:823-825
- Guy de Chauliac, II:414-416
- heart transplants, VII:195, 197
- Lister, VI:1388-1390
- Mayo, VIII:2466
- Paul of Aegina, II:712-714
- Semmelweis, VI:2021-2023

Surrealism
- Appolinaire, VII:82-84
- Bosch, III:72
- Breton, VII:448-451
- Buñuel, VII:505-507
- Cartier-Bresson, VII:594
- Césaire, VII:631
- Dali, VII:827, 829, 830
- Éluard, VII:1074-1077
- Ernst, VII:1098-1100
- Giacometti, VII:1359-1361
- Lacan, VIII:2061
- Magritte, VIII:2349-2353
- Miró, VIII:2546, 2548, 2549
- Nash, VIII:2690
- Nevelson, VIII:2729
- Redon, VI:1855
- Rousseau, VI:1921-1923

Su Shih, II:639
Susquehannocks, IV:81
Sutcliffe, Stuart, VII:226
Sutherland, Graham Vivian, **IX:3587-3589**
- *Bestiary,* IX:3588
- *Burnt-out Paper Rolls,* IX:3587
- *Crucufixion,* IX:3588
- *Thorn Heads,* IX:3588
- *Thorn Trees,* IX:3588

Sutherland, Halliday, IX:3552
Sutherland, Joan, IX:2931
Su Tse-yu, II:855
Su-tsung, II:967
Sutter, John Augustus, V:787
Suttner, Bertha von, **VI:2175-2178**
- *Daniela Dormes,* VI:2175
- *Lay Down Your Arms,* VI:2175, 2177
- *Maschinenzeitalter, Das,* VI:2177

Su Tung-p'o, **II:855-858,** 968
Suvorov, Aleksandr Vasilyevich, **IV:1298-1301;** VI:1305, 1306
Suzuki, D.T., VIII:1745
Svetambara, I:915
Svevo, Italo, VIII:2592
Svoboda, Ludvik, VII:969
Swabian War, III:493
Swan, Joseph Wilson, **VI:2179-2181**
Swedenborg, Emanuel, **IV:1302-1304;** V:67, 1216; VIII:1926
- *Heavenly Arcana, The,* IV:1302, 1303
- *True Christian Religion,* IV:1303

Swedish Tennis Association, VII:370
Swift, Jonathan, IV:220, 984, **1305-1309**
- *Conduct of the Allies, The,* IV:158

Drapier's Letters to the People of Ireland, The, IV:1307, 1308
Examiner, The, IV:1307
Gulliver's Travels, IV:391, 469, 1308, 1309
Journal to Stella, IV:1307
Modest Proposal, A, IV:1307, 1308
*Predictions for the Ensuing Year*IV:1305, 1307, 1308
Tale of a Tub, A, IV:1305, 1307, 1308; V:522
Swimmer, Chief Ross, VIII:2390
Swinburne, Algernon Charles, III:765
Poems and Ballads: First Series, V:1040
Swiss Cottage Fields, V:1114
Swiss Reformation, III:791-794
Syagrius, II:274, 275
Sydenham, Thomas, **IV:1310-1312**
Sykes-Picot Agreement, IX:3931
Sylvester II, II:373, **869-872**
Sylvius, Jacobus, III:755
Syme, James, VI:1388
Symmachus, II:756, 897
symphonies
Barber, VII:191-193
Bartók, VII:210
Beethoven, V:178-181
Berlioz, V:202-206
Bernstein, VII:296
Borodin, V:286-288
Bruckner, V:331-334
Copland, VII:768
Dvorák, V:725-727
Ellington, VII:1068
Franck, V:832-834
Henze, VIII:1634
Liszt, VI:1391-1393
Mahler, VIII:2359, 2361-2363
Mendelssohn, VI:1534-1536
Messiaen, VIII:2503-2505
Milhaud, VIII:2527
Prokofiev, IX:3085-3087
Rachmaninoff, IX:3105, 3106, 3108
Ravel, IX:3129-3131
Rimsky-Korsakov, VI:1889-1891
Schubert, VI:1989, 1995
Schumann, VI:1992-1995
Sibelius, IX:3413-3415
Strauss, VI:2155, 2156, 2158
Tchaikovsky, VI:2198, 2200, 2201
Villa-Lobos, IX:3816
Zwilich, IX:4122, 4123
Syncellus, George, II:903
Syndicat Agricole Africain, VIII:1754
Synoptic Gospels, I:477; VIII:1558
Syon House, IV:9
Syphax, I:535
Syrian Wars, I:64, 717; II:383
Szabolcs, Synod of, II:575
Szell, George, VII:389
Szilard, Leo, IX:3632

Tabari, al-, **II:873-875**
Selections from the Annals of Tabari, II:873, 874
Tabernacles, Feast of, I:332
Tabor, Mount, I:247
Tabor Amendment, IX:3447
Taborites, II:1030, 1031
Tabriz, II:381-383
Tacitus, Cornelius, I:772, **837-840,** 894, 935; IV:304
Agricola, I:136, 838, 839
Annals, I:136, 550, 551, 839; II:903
Dialogue on Orators, I:838, 839
Germania, I:838, 839
Histories, I:839
Tacitus, Marcus Claudius, I:839
Tafari Makonnen. *See* Haile Selassie I
Tafawa Balewa, Abubakar, VII:145, 146
Tafna, Treaty of, V:2
Taft, Robert A., VIII:2298; **IX:3590-3593**
Taft, William Howard, **IX:3594-3597**
Borah, V:280
Brandeis, VII:422, 481
Hand, VIII:1541, 1542
Hughes, VIII:1766
La Follette, VIII:2048
Lathrop, VIII:2097
Roosevelt, IX:3229, 3231
Washington, VI:2337
Taft-Hartley Act, VIII:1867, 2172; IX:3447, 3592
Tagore, Debendranath, VI:1848
Tagore, Rabindranath, IX:3132, 3133, **3598-3602**
Flight of Swans, A, IX:3599
Gitanjali (Song of Offerings), IX:3599, 3601
Gora, IX:3599
Kari O Komal, IX:3598
Religion of Man, IX:3601
Taharqa, I:105, 106
Tahiti, IV:143, 145, 180, 351, 353, 890
Taika Reforms, II:827
Taine, Hippolyte-Adolphe, **VI:2182-2184**
History of English Literature, VI:2182
T'ai-p'ing Heavenly Kingdom, V:1165, 1166
Taiping Rebellion, VI:2260-2262
Taira Kiyomori, **II:881-883**

Taira Tadamori, II:881
Taisho, Emperor, VIII:1678, 1680
Tait, David, IV:875
T'ai Tsu, II:866
T'ai Tsung, **II:876-880,** 1015-1017
  Chen-kuan cheng-yao, II:879
  Li Wei-kung wen-tui, II:879
Taitu, Empress, VIII:1517
Taj al-Mulk, II:679
Taj Mahal, IV:1233
Takauji. *See* Ashikaga Takauji
Takeda Katsuyori, III:571
Takigawa Yukitoki, VIII:1574
Talal, Crown Prince, VIII:1791
Talavera, Battle of, VI:2352
Talbot, Henry Fox, VI:1660
Talbot, Marion, **IX:3603-3606**
  Food as a Factor in Student Life, IX:3604
  Home Sanitation, IX:3604
  Modern Household, The, IX:3604
  More Than Lore, IX:3604
Talenti, Francesco, II:84
Tale of the Heike, The, II:882
Tallchief, Maria, **IX:3607-3610**
Talleyrand, **VI:2185-2188**
Talmud
  Akiba, I:29
  Elijah ben Solomon, IV:432, 433
  Johanan ben Zakkai, I:471-473
  Maimonides, II:620
  Wise, VI:2401
Tambo, Oliver, VIII:2281, 2384, 2386
Tamerlane, II:418, **884-886,** 1022; IV:1232, 1233
Tamm, Igor, IX:3296, 3298
Tammen, Harry, V:532
Tanaka Giichi, VIII:1574
Tananarive accords, IX:3746
Tancred, II:160, **887-889**
Taney, Roger Brooke, VI:2000, 2147-2149, **2189-2193**
Tanganyika African Association, VIII:2773
Tanganyika African National Union, VIII:2773, 2774
T'ang Chien, VI:2260
T'ang Dynasty, II:482-485, 593, 876-879, 918, 1015-1017
T'ang T'ai Tsung, II:484
Tanguy, Julien, V:946
Tanizaki, Jun'ichiro, **IX:3611-3613**
  Chijin no ai, IX:3611
  Diary of a Mad Old Man, IX:3612
  Makioka Sisters, The, IX:3612, 3613
  "Portrait of Shunkin, A," IX:3612
  Some Prefer Nettles, IX:3612
Tannenberg, Battle of, II:1003
Tanutamon, I:106
Tanzimat, V:1207, 1208
T'ao Ch'ien, **I:841-843**
  "Returning to the Farm to Dwell," I:842
Taoism
  Chuang-tzu, I:190-193
  Confucius, I:223
  Lao-Tzu, I:498-500
  Li Po, II:591, 592
  Shih Huang-ti, I:178
Tarbell, Ida, **IX:3614-3617**
  History of the Standard Oil Company, The, IX:3616
Tardieu, André Pierre Gabriel Amédée, VIII:2105
Tariff Reform League, V:464
Tarzan, VII:517, 519
Tashunca-uitko. *See* Crazy Horse
Tasman, Abel Janszoon, **IV:1313-1315**
Tassi, Agostino, IV:317
Tasso, Torquato, **III:710-712;** IV:990
  Aminta, III:710, 711; V:650
  Creation of the World, III:711
  Discourses on the Heroic Poem, III:711
  Jerusalem Conquered, III:711
  Jerusalem Delivered, III:711; IV:990
  Rinaldo, III:710
Tatanka Iyotake. *See* Sitting Bull
Tatars, II:52; III:382; IV:726
Tatti, Jacopo. *See* Sansovino, Jacopo
Tatum, Art, IX:2880
Tawaraya Sotatsu, IV:1041, 1042
taxation
  Akbar, III:6, 7
  Almohad empire, II:5
  Asquith, VII:122
  Cato the Younger, I:166
  Chrétien, VII:681
  clergymen, II:172
  Darius the Great, I:237
  Diocletian, I:265
  Dole, VII:949
  Edward III, II:331
  Frederick the Great, IV:506
  Frederick William, IV:509
  George, V:907, 908
  Hancock, IV:615, 616
  Harding, VIII:1551
  Henry II, II:446, 447
  Hoover, VIII:1729

Joseph II, IV:751
Lavoisier, IV:806
Louis XI, III:435
Maria Theresa, IV:915
Matthias I Corvinus, III:488
Mellon Plan, VIII:2481
Muhammad 'Ali Pasha, VI:1604
nationalization of land, IX:3866
Peasants' Revolt, II:114, 786, 921-923
Persia, II:559
Philip IV the Fair, II:737, 738
Poincaré, IX:3046
Pompey the Great, I:680
Prussia, V:1035
Robespierre, IV:1170
Shays, IV:1239
Townshend Revenue Act, IV:408, 409
Toyotomi Hideyoshi, III:729
Trajan, I:900
Tseng Kuo-fan, VI:2261
U.S. Supreme Court, V:280
Walpole, IV:1402, 1403
See also Stamp Act
Tax Equity and Fiscal Responsibility Act of 1982, VII:949
taxonomy
Agassiz, V:32
Audubon, V:88
Cohn, V:534, 535
Cuvier, V:589-591
Gesner, III:299
Gray, V:979, 980
Linnaeus, IV:846-848
Taylor, Bayard, V:984
Taylor, Frederick Winslow, **IX:3618-3621**
Principles of Scientific Management, The, IX:3619
Taylor, Graham, VIII:2096
Taylor, Jeremy, IV:46
Taylor, John, IV:95
Taylor, Tom
Our American Cousin, VI:2215
Taylor, Paul Schuster, VIII:2084, 2085
Taylor, Zachary, **V:2194-2197**
Clay, V:510
Davis, V:615
Fillmore, V:792, 793
Grant, V:975
Scott, VI:2011
Webster, VI:2345
Tchaikovsky, Peter Ilich, **VI:2198-2202;** VII:884
Manfred, VI:2200
Nutcracker, The, VI:2200; IX:3608
Pathétique, VI:2200
Présages, Les, VIII:2450
Queen of Spades, The, VI:2200
Romeo and Juliet, VI:2198, 2200
Sleeping Beauty, The, VII:155
Yevgeny Onyegin, VI:2198
Teapot Dome Scandal, VIII:1551, 1552
Teasdale, Sara, **IX:3622-2625**
Answering Voice, The, IX:3624, 3625
Dark of the Moon, IX:3624
Flame and Shadow, IX:3624
Helen of Troy and Other Poems, IX:3622
Mirror of the Heart, IX:3625
Potter's Wheel, The, IX:3622
Rainbow Gold, IX:3624
River to the Sea, IX:3624
Sonnets to Duse and Other Poems, IX:3622, 3624
Tecumseh, **VI:2203-2206**
Tefnakhte, I:637, 638
Teilhard de Chardin, Pierre, **IX:3626-3630**
Divine Milieu, The, IX:3628
Phenomenon of Man, The, IX:3628, 3629
Tekakwitha, Kateri, **IV:1316-1318**
Tekere, Edgar, VIII:2648
telegraph
Carnegie, V:420
Colt, V:541
Cooke, V:555-558
Edison, V:743
Henry, V:1094
Kelvin, VI:1269
Lenoir, VI:1343
Maury, VI:1508
Morse, VI:1592-1594
Siemens family, VI:2066
Wheatstone, V:555-558
Telemann, Georg Philipp, **IV:1319-1322**
telescopes
Galileo, IV:521
Lippershey, IV:850-852
Newton, IV:1025
Schmidt, IX:3351, 3352
Tombaugh, IX:3701
television broadcasting
Associated Television Corporation, VII:739
Ball, VII:176-178
Cousteau, VII:781
Garland, VII:1306
Gish, VII:1385
Murrow, VIII:2662, 2664

Parton, IX:2897
Reagan, IX:3138
Walters, IX:3868, 3870, 3871
West, IX:3951
Winfrey, IX:4029-4031
television electronics
de Forest, VII:860
Sony Corporation, VIII:2623, 2624
Zworykin, IX:4125, 4127
Telford, Thomas, IV:203; **VI:2207-2210**
Teller, Edward, VII:301, 302; **IX:3631-3634**
Telneshae, I:784, 785
temperance movement
Anthony, V:61-64
Astor, VII:130
Bright, V:308
Fowler, V:823
Hayes, V:1078
Mann, IV:894
Manning, VI:1477
Nation, VI:1630, 1631, 1633
Picotte, IX:3009
Shaw, VI:2044-2046
Stanton, VI:2111
Stone, VI:2143
Willard, VI:2388-2390
See also Prohibition (of alcohol)
Tempietto, III:582
Temple, Frederick, V:1040
Temple, Henry John. *See* Palmerston, Lord
Temple, Sir William, IV:1305, 1308
Temüjin. *See* Genghis Khan
Ten Commandments, I:563
Tendai sect, II:666
Teng Hsiao-p'ing, VIII:2213, 2214
Teng T'ing-chen, VI:1377
Ten Hours' Act, V:307
Tenka fubu, III:570
Tenkai Togaro, III:679, 680
Tennant, Charles, IV:815
Tennessean, VIII:1431
Tennessee
Benton, V:195
Crockett, V:578
Gore, VIII:1431
Houston, V:1137, 1140
Polk, VI:1802
secession, V:1232, 1233
Tennessee, Army of, VI:2059
tennis
Borg, VII:368-370
Evert, VII:1112-1114
Gibson, VII:1363, 1364
King, VIII:1968-1970
Laver, VIII:2109-2111
Navratilova, VIII:2702-2704
Perry, IX:2979-2982
Wightman, IX:3989-3991
Tennyson, Alfred, Lord, V:966; VI:1462, **2211-2214**
Idylls of the King, VI:2212
In Memoriam, VI:2212, 2213
Maud and Other Poems, VI:2212
Poems by Two Brothers, VI:2211
Poems, Chiefly Lyrical, VI:2211
Princess, The, VI:2212
Tenochtitlán, III:188-191, 377-379, 557
Tensho Shubun, III:679
Ten Thousand, March of the, I:959
Tenure of Office Act, V:1236
Tenzing Norgay, VIII:1662, 1663
Terah, I:5
Terence, I:540, **844-847;** III:155
Andria, I:845
Brothers, The, I:845
Eunuch, The, I:845
Mother-in-Law, The, I:845
Phormio, I:845
Self-Tormentor, The, I:845
Teresa, Mother, **IX:3635-3638**
Teresa, Princess, II:30
Teresa of Ávila, Saint, III:401, 402, **713-716;** VII:568; IX:3507
Interior Castle, The, III:714, 715
Life of the Mother Teresa of Jesus, The, III:714
Way of Perfection, The, III:714
Tereshkova, Valentina, VII:1271; IX:3180, **3639-3641**
Terkhen-Khatun, II:679
Terror, Reign of
Danton, IV:394
Fourier, V:819
Joséphine, V:1246
Lavoisier, IV:807
Marat, IV:912
Marie-Antoinette, IV:920
Michelet, VI:1548
Robespierre, IV:1172, 1176
Saint-Just, IV:1206
Staël, VI:2093
terrorism
Arafat, VII:92, 93
Begin, VII:245
Böll, VII:350, 351

Irish Republican Army, VII:771
Qaddafi, IX:3100
Terry, Alfred H., VI:2072
Terry, Ellen, **VI:2215-2218**
Terry, Megan, **IX:3642-3645**
Approaching Simone, IX:3643
Babes in the Bighouse, IX:3644
Calm Down Mother, IX:3643
Hot House, IX:3642, 3644
Mollie Bailey's Traveling Family Circus, IX:3644
Viet Rock, IX:3643
Tertullian, **I:848-851**
Tesla, Nikola, **VI:2219-2222,** 2360
Tessin, Carl Gustaf, IV:243
Test Acts
Bolingbroke, IV:157
Charles II, IV:284
James II, IV:704, 705
Leeds, IV:821
Oates, IV:1039
Peel, VI:1753
Shaftesbury, IV:1229
Stanhope, IV:1279
Tet Offensive, IX:3823
Teton Mountains. *See* Grand Teton Mountains
Teton Sioux Indians, VI:2070
Tetrapolitana, III:102
Tettenhall, Battle of, II:320
Tetzel, Johann, III:443
Teutonic Order
Alexander Nevsky, II:52, 53
Casimir the Great, II:211-213
Copernicus, III:178
Wladyslaw II Jagiello and Jadwiga, II:1001-1003
Teutons, I:529
Tewkesbury, Battle of, III:268, 343
Texas
Adams, V:24
Austin, V:94-96
Benton, V:196
Burr, V:371
Cabeza de Vaca, III:110, 111
Calhoun, V:395
Clay, V:509
Coronado, III:180
Crockett, V:579
Fillmore, V:793
Hobby, VIII:1703
Houston, V:1137, 1138, 1140
Jackson, V:1198
Johnson, VIII:1866, 1867
Jordan, VIII:1887-1889
Polk, VI:1803
Richards, IX:3169-3171
Santa Anna, VI:1955
secession, V:1138; VI:1338
Tyler, VI:2291
Texas Medley Quartette, V:1240
Texas Revolution, V:94-96, 579, 1137, 1138, 1140
Texas v. White, V:479
textile industry
cotton spinning, IV:59-62
flying-shuttle, IV:769, 770
Hargreaves, IV:623-625
Slater, VI:2074-2076
Tezozómoc, III:555, 556
Thackeray, William Makepeace, V:752
Thales of Miletus, I:50, 51, 53, **852-856,** 955, 972
Thames, Battle of the, VI:1765
Thanh Nien, VIII:1699
Thant, U, **IX:3646-3648**
Thapsus, Battle of, I:167
Thatcher, Charles A., V:715
Thatcher, Margaret, **IX:3649-3653**
Heath, VIII:1608
Major, VIII:2369-2371
National Health Service, VII:306
Thayendanegea. *See* Brant, Joseph
Thayer, Sylvanus, **VI:2223-2225**
Thayer, Webster, VII:1212, 1213; IX:3283
Theagenes, I:280
Theaters, War of the, IV:746
Theatine Order, IV:583, 584
Théâtre-Français, VI:1685
Theatrical Licensing Acts, IV:470
Theatrum Pompeii, I:681
Thebes
Agesilaus II, I:16-18
Akhenaton, I:23
Alexander the Great, I:38
Cleomenes II, I:215
Epaminondas, I:290, 292, 293
Hatshepsut, I:371, 373, 374
Macedonia, I:628
Psamtik I, I:709
Thelwall, John, IV:440
Themistocles, I:199, 788, **857-860**
Thenard, Louis Jacques, V:898
Theobald, Archbishop of Canterbury, II:128, 411
Theoctistus, II:278
Theodatus, Count, II:851
Theodora, II:553-557, 758, 759, **890-893**

Theodore of Mopsuestia, **I:861-864**
On the Incarnation, I:862
On the Twelve Prophets, I:863
Theodoret of Cyrrhus, **I:865-867**
Dialogues, I:866
Reprehensio duodecim capitum seu anathema anathematismorum Cyrilli, I:866
Treatise of Laws, A, I:865
Theodoric Fund, I:254
Theodoric the Great, II:155, 215, **894-898**
Theodosius I, I:862
Theodosius II, I:124
Theodosius the Great, **I:868-872**
Ambrose, I:44, 45
Gregory of Nyssa, I:354
Stilicho, I:825
Ulfilas, I:909
Theoleptus of Philadelphia, **II:899-902**
Theological Declaration of Barmen. *See* Barmen Confession
Theon, I:436, 437
Theophanes Continuatus, II:904
Theophanes the Confessor, **II:903-905**
Chronographia, II:903, 904
Theophilus, I:185
Theophrastus, I:53, 597, **873-876**
Characters, I:539, 873, 875; II:527
De historia plantarum, I:874
Enquiry into Plants, I:874
Metaphysics, I:874
On Stones, I:874
On Winds and On Weather Signs, I:874
Theorell, Axel Hugo Teodor, **IX:3654-3656**
Theosebeia, I:352
Theosophical Society, V:211-213
Therapeutae, I:634
Thermidorians, IV:1207
Thermopylae, Battle of, I:501, 502, 964
Theseum, I:676
Theseus, I:199, 318
Thespis, **I:877-879**
Thessalonica, I:44; II:943
Thessaly, I:629
Thicknesse, Philip, IV:516
Thiers, Adolphe, **VI:2226-2229**
History of the Consulate and the Empire of France Under Napoleon, VI:2228
History of the French Revolution, The, VI:2226
Third Carlist War, V:415
Third International, VII:491
Third Plenary Council, V:919
Third Punic War, I:345, 757, 762
Third Reich. *See* Nazi Party
Third Republic of France
Blum, VII:337
Clemenceau, VII:706
Coubertin, VII:774
de Gaulle, VII:867
Herriot, VIII:1645
Laval, VIII:2106, 2107
Poincaré, IX:3044-3046
Thiers, VI:2226-2229
William II, IX:4004
Third Zionist Congress, VII:484
Thirteenth Amendment, VI:1383, 2137
Thirteen Years' War, II:1002
39 Articles of Religion of the Church of England, III:206; IV:107; VI:1503, 1504, 2063
Thirty Tyrants, I:655
Thirty Years' Peace, I:611
Thirty Years' War
Brandenburg, IV:508
Buckingham, IV:211-213
Condé, IV:341, 342
Ferdinand II, IV:450-452
Grotius, IV:581
Guericke, IV:586
James I, IV:700
Laud, IV:797
Louis XIV, IV:866, 868
Mazarin, IV:945, 946
Pym, IV:1141
Richelieu, IV:1165-1167
Schütz, IV:1222
Sweden, IV:304, 590, 591, 1335-1337
Wallenstein, IV:1396-1398
Thomas, Clarence, **IX:3657-3659**
Thomas, Lowell, VIII:2127
Thomas, Norman, **IX:3660-3664**
Thomas, Saint, **I:880-884**
Thomas, Theodore, **VI:2230-2233**
Thomas, William, V:1142
Thomas à Kempis, **II:906-910**
Imitation of Christ, The, II:904-909, III:594
Modern Devotion, The, II:907
Thomas Aquinas, Saint, **II:911-916**
Albertus Magnus, II:37
Averroës, II:103
Bonaventure, II:163
Gilson, VII:1374-1377
Joyce, VIII:1891
Leo XIII, VI:1349
Maritain, VIII:2425-2427

Raymond of Peñafort, II:777
Scriptum super "Libros sententiarum," II:913
Siger of Brabant, II:830
Stein, IX:3508
Summa contra gentiles, II:913
Summa theologica, II:303, 913, 914, 947, 986; III:334, 768
Vitoria, III:768, 769
William of Auvergne, II:978
William of Auxerre, II:982, 983
William of Moerbeke, II:985, 986
William of Saint-Amour, II:991
Thomas Gallus, II:76
Thomism. *See* Thomas Aquinas, Saint
Thompson, Leonard, VIII:2329
Thompson, Ruth Plumly, V:156
Thompson, Wiley, VI:1695
Thomson, J.J., IX:3277
Thomson, Tom, **IX:3665-3668**
Thomson, Virgil, IX:3513
Thomson, Sir William. *See* Kelvin, Lord
Thoreau, Henry David, V:31, 32, 40; **VI:2234-2237,** 2370
Cape Cod, VI:2235
"Civil Disobedience," VI:2235
Maine Woods, The, VI:2235
"Plea for Captain John Brown, A," VI:2235
"Slavery in Massachusetts," VI:2235
Walden, V:758; VI:2234, 2235, 2237
Week on the Concord and Merrimack Rivers, A, VI:2234, 2235
Thorkell the Tall, II:201, 203
Thorndike, Edward L., **IX:3669-3671**
Teachers Word Book, The, IX:3669
Thorne, George R., VI:2332
Thorpe, Jim, **IX:3672-3676**
Thousand Year Reich, VIII:1695
Thrale, Henry, IV:730
Three Blue Days of 1831, VI:2276
Three Gorges Dam, VIII:2180
Three Henrys, War of, III:333, 538
Three Principles of the People, IX:3579, 3580
Throckmorton, Elizabeth, III:639
Thucydides, I:484, 744, **885-888;** IV:662
Thule, I:732, 733
Thule expedition, IX:3122, 3123
Thurber, James, **IX:3677-3680**
Great Quillow, The, IX:3678
Male Animal, The, IX:3678
Many Moons, IX:3678
"Secret Life of Walter Mitty, The," IX:3678
Thirteen Clocks, The, IX:3678
White Deer, The, IX:3678
Wonderful O, The, IX:3678
Thurii, I:706
Thuringia, II:340, 342
Thutmose I, I:371
Thutmose II, I:371
Thutmose III, I:371, 373, **889-891**
Tiananmen Square massacre, VII:906; VIII:2179
Tiberius, I:134, 152, 153, **892-895**
Tibor de Nagy Gallery, VII:1208, 1209
Ticknor, George, VI:2224
Ticonderoga, Battle of, IV:179
Ticonderoga, Fort, IV:35, 36, 64
Tiepolo, Giovanni Battista, **IV:1323-1326**
Adoration of the Magi, IV:1324
Angel Appealing to Sarah, IV:1323
Apollo Conducting Barbarossa's Bride, Beatrice of Burgundy, IV:1324
Apotheosis of Spain, IV:1325
Banquet of Antony and Cleopatra, IV:1324
Consilium in Arena, IV:1324
Death of Saint Jerome, IV:1324
Fall of the Rebel Angels, IV:1323
Glory of Saint Teresa, IV:1323
Last Communion of Saint Jerome, The, IV:1324
Madonna of Carmelo and the Souls of Purgatory, IV:1323
Neptune Offering to Venice the Riches of the Sea, IV:1324
Phaethon Begging Apollo to Allow Him to Drive the Chariot of the Sun, IV:1323
Power of Eloquence, IV:1323
Repudiation of Hagar, IV:1323
Sacrifice of Iphigenia, IV:1324
Sacrifice of Isaac, The, IV:1323
Story of Scipio, IV:1323
Triumph of the Arts, IV:1323
Virgin in Glory Adored by the Apostles and Saints, The, IV:1324
Tiglathpileser III, I:754
Tigranes V, I:779
Tigranes the Great, **I:896-898**
Tigranocerta, I:897
Tiguex War, III:182
Tilak, Bal Gangadhar, VII:141; **IX:3681-3684**
Tilden, Samuel J., V:1076
Tillich, Paul, VII:1056; **IX:3685-3687**
Tilly, Count, IV:1396
Tilsit Alliance, V:45
Tilsit, Treaties of, V:1033; VI:2115, 2116, 2187
Time magazine, VIII:2260, 2262, 2263
Timon, I:724, 725

Timoshenko, Semyon K., IX:4116, 4117
Timurid Dynasty, II:885
Tin Pan Alley, VII:287, 1347
Tintoretto, **III:717-720;** VII:1359
  Crucifixion, III:719
  Entombment, III:719
  Finding the Body of Saint Mark, III:719
  Last Supper, III:717, 719
  Miracle of the Loaves and Fishes, III:717
  Sacre Conversazioni, III:717
  Saint Mark Rescuing a Slave, III:717
  Saint Ursula and Her Virgins, III:717
  Susanna and the Elders, III:717
  Translation of the Body of St. Mark, III:719
Tippecanoe, Battle of, V:1061-1063; VI:2204
Tippu, IV:368, 369
Tiran, Strait of, VII:855
Tirpitz, Alfred von, **IX:3688-3691**
Tisquantum. *See* Squanto
Tissaphernes, I:32
Titanic, VII:181; IX:3970
Titian, III:60, 306, 598, 717, 719, 720, **721-724**
  Assumption of the Virgin, III:721
  Bacchanal of the Andrians, The, III:721
  Bacchus and Ariadne, III:721
  Gypsy Madonna, The, III:723
  Madonna of the Pesaro Family, The, III:723
  Rape of Europa, The, III:723
  Worship of Venus, The, III:721
Titicaca, Lake, VIII:1659
Tito, **IX:3692-3695**
Titus, I:662, 933, 934
Tlascalans, III:21, 22
Tmutorakan, II:953
Toba-Fushimi, Battle of, VI:1937
Tobey, Henry A., V:715
Tocqueville, Alexis de, **VI:2238-2241**
  Democracy in America, VI:2239
  Old Regime and the Revolution, The, VI:2239
  On the Penitentiary System in the United States and Its Application in France, VI:2238
  Recollections of Alexis de Tocqueville, The, VI:2239
Toghrïl Beg, II:67, 68, 677
Toklas, Alice B., IX:3511, 3513
Tokugawa Bakufu, VI:1936, 1937
Tokugawa Ieyasu, III:728, 730; **IV:1327-1330**
Tokugawa shogunate, III:570-572; IV:1258; V:1117, 1118, 1180-1182
Tokugawa Yoshinobu, VI:1937
Tolbiacum, Battle of, II:275
Toleration, Edict of, III:133; IV:751
Toleration Act of 1689, IV:100
Tolkien, J.R.R., VIII:2168; **IX:3696-3698**
  Hobbit, The, IX:3696, 3697
  Lord of the Rings, The, IX:3697
  Silmarillion, The, IX:3697
  Tree and Leaf, IX:3696
Tolstoy, Leo, V:1101; VI:2177, **2242-2246,** 2269; VIII:1442; IX:2899
  Anna Karenina, VI:2243
  Childhood, VI:2242
  Confession, A, VI:2243
  Death of Ivan Ilich, The, VI:2243
  Kreutzer Sonata, The, VI:2243
  Power of Darkness, The, VI:2243
  Resurrection, VI:2243
  Sebastopol, VI:2242
  War and Peace, VI:1833, 2242, 2243; IX:3087
  What Is Art?, VI:2243
Toltecs, III:529
Tombaugh, Clyde William, **IX:3699-3702**
Tombouctou, III:521
Tomyris, Queen, I:234
tonality
  Berg, VII:271-273
  Boulez, VII:387
  Hindemith, VIII:1670-1672
Tonga, IV:1313
Tonge, Israel, IV:1038, 1040
Tönnies, Ferdinand Julius, **IX:3703-3706**
  Community and Associations, IX:3703, 3704
  Gemeinschaft, IX:3704, 3705
  Gesellschaft, IX:3704, 3705
  Kürwille, IX:3704
  Wesenwille, IX:3704
Tontine Crescent, V:350, 351
Tooke, John Horne, IV:440
Toorop, Jan, VIII:2575
Topa Inca, III:578
Torah, I:330, 471, 472; II:648
Tordesillas, Treaty of, III:262
Toronto *Globe,* V:318-320
Toronto Star, VIII:1624
Torquemada, Tomás de, **III:725-727**
Torretti, V:408
Torrey, John, V:979
Torricelli, Evangelista, IV:586, **1331-1333**
  Opera geometrica, IV:1331-1333
Torrio, Johnny, VII:563, 564
Torstenson, Lennart, **IV:1335-1337**
Tory Party, English
  Anne, IV:52, 53
  Asquith, VII:123

Bevan, VII:305
Bolingbroke, IV:157-161
Brougham, V:314-316
Catholic emancipation, VI:1681
Charles II, IV:285
Defoe, IV:399, 401
Derby, V:653, 654
Disraeli, V:675, 677, 678
George I, IV:531, 532
Heath, VIII:1607, 1608
Kidd, IV:777, 779
Law, VIII:2112
Leeds, IV:821-823
Liverpool, VI:1395
Macmillan, VIII:2340-2342
Palmerston, VI:1719, 1720
Peel, VI:1752, 1753
Shaftesbury, IV:1230
Swift, IV:1307
Walpole, IV:1400-1403
See also Conservative Party (England)
Toscanelli dal Pozzo, Paolo, III:172
Toscanini, Arturo, VII:70, 192; XIII:1747, 1749; IX:3094, 3096, **3707-3710**
Tou Hsien, I:591
Toulouse-Lautrec, Henri de, **VI:2247-2250;** VII:363
Artist's Mother at Breakfast, The, VI:2247
Au Moulin Rouge: La Danse, VI:2248
Cirque Fernando: Circus Rider, Le, VI:2247
Corner of the Moulin de la Galette, A, VI:2248
Englishwoman at the "Star," Le Havre, VI:2249
Examination Board, VI:2249
Goulue au Moulin Rouge, La, VI:2248
Jane Avril at Divan Japonais, VI:2248
Jane Avril at the Jardin de Paris, VI:2248
Jane Avril Dancing at Moulin Rouge, VI:2248
Jane Avril Entering Moulin Rouge, VI:2248
Jane Avril Leaving Moulin Rouge, VI:2248
Jockey, The, VI:2249
Loie Fuller at the Folies Bergère, VI:2249
Portrait of the Artist's Mother Reading, VI:2247
Salon des Moulins, The, VI:2249
Woman with Black Boa, VI:2249
Touré, Ahmed Sékou, **IX:3711-3714**
Tours, Battle of, II:242, 243
Tours, Council of, II:49
Toussaint-Louverture, IV:501, **1338-1341;** VII:633
Townes, Charles, VII:215
Townesend, Stephen, V:362
Townsend, Captain Peter, VII:1062
Townshend, Lord, IV:532, 533, 535, 1278, 1401-1403
Townshend Revenue Act of 1767, IV:408, 409, 615, 616
Towns Improvement Company, V:459
Toynbee, Arnold, **IX:3715-3718**
Study of History, A, IX:3716, 3717, 3762
Survey of International Affairs, IX:3715
Western Question in Greece and Turkey, The, IX:3715
Toynbee Hall, VII:21, 308
Toyoda, Eiji, **IX:3719-3721**
Toyota Motor Company, IX:3719-3721
Toyotomi Hideyoshi, III:570, 571, **728-731,** 1327, 1328
track and field
Coe, VII:725-728
Didrikson, IX:4096
Lewis, IX:2865
Owens, IX:2862-2865
Thorpe, IX:3672, 3674, 3675
Tractarians, VI:1829
Tracy, Spencer, VIII:1639
Trades Union Congress, V:1037; VII:313, 353-356
trade unions. *See* unionism, trade
Trafalgar, Battle of, VI:1636
Trafalgar Square, V:140
Trail of Tears, VI:1911, 2011, 2027; VIII:2389, 2390
Trajan, I:212, 356, 358, 440, 441, **899-903**
Trans-Asiatic Expedition, VII:696
Transcendentalism
Alcott, Bronson, V:37-39
Alcott, Louisa May, V:40
Channing, V:472
cummings, VII:806
Emerson, V:757, 758
Fuller, V:849, 850
Hawthorne, V:1066
Howe, V:1152
Parker, VI:1727-1730
Thoreau, VI:2234-2237
Transcontinental Air Transport. *See* TWA
Transjordan, Hashemite Kingdom of, VIII:1791
Transkei tribe, V:999
Transport and General Workers Union, VII:313-316
Trans-Sahara Expedition, VII:696
Transvaal, VII:376, 377
Trarza, V:763

treason
Burr, V:371; VI:1490
Fries, IV:295
Ludendorff, VIII:2266
Lutuli, VIII:2282
Mandela, VIII:2386
Masaryk, VIII:2441
medieval England, II:331
U.S. Supreme Court, VI:1490, 1491
Treasons, Statute of, II:331
Trent, Council of
Charles V, III:160, 161
Dominic, II:303
Gabrieli, III:282, 283
Greco, El, III:311
Neri, III:551-553
Paul III, III:595, 597
Philip II, III:599
Richelieu, IV:1165
Veronese, III:748
Treppenhaus, IV:474
Tresham, Francis, III:258, 259
Trevithick, Richard, **VI:2251-2254**
Triangle Shirtwaist Factory fire, IX:2962
Tribonian, II:553, 555
trigonometry
Abul Wefa, II:20, 21
Aryabhata, II:89-91
Battani, II:121, 122
Euler, IV:444
Fourier, V:820, 821
Hipparchus, I:407, 409
Khwarizmi, II:564
Napier, III:545
Trinitarianism. *See* Holy Trinity
Trinity. *See* Holy Trinity
Trinity Church (Boston), VI:1882, 1883
Triple Monarchy, VII:1197
Trissino, Count Gian Giorgio, III:580
Troeltsch, Ernst, **IX:3722-3725**
Absoluteness of Christianity and the History of Religions, The, IX:3723
Historicism and It's Problems, IX:3723
Social Teaching of the Christian Churches, The, IX:3723
Trois-Frères caves, VII:457
Trojan asteroids, IX:4039
Trojan War, I:287, 394, 421, 651
Tromp, Cornelus, **IV:1342-1344**
Tromp, Maarten, IV:134, **1342-1344**
Trondheim, II:689
Tropiques, VII:632
Trotsky, Leon, **IX:3726-3729,** 3764
History of the Russian Revolution, The, IX:3728
My Life, IX:3728
Revolution Betrayed, The, IX:3728
What Is to Be Done?, IX:3726
Troy, excavation of, VI:1980-1982
Troyes, Chrétien de. *See* Chrétien de Troyes
Troyes, Treaty of, III:339
Troy Female Seminary, VI:2385, 2386
Trudeau, Pierre Elliott, VII:680; IX:3344, 3345, **3730-3735**
True Whig Party, IX:3757, 3758
Truffaut, François, IX:3159, **3736-3739**
Bed and Board, IX:3738
Breathless, IX:3737
Bride Wore Black, The, IX:3738
Day for Night, IX:3738
Farenheit 451, IX:3737
400 Blows, The, IX:3736, 3737
Green Room, The, IX:3738
Hitchcock, IX:3736
Jules and Jim, IX:3737
Love at Twenty, IX:3738
Mississippi Mermaid, IX:3738
Shoot the Piano Player, IX:3737
Soft Skin, The, IX:3737
Story of Adèle H., IX:3738
Such a Gorgeous Kid Like Me, IX:3738
Two English Girls, IX:3738
Wild Child, The, IX:3738
Trullan Synod, II:824
Truman, Harry S, **IX:3740-3744**
Acheson, VII:17, 18
Attlee, VII:138
Harriman, VIII:1562
Hoover, VIII:1733
Hopkins, VIII:1738
Humphrey, VIII:1784
Lippmann, VIII:2205
Luce, VIII:2263
MacArthur, VIII:2298
Marshall, VIII:2431
military desegregation, IX:3114
Moses, VIII:2635
Nimitz, VIII:2752
Truman Doctrine, VII:315; VIII:1562, 2205
Truth, Sojourner, **VI:2255-2259**
Truth and Reconciliation Commission, IX:3777
Tse Lan, I:188
Tseng Kuo-fan, VI:1362, 1364, **2260-2263**
Tserclaes, Johann. *See* Tilly, Count
Tshombe, Moïse, **IX:3745-3748**

Tsiolkovsky, Konstantin, IX:2777, 2779, **3749-3752**
Tsvetayeva, Marina, **IX:3753-3756**
Lebediny stan, IX:3754
Poema gory, IX:3754
Poema konca, IX:3754
Stikhi k Bloku, IX:3754
Vertsty I, IX:3754
tuberculosis
Behring, V:183
Calmett, VII:546-548
Domagk, VII:952
Ehrlich, VII:1032
Koch, VI:1297-1299
Waksman, IX:3835
Tubman, Harriet, **VI:2264-2267**
Tubman, William V.S., **IX:3757-3759**
Tucca, Plotius, I:927, 928
Tuc d'Audoubert cave paintings, VII:457
Tuchman, Barbara, **IX:3760-3763**
Bible and Sword, IX:3760, 3762
Distant Mirror, A, IX:3762
First Salute, The, IX:3760
Guns of August, The, IX:3760
March of Folly, The, IX:3762
Stilwell and the American Experience in China, IX:3760, 3762
Tudor, Mary, III:195, 293, 655, 733
Tudor family, **III:732-734**
Catherine of Aragon, III:136
Charles I, IV:279
Edward VI, III:237-239
Elizabeth I, III:241-245
Henry III, II:453-455
Henry VII, III:345-347
Henry VIII, III:349, 351
Mary I, III:479-482
Richard III, III:651, 652
Tu Fu, II:592, 593, **917-920**
"Autumn Thoughts: Eight Poems," II:919
"Ballad of the War Chariots, The," II:919
"Brave Adventures," II:917, 918
"500 Words to Express My Feelings when I Went from the Capitol to Feng-hsien," II:919
"Frontier Duties: Nine Poems," II:919
"Hundred Anxieties, A" II:917
"My Thatched Roof Whirled away by an Autumn Gale," II:919
"Poetry Contest after Dinner at the Tso Villa, A" II:918
"Song of the Whiteheaded," II:917, 918
Tugendhat House, VIII:2522
Tuileries Gardens, IV:834
Tukhachevsky, Mikhail, IX:2900
Tull, Jethro, **IV:1345-1347**
Horse-Hoing Husbandry, The, IV:1345, 1347
Tullus, I:703
Tung Chung-shu, I:944
Tunney, Gene, VII:903
Tunstall, Cuthbert, III:735, 736
Tupolev, Andrei Nikolayevich, **IX:3764-3767**
Turenne, Vicomte de, IV:341, 343, 871-874
Turgenev, Ivan, IV:268; VI:1334, **2268-2272**
Fathers and Sons, V:1101; VI:2269
Rudin, VI:2268
Smoke, VI:2269
Sportman's Sketches, A, VI:2268, 2270
Torrents of Spring, The, VI:2269
Virgin Soil, VI:2269
Turgot, Anne-Robert-Jacques, IV:1016, 1017, **1348-1350**
Reflections on the Formation and Distribution of Wealth, IV:1349
Turing, Alan Mathison, **IX:3768-3770**
Turkish Grand National Assembly, VII:134
Turkish National Movement, VII:134
Turkish War of Independence, VII:61
Türkmens, II:68, 69
Turner, Addison, V:1049
Turner, Frederick Jackson, **IX:3771-3774**
Turner, John, VII:681
Turner, J.M.W., VI:1925, **2272-2275;** VIII:2579
Battle of Trafalgar, The, VI:2273
Calais Pier, VI:2273
Dido Building Carthage, VI:2273
Ducal Palace and Bridge of Sighs, IV:244
Fifth Plague of Egypt, The, VI:2273
Fighting Téméraire' Tugged to Her Last Berth to Be Broken Up, VI:2274
Fisherman at Sea, VI:2272
Liber Studiorum, VI:2274
Rain, Steam, and Speed, VI:2274
Snow Storm, VI:2273
Sun Rising Through Vapour, VI:2273
Turner, Nat, V:885; **VI:2276-2278**
Türr Syndicate, VI:1356
Turtle Creek strike, VIII:1880
Tutankhamen, I:23, 25, **904-907**
Tutu, Desmond, **IX:3775-3778**
TWA, VIII:2194
Twain, Mark, V:741; **VI:2279-2283;** VIII:2483
Adventures of Huckleberry Finn, The, VI:2279, 2281, 2282; VII:247; IX:3198
Adventures of Tom Saywer, The, VI:2281, 2282; IX:3198

"Celebrated Jumping Frog of Calaveras County, The," VI:2279
Connecticut Yankee in King Arthur's Court, A, VI:2282
Gilded Age, The, VI:2281
Innocents Abroad, The, VI:2281
Life of the Mississippi, VI:2279
Mysterious Stranger, The, VI:2281
Prince and the Pauper, The, VI:2281
Tramp Abroad, A, VI:2281
What Is Man?, VI:2281
Tweed, William Marcy, VI:1628, **2284-2287**
Twelfth Amendment, IV:719
Twelve, Council of, VI:2414, 2415
Twelver Shi'I Islam, IV:4, 6
twelve-tone composition
Berg, VII:271-273
Boulez, VII:386, 387
Henze, VIII:1633
Schoenberg, IX:3357-3359
Webern, IX:3914-3916
Twelve Years' Truce, III:575; IV:644
Twentieth Century-Fox Motion Pictures, VIII:1630, 2589; IX:3159, 4101
Twenty-eighth Congregational Society, VI:1728
Twenty-fifth Amendment, V:80
Tyler, John, V:509, 582; **VI:2288-2291,** 2345
Tyler, Wat, II:114-116, 786, **921-923**
Tynan, Kenneth, VIII:1818
Tyndale, William, III:193, 654, **735-738**
Obedience of a Christian Man, The, III:736
Parable of the Wicked Mammon, The, III:736
Practice of Prelates, The, III:736
Tyrannio, I:828
Tyre, I:40, 800
Tyre, Synod of, I:322
Tyrkir, II:577
Tyrtamus. *See* Theophrastus
Tzu-ch'u, Prince, I:176
Tz'u-hsi, V:466, 468, 469; VI:1362, 1364, 1365

Uganda-Tanzania War, VIII:2775
Ugo of Segni. *See* Gregory IX
Uitlanders, VI:1875; VII:376
Ujiji, Sea of, V:375
Ulbricht, Walter, **IX:3779-3882**
Ulfilas, **I:908-910**
Ulster, VII:122, 771; VIII:2112
Ulster Volunteer Force, VII:877
Ulyanov, Vladimir Ilich. *See* Lenin, Vladimir Ilich
Umar, V:763, 764
Umar II, II:441
Umayyad dynasty, II:18, 441, 522
Umkonto We Sizwe, VIII:2282, 2386
U.N. *See* United Nations
Un-American Activities, House Committee on
Brecht, VII:445
Chaplin, VII:655
Hiss, VIII:1683-1685
Hughes, VIII:1773
Lang, VIII:2078
McCarthy, VIII:2300-2302
Miller, VIII:2534
Murrow, VIII:2664, 2665
Parker, IX:2886
Reagan, IX:3136
Robeson, IX:3190
Unammuno y Jugo, Miguel de, **IX:3783-3786**
Abel Sánchez, IX:3784
Agony of Chrisitianity, The, IX:3784
Christ of Veláquez, The, IX:3784
Life of Don Quixote and Sancho, The, IX:3784
Nicodemo el fariseo, IX:3784
Peace in War, IX:3784
Saint Manuel Bueno, Martyr, IX:3785
Tragic Sense of Life in Men and Peoples, The, IX:3784
Underground Railroad, VI:1601, 2110, 2264-2267
Unger, Franz, VI:1526
Unified Arab Command, VIII:1793
Union Army
Grant, V:975-978
Hickok, V:1108
Howe, V:1146
Sherman, VI:2057, 2059-2061
Stanton, VI:2106-2109
Webster, VI:2344-2346
Zeppelin, IX:4108, 4109
Union Steel, VIII:2480
unionism, trade
Africa, VIII:1754
Argentina, IX:2969, 2970
Besant, V:212
Bevan, VII:313-316
Carnegie, V:423
China, VIII:2212
Debs, VII:880-882
Disney, VII:940
Ford Motor Company, VII:1187
George, V:907
Gibbons, V:919, 921
Gompers, V:956-958
Guggenheim, VIII:1500
guild socialism, VIII:2093

Hardie, V:1037
Harrison, V:1058
Hughes, VIII:1775
Jaurès, V:1221-1223
Krupp, VI:1303
La Follette, VIII:2048
Matignon Agreements, VII:336
Owen, VI:1710
Perkins, IX:2962
Peru, VIII:1584
Proudhon, VI:1820
Randolph, IX:3114
Solidarity, IX:3844, 3846, 3847
Sorel, IX:3463, 3464
Taft-Hartley Act, VIII:1867, 2172; IX:3447, 3592
United Automobile Workers, VIII:2172; IX:3161-3164
United Farm Workers Association, VIII:1762-1764
United Mine Workers of America, VII:839, 1212; VIII:1879-1881, 2170-2172
Union Pacific Railroad, VIII:1560
Unitarianism
Biddle, IV:126, 127
Channing, V:470, 471
Dix, V:680
Emerson, V:755, 757
Parker, VI:1727, 1730
Ray, VI:1847, 1848
Ricardo, VI:1878
Servatus, III:675-677
Sharp, IV:1237
Unitas Fratrum. *See* United Brethren Church
United African Company, V:953
United Arab Republic, VIII:2694
United Artists Corporation, VII:653, 654; IX:3008, 3009
United Australian Party, VIII:2289, 2290, 2497, 2498
United Automobile Workers, VIII:2172; IX:3161-3164
United Brethren Church, IV:1488, 1490
United East India Company. *See* Dutch East India Company
United Farm Workers Association, VIII:1762-1764, 1934; IX:3163
United Gold Coast Convention, VIII:2762, 2763
Unité d'Habitation, VIII:2138
United Mine Workers of America, VII:839; VIII:1879-1881, 2170-2172
United Nations
Albright, VII:50
Boutros-Ghali, VII:399-401
Bunche, VII:501-503
Bush, VII:520
Casals, VII:608
Charter of the, VII:611, 1109-1111; VIII:1779-1781, 1984; IX:2920, 3861
China, VII:666, 678
Congo, VIII:2562, 2563
Economic and Social Council, IX:2959
genocide, VII:488
Hammarskjöld, VIII:1529-1531
Hiss, VIII:1683
India, IX:2869, 2870
Israel, VII:1000-1002
Japan, IX:3336
Katanga reintegration, IX:3746
Kirkpatrick, VIII:1994-1996
Liberia, IX:3758
Libya, IX:3099
Luce, VIII:2257, 2258
Palestine, VII:91, 502, 854, 855; VIII:2473
Pérez de Cuéllar, IX:2957-2959
Roosevelt, IX:3225
San Francisco Conference, VIII:2572; IX:3476
Saudi Arabia, VII:1118
Smuts, IX:3453
Spain, VII:1201
Thant, IX:3646-3648
Turkey, VIII:1814
Universal Declaration of Human Rights, VII:610-612, 1110; IX:3220
Waldheim, IX:2957, 3841-3843
World War II refugees, IX:3017
United Nations Emergency Force, VIII:1530, 1531
United Officers, Group of, IX:2970
United Shoe Manufacturing Company, VII:419, 422
United Society of Believers in Christ's Second Coming. *See* Shakers
United States, Bank of the
Benton, V:196, 198
Biddle, V:225, 226, 228
Buchanan, V:347
Clay, V:508
Hamilton, IV:610
Jackson, V:1198
Taney, VI:2189
Tyler, VI:2288-2290
United States Air Force, VIII:2554-2557, 2752
United States Army
Gorgas, VIII:1434-1437
MacArthur, VIII:2295-2298
McCarthy, VIII:2301

Marshall, VIII:2429, 2431, 2432
Mitchell, VIII:2554-2557
Patton, IX:2911-2914
Pershing, IX:2983-2985
Powell, IX:3070-3072
Presley, IX:3078
women, IX:3446
Wright brothers, IX:4067
United States Bureau of Reclamation, VI:1812
United States Children's Bureau, VIII:2096, 2097, 2099
United States Civil War
Adams, V:15
Alcott, V:40
Arthur, V:77
Bancroft, V:126, 127
Barton, V:142, 143
Beard, VII:222
Beecher, V:175, 176
Benét's *John Brown's Body,* VII:265
Bierce, V:230
Bingham, V:238
Birth of a Nation, VIII:1480, 1481
Blackwell, V:252
Blaine, V:256
Brady, V:296, 297
Bright, V:307
Bryant, V:344
Buchanan, V:348
Calhoun, V:396
Canada, VI:1437
Carnegie, V:420
Carson, V:432
Chase, V:478
Child, V:491
Cleveland, V:512
Colt, V:542
Cooke, V:551-553
Custer, V:585, 586
Davis, V:614-619
Dewey, V:656
Dix, V:681, 682
Douglas, V:692-694
Dred Scott decision, VI:1999-2001
Eads, V:729, 730
Farragut, V:773, 774
Fillmore, V:792-794
Frémont, V:839, 840, 842, 843
Garfield, V:876
Gibbons, V:919
Godkin, VIII:1400
Grant, V:975-978
Harrison, V:1053
Hay, V:1068
Hayden, V:1072
Hayes, V:1075
Hickok, V:1108
Higginson, V:1110-1112
Holmes, VIII:1720
Homer's art, V:1133
Houston, V:1140
Howe, Elias, V:1143
Howe, Julia Ward, V:1146
Jackson, V:1204-1206
Johnson, V:1232, 1233, 1235-1237
Kemble, VI:1275
Lee, VI:1338-1341
Lincoln, VI:1383
McCormick, VI:1432
McKinley, VI:1453
Morgan, VI:1579
Morse, VI:1594
Morton, VI:1598
Olmsted, VI:1691, 1692
Phillips, VI:1773
Rockefeller, VI:1896
Ross, VI:1911
Saint-Gaudens, VI:1940
Schurz, VI:1996, 1997
Seward, VI:2038
Sherman, VI:2057, 2059-2061
Stanley, VI:2101
Stanton, VI:2106-2109
Stephens, VI:2129-2131
Stevens, VI:2136, 2137
Stowe, VI:2151
Sumner, VI:2172, 2173
Truth, VI:2257
Tubman, VI:2266
Van Buren, VI:2294
Ward, VI:2328
Webster, VI:2344-2346
Westinghouse, VI:2358
Wilkes, VI:2382
Williams, VI:2396-2398
Wilson's *Patriotic Gore,* IX:4014
Wise, VI:2401
Zeppelin, IX:4108, 4109
See also Reconstruction era
United States Constitution. *See* Constitution, U.S.
United States Exploring Expedition of 1838-1842. *See* Wilkes Expedition
United States Geological Survey of Territories, V:1072-1074; VI:1812, 1813, 2328

United States-Japan Security Treaty, VIII:1809, 1810
United States Lawn Tennis Association, IX:3989, 3990
United States Marine Corps, VI:1686; VII:1388; IX:3466, 3467
United States National Park System, VI:1608-1610
United States Navy
Byrd, VII:534-536
Decatur, V:634-636
Dewey, V:656-658
Farragut, V:772-774
Halsey, VIII:1525-1528
Holland, V:1123-1125
Jones, IV:738, 740-742
Kennedy, VIII:1928
Lodge, VIII:2220
Nimitz, VIII:2750-2752
Peary, IX:2941, 2944, 2945
Perot, IX:2973
Perry, Matthew C., VI:1760-1763
Perry, Oliver Hazard, VI:1764-1766
prison system, IX:2853
Rickover, IX:3173-3176
Steichen's photography, IX:3503
Stevenson, IX:3523
Washington Conference on Naval Disarmament, VIII:1767
Westinghouse, VI:2358
Wilkes, VI:2381-2383
women, IX:3446
Wright brothers, IX:4067
United States Open
golf, VIII:1874, 1876, 1877; IX:3041, 3042, 4049
tennis, VII:1112, 1363, 1364; VIII:1968
United States Sanitary Commission, V:1146
United States Signal Corps, VII:102; VIII:2554
United States Steel Corporation, VI:1582; VIII:2480
United States Supreme Court. *See* Supreme Court, U.S.
United States v. Lopez, IX:3144
United Steel Workers, VIII:2172
United We Stand America, IX:2973, 2974
Unity Building, V:56
Universal Christian Conference on Life and Work, IX:3456, 3457
Universal Declaration of Human Rights, VII:610-612, 1110; IX:3220
Universal Negro Improvement Association, VII:668, 1311
Universal Peace Union, VI:1408
Universal Private Telegraph Company, V:558
Uranus, IX:3700, 3701
Urban II, **II:928-931**
Urey, Harold C., **IX:3787-3790**
Planets, The, IX:3789
Urianghad Mongols, II:1022
Urizen, IV:140
Urraca, II:268
Uruk, I:361
Usen, V:915
Utagawa Kunisada, V:1118
U Thant, VIII:2695
Utilitarianism
Bentham, IV:108, 109
Bradley, V:291
Chadwick, V:457-460
Condillac, IV:346
Godkin, VIII:1400
Hobbes, IV:665
Holmes, VIII:1721
Mill, James, VI:1557, 1558
Mill, John Stuart, VI:1559, 1560, 1562, 1563
Place, VI:1787
Sidgwick, VI:2063, 2064
Utrecht, Maria von, III:574
Utrecht, Treaty of, IV:53, 157, 158, 161
Utrecht, Union of, III:575

vaccination
Behring, V:182-184
Pasteur, VI:1747
polio, IX:3305-3307
smallpox, IV:721-723
tuberculosis, VII:546-548
veterinary medicine, IX:3451, 3452
Vaché, Jacques, VII:448
Vagabond King, The, III:766
Vaillant, Édouard, V:1222
Val-de-Grâce, church of the, IV:899, 900
Valdemar I, II:932
Valdemar II, **II:932-934**
Valentinian I, I:44
Valentinian II, I:44, 870
Valentinian III, I:343
Valentinus, **I:911-914**
Valéry, Paul, **IX:3791-3793**
"Fileuse, Le," IX:3791
"Graveyard by the Sea, The," IX:3792
"Introduction to the Method of Leonardo da Vinci," IX:3791
Jeune Parque, La, IX:3792

My Faust, IX:3793
"Narcisse parle," IX:3791
Val-ès-Dunes, Battle of, II:997
Val-Kill, IX:3218
Valla, Lorenzo, **III:739-742**
Adnotationes in Novum Testamentum, III:741
De professione religiosorum, III:740
Dialecticae disputationes, III:740
Elegantiae linguae latinae, III:740
On Free Will, III:739, 740
On Pleasure, III:739
Treatise on the Domination of Constantine, The, III:740
Valley Forge, Battle of, IV:678, 1405
Valley of the Kings, I:904-906
Vanbrugh, Sir John, IV:635-637, **1351-1354**
Relapse, The, IV:1352
Provok'd Wife, The, IV:1352
Van Buren, Martin, **VI:2292-2295**
Bancroft, V:127
Burr, V:371, 372
Clay, V:509
Clinton, V:519
Polk, VI:1802
Vance, Vivian, VII:178
Vancouver, George, **IV:1355-1357;** VI:1257
Voyage of Discovery to the North Pacific Ocean and Round the World, IV:1356
Vandals, I:342-344, 825; II:215
Vanderbilt, Cornelius, **VI:2296-2298**
Vanderbilt, Gloria, IX:3970
Van Dieman, Antony, IV:1313-1315
Vane, Sir Henry, IV:688
Van Gogh, Vincent. *See* Gogh, Vincent van
Vanzetti, Bartolomeo, VII:1212; IX:2885, 3060, 3281-3283
Vanity Fair magazine, VII:809; IX:2884
Vanucci, Domenico Francesco, IV:147
Varangians, II:803, 804, 953
Varazdat, I:780
Vardhamãna, **I:915-917**
Varèse, Edgard, **IX:3794-3797,** 4076
Amériques, IX:3795
Bourgogne, IX:3794
Deserts, IX:3796
Hyperprism, IX:3795
Ionisation, IX:3795
L'Éspace, IX:3795
musique concréte, IX:3795, 3796
Offrandes, IX:3795
Poème électronique, IX:3796
Varius, Lucius, I:927, 928
Varley, Samuel Alfred, VI:2068
Varro, Marcus Terentius, I:335, 659, **918-921**
Antiquitates rerum humanarum et divinarum libri XLI, I:920
Disciplinarum libri IX, I:920
Imagines, I:920
Menippean Satires, I:919, 920
On Agriculture, I:920
On the Latin Language, I:920; III:671
Varus, Publius Quintilius, I:134
Vasa Dynasty, IV:290-292
Vasari, Giorgio, **III:743-746**
Lives of the Most Eminent Painters, Sculptors, and Architects, II:272, 273; III:743-745
Vasily II, III:381
Vasvár, Treaty of, IV:839
Vatican II. *See* Second Vatican Council
Vatican Council, VI:1783, 1784
Vaughan Williams, Ralph, **IX:3798-3800,** 3874, 3875
Fantasia on a Theme by Tallis, IX:3798
Pastoral Symphony, IX:3799
Sea Symphony, A, IX:3799
Vaux, Calvert, VI:1691, 1692
Vauxcelles, Louis, VII:431
Vaux-le-Vicomte, IV:834, 835
Vavilov, Nikolai Ivanovich, VII:224; **IX:3801-3804**
Veblen, Thorstein, **IX:3805-3807**
Engineers and the Price System, The, IX:3806
Imperial Germany and the Industrial Revolution, IX:3806
Inquiry into the Nature of Peace and the Terms of Its Perpetuation, An, IX:3806
Theory of Business Enterprise, The, IX:3806
Theory of the Leisure Class, The, IX:3806
Vecellio, Tiziano. *See* Titian
Vedas, II:89
Vega Carpio, Lope de, IV:235, **1361-1363**
Arcadia, La, IV:1362
Gardener's Dog, The, IV:1362
Justice Without Revenge, IV:1362
Lady Nit-Wit, The, IV:1362
New Art of Writing Plays, The, IV:1361
Sheep-Well, The, IV:1362
Velázquez, Diego, IV:570; **1364-1367;** VI:1837
Bloody Cloak of Joseph, The, IV:1366
Meninas, Las, IV:1366
Surrender of Breda, The, IV:1366
Velbuzd, Battle of, II:843
Velia. *See* Elea
Vendôme, Place, IV:902

Vendôme Column, V:567
Venette, Jean de, **II:935-937**
Chronicle of Jean de Venette, The, II:935
Venice, Republic of
Bayezid II, III:51, 52
Bellini, III:58-61
Canaletto, IV:242-244
Dandolo, II:282, 284
Sansovino, III:664-666
Veronese, III:747, 748
Villehardouin, II:944
Venice, Treaty of, II:284
Venizélos, Eleuthérios, **IX:3808-3810**
Ventose, Laws of, IV:1207
Vercingetorix, **I:922-925**
Verdi, Giusseppe, **VI:2299-2302;** IX:3096
Aïda, VI:2300, 2301; IX:3083, 3093
ballo in maschera, Un, VI:2300
Don Carlos, VI:2300
Falstaff, VI:2300, 2301; IX:3081
forza del destino, La, VI:2300
giorno di regno, Un, VI:2299
I Lombardi alla prima crociata, VI:2299
I masnadieri, VI:2299
Il traviata, La, VI:2300, 2301
Il trovatore, VI:2300, 2301
Macbeth, VI:2299
Nabucco, VI:2299
Oberto, conte di San Bonifacio, VI:2299
Otello, VI:2300, 2301
Requiem Mass, VI:1484, 2300, 2301
Rigoletto, VI:2300, 2301; VII:599
Simone Boccanegra, VI:2300
Verdun, Treaty of, II:229, 600, 740
Verein fur Raumschiffahrt, VII:2778
Vergara, Convention of, V:414
Vergil, I:287, 512, 520, 521, 585, 587, **926-929;** II:288
Aeneid, I:926-928; IV:318; V:205; VII:1250
Eclogues, I:926
Georgics, I:926, 928; IV:566
Vergil, Polydore, III:652
Vergine, Guglielmo, VII:598
Verkade, Jan, VII:910
Verlaine, Paul, VI:1886, 1887
Verlet, Raoul, VIII:2199
Vermeer, Jan, IV:827, **1368-1371**
Allegory of Painting, The, IV:1369
Astronomer, The, IV:1369
Christ in the House of Martha and Mary, IV:1368
Diana and Her Companions, IV:1368
Geographer, The, IV:1369
Guitar Player, The, IV:1369
Love Letter, The, IV:1369
Procuress, The, IV:1368
View of Delft, IV:1369
Verne, Jules, VI:1532, **2303-2306**
Antarctic Mystery, An, VI:2305
Around the World in Eighty Days, VI:2304, 2305
Begum's Fortune, The, VI:2304
Discovery of the Earth, The, VI:2303
Five Weeks in a Balloon, VI:2303
For the Flag, VI:2304
From the Earth to the Moon, VI:2304, 2305
Journey to the Centre of the Earth, VI:2304, 2305
Master of the World, VI:2305
Mysterious Island, The, VI:2304, 2305
Twenty Thousand Leagues Under the Sea, VI:2304, 2305; VII:180
Vernet, Carle, V:910
Vernet, Joseph, IV:1376
Veronese, Paolo, **III:747-749**
Feast in the House of Levi, The, III:748
Triumph of Mordecai, III:747
Triumph of Venice, III:747
Verres, Gaius, I:195
Verrius Flaccus, Marcus, **I:930-932**
De verborum significatu, I:930
Verrocchio, Andrea del, **III:750-753**
Baptism of Christ, III:751
Beheading of Saint John the Baptist, The, III:751
Christ and Saint Thomas, III:751, 752
David, III:750
Equestrian Statue of Colleoni, III:751, 752
Madonna Enthroned with Saints John the Baptist and Donatus, III:751
Portrait of a Woman, III:751
Putto with a Dolphin, III:750
Versailles, Treaty of
Angell, VII:76
Bordon, VII:366
Botha, VII:378
Clemenceau, VII:705
Czechoslovakia, VIII:2442
Erzberger, VII:1102
Hitler, VIII:1694, 1695
Keynes, VIII:1952, 1955
La Follette, VIII:2048
Laval, VIII:2105
Law, VIII:2113
New Zealand, VIII:2445
Poincaré, IX:3044, 3045

Stresemann, IX:3564, 3565
Wilson, IX:4022
Verus, Lucius Aurelius, I:339, 340, 523
Verwey, Jock, IX:3040
Vesalius, Andreas, **III:754-757**
Bloodletting Letter of 1539, The, III:754
De fabrica, III:754
Institutiones anatomicae, III:754
Six Anatomical Tables, III:754, 755
Vespasian, I:472, 483, 484, 663, **933-935**
Vespucci, Amerigo, **III:758-762**
First Four Voyages, The, III:759, 761
Mondus Novus, III:761
Vézère Valley finds, VII:456
Viardot, Pauline, V:968
vice presidency, U.S.
Adams, IV:18
Bush, VII:520, 521
Ferraro, VII:1153-1155
Ford, VII:1181
Garfield, V:78
Gore, VIII:1431-1433
Johnson, VIII:1867, 1868
Nixon, VIII:2758-2760
Tyler, V:509; VI:2288-2291
Van Buren, VI:2293
Vicksburg, Battle of, V:976
Vico, Giambattista, **IV:1372-1375**
New Science, The, IV:1372-1374; VI:1548
On the Study Methods of Our Times, IV:1372
Selected Writings, IV:1372
Victor III, II:928
Victor IV, II:48, 49, 359
Victor Emmanuel, V:447, 448, 881
Victor Emmanuel III, VIII:2668
Victoria, Queen, **VI:2307-2311**
Edward VII:1020, 1021
George III, IV:543
Melbourne, VI:1518, 1519
Palmerston, VI:1721
Victoria, Tómas Luis de, III:107, 108
Victorius of Aquitaine, II:298
Videla, González, VIII:2717
Vien, Joseph, V:610
Vienna
Freud, VII:1224
Haydn, IV:639
Mahler, VIII:2359
Vienna, Concordat of, III:559
Vienna, Congress of
Alexander I, V:44-46
Castlereagh, V:441
Hardenberg, V:1033-1035
Metternich, VI:1545, 1546
Palmerston, VI:1720
Stein, VI:2116
Talleyrand, VI:2187
Vienna, Siege of, IV:840
Vienna Psychoanalytical Association, VII:1225
Viet Cong, VIII:1701; IX:3823
Viète, François, I:274
Viet Minh, VIII:1698-1701; IX:3821-3823
Vietnam Veterans Memorial, VIII:2185-2187
Vietnam War
Acheson, VII:18
Black, VII:322, 323
Calder, VII:540
Chomsky, VII:674, 675
Ford, VII:1181, 1182
Gore, VIII:1431
Greene, VIII:1469
Harriman, VIII:1562, 1563
Hayslip, VIII:1593-1595
Humphrey, VIII:1784, 1785
Johnson, VIII:1867
Kennedy, John F., VIII:1931
Kennedy, Robert F., VIII:1934
King, VIII:1974
Kissinger, VIII:2000
Lippmann, VIII:2205
McCarthy, VIII:2306
Mailer, VIII:2366
Marcos, VIII:2421
Nixon, VIII:2758, 2759
O'Neill, IX:2825
Perot, IX:2973
Powell, IX:3070
Rankin, IX:3119
Sihanouk, IX:3417, 3419
Smith, IX:3448
Terry, IX:3643
Vo Nguyen Giap, IX:3821-3823
Washington Post, VIII:1452, 1453
Vigée-Lebrun, Élisabeth, **IV:1376-1379**
Marie Antoinette and Her Children, IV:1376, 1378
Peace Bringing Back Plenty, IV:1376
Vigilance Society, V:777
Vigilius, II:892
Vikings
Alfred the Great, II:59, 60
Canute the Great, II:201-204
Charles the Bald, II:239
Edward the Elder, II:319-321

Ethelred II, the Unready, II:344-346
Olaf I, II:688-690
Olaf, Saint, II:691-693
Rollo, II:793-795
Rurik, II:804
Villa, Pancho, IX:2782, 2984, **3811-3814,** 4106
Villa Dei, Alexander de, II:757
Village Voice, The, VIII:2365
Villahermosa, VI:1761, 1762
Villa-Lobos, Heitor, **IX:3815-3817**
Bachianas brasileiras, IX:3815
choros, IX:3816
Guia Pratico, IX:3816
Indian Symphony, The, IX:3816
New York Skyline, The, IX:3816
Rudepoema, IX:3816
Villa Mairea, VII:2
Villani, Giovanni, **II:938-941**
Chronicle, II:938, 940, 941
Villani, Matteo, II:940
Villanova, Arnold of. *See* Arnold of Villanova
Villehardouin, Geoffroi de, **II:942-945**
Conquête de Constantinople, La, II:943, 944
Villeneuve, Michel de. *See* Servetus, Michael
Villiers, George. *See* Buckingham, First Duke of
Villon, François, **III:763-767**
"Ballade of the Hanged," III:764
Great Testament, The, III:764, 766
Legacy, The, III:763, 764
Vincennes, IV:312, 314
Vincent de Paul, Saint, **IV:1380-1382**
Vincentians. *See* Mission, Congregation of the
Vincent of Beauvais, **II:946-948**
De morali principis institutiones, II:947
Doctrinale, II:946, 947
Historiale, II:946
Naturale, II:946
Speculum majus, II:946, 947
Vincent of Lérins, Saint, **I:936-938**
Commonitory of Vincent of Lérins, The, I:937, 938
Viner, Charles, IV:129
Vines, Ellsworth, IX:2981
Vining, Elizabeth Gray, VII:41
Viollet-le-Duc, Eugène, IX:2976
violin
Corelli, IV:360-362
Paganini, VI:1711-1714
Stradivari, IV:1281-1283
Vivaldi, IV:1383
Viracocha Inca, III:577
Virchow, Rudolf, **VI:2312-2315**
Virgil. *See* Vergil
Virginia
Bacon, IV:80-82
Brown, V:324
Grenville, III:316, 317
Henry, IV:647-649
Jefferson, IV:716, 718
Lee, VI:1338, 1340
Madison, IV:886
Mason, IV:926-928
Monroe, VI:1571
Powhatan, IV:1122
Smith, IV:1253-1255
Virginia Company, IV:189, 462, 1106-1108
Virginia Declaration of Rights, IV:926
Virgin Lands Program, VII:459; VIII:1962
Virgin Mary, **I:939-942**
Immaculate Conception, II:310, 311; V:10
Visconti, Luchino, **IX:3818-3820**
Damned, The, IX:3820
Death in Venice, IX:3820
Leopard, The, IX:3819
Risorgimento, IX:3819
Rocco and His Brothers, IX:3819
Rosalinda, IX:3819
Terra Trema, La, IX:3818, 3819
Wanton Contessa, The, IX:3819
Visigoths
Alaric, I:342
Attila, I:126
Clovis, II:276
Isidore of Seville, II:518-520
Stilicho, I:826
Theodosius the Great, I:868-871
Ulfilas, I:908-910
Vitellius, I:642
Vitoria, Francisco de, **III:768-770**
De Indis, III:769
Reflectiones theologicae, III:769
Vitruvius, I:76, 77; IV:153
Vitry, Phillippe de, **II:949-951**
Ars Nova, II:660, 661, 949, 950
Roman de Fauvel, II:950
Vivaldi, Antonio, III:285; **IV:1383-1386**
cetra, La, IV:1384
cimento dell'armonia e dell' inventione, Il, IV:1384
estro armonico, L', IV:1383
Four Seasons, The, IV:1384, 1385
Vivarium, II:215, 216
Vladimir I, **II:952-954**
Vladimir-Suzdal, Grand Duchy of, II:52

Vlad Tepes, III:500
Vogue magazine, IX:2884
Volcker, Paul A., VIII:1472
Volger, Georg Joseph, VI:2340
Volkogonov, Dimitri, VIII:1684
Vollard, Ambroise, IX:3252
Voloshin, Max, IX:3753
Voloshinov, Valentin Nikolayevich, VII:152, 153
Volta, Alessandro, IV:523-525, **1387-1391**
Voltaire, **IV:1392-1395**
  Age of Louis XIV, IV:1394
  Alembert, IV:32
  Boswell, IV:175
  Candide, IV:832, 1392, 1394, 1395
  Discourses in Verse on Man, IV:1394
  Elements of Sir Issac Newton's Philosophy, The, IV:344
  Frederick the Great, IV:506
  Henriad, IV:1392
  History of Charles XII, The, IV:1392
  Letters Concerning the English Nation, IV:1392
  Montagu, IV:984
  Oedipus, IV:1392
  Philosophical Dictionary for the Pocket, A, IV:1394
  Poem on the Lisbon Earthquake, IV:1394
  Zadig, IV:1394
Vo Nguyen Giap, **IX:3821-3825**
Voragine, Jacobus de, I:180
Vortigern, I:378, 379
Voting Rights Act of 1965, VIII:1868, 1974
Vuillard, Édouard, VII:362; **IX:3826-3828**
Vyrheid, VII:376
Vytautas, II:1001, 1002

WAAC. *See* Women's Auxiliary Army Corps
Wabash Confederacy, IV:314
Wach, Joachim, **IX:3829-3832**
Wadsworth, Charles, V:669, 670
Wafd Party, IX:4093-4095
Waffen SS, VIII:1668
Wagner, Honus, VII:719
Wagner, Richard, **VI:2316-2320**
  Ban on Love, The, VI:2316
  Bruckner, V:332
  chromaticism, VII:272
  Ehrenfels, VII:1027
  Faust Overture, VI:2316
  Flying Dutchman, The, VI:2316
  Liszt, VI:1393
  Lohengrin, VI:2317, 2319
  Love Feast of the Apostles, The, VI:2317
  Mahler, VIII:2362, 2363
  Mastersingers of Nuremberg, The, VI:2317, 2319
  Nietzsche, VI:1662
  Parsifal, V:1162; VI:1664, 2319; VII:389
  Puccini, IX:3096
  Ravel, IX:3129
  Rheingold, Das, VI:2319
  Rienzi, VI:2316
  Ring of the Nibelungs, VI:2316, 2317
  Schopenhauer, VI:1986
  Schumann, VI:1993
  Shaw, IX:3399
  Siegfried, VI:2319
  Tannhäuser, VI:2317; VIII:2059
  Thomas, VI:2232
  Toscanini, IX:3707
  Tristan und Isolde, VI:2316, 2317
  Twilight of the Gods, The, VI:2319
  Verdi, VI:2301
Wagner Labor Relations Act, VIII:1768
Wagoner, Porter, IX:2896
Wagram, Battle of, V:475
Wainwright Building, VI:2167
Waitangi, Treaty of, V:380
Wakefield, Battle of, III:647
Wakefield, Edward Gibbon, V:722; **VI:2321-2323**
  Letters from Sydney, VI:2321
Waksman, Selman Abraham, **IX:3833-3836**
Walcott, Jersey Joe, VIII:2412, 2413
Wald, Lillian D., **IX:3837-3840**
Walden, Herwarth, VIII:2013
Waldheim, Kurt, IX:2957, **3841-3843,** 3986
Waldrada, II:674
Waldseemüller, Martin, III:761
Wales, Council of, III:235
Walesa, Lech, **IX:3844-3848**
Walker, Alice, VIII:1789; **IX:3849-3852**
  Color Purple, The, IX:3850, 4030
  In Love and Trouble, IX:3850
  In Search of Our Mother's Gardens, IX:3850
  Living by the Word, IX:3850
  Meridian, IX:3850
  Possessing the Secret of Joy, IX:3851
  Revolutionary Petunias, IX:3850
  Temple of My Familiar, The, IX:3850
  Third Life of Grange Copeland, The, IX:3849
  You Can't Keep a Good Woman Down, IX:3850
Walker, Madam C.J., **IX:3853-3856**
Walker, George, V:450
Walker, James J., VIII:2055
Walker, John G., VIII:1435
Walker, William Hall, VII:996

Wallace, Alfred Russell, VI:1421
Wallace, Frank, IX:3949, 3951
Wallace George C., VIII:1785; **IX:3857-3859**
Wallace, Henry A., IX:3662, **3860-3864**
Wallace, Henry C., VIII:1552
Wallace, Sir William, II:185, **955-958**
Wallach, Meier Moiseevich. *See* Litvinov, Maksim Maksimovich
Wallenstein, Albrecht Wenzel von, IV:451, 452, 590, 591, **1396-1399**
Waller, Augustus Volney, VII:1040
Wall Street. *See* Dow Jones Industrial Average; New York Stock Exchange
Walo, V:763
Walpole, Horace, III:652; IV:204, 206
Castle of Otranto, The, V:139
Walpole, Sir Robert, **IV:1400-1404**
Bolingbroke, IV:157-159, 161
Fielding, IV:469, 470
George I, IV:531, 532
George II, IV:535-538
Montagu, IV:984
Pelham, IV:1074-1076
Pitt the Elder, IV:1098
Stanhope, IV:1277-1280
Walras, Léon, **IX:3865-3868**
Elements of Pure Economics, IX:3865, 3866
Walsh, Raoul, IX:3901
Walsingham, Francis, IV:46
Walsingham, Thomas, III:471, 472
Walter, John, II, **VI:2324-2327**
Walters, Barbara, **IX:3868-3871**
Walther, Balthasar, IV:154
Walther, Johann Gottfried, IV:77
Walther von der Vogelweide, **II:959-961**
"I Was Sitting upon a Rock," II:961
"What is Loving?," II:960
"When the Flowers Spring out of the Grass," II:960
Walton, Sir William, **IX:3872-3876**
Belshazzar's Feast, IX:3873, 3874
Façade, IX:3872, 3874
Spitfire Prelude and Fugue, IX:3874
Troilus and Cressida, IX:3874
Walworth, Sir Thomas, II:922
Wampanoag Indians, IV:930-933, 954-956
Wamsutta, IV:931, 932, 954
Wang An-shih, II:840, 841, 855-857, 866, **962-964**
Wang Chin, II:967
Wang Ching-wei, **IX:3877-3880**
Wang Ch'ung, **I:943-945**
Cheng-wu, I:943
Chi-su chieh-yi, I:943
Lun-hêng, I:943, 944
Wanghia, Treaty of, V:582
Wang Hsi-chih, **I:946-948**
Lan t'ing hsu, I:947, 948
Wang Mang, I:590
Wang Pi, **I:949-951**
Wang Wei, I:841; **II:965-968**
Wang Yang-ming, **III:771-773**
Instructions for Practical Living, III:772
Wankel, Felix, **IX:3881-3883**
Warbeck, Perkin, III:346
Ward, Joshua, IV:1182
Ward, Lester Frank, **VI:2328-2330**
Dynamic Sociology, VI:2329
Psychic Factors of Civilization, The, VI:2329
Ward, Montgomery, **VI:2331-2334**
Ward, Nancy, VIII:2389
Wardenclyffe, VI:2220
Wardley, James and Jane, IV:817, 818
Ware, Henry, V:470
Warens, Madame de, IV:1194
Warhol, Andy, IX:3828, **3884-3887**
Andy Warhol's Dracula, IX:3886
Andy Warhol's Frankenstein, IX:3886
Campbell's Soup Can, IX:3885
Flesh, IX:3886
Liz, IX:3885
Lonesome Cowboy, IX:3886
Marilyn Monroe, IX:3885
Trash, IX:3886
Warner, Pop, IX:3674
Warner Brothers, IX:4100
War of 1812. *See* 1812, War of
Warren, Earl, VII:509; **IX:3888-3892**
Warren, John Collins, VI:1597
Warren, Robert Penn, **IX:3893-3896**
All the King's Men, IX:3894, 3895
Approach to Literature, An, IX:3894
At Heaven's Gate, IX:3894
Band of Angels, IX:3894
Brother to Dragons, IX:3894
Cave, The, IX:3894
John Brown, IX:3894
Meet Me in the Green Glen, IX:3894
Night Rider, IX:3894
Segregation, IX:3894
Understanding Poetry, IX:3894, 3895
Who Speaks for the Negro?, IX:3894
Wilderness, IX:3894
World Enough and Time, IX:3894
Warren Commission, IX:3890

Warsaw Pact, VII:969; VIII:1530, 1961
Warsaw Uprising, VIII:1561
Warwick, Earl of, **III:774-777**
Edward IV, III:234
Henry VI, III:342, 343
Henry VII, III:345, 346
Richard III, III:647, 649
Washington, Booker T., **VI:2335-2339;** VII:964
Washington, George, **IV:1405-1408**
Adams, IV:18, 19
André, IV:44
Arnold, IV:66
Cornwallis, IV:367
Fitch, IV:476, 477
Greene, IV:574-577
Hamilton, IV:608
Heth, V:135
Jay, IV:713
Jefferson, IV:718, 719
McGillivray, IV:876
Marshall, VI:1488
Monroe, VI:1571
Peale, IV:1070, 1072
Rochambeau, IV:1174-1176
Ross, IV:1191-1193
Stuart's portrait, IV:1289, 1291, 1292
Wilson, IV:1458
Witherspoon, IV:1469
Wood's paintings, IX:4047, 4048
Washington Conference on Naval Disarmament, VIII:1767
Washington Monument, V:80
Washington Post, The, VIII:1451-1453, 2205
Washkansky, Louis, VII:195, 197
Watergate affair
Bush, VII:521
Ford, VII:1181
Jordan, VIII:1888
Nixon, VIII:2758, 2760
Washington Post, VIII:1453
Waterloo, Battle of, V:942; VI:1617, 1647, 2353
Watson, James D., VII:797; IX:2927, **3897-3900,** 3996, 3997
Double Helix, The, VII:797, IX: 3898
Watson, John C., V:631
Watson, Thomas, III:472
Watson, Thomas A., V:185, 186
Watt, James, **IV:1409-1412**
Arkwright, IV:62
Boulton, IV:182-184
Cavendish, IV:262
Murdock, IV:1008-1010
Roebuck, IV:1184, 1185
Trevithick, VI:2251
Wilkinson, IV:1443, 1444
Watteau, Antoine, **IV:1413-1416**
Gersaint's Shopsign, IV:1415
Gilles, IV:1415
Pilgrimage to Cythera, IV:1414
Venetian Pleasures, IV:1415
Watts, George Frederick, VI:2215, 2216
Choosing, VI:2215
Ellen Terry, VI:2215
Ophelia, VI:2215
Sisters, The, VI:2215
Waugh, Edith, V:1170
Waugh, Fanny, V:1170
Wayne, John, **IX:3901-3904**
Alamo, The, IX:3903
Big Trail, The, IX:3901
Fort Apache, IX:3902
Green Berets, The, IX:3903
Man Who Shot Liberty Valance, The, IX:3903
Quiet Man, The, IX:3903
Red River, IX:3902, 3903
Rio Grande, IX:3902, 3903
Rooster Cogburn, IX:3903
Salute, IX:3901
Sands of Iwo Jima, IX:3903
Searchers, The, IX:3902, 3903
Seven Sinners, VII:932
Shepherd of the Hills, The, IX:3902
She Wore a Yellow Ribbon, IX:3902
Shootist, The, IX:3903
Stagecoach, IX:3902
True Grit, IX:3902, 3903
WCTU. *See* Women's Christian Temperance Union
Webb, Beatrice, VII:308; **IX:3905-3909,** 3939
History of Trade Unionism, The, IX:3907
Industrial Democracy, IX:3907
My Apprenticeship, IX:3908
Our Partnership, IX:3908
Soviet Communism: A New Civilisation?, IX:3908
Webb, Chick, VII:1157
Webb, James Watson, V:191
Webb, John, IV:736
Webb, Sidney, **IX:3905-3909,** 3939
History of Trade Unionism, The, IX:3907
Industrial Democracy, IX:3907
Soviet Communism: A New Civilisation?, IX:3908
Webber, Andrew Lloyd, VII:1060

Weber, Carl Maria von, **VI:2340-2343**
Abu Hassan, VI:2340
Euryanthe, VI:2342
Freischütz, VI:2341, 2342
Konzerstück, VI:2341
Oberon, VI:2342
Peter Schmoll und seine Nachbarn, VI:2340
Weber, Ernst Heinrich, V:781
Weber, Max, IX:3723, **3910-3913**
Economy and Society, IX:3911
Protestant Ethic and the Spirit of Capitalism, IX:3911
Weber, Wilhelm Eduard, V:895
Webern, Anton von, VII:386, 387, 389; IX:3359, 3542, **3914-3917**
Passacaglia Op. 1, IX:3914, 3915
Webster, Daniel, VI:1772, 2075, **2344-2347,** 2375
Webster, John
Duchess of Malfi, The, I:772
Webster, Noah, **IV:1417-1420**
American Dictionary of the English Language, An, IV:1419
Dissertations on the English Language, IV:1419
Grammatical Institute of the English Language, A, IV:1417
Little Reader's Assistant, The, IV:1417
New England Primer, The, IV:1417
Sketches of American Policy, IV:1419, 1420
Weddington, Sarah, IX:3170
Wedgwood, Josiah, **IV:1421-1425**
Address on the Subject of Entering into Service of Foreign Manufacturers, An, IV:1423
Address to the Young Inhabitants of the Pottery, An, IV:1423
Weed, Thurlow, V:792, 793, 984, 985; VI:2037, 2038
Wegener, Alfred, **IX:3918-3921**
Origin of Continents and Oceans, IX:3919
Wei, Lady, I:946
Wei Cheng, II:877, 879
Weigel, Helene, VII:444
Wei Jingsheng, VII:906
Weil, Simone, **IX:3922-3925**
Condition ouvrière, La, IX:3922
Écrits de Londres et dernières lettres, IX:3924
Need for Roots, The, IX:3925
Notebooks, IX:3924
Weill, Al, VIII:2412, 2413
Weill, Kurt, **IX:3926-3929**
Down in the Valley, IX:3928
Eternal Road, The, IX:3928
Firebrand of Florence, The, IX:3928
Happy End, IX:3927
Johnny Johnson, IX:3928
Knickerbocker Holiday, IX:3928
Lady in the Dark, IX:3928
Lost in the Stars, IX:3928
Love Life, IX:3928
"Mack the Knife," IX:3929
Mahagonny Songspiel, IX:3927
One Touch of Venus, IX:3928
Protagonist, Der, IX:3927
Rise and Fall of the City of Mahagonny, The, IX:3927
Seven Deadly Sins of the Petit Bourgeois, The, IX:3928
Sinfonia Sacra Op. 6; *Frauenatz,* IX:3926
Street Scene, IX:3928
Tale of Love and Death of Cornet Christopher Rilke, The, IX:3926
Threepenny Opera, The, IX:3927, 3929
Weimar Republic
Hindenburg, VIII:1674-1676
Hitler, VIII:1694
Niemöller, VIII:2742
Weismann, August, **VI:2348-2350**
Weiss, Carl Austin, VIII:2229
Weiss, Johannes, VII:498
Weizmann, Chaim, VII:252; VIII:2768; **IX:3930-3933**
Welcome House, VII:488, 489
welfare state
England, VII:530; VIII:2094; IX:3908
New Zealand, VI:2017-2019
Stevens, VI:2137
Sweden, VIII:2671-2673
Welfs, II:466, 468, 932
Welles, Orson, VIII:1597; **IX:3934-3937**
Chimes at Midnight, IX:3935
Citizen Kane, VIII:1604; IX:3935
F for Fake, IX:3935
Macbeth, IX:3934-3936
Magnificent Ambersons, The, IX:3935
Othello, IX:3935
Shadow, The, IX:3934
Touch of Evil, IX:3935
Trial, The, IX:3935
War of the Worlds, IX:3934
Wellesley, Arthur. *See* Wellington, Duke of
Wellington, Duke of, V:995; VI:1681, 1720, **2351-2354,** 2393
Wells, H.G., VI:2304; **IX:3938-3940**
Ann Veronica, IX:3938
Anticipations, IX:3939

Experiment in Autobiography, IX:3940
Future in America, The, IX:3939
God, the Invisible King, IX:3939
History of Mr. Polly, The, IX:3939
Invisible Man, The, IX:3939
Island of Doctor Moreau, The, IX:3939
Kipps, IX:3939
Modern Utopia, A, IX:3939
Mr. Britling Sees It Through, IX:3939
New Machiavelli, The, IX:3939
Outline of History, The, IX:3939, 3940
Passionate Friends, The, IX:3938
This Misery of Boots, IX:3939
Time Machine, The, IX:3938, 3940
Tono-Bungay, IX:3939
Wonderful Visit, The, IX:3939
Wells-Barnett, Ida B., **IX:3941-3944**
Welt, Die, V:1104; VII:484
Wenceslaus, **II:969-972,** 1030
Wen-ti, I:431
Wentworth, Lady, IV:765
Wentworth, Thomas. *See* Strafford, First Earl of
Wentworth, W.C., **VI:2355-2357**
Wert, Giaches de, IV:990, 991
Wertheimer, Max, **IX:3945-3948**
Wertheimer, Pierre, VII:651
Wesley, John, **IV:1426-1430,** 1490
Wessex, Godwin, Earl of, II:315, 316, 426
West, Benjamin
Copley, IV:357
Fulton, V:854
Kauffmann, IV:765, 767
Morse, VI:1592
Peale, IV:1070
Stuart, IV:1289, 1290
West, Mae, VII:829; **IX:3949-3952**
Belle of the Nineties, IX:3950
Catherine Was Great, IX:3950, 3951
Come on Up, IX:3950
Constant Sinner, The, IX:3949
Diamond Lil, IX:3949, 3950
Drag, The, IX:3949
Heat's On, The, IX:3950
I'm No Angel, IX:3950
My Little Chickadee, IX:3950
Myra Breckenridge, IX:3951
Night After Night, IX:3950
Pleasure Man, The, IX:3949, 3951
Sextette, IX:3951
She Done Him Wrong, IX:3950
Wicked Age, The, IX:3949
West African Frontier Force, VIII:2269
Western Electric Company, VIII:2623
Western Federation of Miners, V:280
Western Female Institute, V:171
Western Pacific Railroad, VI:2098
Western Reserve Eclectic Institute, V:875, 876
Westinghouse, George, VI:2219, **2358-2362**
Westinghouse Electric Corporation, VI:2360; IX:4125
Westminster, Statute of, VIII:1982
Westminster Abbey
Blake, IV:137
Caxton, III:144
Henry III, II:455
Purcell, IV:1137-1139
Scott, VI:2003
Sharp, IV:1238
Westminster Bridge, IV:243
Westminster Confession, IV:99
Westminster Review, IV:109; V:751
Weston, Edward, VII:809
Westphalia, Treaty of, III:493; IV:304, 305, 342, 508; 644, 946, 1053; VI:2187
West Point, U.S. Military Academy at
André, IV:43, 44
Arnold, IV:66
Bradley, VII:403
Eisenhower, VII:1043
Goethals, VIII:1410
MacArthur, VIII:2295, 2296
Patton, IX:2911
Pershing, IX:2983-2985
Thayer, VI:2223-2225
Wexler, Jerry, VII:1217
Weyden, Rogier van der, **III:778-780**
Descent from the Cross, III:778, 779
Portrait of a Woman, III:779
Entombment, III:779
Madonna with Four Saints, III:779
Whampoa Military Academy, VII:664, 676
Wharton, Edith, VII:1130; **IX:3953-3956**
Age of Innocence, The, VIII:2175; IX:3954
Buccaneers, The, IX:3954
Bunner Sisters, The, IX:3954
Custom of the Country, The, IX:3954
Descent of Man, The, IX:3953
Ethan Frome, IX:3954, 3955
Fruit of the Tree, The, IX:3954
Ghosts, IX:3954
Glimpses of the Moon, IX:3954
Gods Arrive, The, IX:3954
House of Mirth, The, IX:3953, 3954
Hudson River Bracketed, IX:3955

Madame de Treymes, IX:3954
Old New York, IX:3954
Reef, The, IX:3954
Sanctuary, IX:3953
Valley of Decision, The, IX:3953
Wheaton, Henry
History of the Law of Nations, IV:581
Wheatstone, Charles, **V:555-559;** VI:2068; VII:1040
Wheeler, Ralph, IV:196
Wheelwright, John, IV:688
Whewell, William, VI:2063
Whig Party (England)
Addison, IV:26
Anne, IV:52, 53
Bolingbroke, IV:158-161
Brougham, V:314-316
Burke, IV:222
Canning, V:405
Catholic emancipation, VI:1681
Chadwick, V:457, 459
Charles II, IV:285
Cromwell, IV:381
Defoe, IV:401
Derby, V:653
Disraeli, V:677
Durham, V:721, 722
Fielding, IV:470
Fox, IV:479, 481-483
George I, IV:531-533
George II, IV:535
George IV, V:902, 904
Gladstone, VIII:2091
Grey, V:994
Jeffrey, V:1224-1226
Kidd, IV:777, 779, 780
Macaulay, VI:1427-1429
Melbourne, VI:1517-1519
Monmouth, IV:981
Oates, IV:1039
Palmerston, VI:1720
Pelham, IV:1074, 1075
Reynolds, IV:1162
Russell, VI:1930-1932
Seward, VI:2037-2039
Shaftesbury, IV:1228, 1230, 1231
Swift, IV:1307
Vanbrugh, IV:1352
Walpole, IV:1400-1403
Whig Party (U.S.)
Blaine, V:255
Clay, V:509, 510
Crockett, V:578, 579
Cushing, V:581, 582
Fillmore, V:792-794
Greeley, V:984
Harrison, V:1062
Lincoln, VI:1382
Massachusetts, V:125
Polk, VI:1803
Scott, VI:2011, 2012
Stephens, VI:2129
Stevens, VI:2136
Tyler, VI:2289, 2290
Van Buren, VI:2294
Webster, VI:2345
Whipple, George Hoyt, **IX:3957-3960**
Whiskey Rebellion, IV:611, 719
Whistler, James McNeill, **VI:2363-2367**
Arrangement in Grey and Black, No. 1: The Artist's Mother, VI:2364
Harmony in Blue and Gold, VI:2364
Whistler v. Ruskin, VI:2364
Whitaker, Alexander, IV:1106, 1107
White, Stanford, VI:1941
White, Walter, **IX:3961-3964**
Fire in the Flint, IX:3962
Flight, IX:3962
Rope and Faggot, IX:3962
Whitefield, George, IV:429, 1426, 1427
White Friars. *See* Carmelites
White Ghibellines. *See* Ghibellines
Whitehead, Alfred North, **IX:3965-3968**
Adventures of Ideas, IX:3967
Introduction to Mathematics, An, IX:3967
Modes of Thought, IX:3968
Principia Mathematica, VIII:2725; IX:3966, 3967
Process and Reality, IX:3967
Science and the Modern World, IX:3967
Treatise on Universal Mathematics, A, IX:3966
White Lotus Sect, IV:302
Whitewater Development Corporation, VII:715
Whitman, Walt, **VI:2368-2373;** VII:263, 791; IX:3308, 3309
"Child's Reminiscence, A," VI:2370
"Crossing Brooklyn Ferry," VI:2370
Democratic Vistas, VI:2371
Drum Taps, VI:2371
Franklin Evans, VI:2368
Leaves of Grass, V:758; VI:2370, 2371
"O Captain! My Captain!," VI:2371
"Out of the Cradle Endlessly Rocking," VI:2370
Passage to India, VI:2371

Specimen Days and Collect, VI:2371
"When Lilacs Last in the Dooryard Bloom'd," VI:2371; VIII:1672
Whitney, Eli, **IV:1431-1434;** VI:2075, 2076
Whitney, Gertrude Vanderbilt, **IX:3969-3971**
Fountain of El Dorado, IX:3970
Paganism Immortal, IX:3969
Spirit of Flight, The, IX:3971
Titanic Memorial, IX:3970
Whitney Museum of American Art, IX:3969-3971
Whitney v. California, VII:422
Whittaker, James, IV:818, 819
Whittier, John Greenleaf, V:883; **VI:2374-2376**
"Barefoot Boy, The," VI:2375
"Bridal of Pennacock, The," VI:2375
"Christian Slave, The," VI:2375
"Exile's Departure, The," VI:2374
"Farewell of a Virginia Slave Mother, The," VI:2375
Home Ballads and Other Poems, VI:2376
"Ichabod," VI:2375
Justice and Expediency, VI:2374
Lays of My Home and Other Poems, VI:2375
Legends of New England, VI:2374
"Massachusetts to Virginia," VI:2375
"Merrimack, The," VI:2375
"New Wife and the Old, The," VI:2375
"Skipper Ireson's Ride," VI:2376
"Slave Ships, The," VI:2375
Snow-Bound: A Winter Idyl, VI:2376
"Telling the Bees," VI:2376
"Toussaint L'Ouverture," VI:2374
"Within the Gate," V:491
Whittle, Sir Frank, **IX:3972-3975**
Widukind, **II:973-975**
Wieland, Christopher Martin, VI:1294
Wiener, Norbert, **IX:3976-3979**
Wiesel, Elie, **IX:3980-3983**
Accident, The, IX:3980
Beggar in Jerusalem, A, IX:3982
Dawn, IX:3980
Gates of the Forest, The, IX:3980
Jews of Silence, The, IX:3980
Night, IX:3980
Oath, The, IX:3982
Town Beyond the Wall, The, IX:3980
Zalmen, IX:3982
Wiesenthal, Simon, **IX:3984-3988**
Wightman, Hazel Hotchkiss, **IX:3989-3991**
Better Tennis, IX:3991
Wightman Cup, IX:3990, 3991
Wilberforce, William, **IV:1435-1428;** V:378, 379
Wild, Richard, VI:1786
Wilde, Oscar, VI:1750, **2377-2380;** VII:1088, 1367
Guido Ferranti, VI:2379
Happy Prince and Other Tales, The, VI:2379; VII:371
Importance of Being Earnest, The, VI:2377, 2379
Intentions, VI:2379
Picture of Dorian Gray, The, VI:2379
Poems, VI:2377
Salomé, V:163
Wilder, Laura Ingalls, **IX:3992-3994**
By the Shores of Silver Lake, IX:3993
Farmer Boy, IX:3993
First Four Years, The, IX:3993
Let the Hurricanes Roar, IX:3993
Little House in the Big Woods, IX:3992, 3993
Little House on the Prairie, IX:3992
Long Winter, The, IX:3992
On the Banks of Plum Creek, IX:3992
On The Way Home, IX:3992
These Happy Golden Years, IX:3992
West From Home, IX:3993
Wilkes, Charles, **VI:2381-2383**
Wilkes, John, IV:176, 908, 1099, **1439-1442**
Essay on Woman, IV:1440
North Briton, The, IV:1439, 1440, 1441
Wilkins, Sir George Hubert, **IX:3999-4002**
Flying the Artic, IX:4000
Undiscovered Australia, IX:4000
Wilkins, Maurice H.F., VII:797, 798; IX:3897, 3898, **3995-3998**
Wilkinson, James, IV:1094, 1096
Wilkinson, John, **IV:1443-1446**
Willard, Emma, **VI:2384-2387**
Address Proposing a Plan for Improving Female Education, An, VI:2385
Universal Peace, VI:2386
Willard, Frances, **VI:2388-2391**
Willard, Jess, VII:902
Willard, Samuel, IV:1225
William I, II:28, 29
William II, VII:494-496; IX:3689, **4003-4006**
William III, **IV:1447-1450**
Anne, IV:50, 52
Defoe, IV:399
Godolphin, IV:553
Kidd, IV:777
Leeds, IV:823
Locke, IV:857, 858
Marlborough, IV:922-924

Mather, IV:940
Popish Plot, IV:1040
William IV, V:722, 995; VI:2307, 2308, **2392-2395**
William IX, II:336
William X, II:336
William of Auvergne, **II:976-980**
De Universo, II:978
Magisterium divinale sive sapientale, II:978
William of Auxerre, **II:981-984**
Summa aurea, II:982, 983
William of Champeaux, II:10
William of Moerbeke, **II:985, 986**
William of Newburgh, II:293
William of Normandy, II:317, 428, 429
William of Orange. *See* William III
William of Rubrouck, **II:987-989**
William of Saint-Amour, **II:990-993**
Collectiones catholicae et canonicae scripturae, II:992
De periculis novissimorum temporum, II:992
William of Saint-Thierry, **II:994-996**
Enigma of Faith, The, II:995
Expositions on the Song of Songs, II:995
Golden Epistle, The, II:994
Meditations, The, II:995
Mirror of Faith, The, II:995
On Contemplating God, II:994
On the Nature and Dignity of Love, II:994
On the Sacrament of the Altar, II:994
Saint Bernard of Clairvaux, II:994, 995
William of Tyre, II:70
William Rufus, II:73
Williams, Eric, VII:760
Williams, George Washington, **VI:2396-2399**
History of the Negro Race in America, VI:2397
History of the Negro Troops in the War of the Rebellion, 1861-1865, VI:2397
Open Letter to His Serene Majesty, Leopold II, An, VI:2398
Williams, Roger, IV:371, 930-932, **1451-1454,** 1464; IX:2893
Bloody Tenent of Persecution, for Cause of Conscience, Discussed, IV:1451
Bloody Tenent Yet More Bloody, The, IV:1452
Examiner Defended, The, IV:1452
Fourth Paper Presented by Major Butler, The, IV:1452
George Fox Digg'd out of His Burrows, IV:1453
Hireling Ministry None of Christs, The, IV:1452
Mr. Cottons Letter Lately Printed, Examined, and Answered, IV:1451
Queries of Highest Consideration, IV:1451
Williams, Tennesee, VII:795; VIII:2310; IX:3885, **4007-4011**
American Blues, IX:4009
Battle of Angels, IX:4009
Camino Real, IX:4010
Glass Menagerie, The, IX:4007, 4009
Orpheus Descending, IX:4009, 4010
Streetcar Named Desire, A, VII:425; IX:4010
Suddenly Last Summer, IX:4009, 4010
Summer and Smoke, IX:4010
Williams, William Carlos, III:766
William the Conqueror, II:72, 443, 794, **997-1000**
William the Silent, III:574, 575, 600, **781-784**
Willibald, II:167, 168
Willibrord, Saint, II:167, 824, 825
Willich, August, V:761
Willkie, Wendell, VIII:2256
Wilmot Proviso, VI:1803
Wilson, Alexander
American Ornithology, V:86
Wilson, Edmund, VII:1161, 1163; VIII:2304; **IX:4012-4015**
Axel's Castle, IX:4012-4014
I Thought of Daisy, IX:4013
"Man Who Shot Snapping Turtles, The," IX:4013
Memoirs of Hecate County, IX:4013
Patriotic Gore, IX:4014, 4015
"Princess with the Golden Hair," IX:4013
To the Finland Station, IX:4014
Travels in Two Democracies, IX:4012
Wound and the Bow, The, IX:4014
Wilson, Sir Harold, **IX:4016-4019**
Heath, VIII:1607, 1608
Wilson, Sir Horace, VII:645
Wilson, James, **IV:1455-1459**
Wilson, John, IV:688
Wilson, Robert T.
Black Phalanx, VI:2397
Wilson, Woodrow, **IX:4020-4024**
Balch, VII:161
Benes, VII:260
Brandeis, VII:421
Bryan, VII:481
Guggenheim, VIII:1500
Hoover, VIII:1727
Hughes, VIII:1777
Hull, VIII:1779
La Follette, VIII:2048
Lippmann, VIII:2204
Lodge, VIII:2221
Mexican Revolution, IX:3813
Mott, VIII:2639

neutrality declaration, VIII:1396
Roosevelt, IX:3229, 3231
Sargent, VI:1964
Shaw, VI:2046
Stimson, IX:3538
Washington, VI:2337
Wimbledon (tennis tournament)
Borg, VII:368, 369
Evert, VII:1113
Gibson, VII:1364
King, VIII:1968
Laver, VIII:2109, 2110
Navratilova, VIII:2703
Perry, IX:2979, 2981, 2982
Winchester, Statutes of, II:322
Winchester, Treaty of, II:849
Winckelmann, Johann Joachim, IV:408, 410, **1460-1462**
History of Ancient Art, IV:1460, 1461
Reflections on the Paintings and Sculpture of the Greeks, IV:1460, 1461
Windsor, Duke of, **IX:4025-4028**
Windsor, House of, VII:1340
Winfrey, Oprah, **IX:4029-4032**
Beloved, IX:4031
Color Purple, The, IX:4030
Native Son, IX:4030
Oprah Winfrey Show, The, IX:4029-4031
Women of Brewster Place, The, IX:4031
Wingolf Society, IX:3685
Winkler, Paula, VII:484
Winter, Thomas, III:258, 259
Winterfeld, Carl von, III:286
Winter War, VIII:2397, 2398
Winthrop, John, IV:688, **1463-1466**
"Modell of Christian Charity, A," IV:1465
Winthrop, Robert, VI:1772
Wise, Issac Mayer, **VI:2400-2402**
Minhag America, VI:2401
Wise, Stephen Samuel, **IX:4033-4035**
Wister, Owen, V:52
witchcraft trials. *See* Salem witchcraft trials
Witherspoon, John, **IV:1467-1470**
Ecclesiastical Characteristics, IV:1457
Witmer, Lightner, IX:4070
Witt, Jan de, IV:1447
Witta, I:378
Wittel, Gaspar van, IV:242
Wittenberg Concord of 1536, III:102
Wittgenstein, Ludwig, VIII:2607; **IX:4036-4038**
Philosophical Investigations, IX:4037
Tractatus, IX:4036, 4037
Wladyslaw II Jagiello, **II:1001-1004**
Wladyslaw III, III:374, 375
Woffington, Peg, IV:527, 528
Wofford, Chloe Anthony. *See* Morrison, Toni
Wöhler, Friedrich, **VI:2403-2405;** VIII:2713
Wojtyla, Karol Jozef. *See* John Paul II
Wolf, Hugo, V:1163
Wolf, Max, **IX:4039-4040**
Wolfe, Harry Kirke, IX:4070
Wolfe, James, IV:37, 38, 676, **1471-1474**
Wolfe, Thomas, **IX:4041-4044**
Face of a Nation, The, IX:4043
Hills Beyond, The, IX:4043
Look Homeward, Angel, IX:4041-4043
Mannerhouse, IX:4043
Of Time and the River, IX:4042
Stone, a Leaf, a Door, A, IX:4043
Story of a Novel, The, IX:4042
Web and the Rock, The, IX:4041, 4042
Western Journal, A, IX:4043
You Can't Go Home Again, IX:4042
Wolff, Christian von, IV:832
Wolfram von Eschenbach, **II:1005-1007**
Parzifal, II:393, 1005
Schionatulander and Sigune, II:1007
Willehalm, II:1007
Wolfsohn, Leopold, VII:766
Wolie, Ras Gugsa, VIII:1519
Wollman, Elie, VIII:1828
Wollstonecraft, Mary, IV:555-558, **1475-1479;** VI:2048, 2051
Historical and Moral View of the Origin and Progress of the French Revolution, IV:1477
Maria, IV:1477
Mary, a Fiction, IV:1475
Original Stories from Real Life, IV:138
Thoughts on the Education of Daughters, IV:1475
Vindication of the Rights of Men, A, IV:1477
Vindication of the Rights of Women, A, IV:1477; VI:1600
Wolsey, Cardinal Thomas, **III:785-787**
Boleyn, III:66, 68
Catherine of Aragon, III:138
Cromwell, III:208
Fisher, III:264
Gardiner, III:291
Henry VIII, III:349, 351
More, III:534, 535
Woman's Committee of the Council of National Defense, VI:2046
Woman's Journal, VI:2145, 2146

Woman's Peace Party, VII:23
Woman's State Temperance Society of New York, V:61; VI:2111
Women's Armed Services Integration Act of 1948, IX:3446
Women's Auxiliary Army Corps, VIII:1703-1705
Women's Christian Temperance Union, VI:1630, 1631, 2044, 2045, 2388-2390
Women's International League for Peace and Freedom, VII:161, 162, 354
Women's International of Socialists and Labour Organizations, VII:354
women's liberation movement, VII:231; VIII:2536
women's magazines, V:1022-1024; VII:1231
Women's Medical College of the New York Infirmary, V:252
Women's Rights, Declaration of, V:61
Women's Rights Convention, VI:1601, 2257
Women's Social and Political Union, V:778; IX:2871, 2873, 2874
Women's Strike for Equality, VII:1233
women's suffrage
  Addams, VII:23
  Alcott, V:42
  Anthony, V:61-64
  Argentina, IX:2966
  Catt, VII:627-629
  Bondfield, VII:354
  Fawcett, V:776-779
  Hale, V:1024
  Hardie, V:1037
  Higginson, V:1111, 1112
  Howe, V:1145, 1146, 1148
  Lockwood, VI:1407
  Mott, VI:1601
  New Zealand, VI:2018
  Oakley, VI:1679
  Pankhurst, IX:2871, 2873, 2874
  Paul, IX:2919, 2920, 2922
  Rankin, IX:3117-3119
  Shaw, VI:2044-2046
  Stanton, VI:2110-2113
  Stone, VI:2143, 2145, 2146
  Truth, VI:2258
  Turkey, VII:134
  Willard, VI:2388-2390
  Wyoming, IX:3243
Women's Tennis Association, VII:1114; VIII:1969
Women's Trade Union League, VII:160, 353-356
Wood, Grant, **IX:4045-4048**
  American Gothic, IX:4047
  Appraisal, IX:4047
  Daughters of Revolution, IX:4047
  Midnight Ride of Paul Revere, IX:4047
  Parson Weems' Fable, IX:4047
  Stone City, Iowa, IX:4047
  Woman with Plants, IX:4047
Wood, Leonard, IX:3233
Wood, Sidney, IX:2979
Wood, Thelma, VII:201
Woodhull, Victoria, VI:1407
Woods, Frank, VIII:2232
Woods, Tiger, **IX:4049-4051**
Woodstock Music and Art Fair, VIII:1884
Woodville, Elizabeth, III:649, 650
Woodward, Robert Burns, **IX:4052-4055**
Woolf, Virginia, V:330; VII:1193, 1254; VIII:2626; **IX:4056-4059**
  Between the Acts, IX:4058
  Common Reader, The, IX:4058
  Flush: A Biography, IX:4058
  Jacob's Room, IX:4056
  Mrs. Dalloway, IX:4056
  Room of One's Own, A, IX:4058
  Three Guineas, IX:4058
  To the Lighthouse, IX:4056
  Waves, The, IX:4058
  Years, The, IX:4058
Woolner, Thomas, V:1170
Worcester, Battle of, IV:1310
Worchester v. Georgia, VI:2149
Wordsworth, William, V:69, 75; **VI:2406-2409**
  Descriptive Sketches, VI:2406
  Evening Walk, An, VI:2406
  Excursion, The, VI:2407
  Lyrical Ballads, VI:2406-2408
  Michael, IV:566
  Ode: Intimations of Immortality, VI:2407, 2408
  "Ode to Duty," VI:2407
  Prelude: Or, The Growth of a Poet's Mind, The, VI:2406-2408
  River Duddon, The, VI:2407
Workingmen's Concert Association, VII:607
Workman, Fanny Bullock, **VI:2410-2413**
  Algerian Memories, VI:2411
  In the Ice World of the Himálayas, VI:2411
  Sketches Awheel in Modern Iberia, VI:2411
  Through Town and Jungle, VI:2411
Workman, William Hunter, VI:2410, 2412
Works Progress Administration, VII:985; VIII:1736, 1737, 1783, 2023; IX:3224
World Columbian Exposition. *See* World's Columbian Exposition
World Congress for Labor Palestine, VII:252

World Council of Churches, VIII:2743, 2744; IX:3776
World Cup soccer, IX:2950-2952
World Exhibition of 1867, VII:268
World Jewish Congress, IX:3842, 4034
World Missionary Conference, VIII:2639
World's Columbian Exposition
  Burnham, V:367
  Stone, VI:2146
  Sullivan, VI:2168
  Tesla, VI:2220
  Thomas, VI:2232
  Wells-Barnett, IX:3943
  Westinghouse, VI:2360
  Wright, IX:4060
World's Fair of 1893. *See* World's Columbian Exposition
World's Fair of 1937, IX:3252
World's Student Christian Federation, VIII:2638
World's Woman's Party, IX:2920
World War I
  Addams, VII:23, 24
  Allenby, VII:58-61
  All Quiet on the Western Front, IX:3150-3152
  American Expeditionary Forces, VIII:1437, 2555; IX:2893-2895
  Angell, VII:75-77
  Army Air Service, VIII:2554, 2555
  Army Medical Corps, VIII:1436, 1437
  Asquith, VII:122, 123
  Balfour Declaration, VII:174
  Banting, VII:187
  Barth, VII:204
  battlefield injuries, VII:219
  Berlin, Irving, VII:288
  Bernstein, VII:292, 293
  Beust, V:224
  Bondfield, VII:354
  Borah, V:280
  Bryan, VII:481
  Byrd, VII:534
  Canada, VII:365, 366
  Cassin, VII:610
  Catholic Center Party, VII:1102-1104
  Chaplin, VII:653
  chemical weapons, VIII:1510, 1514
  Clausewitz, V:505
  Clemenceau, VII:704
  Conant, VII:749
  conscription, VII:882; VIII:2103; IX:3584, 3585
  Curie, VII:812
  Czechoslovakia, VII:260; VIII:2441, 2442
  Eden, VII:1015
  Edison, V:746
  Faisal I, VII:1122, 1124, 1125
  Fawcett, V:778
  Francis Ferdinand, VII:1197-1199; IX:4005
  German aircraft, VIII:1614
  German High Seas Fleet, IX:3688-3690
  German music ban, IX:3130
  Giraudoux, VII:1379
  Girl Scouts, VIII:2247
  Goethals, VIII:1409
  Goldman, VIII:1413
  Gompers, V:958
  Göring, VIII:1438
  Gorky's propaganda, VIII:1444
  Gramsci, VIII:1460
  Greece, IX:3809
  Grey, VIII:1475-1477
  Gropius's architecture, VIII:1486
  Haile Selassie, VIII:1519
  Harmsworths, VIII:1555
  Hindenburg, VIII:1674-1676
  Hitler, VIII:1692, 1694
  Hobhouse, VIII:1709
  Hoover, VIII:1727, 1729
  Hughes, VIII:1775-1777
  Hull, VIII:1779
  India, VIII:1847
  John XXIII, VIII:1858, 1860
  John Bull, VII:384
  Kitchener, VIII:2003, 2004
  Kokoschka, VIII:2013
  La Follette, VIII:2048
  Laval, VIII:2105
  Lawrence, D.H., VIII:2117
  Lawrence, T.E., VIII:2125
  Léger, VIII:2155
  Lippmann, VIII:2204
  Lloyd George, VIII:2216, 2217
  Ludendorff, VIII:2265-2267
  Luxemburg, VIII:2286
  MacArthur, VIII:2295
  Macmillan, VIII:2340
  Mannix, VI:1480
  Marc, VIII:2405, 2406
  Marne, Battle of the, VIII:1851-1853
  Marshall, VIII:2429
  Mott, VIII:2639
  Mountbatten, VIII:2641
  munitions industry, VII:695
  Mussolini, VIII:2667, 2668
  Nash, VIII:2689, 2690

National Catholic War Council, V:922
National Research Council Fellowships, VII:745
New Zealand, VIII:2445
Oakley, VI:1679
Olympic Games, VII:775
Ottoman Empire, VII:133
Papen, VII:2876
Patton, IX:2911
Pétain, IX:2987-2989
Poincaré, IX:3044-3046
Reith, IX:3146
reparation policies, VII:1104; VIII:1767, 1768; IX:3045, 3046
rocketry, VIII:1396, 1397
Rolls-Royce, IX:3210
Rommel, IX:3213
Sargent, VI:1963
Scheler, IX:3347, 3348
Scotland, VIII:2323
Seeckt, IX:3380-3382
Stimson, IX:3538
Stone, IX:3546, 3547
submarines, IX:3279
Turkey, VII:1078, 1079; VIII:1523
Weber, IX:3911
Whitney's memorial sculpture, IX:3970
William II, IX:4003-4005
Wilson, IX:4021, 4022
Wright brothers, IX:4066
zeppelins, VII:1012; IX:4110
World War II
African Intelligence Department, VIII:2146
Akihito, VII:41
Alanbrooke, VII:45-47
Angell, VII:77
Astor, VII:130, 131
atom bombs, VII:464, 747; VIII:1515, 1801, 2040, 2122, 2337, 2725, 2726; IX:2833-2835, 3376, 3492, 3742
Australia, VII:816-818
Balch, VII:162
Baldwin, VII:170
Beard, VII:224
Blum, VII:337
Bradley, VII:403, 404
Bragg, VII:412
Braudel, VII:436
Britain, Battle of, VII:236
British Fourteenth Army, IX:3435-3437
Burmese Independence Army, IX:3647
Bush, VII:520
Cartier-Bresson, VII:595
Catt, VII:629
Chamberlain, VII:645, 646
Chinese-Japanese War, VII:665
Churchill, VII:693
Czechoslovakia, VII:261, 561
de Gaulle, VII:866, 867
documentary films, VII:1329
Dole, VII:947
Eden, VII:1016
Eisenhower, VII:1043
Franco, VII:1201, 1202
French Resistance, VII:239, 360, 553, 867, 1076; VIII:1872, 2106, 2558; IX:3329, 3330
George VI, VII:1343-1346
German missile program, VII:2777, 2779
Halsey, VIII:1525-1528
Harriman, VIII:1560, 1561
Hatoyama Ichiro, VIII:1575
Heinkel's aircraft, VIII:1615
Hemingway, VIII:1626
Hirohito, VIII:1678, 1680, 1681
Hopkins, VIII:1737
Hull, VIII:1781
India, VII:1283
Ireland, VII:878
Jacob, VIII:1827
Japanese American relocation and internment, VIII:2084, 2085, 2206; IX:3889
John XXIII, VIII:1858
John Paul II, VIII:1862, 1863
Johnson, VIII:1867
Joliot-Curies, VIII:1872
Kawabata, VIII:1914
Keynes, VIII:1954
Kissinger, VIII:1998
Laval, VIII:2105-2107
Libya, IX:3098, 3099
Lindbergh, VIII:2194
Lippmann, VIII:2205
Litvinov, VIII:2210, 2211
Louis, VIII:2243
MacArthur, VIII:2297, 2298
Malraux, VIII:2381
Manchurian takeover, VI:1365
Marshall Plan, VII:315; VIII:1529, 1562, 1696, 2205, 2258, 2431; IX:3862
Matsushita Electric Company, VIII:2458
Mendès-France, VIII:2491
Menzies, VIII:2497
Messiaen, VIII:2503
Milne, VIII:2544
Mitterrand, VIII:2558

Monnet, VIII:2583, 2585
Montgomery, VIII:2602, 2603
Mountbatten, VIII:2643-2645
Murrow, VIII:2664
music business, VIII:1420, 1748
Nimitz, VIII:2750-2752
Palestine, VII:244, 252
Paris Opéra, VIII:2184
Patton, IX:2913
Pearl Harbor attack, VIII:1525, 2172
Pershing, IX:2985
Pétain, IX:2988, 2989
Philippines, VIII:2420
Pius XI, IX:3027, 3028
Pius XII, IX:3030-3032
Rankin, IX:3119
refugees, IX:3017
rocketry, VII:440-442; VIII:1397
Rolls-Royce, IX:3211
Romania, VII:1055
Roosevelt, IX:3225, 3226
Sandburg, IX:3311
Solzhenitsyn, IX:3460
South Africa, IX:3454
Steichen's combat photography, IX:3503
Stevenson, IX:3523
submarines, IX:3174
Tito, IX:3692, 3693
Truman, IX:3742
Turkey, VIII:1813
United Nations Commission on Human Rights, VII:611
War Information, Office of, VII:257
Welcome House, VII:488, 489
Whittle, IX:3974
Women's Auxiliary Army Corps, VIII:1703-1705
Yugoslav Revolution, VII:944, 945
Zhukov, IX:4116-4118
See also Nazi Party
World Zionist Organization, VII:252; VIII:2766-2768; IX:3930-3933
Worlidge, John
Systema Agriculturae, IV:1346
Worms, Colloquy of, III:101, 102
Worms, Concordat of, II:74, 357
Worms, Diet of, III:492
Worms, Edict of, III:445
Wounded Knee, Battle at, VI:2072, 2073
WPA. *See* Works Progress Administration
Wren, Sir Christopher, **IV:1480-1483**
Hawksmoor, IV:635, 636
Mansart, IV:900
Vanbrugh, IV:1354
Wright, Frank Lloyd, VI:2168; VII:325; VIII:2488, 2522; **IX:4060-4063**
Wright, Orville and Wilbur, **IX:4064-4068**
Cayley, V:452
Dunbar, V:714
Heinkel, VIII:1614
Langley, VI:1314
Mitchell, VIII:2554
Otto, VI:1703
Wright, Richard, VII:164; VIII:1788; IX:4030
WSPU. *See* Women's Social and Political Union
Wu, Emperor, I:817, 819, 820
Wu Ch'eng-en, II:485
Wundt, Wilheim, IX:3946, 3947, **4069-4071**
Outlines of Psychology, IX:4070
Principles of Physiological Psychology, IX:4069, 4070
Völkerpsychologie, IX:4070
Württemberg, Duke of, VI:2340
Wu San-kuei, IV:421, 422
Wyatt's Rebellion, III:320, 480
Wyclif, John, II:487-489, 971, 992, **1009-1011,** 1030
De civili dominio, II:1010
Wye River Agreement, VII:93
Wyeth, Andrew, **IX:4072-4074**
Christina's World, IX:4073
Christmas Morning, IX:4073
Hunter, The, IX:4073
Karl, IX:4073
Northern Point, IX:4073
Pantry, The, IX:4073
Public Sale, IX:4072
Revenant, The, IX:4073
Seed Corn, IX:4073
Spring Beauty, IX:4073
Spring Freshet, IX:4073
Thin Ice, IX:4073, 4074
Wind from the Sea, IX:4073
Winter, IX:4072
Wyeth, Newell Convers, IX:4072, 4073
Wyler, William, VIII:1417
Wyndham, Sir William, IV:159
Wynfrith. *See* Boniface, Saint
Wyoming
Calamity Jane, V:390
fur trade, VI:2077, 2078
Ross, IX:3243, 3244
women's suffrage, IX:3243

Wythe, George, V:507
Wyttenbach, Thomas, III:791

Xanthippe, **I:952-954**
Xanthippos, I:740
Xanthus, I:13
Xavier, Saint Francis, III:438, **788-790**
Xenakis, Iannis, **IX:4075-4078**
  Akrata, IX:4077
  Atrées, IX:4077
  Bohor 1, IX:4077
  Cendrées, IX:4077
  Concret PA, IX:4076
  Diomorphoses, IX:4076
  Duel, IX:4077
  Eonta, IX:4077
  Kraanerg, IX:4077
  Métastasis, IX:4075, 4077
  Pithopratka, IX:4076
  Polytope de Montréal, IX:4077
  ST/4, IX:4077
  ST/48, IX:4077
  ST/10, IX:4077
  Stratégie, IX:4077
  Terretektorh, IX:4077
  Vamos Gamma, IX:4077
Xeniades, I:270
Xenophanes, I:596, **955-957**
  Peri phuseos, I:956
Xenophon, I:457, **958-961**
  Anabasis, I:959
  Banquet, The, I:958
  Cyropaedia, I:233
  Defense of Socrates, The, I:958
  Hellenica, I:960
  Institution and Life of Cyrus, The, I:959
  Ways and Means, I:960
Xerox, VII:579, 580
Xerxes I, I:47, 238, 501, 502, 705, **962-966**
X-rays
  Becquerel, V:167
  Bothe, VII:379
  Bragg, VII:410-413
  Broglie, VII:472
  Hertz, VIII:1647
  Hevesy, VIII:1655, 1656
  Hounsfield, VIII:1751-1753
  Lawrence, VIII:2121
  Pauling, IX:2926
  Popov, VI:1806, 1808
  radiation genetics, VIII:2651-2653
  Watson, IX:3897, 3898
  Wilkins, IX:3995-3997

Yaddo, IX:2785, 3061
Yale, Frank, VII:563, 564
Yale University
  Benèt, VII:263
  Boswell, IV:177
  Farrand, VII:1131
  Gibbs, V:923
  Hindemith, VIII:1672
  Hutchins, VIII:1800
  Ives, VIII:1820
  Lin, VIII:2187
  Mather, IV:935, 936
  Sherman, IV:1244
Yalta Conference, IX:3225
Yamani, Ahmad Zaki, **IX:4079-4081**
Yamato clan, II:826
Yamoussoukro, VIII:1756
Yamuna, II:770
Yanayev, Gennady, IX:4087
Yaqut, II:148, **1013-1014**
  Kitab mu'jam al-buldan, II:1013, 1014
  Yaqut's Dictionary of Learned Men, II:1013, 1014
Yaroslav the Wise, II:953
Yates, Robert, IV:609
Yathrib. *See* Medina
Yeats, William Butler, IV:141; VI:1750; VIII:2683; **IX:4082-4085**
  "Among School Children," IX:4083
  At the Hawk's Well, IX:4083
  "Circus Animals Desertion, The," IX:4083, 4085
  "Coat, A," IX:4082
  "Cold Heaven, The," IX:4082
  Countess Cathleen, The, IX:4083
  "Deep-Sworn Vow, A," IX:4083
  "Easter 1916," IX:4083
  "In Memory of Major Robert Gregory," IX:4083
  "Irish Airman Foresees Death, An," IX:4083
  Last Poems and Plays, IX:4083
  Michael Robartes and the Dancer, IX:4083
  "Paudeen," IX:4082
  Responsibilities, IX:4082
  Rose, The, IX:4082
  "Sailing to Byzantium," IX:4083
  "Soldier, Scholar, Horseman," IX:4083
  "To a Shade," IX:4082
  "To a Wealthy Man," IX:4082
  Tower, The, IX:4083
  Vision, A, IX:4083

"Wanderings of Oisin, The," IX:4082
Wild Swans at Coole, The, IX:4083
Winding Stair and Other Poems, The, IX:4083
Yellow Book, The, V:162
yellow journalism
Borden, V:285
Eddy, V:741
Hearst, VIII:1601, 1603-1605
McKinley, VI:1454, 1455
Oakley, VI:1678
Pulitzer, VI:1826
Yellowstone National Park, V:1072-1074
Yeltsin, Boris N., VIII:2010; **IX:4086-4089**
Yen-an Way, VIII:2190
Yen Li-pen, **II:1015-1017**
Eighteen Scholars at the Palace of Ch'in, II:1015
Scroll of the Emperors, II:1015
Yen Li-te, II:1015, 1016
Yen Wu, II:919
Yepes y Álvarez, Juan de. *See* John of the Cross, Saint
Yiddish Scientific Institute, VII:847, 848
YMCA. *See* Young Men's Christian Association
Yo Fei, **II:1018-1020**
Yohai, Simon bar, II:649
Yohannes IV, VI:1537, 1538
Yomiuri Giants, IX:2796-2798
Yom Kippur War, VII:856, 1002; VIII:2474, 2475; IX:3289, 3290
York, Duke of, III:341-343, 345, 346, 657, 774, 775
Yorktown, Battle of, IV:323, 368, 608, 1000, 1174-1176, 1406
Yosemite National Park, VI:1609, 1692
Yoshida, Shigeru, VIII:1575; IX:3336
Young, Brigham, V:840; **VI:2414-2416**
Young, Charles, VI:1262
Young, Lester, VIII:1717, 1718
Young Contemporaries Exhibition, VIII:1711
Young England movement, V:677
Young Germany movement, V:1087
Young Irelanders movement, VI:1682
Young Italy movement, V:932; VI:1514
Young Men's Christian Association, V:711, 712; VI:1575, 1579; VII:477; VIII:2637-2639; IX:3127
Young Turks
Atatürk, VII:133, 134
Enver Pasha, VII:1078-1081
Halide Edib Adivar, VIII:1522-1524
Inönü, VIII:1812
Ypsilanti, Alexander, **VI:2417-2419**
Ypsilanti, Demetrios, **VI:2417-2419**
Yuan Ch'ung-huan, IV:2
Yüan Dynasty, II:566-568, 1021
Yüan Shih-k'ai, VII:687
Yüan Shu, II:841
Yueh-chi, I:494
Yugoslav Communist Party, VII:944; IX:3692, 3693
Yukawa, Hidecki, **IX:4090-4092**
Yung-lo, II:253, 254, **1021-1024**
Yunnan, II:253
Yverdon, VI:1768, 1769

Zaccaro, John, VII:1153-1155
Zacharias, II:824
Zachow, Friedrich, IV:619
Zadar, II:284
Zaghlul, Sa'd, **IX:4093-4095**
Zaharias, "Babe" Didrikson, **IX:4096-4099**
Zahir-ud-Din Muhammad. *See* Babur
Zaïmis, Alexandros, IX:3808
Zalinski, Edmund L., V:1124
Zama, Battle of, I:536, 761
Zambezi River, VI:1399, 1400
ZANLA. *See* Zimbabwe African National Liberation Army
ZANU. *See* Zimbabwe African National Union
Zanuck, Darryl F., XIII:1630; **IX:4100-4103**
Cleopatra, IX:4101
Grapes of Wrath, The, IX:4101
How Green Was My Valley, IX:4101
Jazz Singer, The, IX:4100
Longest Day, The, IX:4101
Public Enemy, The, IX:4101
Zanuck, Richard, IX:4101
Zapata, Emiliano, IX:2782, **4104-4107**
ZAPU. *See* Zimbabwe African People's Union
Zeami Motokiyo, **II:1025-1029**
Kintosho, II:1027
Nogaku koten: Zeami jorokubushu, II:1027
Tochu Zeami nijusambushu, II:1027
Zecca, III:665
Zeckendorf, William, IX:2946
Zedekiah, I:460
Zeeman, Pieter, VIII:2235
Zeffirelli, Franco, IX:3083
Zegzard, Count, II:851
Zemlinksy, Alexander von, IX:3357
Zen Buddhism, II:666, 1028; VIII:1745, 2754, 2755
Zenger, John Peter, **IV:1484-1487**
Brief Narrative of the Case and Tryal of John Peter Zenger, A, IV:1486

Zeno of Citium, I:68, **967-971**
Politeia, I:967, 969
Zeno of Elea, I:597, **972-974**
Zentralschule Laban, VIII:2059
Zephyrinus, I:416
Zeppelin, Ferdinand von, VII:1011; **IX:4108-4111**
Zetkin, Clara, **IX:4112-4115**
Working Women and the Contemporary Woman Question, IX:4112
Zeyer, Julius, VIII:1836
Zhao Ziyang, VIII:2178, 2179
Zhdanov, Andrei, VIII:2377, 2378; IX:3409
Zhemchuzhina, Polina, VIII:2572
Zhukov, Georgy Konstantinovich, VIII:1962; **IX:4116-4120**
Zhukovsky, Nikolay Yegorovich, IX:3764
Zhukovsky, Vasily Andreyevich, V:48
Ziegfeld Follies, IX:3205, 3206
Ziegler, Karl, VIII:2699
Zimbabwe African National Liberation Army, VIII:2647
Zimbabwe African National Union, VIII:2318, 2647-2649
Zimbabwe African People's Union, VIII:2647-2649
Zimri-Lim, I:361, 362
Zincke, Theodor, VIII:1513
Zinj, VIII:2147
Zinzendorf, Graf von, IV:1488
Zionism
Arendt, VII:99, 100
Baeck, VII:150
Balfour Declaration, VII:174
Begin, VII:243
Ben-Gurion, VII:251-254
Brandeis, VII:419, 421
Buber, VII:484, 485
Cassin, VII:610
Eban, VII:1000
Faisal, VIII:1118, 1120
Herzl, V:1102, 1104, 1105
Meir, VIII:2472-2475
Nordau, VIII:2766-2768
Palestine, Conference on, VIII:1118
Weizmann, IX:3930-3933
Wise, VI:2402; IX:4033-4035
Zizka, Count Jan, **II:1030-1032**
Znanya, VII:64
Zoffany, Johann, IV:529
Zola, Émile, **VI:2420-2424;** VII:703
Assommoir, L', VI:2421
Claude's Confession, VI:2420, 2421
Experimental Novel, The, VI:2420, 2421; VIII:2134
Germinal, VI:2421
Madeleine Férat, VI:2420
Nana, VI:2421; VII:119; IX:3157
Quatre Evangiles, Les, VI:2423
Rougon-Macquart Novels, The, VI:2420
Soirées de Medan, Les, VI:2421
Stories for Ninon, VI:2420
Thérèse Raquin, VI:2420
Three Cities, The, VI:2421
Zons, Michael, VI:1702
Zorin, Valerian, IX:3525
Zorn, Anders, VII:1300
Zoroaster, **I:975-977**
See also Zoroastrianism
Zoroastrianism, I:237, 238, 781
Zoser, I:443, **978-980**
Zukor, Adolph, VII:897; VIII:1415, 1417; IX:3006
Zuni, III:181
Zwide, VI:2041, 2042
Zwilich, Ellen Taaffe, **IX:4121-4124**
Cello Symphony, IX:4122
Chamber Symphony, IX:4122
Clarino Quartet, IX:4122
Double Quartet, IX:4122
Einsame Nicht, IX:4121
Fantasy for Harpsicord, IX:4122
Passages, IX:4122
Piano Concerto, IX:4123
String Quartet, IX:4122
Symbalom, IX:4123
Symphony No.3, IX:4123
Symposium for Orchestra, IX:4122
Tanzspiel, IX:4123
Three Movements for Orchestra, IX:4122
Zwingli, Huldrych, III:101, 102, 103, **791-794**
Artikel, III:793
De vera ac falsa religione, III:793
Zworykin, Vladimir, **IX:4125-4128**